GARETH RUSSELL read Modern History at St Peter's College at the University of Oxford and completed his postgraduate at Queen's University, Belfast with a study of Catherine Howard's household. He is the author of two novels set in his native Belfast and several books on royal history. He divides his time between Belfast and New York.

Praise for *Young and Damned and Fair*:

'Scholarly yet highly readable … fresh and compelling … A stunning achievement'
Sunday Times

'Gareth Russell writes with considerable flair and presents a compelling case … Russell expertly tells a tale of jewels and dancing and thrilling trysts that sees Catherine move dizzily towards the block'
Literary Review

'Russell's writing is assured, epigrammatic … he veers with laudable theatricality between the claustrophobic and the panoramic … here is a historian unafraid of the dark, whether of depravity or documentation'
Daily Telegraph

'A timely and powerful re-examin
Gareth Russell has done some be
that Catherine was not as foo
suggested, and that her death wa
her offended husband, purely fo
when historians take the women who have been neglected by history seriously and study their lives rather than accepting stereotypes'
PHILIPPA GREGORY

'*Young and Dam*   phy
should be'   of
                          King

'Russell marries slick storytelling with a great wealth of learning about sixteenth-century personalities and politics. The result is a book that leads us deep into the nightmarish final years of Henry VIII's reign, wrenching open the intrigues of a poisonous court in a realm seething with discontent. At the heart of it all is the fragile, tragic figure of Catherine Howard, whose awful fate is almost unbearable to watch as it unfolds. This is authoritative Tudor history written with a novelist's lightness of touch. A terrific achievement'
DAN JONES

'A magnificent account ... compelling, thought-provoking and above all real ... Catherine Howard and her household are brought to life as never before. Hugely enjoyable'
ADRIAN TINNISWOOD

'This fascinating and ultimately heartbreaking account ... brings to life the cruel, gossip-fuelled, back-stabbing world of the court in which Catherine Howard rose and fell. The uncommonly talented Gareth Russell has produced a masterly work of Tudor history that is engrossing, sympathetic, suspenseful and illuminating'
CHARLOTTE GORDON, author of *Romantic Outlaws*

BY THE SAME AUTHOR

FICTION

Popular

The Immaculate Deception

NON-FICTION

The Emperors: How Europe's Rulers Were Destroyed by the First World War

A History of the English Monarchy: From Boadicea to Elizabeth I

YOUNG
&
DAMNED
&
FAIR

The Life and Tragedy of Catherine Howard
at the Court of Henry VIII

Gareth Russell

WILLIAM
COLLINS

William Collins
An imprint of HarperCollins*Publishers*
1 London Bridge Street
London SE1 9GF

www.WilliamCollinsBooks.com

First published in Great Britain by William Collins in 2017

This William Collins paperback edition published in 2018

1 3 5 7 9 8 6 4 2

Maps and family trees by Martin Brown

Extract from *Die Lorelei* from *Collected Poems and Drawings*
by Stevie Smith, London, Faber and Faber Ltd, 2015.
Kind permission granted by the publishers.

A catalogue record for this book is
available from the British Library

ISBN 978-0-00-812828-9

Printed and bound in Great Britain by
CPI Group (UK) Ltd, Croydon, CR0 4YY

For my grandparents,

Robert and Mary Russell
and
Richard and Iris Mahaffy

An antique story comes to me
And fills me with anxiety,
I wonder why I fear so much
What surely has no modern touch?

… There, on a rock majestical,
A girl with smile equivocal
Painted, young and damned and fair
Sits and combs her yellow hair.

– Stevie Smith, *Die Lorelei*

CONTENTS

ILLUSTRATIONS

Section 1

Section 2

miles
0   50

0   80
km

YORK

Ouse

HULL

PONTEFRACT
CASTLE

North Sea

LINCOLN

Trent

GRIMSTHORPE
CASTLE

COLLYWESTON PALACE

E N G L A N D

FRAMLINGHAM

Severn

Avon

Great Ouse

AMPTHILL

WALTHAM
HOLY CROSS

LONDON

WINDSOR

Thames

OATLANDS
PALACE

CHESWORTH
HOUSE

PORTSMOUTH

English Channel

F
R
A
N
C
E

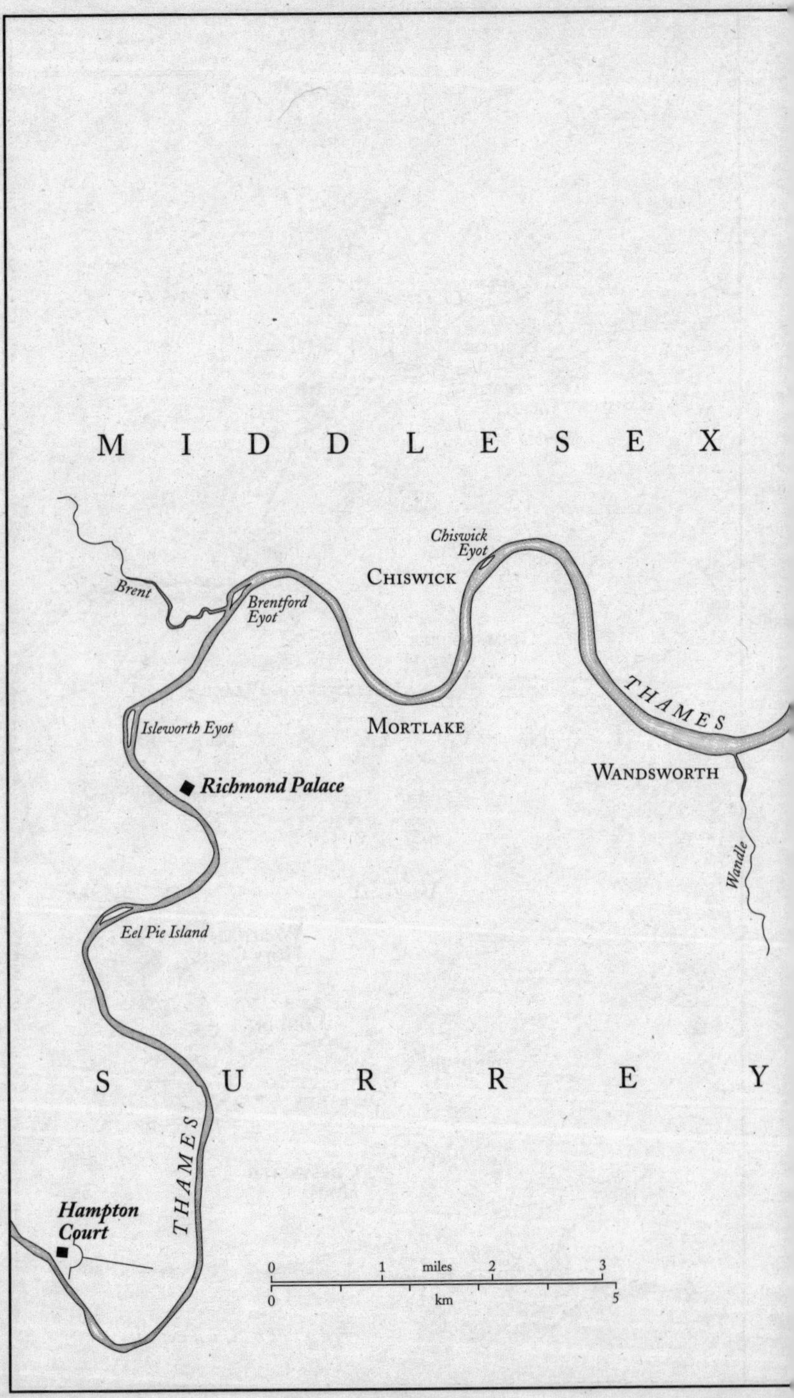

MIDDLESEX

Brent

Chiswick Eyot

CHISWICK

Brentford Eyot

THAMES

Isleworth Eyot

MORTLAKE

Richmond Palace

WANDSWORTH

Wandle

Eel Pie Island

S U R R E Y

THAMES

Hampton Court

| 0 | | 1 | miles | 2 | | 3 |
| 0 | | | km | | | 5 |

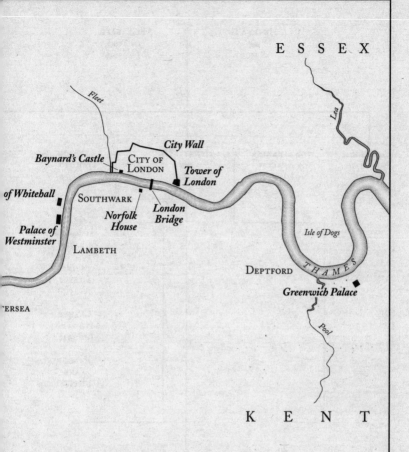

ESSEX

Lea

Fleet

City Wall

Baynard's Castle

CITY OF
LONDON

**Tower of
London**

of Whitehall

SOUTHWARK

*Norfolk
House*

**London
Bridge**

**Palace of
Westminster**

LAMBETH

Isle of Dogs

T H A M E S

DEPTFORD

Greenwich Palace

ERSEA

Pool

K   E   N   T

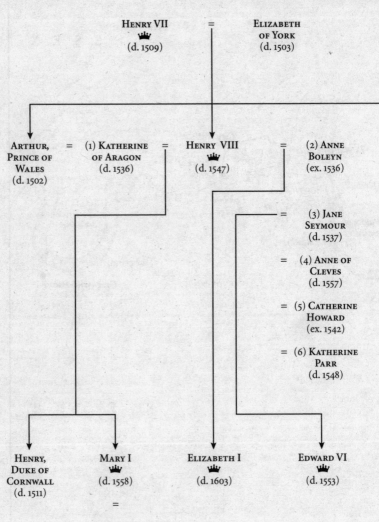

HENRY VII ♛ (d. 1509) = ELIZABETH OF YORK (d. 1503)

ARTHUR, PRINCE OF WALES (d. 1502) = (1) KATHERINE OF ARAGON (d. 1536) = HENRY VIII ♛ (d. 1547) = (2) ANNE BOLEYN (ex. 1536)

= (3) JANE SEYMOUR (d. 1537)

= (4) ANNE OF CLEVES (d. 1557)

= (5) CATHERINE HOWARD (ex. 1542)

= (6) KATHERINE PARR (d. 1548)

HENRY, DUKE OF CORNWALL (d. 1511)

MARY I ♛ (d. 1558)

=

PHILIP II, KING OF SPAIN (d. 1598)

ELIZABETH I ♛ (d. 1603)

EDWARD VI ♛ (d. 1553)

♛ English sovereigns
∗ additional issue, not shown here

The Tudors

(from Henry VII to Elizabeth I)

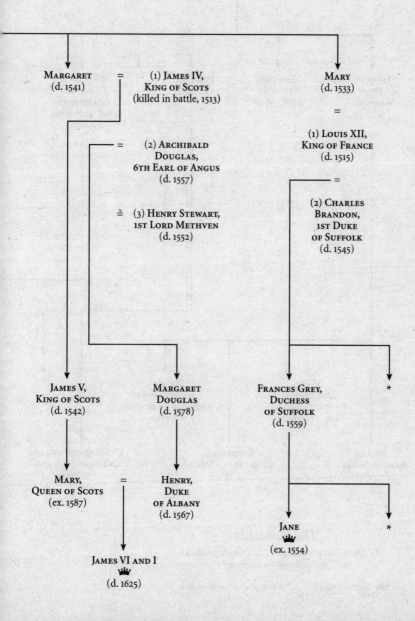

MARGARET
(d. 1541)

= (1) JAMES IV,
KING OF SCOTS
(killed in battle, 1513)

= (2) ARCHIBALD
DOUGLAS,
6TH EARL OF ANGUS
(d. 1557)

≃ (3) HENRY STEWART,
1ST LORD METHVEN
(d. 1552)

MARY
(d. 1533)

=

(1) LOUIS XII,
KING OF FRANCE
(d. 1515)

=

(2) CHARLES
BRANDON,
1ST DUKE
OF SUFFOLK
(d. 1545)

JAMES V,
KING OF SCOTS
(d. 1542)

MARGARET
DOUGLAS
(d. 1578)

FRANCES GREY,
DUCHESS
OF SUFFOLK
(d. 1559)

*

MARY,
QUEEN OF SCOTS
(ex. 1587)

=

HENRY,
DUKE
OF ALBANY
(d. 1567)

JAMES VI AND I
♛
(d. 1625)

JANE
♛
(ex. 1554)

*

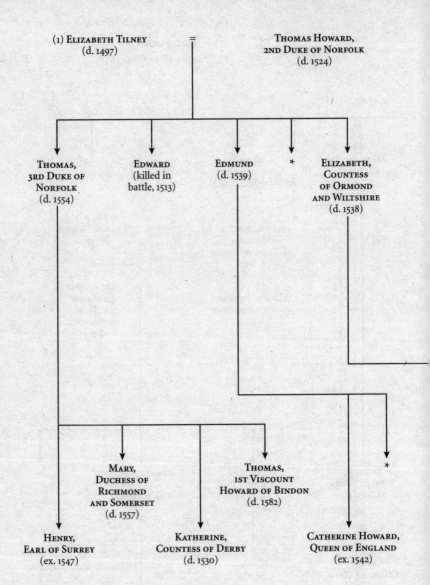

The Howards

(from Thomas Howard, 2nd Duke of Norfolk
to Catherine's generation)

👑 English sovereign   * additional issue, not shown here

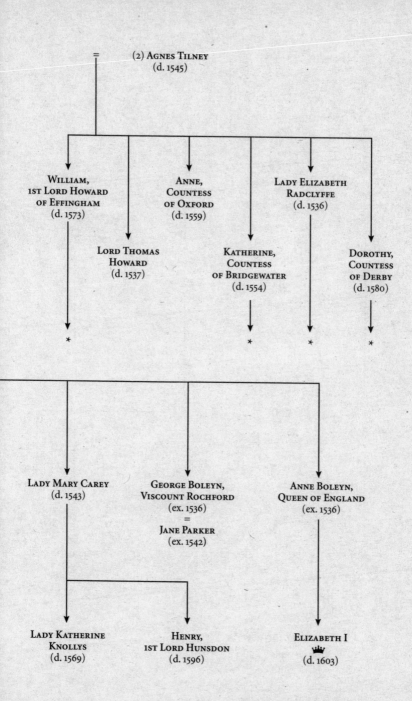

INTRODUCTION

In the Great Hall at Hampton Court Palace, magnificent tapestries depicting scenes from the life of the patriarch Abraham are on display. Every day, hundreds of tourists pass these enormous works of art which cost Henry VIII almost as much as the construction of a new warship. After centuries of exposure, their colours had faded and the bright sparkle of the threads of beaten gold had worn away, until a lengthy conservation project carried out between the Historic Royal Palaces, the Clothworkers' Company, and the University of Manchester offered a reconstruction and an academic paper conveying just how vibrant the tapestries would have been when they were first unveiled. Their detail is extraordinary, mesmeric. The reflections of mallard ducks floating on the ponds are visible, reeds sway in the wind, every face is detailed, sandals and toenails are stitched perfectly, bread in a servant's basket is believably coloured. Crucially, part of the conservation work necessitated turning the tapestries over to look at the threads at the back and see all the ugly, confusing stitch-work that had gone into making the familiar scene on the front possible.

My interest in the story of Henry VIII's fifth wife, Queen Catherine Howard, began years ago and solidified in 2011 when, under the supervision of Dr James Davis at Queen's University, Belfast, I completed my postgraduate dissertation on her household.[1] As with all Henry's wives, Catherine's life had been written about many times in biographies and studies of her husband's reign. In the year of Henry VIII's death, an Italian merchant remarked, 'The discourse of these wives is a wonderful history', an observation that captures why the Tudors remain one of England's most famous dynasties.[2] In Catherine's case, the circumstances of her career had already been dissected in *A Tudor Tragedy: The Life and Times of Catherine Howard*, first published in New York in 1961 and generally judged the standard biography of her. Written by Professor Lacey Baldwin Smith, the central contention of *A Tudor Tragedy* was that Catherine's 'career begins and ends with the Howards, a clan whose predatory instincts for self-aggrandisement, sense of pompous conceit, and dangerous meddling in the destinies of state, shaped the course of her tragedy.'[3]

I intended to use Catherine's sixteen-month period as queen consort as a useful framing device to analyse the queen's household, one of the least-studied but most fascinating components of Henry VIII's court: how it functioned, who populated it, who dominated it, how it was financed, and how it interacted with the wider court.[4] The thesis would place one early modern queen of England, in this case the hapless Catherine Howard, in the context of a life lived not just next to the great men of the early English Reformation but amongst the servants, ladies-in-waiting, and favourites, without whom no great aristocratic lady could function and from whom she was seldom, if ever, separated. I did not, initially, expect to find anything remarkably different about her rise and fall.

Instead, I came to the conclusion that the queen's household had shaped the trajectory of Catherine's career. Popular culture often presents Tudor royal households, particularly a queen's, as beautiful irrelevances. Sumptuously dressed ladies-in-waiting whispering behind their fans, dancing or throwing coy glances, are familiar images of life in the queens' establishments. In many works of fiction, these characters seem to spend a good deal of their time giggling over something which is not credibly amusing. The reality was far more interesting.

Establishing who Catherine's ladies-in-waiting were was a difficult task. The surviving list, which was for a long time incorrectly believed to be a list of women attached to the household of Catherine's predecessor, Anne of Cleves, gives the women by their title or surname, and for a few of the figures I had to undertake some guesswork based on Tudor women with the right background, name, and family ties to court. It was, however, possible to prove that several candidates who are usually identified as her ladies-in-waiting were never in Catherine's service – the 9th Earl of Kildare's daughter, Lady Elizabeth Fitzgerald, was not one of her maids of honour and the 'Lady Howard' mentioned was neither Catherine's stepmother nor one of her sisters, but her aunt by marriage, Lady Margaret Howard (née Gamage). Neither was the Dowager Duchess of Norfolk or the Countess of Bridgewater asked to join the household, despite their closeness to the queen. The more I researched, the more convinced I became that the influence and intentions of Catherine's family had been exaggerated or, at least, misrepresented, and acting on the advice of a professor, I began to consider a full-length study of Catherine's horribly compelling story.

The result, this book, is as much a study of Catherine Howard's world as it is a study of her personal life. Some biographies have a tendency to inflate and isolate their subjects, by endowing them with more importance or independence from the world around them than they actually possessed. The impact of religious changes, international diplomacy, and court etiquette will all be discussed in depth, not just because they are fascinating topics in their own right, but because directly or indirectly they shaped Catherine's story. Like the Hampton Court tapestries, it is the details of the background figures and the threads weaving behind them which together produced the image.

Putting her household, and her grandmother's, at the centre of a biography of Catherine makes her story a grand tale of the Henrician court in its twilight, a glittering but pernicious sunset, in which the king's unstable behaviour and his courtiers' labyrinthine deceptions ensured that fortune's wheel was moving more rapidly than at any previous point in his vicious but fascinating reign. Accounts of the gorgeous ceremonies held to celebrate the resubmission of the north to royal control saw Catherine, the girl in the silver dress, gleaming, Daisy Buchanan-like, safe and proud above the hot struggles of the poor – the perfect medieval royal consort. Until, like a bolt out of the heavens, a scandal resulted in an investigation in which nearly everyone close to Catherine was questioned and which ultimately wrapped itself in ever more intricate coils around the young queen until, to her utter bewilderment, it choked life from her entirely.

The downfall of Catherine Howard took place from 2 November 1541 to 13 February 1542. To narrate and analyse what happened, I have relied on four or five different types of documents. There are the official proclamations and correspondence from Henry's government, principally but not exclusively orders issued by the Privy Council which help establish the broad chronology of Catherine's fall and the Crown's eventual version of events. There are numerous surviving if incomplete transcripts of interrogations held between the first week of November and third week of December 1541, to which we might add the subcategory of the queen's own confessions, framed as letters to her husband. The diplomatic correspondence of the Hapsburg, French, and Clevian ambassadors are invaluable, not least because, while they were initially confused about what was happening, they ultimately left the fullest accounts of events as they unfolded to an outsider's gaze, particularly Charles de Marillac and Eustace Chapuys. Lastly, there are a few surviving letters or chronicles that give clues to the English public's reaction to the affair.

Interpretation of this evidence is fraught with difficulty. Many supporting or referenced documents did not survive the Cotton Library fire of 1731 and some that did were badly damaged by the smoke.[5] That many interviews with those who served either Catherine or her family were conducted but have not survived to the present is proved by the councillors' notes, where they jotted down their intention to summon a witness for a second or third round of questioning, the transcripts of which have since been lost. We know, for instance, that Catherine was rash enough to send Morris, one of her pageboys, to the rooms of her alleged lover Thomas Culpepper with food for Culpepper when he was ill. Yet if young Morris was questioned about what he had brought to Culpepper's rooms, as seems probable, then the transcripts of his interrogation do not survive. Nor do those of Catherine's former secretary Joan Bulmer, who must have been questioned given the fact that she was subsequently incarcerated for her actions. The queen's fleeting mention of Morris's involvement in bringing gifts to Culpepper, usually overlooked, reminds us that numerous members of the household must have been aware, or at the very least suspicious, of the queen's actions and that much of the evidence concerning her behaviour most likely came from sources other than the principals.

The extant records of the interrogations were written quickly, as the deponent gave his or her testimony, and so translating the increasingly illegible scrawl or deciphering the mounting number of abbreviations present their own challenges.[6] Many of these transcripts were translated in full for the first time by David Starkey for his book *Six Wives: The Queens of Henry VIII* (2003). Anyone studying Catherine Howard's life is indebted to Dr Starkey for that, particularly his work on Thomas Culpepper's testimony and Henry Manox's. I wonder if I might have suffered deeply from doubt at my translations of some of Manox's biological vocabulary had I not already known that 'the worst word in the language' had been spotted by another.

Separate to the illegible and the vanished, there is of course the question of intent. A common supposition about Catherine's downfall is that the people who were quizzed lied, because their interrogators or their own panic pressured them into doing so. At least two of the main witnesses were tortured later in the interrogation and one of them almost certainly faced similar horrors earlier. Another witness gave a piece of evidence damning Catherine that can neither be refuted nor verified. It is up to the reader to interpret it as an honest mistake, an accurate testimony, or a lie born of malice or fear.

Yet, even with all these shortcomings, acknowledged and grappled with, there is enough for us to piece together the various stages of the process of Catherine's downfall and its dominant characteristics. Scraps of achingly intimate detail survive – we know that the Dowager Duchess of Norfolk held a candle as she stood over a broken-into chest and the colour of the dress Catherine wore for her final journey by river. Beyond reasonable doubt, what happened in 1541 was not a coup launched with the intention of destroying the queen or her family. Some, if not many, of those involved may have been delighted to embarrass or undermine the Howards, but it was never the primary motivating factor. The government was responding to an unprecedented and unexpected set of developments. In the scrawl of ink on singed or water-damaged pages, amid lists upon lists of questions and the panicked, scratched-out signatures of frightened servants, there is nothing to suggest that Henry VIII's advisers were doing anything other than pursuing the evidence in front of them. Some of their conclusions may have been wrong, but they were not incomprehensible or unreasonable. When torture was used, it did not produce any evidence to contradict the testimonies of those whose bodies had not been brutalised. The fact that Queen Catherine shared a set of grandparents, a husband, and a similar finale with Anne Boleyn has produced a misleading impression that the two queens' fates were broadly similar. To compare them in detail is to produce a study in contrast. The circumstances of Anne Boleyn's downfall are notorious, and the weight of modern academic opinion supports the scepticism of many of her contemporaries about her guilt. Anne's queenship collapsed over seventeen days in May 1536, the evidence against her was given by the only deponent from a background humble enough to allow torture and, as Sir Edward Baynton wrote, in the queen's household in May 1536 there was 'much communication that no man will confess any thing against her'.[7]

The implosion of Catherine's marriage was a very different affair. Three months were taken to determine her fate, Parliament was consulted, embassies were invited to send representatives to the trials of the queen's co-accused, witnesses were fetched back for multiple rounds of questions, and a thorough agenda was set for each interrogation. So the interpretation of Anne Boleyn's downfall as one in which a powerful but divisive queen consort was harried to her death with maximum speed, minimum honesty, and determined hatred has no bearing on her cousin's fate five years later. What happened to Catherine Howard was monstrous and it struck many of her contemporaries as unnecessary, but it was not a lynching. The queen was toppled by a combination of bad luck, poor decisions, and the Henrician state's determination to punish those who failed its king. A modern study of Henry's marriages offered the conclusion that if 'ever a butterfly was broken on the wheel, it must surely have been Catherine Howard', and in the sense that the wheel in question was her husband's government, there was an inexorable quality about the way it turned to crush Catherine after 2 November 1541.[8]

I have spelled Catherine's name with a 'C' to differentiate her from other Katherines in a generation with many. Her name has been given as Katherine, Katharine, Catharine, and Kathryn in other biographies, and standardised spelling was never a sixteenth-century priority. For clarity's sake, Catherine's two stepdaughters are usually referred to here as princesses. Each sister had been styled as a princess from the time of her birth until the annulment of her mother's marriage, after which they were both addressed by the honorific of 'lady', even when they were rehabilitated into the line of succession. During their brother's reign, they were interchangeably referred to by both titles, owing to their positions as first and second in line to the throne, and Elizabeth was often referred to as Princess Elizabeth during Mary's time as queen. To mark them out from the other Marys and Elizabeths, I have decided to err on the side of politesse in giving both women the higher title when they are mentioned in passing. For similar reasons, I have sometimes given the names of foreign princesses in their native language – hence Maria of Austria and Marie de Guise, rather than the anglicised Mary. Where possible, I have tried to be consistent – Maria of Austria was also known as Mary of Hungary, Catherine's sister Isabella is Isabel in some sources. Likewise, the surnames of many of those involved in Catherine's story vary – Culpepper is Culpeper; Dereham is given as Durham, Durant, or Deresham; Edgcumbe or Edgecombe; Habsburg or Hapsburg; Knyvet or Knyvett; Mannox, Manox or Mannock; Damport or Davenport. Where required, I have chosen a common spelling.

I have modernised the spelling in quotations from the original documents. All quotations from the Bible are taken either from the Douay-Rheims or King James editions. I have avoided giving estimations of modern equivalents to Tudor money, since they are often misleading and, at best, imprecise. Prior to 1752, England operated under the Julian calendar, and the new calendar year commenced on 25 March, the Feast of the Annunciation, rather than on 1 January. By our reckoning, Catherine Howard was executed on 13 February 1542, but her contemporaries in England would have given 1541 as the year of her death. Almost all historians give the modern dating and I have followed suit.

Chapter 1

The Hour of Our Death

Renounce the thought of greatness, tread on fate,
  Sigh out a lamentable tale of things
Done long ago, and ill done; and when sighs
Are wearied, piece up what remains behind
With weeping eyes, and hearts that bleed to death.

– John Ford,
The Lover's Melancholy (1628)

A benefit of being executed was that one avoided any chance of the dreaded *mors improvisa*, a sudden death by which a Christian soul might be denied the opportunity to make their peace. So when Thomas Cromwell was led out to his death on 28 July 1540, he had the comfort of knowing that he had been granted the privilege of preparing to stand in the presence of the Almighty. The day was sweltering, one in a summer so hot and so dry that no rain fell on the kingdom from spring until the end of September, but the bulky hard-bitten man from Putney who had become the king's most trusted confidant and then his chief minister[1] walked cheerfully towards the scaffold.[2] He even called out to members of the crowd and comforted his nervous fellow prisoner Walter, Lord Hungerford, whose sanity was questionable, and who had been condemned to die alongside him for four crimes, all of which carried the death penalty. Firstly, he had allegedly committed heresy, in appointing as his private chaplain a priest rumoured to remain loyal to the pope. Secondly, he was accused of witchcraft, by consorting with various individuals, including one named 'Mother Roche', to use necromancy to guess the date of the king's death. Treason was alleged through the appointment of his chaplain and his meeting with the witch, which constituted a crime against the king's majesty. He was also found guilty of sodomy, 'the abominable and detestable vice and sin of buggery', made a capital crime in 1534, in going to bed with two of his male servants, men called William Master and Thomas Smith.[3]

Rumours, fermenting in the baking heat and passed between courtiers, servants, merchants and diplomats who had nothing to do but sweat and trade in secrets, had already enlarged the scope of Lord Hungerford's crimes. The French ambassador reported back to Paris that the condemned man had also been guilty of sexually assaulting his own daughter. It was whispered that Hungerford had practised black magic, violating the laws of Holy Church that prohibited sorcery as a link to the Devil. Others heard that Hungerford's true crime had been actively plotting the murder of the king.[4] None of those charges were ever mentioned in the indictments levelled against Hungerford at his trial, but the man dying alongside him had perfected this tactic of smearing a victim with a confusing mélange of moral turpitudes guaranteed to excite prurient speculation and kill a person's reputation before anyone was tempted to raise a voice in their defence.

The hill where they now stood had been the site of the finales to some of Cromwell's worst character assassinations. It had been there, four years earlier on another summer's day, that George Boleyn had perished before similarly large crowds after Cromwell arranged a trial that saw him condemned to death on charges of incest and treason. The details of Boleyn's alleged treason had been kept deliberately vague during the trial, while the prosecution's fanciful descriptions of his incestuous seduction of his sister had been excruciatingly, pornographically vivid. Boleyn, as handsome as Adonis and proud as Icarus, had defended himself so well against the accusations there had been bets that he would be acquitted.[5] When he was not, when he was condemned to die alongside four other men two days later, no one could risk speaking out for a man found guilty of committing such a bestial act.

Boleyn had died in sight of the Tower's brooding walls, its cupolas and fortifications twin testaments to the inescapably neurotic nature of power. Within the Tower's sheltered courtyards, George's Boleyn's sister, Queen Anne, was executed in a more private setting, before a carefully vetted crowd of around one thousand, which was tiny in comparison to that allowed to gather beyond the walls to watch her brother perish – and now Cromwell and Walter Hungerford.[6] Like Thomas More before her, another political heavyweight in whose destruction Cromwell had been intimately involved, Anne Boleyn had embraced the sixteenth century's veneration for the *ars moriendi* – the art of dying.

The veil between life and death was made permeable by the teachings of Christianity. Everywhere one looked, there was proof of society's lively fascination with the next life. Death was the great moral battleground between one's strengths and weaknesses; the supreme test came when the finite perished and the eternal began. To die well, in a spirit of resignation to the Will of God and without committing a sin against hope by despairing of what was to come next, was a goal endlessly stressed to the Faithful in art, sermons, homilies and manuals. Within the great basilica of Saint-Denis in Paris, the tomb of King Louis XII and Anne of Brittany, his queen, showed the couple rendered perfect in the stonemasons' marble, united atop the monument, their bejewelled hands clasped in prayer, their robes and crowns exquisitely carved; but beneath that sculpture the craftsmen had offered a very different portrait of the royal forms – there, the bodies of the king and queen were shown twisting and writhing in the first stages of putrefaction, their feet bare, their hair uncovered and their flesh pullulating with the onset of corruption.[7] Throughout Europe, these cadaver tombs, the *transi*, were commissioned by the rich and the powerful to show their submission to the final destruction of their flesh and with it the removal of this sinful world's most potent temptations. In corruption they had been born and so through corruption they could be born again.

In the sixteenth century, life was precious, truncated at any moment by plague, war or one of a thousand ailments that would be rendered treatable in the centuries to come, and so the people embraced it with a rare zeal. But living well, as Anne Boleyn had noted at her trial, also meant dying well.[8] Christians were supposed to die bravely because of the surety of mercy that even the weakest and most sinful was guaranteed by their religion, provided he or she had respected its doctrines and honoured its God. Before they were marched to the hill, Cromwell told Lord Hungerford that 'though the breakfast which we are going to be sharp, yet, trusting to the mercy of the Lord, we shall have a joyful dinner'.[9] To the overwhelming number of Henry VIII's subjects, Christianity was not a theory, it was not a belief system, it was not one religion among many – it was, more or less, a series of facts, the interpretation of which could be debated, but whose essential truth was inescapable and uncontested. The result of this way of accepting and experiencing their faith was that sixteenth-century Christians often behaved in ways which were paradoxically far more devout but also far more relaxed than their modern-day co-religionists. The line between sinners and the flock was not so clearly delineated, because even the worst members of society were still, in one way or the other, almost certainly believing Christians. All men were weak, all men would fail, all men would die, all men could be saved.

A celebrated person's execution, their final public performance, was such an exciting event that people made the journey into London especially for it. Vast crowds surged through London, converging on Tower Hill to watch the annihilation of the detested commoner who had somehow risen to become Earl of Essex – a sign of royal favour given to him only a few weeks before he was arrested at a meeting of the Privy Council and taken to the Tower. The last ascent in the life of the Englishman who had risen farther than anyone else in his century were the wooden steps to the scaffold. Thomas Cromwell had not been a popular figure, but royal advisers seldom are. Snobbery played a large role in his reputation – an English diplomat described Cromwell as a man who had been 'advanced from the dunghill to great honour' – but so did his actions.[10] Ruthless, determined, brilliant, and utterly Machiavellian, Cromwell had overseen the destruction of many an aristocratic career and the evisceration of the old religion in England. Many of his opponents blamed him for tearing asunder the spiritual framework that they had lived, and hoped to die, by. The sacraments and liturgies of the Church had given a rhythm to the year, they had bestowed the tools for salvation on the faithful for centuries, and marked every major moment in a Christian's life. In 1536, Cromwell had weathered the Pilgrimage of Grace, a traditionalist uprising which spread through most of northern England and which had demanded his removal from power. However, he could not survive the loss of the king's favour four years later. His enemies surrounded him and he was condemned to death on a long list of crimes that included heresy, treason, and financial corruption.

The crowds entering the capital on 28 July 1540 came from every background, with well-born women wearing veils to shield their faces from the sun, while urchins wore battered hand-me-down cheap leather shoes which prevented their feet from being cut on the animal bones and refuse that littered the city streets. With no rain, the mud in the streets had become a dry dust that would turn into ankle-depth filth when the clouds broke in autumn. The spectators passed through the capital's eighteen-foot high defensive walls via one of the seven gates. Those travelling in from the Hampshire and Surrey countryside entered through Newgate, while those from nearby Smithfield, home to a bustling meat market, accessed the City at Aldersgate. Smithfield also contained London's designated red-light district, the aptly named Cock Lane. Subtlety in the assigning of place names was not a medieval strongpoint. The southwestern city of Exeter had renamed one of its rivers Shitbrook, because of the amount of faeces and waste it contained, and in Oxford, students hoping for an early sexual experience courtesy of the town's prostitutes could find it on Gropecunt Lane, a narrow alley that ran from just opposite the university church of St Mary the Virgin down to the entrance of Oriel College.[11]

Rather more elegant sights awaited those who were travelling towards Cromwell's execution via the Strand, a long straight road lined with the episcopal palaces and impressive homes of the aristocracy. The Strand had been the site of the Savoy Palace, principal residence of Richard II's powerful uncle John of Gaunt, until it was burned down during the Peasants' Revolt of 1381. It was eventually replaced by the Hospital of St John the Baptist, one of the most impressive medical establishments in early modern Europe, founded under the patronage of Henry VIII's father. Near the hospital was one of the Eleanor Crosses, funerary monuments erected by a grief-stricken Edward I in 1290 to mark each of the fourteen spots where his wife's coffin rested on its final journey to Westminster Abbey. This, the last halt before the interment, was now where professional water-sellers took advantage of the area's excellent plumbing, which on occasion pumped the local fountains with wine or beer to celebrate an especially significant royal event – the last time had been for the birth of the heir to the throne, Prince Edward, in 1537. On a hot and busy day like this, as families and groups of friends swarmed towards the Tower, the Charing Cross water-sellers could reasonably have expected to turn a handsome profit.[12]

London in July 1540 was the perfect capital for Henry VIII's domains: a broken society whose fracture lines were both reflected and grotesquely magnified throughout the city. Along the banks of the Thames, formerly semi-rural areas like Deptford and Woolwich were now shipyards for the Royal Navy, where titanic amounts of money poured into the construction of warships designed to repel the French and Spanish, if they ever came. Londoners grumbled at the despoiling of some of the few green areas left to them; they valued their leaf-dappled refuges so much that earlier in the king's reign thousands had rioted over plans to encroach on the area of parkland around Soho, a district which got its name from a traditional hunting cry, 'So, ho!'

Riots were rare in Henrician England, but tensions were constant and none were more intense than those caused by the country's break with Rome. Seven years before Cromwell's execution, the king had repudiated papal authority and embarked upon his own version of the Reformation in what rapidly became one of the least articulate government policies in British history. There was absolutely no clear strategy for where the Church of England should go once it was commanded from London rather than Rome. The king, who had harnessed anti-clericalism in Parliament to secure his dream of annulling his marriage to Katherine of Aragon, had then hurled himself into what initially looked like the wholesale dismemberment of English Catholicism. The severing of obedience to the Vatican was the initial step in a legal, cultural, and economic revolution. The monasteries were dissolved, or pressured to surrender, first the smaller abbeys, then the larger and wealthier. On the eve of the Reformation, about one-third of the land in England belonged to the Church and so the seizure of its assets became an unsavoury bonanza for the government and its supporters, whose loyalty to the regime was often bought with gifts of land taken from the religious orders.

The first human casualties after the break with Rome had been the conservatives who could not in good conscience abjure their oaths of loyalty to the pope. There were some among them who, despite their misgivings, were prepared to acknowledge that canon law just about permitted the king's banishment of Katherine of Aragon and marriage to Anne Boleyn, whom even Thomas More had acknowledged as 'this noble woman royally anointed queen', but under no circumstances could they accept that Henry had the right to make himself Supreme Head on Earth of the Church of England and Ireland.[13] Thomas More, the country's former Lord Chancellor, and the esteemed scholar Cardinal John Fisher went to the block in 1535. The leaders of the Carthusian order of monks were hanged until they were half dead, cut down to be castrated, disembowelled and only then beheaded. The country folk coming into London through Newgate for Cromwell's death had to pass by the looming, grey-stoned edifice of Newgate prison, where three hermits, one deacon and six monks had been stripped, chained to posts with their hands tied behind their backs and simply left to starve to death in their cells, rotting towards martyrdom in excruciating pain and their own gathering excrement. One plucky Catholic lady, a doctor's wife, disguised herself as a milk maid, bribed the guards to let her into the cell and fed, watered and bathed the condemned gentlemen. The gaolers tightened security after the king irritably asked how the condemned men had remained alive for so long.[14]

A few miles to the west of the prison was Tyburn, the site of near-daily executions of criminals – rapists, horse thieves, forgers and murderers. It was here that many of the Carthusian monks met their end after being processed through the streets tied to a wicker hurdle pulled by a slow-moving horse. Back at Smithfield, within sight of the grubby walkways of Cock Lane, Father John Forest had been burned to death atop a pyre that consisted of religious statues, including one of Saint Derfel, taken from a pilgrimage centre in north Wales. There was a hideous poetic irony in using the symbols of pre-Reformation Christianity to incinerate one of its most vocal sympathisers.

For the poorest of the poor, the Reformation initially brought a different kind of martyrdom. Admittedly, the Church had not always done all that it could to alleviate poverty, but as medieval Catholicism's emphasis on charity as a means to secure salvation came under attack by reformers, beggars would have been a depressingly and increasingly familiar sight for the spectators. This was especially true for those from Smithfield whose monastic hospital and poorhouse, St Bartholomew's Priory, had been shut down during the dissolutions, leaving the local poor and invalided defenceless, friendless and often homeless. Throughout London it was the same, with those who had relied on the Church either for charity or work, wandering the streets, joined by the hundreds who poured in from the countryside where the dissolutions had closed off many traditional forms of employment or benefice. Nor were the seized properties being put to edifying use in the post-monastic world. Courtiers, lawyers and merchants who benefited from the government's liberality often turned the former abbeys and churches into stinking tenements, overpacked and overpriced, where families lived in pathetically cramped quarters with rampant disease and indifferent landlords. The church of St Martin-le-Grand was demolished to make way for a tavern; Bermondsey Abbey, where Henry VIII's grandmother Elizabeth Woodville had spent the final few years of her life, became a bull-fighting arena, before it was demolished to make way for the private home of a lawyer who worked on the Court of Augmentations, the legal body set up to deal with former monastic lands; the Priory of St Mary Overy became a bear-baiting pit. Statues of saints and angels had been torn from their niches and burned in a crusade against the old ways; yet even with such zeal from the iconoclastic reformers, clear religious policy, vital in an age which still carried the death penalty for heresy, proved elusive.

Thomas Cromwell, rising to power during the break with Rome and then securing his position at the king's side thanks to his indefatigable work on the dissolutions, was seen as the Reformation's henchman by its opponents and 'an organ of Christ's glory' by its supporters; he seems to have believed in the Reformation's mission and to have risked much to support those who shared his spirituality.[15] Whether he was as indifferent to its human cost as is usually supposed is unclear, but that he never shirked from unpleasant tasks is certain. The quartered limbs and parboiled heads of dead traitors were on prominent display throughout the capital, with the skulls of the most famous offenders sitting atop pikes that jutted out over the nineteen arches of London Bridge. They would stay there until they had been stripped clean by birds and the elements.

Bile and viciousness increased on both sides of the confessional divide as the king, with God in one eye and the Devil in the other, brooded like Shelley's Ozymandias over a kingdom riven by divisions. Who was in and who was out at the centre of government changed constantly and, unlike most of his predecessors, Henry VIII seemed to want his fallen favourites to vanish into the vast silence of mortality rather than simply leave the sunlight of his presence. Cromwell had previously helped arrange the exits of other favourites, now he was enduring the same agony.

We may know now that the Tudor dynasty was successful in holding on to power, and in preventing both civil war and foreign invasion, in the same way we know that the United States and her allies prevailed in the Cold War, but those attending Cromwell's execution had no such assurances, and paranoia was rampant, a communal insecurity for which the king's glamorously bizarre behaviour must bear a large portion of the blame. To have embarked upon something as seismic as the schism with the Vatican without having a clear strategy for the years ahead was foolish, but to then change his mind as often as he did with something as sacred and vital to his people's understanding of themselves was criminally incompetent. When Henry VIII had exhausted the wealth of the Church, he began to lose interest in the Reformation; his natural conservatism reawakened and he was appalled by the many Protestant sects that were using the newfound availability of the Bible to interpret God's Word for themselves, in many cases reaching conclusions that Henry regarded as rank heresy. The pendulum began to swing in the opposite direction, with legislation known as the Six Articles reaffirming the government's commitment to Catholic theology. Protestants nicknamed the laws 'the whip with six strings' and the arrests of religious radicals began once their patron, Cromwell, was no longer in a position to protect them. At Smithfield, the local authorities were busy setting up another pyre to burn three Lutherans, Robert Barnes, Thomas Gerard and William Jerome, who had once preached their gospel with Cromwell's support. They were to die on the 30th, two days after Cromwell. With intimidation, espionage, cancerous fears of enemies foreign and domestic, and bitter sectarian tensions, Henrician England and Ireland were countries tottering permanently on the edge and many blamed Thomas Cromwell for organising the march to the precipice.

In the countryside, beyond the stench and sweat of the crowd assembled to watch Cromwell's and Hungerford's deaths, Edmund Bonner, Bishop of London, prepared to preside over the king's wedding service to Catherine Howard. The pretty palace of Oatlands sat in a rolling deer park, its loveliness marred only by the building work that the king, with his passion for architecture, had ordered three years earlier when the manor had come into his possession.[16] A fortune was spent on transforming the seldom-used Oatlands into a retreat fit for the sovereign – an octagonal tower, still a work in progress on the day Cromwell was struck down, was added to the courtyard. Terraced gardens were constructed with multiple fountains, each one an enormous extravagance splashing cooling streams of water. An orchard, its mature trees groaning under the weight of fruit, offered shade to the heads of courtiers and servants, as they endured the stifling heat. The trees were old, but the orchard was not. They had been uprooted from St Peter's Abbey at nearby Chertsey, a nine-century-old monastery founded by Saint Erkenwald, one of the earliest bishops of London, and brought to grace the king's gardens when the abbey was shut down, its brothers expelled and its possessions stripped by Cromwell's inspectors. The stones that built the little palace's extension had come from the Augustinian priory at Tandridge as it was pulled down to make way for aristocratic demesnes. The price paid by many of his subjects for the king's religious revolution weighed heavily and silently on Oatlands, but as thick carpets from the Ottoman Empire, chairs upholstered in velvets and cloth of gold, gilt cups, bejewelled table services, and beds hung with cloth of silver were all processed into Oatlands, there was little outward sign of the stresses and tribulation that had gone into making it suitable for the royal household.[17]

An Oxford graduate in his early forties, Edmund Bonner had risen from relative obscurity, which encouraged accusations that he had been born out of wedlock, to become England's ambassador to France and, after that, Bishop of London.[18] He had secured both his ambassadorship and episcopacy through Thomas Cromwell's patronage, yet like everybody else he had abandoned Cromwell in his hour of need. The latter's frantic letters from prison, entreating royal mercy from Henry, written in a disjointed and panicky mess compared to his usual precise calligraphy, had gone unanswered, as Cromwell's former dependants turned their faces from him, as if he had never existed.

We cannot say for certain where in Oatlands Catherine Howard resided during her wedding visit. Recent excavations of the palace have given us a better picture of its layout and the safest guess would be that her rooms were in the queen's apartments, located in the palace's southern towers between the inner and outer courtyards. From any eastern- or western-facing windows above the quadrangle, she would have had beautiful views of either the orchard with its purloined apple trees, the octagonal dovecote or the ornamental gardens circling the fountains. From just above the entrance to the inner courtyard, she would have been able to see the ramp that had recently been installed to help her husband-to-be mount what must have been a particularly sturdy steed. Beyond the walls lay the deer park where she and the king would spend a few days of hunting as part of a ten-day honeymoon.

She was in her late teens, slender, like most of the Howard women, with a 'very delightful' appearance, according to the French ambassador.[19] The court's temporary reduction in size and then its removal to the relative obscurity of Oatlands fuelled speculation that she was already pregnant; Catherine's petite frame gave the lie to the story, but it would be weeks before she was unveiled to the public again and the stories could finally be put to rest.[20] Sixteenth-century weddings were not usually romantic occasions and the modern idea of writing one's own vows or of putting the couple's affection for one another at the centre of the ceremony would have struck Catherine and her contemporaries as bizarre. It was, like an execution, a formal occasion governed by established precedent; there was a proper way of doing things and as she made her way down to the recently renovated chapel near her husband's tower to stand in front of Edmund Bonner, Catherine, keen to adhere to etiquette after a lifetime spent learning its nuances, had no intention of making a mistake.

The king had arrived at Oatlands earlier that day. Lucrezia Borgia's twenty-three-year-old son Francesco, Marquis of Massalombarda, had been visiting London for the last week and he was due to leave that evening; the king had entertained him with visits to his palaces at Greenwich and Richmond and given him two fine horses as a parting gift.[21] It was unusual for a traveller to begin a journey in the evening when visibility was poor, so perhaps the marquis had delayed his departure to make sure he witnessed the executions on Tower Hill. If he did attend, his status would have vouchsafed for him a place at the front of the crowd.

Much as a hush falls when a bride enters a church, a silence settled over the spectators as Cromwell began his final speech.[22] He delivered it perfectly, thanking God for allowing him to die this way, in full knowledge of what lay ahead, and confessing readily that he was a wretched and miserable sinner who had, like all Christians, fallen short of the standards hoped for by Almighty God: 'I confess that as God, by His Holy Spirit, instructs us in the truth, so the devil is ready to seduce us – and I have been seduced.' Then he began to pray – for the king, for 'that goodly imp' the heir apparent – and to ask for prayers for himself, though as a reformer he was careful not to ask for prayers for his soul after he was dead but solely 'so that as long as life remaineth in this flesh, I waiver nothing in my faith'.[23]

As Catherine, her throat now glittering with pieces from the royal collection, knelt before Edmund Bonner, Cromwell knelt in the sawdust of the scaffold and prayed aloud, 'O Lord, grant me that when these eyes lose their use, that the eyes of my soul might see Thee. O Lord and father, when this mouth shall lose his use that my heart may say, *O Pater, in manus tuas commendo spiritum meum.*'[24] Hungerford, his sanity now snapped entirely, kept interrupting, writhing and screaming at the executioner to get on with his bloody business.[25] Henry Howard, Earl of Surrey, stood at the forefront of the crowd and watched the scene without pity. He was missing his cousin's wedding to be here to see his family's *bête noire* finished off. Later that day, he could not conceal his good mood. It felt to him like a settling of scores: 'Now is the false churl dead, so ambitious of others' blood.'[26]

More of the Howards may have been at Oatlands to help Catherine, steady any nerves and, as ever, offer advice. A few days earlier, in preparation for the wedding, the king had granted Catherine's eldest brother Charles five properties in London, while their half sister Isabella got a manor house in Wiltshire and all the lands that had once belonged to Malmesbury Abbey. As a gift for performing the service, Bishop Bonner's debts were paid off by the royal household and he was given a set of gold dining plate that had been confiscated from his predecessor during the dissolutions.[27] The newly enriched Isabella, wife to the queen's vice-chamberlain, was almost certainly in attendance in her capacity both as Catherine's sister and lady-in-waiting. This was the second queen Isabella would serve and her husband's fifth. Both were too clever to give any thought to the merry-go-round of queens consort, or rather, any voice. A woman would soon be imprisoned for asking of the king: 'How many wives will he have?'[28]

At the Tower, Lord Hungerford's wish that the headsman should acquit his task quickly was not to be fulfilled. Edward Hall described Cromwell's executioner as 'ragged [and] butcherly', who 'very ungoodly performed his office'.[29] No more details are provided about what went wrong with the beheading, but rumour began with the claim it had taken three strokes to cut through the minister's thick neck. By the end of the month, entertainment had triumphed over plausibility with stories that it had taken two headsmen half an hour to kill him and allegations that Cromwell's enemies, who had been seen banqueting and celebrating throughout the week preceding his death, had taken the executioner out to feast him the night before, to get him drunk and hope that with a hangover he would give Cromwell as painful a death as possible. All we know for certain is Edward Hall's remark that the executioner had carried out the task in an 'ungoodly' manner and that afterwards Cromwell's head was taken with Lord Hungerford's to gaze and rot from the top of the pikes at London Bridge.

From the little chapel at Oatlands and the imposing towers of London, bells tolled out to mark a wedding and a death. Bells still tolled too every second day of November, the Feast of All Souls, the Catholic Day of the Dead, when Christ's flock on earth were compelled to remember their brothers and sisters in the faith who had gone before them. They would toll again on the fifteenth day of August, the Feast of the Assumption, to mark the entry of the Virgin Mary into Heaven, there to be crowned its queen, as foretold, so the Church taught, in the visions of Saint John in the Book of Revelation.[30] Celestial queens had not yet been abolished, despite the best efforts of the Protestant evangelicals and the man who had fallen on Catherine's wedding day. But in a world where statues of Our Lady could be taken from Norfolk and torched in front of large London crowds with Cromwell watching on, it did not seem as if the Virgin Mary was any more secure on her throne than Katherine of Aragon or Anne Boleyn had been on theirs. It was an age of uncertainty and terrifying possibilities, and Catherine Howard was now its queen.

Chapter 2

Our Fathers in Their Generation

Let us now praise men of renown,
and our fathers in their generation.

– Ecclesiasticus 44:1

The first recorded mention of Catherine Howard, born as she was in the decade before the government made mandatory parish-level records of each baptism, comes from a will.[1] Her maternal grandmother, Isabel Worsley, left a bequest, 'To Charles Howard Henry George Margaret Catherine Howard XXs [twenty shillings] each.'[2] It is a very quiet entrance for a future queen of England – Catherine is even upstaged in the concluding half of the sentence by her younger sister Mary, who, as Isabel's goddaughter, received a more substantial bestowal of £10.[3] Yet it is from the Worsleys and their kin that much of the relevant evidence about Catherine's early years originates.

Beyond its object as a matter of general historical interest in showcasing how prosperous members of county society chose to dispose of their earthly possessions on the eve of the Reformation – rather touching is Isabel's stipulation that every housewife in Stockwell, part of Isabel's home parish of Lambeth, should receive a gift of linen worth twelve pence or, failing that, a monetary gift of the same amount; likewise her decision to set aside £6 to repair a local highway – the will, which went to probate on

26 May 1527, proves that Catherine had been born, with time to spare for a younger sister, by the spring of that year.[4] As with all four of Henry VIII's English-born wives, and many of their contemporaries, we are left to guess when they arrived in the world using fragmentary evidence provided by throwaway or contested remarks from those who knew them or saw them, personal letters, family wills, and comments in contemporary memoirs or chronicles. The analysis of these documents has thus produced a broad spectrum of supposition. In Catherine's case, suggestions for her birthdate have run the gamut from 1518 to 1527. The promotion of the former date seems motivated mainly by a desire to rehabilitate a particularly dubious portrait, which will be discussed subsequently, while support for the later years partly derives from the account of a Spanish merchant living in London late in Henry VIII's reign, who described Catherine as 'a mere child' at the time of her marriage in 1540.

While both Catherine and her younger sister are mentioned in Isabel's final testament of 1527, they are absent from the will of her husband, Sir John Leigh, which is usually dated to 1524. Their three brothers, Charles, Henry, and George, are mentioned in both.[5] The year 1525, which leaves time for a younger sister to be born and named as Isabel's goddaughter by 1527, has thus gained understandable acceptance as Catherine's most likely date of birth in several recent accounts of her career.[6] Critics of this conclusion point out that the two sisters' absence from Sir John's will proves nothing, because in a patriarchal society like early modern England, it would be unusual for very young female members of a family to be mentioned in the wills of male relatives.

In fact, both conclusions are arrived at by misreading John Leigh's testament. While codicils pertaining to the distribution of some parcels of land were added in August 1524, the will itself was actually written nearly a year earlier, and dated 16 June 1523. If the Leighs' documents are to be used as bookends for Catherine's arrival, they establish a date between the summer of 1523 and the spring of 1527. Furthermore, far from focusing solely on the male members of his line, John Leigh made numerous gifts to young female members of his extended family, including all Catherine's elder half sisters. They, admittedly, were Leighs, but it seems unlikely that John Leigh would also include all Catherine's Howard brothers and neglect to mention her at all, unless she was extremely young, a tentative conclusion that leaves us free to accept the one specific contemporary comment on her age, made by the French diplomat Charles de Marillac, who met Catherine on several occasions in 1540 and 1541, and believed that she had been eighteen years old in 1539–40.[7] Catherine and de Marillac attended several hunting trips together in the summers of 1540 and 1541, and this seemingly decisive statement from someone well placed to know dates her birth to 1520 or 1521. De Marillac's credibility is allegedly undercut by the claim that he believed Anne of Cleves to be thirty in 1540, when she was in fact twenty-four, but an examination of the relevant letter shows that on the subject of Anne's age, de Marillac wrote, 'Her age one would guess at about thirty.'[8] An unchivalrous comment, but not necessarily an inaccurate one.[9] It may very well be that, with Catherine, de Marillac was again basing his estimate on how old she looked.

De Marillac's estimate of Catherine's age gains more credibility upon examination of the ages of Catherine's peers when she joined the court as a maid of honour in 1539. None of the girls who served alongside her was born before 1521, the date of birth for Anne Bassett, the most senior of the group, who had been at court since 1537. One of the girls who joined at the same time as Catherine, her second cousin Katherine Carey, was born either in 1523 or 1524, and while we do not have precise dates for the others, all those who joined within twelve months of Catherine were definitely born at some point in the early-to-mid-1520s.[10] The implication that Catherine, coming from a similar background into the same position, was five or six years older than the rest – or even three years older than the already established Anne Bassett – stretches credulity. When combined with the evidence of John and Isabel Leigh's wills, Charles de Marillac's indirect guess of about 1521 rules out a date as late as 1525, and the biographical details of the other half-dozen or so maids of honour similarly discredit one as early as 1518. None of this is definitive, but when set alongside other circumstantial evidence from Catherine's life, it suggests 1522 or 1523 as the most probable years of her birth.[11]

Where she was born is more easily established. Most accounts of Catherine's life state that her place of birth is a mystery, but in fact regardless of when she was born, it was almost certainly in the parish of Lambeth in the county of Surrey, just south of London.[12] Before she was born and throughout her childhood, her father Edmund served as a justice of the peace for Surrey, charged with the 'conservation of the King's peace' and to 'punish delinquents … [and] hear and determine felonies' in the king's name.[13] Directives to him from the Privy Council, issued on either side of Catherine's birth, as well as evidence from family accounts, place him specifically in Lambeth – for a time, he lived in a house on Church Street, part of what is now Lambeth Bridge Road.[14] Several members of Edmund's family had homes in Lambeth, most prominently Norfolk House, a mansion renovated at the command of Edmund's father which subsequently functioned as the Dukes of Norfolk's main residence near the capital.[15] For a Howard, Lambeth was the most logical place in Surrey to set up residence, and as further examination of his finances make clear, by the 1520s Edmund could only, indeed barely, afford one establishment, so it is highly unlikely that Catherine could have been born anywhere else. It was from his father that Edmund acquired his home on Church Street.[16]

Lambeth was, to use a modern term but ancient concept, a place of high property prices, favoured by the elite for its proximity to Westminster and the court, and in 1522 the Howards began construction of a family chapel within the pretty riverside church of St Mary-at-Lambeth. That chapel has now all but vanished, although the church itself remains, significantly renovated by the Victorians and preserved as a horticultural museum. As in Catherine's lifetime, the building nestles in the shadow of

Lambeth Palace, principal residence of the archbishops of Canterbury.

In the 1520s, the Church prohibited even the grandest families from carrying out private christenings in the intimate chapels that were ubiquitous in any aristocratic dwelling. Baptism inducted a soul into the community of the faithful, and so unless the baby looked likely to die shortly after its birth, the clergy insisted that christenings could only be carried out at the local parish church. Given her father's residency as a JP for Surrey and her family's ties to St Mary's, then the local parish church, it is more than probable that shortly after her birth, Catherine was brought to its porch by her godparents and midwife.[17] Regrettably, there is no record of who they were.

Baby Catherine had no right to look upon the interior of the church proper until she had been baptised. The local priest arrived in the porch to greet the baptismal party, which, as was customary, did not include the parents.[18] He inquired after the child's gender. When they told him that they had brought a girl, the padre placed Catherine on his left side – boys went to the right. As the door into the interior opened, the sign of the cross was made on Catherine's forehead, and the priest, his hand resting on her forehead, asked her name. After answering 'Catherine', her godparents handed the priest some salt and he put a little into Catherine's mouth. Prayers were intoned over her during the 'exorcism of the salt', a symbolic banishing of the taste of sin that the Devil had brought to Eden, and the sign of the cross was made over her forehead twice more. More homage was paid to Holy Scripture when the priest spat into his left hand, dipped the thumb of his right hand into the spittle, and rubbed it onto Catherine's nose and ears to remind the party of how Christ had healed a deaf and dumb man who sought His aid.[19] As the sign of the cross was made on Catherine's tiny right hand, the priest told her that all this was done 'so that you may sign yourself and repel yourself of the party of the Enemy. And may you remain in the Catholic faith and have eternal life and life for ever and ever. Amen.'[20] Now, at last, she could enter the hallowed ground, and before she passed from porch to church, the priest announced, 'Catherine, go into the temple of God.'

The clergyman, the baby, and her guardians took a few steps to the font, where Catherine was stripped of her christening robe and her godparents answered questions on her behalf, confirming not just her admission to the Catholic faith but also their role as sponsors of her spiritual development. Even if they did not speak Latin, the adults knew enough from a lifetime of services in that language to respond with '*Abrenuncio*' when the priest asked, '*Abrenuncias sathane?*' After renouncing the Devil, they responded with the same answer to the question, '*Et omnibus operibus eius?*' ('And all his works?') Likewise for the final question, '*Et omnibus pompis eius?*' ('And all his pomp?') With oil on his fingers, the priest made the sign of the cross on Catherine's chest and back, before asking the godparents, '*Quid petis?*' They answered that they sought '*Baptismum*'. To clarify that they wished to see her admitted to the eternal Church, the priest pressed, in ecclesiastical Latin, '*Vis baptizari?*' ('Do you wish to be baptised?') And they answered, simply, '*Volo.*' ('I do.') The priest then shifted Catherine in his arms so that her head faced the east, and he intoned the words, '*Et ego baptizo te in nomine patris*' just before he fully submerged her in the holy water. ('And I baptise you in the name of the Father.') Then he plucked the infant from the font, turned to face the south, immersed her again in the name of the Son and then, this time upside down, in the name of the Holy Spirit. Finally, the priest passed what was quite probably a crying baby into the arms of her most senior godparent, who held Catherine as she was bundled into a chrisom, a hooded robe that covered her forehead and body to preserve the signs of her baptism.

Her godparents held a candle in Catherine's little hands as the priest prayed, 'Receive a burning and inextinguishable light. Guard your baptism. Observe the charge, so that when the Lord comes to the wedding, you may be able to meet him with the saints in the hall of heaven.'[21] That duty was stressed to the godparents, who were also enjoined to make sure she knew her

Our Father, Hail Mary, and Apostles' Creed. Catherine was taken home in the borrowed chrisom; her mother would return the garment when she was ready to rejoin society.

Within a year or so of her birth, Catherine's father joined most of the other Howards at Framlingham Castle in Suffolk for his father's funeral. In May 1524, there was little outward sign that they all stood on the precipice of an unfamiliar world. The Reformation, the real undertaker of the Middle Ages, was not quite seven years old, and its influence had yet to be significantly felt by the majority of Tudor subjects. There was no deviation from the centuries-old Catholic liturgy as the Howards gathered to bury their patriarch, and saviour, Thomas Howard, 2nd Duke of Norfolk, dead at the age of eighty in the county of his birth.[22]

Unlike a christening, most aristocratic farewells in the sixteenth century were neither an intimate affair nor a single ceremony. The late duke had nine surviving children by the time he died in May 1524, several of whom had children of their own, giving Catherine kinship to most of the great landed families.[23] Catherine's aunt Elizabeth was married to Sir Thomas Boleyn, head of one of the wealthiest families in Kent and currently in pursuit of his right to succeed his Irish grandfather as Earl of Ormond.[24] Anne Howard was already a countess through her marriage to the head of the de Vere family. In the months preceding the duke's death, Edmund's unmarried sisters were affianced, and the fractious negotiations concerning their dowries and widows' rights were tidied up. The second youngest, also confusingly christened Elizabeth,* was betrothed to the heir of Lord Fitzwalter, another prominent East Anglian landowner.[25] Katherine, the youngest and fieriest of the late duke's daughters, was accompanied to the funeral by her

---

* To have two children with the same name was not unusual in an era with a relatively limited pool of Christian names and a custom for allowing godparents to pick a name at the christening ceremony. The 2nd Duke of Norfolk had two sons called Thomas and two daughters called Elizabeth. The aristocratic custom of a plethora of cosy nicknames arose from necessity's proverbial role as the mother of invention.

handsome if equally temperamental fiancé Rhys, scion of a successful political family in south Wales – Rhys had an ailing grandfather who was not expected to live much longer.[26] In Wales, the young man was known as Rhys ap Gruffydd, but the English often preferred to anglicise the couple's surname to 'Griffiths'.[27] The only Howard sister left unattached at the time of their father's funeral was Lady Dorothy, but her father had 'left for her Right, good substance to marry her with', and the family eventually arranged a wedding with the Earl of Derby.[28]

That will left Edmund's stepmother Agnes as one of the wealthiest independent women in England. As dowager duchess, she would no longer have access to Framlingham Castle as her home, but she had periodic use of Norfolk House in Lambeth and full-time access to a sizeable country estate near the village of Horsham in Sussex. With the exception the eldest son, none of the old duke's surviving children, including Edmund, expected much of a windfall from their father's final testament. While provisions were usually made to fund younger sons' education or early careers, to prevent the destruction of the family's patrimony by generations of division by bequests, the nobility endeavoured to pass the inheritance more or less intact to the next in line.[29] The other siblings' absence from the will was not therefore a matter for shock or confusion; younger sons could and often did parlay their family name and connections into successful careers of their own. One of the most remarkable aspects of the system was the extent to which even those left out of the posthumous treasure trove seemed to support it as necessary for the common good.

However, two of the Howard siblings had reason to rue the custom that dictated an undiluted inheritance for the new patriarch: Edmund and Anne, both of whom had come to rely on their father's help.[30] Anne was trapped in a miserable marriage to the twenty-five-year-old Earl of Oxford, who, two years earlier, had been sent to live in his father-in-law's household like an errant child when the royal court decided that his immoderate drinking, dereliction of duty, and reckless spending were besmirching one of the oldest names in the country.[31] With the duke dead, the chances of the adult earl being allowed to return to his hedonism were much improved, and Anne, like most wives, remained dependent on her husband's generosity.[32] For Edmund, his father's death robbed him of his principal benefactor and patron, adding to the financial worries afflicting him at the time of Catherine's birth.

In addition to a very large family, their surnames reading like a who's who of Henry VIII's England, the Duke of Norfolk's funeral was also attended by thousands of others, including 'many great Lords, and the Noble men of both Shires of Norfolk and Suffolk', who arrived at Framlingham to pay their respects to the old duke and solidify ties to the new.[33] The kaleidoscope of different servants' liveries danced through the other guests, the priests, monks, guards, squires, and common people who gathered in the shade of the castle's walls or lined the route to the Benedictine priory at Thetford, where the duke's tomb had been prepared.

When Framlingham's gates, crowned by the Howard coat of arms, swung open, the long cavalcade of choreographed grief snaked its way under the arch and down the hill, passing two artificial lakes, with a dovecote on the manmade island in the middle of the largest body of water. Combined, Framlingham's two lakes, which were constructed after the damming of a nearby stream, covered nearly twenty-three acres, a perfect reflecting pool for the castle's thirteen towers, slightly lowered on the Howards' order to further emphasise the impressive size of the walls. Fashionable red brick extensions, remodelled gardens, new chambers, and the latest in Renaissance design had also been added at the family's instructions.

As was customary for the aristocratic elite, a wax effigy topped the duke's bier, rendered as lifelike as possible by the artisans entrusted with the task. One hundred smaller wax effigies had been placed beneath it, representing those who mourned, while space for 700 candles had been set aside, so that even when it travelled at twilight or rested at night, the Duke of Norfolk, and through him the House of Howard, could be illuminated for those hoping to catch a glimpse. Four hundred men, hooded as a sign of mourning and penitence, were assigned to carry torches. Ten thousand people received charitable bequests under the terms of the duke's will, with the money paid out at the time of the funeral in the hope of encouraging prayers for his posthumous redemption, as well as to display the largesse that the aristocracy prided themselves on. In total, the funeral cost nearly £1,300, at a time when the average weekly income of a skilled worker was about twenty-six pence, and pre-decimalisation of the currency there were 240 pence in every pound.[34]

The Howards' quartered coat of arms was displayed on pennants and a thousand cloaks throughout the parade. Four lions could be found on the shield and one as the crest, the motif broken in the third quarter by a chequered blue-and-gold field that advertised their possession of the earldom of Surrey. The first quarter had the original Howard coat of arms scaled down to make room for the arms that proclaimed their descent from King Edward I, in the second quarter, and beneath that, the earls of Arundel.

No less than many of their contemporaries, Catherine's family were fascinated with the tangled limbs and roots of their family tree. She could claim distant descent from Adeliza of Louvain, a twelfth-century queen who was subsequently the Countess of Lincoln and Arundel.[35] Later generations of the Howards eulogised Adeliza, with only marginal exaggeration, as 'a Lady of transcendent beauty, grace and manner, of peculiar gentleness of disposition, added to true virtue and piety'.[36] However, there were other less exalted ancestors who had played a more deliberate role in pushing the Howards to the apex of English society – the first recorded mention of the family places them to the village of East Winch in Norfolk, about three centuries before Catherine's birth. From there, a family associated with law and commerce had risen through a shrewd policy of exemplary civil service, coupled with unions with the daughters of similarly wealthy businessmen and, eventually, the sons and daughters of the local nobility. They had been introduced to the court of King Edward I and used their money to raise troops for the king's wars and those of his son, Edward II.[37] In the fourteenth century, they had married into the powerful de Mowbray family, which eventually brought them the dukedom of Norfolk after they continued to serve the Crown and, crucially, supported the winning side in the dynastic conflicts of the 1400s.

Their luck seemed to have deserted them when the first Howard duke, John, enjoyed his new dukedom for just over two years, until he was killed supporting King Richard III at Bosworth Field in August 1485. That battle brought the Tudors to power after decades of exile on the Continent, and unsurprisingly they took a decidedly dim view of the Howards' Ricardian loyalties. Fortunately, unlike Edward IV or Richard III, Henry VII understood that irreversible punishments turned the aristocracy into implacable enemies. Instead of destroying the Howards, he therefore decided to demote them and then promote them again, at his pleasure. Luckily, the Howards had not lost their genetic knack for climbing and they proved adept at playing the unpleasant game the new king set for them.

John Howard's heir and Catherine Howard's future grandfather, thirty-nine-year-old Thomas, had also fought for King Richard III at Bosworth. Unlike his lord father, he was wounded but survived the battle.[38] Much was made later of Thomas's insistence that he would always fight for England's true king, regardless of who that king was, but even such protestations of patriotic zeal made over Richard III's not-quite-cold corpse were insufficient to convince the Tudors that Howard should go unpunished.[39] Henry VII could not afford to be seen as weak, particularly where the aristocracy was concerned. His late uncle, the deeply unfortunate Henry VI, had ended his life deposed and murdered in the Tower of London. For a medieval king, unfettered mercy could create as many problems as unchecked tyranny. Thomas Howard was therefore temporarily banned from inheriting his father's titles, a large slice of the Howard fortune was handed over to the Tudor loyalist, the Earl of Oxford, and Howard himself was sent to the Tower of London, where he spent the next three years as a prisoner.[40]

Having shown the potential of the stick, Henry VII moved to the carrot. In 1489, Thomas was allowed once again to style himself Earl of Surrey, a subsidiary title previously used as a courtesy by the Duke of Norfolk's eldest son and heir. Two years earlier, Thomas had an opportunity to gain his freedom from the Tower during the Earl of Lincoln's ill-fated rebellion against Tudor rule. He wisely chose to stay put to demonstrate that he remained faithful to his king, even while a prisoner – a decision for which he must have given hearty thanks after Henry VII remained secure on his throne and Lord Lincoln ended his life as a sword-pierced corpse.[41] When Thomas was eventually released from the Tower, he further proved his fidelity by helping to suppress anti-taxation riots in Yorkshire and deputising for the king's son, Prince Arthur, who, at the age of three, was understandably considered too young to police the Anglo-Scottish border himself.[42] In return for each act of service, another title, another piece of land, another sign of royal favour, was handed back to the Howards. Thomas's first wife, Elizabeth, became a lady-in-waiting to the new queen, Elizabeth of York, and eventually godmother to the king and queen's eldest daughter, Princess Margaret.[43] The Howard children were allowed to come to court, and the boys were given positions in the royal households.[44] The message from the Tudors' throne was clear, if not always easy to follow. Where Edward IV had turned the Howards into enemies whose only chance of prosperity lay with toppling his lineage, Henry VII had turned them into servitors whose hope lay in doglike obedience.[45]

Thomas Howard's tribe of children were expected to do their part in the rebuilding of the family – either through royal service, advantageous marriages, or both. The most spectacular match was that of the family's heir, young Thomas, who married Henry VII's sister-in-law, Anne of York; when she died in 1511, Thomas wed Henry VIII's cousin, Lady Elizabeth Stafford, the younger sister of the Duke of Buckingham.[46] The marriage of two of the Howard sisters, Elizabeth and Muriel, to members of relatively 'new' families like the Boleyns and the Knyvets, might seem curious given the numerous subsequent accounts of the era that describe them as families of knights or country gentlemen, apparently far removed from the aristocratic pedigree the Howards had built for themselves. However, the idea of a binary of gentry and aristocracy is a misleading modern conceit. The few centuries before Catherine's birth had seen enormous changes in the personnel of the elite – of the 136 lords who attended Parliament at the end of the thirteenth century, the direct descendants of only sixteen of them were around to perform similar duties at the start of the sixteenth.[47] The aristocratic caste was simply too narrow to socialise or marry solely within itself, particularly if it is defined as those in possession of, or the offspring of someone with, one of the five titles of the nobility – in ascending order in England, baron, viscount, earl, marquess, and duke, or their female equivalents, baroness, viscountess, countess, marchioness, and duchess. In everyday social interactions, the nuances of aristocratic etiquette drew little distinction between the children of respected gentry families and those from certain families in the nobility – for instance, the offspring of a viscount, a baron, or a gentleman were not entitled to style themselves 'lord' or 'lady', unlike those born to a duke, marquess, or earl.

To give an idea of how small the high nobility was as a group, compared to the thousands who thronged the court and enjoyed a privileged lifestyle, by 1523 there were only two dukes, one marquess, and thirteen earls in the combined English and Irish peerages.[48] Of those sixteen, fewer than half possessed a title that had been in the family for more than three generations. The idea of being 'gently born', meaning into a class of landowners who did not have to till their land themselves in order to generate an income from it, bonded the English upper classes together far more than a distinction between who was technically an aristocrat as opposed to a member of the gentry. Families like the Arundells, who owned 16,000 acres in the south-west, were technically 'only' gentry, but they were still referred to as a 'great' family by their contemporaries, and like most upper-class clans they benefited from their peers' tendency to count the maternal ancestry as being equally important as the paternal.[49] There was certainly a pecking order, and under Henry VIII it worked in the Howards' favour, but, as ever, people tolerate in their friends what they deplore in their enemies, and it was often only once people quarrelled over other things that truly vicious hauteur reared its head.[50]

The Howards' return to the dukedom they had lost at Bosworth was accomplished after twenty-nine years when, in 1514, Henry VIII restored the title in recognition of Thomas Howard's leadership of the English forces at the Battle of Flodden. Thomas Howard certainly showed no sense of snobbery towards his sons-in-law, and they seem to have been promoted and patronised alongside his own boys.[51] In his old age, those men continued to rise after he effectively retired from public life, spending most of his time, in his family's words, at the 'Castle of Framlingham, where he continued and kept an honourable house unto the hour of his death. And there he died like a good Christian prince.'[52]

At the burial ceremony itself, the priest chose to deliver his sermon on the text 'Weep not: behold, the Lion of the tribe of Judah, the Root of David, hath prevailed.'[53] Tribes, lions, and tenacity spoke to the Howards' souls. As the padre reached the crescendo of his terrifying homily, mixing panegyric with eschatology, the individual with the eternal, several of the congregation became so unsettled and afraid that they left the chapel. Once the hardier mourners had departed at a more decorous pace, the workmen arrived to begin construction of the duke's unique monument. From an incarcerated traitor to the king's right hand for defence of the realm, and paterfamilias of one of the largest aristocratic networks in northern Europe, was an extraordinary trajectory for any life, yet the duke died apparently torn between pride at his accomplishments and concern that in years to come observers would assume the worst regarding his loyalty in shifting allegiance from Edward V to Richard III to Henry VII. To prevent this, his tomb boasted a lengthy carved account of his life,

which constantly stressed his service to the Crown, irrespective
of its incumbent. Over a year later, long after Edmund had
returned to Lambeth, his wife, and their growing brood of children, work on the tomb was complete and Catherine's grandfather rested in splendour.[54]

Chapter 3

Lord Edmund's Daughter

Anger makes dull men witty, but it keeps them poor.

– Elizabeth I (1533–1603)

Edmund Howard cannot have been thrilled at the arrival of another daughter. Girls required dowries and Edmund was already struggling financially. Catherine had the bad luck to be born to a man who peaked long before he became a father. Edmund was a toxic combination of corrupt, unstable, and pathetic, but he had not always been that. Those who knew him in his youth described Catherine's father as 'a courage and an hardy young lusty gentleman'.[1] One of seven sons, but the third to reach adulthood, he had his father's and brothers' athletic capabilities, but lacked their acute social intelligence. He had spent most of his childhood at court as a pageboy in the service of King Henry VII, like his elder brother Edward, and the upward trajectory of his family after Bosworth seemed to promise a life of plenty. During the festivities for Henry VIII's coronation in 1509, Edmund and his two elder brothers were part of a group of 'fresh young gallants and noble men gorgeously apparelled' who were asked to lead a tourney at the Palace of Westminster.[2] The roll call of those invited to fight alongside him suggests that only the best jousters were chosen, and with good reason, given how much had been spent.

Jousting mingled with a pageant was a relatively new kind of entertainment at the English court, with its combination of set pieces atop moving stages, music, dialogue, and mock combat. In Europe, it had long ago been transformed into an art form, with some celebrations recreating the city of Troy or the twelve labours of Hercules, complete with mechanised monsters and giants. Artistic ingenuity rubbed uneasily with a sportsman's zeal, and it was not always clear how choreographed the fighting should be. At a tournament performed before Pope Clement V, even the horses had been reduced to moving props manoeuvred by six men concealed beneath cloth; a recent pageant for Cesare Borgia in the city of Ferrara saw the 'dead' combatants fall to the ground in a beautifully executed dance, before standing to take their bows. In contrast, an entertainment in honour of Queen Isabeau of France saw real knights sparring in front of the royal party for several hours.[3] In England, the men of Henry VIII's court seemed keener to follow the French example than the Italian.

Rather than a typical outdoor arena, like those used for a joust, the men fought in an elaborate fairy-tale set, as members of the court looked on and placed bets. A miniature castle had been built within the courtyard – miniature, at least, in comparison to its inspiration. Tudor roses and engraved pomegranates, Katherine of Aragon's device, lined its walls, while a fountain splashed water in front of it. In the spirit of Sybaris, the little castle's gargoyles spouted red, white, and claret wines to the delight of the audience. The entirely artificial ivy that wrapped this *folie* was 'gilded with fine gold'. Edmund, by no means the least competitive of the group, rode forward from the castle to ask the king's permission to fight for the honour of the court *belle* who had been given the role of Pallas Athena, the chaste embodiment of wisdom. Royal permission gave way to a testosterone-fuelled spectacle of egotism. The participants' vitality and their determination were well matched, and the joust only halted at nightfall. The next day, the king and queen prevented the match resuming by stepping in to pre-emptively select the winners for themselves.[4]

In the years to come, the court lost none of its allure for Edmund. A brief, half-hearted and failed attempt to pursue a legal career did not get much further than enrolling in London's prestigious Middle Temple in 1511.[5] Within ten days of his admission to the Temple, Edmund was back at court to participate in another set of jousts, this time to mark the birth of the Duke of Cornwall, the king's short-lived son and heir. Henry VIII, a tall and muscular youth blessed with the good looks of his grandfather Edward IV, was, at nineteen, keen to participate rather than simply observe as he had two years earlier.[6] In recognition of Edmund's skills, he was asked to lead the defenders; his brother-in-law, Sir Thomas Boleyn, was on the same team, as was Charles Brandon, the king's handsome and womanising favourite. Once again, the royal household spared no expense to celebrate such an important event. The queen and her ladies gazed down from a box hung with arras and cloth of gold on a forest crafted from green velvet, satin, and 'silks of divers colours', complete with artificial rocks, hills, dales, arranged flowers, imported ferns, and grass. In the middle of the forest, the workmen had rendered another miniature castle 'made of gold'. A manmade lion, 'flourished all over with Damask gold', and an antelope clothed in silver damask were flanked by men disguised as wildlings from a mythical forest, who escorted the bejewelled beasts as they dragged the final pieces of the pageant into place in front of the queen. Horns blasted, and parts of the set fell away to reveal four knights on horseback 'armed at all places, every of them in cloth of gold, every of them his name embroidered'. These were Edmund's opponents, the challengers, and their captain was the young king, joined by another of Edmund's brothers-in-law, Sir Thomas Knyvet, and a clique of companions, all of whom had been given aliases that married amorous devotion with masculine honour. The king led the charge with his pseudonym of Coeur Loyale ('Loyal Heart'), while Sir Edward Neville, another teammate, got 'Valiant Desire'.[7] Knyvet, who got the part of Ardent Desire, joked that his character's name would be better suited to his codpiece.[8] The sounds of the trumpets gave way to the beating of the drums that announced the arrival of these challengers, dressed in armour and crimson satin.

Edmund's slot came on the following day, 13 February, when the entertainments began with Thomas Boleyn and the Marquess of Dorset arriving in the costumes of pilgrims en route to the shrine of Santiago de Compostela, a holy site in the queen's Spanish homeland reputed to be the burial place of Saint James the Apostle. They knelt before the 'mighty and excellent princess and noble Queen of England' to ask permission to joust in her presence; the queen graciously acquiesced and her husband returned to the fantastic tiltyard.[9] An account of the joust, containing a tally of the scores of each knight, divided along the lines of their respective teams, survives today in the Bodleian Library at Oxford. In thin scratches of black ink, it lists Edmund Howard's mistakes.[10]

The athletic Charles Brandon parried well, superbly in fact, but after an acceptable length of time in the tilt, without fail he yielded to the king by a margin or tied with him, a masterstroke of hail-and-hearty camaraderie that suggested that when the king triumphed it was because he was the better sportsman. Every one else followed suit and let the king win, except Edmund, who beat him every time. Lances splintered and sweat-drenched men cried out, while noblemen and 'well-apparelled' servants watched as Edmund Howard repeatedly sent the nineteen-year-old monarch crashing to the ground.[11] It was said that a banquet afterwards ended with 'mirth and gladness', but that was mainly because the decision to let some of the common people take away as souvenirs the solid gold letters and decorations hanging from the courtiers' costumes had resulted in poor Thomas Knyvet practically being stripped naked by zealous trophy hunters.[12]

Nearly all the men who participated in the Westminster jousts of February 1511 went on to rise further in the king's graces, with the exception of Edmund. Three months later, Edmund was not asked to join in another set of jousts at the king's side, while his elder brothers and his brothers-in-law were. Two years after those Westminster jousts, and the funeral of the little baby prince they had celebrated but who did not live to see his eighth week, the king went off to war against France, and he did not invite Edmund to accompany him. Henry VIII's dreams of recapturing the martial glory days of Edward III or Henry V proved costly to the Howard family – Edmund's elder brother Edward, who had become a favourite of the king's, drowned in a naval battle against the forces of Louis XII. Despite the attacks Edward had led against Scottish ships, King James IV chivalrously told Henry VIII in a letter that Edward Howard's life and talents had been wasted in Henry's pointless war.[13] Edmund's brother-in-law and former jousting companion, Thomas Knyvet, was likewise lost at sea when his ship went up in flames at the Battle of Saint-Mathieu. Knyvet's widow and Edmund's sister, Muriel, died in childbirth four months later. Another of Edmund's brothers, Henry, seems to have died of natural causes the following February, and been buried at Lambeth, less than a year after the death of another brother, Charles.[14]

The war that took his brother's life provided Edmund Howard with the opportunity to achieve the high point of his career. In the king's absence, the northernmost English county of Northumberland was invaded by Scotland, France's ally, who 'spoiled burnt and robbed divers and sundry towns and places'.[15] It was quite possibly the largest foreign army ever to invade English soil – 400 oxen were needed to drag the mammoth cannon across the border.[16] Queen Katherine of Aragon, left behind as regent, 'raised a great power to resist the said King of Scots', and placed it under the command of Edmund's father.[17] Katherine had been forced to marshal an army quickly, and they were bedevilled by the war's ongoing problem of poor supplies. By the time they actually engaged the Scots, many of the 26,000 English soldiers had been without wine, ale, or beer for five days.[18] In an age when weak ale, or 'small beer', was often supplied to prevent people drinking from dubious or unknown water supplies, its absence as the army moved north was felt keenly.[19]

At the Battle of Flodden, which took place on 9 September 1513, Edmund was given command of the right flank on the 'uttermost part of the field at the west side', with three subordinate knights serving as lieutenants over fifteen hundred men, mostly from Lancashire and Cheshire.[20] When they were 'fiercely' attacked by the soldiers of Lord Hume, Edmund's personal standard, and his standard-bearer, were hacked to pieces on the field, at which point most of Edmund's men turned and fled.[21] If his talents as a leader failed, his courage did not. With only a handful of loyal servants remaining by his side, Edmund was 'stricken to the ground' on three separate occasions. Each time, according to a contemporary account, 'he recovered and fought hand to hand with one Sir Davy Home, and slew him'.[22] A wounded soldier called John Heron returned to fight at Edmund's side, declaring, 'There was never noble man's son so like to be lost as you be this day, for all my hurts I shall here live and die with you.'[23] Edmund's life was only saved by the arrival of cavalry headed by Lord Dacre, who rode in 'like a good and an hardy knight' to rescue Edmund from annihilation and bring him through the cadavers to kneel at his father's feet, where he learned that 'by the grace, succour and help of Almighty God, victory was given to the Realm of England' and received a knighthood, an honour bestowed on about forty-five of his comrades who had also shown exceptional bravery in the melee.[24]

The scale of the Scottish defeat stunned as much as their mighty guns had when they first crossed the border – the corpse of King James was found 'having many wounds, and naked', lying in egalitarian horror with about eight thousand of his subjects, including nine earls, fourteen lords, a bishop, two abbots, and an archbishop.[25] There was hardly a family in the Scottish nobility who escaped bereavement after Flodden; particularly heartbreaking was the example of the Maxwell clan – Lord Maxwell fell in combat within minutes of all four of his brothers.[26] In the immediate aftermath of the carnage, many English soldiers were spotted wearing badges that showed the white lion, the Howards' heraldic crest, devouring the red lion, an ancient symbol of Scotland.[27] English writers later praised the Scots' 'singular valour', but at the time soldiers on the field were so repulsed by the violence that they refused to grant amnesty to the captured prisoners.[28] Queen Katherine shared the attitude of the troops with the victorious lion badges. Edmund's father wanted to give King James's remains a proper burial; he, and several councillors, had to talk the queen out of her original plan of sending the body to Henry as a token of victory. The queen relented. She dispatched James's blood-soaked coat to her husband instead of his body and jokingly cast herself as a good little housewife in the accompanying letter, which contained the rather repulsive quip, 'In this your grace shall see how I can keep my pennies, sending you for your banners a King's coat. I thought to send himself unto you, but our Englishmen's hearts would not suffer it.'[29]

Flodden provided the exorcism for Bosworth, and a few months later, on the Feast of Candlemas, the Howards' dukedom was restored to them.[30] Edmund's bravery was commented upon by his contemporaries, but an anonymous and spiteful letter, regaling the king with the story of how Edmund's men had deserted him, 'caused great heart burning and many words'.[31] The king was furious, and it took a lot for his courtiers to calm him down to the point where he ruled that no one should be punished for the crime and humiliation of flight from the field. Nonetheless, the deliberately leaked news meant that there was no escaping the fact the Edmund's division had been the only section of the English forces to sustain a defeat at Flodden. This might explain why Edmund's sole reward from the Crown was a daily pension of three shillings and four pence, an amount that could generously be described as nominal.[32]

Still, he was able to bask in the reflected glow of his father and benefit from the general climate of exultation, or relief, after the battle. In the autumn of the following year, the government gave Edmund £100 to equip himself in suitable finery for jousting at another major royal event, the marriage of the king's youngest sister to King Louis XII of France, as the living seal on the post-war treaty. In Edmund's own words, he was 'to prepare myself to do feat of arms in the parts of France at jousts and tourneys' during the celebrations.[33] In a theme that was to repeat itself throughout most of their subsequent diplomacy, the English and French vied to outshine one another, with the result that peace between them was less bloody but hardly more cordial than war. Edmund was sent with his father, stepmother, and half sister, the Countess of Oxford, in a delegation that included a hundred horses, numerous retainers, and suitably lavish outfits to conform with the government's request that everything should be done to advertise the wealth of Henry's kingdom.[34]

At least by then Edmund had steady employment as a justice of the peace in Surrey, thanks in no small way to his family's influence there.[35] Tasked with preserving order in the localities, the JPs and their deputies were supposed to arrest criminals, keep a watch on troublemakers, maintain law and order, supervise foreign nationals, levy fines, and make sure food prices were being set at a fair rate. For the next few years Edmund appears in government documents arranging for safe conduct for a group of Prussian friars on a pilgrimage to Scotland, interrogating six suspected French spies, adjudicating on the alleged kidnapping of a maid by her employers who disapproved of her choice of husband, confining a constable called William Bever to the stocks on Lambeth High Street as punishment for ransacking a man's house in the search for French agents, and obeying government orders to carry out a hunt for vagrants.[36]

Approaching forty, he found a wife in Joyce Leigh, a widow with five children from her first marriage to another local official.[37] Joyce, whom the Howards tended to refer to by the slightly grander name of 'Jocasta', was nearly the same age as her new husband; she had first been married off at the age of twelve, then left a woman of substance by both her father and her first husband.[38] Her money as well as her standing within the Lambeth community were useful to Edmund, since by 1514 there were signs that he was accumulating debts and that the blue-blooded security conveyed by his visit to France for the royal wedding was a slowly unravelling illusion.[39]

In November 1519, shortly after his marriage to Joyce, riots in Surrey resulted in Edmund being hauled in front of the Star

Chamber, a panel set up to administer justice to the kingdom's elite if there was a fear that common courts and judges might be too intimidated to hand down a fair sentence on a nobleman. As a body, the chamber was particularly concerned with the maintenance of public order. Consisting of legal experts from the common courts and members of the Privy Council, the royally appointed body of men that still constituted the main organ of government in early Tudor England, the Star Chamber could pass its defendants over to the commons if they felt their misdemeanours constituted crimes that could and should be adequately and publicly punished. The Star Chamber played on concepts of honour and the corresponding power of shame to bully errant peers into compliance. Even if they were pardoned, as many of them were, the summonses alone were enough to set tongues wagging.

The relationship between rulers and ruled in Tudor England was characterised by elaborate anxiety. Political theorists, such as Sir Thomas Elyot who published his treatise on good government in 1531, preached that 'everything is order, and without order nothing may be stable or permanent'.[40] This belief was occasionally both shaken and strengthened by the fact that the century proved to be one of social mobility, wider literacy, growing towns, and an expanding population. Elite views of social unrest were inevitably influenced by their own childhood curriculums that were generally heavy on the classics, in which rebellion was cited as a chief cause for the fall of Ancient Rome, encouraging a belief that popular protest led to mob rule, 'which of all rules is most to be feared'.[41] No one wanted the poor to be miserable, but nearly everyone wanted them to be obedient. In both town and countryside, outdoor and entertaining activities were encouraged in every season, because it was understood that people needed to enjoy themselves and, in doing so, dissipate their energy.

The belief that the plebeian urban classes were naturally credulous, easily distracted, and prone to overreaction placed the blame for any outburst of civil unrest squarely on the shoulders of their immediate superiors. Edmund and a colleague 'were indicted of riots, and maintenance of bearings of diverse misdoers within the county of Surrey'.[42] The recent disturbances in the county were a poor reflection on the king's deputies, and Edmund's fiery temper, or ill standing with the sovereign, did not help. Both defendants were shamed but pardoned, while another, Lord Ogle, was passed over to the common courts after riots blamed on his dereliction of duty resulted in the death of a bystander.[43]

The years following the Star Chamber hearing saw Edmund's career stagnate and his debts increase. Joyce Howard's properties were mortgaged and remortgaged, despite opposition from her mother and stepfather. Years earlier, after the death of Joyce's father, Richard Culpepper, who had been a wealthy landowner in Kent, her mother Isabel had remarried to Sir John Leigh then swiftly arranged a wedding between Joyce and John's younger brother, Ralph. This meant that John and Isabel had a doubly vested interest in monitoring Joyce's inheritance, with Isabel mindful of the Culpepper estates and John equally concerned about the disposal of the Leigh bequests from Joyce's first husband.[44] The couple evidently came to distrust Edmund Howard, and both their wills attempted to limit his ability to interfere in their daughter or grandchildren's inheritance.

This distrust was not entirely undeserved – Edmund's debts had all but taken over his life by 1527. Despite being a public figure tasked with the maintenance of the law, on one occasion Catherine's father had only dodged arrest as a debtor thanks to a tip-off from a friend.[45] Aristocratic poverty, of course, was not quite the same as the agony of the actual condition, and the names of at least two of Lord Edmund's servants crop up in subsequent correspondence.[46] But by the end of the 1520s, he was undeniably struggling and badly so, to the extent that he began to borrow heavily from his friends, even persuading one, John Shookborough, to stand as surety for his debts.[47] The idea of getting another job, a profession that would pay a consistent wage, was considered abhorrent, something that would bring 'great reproach and shame to me and all my blood', in Edmund's words. At least on the surface, he claimed to resent the position he was born into, citing his aristocratic heritage as something that had condemned him to a life of genteel struggle.

Perhaps such woeful excuse-making was why his relatives' aid seems to have dried up between 1524 and 1531, a time when Edmund became increasingly desperate. During one spell of hiding to avoid the possibility of being apprehended by his creditors, he sent his wife to petition Cardinal Wolsey, the king's then chief minister, on his behalf. According to his accompanying letter to the cardinal, unless Edmund received financial help he would either have to seek sanctuary in a religious institution or flee abroad. The panic and unhappiness apparent in Edmund's letter remains uncomfortable to read. Quotations from it are usually cited in the various biographies of Catherine, but it is by reading the majority of the text – including his astonishing offer to serve on a mission to the Americas – that one can fully appreciate the depth of Edmund Howard's desperation. Addressed to 'My Lord Cardinal's Grace', in haste, it reads:

> My duty remembered, humbly I beseech your grace to [be] my good Lord, for with out your gracious help I am utterly undone. Sir so it is that I am so far in danger of the King's laws by reason of the debt that I am in, that I dare not go a broad, nor come at mine own house, and am fain to absent me from my wife and my poor children, there is such writs of executions out against me; and also such as be my sureties are daily arrested, and put to great trouble, which is to my great shame and rebuke. Sir there is no help but through your Grace and your good mediation to the King's Grace, in the which is my singular trust: and your gracious favour showed unto me ... shall not only be meritorious but shall be the safeguard of my life and relief of my poor wife and our ten children, and set me out of debt. And humbly I beseech your Grace for such poor service as I have done the King's Grace, and trust for to do, that I be not cast away;

and if the King's Grace or your Grace should command me
to do any service I would trust to do acceptable service; and
liver I had to be in his Grace's service at the farthest end of
Christendom than to live thus wretchedly, and die with
thought, sorrow and care. I may repent that ever I was
nobleman's son born, leading the sorrowful life that I live,
and if I were a poor man's son I might dig and delve for my
living and my children and my wife's, for whom I take more
thought than for my self: and so may I not do but to great
reproach and shame to me and all my blood. Sir if there be
any creature living that can lay to me other treason, murder,
felony, rape, extortion, bribery, or in maintaining or
supporting any of these, and to be approved on me, then let
me have the extremity of the King's laws; and I trust there
shall none lay against me any thing to be approved to my
reproach but only debt. Sir I am informed there shall be a
voyage made in to a newfound land with divers ships and
captains and sogears [soldiers or sea-goers?] in them; and I
am informed the voyage shall be honourable and profitable
to the King's Grace and all his realm. Sir if your Grace think
my poor carcass any thing meet to serve the King's Grace in
the said voyage, for the better passion of Christ be you my
good lord there in, for now I do live a wretched a life as ever
did gentleman being a true man, and nothing I have to live
on, nor to find me my wife and my children meat or drink;
and glad I would be to venture my life to do the King's
service, and if I be put there unto I doubt not but I shall do
such service as shall be acceptable and redound to his
Grace['s] honour. And Sir I have nothing to lose but my life,
and that I would gladly adventure in his service trusting
thereby to win some honesty, and to get somewhat toward
my living; and if it shall please the King's Grace to have my
body do him service in the said voyage, humbly I beseech
your Grace that I may know your pleasure therein. Sir I
ensure you there shall be nothing nor nother friend nor kin
let me, but with a willing heart I will go, so it shall stand

with the King's pleasure and yours. The King's Grace being so good lord to me through your good mediation ... and assign my bill the which I now do sue for, or to set me out of debt some other ways. Sir I beseech your Grace to pardon me that I came not to your Grace myself according to my duty, but surely Sir I dare not go a broad, and therefore I have been thus bold to write to your Grace. All the premises considered I humbly beseech your Grace to be my good lord, for the passion of Christ and in the way of charity and piety. I beseech your Grace to pardon me for this my bold writing, but very poverty and need forceth me thus to do, as knoweth our Lord Jesus, who have you in his blessed tuysseone. Written with the hand of him that is assuredly yours, Edmund Howard, Knight.[48]

If help did come from Wolsey, it was piecemeal. Edmund was head of a large household, which added to his financial woes. The elder girls, Isabella and Margaret, along with Catherine's full siblings Charles, Henry, George, another Margaret, and their younger sister Mary, were all still living at home. Interestingly, a later survey also mentions Jane Howard, a sister born after Mary, who, if she existed at all, must have been born after 1527 and died in infancy, perhaps sometime after 1530.[49] Catherine's two eldest half brothers, John and Ralph, had moved out when she was a child. On turning twenty-four, John inherited a manor in Stockwell from his grandfather, and Ralph had been left a trust fund to finance his training as a lawyer in London. Her half sister Joyce was also married and out of the house.[50] Even by including Jane, Edmund's claim that he had to maintain ten children in 1527 does not seem to be entirely accurate, but debt seldom stimulates a compulsion toward honesty.

Catherine's early life is thus difficult to trace – one of the youngest in a large family amid a wealth of contradictions. She possessed one of the most respected surnames in the country, but at least initially it brought her little in terms of material comfort or security. Her father was theoretically one of the pillars of the local community, but in practice he spent most of her childhood hiding from his creditors and resorting to increasingly desperate methods to get his hands on the money they needed. Whether her time in her father's household was happy or not, we have no way of knowing. It was certainly short. Her mother died in about 1528 or 1529 and her father swiftly remarried, to another widow, Dorothy Troyes. This marriage, too, seems to have been short, since Dorothy's will was made in the early summer of 1530, by which point Catherine's first cousin, Anne Boleyn, was firmly established at court as queen-to-be.[51] Anne possessed the natural assertiveness that bordered on bossiness common in someone who was often found, or believed herself, to be more competent than those around her. She set out to find her hapless uncle Edmund a job, and when the death of Sir William Hussey opened up a vacancy for the post of comptroller to the civic authorities at the port of Calais, she pounced.[52] Putting Edmund in the post of comptroller with its heavy financial duties was a little like putting the poacher in charge of the game. With unintentional irony, the decision was finalised on April Fool's Day 1531.[53]

For Edmund, the chance to get safely across the Channel could not have come at a more opportune time. Within a few months of his departure, his friend John Shookborough had been arrested as guarantor for Edmund's debts. Realising that the net was closing around him, and horrified to discover the extent of his friend's financial deceptions, Shookborough tried to catch the attention of Thomas Cromwell as he attended Mass at the Augustinian friary near his home in Austin Friars, hopeful that a message could be passed on to the court through him. Unfortunately, Cromwell did not see Shookborough in the crowd, and as the latter returned into the city, he was arrested for £26 of Lord Edmund's debts. In a letter to Cromwell he admitted, 'I am surety for more, and dare not go abroad in the city.' To avoid prison, Shookborough had to pledge two of his family's best items of clothing to the creditors, and he offered Cromwell a gelding 'for your favour' in helping him out of the mess in which friendship with Edmund had landed him.[54]

Edmund arrived in Calais on St Nicholas's Day 1531, amid the December chill, with an introductory letter from Anne Boleyn clutched in his hands. He took it to the town's vice treasurer, Thomas Fowler, who was canny enough to realise the tacit instructions implicit in Anne's avalanche of complimentary charm: 'At his coming here on St Nicholas Day,' he told his brother, 'he [Edmund] brought me a letter from my lady Anne, directed to you and me, which my lord commanded me to open, giving us great thanks for our kindness to my lord Edmund.'[55]

At some point between April and December 1531, between the announcement of Edmund's new post and his assumption of his duties, his household in Surrey was broken up. Two of the girls were married – Isabella Leigh to Sir Edward Baynton, a widowed courtier with seven young children, and Margaret Howard to Thomas Arundell, a close friend of the Earl of Northumberland and son of a Cornish gentry family who were wealthy enough not to need a sizeable dowry.[56] Edmund's other children were old enough to begin the process of education in another's household; we do not know where the others went, but both Catherine and, at some unknown point, her brother Henry, were invited to live as wards of their wealthiest female relative, the Dowager Duchess of Norfolk.

Chapter 4

The Howards of Horsham

But oh, young babies, whom blood … hath endowed
with grace, comeliness, and high ability … it were
great pity but that ye added to sovereign beauty
virtue and good manners.

– Dr Furnivall, 'The Babees' Book or A Little
Report on how young people should
behave' (*c.*1475)

When Catherine Howard arrived in the Sussex village of Horsham
in 1531, she had every reason to feel thankful for the fact that her
gender had spared her a grammar school education similar to
those endured by her grandfather and many of her peers.[1]
Contemporary gossip was rife with horror stories of how young,
upper-class boys were disciplined at their boarding schools – the
philosopher Erasmus of Rotterdam relayed tales of students
beaten nearly to the point of unconsciousness by their masters,
forced to swallow salt, vinegar, or urine as a form of punishment,
and how the schools ran on 'howling and sobbing and cruel
threatenings'.[2] When Elizabeth I, 'being a learned Princess',
visited Westminster School a few decades later, schools' reputation for unchecked corporal punishment was so widespread that
she bypassed the official meet-and-greet to talk directly to one
pupil 'of a fair, and ingenious countenance'. The queen stroked

the young man's head and 'demanded him to tell her how often he had been whipped'. The boy paused, but 'being witty' he answered the royal query by quoting Virgil's *Aeneid*, 'Most gracious Queen, you do desire to know, / A grief unspeakable and full of woe.'[3]

Instead, Catherine, about eight or nine years old in 1531, could expect her education to be conducted privately through a set of tutors chosen by her grandmother, whose principal manor, Chesworth House, sat on the edge of Horsham village, where life continued in much the same way as it had for decades. The Howard influence in Horsham remained strong. They hand-selected its Member of Parliament, often predictably picking a member of their extended family. The provisions needed to feed, clothe, and heat the dowager and her staff accounted for a significant chunk of the area's economy, a relationship replicated across Tudor England, where the nobility stimulated and sustained the employment of tens of thousands of people – not just those who farmed and traded in the supplies they needed, but also those who served them. From the figures available to us, it seems that nearly two-thirds of people aged between fifteen and twenty-four worked as servants in this period, either to the aristocracy or to the middle classes, and somewhere between a quarter and half of the total population were in domestic service at some point in their lives.[4]

Like most girls with a similar background, Catherine had grown up with servants, but the sheer number she saw as she was led across the drawbridge of her grandmother's pretty moated manor at Chesworth could not have been a familiar sight.[5] Even if widows usually kept smaller households than a married noble-woman, the scale of the dowager's establishment would have been difficult to comprehend for a young girl who had spent her infancy at the mercy of her father's financial fluctuations. As the fourth highest-ranking woman in the kingdom, Agnes Howard did not keep a small household.[6] It would have been considered unseemly for her to do so. Etiquette guides from the time suggested it was appropriate for a duke or duchess to have about

240 servants.[7] As with most manners manuals, this was only a guideline, and some peers, such as the late Duke of Buckingham who employed nearly 500, preferred to live on the larger side.[8]

In the courtyard at Chesworth House, or Chesworth Place as it was sometimes known, Catherine got her first sight of the dozens of men and women who attended her grandmother.[9] The chief household officers, like the steward who essentially ran the establishment, the treasurer, and the chaplain, Father Borough, who looked after the house's religious valuables and spiritual needs, wore cloaks sporting the dowager's personal coat of arms in bright threads as they walked to or from their offices, all of which were located within the house proper. The chaplain's deputy, the almoner, was in charge of arranging for charity to be given to the local poor and for any food that was left uneaten to be distributed at the manor gates. Valets, whose job was very different to their more famous Edwardian counterparts, might be on their way to check on the grain stock in the stables, while young grooms cleaned out the stalls nearby. Little pageboys, the only servants likely to be on a pittance of a salary or none at all, ran through the house carrying messages, fulfilling errands from their superiors, and trying to find time to attend training to work in another part of the household once they were older. The servants certainly had enough tasks to keep them occupied. Chesworth had its own orchard, slaughterhouse, large kitchens, a pantry to oversee the production and storage of bread, a buttery that stored the manor's ale, beers, and wine, and a great hall where the household dined and the dowager could entertain her guests. A career in service was not considered in any way demeaning – society was hierarchical, and the rewards and security offered by employment with the aristocracy were substantial. All the servants wore uniforms and they were expected to conform to expectations that a good servant should be 'neatly clad, his clothes not torn, hands and faces well washed and head well kempt'.[10]

As Catherine was ushered down Chesworth's long corridors, the signs of her grandmother's fortune were everywhere. This was a woman so wealthy that she kept £800 in silver around the house in case of an emergency; to give an idea of the scale of that hoarding, one of Catherine's aunts had been expected to maintain a family and a household on about £50 a few years earlier, another lived comfortably on £196.[11] Cleaners bustled around placing reeds and rushes on the floor or sweeping them away for hygiene's sake once they became too dirty. When they entered the dowager's presence, Catherine and her brother were expected to bow or curtsey and to repeat that action in miniature every time she asked them a question, 'otherwise, stand as still a stone'.[12] Like their servants, they were taught that it was impolite to sigh, cough, or breathe too loudly in the lady of the house's presence.[13]

The abundance on display at Chesworth underscored why Edmund Howard was considered such a failure by his contemporaries. Consumption and display were part of the nobility's duty, a clause in the social contract, by which they generated work for those around them and upheld the class system whose origins were believed to mirror Heaven's. As part of his Christmas celebrations a few years earlier, Catherine's uncle Thomas, Duke of Norfolk, had hosted a dinner for 580 guests one night and then another for 399 five days later.[14] A frugal aristocrat was a source of universal contempt in the sixteenth century; an indebted one even more so.

The Dowager Duchess of Norfolk was only fifty-four years old when Catherine first came into her care. The daughter of two gentry families from Lincolnshire, Agnes had come to the late duke's attention when his first wife, Agnes's kinswoman, passed away. Agnes's brother Philip had then been the duke's steward, a position often given to members of one's extended affinity, and despite – or because of – the fact that he was nearly thirty-five years older, the duke was sufficiently smitten with Agnes's charms to marry her regardless of the fact that she brought him little in the way of a dowry. She was thus technically Catherine's step-grandmother, since Edmund was born from the duke's first marriage.

Agnes's late husband had left her twenty-four manors, and the tetchy, opinionated dowager used them to finance a life of luxury and convenience, expressing her opinions as and when they came to her. She wrote chatty letters full of unsolicited medical advice to Cardinal Wolsey, perhaps patronised poets including, quite possibly, the famous John Skelton, and made sarcastic quips at the expense of everyone from the royal court to her stepson the Duke of Norfolk.[15] During an outbreak of the plague in 1528, she told a visitor that the reason the sickness had affected some of the duke's servants was the slipshod management of his household staff.[16] Time was to show that Agnes did not have a firm hand on the rudder of her own retinue either, but like most witty people she did not let accusations of hypocrisy stand in the way of a memorable put-down. She was a generous employer, an inveterate gossip, and conscious of the magnificence of her position – one of the many jewels she owned was a personalised initial 'A', crafted from pearls and set with diamonds.[17] To her wards, the dowager duchess was a strict but inconsistent guardian. The pearls, the diamonds, and the lady herself were often away from Catherine for extended periods, mainly at court.[18]

In the meantime, Catherine settled into life at Chesworth and its acres of fine deer-hunting country.[19] Our image of a rough-and-tumble Tudor England, replete with belching men with earthy appetites gnawing at chicken legs, and buxom serving wenches, is not a world that Catherine or her contemporaries would have recognised. From infancy, she was expected to learn etiquette and to behave appropriately. Guides and manuals from the era laid out in great detail how the children of the gentry and nobility should behave from the moment they woke up in the morning – 'Arise from your bed, cross your breast and your forehead, wash your hands and face, comb your hair, and ask the grace of God to speed you in all your works; then go to Mass and ask mercy for all your trespasses. When ye have done, break your fast with good meat and drink, but before eating cross your mouth, your diet will be better for it. Then say your grace – it occupies but little time – and thank the Lord Jesus for your food and drink. Say also a *Pater Noster* and *Ave Maria* for the souls that lie in pain' – to how long they should nap and how they should enter a room.[20] When Catherine was brought into her grandmother's company she was expected to 'enter with head up and at an easy pace' and say 'God speed' by way of greeting, before sinking into a curtsey.[21] Obeisance was worked on ad nauseam. A clumsy dip was an embarrassment that no girl could afford in Tudor high society; one Howard had a servant repeat a perfect bow a hundred times after the poor man had been in such a rush that he admitted his previous attempt had been made on 'a running leg'.[22] Catherine was told to look straight at whoever was speaking to her, to listen carefully to whatever they were saying, to make sure they knew that she was paying attention – 'see to it with all your might that ye jangle not, nor let your eyes wander about' – and 'with blithe visage and diligent spirit' set herself to the task of being as charming and interesting as possible. Her anecdotes and stories should be entertaining and to the point, since too 'many words are right tedious to the wise man who listens; therefore eschew them'.[23] Above all, she must learn to act like a lady in front of her relatives – to stand until they told her otherwise, to keep her hands and feet still, never to lean on anything, or scratch any part of herself, even something as innocuous as her face or arms.[24]

This curriculum was part of the rationale behind the farming out of English aristocratic children to their relatives, a custom which foreign visitors often found peculiar. It was believed that parents might spoil or indulge their own children and thus neglect their education. Even if Edmund had not gone to Calais, Catherine would at some point probably have found herself attached to the dowager's household. It was not just her new home, but her classroom and her finishing school where she would learn by example to behave like the great ladies of her family. Like the generation before her, Catherine was taught that good manners were essential to 'all those that would thrive in prosperity'.[25] Etiquette was drilled into her at a young age and into hundreds of other girls just like her. One of her cousins was praised for being 'stately and upright at all times of her age' and never 'diminishing the greatness of birth and marriage by omission of any ceremony'.[26] There were rhymes to help her remember the rules of *placement*, books aimed at children and adolescents that stressed how rude it was to point or to be too demonstrative in conversation – 'Point not thy tale with thy fingers, use not such toys.' There were rules that would hardly be out of place in a modern guide, such as enjoinders to keep one's hands 'washèd clean / That no filth in thy nails be seen', not to talk with your mouth full, to keep cats and dogs away from the dinner table, and to only use one's best dinner service for distinguished guests; but there were also instructions on where to put cutlery, how to cut bread (it was never to be torn with the hands), and a culture that almost elevated propriety into a religious duty.[27] One children's textbook on the proper way of doing things began with:

> Little children, draw ye near
> And learn the courtesy written here;
> For clerks that well the Seven Arts know,
> Say Courtesy came to earth below,
> When Gabriel hailed Our Lady by name,
> And Elizabeth to Mary came.
> All virtues are closed in courtesy,
> And vices all in villainy.[28]

They were lessons that Catherine swallowed whole. For the rest of her life, she remained devoted to the niceties. Few things seemed to cause her greater stress or anguish than the fear that she might make a mistake in public. She seldom did. Compliments on her polite gracefulness followed her into the grave.

This decorum subjugated and elevated Catherine, for while it kept her firmly kowtowing at the feet of her guardian, it also affirmed her superior position to those around her. Since the Victorian era, when the cult of domesticity was at its height, many writers have bewailed Catherine's childhood as one of gilded neglect in which the poor young girl was cast adrift by a 'proud and heartless relative' to live amongst a group of servants who delighted in corrupting her.[29] However, on looking closely at all the available evidence that has survived from Catherine's life at Chesworth House, it is difficult to escape the conclusion that throughout her time there she was treated differently to the other young people. In almost every instance, it was Catherine who remained in control of her roommates, Catherine who confidently issued orders and had access to all the chambers and keys of the mansion. If she or her brother Henry entered a room, the servants were supposed to back away discreetly. This did not mean that they flung themselves against the wall, more that they gave them space, and they were expected to continue paying them attention for as long as they were speaking.[30] Catherine was initially one of only two people under the roof who was the grandchild of a duke, and the deference she was shown throughout her childhood, even by those she counted as close friends, nurtured her confidence and habit of command.

When the household ate, Catherine and her brother were on display, both before the rest of the household and under the watchful eye of the dowager or, if she had gone to court, her steward. At meals, often taken in the Great Hall, if the dowager was present and showed Catherine a sign of affection, such as allowing her to take a drink from the same cup, Catherine knew to reach out with both hands as she took it, then to pass it back to the servant who had brought it over to her. Even if there were no guests and the duchess chose to dine more privately, her establishment sat in order of precedence. Before Catherine and her family arrived in the hall, the tables were wiped down, then three layers of fresh linen were spread, with care taken to ensure each hung evenly. Eight loaves of the best bread to come out of the bakery that day were put at the top table, while servants with napkins slung from their necks to their arms covered the dowager's cutlery with a cloth until she was ready to use it. If a servant was in doubt about the way to fold the linen or wrap the bread before consumption, there were etiquette manuals for that, as well. Basins with hot and cold water for washing one's hands were brought out and last-minute checks conducted to make sure the salt was 'fine, white, fair, and dry' as required.[31] The dowager's carvers would sharpen their knives before the meal, politely holding them with no more than two fingers and a thumb when it came time to carve the meat. It was a time that regarded carving as an art, with textbooks produced specifically to discuss the correct way to slice and serve.[32]

One place where etiquette did relax was the maidens' chamber, the room where Catherine slept, in essence a form of dormitory, such as might be found in a traditional boarding school. Certainly, the maidens' chamber engendered similar feelings of camaradèrie and corresponding lack of privacy. Bedrooms were a rare luxury in Tudor households; sharing beds was common and sleeping in group accommodation even more so. (The dowager's dependants were lucky to have beds; many lesser households handed out straw mattresses and glorified sleeping bags.) In the maidens' chamber, Catherine bunked down with other young women in her grandmother's care and service. She befriended the forceful and brash Joan Acworth, who had a string of beaux and the confidence of a girl who expected life to treat her well; there was also Alice Wilkes, who seems to have enjoyed agreeing with the prejudices of whoever she was gossiping with at the time, as well as girls related to the dowager's natal family, such as young Katherine Tilney. With these comrades, Catherine wiled away an unremarkable early adolescence. Some of her friends, like Joan, were a few years older, others were the same age or a little younger.[33]

For almost half a century, our views on medieval and early modern childhood have been influenced by the work of the late French historian Philippe Ariès, whose book *Centuries of Childhood: A Social History of Family Life* argued that childhood was a relatively modern concept, alien to the Middle Ages or the sixteenth century with their detached style of parenting that sought to accelerate an infant's path to adulthood.[34] This theory has been comprehensively debunked in recent years, and ample evidence survives, both in the relevant documents and from excavated toys belonging to medieval children, to prove that they were recognised as a separate category. Games and dolls existed for children; there were debates on the different stages of infancy; the Virgin Mary and Saint Nicholas were popular heavenly protectors of the young. By the standards of many people at the time, Catherine enjoyed a youth that could be described in positive terms – if not as idyllic, then certainly as privileged, affectionate, and happy. She was sincerely liked by many of the people at Chesworth, who appreciated the loyalty she showed towards her family's servants, the effort she exerted to help them, her high spirits, her generosity, and her sense of mischief and fun. Life could of course be cut short in infancy, and youth could be butchered by an arranged marriage, but in Catherine's case there is no reason to believe that she endured an unhappy or neglected childhood or adolescence.

Festivals, usually religious ones, shaped the calendar. The feast of St George, England's national saint, and May Day, the start of summer, brought a flurry of celebrations. The twelve days of Christmas, from Christmas Day to the Feast of the Epiphany, were an especially busy time. The Christmas log, usually ash emitting a festive green flame, burned in the great fireplace,[35] and carols, their melodies faintly reminiscent of a dance, replaced the usual, more sombre hymns. Fine food was laid on by and for the dowager's staff; wine, ale, and mead fuelled the party spirit – the English had a reputation for being great drinkers – while entertainments marked each passing day. Midnight Mass on Christmas Eve was a tradition that stretched back a millennium by the time Catherine huddled inside the local chapel to commemorate the Saviour's arrival. A troupe of itinerant actors might arrive, or have been sent for, to perform a nativity play, another tradition which has survived but evolved to the present day. Symbolism and sentiment pervaded a Tudor Christmas – the holly hung throughout the house emphasised the presence of Easter in the Christmas story, sorrow amid joy, with the holly's prickles alluding to Christ's crown of thorns at His crucifixion, and its berries to His spilled blood. Saint Francis of Assisi had taught that even animals should share in the joyfulness of the season, originating the custom that cattle, horses, and pets should be given extra food on Christmas morning, and sheaves of corn should be left out to feed the birds struggling through winter.[36]

In the manor house's rooms, boughs were built and hung by servants and members of the family. Evergreens were bound together and little gifts wrapped around them, with holders for candles added before the whole thing was hoisted high enough for people to stand underneath it. Mistletoe dangled from the centre of the bough, thus explaining its nickname 'the kissing bough'. The evergreen bough's candles were lit for the first time on Christmas Eve, then again every night until Twelfth Night, the colloquial name for the Feast of the Epiphany, when the Magi had arrived at the manger in Bethlehem.[37] The boughs were a source of mirth and merriment throughout Yuletide, with mummers or musicians often ending their performance beneath them for comic effect or hopeful flirtatiousness. Unfortunately, Catherine soon took to kissing musicians, in other parts of the house, without the excuse of Christmas revelry.

To tell the story of Catherine's early romances and the role her family's servants played in them, it is necessary to introduce her aunt, Katherine, a regular presence after Catherine left Edmund's care but one who has hitherto been almost completely ignored in most accounts of Catherine's life. The elder Katherine Howard's impact on the journey of the younger was significant, and both began spending more time with the dowager in the same year. Katherine's betrothal to Sir Rhys ap Gruffydd before her father's funeral in 1524 has already been mentioned; the marriage ended in a tragedy that nearly destroyed Katherine.

A year after her father's death and a few months into her marriage, the elder Katherine Howard's grandfather-in-law died. An early supporter of the Tudor claim to the throne and a stalwart loyalist ever since, the old man's position as the monarchy's satrap in south Wales was expected to pass to his grandson and heir, Rhys, who was in his early twenties.[38] However, mourning had barely concluded before the government appointed the thirty-six-year-old Lord Ferrers instead. The decision was widely perceived as a humiliation for a family who had devoted their lives to serving the Tudors, and the sting worsened when young Rhys was excluded from the council that advised the royal household's outpost in Wales. The marriage between Katherine and the attractive but hotheaded Rhys was a happy one, and she was outraged on her husband's behalf, particularly since she believed that the decision to elevate Lord Ferrers, who had, after all, been judged too incompetent to serve as her brother's successor as Lord Lieutenant of Ireland four years earlier, was part of a deliberate policy to humble her husband's family.[39] When Rhys and two of his servants were set upon by an unknown gang as they travelled past Oxford University, she began to suspect that Ferrers meant to harm or kill him.[40] Rhys and his family were popular in Wales; a contemporary noted that 'the whole country turned out to welcome him, and this made Lord Ferrers envious and jealous'. When Ferrers overplayed his hand and arrested Rhys for disturbing the peace, Katherine rallied hundreds, including the Bishop of Saint David's and many representatives of the local gentry, who marched with her on Carmarthen Castle.[41] Katherine threatened the castle under cover of darkness, making sure to display her strength through the guise of delivering a message that asked for her husband and his men to be freed. If they were not, then she promised Ferrers that her men would burn down the castle door to fetch them, a threat which rather undercut her claims that she had no intention of causing further disturbances. Ferrers managed to disperse Katherine's supporters, but the lull was temporary. Chaos began to spread in the region. Servants of the two factions were ambushed and killed, Rhys was freed, only to be taken once more, Katherine and her men attacked one of Ferrers's homes, lives were lost and property ruined. In his letters to his superiors in London, Lord Ferrers described Katherine and Rhys as leaders of a 'great Rebell[ion] and Insurrection of the people'.[42]

Eventually, Rhys was arrested one last time and brought to London to stand trial for treason. He was accused of discussing prophecies that concerned the downfall of the king and of conspiring with Scotland to foment another invasion. One of his own servants provided evidence against him. The case, which resulted in a conviction, was overseen by an on-the-rise Thomas Cromwell, who also helped to arrange some of the logistics of Rhys's execution on 4 December 1531. It is unclear to what extent Rhys had been driven to contemplate allying with a foreign power in order to recapture his family's position in south Wales; the common view at the time seems to have been that he was 'cruelly put to death, and he innocent, as they say, in the cause'.[43] Allegations of financial corruption, his feud with Lord Ferrers, and the resultant threat to peace in Wales made his destruction a matter of convenience for the central government.

While we may never know exactly how much his own actions brought about Rhys's death, we can be certain of the devastating effect it had on his widow. She had been intimately involved in her husband's quarrel, and so the possibility that she would be accused of complicity in his alleged treason was tangible. Left to forge prospects for their three young children – Anne, Thomas, and Gruffydd – and fearful for herself, Lady Katherine followed in the footsteps of her elder brother Edmund and flung herself on the mercy of their niece, Anne Boleyn.[44] Once again, the family's dark-eyed golden girl did not disappoint.[45] She may even have tried to limit the damage for her aunt and young cousins shortly before Rhys's execution. Rhys had been attainted at the time of his conviction, meaning that the Crown could seize his goods and property, but his act of attainder specifically and unusually made provisions for his widow, who was left with an annual income of about £196.[46] If Anne could not save Rhys, she worked hard to salvage his family's situation. It is incorrect that his two boys, both under the age of seven, were packed off to live in the care of another family, as has been stated. All three of the siblings stayed in their mother's care, and she swiftly married Lord Daubeney, a widower nearly two decades her senior. Anne Boleyn had not had much time to deploy her matchmaking skills, and the sickly Daubeney was hardly as easy on the eye or heart as Rhys had been, but he enjoyed royal favour, and in such pressing circumstances that was more important than personal preference.[47] A few years later, Daubeney was created Earl of Bridgewater by Henry VIII, making Katherine a countess, but the marriage that saved her from going under with her first husband was not a happy one.* It was mutually miserable to the point that within three years the pair were living apart and complaining about one another to anyone who would listen.[48] The countess's sons joined Catherine as their grandmother's wards, though they had ample opportunity to see their mother who, accompanied by her maid, Mistress Philip, began to spend much of her time residing with her mother.[49]

The countess's case showed the extent to which the new queen's loyalty to her family could prove invaluable. It was not the same thing as infallible – she had saddled Edmund with a job for which he was manifestly unqualified and Katherine with a husband she came to loathe – but in difficult circumstances, Queen Anne was a worthwhile ally. Young Catherine was one of dozens of the queen's cousins, nieces, aunts, uncles, and extended relatives who would look to her for advancement, especially in bringing them to court to serve her in lucrative obedience. In Calais, rumour had it that Catherine's father did not plan to live out his life as a comptroller but 'hopes to be here in the court with the King or the Queen, and have a better living'.[50] But court gossip was vicious and mercurial, savaging those it had once nurtured. Just as an anonymous letter years earlier had damaged Edmund's standing in the aftermath of the Battle of Flodden, whispers on the court grapevine tried to harm the countess. 'I have none to do me help except the Queen,' she wrote in a letter, 'to whom am I much bound, and with whom much effort is made to draw her favour from me.'[51] The more Howards around Anne, the better, and even if she was not destined to serve at the queen's side, Catherine needed to continue learning the courtly graces. She was not going to spend her whole life at Chesworth House.

---

* Lord Daubeney was not elevated to the earldom until 1538. However, for clarity's sake, especially in differentiating her from her niece, the elder Katherine Howard will usually be referred to as 'the countess' from now on.

On 2 May 1536, the ground shifted beneath the family in the most devastating fashion since their defeat at Bosworth. Shortly after lunch, Queen Anne Boleyn was arrested and rowed upriver to the Tower of London, where, seventeen days later, she bowed off the earthly stage after tucking the hem of her dress under her shoes, hoping to preserve her dignity once her body collapsed forward into the straw.[52] Two days earlier, another of Catherine's cousins, Lord Rochford, perished as collateral damage in the quest to ruin the queen, along with Sir William Brereton, a Welsh landowner who had once been supported by the countess's first husband.[53] In seventeen days, the Howard women had been robbed of their most celebrated kinswoman, and while it is tempting to think that the people at Chesworth spoke of Anne's fate in much the same horrified, incredulous way as distant relatives like the Ashleys or the Champernownes seem to have, it is equally possible that Catherine's friends discussed the events of 1536 with the same unthinkingly gleeful acceptance that greets so many political or royal scandals, no matter how improbable their details.[54] The government's version of events that had Anne as a bed-hopping, murderous adulteress certainly made for a good story, so good in fact that its manifest falsities still cling to popular perceptions of its victims, almost five hundred years later.

If the family was not already nervous enough, within weeks of the queen's execution Catherine's younger uncle Thomas was also sent to the Tower, after his secret betrothal to the king's niece, Lady Margaret Douglas, was discovered.* The king was apoplectic and chose to see the romance as part of a plot to place the Howards closer to the throne.[55] The couple were separated and while Margaret was eventually released, Thomas died of a fever after eighteen months in prison. His body was handed back to the dowager, who was granted permission to bury her son next

---

* This was not the Duke of Norfolk, but his younger half brother with the same name, Lord Thomas Howard. In the same year, another of Agnes's children, her daughter Lady Elizabeth Radclyffe, died of natural causes.

to his father at Thetford on condition that 'that she bury him without pomp'.[56]

Throughout the scandal caused by Thomas's elopement, the Pilgrimage of Grace rebellion convulsed the north of England. Thousands rose in protest at the closure of the monasteries and the gathering pace of religious revolution. Even a young girl growing up in a country house in the south cannot have missed the changes affecting England after the break with Rome. Catherine's family were initially sympathetic to the king's quarrel with the pope, but by 1536 they were beginning to feel a mounting sense of dread. Edmund Howard had sworn the mandatory oath acknowledging the king as head of the Church in 1534, yet a few years later he and his colleagues in Calais were accused of failing to implement the king's latest spiritual policies.[57] Even the late queen, the alleged harbinger of the English Reformation, had shown signs of swinging towards theological conservatism in the months before her death.[58] When news of the northern uprising reached Horsham, the dowager showed herself supremely reluctant to honour her feudal obligations and provide men to help suppress it.[59] Her sons and stepsons felt differently, perhaps mindful of their precarious position in the king's favour after the events of the summer, and it was Lord William Howard who eventually had the lucky honour of kneeling at Henry's feet with the news that the north had submitted.[60]

At this point, Catherine was about thirteen or fourteen years old. Sometime between her cousins' executions and her uncle's death, she began formal music lessons. Thirteen was a little late to start the music lessons that many children in her position had been taking from the ages of six or seven, so it is possible that she had some lessons earlier, though Catherine's formal education does seem to have been somewhat neglected. Unlike several of her relatives, she was never singled out for praise for her musical or literary abilities. By the autumn of 1536, her schooling had focused on teaching her how to read, write, walk, talk, stand, dance, and move in a way guaranteed to please her contemporaries, but not much else.

Her principal music teacher was a young man called Henry Manox, brought in by the dowager, possibly on the recommendation of his kinsman, Robert Damport, who was already in her service.[61] Manox deviated little from the stereotype of an arrogant, young, emotionally impulsive musician. He set the mould for the type of man Catherine was subsequently drawn to – handsome, cocky, more brawn than brain, and passionate to the point of possessive. Several of Catherine's friends already had romantic entanglements with the young gentlemen of the household – as with most establishments before the late seventeenth century, women were in the minority on the dowager's staff – and Catherine and Manox began a flirtation that eventually progressed to kissing and fondling. In modern parlance, they fooled around but did not go all the way.[62]

This relationship forms the first piece of 'evidence' in a recent theory about Catherine's life, namely that she was the victim of repeated sexual abuse throughout puberty, with Manox being the first of several men to groom her.[63] Variations on this narrative describe Manox as a predator or simply the first in a succession of men, such as Francis Dereham, who repeatedly raped her. The latter interpretation can only be sustained by either wilful or accidental ignorance of almost every piece of relevant surviving evidence. It requires misrepresenting Catherine's personality, disregarding the biographical details of everyone around her, and twisting beyond recognition every comment made by most of the people who knew her. This is not to suggest that such abuse did not happen – the young Elizabeth I was molested and horribly manipulated by her stepfather, Thomas Seymour, in a relationship that was not just quite clearly one we would characterise as abuse, but which was described as such in contemporaries' vocabulary for it.[64] Cases of child abuse were reported and prosecuted, and the concept was understood in the early modern era, so it is untrue to say that there was no perception of victimhood or coercion.[65] The memoirs of the fourteenth-century merchant's wife Margery Kempe recounted an argument that contained a threat of what would now clearly be recognised as marital rape, if the husband did not get what he wanted.[66] Admittedly, Catherine herself would later claim that she had been forced into sexual relations at this stage in her life, but it can be shown that she was lying, and doing so in desperate circumstances.[67] Against that claim, which no one at the time believed, there is a mountain of precise evidence, from those who knew her and from the men involved, about when her relationships began, how they began, their consensual basis, and above all, Catherine's role in ending them when she lost interest.

The idea of Henry Manox as a paedophile preying on his young charge is a grotesque one, but mercifully without any supporting detail. Manox certainly put Catherine under pressure to consummate their relationship and reacted crudely when she ended things between them, but none of this supports a hypothesis of sustained and deliberate abuse. In the first place, we do not know Manox's date of birth, and given the average age of the group he consorted with, he was likely to have been five years older than Catherine at the very most. Furthermore, the scenario of Manox using their lessons to bully her into a sexual relationship is undercut by reading transcripts from the investigations of 1541, which prove Catherine's lessons were actually taken by two teachers at the same time – Manox and another man, Barnes – during which Catherine would have been chaperoned.[68] However, if not horrible, their relationship was nonetheless inappropriate, on several levels.

Catherine began her lessons with Manox and Barnes in 1536. The attraction between Catherine and Manox seems to have been relatively slow-burning, but eventually the couple were sending each other little gifts, with a young maid called Dorothy Barwick being the first to carry tokens on Catherine's behalf.[69] Manox later claimed that 'he fell in love with [Catherine] and she with him', but that was not how others remembered it.[70] More honestly and less nobly, he and Catherine found each other very attractive, and the taboo nature of their affair, particularly the difference in class, added a certain inevitable spice. To meet up alone and outside their lessons would have required significant skills of subterfuge. Catherine did not bring Manox into her shared dormitory, so where they found the time and venue to progress along the bases of physical intimacy is anybody's guess. They had perhaps been meeting on several occasions when the dowager discovered them kissing in an alcove near the chapel one afternoon. She slapped Catherine two or three times and reiterated that they were never to be left alone together.[71] They did not obey her, but they had the sense to become more discreet. While it remained an open secret to many other people at Chesworth, they subsequently and successfully hid their relationship from the dowager.

They were still seeing each other in early 1538, when a young woman called Mary Lascelles arrived to serve in the household on a regular basis.[72] She was working as a nursemaid to one of Catherine's infant cousins when the child's father, Lord William Howard, the dowager's youngest surviving son, began to spend more time in his mother's household.[73] Tudor house guests sometimes stayed longer than modern tenants, so their servants ended up living and serving alongside the owner's. Lord William, a diplomat and soldier, had recently been widowed and married again, to Margaret Gamage, the daughter of a Welsh landowner. He had one daughter, Agnes, from his first marriage and at least one son from his second by 1538. Mary the nursemaid was a prim young girl from a family who took the Reformation very seriously, and she was horrified at what she heard about her master's niece – two fellow maids, Isabel and Dorothy, admitted to her that they had been carrying messages and love tokens from Catherine to Manox.

Concerned, Mary reached out in a spirit of servant solidarity to Manox to warn him of the danger he was in. She told him that if he had any plans to marry Catherine, they were impossible as 'she is come of a noble house and if thou should marry her some of her blood would kill thee'. Manox was contemptuous: 'Hold thy peace, woman. I know her well enough.' With maximum honesty and minimal charm, he explained, 'I have had her by the cunt and she hath said to me that I shall have her maidenhead though it be painful to her, not doubting but I will be good to her hereafter.'[74]

Manox's boast shot through the gossip network of the house, flying with rumour's customary unerring skill right to the ears of its subject. Catherine's heart was not exactly warmed when she heard what Manox had said about her, and she ended their affair, even in the face of Manox pleading that he 'was so far in love with her that he wist [knew] not what he said'.[75] Catherine, by then fifteen or sixteen, was disbelieving and unimpressed. She was firm to the point of brutal in her bad temper. During their argument, she pointed out, 'I will never be nought with you and able to marry me ye be not.'[76] This comment is usually interpreted by historians as an example of snobbery on Catherine's part – a wounding reminder that their respective backgrounds made the idea of marriage absurd. Had Catherine meant to make that point, she would have been unkind and accurate. In fact, it seems that she was actually being more specific. Manox could not marry her because he was already engaged to somebody else or already married. Catherine's uncle William is mentioned calling 'on him [Manox] and his wife at their own door' shortly after Manox's liaison with Catherine ended.[77] That Manox was engaged at the time he became involved with Catherine and married shortly after would explain both their comments about the improbability of their dalliance ending in marriage and her decision to keep their physical intimacy in check. If Catherine did intend to lose her virginity to Manox, despite her reticence, his comments about her and his fiancée gave her the motivation to end things before they went any further. All her life, Catherine hated to be humiliated and reacted strongly when faced with disrespect or embarrassment.

A few days after their quarrel, Catherine had softened and agreed to hear Manox out one last time. The two went for a stroll in the duchess's orchards. Manox seems to have mistaken this promenade as a sign that the relationship might soon be back on track, but it was only well-meaning politesse on Catherine's part. Her mood had altered, but her mind was made up, and not long after that she found a replacement for Manox in the form of Francis Dereham, her grandmother's secretary.

Chapter 5

Mad Wenches

For among all that is loved in a wench chastity
and cleanness is loved most.

– Bartholomew of England,
De proprietatibus rerum (*c.*1240)

Catherine never could make a clean break of things. Time and time again, she went back to pick at a wound, drawn irresistibly to the drama of the supposed farewell or the intimacy of an emotional conversation. Her tête-à-tête with Manox in the orchard only a few days after she broke off their relationship was the first recorded instance of a trait that left too many of her actions open to misinterpretation. As Manox nursed hopes of reconciliation, Catherine entered a more adult world. The dowager's household began to spend more time at Norfolk House in her home parish of Lambeth, the Howards' recently completed mansion on the opposite side of the river to Whitehall, the king's largest and still-expanding palace. There, Catherine began to see more of the relatives who lived in the capital or at court – her elder half sister, Lady Isabella Baynton, visited the dowager, and their brother Henry had married and brought his new wife to live with him.

Catherine conformed to general contemporary ideals of beauty, which praised women who had 'moistness of complexion;

and [are] tender, small, pliant and fair of disposition of body'.[1]
Contrary to the still-repeated tradition that she was 'small, plump
and vivacious', the few surviving specifics about Catherine's
appearance describe her as short and slender.[2] A former courtier
subsequently described her as 'flourishing in youth, with beauty
fresh and pure'.[3] She was comfortable with admiration and attention. Manox was not the only servant who was smitten; a young
man called Roger Cotes was also enamoured.[4] As she got older,
Catherine was given servants of her own, including her roommate Joan Acworth, who became her secretary. How much
correspondence Catherine actually had at this stage in her life is
unknown, but it clearly was not enough to create a crushing
workload for Joan.

It was through her secretary-cum-companion that Catherine
found Manox's successor. Francis Dereham was good-looking,
confident to the point of arrogance, and a rule breaker who
possessed a blazing temper which Catherine initially chose to
regard as thrilling proof of his affection for her. He was also a
'ladies' man', who had already notched his bedpost with several
fellow servants, including Joan Acworth.[5] Their fling had since
ended, and Joan cheerfully moved on, even singing his praises to
Catherine, who began to show an interest in him in the spring of
1538 – at the very most within a few weeks of ending things with
Manox.[6]

By then, Francis had been in the dowager's service for nearly
two years.[7] Distantly related to her, he was the son of a wealthy
family in the Lincolnshire gentry where he learned the upper-
class syntax and mannerisms necessary to pass as one of the club.[8]
The dowager was fond of Francis, and he eventually carried out
secretarial work for her. When he first arrived at Chesworth
House, he and his roommate Robert Damport were given tasks
like buying livestock for the household, perhaps a boring pursuit
but an important one considering that many aristocratic households spent nearly one-quarter of their expenditure on food.[9]
Dereham and Damport were sent to get animals ready for the
annual cull on Martinmas, a religious festival that fell every year

on 11 November. Not all the livestock were killed then, and it is not true that most meat served in winter was heavily salted or covered in spices to hide its decay; households generally fed the animals intended for table with hay throughout the colder months to keep the food as fresh as possible.[10]

One of Francis's closest friends in the household was his wing-man Edward Waldegrave, who gamely chased the friends of Francis's lovers and helped organise nighttime visits to the maidens' chamber, arriving with wine, apples, strawberries, and other treats pinched from the kitchens. Talking, drinking, and flirting continued into the small hours, often to two or three o'clock in the morning, and if anyone from downstairs unexpectedly came to inspect, there was a small curtained gallery at the end of the maidens' chamber where the men could hide until danger had passed. The idea to hide them in there was Catherine's.[11] She was not the only girl with a sweetheart – for instance, Francis's friend Edward was courting one Mistress Baskerville. To make the numerous rendezvous easier, Catherine took the initiative and sneaked into her grandmother's room one evening, stole the relevant key, had a copy made, and then ensured the door to the staircase that led to the maidens' chamber was unlocked after the dowager went to bed.[12]

Within a couple of months of seeing Dereham, the reluctance Catherine had expressed to Manox about losing her virginity had evaporated. She and Francis began lying on her bed during the clandestine parties; this progressed to kissing, foreplay, and then sex. There was not much privacy in the maidens' chamber, but Catherine was 'so far in love' that it did not seem to deter her.[13] One of the dowager's maids, Margery, who later married another servant in the household called John Benet, spied on them and saw Francis removing Catherine's clothes. Later, Francis told Margery that he knew enough about sex to make sure Catherine did not end up pregnant.

In much the same way as life in university halls can erode a sense of propriety, years in the maidens' chamber left the girls feeling extremely comfortable in one another's presence. When the bed hangings were pulled shut, the noises the couple made left no doubt about what they were doing. Their lovemaking was so energetic that their friends took to teasing Francis about being 'broken winded' once it was over.[14] The pair were drunk on one another, kissing and cuddling like 'two sparrows', and the memories of the people who saw them in 1538, written down in 1541, prove beyond a shadow of a doubt that their relationship was consensual.[15] It has already been mentioned that it was customary for young people of the same sex to share a bed – in the way Francis did with Robert Damport – and on several occasions, perhaps after too much of the purloined wine, another girl was in the bed when Francis and Catherine began foreplay.[16] Alice Wilkes was so irritated by the couple's 'puffing and blowing' that she insisted on switching beds to get a better night's sleep.[17] Alice, who was soon to marry another member of the household called Anthony Restwold, tried to speak to Catherine about the terrible risks she was taking. Any girl would find herself ruined by a pregnancy out of wedlock, let alone the Duke of Norfolk's niece. Catherine dismissed her concerns by pointing out that 'a woman might meddle with a man and yet conceive no child unless she would herself', much the same stance taken by Francis in his earlier conversation with Margery.[18] A rebuffed Alice then shared her fears with Mary Lascelles, who had held a low opinion of Catherine ever since she found out about her involvement with Henry Manox. 'Let her alone,' she advised, 'for [if] she hold on as she begins we shall hear she will be nought in a while.'[19]

Mary Lascelles's sour-sounding reflection on Catherine's impending comeuppance was based as much on hard-nosed pragmatism as on religious sensibility. Lascelles's advice to Henry Manox about the consequences of becoming involved with a noble girl showed that she appreciated the practical dangers implicit in these kinds of upstairs–downstairs romances. The potential consequences of sin were awful, particularly in a society where God was liable to prove far more forgiving than His earthly flock. Religion was omnipresent in Catherine's world. It was not separated from the world, but rather it influenced everything in society, from the ecstatic to the banal, and was in its turn influenced – sixteenth-century villagers playing football after Mass sang songs celebrating the skills of Saint Hugh of Lincoln in bouncing the ball up and down from the tips of his toes.[20] Eroticism and sexuality could be incorporated into the Divine as much as the mundane. Christianity's blushes about nudity were at least a century away – prayer books handed out to children might show a naked Bathsheba bathing in the moonlight; icons of pure and brave Saint Agatha often depicted her bare breasts seconds before the pagan Romans tore them from her as part of her martyrdom; the loincloth-wearing Saint Sebastian was usually shown as lean and muscular as the arrows of the unbelievers pierced him for his faith in Christ.[21]

None of these devotional images were supposed to excite lust, of course, but nude images, no matter how holy their intent, at the very least ran the risk of provoking impure thoughts in some of their audience, and this reflected a society in which theological teachings on sexuality were often torturously contradictory. There were tensions between, and within, theological writings on sex and medical thoughts on the same subject. Views on what constituted a danger to one's spiritual or physical health swung depending on which writer you consulted: a monk from the Franciscan order, for instance, was historically likely to be less censorious than one from the Dominican tradition. Medical wisdom held that 'men fall into various illnesses through retaining their seed with them', while in Catherine's lifetime the Bishop of Rochester argued that an orgasm damaged a man's health more 'than by shedding of ten times so much blood'.[22] A large part of the dichotomy stemmed from the age-old question of whether sex was something to be enjoyed or endured and if, in circumstances such as marriage or procreation, it might become something praiseworthy. The philosopher Sylvester Prierias Mazzolini, who died around the time of Catherine's birth, argued that any deviation from the missionary position was a contraceptive, itself a sin, and that the pursuit of sexual pleasure, even within wedlock, was fundamentally dangerous. Couples who were engaged often began a sexual relationship before the actual wedding service, a custom with which certain members of the priesthood had no quarrel but others found to be objectionable.

Almost none of Catherine's contemporaries disregarded the Church's teachings on sex in their entirety, but equally there is plenty of evidence that very few accepted them in full. Moralists noted with concern, disappointment, and apparent surprise that very few men admitted to masturbation when they confessed their sins.[23] The suggestion that couples should wait three days before consummating a marriage was almost universally ignored.[24] Clerical tomes lambasted homosexual activity, masturbation, foreplay, oral sex, and anal sex, lumping them all together as sodomy, but even here there were inconsistencies. For every morality guide that ranked homosexual sex in the same category of vice as masturbation, there were others that ranked it just above bestiality, such as the manual written to help confessors in the assigning of penance which carefully ranked every sexual transgression from the least severe (an unchaste kiss) to the worst (bestiality). In the same list of ascending vice, incest was number eleven, while masturbation was jarringly ranked as number twelve, which was four ranks worse than the rape of a virgin, itself classed as marginally worse than the rape or abduction of a married woman. Many lay Christians found these debates absurd and correspondingly ignored thundering assertions like the one that claimed that if a sinner 'has foully touched his own member so that he has polluted himself and poured out his own semen, this sin is greater than if he had lain with his own mother'.[25]

However, even if people did not always pay attention to the obsessively detailed denunciations from the guardians of sexual morality, there was still widespread acceptance of the importance of chastity, especially in women, and a belief that sexual inter-course created a bond between two people that could not easily be broken. Medicine taught that women were more lustful than men, more illogical, more emotional, and more susceptible to biological impulses. Female orgasm was believed to be desirable in securing a conception, perhaps one of the few pieces of medical advice that worked in a woman's favour in the 1530s. The rest seemed to focus either on their emotional volatility or the horrors that sex could inflict on them – childbirth, after all, killed many, and contemporary textbooks acknowledged that some women endured great pain during sex itself, perhaps because of a prolapsed uterus or some other infirmity, when 'such women cannot endure a man's penis because of the size of it, and sometimes they are forced to endure it whether they would or not'.[26]

A woman's life could be ended or ruined by the consequences of sex, a point which was constantly stressed in the hope of encouraging restraint. Virginity, or perhaps more accurately an unsullied reputation, was the most valuable part of an aristocratic lady's social armour. Without it, she was a defenceless and easy target. Catherine was clearly enjoying her sexual relationship with Francis, while doing her research in how to avoid becoming a mother. Her boast that she knew how to 'meddle' with a man without risking pregnancy suggests that she knew something about oral sex – number fourteen in the aforementioned confessors' manual, between having sex outside the missionary position and homosexuality – or the other rudiments of sixteenth-century contraception. In the rural idyll at Horsham or behind the walls of her grandmother's London mansion, it was easy to make the mistake of thinking that biology and the disapproving stares of Mary Lascelles were her greatest threats.

Before the dowager arrived at her pew for morning Mass, her servants gathered the usual pile of letters left there as petitions for her. After a service at Lambeth, one note brought a nasty surprise: it claimed that if the dowager went up to the maidens' chamber half an hour after her usual bedtime 'you shall see that which shall displease you'.[27] The dowager 'stormed' in a rage and only through sheer luck did the girls manage to hide the worst from her. Perhaps it was one night where only a few couples were meeting or most of the men managed to make it into the curtained gallery in time. In any case, the duchess did not discover that Catherine was seeing Dereham. The note was opaque enough for the dowager to think that it referred to another young man called Hastings, whose flirtatious interest in one of Catherine's roommates had already been noticed. Catherine did not think the tip referred to Hastings, and she was angry enough at the potential embarrassment to break into the dowager's rooms again, steal the letter, and take it straight to Francis, who agreed that Henry Manox must have written it, perhaps with the help of one of his friends. Apparently, Manox had wanted to ruin Dereham without ruining his own chances with Catherine. True to form, Francis was almost as angry as the dowager, if for very different reasons. He found Manox and proceeded to hurl insults at him.[28] The two men may have been friends before, since one of Francis's complaints was that the letter proved Manox had never loved him or Catherine.

Arguments about who had incited the wrath of the dowager eventually reached the ears of Lord William, who was irritated by the atmosphere in the house and went to Manox's accommodation to add a second dose of criticism, rather awkwardly bringing the news up in front of Manox's wife. William was unimpressed by Manox's churlish troublemaking, as he saw it, and perhaps by the abuse of his position in flirting with Catherine. He was equally bored by the gossiping about it in the maidens' chamber and the he-said-she-said resulting from the dowager's discovery: 'What mad wenches!' he said. 'Can you not be merry amongst yourselves but you must thus fall out?'[29] Lord William's anger understandably frightened Manox more than Francis Dereham's. Not long after the contretemps, Manox left the dowager's service to work for another family in Lambeth.[30] In regards to the temporarily strained environment in the house, Catherine's glamorous aunt, the countess, was more sanguine when the scandal broke: the only advice she gave her niece was that staying up too late would 'hurt her beauty'.[31]

While Catherine's guile and Francis's bravado saved them and their friends from the worst of her relatives' suspicions, they were so obviously obsessed with each other that the dowager eventually noticed.[32] She may actually have been the last person in the house to know – even John Walsheman, the dowager's elderly porter, realised before she did.[33] Years of being told to look at Catherine, to watch her and defer to her, meant that almost everyone in the household knew what their mistress's granddaughter was doing. The grooms who worked in the dowager's chambers knew what was going on, which was unsurprising given that their female colleagues, the dowager's maids (known as chamberers), including Dorothy Dawby, who was carrying messages and gifts between the lovers, and the disapproving Mary Lascelles, who had recently been promoted from the nursery, were also aware of the situation.[34] The dowager's other maids, Lucy and Margery, were talking about the affair, as was the maid Mistress Philip, who brought the news to her mistress, the Countess of Bridgewater.[35] Catherine's uncle William and his wife, Lady Margaret Howard, also knew, with Margaret apparently spotting the obvious signs of infatuation and discussing it with her husband, whose fondness for Dereham prevented him from reacting aggressively or from inquiring too closely into what was happening.[36] Andrew Maunsay, another servant, remembered later that 'a laundry woman called Bess' knew about the liaison too – an oddly specific memory which raises the possibility that Catherine needed a laundress who could clean her sheets more often than usual, without telling the dowager.[37]

Since aristocratic households kept secrets with the same discretion as a modern workplace or high school, perhaps what was most remarkable about Catherine's summer romance in 1538 was that nobody else tried to inform the dowager about it after Manox's botched attempt to exact revenge. Catherine benefited from the affection she inspired in many of those around her, while those who did not care for her, such as Mary Lascelles, were too afraid to spill her secrets to the dowager. The duchess's suspicions were only confirmed one afternoon when she walked in on Catherine and Francis wrapped in each other's arms, chatting with Joan Acworth, who was acting as Catherine's woefully inept chaperone. The last time she had caught Catherine in an embrace, the dowager had slapped her. This time, her blows fell with a more democratic energy – she punched Catherine, Francis, and Joan, then launched herself headlong into a tirade.[38] Back in her rooms, she raged to her sister-in-law and companion, Malyn Tilney. Malyn seemed to know or suspect what was going on with Catherine, but chose tact over honesty in dealing with Agnes's anger and apparently encouraged her belief that what she had just witnessed was the worst of it. Eventually, the dowager calmed down and contented herself with comments that evolved from acid to arch to accepting and finally to amusement. When anyone asked where Francis was, she replied with comments in the vein of 'I warrant if you seek him in Catherine Howard's chamber ye shall find him there.'[39]

The fact that Dereham, like Manox before him, was able to keep his job was a poor reflection on the dowager's acquittal of her position as a guardian. Properly, either he would have been dismissed or Catherine would have been sent to stay with another relative until the infatuation had passed. Agnes may have failed to act out of a desire to avoid embarrassment for herself – after all, how could she explain the problem without admitting her own dereliction of duty? She was anxious that none of the other girls should breathe a word about it to Catherine's uncle William and confided these worries to her chaplain, Father Borough.[40] At what point she figured out that one of William's own servants, and his wife, had passed on the household gossip about Francis and Catherine is unclear. For quite some time she seemed to believe, or chose to, that it was only a mutual crush that would soon blow over. Katherine Tilney, who slept in the maidens' chamber, stated later, and stood by her testimony, that the dowager duchess never knew the relationship had been consummated or that there was talk in the house of the couple making it to the altar.

Francis encouraged the idea of a wedding. When a friend asked him if he would 'have' her, meaning marry her, Francis replied, 'By St. John you may guess twice and guess worse.'[41] The gifts passing between the couple took on a domestic character. Catherine gave him bands and sleeves for a shirt; at New Year's he gave her a gift of a heartsease, a wild pansy with yellow and purple markings, crafted from silk for her to wear. Dereham was with her almost constantly; they nicknamed each other 'husband' and 'wife', and he lounged 'on one bed or another' to talk to her in the maidens' chamber and constantly brought up 'the question of marriage'.[42] When his friends teased Francis about how he could not kiss Catherine often enough, he bantered back by asking why he should not kiss his wife. According to her own recollections a few years later, Catherine did not correct him but instead winked and whispered, 'What if this should come to my lady's ear?'

She was still careful to keep the details from her grandmother. She would not wear the lovely silken flower until she persuaded a family friend and visitor, Lady Eleanor Brereton, to tell the dowager that she had given the bauble to Catherine as a gift.[43] The silk flower was a token Catherine appreciated, and she wanted more. Catherine's love of clothes and fashion developed, although like most young unmarried girls from the same background, she had almost no money of her own. She had enough pocket money to go to Mrs Clifton, a housewife in Lambeth who embroidered for her one of Francis's shirts that he had received as a present from the dowager at New Year's. When Francis told her about a hunchbacked lady in London who was said to be a skilled needlewoman, particularly with silk, Catherine was so keen to commission some pieces that Francis offered to lend her the money to buy another silk flower. At a later date, he bought her the fabric she wanted to make a new headdress. He considered it a gift; Catherine intended to pay him back. She took the cloth to the diminutive Mr Rose, her grandmother's embroiderer. Trusting in his good taste and perhaps not too interested in the precise details beyond securing the desired colour and fabric, Catherine did not give Rose specific instructions beyond what kind of hat she wanted. When it was ready, she regretted her lack of specification. Francis loved the Freer's knots, symbols of constant love that Rose had stitched into it, but Catherine was less enthused.

She was starting to withdraw from him. Francis's ardour was suffocating, his attentiveness more possessive than protective, and his volatile temper now struck Catherine as a predictable and irritating liability. After their few months together, Francis Dereham was stripped of his appeal. To his frustration, she evaded giving him a firm answer about a wedding. Their marital pet names for each other fell by the wayside, as Catherine tried to slow down Francis's march to the altar. At the time, a pre-contract referred to a commitment between two people who were pledged to marry at a future date. With it in place, many couples began to sleep together, partly because of the belief that sex created a bond as unbreakable as marriage. Obviously, in practice it did not always work that way, but pre-contracts were a serious business, especially for the upper classes. One could be disinherited if evidence was found or manufactured suggesting a parent had been pre-contracted to someone else before their marriage, thus rendering their future children bastards in the eyes of the law.[44] A real problem lay in the fact that the details of what constituted a pre-contract were infamously blurred, not least because there was no real requirement for them to be written down. At what point did talk of marriage become an unbreakable pledge? As far as Francis Dereham was concerned, he and Catherine were bound to one another. She, it seems, did not view the situation in quite the same way.

On 19 March 1539, her father died.[45] After his second wife's death, Edmund had married Margaret Jennings, a forceful lady who rather ruled the roost at their home in Calais.[46] His last few years had been plagued by bad health and the monetary problems he had tried so hard to escape. One evening, shortly before he was due to arrive as a dinner guest of Lord and Lady Lisle, he had to send a letter to his hostess, addressed with the words, 'To the Right Honourable the Viscountess Lisle this be delivered – Haste, post haste, haste, for thy life.' In it, he confessed that he could not attend because the medicine he was taking to cure the pain of kidney stones 'made me piss my bed this night, for the which my wife hath sore beaten me, and saying it is children's parts to bepiss their beds'. There is a commendable sense of undaunted humour in Edmund's letters, perhaps a clue to some of the qualities that had won his contemporaries' praise so many years ago. It was Lady Lisle who had recommended the medicine that made him so ill – 'You have made me such a pisser,' he joked, 'that I dare not this day go abroad [outside], wherefore I beseech you to make mine excuse to my lord ... for I shall not be with you this day at dinner.'[47] Two years before he passed away, his colleagues in Calais had voted to elect him their mayor, a move that surprised everyone and raised a few eyebrows in London. Those on the ground in the town advised the government to approve the election, as they customarily did, because the result had been a popular one with 'the Caliciens'.[48] Evidently, in his new home Edmund had managed to build up a decent supply of goodwill, but when the letter announcing the election was read out to the king, he 'laughed full heartily' and vetoed it. Thomas Cromwell was ordered to write to the burgesses and aldermen of Calais to inform them 'that the King's Majesty will in no wise that my Lord Howard be admitted unto the Mayoralty'.[49] A few months after the king torpedoed his career, Edmund's religious conservatism got him into trouble.[50] Then, on St Joseph's Day, a long and frustrating life came to its end.

Catherine almost certainly saw her father again shortly before his death. The previous spring, he had returned to England, and Lambeth, to act as one of the chief mourners at the funeral of his younger sister Elizabeth Boleyn, Countess of Ormond.[51] Elizabeth was buried in the Howard crypt in St Mary-at-Lambeth, so it is highly probable that Catherine and others from Norfolk House made the short journey to attend. This would have been the first time father and daughter had seen one another in nearly seven years, and it does not seem as if Edmund permanently relocated, firstly because the hoped-for job at court never materialised and secondly because he could not stay while he remained in debt to so many people. His death in 1539 made Catherine an orphan, and the responsibility to find her a good position in life rested even more with the other Howards. Luckily, an opportunity presented itself, which would also have the added advantage of getting her away from Francis Dereham. Her uncle William had been involved in several missions abroad to scout eligible princesses for Henry VIII. By summer 1539, he was well placed to know that the queen's household was going to be revived to serve the Duke of Cleves's younger sister, Anne, who would arrive in England for her wedding within the year. The Duke of Norfolk and his allies at court were unenthusiastic about the king's choice. Many of them would have preferred an alliance with the French or the Hapsburg Empire, whereas the queen-to-be's relatives were part of a German cabal against Europe's most powerful family. Even more upsettingly, the match was seen as a victory for its chief architect, Thomas Cromwell. Politics aside, the queen's household was an ideal place for a well-bred young girl, particularly if she still needed a husband, since she would be introduced to the most eligible men in the country. Catherine's uncle Norfolk sent word to Norfolk House that Catherine had been selected to join the court as a maid of honour.

The fantastic new life opening up in front of her gave Catherine the push she needed to break things off with Francis. As with Manox, the two talked things over in the orchard at Lambeth. Francis claimed later that Catherine wept hysterically, sobbing that she had to obey her family's orders. In her memory, she lost her temper at his numerous agonised questions about his future – she replied that he 'might do as he list', since his plans were no longer her concern.[52] Both versions of their conversation may contain some element of truth. Perhaps Catherine did weep at seeing how upset he was – it is entirely possible to feel grief for a relationship that one nonetheless intends to end. The hesitation or mixed emotions resulted in another failure to drive the point home. She did not make clear to Francis that she considered this a permanent goodbye, nor did she state firmly that she had never considered their talk of marriage to constitute a binding pre-contract. Francis, who was both enraged and devastated by this turn of events, still believed there was a chance he would one day be Catherine's husband.

Chapter 6

The King's Highness
Did Cast a Fantasy

And it came to pass in an eveningtide, that David arose
from off his bed, and walked upon the roof of the king's
house: and from the roof he saw a woman washing herself;
and the woman was very beautiful to look upon. And
David sent and enquired after the woman. And one said,
'Is this not Bathsheba ...?'

– 2 Samuel 11:2–3

Catherine's arrival at the Tudor court was made possible by royal deaths and the fluctuations of international diplomacy. Two years before Catherine left the dowager's care, Queen Jane Seymour died shortly after giving birth to a son who, to the relief of nearly everybody, survived. The queen's funeral and the hunt for her replacement were not separated by a significant passage of time.[1] English diplomats were mobilised to find the king a wife and, through her, an alliance for a country that had found itself politically isolated since the break with Rome. Several princesses were considered, with the daughters of the Hapsburg and Valois families the front runners for most of the negotiations, as a bride from one of the two continental rivals seemed like the obvious choice. Catherine's uncle William was dispatched to France to keep an eye on Marie de Guise, the twenty-four-year-old widow of the Duke of Longueville.[2] The French were increasingly offended by King

Henry's demands to see the lady before he married her, until the exasperated French ambassador in London felt the need to point out to Henry that the well-born women of his country were not accustomed to being appraised like horses at market.[3] Marie eventually dropped out of the race to marry the King of Scots, and her younger sister Renée, who was also considered, took the veil.[4] After her, the favourite was Christina, a seventeen-year-old Danish princess who had lived in exile since her father's deposition. On her mother's side, Christina was a Hapsburg, and she had been under their care since Queen Elisabeth's death in 1526. Married at thirteen and widowed at sixteen, Christina of Denmark was still wearing mourning for her husband, the Duke of Milan, when English envoys began to court her by proxy for their master. Letters to Cromwell and the king described her as 'a goodly personage of excellent beauty'; her dimples were lauded along with 'the great majesty of her bearing and the charm of her manners', as well as her faint lisp which 'doth nothing misbecome her'.[5]

Amid the dimple praising, the English diplomats seem to have underestimated Christina's intelligence. She came from a family of clever and self-assured women. When an envoy told Christina that Henry VIII was 'the most gentle gentleman that liveth, his nature so benign and pleasant that I think no man hath heard many angry words pass his mouth', the princess struggled to keep a straight face.[6] Like the French court before them, the Hapsburgs were left cold by Henry's wooing techniques. His belligerence on the subject of the pope's authority, which both the Hapsburg emperor and the King of France still acknowledged, irritated almost as much as the superior and slightly hectoring tone he used in his correspondence. Even as Henry was inaccurately claiming that his hand in marriage was desired by all the great powers of Europe, his representatives noticed that whenever they sought a subsequent audience with Christina, she had scheduled yet another fortuitously timed hunting trip with her aunt, the Dowager Queen of Hungary.[7]

For most of Henry VIII's reign, England's foreign policy had been predicated on the assumption that France and the Hapsburg

Empire would always be in a state of enmity, with England able to alter the balance in favour of one or the other. France, ruled by the womanising François I, had been alarmed by the increase in Hapsburg power when his contemporary Charles V inherited the central European territories of his father's family and the expanding Spanish empire of his mother's. The emperor's attempts to dominate the northern half of the Italian peninsula as thoroughly as he did the southern became the two countries' central point of contention, aggravated by personal rivalries and decades of hostility. Then, in the summer of 1538, the two monarchs signed a ten-year truce which received the blessing of Pope Paul III, who, a few months later, published a bull excommunicating Henry VIII for his schismatic disobedience and iconoclasm.[8] For the English government, a rapprochement between the empire and the French was as unwelcome as it was alarming. At best, there was a concern that the alliance might provide aid or encouragement to discontented aristocrats in Ireland, who were opposed to the king's religious policies.[9] At worst, there was the terrifying possibility that the former enemies would invade England themselves and punish a king who had, in one cardinal's words, 'rent the mystical body of Christ which is His Church'. Fear of attack produced stories that the country would be divided, with the French occupying Wales, Cornwall, and the southern shires, while the emperor annexed everything north of the Thames.[10]

To defend the realm, strongholds were built along the coastline, from Berwick in the northeast to Falmouth in Cornwall. The king inspected many of them personally, while the Earl of Hertford was sent to assess the fortifications in Calais, where the French would certainly attack first.[11] The suspicion that the pope had 'moved, excited and stirred divers great princes and potentates of Christendom, not alonely to invade this realm of England with mortal war, but also by fire and sword to extermin[ate] and utterly destroy the whole nation' helps to explain not just the nervous atmosphere in London but also the slew of arrests and interrogations, subsequently known as the White Rose Affair, which affected Catherine's family and took place around the time she began her relationship with Francis Dereham.[12]

Margaret Pole, Countess of Salisbury, was an aged grande dame of the English aristocracy when she was arrested. A niece of two kings, Edward IV and Richard III, cousin of Henry's late mother Elizabeth of York, and godmother to his eldest daughter, she was 'the last of the right line and name of Plantagenet', the royal family who had ruled England in one form or another between 1154 and 1485.[13] Her third son, Reginald, had never accepted the legality of the break with Rome and chose life abroad, where he became a cardinal who wrote stinging tracts criticising Henry VIII's morals and policies. Henry knew that Reginald Pole was actively encouraging the papal initiative for a joint Franco-Hapsburg invasion, which was especially worrying given that his mother, who was the fifth or sixth richest person in England, had sizeable estates on the southern coast.[14] If imperial troops landed there, Henry suspected that her loyalty could not be counted upon.

One of the Poles' servants betrayed the family by revealing that they were still in contact with the traitorous Reginald and that they had warned him about English plots to have him assassinated. The government homed in on the Countess of Salisbury's youngest son, Sir Geoffrey Pole, and questioned him relentlessly. The Poles had certainly been indiscreet – at home, they had lamented the destruction of the monasteries and 'plucking down of the Abbeys' images', and criticised the king's dishonesty in how he had negotiated with the northern rebels of 1536. One of their cousins had described Henry as 'a beast and worse than a beast', and Geoffrey's eldest brother, Lord Montagu, had commented hopefully on the life-shortening potential of the king's infected leg after an ulcer had closed over earlier that year and, for ten days, the monarch writhed in agony.[15]

Under interrogation, Geoffrey provided enough evidence to destroy them all except, frustratingly for the government, his mother. It was not through lack of trying on their part. An unsubstantiated contemporary rumour claimed that Thomas Cromwell threatened Geoffrey Pole with torture.[16] Sir Geoffrey insisted that while his family regretted the changes to the Church, they had never imitated Reginald by plotting the king's deposition. A particularly horrible aspect of the case was the poor man's attempt to exonerate even as he accidentally condemned. He affirmed or confessed conversations that the government used as evidence of treason, which he relayed to prove nothing more serious than private dissatisfaction. There were more arrests, more interrogations, and on 9 December 1538, Geoffrey's eldest brother was executed alongside their kinsmen, the Marquess of Exeter and Sir Edward Neville. Three of their servants were hanged, then drawn and quartered, their limbs displayed throughout London, and the Countess of Salisbury was attainted and imprisoned in the Tower. In an age when self-destruction was regarded as a mortal sin, a guilt-addled Geoffrey made several suicide bids – twenty days after his brother was beheaded, he attempted to suffocate himself in his cell at the Tower.[17] He was pardoned in recompense for his testimony and eventually went abroad, where he was reunited with his brother Reginald, who had to take care of the broken man for the rest of his life.[18]

Worryingly for the Howards, they heard later that when the Marquess of Exeter's wife had been brought in for questioning, Cromwell had spent a great deal of time trying to get her to incriminate the Duke of Norfolk. Luckily for them, Lady Exeter held firm in denying that Norfolk had anything to do with her husband's alleged politics, but the duke did not forget, or forgive, Cromwell's attempts to implicate him during the White Rose Affair.[19] The deteriorating relationship between the duke and Henry's chief minister helped shape Catherine's career when she arrived at court a few months after Lord Exeter's execution.

Within court circles, at least officially, the reaction to the cull was to express 'how joyful tidings it must be to all Englishmen to know that such great traitors have been punished'.[20] Unofficially, by the time Catherine was spending more time near the capital, the government seems to have been aware of how badly the executions had played with the public. No firm reason for the deaths had been given. Beyond warning a close relative of a plot to murder him, the Poles did not seem to have had any communication with a foreign power. The secrecy of Lord Exeter's trial invited suspicion, as did Cromwell's attempts to magnify their crimes beyond what they had been accused of, or even what was credible.[21] No one seriously believed that Lord Exeter had been plotting to murder the king and all his children or the king's claim that the Poles, the Nevilles, and the Courtenays had been plotting treason for a decade.[22] When yet more court figures, including the king's longtime friend Sir Nicholas Carew, were publicly executed in the aftermath of the White Rose intrigue, Cromwell had one of his employees, Richard Morrison, publish a defence of the purge, entitled *An invective against the great and detestable vice, treason, wherein the secret practices, and traitorous workings of them that suffered of late are disclosed*. Yet still it offered no clear details of the alleged conspiracy, beyond insisting that the accused were papists.[23]

As the limbs of the Poles' dead servants rotted in the streets, the public mood was one of thinly veiled disquiet. There was discontent about impending tax increases, preparations against the possible invasion, and continuing religious tensions.[24] Food prices were rising in the west of England, the decision to cut the number of saints' days was unpopular in dioceses in the south, and, as if to give credence to the worst fears about the international situation, the king, flanked by his courtiers, inspected parades of troops mobilised to guard the capital if the kingdom was attacked.[25]

It is inconceivable that Catherine would not have heard of the White Rose Affair – the questions about the conservatism of her uncle were enough to make the Howards uneasy – but how much she knew about the rest of the problems facing the country in 1538 and 1539 is unclear. She was young, privileged, and politically sheltered. It is quite possible that many of the nuances, and much of the unhappiness, bypassed her completely. The rising cost of food in Bristol was unlikely to disturb a girl laughing, flirting, and crying behind the red brick walls of Norfolk House.

One event that she cannot have missed was the death of the Hapsburg empress consort, which occurred during Catherine's final irritation-filled months with Francis Dereham. Weakened by a miscarriage, the Empress Isabella had succumbed to a fever, possibly influenza, at the age of thirty-five, and one Spanish courtier observed that 'to describe the sadness which His Majesty felt at her tragic death will need many pages'.[26] Royal etiquette was inviolable, unaffected by passing trivialities like the threat of war or diplomatic crises, so when news arrived of Isabella of Portugal's death in Toledo, the Tudor court acted as if the spouse of a cherished ally had passed away, rather than the empress of a country expected to invade within the year. Henry ordered his court to wear mourning for fifteen days, and a service was organised at St Paul's Cathedral, which began with five heralds carrying banners of the Virgin Mary and St Elisabeth, the late empress's patron saint. The archbishops of Canterbury and York participated, and both the country's surviving dukes, five earls, and Thomas Cromwell attended, along with the Lord Mayor of London and all his aldermen, dressed in black robes. Their attire blended in with the dark velvet and hangings that covered the enormous church, broken only by the light of the candles, the golden letters reading *Miserere mei Deus* on the empty hearse, and the colourful Hapsburg coats of arms, which had been installed especially for the service. No one in the capital could escape the obsequies for the empress – every parish church in London was ordered to light candles and sing a requiem for her.[27] St Mary-at-Lambeth, the church that stood less than a minute's walk from the dowager's town house, was not exempt.

Beneath the façade, diplomatic tensions simmered. English councillors noted that the French and imperial ambassadors turned up to the service at St Paul's together, a pointed display of their countries' continued amity, and King Henry sent his Lord Chancellor to represent him, rather than attend in person. Even less tactfully, eleven days after the service the king and various members of his entourage were in public to watch a performance on the Thames in which two galleys engaged in a mock battle that culminated with actors dressed as the pope and the college of cardinals losing and being tossed into the river. The disgusted French ambassador refused to attend a spectacle he described as a 'game of poor grace'.[28]

The anti-papal river pageant took place in June 1539, probably before Catherine joined the court. Her debut and the months immediately after are the least documented part of her adult life.[29] Nonetheless, it is possible to piece together a broad picture of events in the final third or quarter of 1539, beginning with the acceleration of the king's plans to marry again that ultimately brought Catherine to court for the first time as a maid of honour.

The invasion threat settled the choice of who would be the next queen consort. The English ambassador to Paris reported home that the Queen of France, a Hapsburg archduchess by birth, was doing everything in her power to strengthen the alliance between her husband and her brother.[30] Accepting that the Franco-Hapsburg pact could not be broken for the time being, Henry decided to look for friends elsewhere. Englishmen at the imperial court noticed that the emperor could not mask his irritation at news that Henry VIII had sent a delegation to meet with King Christian III in Copenhagen – years earlier, Christian had deposed the emperor's brother-in-law and driven the then Danish royal family into exile, including the aforementioned Princess Christina.[31] Riling the Hapsburgs temporarily became the driving force behind English foreign policy, and it was in this mood that attention turned to Duke Wilhelm of Cleves, a German nobleman who was involved in a territorial dispute with the emperor over possession of the county of Gueldres. His eldest sister, Sybilla, was married to the head of the Schmalkaldic League, a federation of German rulers who were generally sympathetic to the Reformation and wary of the Hapsburg emperor who technically remained their overlord. An alliance with the league, through one of Sybilla's unmarried sisters, meant that if the empire and France attacked, England would have allies who could distract them by starting a war in the Hapsburgs' German territories. In the first week of October 1539, the negotiations ended with the announcement that Henry VIII would marry the Duke of Cleves's middle sister, Anne.[32]

Once the tentative timetable for the royal wedding had been established, more and more women returned to court to take, or seek, their places in the re-formed household. Catherine was still in her grandmother's care by the first week of August, when her name is absent from a thank-you note signed by ladies of the court to the king, after they were taken to Portsmouth for a banquet and tour of the navy's new ships.[33] Further circumstantial evidence suggests that she should have been at court by 5 November, when the king announced that he expected his fiancée to arrive in the next twenty days.[34] That optimistic estimate was defeated by the atrocious weather conditions which delayed the princess's arrival by a month, but the king's hope suggests that Catherine and many of the other ladies had already arrived in the palace. Preparations for the future queen's numerous official receptions had started by 24 October, which supports a timeline that has Catherine ending her romance with Francis Dereham in the late summer of 1539 and arriving at court before the autumn.

By Catherine's own admission, she was keen to go. She later told the Archbishop of Canterbury, 'all that knew me, and kept my company, knew how glad and desirous I was to come to the court'.[35] Many of her friends were also leaving the dowager's household – Joan Acworth became Joan Bulmer and moved north to York to live with her husband, along with one of the dowager's maids who had married a city official there. Lord William found a new job for Alice Wilkes as she prepared to marry Anthony Restwold, who planned to join the administration in Calais. The disapproving Mary Lascelles became Mary Hall after she married and moved to Sussex. Dereham's friend Edward Waldegrave was, like Catherine, entering royal service by joining the household of the infant Prince of Wales.[36] Some of the old group remained in the dowager's service, including Robert Damport and, to his immense frustration, Francis Dereham.[37]

Catherine's enthusiasm for entering the glamorous uncertainty of palace life was not shared by everybody. Some peers, such as the earls of Arundel and Shrewsbury, were notably infrequent attendees, preferring to leave the necessary networking to their relatives. Poets like John Skelton and Thomas Wyatt, who knew the court well, mercilessly satirised its mores. One of Wyatt's most severe criticisms of his fellow courtiers was the way in which daughters, sisters, and nieces could be farmed out for their family's political advantage.[38] In the oft-repeated narrative of Catherine's life, this was her fate – brought to court and groomed by her relatives to seduce the ageing king, maximise their influence over him, weaken Queen Anne's position, and in doing so destroy Thomas Cromwell, the architect of her marriage. The chronology of Catherine's rapid rise to prominence does not support this narrative, nor do the memories of those who knew her. Rather, it seems to have been coincidence, not design, which first brought Catherine into the limelight.

The dowager duchess did not accompany Catherine to court, but Norfolk House was close enough for the girl to visit and for the dowager to keep informed of what was going on at court.[39] On several subsequent occasions, the dowager expressed variations on the remark 'that the King's highness did cast a fantasy [attraction or fancy] to Katharine Howard the first time that ever his Grace saw her'.[40] The dowager made her claims in conversation with several of the king's councillors in 1541 and tellingly they did not correct her – they simply wanted to know who had told her.[41] Her recollections suggest that the king's initial attraction to Catherine was a spontaneous case of lust at first sight.

Throughout his life, Henry VIII was fascinated by the story of King David, the Old Testament hero who, while flawed, nonetheless fulfilled God's plans for him. Over the course of his reign, Henry paid for three series of tapestries that depicted scenes from David's life.[42] According to the Bible, in middle age David spotted a young beauty called Bathsheba bathing one evening, was overcome with lust, and ruthlessly pursued her until she became his queen.[43] Given his fascination with King David and his subsequent marriage to Catherine, the dowager's claim that he 'cast a fantasy' on their first meeting might suggest a similarly single-minded pursuit. However, if Henry did notice Catherine when she was first presented at court in the autumn of 1539, any flirtation seems to have been obvious, if the dowager duchess is to be believed, but short-lived. After that first meeting and perhaps some subsequent slightly lecherous displays of fondness towards her when she was in his company, there are no further signs of royal interest in Catherine for several months. Considering that Anne of Cleves had not yet arrived in England and the king had such high hopes for his forthcoming marriage to her, it would be odd if the Howards had planned to put Catherine in the unenviable position of being her employer's competition, especially when all the signs initially suggested that Anne would enjoy her husband's support and affection.[44]

Instead, Catherine settled down to life in the queen's household, something that cannot have been too onerous considering their mistress was still on the other side of the North Sea. All the other ranks of ladies-in-waiting were either married or widowed. Catherine's immediate companions were the other maids of honour, young and unmarried girls like herself from a noble background who had been sent to court to serve the future queen, who would act as both their chaperone and matchmaker. Catherine was joined by her second cousin Katherine Carey, the eldest child of Anne Boleyn's sister Mary, and Mary Norris, who had been the Duke of Norfolk's ward ever since her father was executed for treason in 1536.[45] Earlier that year, Mary's brother had managed to win back some of the estates that had been confiscated by the Crown at the time of their father's death, and her admission to court was another sign of their reviving fortunes.[46] The final maid of honour we can be certain of was Anne Bassett, who was very pretty and fluent in French and English, but struggled with writing the latter to the extent that she used a scribe for letters home.[47] Anne, whose stepfather, Lord Lisle, was King Henry's uncle, was the only one of the maids to have lived at court before – she had joined Jane Seymour's household shortly before her death.[48] Since her parents lived in Calais, Anne spent the next two years residing at court or in the homes of her well-connected mother's many friends. That autumn, she had gone to her cousin's house in the country to recuperate from a cold before returning to London.[49] She certainly knew how to talk like a courtier – she had been part of the group of ladies invited to a banquet on some of the new warships at Portsmouth. As part of their thanks to the king, they wrote, 'We have seen and been in your new Great Ship, and the rest of your ships at Portsmouth, which are things so goodly to behold, that, in our lives we have not seen (excepting your royal person and my lord the Prince your son) a more pleasant sight.'[50] Along with the French phrases and little Latinisms with which courtiers liked to liberally pepper their conversations, Catherine was also going to have to learn the knack of laying flattery on with the proverbial trowel.

The period between Queen Jane Seymour's death on 24 October 1537 and the king's marriage to Anne of Cleves on 6 January 1540 was the longest period in Henry VIII's reign in which he was without a wife. The queen's household was a lucrative source of aristocratic employment, and its absence in those years had been felt both by the young women who hoped to come to court and by their parents. However, when Henry began to reconvene the household in 1539, he did so after a recent batch of reforms that sought to limit its size. The aristocrats' jockeying for places attempted to circumvent the monarch's decision, trying everything from milking family connections to sending thoughtful personal presents to those who might help them.[51] Anne Bassett was sent into the royal presence with a gift of the king's favourite marmalade as an accompaniment to a request that her younger sister be allowed to join the household. Reading Anne Bassett's letters to Calais, it is clear that her mother, Lady Honor Lisle, had been applying pressure to her daughter to be successful in her petition. Anne, dictating to a scribe, reported that she had 'presented your codiniac [marmalade] to the king's highness and his grace does like it wondrous well, and gave your ladyship hearty thanks for it', but given the number of requests the king was receiving, Anne Bassett apologetically told her mother that she had not been able to press her sister's suit for 'fear how his grace would take it'.[52] The palace, at least initially, stood firm and the cap on numbers was maintained.[53]

The maids of honour, who were the lowest rank in the queen's 'above stairs' household, bar the chamberers, were out of bed at about six or seven o'clock in the morning to supervise the chamberers, maidservants who would light the fires in the queen's apartments and clear away the collapsible beds or mattresses that many of the servants slept on during the night. Once the queen arrived from Germany, Catherine and her colleagues were expected to accompany her to Mass and attend to her during her meals. Catherine's place in the household gave her access to the privy chamber, the queen's private rooms, which very few courtiers ever saw. Entry to them was controlled by well-placed servants who acted like watertight doors shielding the royals from the never-ending crowds of petitioners and place seekers who thronged the public rooms. Tudor palaces were constructed with this limiting of access in mind. The queen's public apartments, where she granted audiences and hosted foreign dignitaries, were separated from her privy rooms by a short gallery that ensured that even when the doors opened from the public rooms, the crowds still could not glimpse into the royals' private chambers. Servants sped up and down stairs to this gallery, bringing up plates of food from the queen's privy kitchen, which then had to be handed over to the maids of honour, pages, or chamberers, who would take the plates from them at the privy apartment doors. The same routine was repeated when clothes were ordered up from Her Majesty's cavernous wardrobe. The maintenance of the queen's wardrobe required soft brushes, and furs in particular had to be properly cleaned at least once a week, even if she was not using them, 'for moths be always ready to alight in them and engender'.[54]

The gallery had two little rooms jutting off from it – one held a small altar and the other, separated by a lattice grille, contained a prie-dieu. The queen went there to hear Mass every day, accompanied by a few of her maids of honour. The queen's priests were not technically members of her elite privy chamber staff, and so to prevent them or their altar boys entering the inner sanctum, a small devotional space was set aside in the gallery. It was only on holy days that the queen joined her husband to progress through the throngs of courtiers to attend Mass in one of the palace's public chapels.[55]

Along with memorising the complex rules of who could pass through which door and no further, maids of honour were expected to look the part. They were to be stylish enough to complement their mistress without outshining her. Catherine's early purchases during her time with Francis Dereham showed her appreciation for fashion, but life at court required more than a few tasteful silk flowers. The court was obsessed with appearances and everyone wanted to make sure their clothes advertised their position in the hierarchy. Pins held together the voluminous folds of noblewomen's dresses – the king's eldest daughter ordered 10,000 of them for her wardrobe – and the extortionate cost of the dresses meant that hand-me-downs were greatly appreciated.[56] Catherine's family were expected to provide for her when she made her debut, particularly her wardrobe, but as an unmarried girl she was also one of the few ladies in the queen's service who received a salary. She and the other maids of honour received £10 a year, a sum she immediately used to pay back Francis Dereham what he had loaned her to buy some clothes in Lambeth.[57] It was a further indicator of her desire to move on from their relationship.

Discipline was harsh in the royal household, with a warning for the first offence and dismissal for the second.[58] Many of the palace's rules were hygiene related – residents were forbidden from leaving half-eaten food or dirty dishes around, and if any were found the servants had to clear them away immediately.[59] Urinals were built near most of the major courtyards, though as any attendee at a modern festival or large-scale outdoor event will know, even the most adequate provisions did not always satisfy men who were either in a rush or drunk. To combat this, palace officials at Greenwich daubed white crosses on some of the palace's outer brickwork, counting on the fact that the symbol of Christ's crucifixion would prevent anyone from defacing it. For Catherine, the proper toilets were called the 'common house of easement', a large building where the toilets were covered by a plain piece of wood with a hole over a large tank. Depending on how old the palace was, the tank's contents were either periodic-ally flushed away or cleared out by a gang of labourers once the court had moved on to another residence. In the newer or reno-vated buildings, water from the palace moat was used to flush, but pipes ensured the filth was taken away from the moat itself, which was kept clean as a breeding ground for carp and other fish that ended up on the palace tables.[60]

Although Catherine had grown up in the aristocracy and its households, nothing in her past could have prepared her for the splendour of palace life. In terms of size and magnificence, the English royal establishment had no peer in the British Isles. Her own family's vast wealth paled in comparison to the king's. One modern estimate puts Henry's income at nearly forty times the Duke of Norfolk's.[61] The court was the great theatre of political display, and under Henry VIII it seemingly had enough funds to glitter. Foreign visitors remarked that the prettiest of the king's houses were Greenwich Palace, Hampton Court, and Windsor Castle, but his favourite residence was also his largest, the Palace of Whitehall, which in 1539 was still sometimes referred to in courtiers' conversations by its old name of York Place.[62] A sprawling complex of buildings, Whitehall was the largest palace in Europe, and it only yielded the accolade to Versailles after an accidental fire in 1698. It stood, like nearly all of Henry's largest homes, on the bank of the Thames, and when Catherine first arrived there as a resident in the autumn of 1539, preparations were under way for a series of renovations and expansions, including the construction of a set of riverside rooms for the king's eldest daughter.[63] The expansion of Whitehall would cost nearly £30,000. To put the scale of its expense into context, the construction of the entirety of the king's fabulous new hunting lodge at Nonsuch had finished at £24,500. For the palace expansion 12,600 yards of land were reclaimed from the Thames via a 700-foot stone dyke that would help create the space needed for the new gatehouse, banqueting hall, outdoor preaching auditorium, orchards, and enlarged gardens. Whitehall already had the largest set of royal apartments in England, four tennis courts, two bowling alleys, and a tiltyard. An entire suburb of Westminster had been bought up and demolished to make room for its twenty-three acres – compared to six at Hampton Court. It was so large that a gatehouse was necessary to straddle the busy London street that divided the park side, with most of the palace gardens, from the public rooms, stables, and accommodations on the other side.[64]

Life in this splendid maze brought Catherine into more regular contact with other members of her family. Her elder half sister Isabella was also in the queen's household, as one of the ladies of the privy chamber, an elite band of eight who helped the queen to dress and tended to her in her most intimate moments. Isabella and her husband, Sir Edward Baynton, who was to serve as vice chamberlain of the same household, were beneficiaries of sustained if restrained royal favour, having received two countryside properties in grants earlier that year.[65] Catherine's paternal uncle the duke was still a vital man at the age of sixty-six and a prominent presence at court. The Howard fortunes had admittedly stuttered after the execution of Queen Anne Boleyn and then Lord Thomas's elopement with the king's niece, but the duke's military and diplomatic skills meant the government had come to rely on him again after the Pilgrimage of Grace and during the attempts to prevent an invasion. His ability to win three of the maids of honour places for members of his affinity reflected his continued influence at court, as did his pension from the French government, letters from petitioners, such as those who hoped he could use his position to save the monastery of Our Lady in western Ireland, and his regular attendance of the Privy Council.[66]

Catherine did not know this uncle, with his patrician nose and thin lips, as well as she knew her uncle William or her aunt

Katherine, Countess of Bridgewater, but she would have been presented to him before he brought her to court. Sometimes, when it was too dark for him to travel back from any business in Lambeth safely, the duke was invited to stay at his stepmother's house, but he was not as close to Agnes as her own children were.[67] His marriage to the late Duke of Buckingham's daughter was unhappy enough to warrant comparisons to Jason and Medea, and there were contested allegations that Norfolk had beaten his wife along with the uncontested fact that he was now living in sin with a mistress called Bess Holland.[68] To his wife's distress, their three surviving children – Henry, Mary, and Thomas – had all sided with their father, although it seems that the eldest at least did so under duress.[69] The eldest two were regular fixtures at court by the time Catherine joined it. Henry Howard, the duke's twenty-two-year-old heir apparent, enjoyed the courtesy title of Earl of Surrey, but his father kept a tight control of the purse strings, which might explain why he was able to win his son's loyalty.[70] Surrey was married in his teens to the Earl of Oxford's daughter, and she was pregnant with their fourth child when Catherine went to court for the first time.[71] A superb horseman and intellectually brilliant, Surrey was a celebrated poet who helped pioneer several new verse forms in English, most notably blank verse and the English sonnet.[72] Like many of his relatives, he had a flammable temper, unassailable pride in his ancestry, and the same views about the damage being done, as they saw it, to the social hierarchy by men such as Thomas Cromwell. Unlike his father, Surrey's religious views leaned towards reform.

His younger sister, Mary, had been married at fourteen to the king's bastard son, the Duke of Richmond, and became a widow at seventeen when her husband was left sufficiently weakened by a virus to succumb to a subsequent bacterial infection.[73] Mary was as bright as her brother, which meant that her father thought she was too clever for a woman. Compared to Catherine, her education had been exhaustive. She was also attractive and tenacious – since her husband's death, Mary and her family had been fighting to get the widowhood settlement promised to her at the time of the marriage. As Dowager Duchess of Richmond and Somerset, she was owed an annual income of £1,000 from the government, but because the marriage had never been consummated, owing to the couple's youth, the king claimed that there was some doubt about whether Mary had any right to the inheritance.* He turned the matter over to a panel of lawyers and judges, even though all impartial experts, including the Archbishop of Canterbury, believed that Mary was owed the money as Richmond's widow, with or without a consummated marriage.[74] Since no attempt was ever made to take the titles she acquired through marriage from her, the king may have known they were right and simply did not want to part with the money. A year before Catherine left Norfolk House, there had been talk of marrying the lovely Mary to Sir Thomas Seymour, the late queen's brother. Mary, it seems, had resisted because she suspected that a remarriage would not only cost her the rank of a dowager duchess, twice over, but also diminish her chances of getting the revenue promised to her in 1533.[75] In 1539, she too was appointed to the new queen's staff, though given her rank as a duchess she joined it as one of the great ladies, the six highest-ranking members of it after the queen. She was, at this stage at least, still far above her cousin from Lambeth.

With Francis Dereham back at Norfolk House, Catherine enjoyed a new flirtation that winter. Thomas Culpepper was the son of a gentry family who had rebelled against Richard III, which meant they were well placed to enjoy royal favour after the Tudors came to power. Catherine's mother had been a Culpepper, but subsequent accounts of Catherine's career that describe Thomas as her

---

* Although marriages did take place and were often consummated at fourteen or fifteen, several dynasties gave credence to the argument that overexertion in the marital bed could harm an adolescent male's health. The premature deaths of heirs to the English and Spanish thrones had previously been attributed to this, which might explain why Henry Fitzroy and Mary Howard were kept apart during their short marriage.

cousin are incorrect. There were several branches of the Culpeppers, and Thomas was one of the Bedgebury Culpeppers, meaning that he and Catherine were sixth cousins. Even in the world of sixteenth-century kinship where the word 'cousin' was stretched to elastic limits, they hardly qualified as related.

He was exactly her type. He served as one of the king's gentlemen of the privy chamber, all of whom, according to the household's ordinances, had to 'be well-languaged, expert in outward parts, and meet and able to be sent on familiar messages'.[76] He was handsome, athletic, and if he had any insecurities, they were extremely well hidden. Even some relatively prim women seemed to forget themselves in Culpepper's company – Anne Bassett's mother, Lady Honor Lisle, coyly sent him her colours to wear during a jousting tournament, accompanied by a letter confessing she had never done anything like that before.[77] In his younger days Culpepper had served as one of Lord Lisle's servants and apparently flirting with his master's wives was a habit he never grew out of.

An inventory of his possessions taken in 1541 shows that Culpepper was a dapper dresser with 'numerous gowns, coats and other articles of apparel'.[78] The king, who liked to be surrounded by men younger than himself, perhaps in an attempt to recapture something of his own vanished youthfulness, adored him, and the profitable side to royal employment ensured that the unmarried Thomas was a wealthy man by 1539. He owned several properties, including lands from a shuttered monastery in Kent, seven manors, and a fifteen-roomed townhouse at Greenwich. Like many young men, he seemed slightly more interested in clothes and other immediate outgoings such as gambling and high living than in long-term investments. He did not spend much on decorating the townhouse, which was described as having 'hangings (mostly old) and some very scanty furniture in hall, parlour, and 13 other chambers and a chapel'.[79] Given that he spent most of his time at court, perhaps he felt decorating was an unnecessary expense.

He noticed Catherine shortly after her arrival at court. They were both young, unattached, and good-looking. They flirted and he pursued her. Catherine demurred, apparently holding Thomas at arm's length. Thomas was persistent, and he told Catherine that he loved her. Their attraction to one another became a topic of conversation between Catherine and the other maids of honour. When she was in Thomas's company, Catherine flirted but apparently hid the depth of her feelings. From remarks he made a year later, it seems clear that he wanted and expected a sexual relationship, which did not occur.[80] Thomas, who expressed love more easily than he felt it, did not deal well with sexual frustration, and so he moved on to somebody else, an unexpected turn of events that caused Catherine to break down in tears in front of her fellow maids. The rejection certainly came as a jolt to someone who had only ever been the object of lavish, even cloying, devotion and pursuit. Prior to Culpepper, Catherine had always been the one to end her relationships, and she had never been replaced by another woman. Henry Manox had apparently even ranked his fiancée after Catherine. Thomas's rejection was thus a new and unwelcome sensation for Catherine, made worse by the fact that she does seem to have developed genuine feelings for him.

Courtiers, like servants and politicians, gossiped only a little less than they breathed, and rumour's ability to report and magnify meant the news reached Francis back at Lambeth. He stormed up to court demanding to know if it was true that Catherine was going to marry Culpepper. They quarrelled, with Dereham predictably insisting that she belonged with him. Catherine, who had already shown her ability to be brutally honest when sufficiently riled, was firmer with him than she had been when they last spoke. 'What should you trouble me therewith,' she asked, 'for you know I will not have you; and if you have heard such report [about Culpepper], you heard more than I do know.'[81] Dereham returned to Lambeth, where he demanded to be released from the dowager's service if it meant living there without Catherine. The dowager thought his desperation would blow over and refused his request.[82]

By December, Anne of Cleves was at last on her way to England, and the king was impatient to see her for the first time.

He wanted her to travel by sea, but the court in her native Düsseldorf preferred her to make the journey most of the way by land. The winter seas would be treacherous, and Anne was 'young and beautiful, and if she should be transported by seas they fear how much it might alter her complexion. They fear lest the time of the year being now cold and tempestuous she might there, though she were never so well ordered, take such cold or other disease, considering she was never before upon the seas, as should be to her great peril and the King's Majesty's great displeasure.'[83] Moving the princess and her retinue by land meant travelling through Hapsburg and French territory, since the Netherlands were governed by the emperor's younger sister Maria of Austria, Dowager Queen of Hungary, who acted as regent on her brother's behalf.[84] Parading the symbol of the alliance against him through the emperor's dominions struck Henry as a bad idea, and he feared that his fiancée might be detained in order to prevent the marriage. He did not count on the Hapsburgs ladies' compulsive good manners. Maria promised to 'see her well treated in the Emperor's dominions' and made good on her word when she dispatched a nobleman to escort Anne and her retinue en route to her wedding, 'although it displease them', as an Antwerp-based merchant remarked.[85]

Thomas Culpepper was sent across the Channel as part of the delegation to welcome Anne when she reached Calais, but they found themselves trapped there with her as storms prevented a return journey. As bitter winds and sleet lashed England, Catherine waited for the woman she was to serve.[86] A letter managed to get through from Anne Bassett's mother, who was hosting the future queen in Calais, which brought the welcome news that the princess was 'good and gentle to serve and please'.[87] The courtiers and officials were less inclined to be adventurous than the merchants who tried to make it back to England, so letters got through long before Anne did. Finally, two days after Christmas, the weather lifted long enough for her to board a ship 'trimmed with streamers, banners and flags' and cross from Calais to England.[88]

Chapter 7

The Charms of Catherine Howard

The charms of Catherine Howard, and the endeavours
of the duke of Norfolk and the bishop of Winchester,
at length prevailed.

– Gilbert Burnet, Bishop of Salisbury,
*The History of the Reformation of the
Church of England* (1679)

On 4 January 1540, Catherine stood outdoors in the cold afternoon air wearing a new gown, her face framed by a French hood,
a round headdress that curved around the back of the head with
a veil flowing down behind it. This was to be her first glimpse of
her employer, and the ladies and maids were expected to start
serving immediately. Before they saw Anne of Cleves, Catherine
and all the other members of the queen's household had to listen
to an oration delivered in Latin by Dr Daye, the queen's almoner,
which was answered in a similar style by a representative of the
Duke of Cleves. Two of the king's nieces, Lady Margaret Douglas
and her twenty-two-year-old cousin the Marchioness of Dorset,
led a delegation of ladies from the high nobility to greet their
mistress as she stepped out of the carriage 'she had ridden [in] all
her long journey'. Anne of Cleves was twenty-four, tall and
dignified, with a swarthy complexion and a prominent nose.
After another round of presentations to the princess, 'she with all

the Ladies entered the tents, and there warmed them a pace'.[1] For the first week after her arrival in England, she wore the opulent yet unflattering fashions of her homeland, to the distress of her attendants and courtiers, who described German fashion as 'monstrous habit and apparel'.[2]

A blast of trumpets outside the tent announced the approach of the king on horseback, accompanied by his councillors, his gentlemen attendants, bishops, and nobles. The new division of the royal bodyguard, the Gentlemen Pensioners, were on hand, along with ten young footmen, garbed in gold, who stood nearest the king, assisted by pages dressed in crimson velvet. Anne, flanked by Catherine and her other women, emerged from the tent wearing a dress of cloth of gold with a pearl-encrusted bonnet on her head. She was helped into a saddle decorated with heraldic devices associated with her family in Cleves and rode over to her husband, who cut no more of a minimalist figure with the buttons on his purple velvet coat made of pearls, rubies, and diamonds, and the handle of his sword glittering with the numerous emeralds attached to it. As Henry and Anne spoke, the crowds who had gathered to watch them began to cheer. In the words of one Member of Parliament, 'O what a sight was this to see so goodly a Prince & so noble a King to ride with so fair a Lady of so goodly a stature & so womanly a countenance ... I think no creature could see them but his heart rejoiced.'[3]

For the journey to Greenwich Palace, where the royal wedding was to take place two days later, Catherine and the other gentlewomen were put in carriages and taken in procession with the other attendees. As they travelled, the queen's ladies 'beheld on the wharf how the Citizens of London were rowing up & down the Thames' with banners and flags streaming from barges out to celebrate, despite the chill. Once they were behind the palace walls, Henry accompanied Anne and her servants to her private apartments, from where they could hear cannons in the City firing welcoming salutes.

* * *

Catherine spent the next month of her life at Greenwich, a river-front palace of red brick. The queen's apartments overlooked the west side of the inner courtyard, and it was from there on 6 January, the Feast of the Epiphany and the last of the traditional twelve days of Christmas, that Catherine helped escort the queen to her nuptial Mass.[4] Royal weddings in Tudor England were not usually great state occasions. The last public royal union had been Prince Arthur's four decades earlier, and apart from Mary I's marriage to Prince Philip of Spain in 1554, all subsequent British royal weddings took place in relatively private palace chapels until the children of King George V decided tentatively to embrace the media age in the 1920s.[5] Henry VIII's fourth wedding was conducted in the queen's closet at Greenwich at eight o'clock in the morning. He wore cloth of gold, decorated with silver flowers, and a crimson satin coat clasped by diamonds. The bride came in another cloth-of-gold gown, with decorative flowers crafted from pearls; her long blonde hair hung loose, topped by a small crown, and she wore a necklace full of 'jewels of great value'.[6] Count von Overstein, a nobleman in her brother's service, gave her away, and Mass was celebrated by the Archbishop of Canterbury.[7] When it was over, the dukes of Norfolk and Suffolk escorted the new queen back to her rooms, where Catherine and all the other women of the household kept her company while the king went to change his outfit.

The wedding afternoon was taken up with a procession and the royal couple's first public meal together as husband and wife, followed by enough time for the queen to change into a dress trimmed with ermine, which she wore to Evensong with her ladies. That night, the court was entertained with banquets and dancing before the king and queen were ceremonially put to bed. The drapes were closed, the servants retreated, and, so everyone assumed, the deed was done. Five days later, with snow still on the ground, Catherine and the other women saw Queen Anne in English attire for the first time when they accompanied her to a celebratory joust.[8] Those around her judged the sartorial change a huge improvement 'which so set forth her beauty and good visage, that every creature rejoiced to behold her'.[9]

The chronicler's rhapsody about Queen Anne's beauty at the joust may have been the result of florid patriotism rather than honest reporting. By the time the court moved to Westminster on 5 February, no one in it could have missed the rumours about the king's latest wedding night. The whispers had even reached the ears of the Queen of France. Thomas Cromwell, who obviously had a vested interest in seeing the marriage work, thought Anne had 'a queenly manner', and many people, including the French ambassador, agreed that her carriage and manners were commendable, though revealingly the latter reported it in the context that 'people who have seen the lady close say that she is neither as young as was expected, nor as pretty as she was reported to be. She is tall, and her face and carriage have a force in them which shows she is not without mind. The spirit and sense will perhaps supply the deficiency of beauty.'[10]

Initially, a date in February had been mooted for Anne of Cleves's coronation. That was then pushed back to Whitsuntide, in early summer. On 22 February, Marie de Guise was crowned queen consort in Scotland at Holyrood Abbey, an event which may have exacerbated Anne's worry about why her own had not been arranged. She dropped heavy hints about it to some of the king's councillors when they called on her in early spring, by which point they must have known that there would never be a coronation.[11] Some of the gentlemen in the king's privy chamber had started to criticise earlier reports from Cleves that had praised Anne's beauty. Her later reputation as the 'Flanders Mare', a grotesque caricature of ugliness, is the product of imaginative histories written in the eighteenth century, but it does seem that she failed to live up to expectations.[12] When she first landed in England, Henry had ridden in disguise to surprise her. Anne was the first foreign princess to arrive in the country to marry a reigning English monarch since Margaret of Anjou wed Henry's great-uncle Henry VI, ninety-five years earlier. Henry VI had gone disguised as a messenger to Southampton to deliver a letter from himself to Margaret, who, unfortunately for the hoped-for moment of a romantic recognition, assumed he actually was a servant and kept him kneeling while she absentmindedly read his letter.[13] Anne of Cleves's first encounter with her husband was even less encouraging. She failed to pay much attention to the corpulent messenger in front of her, and when he tried to get her attention by kissing her she, naturally, recoiled.[14] Henry was disappointed by her behaviour and her appearance. In a conversation with the papal nuncio, the Queen of France, Eleanor of Austria, remarked 'that the new Queen [of England] is worthy and Catholic, old and ugly'.[15] Eleanor must have received her report from the French ambassador to England because she was able to tell Cardinal Farnese about Anne's unflattering Teutonic wardrobe, which had been described in a letter to Eleanor's husband, along with de Marillac's description of Anne as 'tall and thin, and not particularly pretty'.[16] Amid dripping disdain for the English court's mimicry of her own, Queen Eleanor managed to correct the English accounts that had Anne improving herself via English fashion. The styles *en vogue* at Henry VIII's court may be popular with the English nobility, but they had originated in France.

At some point, a few of Queen Anne's ladies took it upon themselves to find out exactly what was happening in the royal marriage. A well-aimed compliment would bring information, through the queen's denial or acceptance of it, and one afternoon while Anne was with three of her women – the Countess of Rutland and the widowed ladies Edgecombe and Rochford – they expressed the loyal hope that she might soon be pregnant and give birth to a Duke of York, a title that had been given to second sons in the royal family since the reign of Edward IV.[17] The queen took the bait by saying she was certain that she was not pregnant and stuck to it even when the women gamely pressed her on how she could be absolutely certain. Faced with the queen's persistence, Lady Rochford joked, 'By Our Lady, I think your Grace is a maid still indeed.' The queen answered, 'How can I be a maid and sleep every night with the King?' Lady

Rochford made the obvious jest of how a bit more than sleep was required to make a prince, but Anne did not seem to know how much more – 'When he comes to bed, he kisses me and taketh me by the hand and biddeth me, "Goodnight, sweetheart"; and in the morning kisses me and biddeth me, "Farewell, darling." Is that not enough?' Confronted by the queen's naïveté, Lady Rutland stopped laughing and replied, 'Madam, there must be more than this, or it will be long ere we have a Duke of York.'[18]

Queen Anne's ignorance of sex and conception still stuns and confuses. On the one hand, it is perfectly believable that a woman who had been brought up with a limited education, no knowledge of music or dancing, who spoke and understood no language except German when she was shipped off to England, and who had spent her entire life under the watchful eye of her adoring but strict mother, could have been innocent enough to think that sharing a bed with a man constituted full marital intimacy.[19] Especially since, at a later date, Henry admitted that he had gone so far as digital penetration which, to a very innocent person, might conceivably equate with consummation. On the other, there is the possibility that Anne of Cleves was playing up her simplicity to escape from embarrassing conversations. It is worth noting that despite asking, 'Is that not enough?' at the end of the conversation, she had insisted at the start of it that she knew that she could not be pregnant.

In her short career as queen, Anne of Cleves elicited great praise for her public behaviour, and several sources confirm that she managed to make herself very popular with the people of London.[20] Her correspondence with her family revealed how happy she was in 'such a marriage that she could wish no better'.[21] She tried to learn English as quickly as she could, and was apparently successful in her endeavours since she had mastered it by the end of 1540.[22] She asked to be taught the rules of the card games her husband enjoyed, and she sought advice on how she could make herself more agreeable to him. Deciphering much of Anne's behaviour, including the aforementioned conversation with her ladies-in-waiting, is frustrated by the same problem facing the French ambassador when he explained to his master that it was impossible to tell if Anne's preternatural calm and good nature were the result of 'either prudent dissimulation or stupid forgetfulness'.[23] She was capable of losing her temper, and during one very mild disagreement, Henry complained that she 'began to wax stubborn and wilful', which suggests that she was not quite as docile as she pretended.[24] There were also some indicators that she understood that she was in difficulty, without perhaps realising until the final move that she had lost before she started playing.

After the farce of their first meeting, Henry VIII had entered into their marriage determined to dislike her, and the intention created the reality. Before Anne arrived, the Archbishop of Canterbury had tried to warn Cromwell that an arranged marriage was a risk for someone like Henry, who set such high store on his personal happiness. It would be 'most expedient the King to marry where that he had his fantasy and love, for that would be most comfort to his Grace', advice which Cromwell ignored.[25] Henry even tried to get out of going through with it on the morning of the wedding, asking, 'Is there no remedy but to put my neck in the yoke?' before Cromwell reminded him that jilting Anne meant losing the alliance.[26]

He was right. As long as the pact between the Hapsburgs and the French monarchy remained, England could not sacrifice its ties to Queen Anne's family. Cleves still seemed like a valuable ally, particularly after another nosedive in relations between the English court and the emperor's.[27] The latter had chosen not to wear his insignia as a member of the English Order of the Garter on St George's Day, as was customary, a fact not missed by the English, who complained about it later to his ambassador.[28] In Spain, then part of the Hapsburg Empire, several men under the protection of the English Crown had been tossed into the gaol cells of the Inquisition.[29] The English ambassador, Sir Thomas Wyatt, who suspected the men had been imprisoned in retaliation for his country's alliance with Cleves, had an audience with Charles V in which he mistakenly used the word 'ingratitude' to describe the emperor's attitude towards Henry.[30] Charles, whose letters from his servants were often addressed to 'His Sacred Imperial and Catholic Majesty', and whose dominions stretched from the Americas to the Alps, had been listening politely to Wyatt but 'then stopped him, and made him repeat it, asking who it was he charged with ingratitude'.[31] When Wyatt failed to take the hint and repeated his faux pas, the emperor made it very clear to Wyatt that 'he owed his master nothing, and the term ingratitude could only be used by an equal or a superior'. His Sacred Imperial and Catholic Majesty proceeded to take several swipes at Henry's concept of justice, which caused Wyatt to behave even more rudely.

Manners were apparently not high on the list of English diplomatic priorities that winter. On 2 February, the French ambassador visited Henry and asked him to recall his representative in Paris.[32] The Bishop of London had spoken to King François in an offensive manner and the latter wanted him 'replaced by a more prudent and wiser' envoy.[33] The French would not let the matter drop, and to appease them Henry eventually decided to appoint Sir John Wallop. In France, the outgoing ambassador, the obstreperous Bishop Bonner, reported that 'more [honour] is now made to the queen than heretofore'.[34] The French courtiers' attention to their Hapsburg queen suggested that the alliance with the emperor was still strong, but the English also received some intelligence from other sources about cracks that were beginning to appear over the possession of Milan, which the empire had and the French wanted. Sensing an advantage, Catherine's uncle Norfolk left London quietly on the king's orders on 12 February, just as the weather was beginning to thaw, and reached the French court four days later.[35] His mission was to weaken François's trust in the emperor by playing on anxieties about Milan and liaising with courtiers who might be privately hostile to the pact with Austria.[36]

In this he had no better ally than the French king's elder sister Marguerite, Queen of Navarre. Navarre, a small kingdom straddling what is now southwestern France and northwestern Spain, had been absorbed by the Hapsburg Empire, a development that unsurprisingly left Marguerite less than enthusiastic about her brother's diplomatic volte-face. She met with Norfolk and bombarded him with advice – the King of England should grease the palms of those who could help him, including François's two sons, who had already received expensive gifts from the emperor.[37] They should counteract Queen Eleanor's influence by winning the support of the king's mistress, the Duchess of Etampes. Norfolk was sceptical about that last recommendation because he 'thought it strange to seek anything at such a woman's hand', but Marguerite assured him that she spoke from personal experience, 'as she was compelled to do it herself'.[38] Norfolk, who thought Marguerite was 'the most frank and wise woman he ever spake with', began gift hunting for the princes and courting the favour of Madame d'Etampes, who was certainly open in her requests for payment – Henry VIII had to buy her two stallions – and Norfolk returned to England at the start of March impressed, and perhaps surprised, at the influence a royal mistress could wield.[39]

Nineteen weeks passed between Norfolk's return and Catherine Howard's wedding. It was assumed, then and later, that Norfolk was the 'author of this marriage' in conjunction with his ally Stephen Gardiner, the conservative Bishop of Winchester, who used Catherine to facilitate the downfall of Thomas Cromwell.[40] Catherine's rise coincided with and influenced Cromwell's demise, but the extent to which she was deliberately and completely used to further her uncle's goals is difficult to gauge.

Ten years earlier, Norfolk had liked and even supported Thomas Cromwell.[41] He had shared bawdy jokes with him about a serving girl's 'tetins' and described himself as 'your poor assured friend'.[42] Since then, jealousy and political differences had divided them. Norfolk could not forgive Cromwell's attempts to get the Marchioness of Exeter to incriminate him when she was interrogated during the White Rose Affair.[43] Above all, Norfolk was too good a servant to the king to remain loyal to any man who lost his favour, which was Cromwell's fate in the spring and early summer of 1540. Stephen Gardiner, the son of a cloth merchant from Bury St Edmunds, was as clever as Cromwell, only moderately less ruthless, and substantially less charming. He had excelled in his legal studies at Cambridge and come to the court's attention in the early 1520s. He subsequently represented Henry in missions to France, Rome, and Venice, debated the merits of ecclesiastical versus classical pronunciation of ancient Greek, and served for a time as the king's principal secretary. Although he had written books defending the break with Rome, by 1539 continental Protestants detested him – even Martin Luther knew of, and worried about, his prominence in the English government.[44] At home, Gardiner was dogged by accusations that he remained a papist at heart, and during Lent 1540 a radical preacher called Robert Barnes publicly accused him of it.[45] Barnes had previously enjoyed Cromwell's protection, but when Gardiner went to the king to protest this slander, Henry allowed him to bring Barnes in for questioning.[46]

By 3 April, Barnes and two of his colleagues, William Jerome and Thomas Gerrard, were in the Tower. Barnes had not just insulted Gardiner but slandered the Virgin Mary, allegedly proclaiming that she had only been worth something when she was pregnant with Christ, otherwise 'our Lady was but a saffron bag'.[47] He denied that specific allegation, but he was not quite so definite when it came to refuting the charge that he had argued that a government had no right to 'make laws that rule men's consciences'.[48] William Jerome's sermons had sailed dangerously close to supporting the doctrine of predestination, a belief that the majority of English people still regarded as heresy. Cromwell's association with these men tainted him at a time when he was already vulnerable, and Gardiner, whose skills as an interrogator were considerable, was determined to make the most of the opportunity.

Before Gardiner struck against them, English reformers and radicals had their hopes raised by the king's marriage to 'a pious woman, by whom, it is hoped, the Gospel will be diffused'.[49] Unfortunately for them, they overestimated the queen's influence and her allegiance to Protestantism. The Queen of France was closer to the mark when she identified Anne of Cleves as a Catholic whose family, like Henry, had quarrelled with the pope.[50] Raised hopes perhaps inevitably led to raised voices, and the three men had preached sermons that stepped far beyond what Henry's government was prepared to tolerate. By Easter, many English evangelicals seem to have realised their mistake. On 12 April another Protestant clergyman in Gardiner's custody committed suicide by hanging himself in his cell.[51] After Cromwell was gone, some of the fiercer sort of Protestants chose lives or careers abroad.[52]

In this ugly battle, Henry's physical attraction to Catherine was obviously very useful to Gardiner and the duke. Subsequent accounts of her rise to the throne often cast Norfolk and Gardiner as an unsavoury cross between Catherine's chaperones and her pimps, hosting banquets at which they pushed a singing, smiling Catherine into the king's sights. Gardiner's modern biographer, Glyn Redworth, has cast doubt on this version of events, and there is room for scepticism, not least because this narrative of Catherine's rise is too neat.[53] The dowager duchess's previously mentioned recollection of Henry's instant attraction to Catherine provides evidence that the initial stage of their relationship was spontaneous and apparently inconsequential. The likelihood is that the king flirted with Catherine, probably quite obviously, but the impending arrival of Anne of Cleves made it little more than a social diversion. Once the king decided that he 'abhorred' his new wife, his interest in Catherine revived.[54]

That Norfolk was responding to circumstances as they unfolded is supported by the fact that he clearly knew very little about his niece. There is, for instance, absolutely nothing to suggest that he was aware of her previous romances with Henry Manox or Francis Dereham. The dowager did not rush to enlighten him. If the Howards had wanted to entice Henry VIII, they would not have chosen Catherine. She was damaged goods. Had they been as Machiavellian as the usual presentation of them suggests, at some point in the vetting process either the dowager duchess or the Countess of Bridgewater could have pointed out that elevating Catherine would put them all at risk in the long run. Rather, the king's infatuation seems to have caught them all off-guard, and while her family seem to have played the hand dealt to them – they would have been foolish not to – that is not the same thing as stacking the deck.

Confronted with the king's frequent demands for her company, Catherine sought the wisdom of her relatives. They gave her advice on the proper way to behave when she was with him, 'in what sort to entertain the King's Highness and how often', as it was put later.[55] On one of her trips back to Lambeth to visit her grandmother, Catherine discovered that Francis Dereham had absconded without telling anyone where he was going. The dowager asked her if she knew where he had gone, but she answered, probably quite truthfully, that she had no idea.[56] After he heard about the king's interest in his beloved, Francis confided his despair to a friend, and since the indulgent dowager consistently refused to give him permission to leave, Francis had taken matters into his own hands and fled.[57] He had called on Catherine before he left and gave her £100 of his savings to look after in his absence. If he did not return, he told her she could do what she liked with the money. Thoroughly unmoved by these cryptic and melodramatic comments, Catherine asked where he was going but did not press him when he refused to answer her. At Norfolk House, she asked their old friend Katherine Tilney of Francis's whereabouts, but like Catherine and the dowager, Tilney had no idea.

The precise chronology of Catherine's affair with the king is unclear. A few clues are provided in grants made to her by the royal household, one of which made Catherine a woman of moderate means in her own right – at the end of April, the goods of two condemned criminals, a father and son both called William Lidbeter, who had been convicted of murder, were signed over to her.[58] By modern standards, the second-hand goods of two killers might lack in romance, but the Tudors were incorrigible recyclers. In May, the king bought her twenty-three brand new quilts of sarsenet, a light silk, which was perhaps a welcome choice of fabric given the mounting temperature in the capital.[59]

At some point, her family decided to move Catherine and her silk quilts back to Lambeth for propriety's sake. During her courtship with the king, Anne Boleyn had insisted on being accompanied by her mother for a chaperone, while Edward Seymour and his wife fulfilled the honours for an unmarried Jane in 1536. Henry's barge, the *Lyon*, was difficult to miss given its size and gilding, so when he began paying evening visits to Lambeth, people talked, and when the official reason was that the king had called to pay his respects to the Dowager Duchess of Norfolk, they guffawed.[60] Whether the relationship with Catherine was sexual at this stage is unknown. The royal barge's visits provoked gossip, but Henry was historically impressed by women who preferred to wait for a wedding ring. If Catherine was his mistress, or if she would have become his mistress had the relationship lasted much longer, is unclear. A London merchant with ties to the court heard the affair was 'whispered by the courtiers, who observed the king to be much taken with another young lady of very diminutive stature'.[61] Queen Anne found out about the liaison and confided her unhappiness on 20 June to a fellow Clevian called Karl Harst, who lived in London. By that stage the king's relationship with Catherine was well advanced, and events in Europe had combined with those in London to make the young, lovely, 'diminutive' and vivacious Catherine a serious contender for Anne's crown.

Yet even with these setbacks, Henry's interest in Catherine and Gardiner's detention of the preachers, Cromwell's fate was not a foregone conclusion. His downfall was more of a cockfight than a fox hunt. Up until the very last moment, it was not clear to outside observers who would emerge as victor.[62] At the start of March, the Earl of Essex broke his neck in a riding accident, and instead of the title passing, as expected but not confirmed, to his son-in-law, it went to Thomas Cromwell two weeks after his three former protégés ended up in the Tower.[63] When one of the Duke of Norfolk's servants died, Cromwell tried to have the duke kept from the king's presence on the grounds that the man might have been a victim of the plague. Norfolk pointed out that there had been fourteen other people living with the man at the time, none of whom had subsequently fallen sick, and even if it had been the plague, the duke had been miles away when the death occurred.[64] As part of the counter-attack against his opponents, Cromwell arrested the conservative Bishop of Chichester, then made heavy hints that five more bishops who were suspected of secret loyalty to Rome would soon be taken.[65] Given the allegations of papism already made against Gardiner, it was not difficult to guess who one of the five might be.

One victim of Cromwell's counter-attack was Catherine's fellow maid of honour, Anne Bassett, who was interrogated but released after her stepfather Lord Lisle was imprisoned in the Tower. He was accused of papism and potentially treasonous communications with hostile foreign powers. Bassett's mother, who suffered a nervous breakdown when her husband was taken, had been seen throwing potentially incriminating letters 'into the jaques', that is, the toilets.[66] Lord Lisle's detention was a setback for Cromwell's opponents, but they rallied quickly. Norfolk had already asked for a commission to investigate heresy in the Pale of Calais, where Lord Lisle had served as governor, and he used his investigation to furnish the king with proof that Cromwell had been influential in allowing radicals and suspected heretics to escape to the colony.[67] Of the thirteen men who were shipped from Calais back to London to stand trial for heresy in the spring of 1540, five of them had previously been recipients of Cromwell's patronage. Over the previous few years, a significant amount of Henry's attention had been spent trying to crush 'the sedition likely to arise from the diversity of opinion in religion', and Norfolk's hunt in Calais suggested that Cromwell had been thwarting that objective.[68]

The atmosphere in the palace was nightmarish, and another member of the queen's household fell victim to the tit for tat when one of the grooms, a young man with the surname Mandeville, was hanged for sacramentarian heresy (the Protestant belief that the Eucharist during Holy Communion was purely symbolic rather than the older belief that, through the miracle of transubstantiation, it became the Body and Blood of Christ).[69] Watching from the sidelines, the French ambassador concluded, 'things are brought to such a pass that either Cromwell's party or that of the Bishop of Winchester must succumb'.[70]

At the time of his wedding in January, Henry had justified going through with it because to abandon Anne would 'be a mean[s] to drive her brother into the hands of the Emperor and the French king'.[71] By the end of spring, Cleves had transformed from an asset into a liability. English spies reported that the anti-Hapsburg clique at the French court was gaining ground.[72] Marguerite of Navarre defended King Henry in her conversations, and the English received signs that Queen Eleanor was the only member of the French royal family intent on preserving the alliance with the emperor.[73] A servant of Catherine de Medici, the dauphine of France, arrived in London with messages for Henry from the dauphine, Madame d'Etampes, and Queen Marguerite.[74] While he could not take any action that publicly contradicted his father's policy, the presence of his wife's servant in London strongly suggests that the dauphin's views correlated, in this instance, with his aunt's. At the same time, English fears that the Duke of Cleves's aggression might drag them into a war over the issue of Gueldres solidified.[75] The emperor warned Henry 'not to interfere between him and his subject', by which he meant the Duke of Cleves, who was technically his vassal, and following his suppression of a rebellion against his rule in Ghent, there were concerns that the emperor would now turn his attention to Cleves.[76] The treaty between England and Cleves was mutually defensive, but the English had only ever intended it to be invoked if they were attacked. As the emperor's alliance with France cracked open over the issue of Milan, Henry VIII could safely wash his hands of his in-laws.[77] In May, he informed the emperor that he had no intention of declaring war on Cleves's behalf.[78] At the same time, noblemen from the empire, such as the Prince of

Salerno and the Marquis of Massalombarda, received the emperor's permission to visit England, albeit in a private capacity.[79]

With the alliance gone, Queen Anne's position was no longer tenable. On 22 May, Henry received news that a prince, the Duke of Rothesay, had been born in Scotland as heir to Henry's nephew, King James V. James wrote to his uncle that God, in His great goodness, had sent 'a son and prince fair and lively to succeed to us and this our realm'.[80] There was no chance of Henry fathering a spare prince if he remained trapped in a marriage to a woman he considered useless and repellent. He desperately wanted to get out. Years later, Bishop Gardiner believed that it was this failure to arrange a dignified divorce for the king that sealed Cromwell's fate.[81] One of his colleagues warned the minister, 'For God's sake, devise for the release of the king; for, if he remains in this grief and trouble, we shall all one day smart for it.'[82] In one of the rare missteps of his career, Cromwell would not accept defeat.[83] Quite possibly, the prospect that Norfolk's niece would become queen in Anne's place compelled him to try shoring up the marriage to the extent of giving the queen advice, via her servants, on how to make herself more alluring to her husband.[84] That apparent dereliction of duty, when combined with his links to radical preachers, the campaign against him by his rivals, and the breakdown of the Franco-Hapsburg alliance, left Cromwell fatally vulnerable.[85] Henry did not forgive failure easily, and embarrassment even less so. Cromwell was arrested at a council meeting on 10 June, where Norfolk, along with some of Cromwell's former friends, helped tear decorations from his coat and joined in the cries of 'Traitor!' as the minister was taken to the Tower. Observing Cromwell's ruin, the French ambassador wrote, 'They had only reduced thus a personage to the state from which they raised him and treated him as hitherto everyone said he deserved.'[86] Cromwell, or 'Thomas Essex', as he had proudly taken to signing himself a few weeks earlier, had been completely forsaken. As the ambassador noted, the only courtiers left 'on his side [are] the archbishop of Canterbury, who dare not open his mouth, and the lord Admiral, who has long learnt to bend to all winds, and they have for open enemies the duke of Norfolk and the others'.[87]

Under the guise of trying to protect her and her servants from any possible outbreak of plague in the heat, Queen Anne's household was sent to Richmond Palace on the outskirts of London. It was a ruse to get her away from the king before the divorce proceedings began, or technically, the annulment, since Henry insisted the marriage had never been legal in the first place. Catherine stayed with her family while the council prepared to dissolve the king's marriage. As a young girl, Anne of Cleves had been betrothed to the Marquis de Pont-à-Mousson.[88] Despite having received the documentation which proved that the nature of that pre-contract had left both parties free to wed elsewhere, the English government insisted that this engagement meant Anne was never legally free to marry Henry VIII.[89] They had known all about the pre-contract early on in negotiations for her hand and pressed ahead rather than angling for Anne's youngest sister, Amelia, which they could have done if they had considered the impediment serious enough.[90]

To justify divorcing Anne, Henry fired out reasons like an erratic machine gun – his reluctance on his wedding day showed that he had been coerced into the marriage with a woman he 'liked so ill he was sorry she had come', his inability to consummate the match was described in detail, as were his subsequent wet dreams to prove he could and should marry somebody else.[91] A delegation was dispatched to Richmond to deliver the news to Anne that she was no longer queen, through her translator, 'who did his part very well'. The king's representatives reported that the queen took the news 'without alteration of countenance' and that she replied, through her official, 'that she is content always with your Majesty'.[92] In fact, as subsequent events were to show, Anne felt utterly humiliated.[93] Her earlier quiescence may have been because she genuinely did not understand that the decision had already been reached, and when she realised that she was definitely being divorced, Karl Harst remembered, 'Good Lord, she made such tears and bitter cries, it would break a heart of stone.'[94]

The three ladies-in-waiting who had joked with the queen about her lack of pregnancy during Lent testified to what she had said. The courtiers who had once been mortified about the king's frankness on the subject now fell over themselves to relay what had gone wrong in the royal bed – the king's physician, Dr Butts, confirmed the monarch's wet dreams but inability to perform with the queen; the Earl of Southampton apologised for praising Anne's looks so highly when he met her in Calais, though in his own defence he pointed out that considering he was escorting her to her wedding he felt that 'it was no time to dispraise her'; Sir Anthony Browne, who witnessed the couple's first meeting at Rochester, confessed that he had suspected from that point onwards that the king disliked her, and another gentleman of the privy chamber, Sir Anthony Denny, described the king's revulsion for his wife's drooping breasts, because the king had it in his head that saggy or large bosoms were a sign that a woman was not a virgin.[95] A remark by the late Lady Browne, who had told her husband 'how she saw in the Queen such fashion and manner of upbringing so gross that in her judgement the king should never heartily love her', was one of the milder insults tossed around during the inquest.[96] Anne's appearance, her personal hygiene, upbringing, and her most intimate parts were traduced to make sure the annulment went through. When asked about the non-consummation of the marriage, Henry could not answer in a simple affirmative; he constantly qualified it with aspersions such as 'if she brought her maidenhead with her' he 'left her as good a maid as [I] found her'.[97]

On 9 July, two archbishops, sixteen bishops, and 139 clergymen declared the marriage between Henry VIII and Anne of Cleves null and void on grounds of non-consummation and pre-contract.[98] Four days later, their decision was ratified by Parliament, which then made itself even more useful by rushing through a special act that permitted the king to marry a woman whom he had previously had sexual relations with or with any of her close relatives.[99] The act served as a legal exorcism for the ghost of Anne Boleyn.[100] The councillors could breathe easily, having made good on their promise to Henry at the start of the divorce proceedings – that they would secure 'your Highness's virtuous desire'.[101] Anne of Cleves's obedience was rewarded by a king anxious to show his generosity to the world and buy her silence. She was given an honorary position in the royal family, ranked above everyone except the king's children and his future wife, accorded the legal rank of one of his sisters, a sizeable entourage of servants, Henry VII's palace at Richmond, Anne Boleyn's childhood home at Hever Castle, and multiple smaller estates to supplement her income, as well as plate, jewels, clothes, and furniture for her houses.[102] In return for this, she was required to go quietly and write letters to her relatives in Europe lauding Henry's chivalry and the justice of her annulment.[103] She must also reside in England for the rest of her life, and her servants were asked to keep an eye on her, open her correspondence, and report if she ever attempted to take a lover or find another husband.[104] Nobody could replace the king, even with someone he had never wanted. Anne herself was fulsomely obedient: when her brother wrote to her, she sent the letters for inspection to Henry, who then sent them back to her.[105]

As Anne of Cleves began her new life, a betting Londoner's money was with the rumour heard by one of the diplomats, that 'it is commonly said that this King will marry a lady of great beauty, daughter of Norfolk's deceased brother'.[106] A few weeks before the divorce, lawyers working on the case had leaked news that Catherine was the intended replacement, when one of the team raised the possibility that 'the King could not marry the Lady Howard [*sic*], because she and Queen Anne [Boleyn] were in the second degree of blood', a point which necessitated the subsequent dispensation.[107]

Writing a century later, the Bishop of Salisbury saw the circumstances of Catherine's rise and Cromwell's fall as proof of the power of political faction at Henry VIII's court. In this version of events, the king had been manipulated by a young girl who fulfilled her family's agenda as they and their allies found, or manufactured, evidence against their opponents. This faction used Catherine's sexuality to unseat a queen supported by one of those opponents and in doing so secured his ruin and their triumph. He concluded, 'The charms of Catherine Howard, and the endeavours of the duke of Norfolk and the Bishop of Winchester, at length prevailed … [and] thus fell that great minister, that was raised merely upon the strength of his natural parts.'[108] It is an arresting but misleading narrative.

An octagonal tower stood in the grounds of the Palace of Whitehall. It was the court's cockfighting arena. It was built in 1533 and inside there were three tiers of seats for the spectators who would gather to watch as two aggravated birds tore each other to shreds. The queen's viewing gallery had originally been constructed for Anne Boleyn, and its location, with obstructed views, suggests that the late queen had not particularly enjoyed this blood sport.[109] Her husband was more enthusiastic, to say the least. The king's chair sat on top of the birds' cages. On Henry's nod, the grilles were raised and the contestants darted out into the pit.

Henry VIII was adept at letting his servants appear to pursue their own agendas when in fact they corresponded closely with his own. When they appeared to put anyone's needs before his own, when they bungled badly, or if they pursued a policy that upset or embarrassed Henry, as Cromwell did in 1540, he lifted the cage doors. Many of the leading nobles of Henry VIII's court detested his policies at one point or another, but not once did they side with a rebellion against him. Henry let them get away with comparatively little things, but obedience and fear were too ingrained in most for them to strike out from their sovereign. As the former Bishop of Worcester had stressed, 'When the king's Majesty himself commandeth me to do so, then I will do it, not afore.'[110] Technically, Thomas Cromwell, like Lord Exeter, Anne Boleyn, and Cardinal Wolsey before him, was destroyed by others, but only once the king signalled that it was time for the game to start.

Chapter 8

The Queen of Britain Will Not Forget

I met a Traveller from an antique land,
Who said, 'Two vast and trunkless legs of stone
Stand in the desert. Near them, on the sand,
Half sunk, a shattered visage lies, whose frown,
And wrinkled lip, and sneer of cold command,
Tell that its sculptor well those passions read,
Which yet survive, stamped on these lifeless things,
The hand that mocked them and the heart that fed:
And on the pedestal these words appear:
"My name is OZYMANDIAS, King of Kings.
Look on my works ye Mighty, and despair!"
No thing beside remains. Round the decay
Of that Colossal Wreck …

– Percy Bysshe Shelley,
'Ozymandias' (1818)

Oatlands Palace, one of Henry's favourite spots for hunting, lay within the Hampton Court Chase, a 10,000-acre private royal hunting route linking several palaces and lodges, which had recently been completed at enormous cost because, as his councillors explained after his death, 'his Highness waxed heavy with sickness, age and corpulences of the body, and might not travail so readily abroad, but was constrained to have his game and pleasure ready at hand'.[1] It was there that Henry planned to spend what we might call his honeymoon.

Catherine can not have seen much of her fiancé in the run-up to the wedding. He remained in London for most of July to host the visitors from the empire, then to testify to the illegality of his marriage with Anne of Cleves. Catherine's wedding was even more private than Anne's, and the formal announcement was not made until 8 August.[2] In the meantime, there were rumours in London that Catherine was already pregnant, and derogatory comments were making the rounds at foreign courts, fuelled by their respective ambassadors' assessment of the situation, which included the guess that the wedding only took place because Catherine had found herself enceinte.[3]

By marrying Catherine, Henry VIII achieved the dubious distinction of becoming the most married Christian monarch in European history – the previous record had been held by Emperor Charles IV, who had managed to avoid Henry's reputation for matrimonial misadventures by the natural deaths that resulted in three of his four wives predeceasing him.[4] Despite their relief that Cleves had lost its most powerful protector, at the Hapsburg court Henry's latest matrimonial hiccup was cited as proof that murky and megalomaniacal morals had been the real reason for his rupture with Rome. In a letter to the emperor's secretary, a Spanish governor wrote, 'A very good joke of the king of England again divorcing his Queen. Not in vain does he pretend and assume spiritual authority that he may at will decide upon matrimonial cases whenever he himself is concerned. Although this is a wicked and abominable thing to do, yet it must be owed that concerning – as it does the duke of Cleves – the Queen's brother, it is not so bad after all.'[5]

While the king was preparing to welcome the Marquis of Massalombarda, Catherine received a letter from her old friend, secretary, and ally in mischief, Joan Acworth, now Joan Bulmer following her marriage to a small landowner from York.[6] A knight in the dowager duchess's service, Sir George Seaford, had recently called on Joan during his visit to the city. Seaford told her about

Catherine's impending marriage, and Joan was not slow to put ink to paper asking for permission to join her in London. As her letter makes clear, she did not enjoy married life and she trusted in Catherine's newfound influence to rescue her from it.

If I could wish you all the honour, wealth, and good fortune you could desire, you would neither lack health, wealth, long life, not yet prosperity. Nevertheless, seeing I cannot, as I would, express this unto you, I would wish these my most hearty salutations might you to know, that whereas it had been shown unto me, that God of his high goodness hath put unto the knowledge of the king a contract of matrimony that the queen hath made with another before she came into England, and thereupon there will be a lawful divorce had between them; and as it is thought that the king of his goodness will put you in the same honour that she was in, which no doubt you be worthy to have, most heartily desiring you to have in your remembrance the unfeigned love that my heart hath always borne towards you, which for the same kindness found in you again hath desired always your presence, if it might be so, above all other creatures, and the change of fortune that hath brought me, on the contrary, into the utmost misery of the world and most wretched life. Seeing no ways, then, I can express in writing, knowing no remedy out of it, without you, or your goodness, will find the means to get me to London, which will be very hard to do; but if you write unto my husband and command him to bring me up, which I think he dare not disobey, for if it might be, I would fain be with you before you were in your honour; and in the mean season I beseech you to save some room for me, what you shall think fit yourself, for the nearer I were to you the gladder I would be of it, what pains soever I did take. I would write more unto you, but I dare not be so bold, for considering the great honour you are towards, it did not become me to put myself in your presence; but the remembrance of the perfect honesty I have always known to be in you, and the report of Sir George Seaford, which hath assured me that the same thing remains in you still, hath encouraged me to this.

Whereupon I beseech you not to be forgetful of this my request for if you do not help me, I am not likely to have worldly joys. Desiring you, if you can, to let me have some answer of this for the satisfying of mind, for I know the queen of Britain will not forget her secretary, and favour you will show.

Your humble servant,
With heart unfeigned,
Jone Bulmer[7]

Given Joan's behaviour at Horsham and Lambeth, many historians have wondered why Catherine agreed to her request and appointed someone who had the potential to cause her so much harm. Looking at the letter, it is understandable why some subsequent writers have been quick to think that Joan's effusive humility masked 'a subtle form of blackmail'.[8] Phrases such as 'I would write more unto you, but I dare not be so bold,' her confidence that 'the queen of Britain will not forget her secretary,' and the slightly commanding tone in which she instructed Catherine on how to summon her to court could be interpreted as Joan applying pressure to ensure that Catherine answered her, rather than the sentiment she doused the letter in. One of Queen Anne's maids of honour, Mary Norris, was leaving court to marry Sir George Carew, a soldier who later drowned when the warship *Mary Rose* capsized in 1545, and Mary's departure left a vacancy, although since Joan did not come from an aristocratic background and was now married, that particular place could not pass to her.[9] In a better mood, the king was also beginning to relax the cap on numbers in the queen's household, which theoretically gave Catherine the leeway she needed to appoint former companions like Joan. The first beneficiary of this expansion was Catherine's distant cousin and childhood companion, Katherine Tilney, who was brought to court as one of the chamberers.

In themselves, such appointments were typical and invited no suspicion at the time. The noble mind-set in 1540 was still predominantly feudal. The promotion of families who had served or were tied to one's own was the sine qua non of aristocratic employment. Everything turned on the idea that there was an inextricable link between loyalty, service and obedience and protection, patronage, and generosity. Not long before, Catherine's uncle William had helped find a new job for Alice Wilkes when she wanted to move on and get married.[10] When Sir George Seaford brought her the news that her old superior was only a few weeks away from becoming queen, Joan Bulmer was well within her rights to ask for a place at her side. She can hardly be blamed for wanting to join the queen's household, which, if light on salaries, was heavy on kickbacks. Household employees had plenty of opportunities to enrich themselves through selling their influence to outsiders. In 1545, a man called Clement Throckmorton, who worked as the queen's cupbearer, was able to pay £654 for lands in Worcestershire and Warwickshire, a sum that even a nobleman might have hesitated at.[11]

Catherine's response to Joan Bulmer does not survive, but on the basis of the latter's letter some historians have presumed that Joan was appointed to Catherine's household, as the first example of the queen's stupidity in stuffing her household with friends and relatives, many of whom would have been better left in the past. The belief that Joan was invited to court in 1540 has led to other theories about how Catherine ran her household and why her queenship ended in the way that it did in 1542. Joan Bulmer's admission to the household has been repeated in nearly every biography of Catherine written for the last century and a half, but Joan's petition to 'the queen of Britain' is a cautionary lesson in the power of assumption and repetition during research, because there is no evidence that Joan Bulmer re-entered Catherine's service after she married the king.

When former servants of the dowager duchess who had subsequently transferred to Catherine's household are mentioned in the surviving interrogation records of 1541, it is often with the suffix of 'now servant to the Queen' or 'now chamberer to the Queen'. In the same documents, Joan is simply referred to as 'Young Bulmer's wife'.[12] In a letter to one of the English ambassadors to France, the king's councillors stated that Catherine had hired 'to be one of her chamberers, one of the women' from Horsham, who, in earlier documents from the month in question, was named as Katherine Tilney.[13] When Joan was quizzed about Catherine in 1541, she was only asked about Catherine's life before marriage, and during a later round of interviews she is grouped in the transcripts with people such as Mary Lascelles, Catherine's sister-in-law Anne Howard, or Dereham's friend Robert Damport, none of whom served in the queen's household.[14] While most of this evidence is circumstantial, the failure to ask Joan any questions about Catherine's life after she married the king suggests that her request to come to court in July 1540 had still not been granted by November 1541.

Joan Bulmer had been wrong when she described Catherine as 'the queen of Britain' – she was only Queen of England in 1540, if Britain was taken by its proper meaning, the islands rather than any one part of them – but she was right, if not in the way she hoped, when she fawningly suggested that Catherine 'will not forget'. Accepting that Joan was not successful in her petition helps give a clearer picture of what the Howards were doing in the wake of Catherine's unexpected and meteoric ascent. We know from one specific piece of evidence from later in Catherine's career that when it came to the appointments of ghosts from her life at Chesworth, the young queen turned to her grandmother and her aunt. The old aristocratic anxiety over what the servants knew festered in the dowager and even more so in the Countess of Bridgewater.[15] The downfall of the Countess of Salisbury and the rest of the Pole family in 1538 had commenced when a servant divulged details of their private conversations. During the final days of Anne Boleyn, her enemies had tried to bully one of her favourite maids.[16] Catherine's uncle William and his wife Margaret knew something about her earlier romances, but based on the evidence imparted later, their role seems to have been far more passive than the dowager duchess's or the Countess of Bridgewater's. They were the two who knew the most, and the countess was the one most preoccupied by the damage servants could cause – her first husband's path to ruin had been marked at every stage by it. During the early stages of his feud, Rhys had accused three of his late grandfather's servants of 'crafty and untrue means' in embezzlement after they abandoned the family to join the household of his enemy, Lord Ferrers.[17] At his trial for treason in 1531, one of Rhys's dependants, James ap Gruffydd ap Hywel, testified against him and, according to the countess, committed perjury by doing so. The countess did not forget the circumstances of her first husband's death, and a family tradition maintained that she spent several years trying to prove that another former servant, Edward Llwyd, had accepted a bribe of 500 marks in return for also providing evidence for Rhys's prosecution.[18]

The dowager and the countess's decision to find jobs for nearly everyone who knew enough to destroy Catherine is usually dismissed as 'dangerous idiocy'.[19] But the truth is that they took their time, with a policy that aimed to charm the witnesses by arranging audiences with Catherine, but as part of a wider strategy to keep the most dangerous, or indiscreet, away from regular attendance at court. It was still a risk-filled strategy, but that does not mean it was axiomatically stupid. All the Howard ladies had to go on was the evidence of past crises, such as servants' roles in the destruction of the countess's first husband in 1531 or the Poles in 1538. In July 1540, Catherine's family did not know if or how disaster would overtake them, simply that it might and that somehow they had to at least try to prevent it. The unknowns were the servants and companions who had witnessed Catherine's romance with Dereham at first hand. Short of sliding into the worst kind of moral depravity and having them all killed, the Howards had to prevent their former retainers from blabbing to the wrong people. If all the witnesses had a vested interest in seeing Catherine remain undamaged by her past, then there was less chance of anyone going to the council with the information that Catherine had not been a virgin when she married the king. The Howards did not appoint the Chesworth alumnae en masse, and it was only in August and September of the year after Catherine's marriage that there was a steady trickle of former Lambeth or Chesworth employees entering the royal household or being invited to visit as the queen's guests. There is enough evidence left to us to support the theory that the Howards who knew something about Catherine's affair with Dereham – the queen herself, the dowager duchess, the Countess of Bridgewater, her brother Lord William, and his wife Margaret – decided to proceed with caution.[20] Each appointee was treated differently – Katherine Tilney, who knew more than anyone at Chesworth since she had actually been in the bed one night when Francis and Catherine began canoodling, was a safe early appointment because of her blood relationship to the queen and the dowager duchess. Joan Bulmer did not exhibit any clear animus to Catherine in 1541, which raises the possibility that she was fobbed off with the promise that she would be sent for in due course, a strategy which the Howards repeated later.[21]

One more factor is important in understanding the policy embarked upon by Catherine's childhood guardians in 1540. They were solely concerned with containing the matter of Francis Dereham. Although most modern accounts of Catherine's career state that she also appointed Henry Manox to her staff as a musician, they are incorrect, and interviews from November 1541 clearly show that he was still living and working in Lambeth.[22] Manox was completely overlooked, as were any of the girls who had not shared the maidens' chamber with Catherine, most damagingly the censorious Mary Lascelles, who had served as nursemaid to Catherine's young cousin Agnes. Manox and Catherine had never consummated their relationship, and it was highly unlikely that she ever confessed to her grandmother or aunt about how far they had gone physically, with the result that they seem to have dismissed it as a matter of no real importance, or else forgotten it entirely. Dereham, on the other hand, had spoken of marrying Catherine; he had made a spectacle of himself when she left him for life at court, and there were plenty of people, from the countess's maid to the dowager's porter, who knew about the liaison. If anyone repeated Dereham's claim that he and Catherine were legally pre-contracted in the fullest sense possible, then she could be divorced by the king and ruined. Dereham – who was God knows where when Catherine walked down the aisle – would still have to be taken care of as the most dangerous and unreliable witness of all, if he ever returned.

Only a few ladies and gentlemen of the privy chamber were present as witnesses as Henry and Catherine stood before Bishop Bonner. As at her baptism, the Church required a declaration of consent and both answered that they wished to be married. Henry, his high voice issuing from thin lips, vowed, 'I, Henry, take thee to my wedded wife, to have and to hold from this day forward, for better or worse, for richer for poorer, in sickness and in health, till death do us part, and thereto I plight thee my troth.' Catherine replied, 'I, Catherine, take thee to my wedded husband, to have and to hold from this day forward, for better for worse, for richer for poorer, in sickness and in health, to be bonny and buxom in bed and at board, till death us do part, and thereto I plight thee my troth.' As her slightly longer vow made clear, a wife had a certain set of duties and emotional obligations when it came to serving her husband. When the ring slid over her slender finger, guided by the bejewelled and plump hands of the forty-nine-year-old groom, she became his property. A king ruled over his subjects, but they were not his possessions; in contrast, a wife had no separate legal identity to her husband and could not even leave a will of her own until she became a widow. Marital rape was regarded as an oxymoron, and domestic abuse was frowned upon only if it reached the stage where the wife's health or life were endangered.

If her wedding night at Oatlands was the first time Catherine slept with Henry VIII, she cannot have had a particularly pleasant evening, even disregarding the necessary inconvenience of pretending to lose her virginity. Since his third marriage, Henry's physical appetite had grown, his sporting capacities had faded, and his waist had expanded. An ulcer on his leg regularly oozed pus. Rather than heal, it periodically closed over. When that happened, Henry's face became discoloured with the pain he endured.[23] Mercifully for Catherine, the man in the long embroidered nightgown who climbed into bed next to her was not syphilitic, despite how frequently that has been asserted in the years since his death. The idea that Henry had syphilis was not suggested prior to an article published in 1888, which did not make much of an impact until its findings were revived in 'The Medical Problems of Henry VIII', a piece written by the Danish historian Ove Brinch in 1958. Brinch argued that some portraits from later in Henry's life show a ridge in the nose consistent with a syphilitic gumma.[24] Syphilis was a relatively new phenomenon in the sixteenth century, the cause célèbre of early modern diseases, with the result that when it appeared it was hardly ever misdiagnosed and it was nearly always treated with mercury. None of Henry VIII's medical records, which survive intact, contain bills or lists of mercury. Furthermore, he did not exhibit many of the symptoms associated with secondary or tertiary syphilis.

Along with its fixture in popular culture, the syphilis myth was recently resurrected in biographies of Anne Boleyn and Catherine, despite having been conclusively disproved decades ago when Henry's medical history was thoroughly examined in two mid-century texts – Frederick Chamberlin's *The Private Character of Henry the Eighth* (1932) and Sir Arthur MacNalty's *Henry VIII: A Difficult Patient* (1952).[25] Chamberlin compiled a full medical report on Henry's physical symptoms, his wives' miscarriages, his children's health, and the medical treatments he received, and sent it to medical experts in Britain and the United States with the request that they return an opinion on whether it was possible, in light of what they had read, for Henry VIII to have suffered from syphilis. Sir D'Arcy Power, vice president of the Royal College of Surgeons, wrote back that 'there does not seem to be the least reason, on the surgical side, for supposing that he ever had syphilis'. John Whitridge Williams, professor of obstetrics at Johns Hopkins University in Maryland, replied that 'there is nothing in the histories of either Mary or Elizabeth [Henry's daughters] to indicate that they had congenital syphilis'. Dr Eardley Lancelot Holland, editor of the *Journal of Obstetrics and Gynaecology of the British Empire*, told Chamberlin that in his opinion 'it is improbable that Henry suffered from syphilis', and Professor Philip F. Williams at the University of Pennsylvania concluded that any evidence trying to link Henry with the disease was 'insufficient' to support a diagnosis.[26]

Were there other problems for Catherine to deal with on her wedding night? Henry's private life was so improbable that it has provoked many theories as possible explanations, some more plausible than others. One which has gained widespread credence in academic accounts of Henry's life over the last fifty years is the idea that Henry was more or less impotent after he entered middle age. This is a more tenable theory than the one that posits he was syphilitic. The more thoughtful exponents of the impotence theory argue that the psychological pressures to sire an heir led to physical problems masked by a larger-than-life personality, which, according to one of Henry's recent biographers, 'covered up this weakness with male braggadocio'.[27] There were moments when the mask seemed to slip. When the Hapsburgs' ambassador made an innocuous comment about small families, the king shouted, 'Am I not a man? Am I not? Am I not?'[28] Another piece of evidence central to a discussion of the king's bedroom problems is Anne Boleyn's alleged complaint to her sister-in-law that sex with the king was not enjoyable, but at least it did not last very long.[29] Much of Henry's behaviour seems explicable when looked at in this light, from minor details in his everyday appearance – even someone ambivalent about the nuances of Freud might wonder at the increasing size of the king's codpieces – to the public humiliations of his first, second, and fourth wives and the neurotic preoccupation with sexual performance that pushed him to flout convention by choosing wives he already knew himself to be attracted to.

Speculation about Henry's poor performance as a lover has resulted in several other theories about the king and his marriages, the oddest of which is the claim that his wives, faced with their husband's impotence, took to adultery to provide an heir and save themselves. This theory holds water only if the essential facts of sex, impotence, and conception are ignored. If Henry had been impotent, he would have known that his wife's pregnancy was the result of infidelity. Even if Anne Boleyn did admit to her sister-in-law that she did not enjoy sex, and whether she ever said it is contested, her comment did not imply that Henry was impotent. If anything, it confirmed the opposite.

If Henry was affected by intermittent erectile dysfunction rather than long-term impotence, any wife tempted to stray for the sake of a child would have been more sensible to cling to the hope that her husband would perform again soon, as he clearly had performed at one time with all of them, except Anne of Cleves. Childlessness might end a queen's career; adultery certainly would. In light of Henry's obesity in later life, flagging sexual performance was inevitable, but it is difficult to see much evidence of impotence in his relationship with Catherine.

No joint portrait of Henry and Catherine as man and wife was ever painted to celebrate their marriage – the fashion for such portraits did not take off in England until the reign of the happily married Charles I in the following century – but Henry certainly emerged from his fifth bridal chamber in far better spirits than those in which he had emerged from his fourth.[30] Marital bliss was very much the mood as he and Catherine set off on a ten-day hunting trip through the new Court Chase. Catherine had married a man who, while much older than her and putting on weight, was still an impressive figure; or perhaps it would be more accurate to describe his appearance as inspiring, not just in terms of his height and confidence, but also in the way he could give her everything she had ever wanted – jewels, land, money, limited power, and significant influence. Having only had space in the palace stables for one horse of her own when she was a maid of honour, Catherine now had her own master of the horse, the ambitious and athletic John Dudley, who oversaw everything to do with the steeds a queen had access to.[31] Henry VIII often sent to Europe for the best horses for the royal studs and stables. Palfreys, generally agreed to be the finest kind of riding horse for a lady, were ranked in the stables according to which of the five shades of the desired grey they sported. Surviving inventories list royal saddles covered with silk or fine leather, with black-silk-and-gold reins and copper-fringed buttons and tassels.[32]

One place the newlyweds could have visited en route back to London was Henry's latest hunting lodge with the none-too-subtle name of Nonsuch, inspired by and built to eclipse the French royal family's châteaux in the Loire Valley, such as Amboise or Chenonceau. Construction on Nonsuch had started two years earlier and was almost completed by 1541, though some parts of the palace were not finished until 1545. Its cost and magnificence did not translate into a large palace: it had only one public reception room. Its primary purpose was to accommodate the king and his riding household, the reduced entourage he took with him on small hunting trips such as the one with Catherine in 1540.[33]

Nothing survives of Nonsuch today – by the time it was gifted to the Queen Mother Henrietta Maria, in 1660, it was already beginning to crumble.[34] Part of the reason why Nonsuch was in such a shambolic state by the time it passed to Henrietta Maria was doubtless the neglect it had suffered during and after the English Civil War, but far more harm was done by the way in which it and nearly all Henry VIII's palaces had been built. During the reign of his youngest daughter, Henry had acquired a posthumous reputation in England as 'a perfect Builder as well of fortresses as of pleasant palaces'.[35] At the start of Elizabeth's reign, her father's palaces still retained their splendid appearance and stood as expressions of Henry's interest in architecture, masonry, and the arts. They suggested that he had been the multi-faceted Renaissance prince he aspired to be. However, with the exception of a few wine cellars now occasionally used by the Ministry of Defence to host receptions, the only bit of Whitehall Palace that survives today is its banqueting house, which was built on the orders of James I. When most of the rest of the palace burned down in an accidental fire in 1698, its sturdiest buildings were those which had been added by the Stuarts. Hampton Court, the largest surviving Tudor palace, had its foundations laid under the watchful aegis of Cardinal Wolsey, and St James's Palace, which also remains, was a lesser residence that may ironically have weathered the centuries ahead because Henry did not take much interest in it while it was being built.

The other palaces' long-term problems reveal a great deal about the king's mind and capabilities. Henry was impatient to see his ideas realised, and he had no interest in allowing them the time they needed to be well executed. The royal household's accounts are littered with overtime payments to workmen who toiled through the night once the king had decided that he would be inspecting his latest renovation in a few days, weeks if not months before he should have. Charcoal braziers were dashed around the palaces to dry the paintwork as the king approached.[36] Under pressure from the king, the decoration of the palaces was perfected at the cost of their longevity, and the workmanship in most of Henry VIII's homes was in fact slipshod, rushed and insufficient, which is why so few of them managed to last much more than a century. The same was true of the fortresses he had ordered when he feared an invasion. The French ambassador, who saw some of them, remarked that they looked impressive but he doubted how strong they were, given the haste in which they had been built.[37]

Catherine's honeymoon played out in a mood of sticky somnolence. The fiction of plague as an excuse to move Anne of Cleves to Richmond had become a reality as England struggled with drought and stultifying heat. One MP wrote later that in the summer of 1540 there was suffering 'universally through the realm [and] great death, by reason of new hot agues and Fluxes, and some Pestilence, in which season was such a drought, that wells and small rivers were clean dried, so that much cattle died for lack of water: and the Thames was so shallow, and the fresh water of so small strength, that the Salt water flowed above

London bridge'.[38] Henry, however, did absolutely nothing, and it was left to urban authorities to organise penitential parades through the streets, begging God to send them relief and rain.[39] The king's indifference to his subjects' needs was a long-running theme in his reign. He had, after all, pitched them headlong into a generation of political instability, and unlike his great-uncle, father, and two daughters, he never pushed forward any legislation which could improve his subjects' lot in life. Today, there is an oft-repeated view that Henry VIII was a popular monarch, because his people admired his flamboyant personality and possibly exaggerated machismo, but the sources from the time record complex attitudes that veered from loyalty through frustration to outright loathing in almost equal measure. A year before Catherine's wedding, one of her countrymen remarked that 'if the King knew every man's thought, it would make his heart quake'.[40] In the sixteenth century, it was a rare man who could unite the vanguard of the Protestant and Catholic reformations, but Henry VIII managed to be hated by both sides. The German reformer Philip Melanchthon described him as 'the English Nero' and prayed 'May God destroy this monster!'; another called him 'godless', while an Italian Catholic priest concluded that because of Henry, 'never before was Christianity in such turmoil as today. The King of England triumphs in his ruin.'[41] In Ireland, priests denounced him as the 'worst man in the world'.[42]

A few weeks after Catherine's wedding, the celebrant vividly and horribly demonstrated his repudiation of his former patron Cromwell by overseeing the arrest, torture, and trial for heresy of a fourteen-year-old apprentice boy called Richard Meekins. Meekins's burning stunned a city that had already witnessed more than its fair share of horrible and controversial exterminations.[43] There was a sense in London of repulsed malaise at the cost of Henry's religious policies. Meekins's only crime was having heard Protestants speak against the Mass, at a time when Henry's government had allowed them to do so, and then to gullibly repeat what they said to someone who, in their turn, reported it to the diocesan officials. Henry's religious policy had changed and what was once publicly preached had now been deemed heresy. Reacting to the events of the summer of 1540, a Huntingdonshire man called Robert Swinerton was hauled before the council for saying, 'O Jesus, what a world is this that so many men shall die, and all for one man's sake!'[44] In London, people jokingly asked if the two-year-old Prince of Wales, whose mother had died after giving birth to him, would turn out to be as great a murderer as his father since 'he must be a murderer by kind for he murdered his mother in his birth'.[45]

Like all those around Henry, Catherine was careful to express her views of her husband only in terms of the most abject obedience and adoration, but there are comments from those who knew Henry's courtiers, but were not courtiers themselves, that this was play-acting. Even some comments made by Catherine in future conversations with Thomas Culpepper suggest that she was deeply afraid of the king. The Prince of Salerno, an Italian nobleman who spent just over a week at Henry's court a month before Catherine's wedding, held his peace while he was in London, but even Henry's generosity could not sway the prince's opinion of him. Salerno later told his countrymen that the king was 'like a pig', and he was even less impressed by the environment at court. He felt that he had been treated like a spy, with the courtiers' good manners failing to mask the sense of eyes at keyholes and ears behind the walls. No wonder Salerno had been treated like a spy; at Henry VIII's court, nearly everyone was. The French ambassador had informants watching the Duke of Norfolk and the king's eldest daughter, servants stole letters, sensible people wrote in ciphers, and the Hapsburgs' ambassador knew that an Italian physician who dined with him was 'the King's spy … I had no difficulty in guessing, by various loose remarks he made, who had sent him on to me'.[46] The Prince of Salerno blamed the king for the atmosphere. 'Everything is descending into chaos,' he wrote of his time in England, 'and it seems like Hell.'[47]

Salerno's view was held, in one way or another, by most Europeans who encountered Henry in his later years. Two days before Catherine's honeymoon ended, the French ambassador to

England, Charles de Marillac, gave his unvarnished assessment of Henry VIII to his superior, the Constable de Montmorency.[48] It is perhaps one of the most detailed and honest accounts of Henry's rule by a contemporary:

First, to commence with the head, this Prince seems tainted, among other vices, with three which in a King may be called plagues. The first is that he is so covetous that all the riches in the world would not satisfy him. Hence the ruin of the abbeys, spoil of all churches that had anything to take ... Hence, too, the accusation of so many rich men, who, whether condemned or acquitted, are always plucked; and it is unlikely that he should pardon the living who troubles even the dead, without fearing the offence to the religion of the world which reveres them as saints, witness St. Thomas of Canterbury, who, because his relics and bones were adorned with gold and jewels, has been declared traitor. Everything is good prize, and he does not reflect that to make himself rich he has impoverished his people, and does not gain in goods what he loses in renown. As it seemed difficult to attain his desires after withdrawing obedience from the Holy See, he got preachers and ministers to persuade the people that it was better to employ the Church revenue on hospitals, colleges, and other foundations tending to the public good than to fatten lazy and useless monks. Having under this pretext taken to himself what had been consecrated to God, when the same preachers and ministers exhorted him to fulfil his duty and remit it to better uses they have been condemned and burnt as heretics, as they said at their execution, to the scandal of everyone. And although they well deserved to be the end of that of which they had been the beginning, still, those who commanded them are not free from blame, for, if they showed repentance for what was done, they should restore what they have demolished; but they easily find a thousand ways to take things to themselves and not a single one to give them up.

Thence proceeds the second plague, distrust and fear. This King, knowing how many changes he has made, and what tragedies and scandals he has created, would fain keep in favour with everybody, but does not trust a single man, expecting to see them all offended, and he will not cease to dip his hand in blood as long as he doubts his people. Hence every day edicts are published so sanguinary that with a thousand guards one would scarce be safe. Hence too it is that now with us, as affairs incline, he makes alliances which last as long as it makes for him to keep them.

The third plague, lightness and inconstancy, proceeds partly from the other two and partly from the nature of the nation, and has perverted the rights of religion, marriage, faith and promise, as softened wax can be altered to any form.

The subjects take example from the Prince, and the ministers seek only to undo each other to gain credit, and under colour of their master's good each attends to his own.[49]

Two days after this letter was written, Catherine made her first public appearance as queen consort at Hampton Court Palace.[50] The news of the royal wedding was announced there at the same time.[51] A week later, on the Feast of the Assumption, she was included in the prayers for the royal family for the first time.[52] In the descent into the chaos described by the Prince of Salerno, the office had already seen one queen banished into internal exile after twenty-three years of marriage, a second publicly butchered on charges that would have raised eyebrows at the court of Agrippina, a third who lay dying while her husband debated whether to cancel his hunting trip to Esher, and a fourth who had been metaphorically stripped bare before the public as every fold, sag, and blemish was discussed in excruciating detail to justify why she was too grotesque to please her husband.[53] Just over a year later, the Privy Council claimed that everyone had expected Catherine to succeed where the others had failed because 'after sundry troubles in marriage', Henry had found in her 'a Jewel for womanhood'.[54]

Chapter 9

All These Ladies and My Whole Kingdom

I am a spirit of no common rate;
The summer still doth tend upon my state;
And I do love thee: therefore, go with me;
I'll give thee fairies to attend on thee,
And they shall fetch thee jewels from the deep,
And sing while thou on pressed flowers dost sleep …

– William Shakespeare,
A Midsummer Night's Dream (*c*.1595)

One heavily romanticised version of Catherine's ascent claimed that Henry first noticed her when she was serving in the nursery of his two-year-old son, Edward. Visiting his child one afternoon, the king spotted Catherine curtseying with the rest of the women. He marched over, raised her to her feet, and told her, 'Catherine, from henceforward, I wish you never to do that again, but rather that all these ladies and my whole kingdom should bend the knee to you, for I wish to make you Queen.' Catherine made a suitably self-effacing response, as virtuous maidens inevitably did, and the king 'sent for the Bishop of London to come and marry him' that very same day.[1]

The story is fiction. Despite living in London at the time, the Spanish merchant who wrote it managed to get the order of Henry's marriages to Anne of Cleves and Catherine in reverse order. His account does nonetheless capture something of the suddenness with which Catherine made the transition from courtier to queen consort. Compared to her immediate predecessors, she had comparatively little experience of life at court before becoming one of its principal figures: Katherine of Aragon had been Princess of Wales and then dowager princess for nearly eight years by the time she became queen in 1509; for most of her childhood Anne Boleyn had lived in the household of the Queen of France, then the Queen of England's from 1521 to 1527, and enjoyed her own household as de facto first lady throughout the six years of the king's first annulment; and Jane Seymour had served in the households of both Queen Katherine and Queen Anne. Catherine, in contrast, was a resident at court for no more than eight months by the time she became queen – a short apprenticeship before being promoted to the top job.

Catherine's household was a vast entity with a corresponding income. She and her servants had access to her own granary, bakery, brewery, buttery (to dispense wine and ale to the staff), cellar, garderobe of spices, a chaundry (to allocate the candles and tapers for the queen's rooms and those rationed to her retainers), a ewery to house her table linen, and a private kitchen which was supplied by her own slaughterhouse, scullery, and wood yard. There were some hardships, admittedly, since unlike the king, the queen had to make do without her own confectioner or a wafery, a specific department set aside to take care of her biscuits. Her kitchens also lacked a separate department for poultry, meat, and fish.[2] Within each of these departments, there were different staff members and competing agendas. Maintaining goodwill in the queen's household required a nimble grasp of decorum to avoid giving offence, and even the queen had to respect that. For instance, when a bill came into the household from an apothecary, it was considered a faux-pas if the queen signed it. Payment should be authorised by her vice chamberlain, Sir Edward Baynton.[3]

On the male side of her staff, Catherine had ten officers of her household, headed by her chamberlain Thomas Manners, 1st Earl of Rutland, a peer who was roughly the same age as her husband and who delegated most of his work to Baynton. There was also a clerk of the Queen's Council; a serjeant at arms; a clerk in charge of her wardrobe; eight titled positions in her stables; two wardens attached to her wardrobe; two sewers of her chamber, who had the job of tasting her food and guiding her guests to sit in the proper spots at dinner; four gentlemen ushers; two gentlemen waiters; twenty-one grooms; three pageboys, who carried out odd jobs and errands; four footmen, seven yeomen, and two grooms extraordinary for busy occasions in the queen's household; two men who cleaned and arranged Catherine's litter when she travelled; and seven sumptermen, who packed and led the workhorses when the court moved to a different residence.

While these male servants were vital to the running of the household, it was the ladies, as those who came into regular contact with the queen, who were the most important people in the establishment. These thirty-four women, excluding laundresses and kitchen staff, were grouped into five ranks – six great ladies, four ladies, and four gentlewomen of the queen's privy chamber; nine ladies of exalted rank; five maids of honour; one 'mother of the maids', who watched over the maids of honour on the queen's behalf; and four or five chamberers.[4]

Of these women, the six great ladies were the women with the least day-to-day interaction with Catherine. As their collective name suggests, they were drawn exclusively from the icing on the upper crust. At the start of her queenship, this group consisted of the king's niece Lady Margaret Douglas; Catherine's cousin Mary Fitzroy (née Howard), Dowager Duchess of Richmond and Somerset; her uncle William's wife, Lady Margaret Howard; Katherine Brandon (née Willoughby), Duchess of Suffolk; Mary Radclyffe (née Arundell), Countess of Sussex; and the king's former mistress, the lovely Elizabeth (née Blount), Lady Clinton, mother of the late Duke of Richmond. Shifts and positions in the queen's households were frequently adjusted to suit its members' pregnancies, and the great ladies as a group were often thinned out by the requirements of childbed. The Countess of Sussex left royal service to give birth to her son, Lord John Radclyffe, around the same time that Lady Clinton departed and never returned after she died giving birth to a daughter.[5] The other great ladies were only required on state occasions, when their rank was used to convey the government's respect for its visitors.

Etiquette elevated Catherine as queen in the same way but to far greater heights than it had every day since her childhood. When she sat in public or in her apartments, her chair was canopied by a cloth of estate. Everyone around her had to 'stand still as a stone' until she spoke, according to the strictures of an etiquette manual.[6] Before she entered a public space, her servants cleared a route for her. In her guard chamber, her yeomen ushers were on hand to gently whisper advice and 'receive, teach, and direct every man' about the intricacies of court decorum.[7] When Catherine sneezed, a forest of caps undulated in the air from her male servants and all, regardless of gender, politely blessed her.[8]

When she awoke, usually at about seven o'clock in the morning, she was greeted by the women who had, until June, been her superiors. Once, she had been expected to stand and curtsey when they entered a room. Now, as they dressed her and prepared her for her day, they were her underlings. They placed a footstool beneath her feet as they combed her hair.[9] The girl who less than a year ago had been borrowing money to pay for a few silk trinkets now waited while the bejewelled hands of a countess fastened a diamond-and-pearl crucifix around her throat. The morning toilette was always performed by the ladies of Catherine's privy chamber. Theoretically, they ranked beneath the great ladies, but in practice they were far closer to the queen, because of the intimate nature of their tasks. They consisted of four ladies, born or married into the nobility, and four married gentlewomen.[10] The neat division in the group was supposed to allude to the support of both nobility and commoners for their sovereign's wife, part of the constant play on symbolic gestures to confirm acceptance of the status quo in early modern politics.

Nearly all the women of Catherine's privy chamber were significantly older than her. Her half sister Isabella Baynton was a mother and stepmother. Two of the ladies, Lady Rochford and Lady Edgecombe, were widows – Jane Boleyn, Dowager Viscountess Rochford, was in her mid-thirties, and Katherine, Dowager Lady Edgecombe, was in her forties.[11] Their colleague Eleanor, Countess of Rutland, was about the same age as Lady Rochford. She was a Paston by birth, a long-established family of the Norfolk gentry who, decades earlier, had detested the Howards as aggressive arrivistes.[12] Those quarrels were long dead by 1540. Lady Rutland had the easy grace and casual generosity of someone who was born into great money and married more. Her husband was an old jousting buddy of the Duke of Suffolk, and the countess had named their daughter, born a year earlier, in honour of the Duchess of Suffolk, another of Catherine's ladies-in-waiting.[13] Lady Rutland was effusively polite, a hostess par excellence: at the family's country seat of Belvoir Castle she had the servants keep a room ready specially for the Duke of Suffolk, a frequent visitor, as was the Countess of Westmorland, the king's kinswoman.[14] Like many socialites, Lady Rutland stood at the centre of a vast network of patronage and mutual favours, under-scored by frequent gifts and notes dripping with gratitude and hyperbolic affection.[15] Presents among the Tudor aristocracy could be anything – those exchanged between courtiers during Catherine's career included stags killed and sent as a gift from the hunter, golden brooches with scenes from the life of Saint John the Baptist, pieces of furniture, hawks and other prized birds, shirts stitched by the giver, French wine and other delicacies for a friend's table like quails, baked partridge, herring, carp, and marmalade.[16] Even eye medicine was dispatched, with noble-women such as Catherine's grandmother and Lady Lisle priding themselves on their apparent expertise.[17] In the treacherous and fraught world of the court, the Countess of Rutland's good stand-ing with her peers was a testament to her charm. When Anne Bassett's younger sister found that she was to complete her education at the house of a family friend, she was relieved to be sent to Lady Rutland rather than the Countess of Hertford, since Lady Rutland treated her wards like daughters, while Lady

Hertford treated them like servants.[18] Queen Catherine clearly grew fond of her as well and gave her a necklace from her own collection.[19]

Catherine had enough jewellery to be generous with it. So much was flung at her in the opening months of her queenship that she may have struggled to keep up with it all. The glittering avalanche began with the official pieces which decorated the necks of her predecessors, and they were soon augmented by new trinkets from the king. When the ladies dressed Catherine in the morning, they might help her into one of the three 'upper habiliments' (the outward part of a dress) she had recently received, decorated with eight diamonds and seven rubies each.[20] Her clasps were capped off by emeralds, her buttons were set with diamonds, and for her brooches rubies were crafted into the shape of flowers, then trimmed with diamond and pearl petals.[21] If something was still felt to be missing from the top of her outfit, there were dozens of other brooches to choose from, like one of black agate that showed scenes from the Passion of Christ on one side and the Resurrection on the other, with rubies and small diamonds scattered around the base.[22] There were earrings and French hoods trimmed with gold. She had seven diamond-and-gold rings.[23] The ladies of the privy chamber circled Catherine's little waist with golden girdles or double rows of pearls routinely interrupted by rubies.[24] From these, it was fashionable to hang pomanders that contained pleasing scents in the bottom capsule, or little books at the end of a golden chain. As queen, Catherine's dangling books included one that had belonged to Jane Seymour with a gold enamelled cover and a clock set into it – 'upon every side of which book is three diamonds, a little man standing upon one of them, four turquoises and three rubies, with a little chain of golden hanging at it'. If that did not suit on a particular day, there was another gold book garnished with twenty-seven rubies, another 'having a fair sapphire on every side and viii rubies upon the same', or the ruby quota could be increased by selecting a gold-trimmed book 'containing xii diamonds and xl rubies'.[25]

Care of the jewels was entrusted to another of the privy chamber women, Mrs Anne Herbert, who had ginger hair, a clear complexion, a prim smile and, by the time of Catherine's wedding, a growing belly.[26] Anne Herbert was a career courtier and the daughter of two more. Her mother had been a lady-in-waiting to Katherine of Aragon, her paternal grandmother had served Richard III's queen, and her paternal great-grandmother had been a member of the royal household in the mid-fifteenth century.[27] Born Anne Parr in 1515, she had joined Anne Boleyn's retinue shortly after her mother's death left her an orphan in 1531, and taken an oath of loyalty to Jane Seymour when there was a change in command in 1536, shortly before her own marriage to William Herbert, an insatiably ambitious Welsh soldier who had a contested claim to the defunct earldom of Pembroke.[28] Technically, there was a male officer to monitor Catherine's jewels, but the day-to-day running of the queen's household was a study in the art of delegation. It was Anne Herbert who sent for pieces from the wardrobe, liaised with the relevant clerks, and dispatched the items that would not be used for a while into storage at Baynard's Castle in London, where most of the queen's wardrobe went if she was unlikely to use pieces for a few weeks.

The other women of the privy chamber were Anne Herbert's kinswoman, Mrs Elizabeth Tyrwhitt, Mrs Joyce Lee, and Mrs Susanna Gilmyn.[29] The latter was a talented artist, born Susanna Horenbout in the Netherlands; her brother was the portraitist Lucas Horenbout, and as a young woman her images of Christ had been praised by Albrecht Dürer, who admitted surprise that a woman had been capable of creating such beauty. Susanna's first husband was John Parker, the man in charge of the maintenance of the Palace of Westminster, and after his death she married a London merchant, John Gilmyn, in September 1539. Life had never given Susanna as many opportunities as it had her brother, but she was well liked and respected by many of her contemporaries, including Henry VIII's daughter Mary, who gave her a gift of twelve yards of black satin in 1544.[30] She had come into the queen's household thanks to her fluency in German, which she used to help Anne of Cleves with her English, but like the rest of the Privy Chamber women, Susanna remained to serve Catherine after Anne's rustication.[31]

These women orbited Catherine, and their daily duties were arranged in something like shifts, since all eight were seldom needed at one time. If she wanted to take a nap after dinner, the ladies were ready with water and towels to refresh her when she woke, though contemporary guides discouraged too much sleep during the day on the grounds that it 'dulls the wits and hurteth the brain'.[32] When she wanted to bathe, they arranged it and waited on her throughout. At Hampton Court, hot and cold running water was pumped through golden taps into a sunken stone bathtub for the king or a lead-lined one, draped in linen, for the queen. At Whitehall, there were stoves to make sure the royal bathrooms never became too cold.[33] The dozens of linen towels, bathrobes, curtains, and cloths used during the queen's baths were passed to the household's team of laundresses, while her bedsheets and menstrual cloths, strips of fine Holland linen, were sent to the queen's personal laundress.[34] Life as queen removed discomfort even from the mundane. Catherine would never again have to visit the 'house of easement' with its utilitarian rows of toilets. Instead, she was accompanied to her stool chamber, with its crimson velvet canopy, by one of the privy women, who left her while she used a toilet capped with a crimson velvet seat.[35] When she was finished, a red silk cloth was tied over it and pinned down with gilt nails. Later, another servant would arrive to open up the wooden box, take out the removable pan, empty it, clean it, and replace it.[36]

Apparently, the ladies of the privy chamber did not much care for the house of easement, either, and they were not above using their position to secure some privileges of their own. The queen's closed stool cost more than her vice chamberlain received in annual salary. Nevertheless, the household paid for six for the privy women. Some of these presumably made their way to the double lodgings, two rooms allocated to ladies of the queen's privy chamber, each with a fireplace and a separate 'garderobe' where the new toilets could be placed.[37]

Once Catherine was dressed, the maids of honour carried out the tasks she had once performed for Anne of Cleves. They gave her one of her three private prayer books and then, carrying her beads and cushions, accompanied her from her privy chambers into the little gallery where she could listen to Mass being celebrated by one of her four chaplains from behind a grille. While she was at prayer, the chamberers went into her bedroom to strip the clothes off her bed, lightly beat the feather bed to plump it for her, changed the sheets if they were not clean, and then rearranged everything, finishing with the cushions and pillows. They would then check her carpets, tapestries, and room cushions to see if they were clean and send for someone if they thought the fire in the grate, if lit, was about to die out.[38]

After Mass, the maids of honour accompanied Queen Catherine back to her privy apartments. There was a high turn-over in the maids of honour who were after all at court with the goal of securing a husband. Katherine Carey had been the first maid to depart when she left Queen Anne's service shortly after Easter to wed Francis Knollys, who brought her to his family's manor house in Oxfordshire, where she began the business of giving birth to the first of their sixteen children.[39] Mary Norris had married Sir George Carew. Catherine gave Mary Carew a necklace as her wedding present.[40]

It was only Anne Bassett who remained to walk a few decorous steps behind her former-colleague-turned-mistress. The arrest of her stepfather for treason and her mother's subsequent mental collapse left Anne financially shipwrecked, dependent on the generosity of her superiors or extended relatives and, without a dowry, bereft of any real chance of a proposal. She was now flanked by newcomers – Margaret Garneys, Margaret Copledike, and Damascin Stradling, whose Welsh mother was kin to the queen's aunt, Lady Margaret Howard. Even they did not stay for long, and within a year Margaret Garneys had married Walter Devereux, Viscount Hereford, a match that cannot have been approved of by the queen's aunt, Lady Bridgewater, since before being elevated to the viscounty of Hereford, Walter Devereux had been Lord Ferrers, the man who had quarrelled with, and arrested, the countess's first husband, Rhys ap Gruffydd. A replacement maid of honour was Dorothy Bray, one of the younger daughters of the recently ennobled Lord Bray. In later life, Dorothy had a reputation as something of a bluestocking – in Queen Elizabeth's reign, she kept two hundred books in her private rooms at her London mansion. In Catherine's time, a young and ebullient Dorothy balanced any nascent literary interests with a flare for romances which seemed to remind the queen of her younger self.[41]

Catherine's fifth maid of honour is listed as 'Lady Lucy' in the accounts, and she must have been Lady Lucy Somerset, the eldest daughter of the Earl of Worcester, who was the only peer with a daughter called Lucy in 1540.[42] A great-granddaughter of Edward IV on her mother's side, she was born sometime around 1524, which made her roughly the same age as the rest of the young girls who were sworn in as maids of honour between 1539 and 1541.[43] Lucy's stepmother had been a favourite lady-in-waiting of Anne Boleyn's and had retired from court life after that queen's execution.

If, during the day, Queen Catherine wanted some semblance of privacy, she could retreat to her closet. It was a small and intimate room where the queen could go to read or write letters or conduct private conversations. Her closet would have been the most probable place for her to chat with her grandmother or aunts if they needed to speak with her. They remained in regular contact. It was also where she could summon her secretary when they were going over her correspondence. Because of this, the closet featured prominently in lurid sixteenth-century fantasies of libidinous secretaries seducing their wealthy patronesses. Ordinarily, a private meeting between two people of the opposite gender was considered inappropriate, but a great lady could not expect to discuss her communications in public, giving rise to the habit of the secretary conferring with his employer in her closet. Filthy puns on secretaries having a key to the most private lock abounded. Nor were noblemen exempt from the deluge of winking innuendo about the closets. Some complained that 'jealous women and some men' were apt to think that a man who spent a great deal of time in the closet with scholars he patronised or male secretaries he employed must 'useth his servants in his chamber'.[44]

Catherine generally preferred company to solitude, and the nine 'ladies of exalted rank' provided her rooms with a constant hum of activity.[45] Favoured guests were often entertained in the queen's galleries, which, like her gallery at Hampton Court, usually had a view of the gardens and were stuffed full of folding chairs and card tables, their walls hung with portraits and tapestries. Maids of honour stood nearby with basins and ewers so the queen's guests could wash their hands, while gossip and ideas passed back and forth among the women gathered around the tables.[46]

Cliques are unavoidable in any large establishment, and Catherine's household was no exception. One group orbited the Duchess of Suffolk, whose religious sympathies lay increasingly with Protestantism. It was a circle of palace intellectuals, with the ladies debating religion, financing scholars at Oxford or Cambridge, translating books on theology, or even writing their own. A few years later, several women in this group would risk their lives to support a young female Protestant preacher, though they ultimately failed to save her from death in the flames. Lady Joan Denny, whose husband Anthony was one of the gentlemen of the king's Privy Chamber, was an enthusiastic patron of the new learning. She was also reputed to be one of the most intelligent of Catherine's ladies-in-waiting, as well as very beautiful.[47] Like many women in Catherine's household, Lady Denny was often prepared to go further than her husband in matters of religion, and the cloistered environment of the queen's rooms gave her the opportunity to do so. While the crackdown on the theological independence of the queen's household began several years after Catherine's career ended, the provocation developed throughout her time as consort. The Duchess of Suffolk named her pet dog 'Gardiner'; that way the ladies could order at least one Gardiner to desist from making such a mess.[48] There is no record of Catherine being particularly close to this set of women – who included her cousin the Dowager Duchess of Richmond, Anne Herbert, Elizabeth Tyrwhitt, and the shy Lady Jane Dudley, whose husband Sir John served as Catherine's master of the horse – however there is also nothing to suggest any animus, and Catherine seems to have got on quite happily with these women, who gave her every outward sign of deference.[49]

She remained close to Katherine Tilney, her old friend and bedmate from Chesworth, who now served as one of her chamberers. It was Tilney, or one of her colleagues, who opened the door at six o'clock in the evening when Sir Thomas Henneage, one of the king's gentlemen, arrived with a report on how the king's day had gone. Sir Thomas's wife, Lady Katherine Henneage, served as one of Catherine's nine ladies attendant, and the couple lived together in court accommodation. At Hampton Court they had a fine two-storey brick house in the palace grounds. The king did not visit his wife every day, but if Henneage informed Catherine that the king would dine with her that evening, the meal usually served as a prelude to sex, which took place in her apartments.[50] On these occasions, none of Catherine's ladies or gentlewomen of the privy chamber would sleep in a pallet bed at the foot of hers, as they usually did. Instead, she would be left alone with her husband.

Catherine's husband was born on 28 June 1491, the third child and second son of Henry VII and his queen, Elizabeth of York. The dynasty's grasp on power was not yet six years old, and Henry's earliest public appearances, like his investiture as Duke of York on his third birthday, aimed to appropriate the legacy of the Tudors' predecessors and discourage the dwindling number of Yorkists who hoped that fortune's wheel might turn again in their favour. His Welsh father was tall, lean, and athletic, with dark hair and watchful brown eyes. As he grew, young Henry looked far more like his mother's side of the family – fair hair, muscular build, and a height that made him about a head taller than most of his contemporaries. He spent most of his childhood in the same household as his sisters Margaret and Mary, two of the four siblings who survived the perils of infant mortality to make it past their fourth birthdays. He charmed nearly everybody he met – the European philosopher Erasmus of Rotterdam was formally presented to Henry when he visited England in 1499, and in 1501 Henry escorted Katherine of Aragon down the aisle of St Paul's Cathedral at her wedding to his eldest brother, Arthur. On both occasions, the prince's dignity and confidence won praise.[51]

Shortly before his eleventh birthday, Henry's life changed irrevocably when Arthur died during an outbreak of the sweating sickness. Arthur's sixteen-year-old widow had also been infected, and for a few weeks her life hung in the balance. When she recovered, the preservation of the Anglo-Spanish alliance prompted a petition to the Vatican for the pope to dispense the biblical prohibition of a brother marrying his spouse's widow.[52] Julius II obliged, since there was some confusion among experts in exegesis about the Bible's intentions – it was banned in Leviticus, but permissible in Deuteronomy – and similar dispensations had already been granted for families across the social spectrum in Christendom, including Katherine of Aragon's.[53]

Post-natal complications carried off Henry's mother less than a year after Arthur's passing. There was talk of his father's remarriage to the Dowager Queen Giovanna of the Naples, and English diplomats tried to inspect her gowns to see 'her breasts and paps, whether they be big or small', but the Neapolitan match came to nothing, and a darker, more repressed atmosphere settled over the royal family's daily lives.[54] Henry VII's popularity diminished with each new tax hike and as the new heir Henry was guarded by his father with a zeal that the Spanish ambassador characterised as obsessive.[55] His eldest sister travelled north to marry King James IV of Scots, despite her grandmother's fears that a thirteen-year-old was too young for wedlock.[56] Henry's father briefly considered breaking off the proposed marriage between Henry and Katherine of Aragon, who was still living in London in increasing unhappiness at the delay, and feelers were put out about the possibility of a match with the Archduchess Eleanor of Austria. Those plans came to nothing when Henry VII succumbed to tuberculosis on 23 April 1509. The new king made it clear that he wanted to marry Katherine at the first available opportunity, and Eleanor of Austria went on to marry François I of France.[57]

Katherine of Aragon's happiness that her seven years of uncertainty were over was in step with the general mood at Henry VIII's accession. Diplomats gushed about a king who was 'much handsomer than any sovereign in Christendom'; courtiers wrote to friends abroad that 'everything is full of milk and honey and nectar'; it was 'the prettiest thing in the world to see him play' tennis, and in physical competitions he 'surpassed them all, as he surpasses them in stature and personal graces'.[58] Henry was fluent in Latin and French, had a working knowledge of Italian, possessed an imperfect if passionate interest in engineering and architecture, dabbled in mathematics, Spanish, astronomy, classical Greek, and he was a superb musician. He performed his own compositions before a court that Queen Katherine described as one of 'continual feasts'.[59]

Capable of parroting, expanding, or critiquing another's thoughts, but incapable of developing many that were uniquely his, Henry VIII was intellectually skilled, but not brilliant. In itself, that is hardly a great failing or even an insult, but it became a problem because Henry failed to recognise his own limitations. Throughout his life, the majority of Henry's troubles were caused by the fact that he constantly overestimated himself. On several occasions during the first decade of his reign, he leapt into hugely expensive wars on the Continent after repeatedly trusting in the good intentions of allies, including his father-in-law King Ferdinand, who used England to distract the French long enough to achieve his own goals, then pulled out of the war and left England to fight on alone.[60] Henry's foreign policy was an unending catalogue of aggression, duplicity, myopic eagerness, expense, and defeat. Even his infrequent victories in France carried more than a whiff of Pyrrhus when they conquered towns that proved so costly to defend that in his son's reign they eventually had to be handed back to the French.

The universal acclaim for the pulchritudinous prince of 1509 began to dry up as he was played for a fool by men who were ostensibly his allies, and it evaporated after his quarrel with the papacy. Henry insisted that the death of his son, the Duke of Cornwall, in 1511, and the deaths in utero or shortly after birth of the boy's male siblings proved that the royal marriage was a contravention of biblical law. Initially, there was no reason to believe that the Vatican would put up too much resistance to the king's request for his marriage to be dissolved. Popes were often prepared to grant annulments to childless emperors, kings, and princes if it meant preventing the ensuing unrest of a succession crisis. Thirty years earlier, Pope Alexander VI annulled the marriage of King Louis XII of France to the childless Queen Jeanne on grounds that could kindly be considered tenuous, to pave the way for Louis's marriage to the Duchess of Brittany. Queen Jeanne, who had contested her husband's blatantly dishonest account of their private lives, had to accept the pope's decision, retired to a convent, and subsequently founded an order of nuns dedicated to the Immaculate Conception of the Virgin Mary. It was hoped that the equally pious Queen Katherine might follow suit if Pope Clement VII performed a similar service for Henry VIII.

Unfortunately, Henry seemed to think the best way to crack a walnut was to drop a brick on it. He wanted the annulment granted on the grounds that the previous pope had exceeded the limits of his office in dispensing what could not be dispensed, namely the word of God. This required Clement VII to curtail the past and future powers of his own office, a prospect which became even less tempting when the queen's Hapsburg relatives stepped up their pressure on the pope to support her. Attempts via the papal nuncio to persuade Queen Katherine to mimic the actions of Jeanne of France, by stepping aside and taking the veil, were scuppered by the lady herself, who was determined to fight her proposed demotion every step of the way.

By this stage, Henry was no longer able to keep pace with his younger self, who had spent his summers 'shooting, singing, dancing, wrestling, casting of the bar, playing at the recorders, flute and virginals, and in setting of songs, making of ballads ... jousts and tourneys'.[61] His youthful prettiness had settled into an impressive and mature presence by the time he turned forty in 1531, captured in Joos van Cleve's portrait of him, which shows a confident monarch piously clutching a scroll with an extract from the Gospel according to Saint Mark, 'Go ye into all the world, and preach the gospel to every creature.'[62] An evangelist monarch was how Henry saw himself as his frustration with the pope turned to anger. Anne Boleyn was the most prominent person close to the king whose Catholicism was tinged with enough sympathy with the cries for reform and the protests of Martin Luther to make her a powerful critic of Clement VII's inaction, but she was not the only one. The break with Rome was solidified by 1533, the same year as the new Archbishop of Canterbury ruled in Henry's favour, dissolved the marriage to Katherine of Aragon, and crowned Anne Boleyn at Westminster Abbey. Three years later, Anne was dead on manufactured charges of adultery and treason, and within eighteen months her successor had followed her into the grave, twelve days after giving Henry the legitimate son he needed.

As dissatisfaction turned to protest, the death toll in England mounted in opposition to the religious changes. The northern rebellion of 1536 may have had the potential to bring Henry's entire regime crashing down around him had the palace-bound aristocracy not remained loyal to their king.[63] Earlier that year, Henry had been competing in a jousting tournament when he was thrown from his horse and knocked unconscious. That incident has featured prominently in several theories that seek to explain the increasing terror of Henry's final decade in power by postulating that he suffered sufficient brain damage from the fall to bring about a decisive and terrible shift in character.[64] There have also been suggestions that Henry perhaps suffered from a genetic disorder such as McLeod syndrome, which usually accelerates in middle age, when it can cause heart failure, physical pain, and behavioural changes, or Cushing's syndrome, which can cause skin to heal poorly, a possible explanation for the problems Henry endured as a result of his leg ulcer, along with high blood pressure, abdominal obesity, migraines, exhaustion, and painful deposits of fat between the shoulder blades.[65]

Many of the modern speculations on the symbiosis between Henry VIII's mental and physical health are well written, well researched, and thought-provoking. They are inevitably based on speculation, since the surviving records make it far easier to rule out what Henry VIII did not suffer from than to diagnose what he did endure. It is possible that he suffered from a severe illness in the later years of his life – type 2 diabetes would explain many of his ailments and fit with his increasingly unhealthy lifestyle – but there is a fundamental flaw in the argument that a medical explanation is needed to explain why the latter half of Henry's reign was more bloody than the earlier years.[66] The break with Rome created a trauma in the body politic, even for those who were enthusiastically in favour of it and were later appalled by the government's exploitation of it. After 1533, a king who detested disobedience had embarked upon a policy that was controversial enough to generate a lot of it. Yet his execution of his father's unpopular advisers Richard Empson and Edmund Dudley in 1510 and the destruction of the Duke of Buckingham in 1521 showed that Henry had always been capable of morally and legally questionable savagery. Henry VIII was a man who had somehow gone rotten without ever being ripe.

After the tangible disappointment of having no heir was banished by Prince Edward's birth in 1537, words and images flowed from the pens of Tudor servants and wrapped themselves around Henry VIII, casting him as the father of his people, the custodian and dispenser of true religion in the ilk of Old Testament hero-kings like Asa or Jehoshaphat. Frontispieces in new editions of the Bible portrayed the bearded king handing down the gospel to his grateful subjects, flanked by wise and demure councillors. The overwrought rhetoric was the product of a stomach knot of fear which never quite left the illustrated councillors' real-life counterparts, as they struggled to serve a consistent inconsistency. Henry VIII's government may have appeared as one of brutal lunacy to frequently appalled foreign observers, but those close to Henry were often as dazzled by his charisma as they were terrified by his chilling cruelty to those who disappointed him. The king's manners were flawless, his charm and munificence capable of eliciting compliments even from those diplomats who were usually revolted by him. He was large but not yet obese, and so there was still an air of majesty about him rather than bloated despotism. The physique helped distract from the fact that the king was a pathological hypochondriac, paradoxically laying waste to his own health with mounting portion sizes and too much alcohol at his meals. Despite his pious protestations about marrying her for the sake of his country, at the time of his wedding to Anne of Cleves, Henry appeared obsessed with romantic love, and at least one of his courtiers seemed to hold the private opinion that he was shirking a prince's duty by expecting to marry as happily as an ordinary gentleman.[67] This was the man who visited Catherine's apartments at night and on whom she was completely dependent.

Curfew for the queen's staff was at nine o'clock. If Catherine was hungry, and the king had chosen not to visit her, the maids usually brought her a bedtime snack in the hour before curfew.[68] Leaving the food, they curtseyed out of her presence and left her in the enormous canopied bed, while a lady-in-waiting slumbered nearby in case the queen needed anything in the small hours. Given her newfound position as head of the largest female-dominated domestic establishment in England, Catherine seemed lucky to have spent most of her formative years in a large female-dominated establishment like the Dowager Duchess of Norfolk's. Unfortunately, Catherine's childhood and adolescence at Horsham and Lambeth were to shape her subsequent career in predominantly negative ways. Her education had rendered her poised, elegant, and immaculately mannered, with a talent for music and dancing that equipped her to succeed in a court with a king who loved the former and had once excelled at the latter, but it had also left her woefully unprepared for a position that required her to psychologically distance herself from her daily companions. Her youthful romances and easy dominance of her friends at Horsham gave her a taste for gossip and backstairs intrigue which she never had a chance to grow out of. The examples of her friends' behaviour and the extent to which she had escaped censure at Chesworth and Lambeth had also desensitised her to the opprobrium that such behaviour could elicit in other environments.

Separate to that and with their own potential to harm her were attitudes within the court towards the institution of the queen's household. Both Katherine of Aragon and Anne Boleyn been criticised for the secretive natures of their households and the dangerous independence of the female bonds established within them – Katherine from her reliance on one of her disreputable confessors and Anne through her closeness to various ladies-in-waiting – which invited suspicion and resentment from the male courtiers and even the household's own members.[69] The climate of self-scrutiny in the household was almost as intense as the watchful stares from outsiders. Household members were encouraged to report colleagues who slept in or broke curfew to the vice chamberlain.[70] Servants noticed if a male retainer stayed too long at the dinner table after the food was cleared away, since the right to dally was reserved solely for officers of the household.[71]

In a world sealed within the walls of a palace and moderated by decorum and hierarchy, arguments were magnified and the seemingly trivial crushed friendships and reputations. Feuds were endemic. The Countess of Sussex, once a benefactress, regarded Anne Bassett with cold dislike, and while a mutual friend's letter does not give us the cause of the dispute, it confirms that 'though the matter is forgiven, she has not forgotten it'.[72] Queen Catherine, significantly younger than any of Henry's previous queens and with the least experience of life at his court, bar Anne of Cleves, had inherited a household, newly formed and swiftly transferred from one mistress to the other, which knew many secrets and was constantly suspected of knowing more.

Chapter 10

The Queen's Brothers

> The many pleasures that I bring
> Are all of youth, of heat, of life and spring …
> We see, we hear, we feel, we taste,
> We smell the change in every flow'r,
> We only wish that all could last,
> And be as new still as the hour.
>
> – Ben Jonson,
> *The Vision of Delight* (1617)

The least used part of Catherine's arsenal of jewellery was the crown inherited from her predecessors. Its sapphires, six large and many small, twinkled next to thirty-two pearls, capped by a gold cross with an inset diamond. Its golden base, decorated with six gold-sapphire-and-pearl crosses, was lined by a cap of purple velvet that made it more comfortable to bear.[1] Crowns were generally only worn on state occasions, which diminished in number and certainly in splendour as the king continued to haemorrhage funds over the course of his long reign. Shortly before his marriage to Catherine, Henry had asked Parliament for more money, a request that raised eyebrows, but few voices, given how much the government must have pocketed from the dissolution of the monasteries.[2] The inheritance left by Henry VII had long ago been damaged by the reign's earlier squabbles with France and Scotland. Yet even if there had been more ready cash, Catherine's crown would have likely remained purely ceremonial.

Historically, Catherine's tenure as queen consort occurred at the end of a long period of decline for the office in England. Today, she and Henry's five other wives are among the most famous queens in English history, but they certainly were not the most powerful. The political clout and relative independence of the Anglo-Saxon and Norman consorts in the tenth, eleventh, and early twelfth centuries dwarfed that of their successors. This decline in power seems to have begun under Henry II, who drove his wife Eleanor of Aquitaine to rebellion by constantly sidelining her from the government of her own duchy. By the thirteenth century, queens who pursued their own agendas were often criticised as acting ultra vires, and fifteenth-century consorts, particularly Margaret of Anjou, who played a pivotal role in the early Wars of the Roses, were generally exonerated by their supporters on the grounds that kingly incapacity had made their assertive actions necessary. The implication of such a defence was that under normal circumstances, no good queen would dream of adopting such a stance.

The Tudors had intensified this trend by altering and then abandoning the traditions surrounding a queen consort's coronation. Prior to Henry VII, English queens were usually crowned shortly after their weddings, if they married a reigning monarch, or at the first available opportunity following their husband's succession. There were only two exceptions – Edward I's second wife, Marguerite of France, who was never crowned, and Edward III's queen, Philippa of Hainault, whose delayed coronation was generally blamed on her mother-in-law, Queen Isabella, who had to buckle once Philippa became pregnant.[3] Any other significant delays, like Matilda of Flanders's in 1068 or Eleanor of Castile's in 1274, were because the queen in question had been away from England when her husband became king. Excepting Philippa of Hainault, there was no suggestion of waiting until a queen was with child, much less until after she had delivered, before organising her coronation. In contrast, Henry VII married Elizabeth of York at Westminster Abbey in January 1486, but she was not crowned until November 1487, by which point she had already given birth to her husband's heir.

By waiting twenty-two months after their wedding and nearly two years after his own coronation, Henry VII had tried to distance himself from the suggestion that he owed his crown to his marriage to Elizabeth, who was the niece, sister, and daughter of his three immediate predecessors. A promise to marry her had been an incentive for many people to support Henry Tudor's bid for the throne in 1485, but after he triumphed Henry was nervous at any implication that it was Elizabeth's hand rather than his own victory in battle and distant descent from Edward III that had secured his kingship. The corresponding delay in Elizabeth of York's coronation marked a significant break with the customs of the last five centuries. It suggested that the queen's role was optional and her coronation a conditional that should only be brought about if she fulfilled her part of the bargain in providing the kingdom with an heir. The mystical investiture, with its oils, incense, pageantry, chants, and primal, evocative ritual, that had for centuries cast England's queens as earthly handmaidens of the Virgin Mary was debased by the demands of realpolitik, and while Henry VIII did return to the medieval norm by having his first two wives crowned at the first available opportunity, after 1533 he reverted to the example of his father. It may have been the expense involved in a coronation which prompted this, although it is revealing that talk of crowning the wives that followed only surfaced once they were thought to be pregnant. Henry VIII's first wife had occasionally outshone him, his second wife argued with him, and his third was reminded 'not to meddle in his affairs', lest she meet the fate of the last queen who had debated with him.[4] He had no interest in elevating his wife through a public ceremony which gave her an identity that was uniquely special. In the final decade of his life, the greatest attribute Henry prized in his wives was an obedience as total as he expected from his subjects. In this regard, Catherine Howard was suited to the position she acquired in 1540. If the queen's role was to greet dignitaries and shine like an ornament at the king's side, then Catherine was, at least on the surface, the perfect candidate.

For the first few months of her marriage, Catherine was not yet immersed in the official functions of a queen consort.[5] After a brief stop at Hampton Court for her official proclamation, Catherine stayed away from London for the rest of summer and all of the autumn. From summer to Michaelmas, many courtiers were given permission to go home to tend to their estates in the country. The French royal household had the same custom, and in the interim Henry wanted to enjoy a reduced household, greater freedom, and blue skies by hunting deer and, when that season passed, hawking.[6] With Henry, Catherine moved from one smaller home to another, through Reading, Grafton, Ampthill, Dunstable, and St Albans, to grander houses like the More, before she and the king returned to Windsor Castle on 20 October.[7]

Their eight-day stay at Reading was a reminder, if anyone cared to be reminded, of the recent gruesome past. The last abbot of the now abandoned monastery had been hanged, drawn, and quartered for treason ten months earlier.[8] Some of his confiscated land and possessions were deeded to Catherine five months after her visit to Reading.[9] Grafton Regis manor in Northamptonshire had more pleasant associations – tradition had that it was at Grafton that Henry's maternal grandparents had eloped in 1464, giving England its first native-born queen consort since the eleventh century. Henry had bought the house from his cousin, the Marquess of Dorset, in 1526 and spent a significant sum renovating and expanding it. Catherine benefited from the refurbishment, and her rooms had views over the idyllic countryside with the 'pleasant and healthful' airs Grafton was praised for.[10]

After eight days there, they moved on to Ampthill, another royal hunting lodge with a reputation for clean airs and smells. From the great bay windows and stone towers, Catherine had a view of the little market town that sloped down the hill into the valley and the forests that stretched out behind the castle. At

Currently housed in the Metropolitan Museum, New York, this portrait of a seventeen-year-old courtier may depict Catherine Howard.

ÆTATIS·SVÆ·XVII

Identified as Catherine Howard in the early twentieth century, the lady in this portrait by Holbein is far more likely to be Thomas Cromwell's daughter-in-law, Elizabeth, or Jane Grey's mother, Frances.

A miniature, also by Holbein, showing a lady wearing jewels from the royal collection. It may be a portrait of Catherine, painted around the time of her marriage.

The ruins of Framlingham Castle, the Howard family's one-time seat in Suffolk.

The former Church of Saint Mary-at-Lambeth, the site of many Howard burials and, almost certainly, Catherine's christening.

Catherine's childhood guardian Agnes Howard, Dowager Duchess of Norfolk. One of the wealthiest women in the country, Agnes's love of gossip and intrigue brought her close to total ruin.

ANNA · BOLINA · · ANG · R

Catherine's glamorous but divisive cousin, Anne Boleyn, who was executed in 1536. The two women shared a sense of elegance and confidence, but Anne was substantially more intelligent.

The influence on her life of
Catherine's uncle Thomas, 3rd
Duke of Norfolk and head of
the Howard family, has been
greatly exaggerated. Evidence
suggests that he knew, and
understood, his niece poorly.

A diplomat and a soldier, Lord William Howard was the uncle who knew Catherine best. For most of her queenship, he served as one of the English ambassadors to France.

A portrait believed to be of the devout Margaret Pole, Countess of Salisbury, who was accused of treason and imprisoned in 1538. Her interrogators attempted, but failed, to implicate Catherine's family in her disgrace. Three centuries after her death, Lady Salisbury was beatified by Pope Leo XIII.

Catherine's second cousin, Katherine Carey – they joined the court at the same time as maids of honour. Carey married soon after their début and she is shown here, during one of her sixteen subsequent pregnancies. She was later a favourite lady-in-waiting to Queen Elizabeth I.

Catherine initially served in the household of Henry VIII's fourth wife, Anne of Cleves. Many of Anne's ladies-in-waiting regarded her German dresses as ornate, but hideous.

Thomas Cromwell, Henry VIII's chief minister, was executed on Catherine's wedding day in 1540. The Duke of Norfolk was active in the plots against him.

Ampthill, her lady-in-waiting Anne Herbert turned over the keys for Catherine's jewellery caskets to her colleague Elizabeth Tyrwhitt, who was to oversee day-to-day management of the jewels for the next four months, while Anne was absent from court to have her first baby.[11] As Anne Herbert left, Catherine and the other women congregated in a stand in the castle grounds where they could relax and watch the hunting on any day when the queen did not feel like participating. Servants brought them drinks and snacks as the unbroken sunlight shone through the stand's glass windows, which had been added six years earlier for the comfort of Anne Boleyn and her women.

Catherine and Henry stayed at Ampthill for just over three weeks, then moved on to spend the night at Dunstable, which had two shuttered monasteries, followed by a two-night stopover in St Albans, before the More came into view and the party could be let loose on the five hundred or so deer living on the estate. The difference in the king's mood now that he was free from Anne of Cleves was obvious.[12] 'The King has taken up a new rule of living,' wrote one diplomat – Henry rose between five and six o'clock in the morning, heard Mass in private at seven, and went out riding until dinner, which was served at ten in the morning.[13]

At the More, Catherine's servants unpacked her things and set out her furniture in her one public room – her presence chamber – and in her private rooms, like her dressing room (known as a 'raying room' in the sixteenth century), her privy chamber, her bedroom, her closet, and her watching room, a reception room. The servants moved up and down two staircases with white walls and yellow ochre details, set aside exclusively for the queen's household. Her watching room had the same decorative patterns and colour scheme; it gave Catherine views of the moat, where her husband and his men liked to fish when they were not hunting, and gardens also overlooked by a 253-foot private gallery, from the windows of which the king practised his shooting.[14] He may have practised with arrows, but Henry and his companions were some of the few men in England who had the money to pursue the new pastime of shooting with pistols. Man-shaped targets had already been made by one of the king's joiners for Henry to practise against.[15] As the baking summer turned into a more endurable autumn, there were also games of tennis, and bowls, archery and more fishing, especially when fish had to be substituted for meat on Fridays. The king even occasionally enjoyed sawing blocks of wood or turning his hand to blacksmithing.[16]

In late August, the French ambassador was invited to join the king and queen for a few days at the chase. Charles de Marillac was an urbane and acerbic French clergyman in his late twenties who had previously trained as a lawyer and represented his master at the court of Sultan Süleyman the Magnificent in Constantinople. The hunting trip gave the ambassador the opportunity to observe Catherine properly for the first time.[17] From his sources in London, he had heard that Catherine was 'a lady of great beauty', but in person he thought she was 'graceful rather than beautiful', a dissenting view since others tied to the court described her as possessing 'blazing beauty'.[18] William Thomas, a man then in service to the king's master of the horse, considered Catherine 'a very beautiful gentlewoman'.[19] De Marillac observed that 'the king is so amorous of her that he cannot treat her well enough'. That devotion was sensibly reciprocal: the queen had chosen as her personal motto a prostrate declaration of adoring obedience, 'No other will but his'. De Marillac gave it in French in his letter, '*Non autre volonté que la sienne*', but we do not know if that was simply his translation or if, like many queens, she chose to have her device in another language.[20] There is no record of her heraldic device which replaced Anne of Cleves's in the palaces. In early 1541, Galyon Hone, the king's glazier, was paid for the installation of the queen's arms in stained glass in some of the royal lodgings, but thanks to the thoroughness with which they were erased when she fell from favour, we do not know what they were. Traditionally, a queen consort would have a coat of arms and one or two heraldic beasts, often from mythology, which conveyed a political or dynastic message. In Catherine's case, it may be that she simply preferred to use the

Howard arms combined with the royal crest, and when it came to badges and creatures, it is possible that, like Anne Boleyn, who had occasionally used the male griffin associated with her family's Irish peerage of Ormond, Catherine opted for animals that had traditionally appeared in the Howards' heraldry.[21]

On the basis of their meeting at the hunt, subsequent accounts of Catherine's career claimed that de Marillac gave the young queen credit for reintroducing the French hood and other Gallic fashions which had been popularised by Anne Boleyn and thus apparently discouraged by Jane Seymour. However, Henry VIII's inventories show that Queen Jane owned French hoods, and other accounts mention women of the court wearing them before Catherine became queen, including at Anne of Cleves's arrival in January 1540.[22] It was later writers who made this mistake in attribution, not de Marillac, since as regards Catherine's dress sense his letter simply states, 'She and all the Court ladies dress in French style.'[23]

Another myth from this period in Catherine's life is that her husband gave her the nickname *Rutilans rosa sine spina* ('The dazzling rose without a thorn').The legend, which originated in a bestselling nineteenth-century account of English queens, was based on a coin minted in Henry's reign with the king's coat of arms on one side and a rose with the aforementioned motto in Latin on the other.[24] Alas for the romantic fable which claimed the coin was struck in Catherine's honour shortly after her honeymoon, the rose motto did not refer to any of Henry's wives but to the king or, rather, to the dynasty. The Tudor rose was the flower without a thorn, a royal succession that would inflict no more wounds on the nation. Coins bearing this device were first issued in 1526. There is no contemporary account of Catherine being referred to by this nickname, likewise for the story that she chose the rose as her personal crest after the coin went into circulation.[25]

Although the coin was not one of them, Catherine did receive gifts from her rejuvenated husband as they hunted, including three golden belts for her wardrobe and a brooch with scenes from the life of Noah crafted from thirty diamonds and fifteen rubies.[26] Serious politics were abandoned as a preferred topic of conversation, except inside the great chambers where the Privy Council met.[27] After the stress of the previous year, the rest of the royal household seemed eager to forget matters of state and focus instead on the constant entertainments thrown in Catherine's honour. 'Nothing [is] spoken of here,' de Marillac wrote, 'but the chase, and the banquets to the new Queen.'[28]

A typical day at the hunt began with Catherine arriving at the meet in a velvet riding jacket, dress, gloves, and cap, a style that had allegedly been introduced to England by Richard II's queen, Anne of Bohemia. Picnics were organised for the courtiers, while scouts beetled to and from the master of the game with reports about where the best prey was hiding. Contemporary fashion for the gentlemen who escorted Catherine and her ladies from one activity to another was designed to flatter any man with an athletic build, particularly the hose which ran up a man's leg in fabric cut on the bias to cling. The detachable codpiece, padded more with each new fad, was still the subject of ribald teasing and puns in court circles.[29] Some of the ladies perched around the refreshments before the hunt wore gowns in a simpler style and a looser cut; they were the women who took the chase more seriously and intended to keep pace with it. Nearby, Irish greyhounds, the most expensive breed, lounged in the sun, their collars marked with their owner's initials glinting in the light. When the horns sounded, the hounds leapt up for the pursuit. Catherine, with her embellished spur, was helped into her saddle, and the party rode off in chase of the stag, the in-season quarry that was often seen as the most 'noble' kill, hence the tradition of its head being mounted on the wall in a hall. In the evenings, there were banquets and dancing.[30]

Some of the courtiers seem to have been carried away by the convivial atmosphere. The king's former brother-in-law, Sir Thomas Seymour, was expected to receive a heavy fine for brawling within the confines of the court, something that was strictly forbidden, and on 18 September Catherine's brother-in-law and vice chamberlain, Sir Edward Baynton, was given orders, along with sixteen other household servants, to make sure that members of both the king's and queen's households remembered to behave in 'sober and temperate order' when they were in the royal apartments.[31]

One person who was not there to enjoy the halcyon days of Catherine's early queenship was her uncle the duke. Like many nobles, Norfolk went home in the late summer and early autumn. He did not rejoin the court until 21 November, when he briefly attended a Privy Council meeting at Windsor Castle, then left the next day to interrogate Lord Leonard Grey, the disgraced former Lord Deputy of Ireland, who was in the Tower charged with treason.[32] In late December, the duke was still allowed to skip council meetings to tend to affairs on his estates, and his prolonged absences from court for most of Catherine's first six months as queen upsets the traditional image that has Norfolk pulling the strings of a willing puppet to ensure that Catherine's queenship functioned as a gaudy free-for-all for her relatives.[33] Clearly Norfolk felt comfortable enough in his position to take time away from palace life, when previously the thought of doing so had caused him anxiety, particularly as his rivalry with Cromwell escalated. Watchers of the royal court had a long history of exaggerating the importance of the queen consort's family, since they assumed a queen 'always exerted herself to aggrandise her relations'.[34] Admittedly, several had, since custom and concepts of loyalty encouraged it. Henry's grandfather, King Edward IV, had defended his generosity to his wife's family on the grounds that it was 'most reasonable that we should do more than for others who are not so nearly connected with us', but Henry VIII was never as close to his in-laws as earlier kings like Edward IV or Henry III.[35]

Relatives by marriage who did receive promotions through their ties to Henry VIII were usually men who already had long careers of service to the Crown or who capitalised on royal intervention to swing a long-running dispute in their favour – hence Thomas Boleyn was finally able to settle his legal pursuit of his late grandfather's earldom of Ormond in 1529, after the case had dragged on for fourteen years, and William Parr recovered his father-in-law's earldom of Essex in 1543, three years after the latter's death. There also seems to have been a tentatively proportional relationship between rewards and talent for a queen's relatives. For instance, Jane Seymour's cleverest brother, Edward, received far more by way of promotions, missions, and influence than his more impulsive sibling Thomas. Similar trust was shown in George Boleyn and William Herbert, Katherine Parr's brother-in-law. If her relatives were not deemed talented enough, Catherine did not possess the influence necessary to promote them into government. A few years later, courtiers agreed that Katherine Parr's brother had done better out of his sister's marriage to the king than the Howard brothers had in 1540.[36] That is not to say that Catherine's family received nothing. Her uncle's ally Stephen Gardiner got the chancellorship of his alma mater, Cambridge, from the deceased Cromwell, and Catherine's cousin Lord Surrey was made a member of the Privy Council.[37] The queen's half sister, Lady Isabella Baynton, and her two children both received 100 marks from the king as a gift, and Catherine and Isabella's brother George was given the same amount as an annual pension.[38] Charles Howard received a few properties from the king, £100 a year, a licence to import 1,000 tons of Gascon wine and French timber, and a place as a gentleman of the Privy Chamber. But in comparison to the treasures that were heaped upon them in popular legend, the Howards were left wanting. When Catherine's elder sister, Lady Margaret Arundell, came to London with her husband in October 1540, they chose to stay as guests of Sir Richard Rich in his townhouse at Smithfield, which not only suggests that Catherine was not particularly close to this sibling but also that the Arundells did not expect to benefit from the munificence of the royal household.[39]

Henry Howard, the brother Catherine had spent most of her time with when they had both been attached to the household of the dowager duchess, does not seem to have joined their other brothers at court, at least not on a permanent basis, for reasons which are unknown. Henry Howard was already married, while the other two were not.[40] George, who had the longest career at court, was the youngest of the brothers and he had inherited their father's skills as a jouster.[41] Luckily, the king was too out of shape to joust by 1540, which removed the possibility that George might harm his prospects with the same lack of tact as Edmund had displayed thirty years earlier.[42] George Howard's position in his brother-in-law's service is difficult to specify. A grant made to the two brothers a year after their sister's wedding refers to Charles as a 'gentleman of the Privy Chamber' and George by the Latin description *'chironorum nostrorum'*, an example of the court's tendency to refer to its members in vaguely classical terms. As a colloquialism, it could just about be taken as the Latin equivalent of 'our right-hand man', but that would be to vastly overstate the importance of the queen's youngest brother. In Ancient Rome, a *chironorum* was a public newsreader, a kind of town crier whose proclamations of the news were accompanied by explanatory hand gestures, and *'chironomos'* could mean one who gesticulated according to the rules of a particular art or style. From there, a logical deduction would be a herald, but George's name does not appear in *The College of Arms* volume in *Survey of London*, which lists all the heralds who served Henry VIII. The closest position one can find that makes sense is a sewer in the king's household, an attendant who oversaw the arrangement of the king's table at meal times, tasted and served his dishes, and oversaw the *placement* of his guests. A working knowledge of etiquette was essential for the execution of this post, ensuring the appointment of young gentlemen, like George Howard.[43]

Charles Howard seems to have had the Howard charisma seeping out of his fingertips, and if he was not quite the stuff of the council chamber, he at least fitted in perfectly to the merrymaking routine that dominated the court in the latter half of 1540. His place as a gentleman of the Privy Chamber implies that he had the skills required in most of his colleagues – to be articulate, charismatic, and sporting – and he soon put those qualities to use by flirting with the king's twenty-five-year-old niece, Lady Margaret Douglas, who had already incurred her uncle's displeasure by eloping with Charles and Catherine's late uncle, the unfortunate Lord Thomas Howard, who had died of a fever in the Tower four years earlier.

Margaret Douglas was the only child of Henry's elder sister Margaret, Queen Mother of Scots, and her second husband, Archibald Douglas, 6th Earl of Angus. She had spent most of her childhood in France, after her father snatched her from her mother's care during their acrimonious separation, and then most of her adulthood in England, where she had lived with various members of the court, including her cousin Princess Mary, and then with Anne Boleyn, who seemed to like her. A French diplomat who saw her during Anne Boleyn's tenure described Margaret as 'beautiful and highly esteemed here'.[44] Owing to her mother's rank, Margaret Douglas was sometimes inaccurately referred to by foreign visitors to Henry's court as 'the Princess of Scotland', but since a royal title could not pass down through a foreign-born female who had remarried, Margaret Douglas was instead technically a member of the Scottish nobility who, in London, enjoyed the privileges of an extended member of the English royal house, including double lodgings at most of the palaces.[45] Her secret betrothal to Catherine's uncle Thomas in 1536 had earned Margaret a spell in the Tower as well and rustication from court which only ended when the birth of her cousin Prince Edward bumped her so far down the line of succession that her uncle relaxed enough to bring her back. In October 1538, the king had reminded Margaret of her purpose when she was dangled on the international market as bait in a last-ditch attempt to prevent Charles V's impending alliance with François I.[46]

At the time of her restoration to her uncle's favour, Margaret was so relieved that she wrote, 'I pray our Lord sooner to send me death than that' – meaning a return of the king's anger.[47] Her affair with Thomas Howard had been decried by her contemporaries as a 'presumptuous act [and] he was attained of treason ... and so he died in the Tower, and she was long there as prisoner'.[48]

Either Charles Howard was sufficiently enthralling to override this warning, or Margaret's own irrepressible confidence produced a spell of amnesia, because by 1541 the lady with the 'pretty face, a very beautiful complexion [and] well-proportioned physique', as judged by the Venetian ambassador, was once again romantically involved with a member of Catherine's family.[49]

There is some confusion about when this affair was discovered, and several modern accounts repeat that the king found out about it when he and Catherine reached Windsor Castle on 20 October 1540. He allegedly banished Margaret to another spell of house arrest at the disused abbey of Syon; Charles tactfully decided to pursue a military career abroad, and Margaret was only moved from Syon to make way for Catherine herself in November 1541.[50] The evidence indicates that Margaret was still a member of Catherine's household at this stage, when she is mentioned as joining the Dowager Duchess of Richmond on a visit to the Howards' mansion at Kenninghall in Norfolk. Nor does Charles Howard seem to have fled the country in autumn 1540, since grants were still being issued to him as a member of the Privy Chamber in July 1541.[51]

The confusion over the liaison's dates may have arisen either from Margaret's earlier detention at Syon in 1537 or from the fact that upon returning to Windsor in October 1540, Charles de Marillac observed that the king was in a poor mood, which his ministers could not explain.[52] As Henry raged in his apartments, for whatever reason, rain was at last falling over England. The miserable drought had broken around Michaelmas, the feast of St Michael the Archangel that was typically associated with the harvest.

When Margaret Douglas and Charles Howard began their affair is even harder to pinpoint than when it ended. Orders from the council in November 1541 suggest that it may have been an open secret for some time, at least among members of the queen's household, and it is difficult to believe that Catherine herself was unaware of her brother's liaison. Of course, it is not impossible that Charles could have kept such a secret from a sibling, but later events indicate that Catherine kept her finger firmly on the pulse of court gossip. Even if we accept that she did not know, or suspect, what was happening between her brother and one of her ladies-in-waiting, there were others at court who had long-standing concerns about the role of the queen's household, who were liable to see validation of their worries in Charles and Margaret's affair. Among those keeping a close eye on Catherine's intimates was her brother-in-law Sir Edward Baynton, who was significantly older than them, born circa 1495, and who had served in the queen's household since Katherine of Aragon's time.

Baynton had risen to the position of vice chamberlain and he had managed to keep the king's favour for over a decade. In 1540, along with his eldest son, Andrew, he received a grant of land, a dissolved monastery's, from the Court of Augmentations in September, part of several gifts the Bayntons received from the Crown over the years.[53] Despite the relative longevity of his service, Baynton had a strong antipathy towards what he saw as feminine independence under the protection of the queen's household.[54] In 1536, he had provided the then Lord Treasurer, William Fitzwilliam, with a list of women favoured by Queen Anne Boleyn and helpfully offered to apply pressure to them himself to elicit evidence that might help condemn the queen at her trial.[55]

Baynton's eagerness to assist Cromwell and Fitzwilliam in their 1536 case against his employer, who had once generously loaned him nearly £200, suggests how flimsy the oaths of loyalty could be within the queen's household, particularly across the gender divide.[56] From Baynton's point of view, the refusal of the women to cooperate with his requests for testimony and, in particular, the obstreperous loyalty of Margery Horsman, one of Boleyn's favourite maids, indicated how dangerous the ties of allegiance could be within the women of the household. Even in happier times, Baynton had been quick to criticise the frivolity of Anne's ladies and the cavalier attitude towards men that the household supposedly encouraged. In a letter to Anne Boleyn's brother, Lord Rochford, Baynton wrote, with more than a touch of the killjoy: 'As for pastime in the queen's chamber, [there] was never more. If any of you that be now departed have any ladies that ye thought favoured you and somewhat would mourn at parting of their servants, I can no wit perceive the same by their dancing and pastime they do use here, but that other take place, as ever hath been the custom.'[57]

Nor was Baynton alone in his concern that the women in the household were behaving inappropriately under the protection of the queen and in the absence of a stabilising male authority. Katherine of Aragon had been separated from one of her favourite female attendants when the latter was accused of encouraging the queen's unhappiness at her husband's adultery, and Sir Anthony Browne, the king's master of the horse, had quarrelled with his sister Elizabeth, Countess of Worcester, over the freedom she enjoyed when she served Anne Boleyn and the subsequent estrangement her residency in the household had apparently created with her husband.[58] Queen Anne had not only paid the countess's midwifery bills, but loaned her £100 without Lord Worcester's knowledge.[59] It may have been that, like Joan Bulmer in 1540, the Countess of Worcester hoped to exploit the anomalous position of the queen's household to extricate herself from an unhappy domestic life, fuelling the neuroses of men like Baynton and Browne.

The rumours about Margaret Douglas and Charles Howard helped focus attention on the queen's household, and although Queen Catherine escaped censure for her brother's behaviour in 1540–41, she also seems to have failed to realise that tolerating such behaviour would never reflect well on her. In the early winter of 1540, her confidence was understandable. She seemed secure to the point of being untouchable. Less than two weeks after the rain returned, de Marillac reiterated in his letters that 'the new Queen has completely acquired the King's grace, and the other [Anne of Cleves] is no more spoken of than if she were dead'.[60]

Chapter 11

The Return of Francis Dereham

For my sweet thoughts sometime do pleasure bring:
But by and by, the cause of my disease
Gives me a pang that inwardly doth sting,
When that I think what grief it is again
To live and lack the thing should rid my pain.

– Henry Howard,
Earl of Surrey (d. 1547)

From its earlier days under the Norman and Plantagenet kings, the queen's household had derived its income from a set of properties that funded her lifestyle as well as her political or charitable activities. Individual queens had access to different perks, exemptions, and parcels of land, and there was usually an undignified scramble over how to fund a dowager if there was more than one queen alive early in a reign, but by and large the portfolio was passed from one generation to the next. Medieval queens consort who possessed ambitious or aggressive agendas, such as Henry III's wife, Eleanor of Provence, were often strapped for cash, but otherwise the long-term dilution of a queen consort's independence at least helped stabilise their finances. Catherine's lands included six castles and more than one hundred manors, mills, farms, parks, and forests that were rented out to generate about £3,352 per year.[1] Henry VIII's first two wives had been given more or less the same estates once owned by Henry's mother, but the dissolution of the monasteries helped swell Queen Jane Seymour's coffers.[2] Like Queen Jane, Catherine became the passive beneficiary of the misfortune of others when she received manors and estates left by Cromwell, Lord Hungerford, and the Marquess of Exeter, more from the recently executed abbot of Reading, and some confiscated from the still-living but ruined Countess of Salisbury, who had remained in the Tower since her incarceration during the White Rose intrigue.[3]

These properties made the queen consort one of the greatest magnates in the kingdom. Anne Boleyn, who had also held lands in Wales in her capacity as Marchioness of Pembroke, and Katherine Parr, who followed Catherine, took their duties as landowners seriously, and they were heavily involved in the running of their estates, in contrast to Catherine, who passed many of the responsibilities on to others.[4] However, Catherine's failure to assume as proactive a role in her finances as Anne Boleyn or Katherine Parr, both of whom had some relevant experience in the management of their estates before they became queens, need not be interpreted as crass indifference, especially in light of her ignorance when it came to land management.

Responsibility for caring for her estates fell to the Queen's Council, which consisted of her receiver, surveyor, attorneys, solicitors, auditors, and the clerk of the council. They met at Westminster under the leadership of Catherine's chancellor, Sir Thomas Denys.[5] From their offices, the council could summon, in the queen's name, tenants whose rents to the household were in arrears. Those tenants could then either negotiate an extension or pay when summoned, options sadly unavailable to the silkwomen and tailors who complained about how slow the council was in settling its own outstanding bills.[6] Queen Catherine was not close to her councillors, and she made no effort to help Thomas Smith, her clerk of the council, when he earned himself a spell in the Fleet prison in London for quarrelling within the confines of the court.[7]

Catherine was, at heart, a pragmatist. It was how she approached the public execution of her queenship. Her failure to help Thomas Smith indicates her streak for self-preservation. Smith had been accused of papist sympathies, apparently evident in an exchange of insulting poetry with William Grey, a former servant of Thomas Cromwell.[8] Whether Catherine acted out of studied or genuine ambivalence, her disregard for Smith's plight reinforces the view that she was not a political queen. Unlike Anne Boleyn, or later queens consort such as Katherine Parr, Henrietta Maria of France or Caroline of Ansbach, Catherine had no clear political or religious agenda. Any books dedicated to her during her time as queen, such as the English translation of a German medical textbook on midwifery, were devoid of overt political or religious tones and seem to have been dedicated to her solely because of the position she occupied, rather than any expressed interest on her part.[9]

However, she may have attempted to exert some political influence very early on in her career. A tantalising glimpse of her nascent ambitions comes via her letter to Thomas Cranmer, the Archbishop of Canterbury, penned shortly before her wedding, in which she assures the archbishop that he will not suffer once she replaces Anne of Cleves. She promises him 'you should be in better case than ever you were', which simultaneously suggests an overestimation of her power and her refusal to play at factional politics, since Cranmer was regarded as one of the key advocates of reformism and had been a close ally of Thomas Cromwell's.[10] It is quite possible, even probable, that some of her relatives advised Catherine to make some gesture of goodwill to Cranmer, who was one of the councillors genuinely and consistently liked by Henry VIII, but her implication that she would have the power to make him more prosperous than he had been before was absurd. At some point, very early on, Catherine learned her lesson. Henry was not above reminding his wives, as he once had Jane Seymour, to keep out of affairs of state.

As a result, Catherine's focus narrowed, and she seems to have taken an aggressive delight in playing the role of Lady Bountiful by helping her servants. A surviving letter to Catherine from Edward Lee, Archbishop of York, is a regretful response to her request that he accept one of her chaplains as an archdeacon. As a landowner in the region Catherine technically had the right of advowson – to nominate someone for a vacant ecclesiastical post – but it seems that in her zeal to help her chaplain she may have overreached. The popular fantasy of being a queen is one that carries with it the promise of a life without restrictions, when, in reality, it contains more. Archbishop Lee told Catherine that 'I never granted advowson saving at the King's command, but one, which I have many times sore repented,' and while he acknowledged her complaint that he had not properly responded to an earlier letter she had written on behalf of another clergyman in her household, Dr Mallett, he reminded Catherine, perhaps a tad pointedly, that not only had she unhelpfully failed to specify which dependant she wanted to nominate as archdeacon, but that the archdiocese had already given a nod towards the queen's household when it had promised Catherine's chaplain, Dr Lowe, a living that would bring him an extra £40 once it became available.[11]

Catherine had the personality traits nurtured by lifelong popularity among her peers, including an affable bossiness that became tart when defied. Years earlier, Catherine had been quick to rebuke Henry Manox for embarrassing her in his conversations with Mary Lascelles. Her exchange with the Archbishop of York displayed her insistence, perhaps to the point of sensitivity, on respect from those around her, as well as her tendency to back down when presented with a satisfactory explanation. If an argument persisted and no apology was offered, a less pleasant side of Catherine's character revealed itself.

That autumn, a series of slights came from her eldest stepdaughter, Mary, the only surviving child of Henry's first marriage. Mary, who was referred to as 'the princess' by her Hapsburg relatives but who had been legally classed as 'Lady Mary' since her father disinherited her at the age of seventeen, disliked her new stepmother and she was not blessed with gifts of subtlety any more than Catherine was with patience in the face of an insult. This was not how Mary had treated Anne of Cleves, and someone who had been at court was able to tell Catherine that Mary had also been more respectful towards Jane Seymour. Mary Tudor was a clever woman, fluent in several languages. Like many upper-class women who benefited from a Renaissance education, she was as comfortable choosing jewels and gowns as she was translating books of theology, a task which presented a pleasant challenge for someone who was a good linguist, if somewhat shaky on the finer points of grammar.[12] However, if she was clever, Mary was not always wise, and she badly underestimated the new queen's temper.

In a letter from 5 December, the emperor's ambassador to London informed Mary's cousin, Maria of Austria, Dowager Queen of Hungary: 'The Princess, having heard from me that the attempt lately made to take away from her two of her maid servants proceeded entirely from this new queen, who was rather offended at her not treating her with the same respect as the two preceding ones, has found some means of conciliation with her, so that she thinks that for the present, at least, her two maids will not be dismissed from her service.'[13]

A subsequent letter, written by the ambassador two months later to the dowager queen, indicates that the reconciliation between Catherine and Mary only lasted a few weeks, at the very most, and when it broke down Catherine made good on her threat. On 6 February 1541, the ambassador told Maria that her cousin was 'thank God, in good health just now, though exceedingly distressed and sad at the death of one of her favourite damsels, who has actually died of grief at her having been removed from her service by the King's order'.[14] While he did not specifically state that the deceased woman was removed from Mary's service at the queen's behest, the dismissal so soon after it was raised as a threat by Catherine, and the fact that Mary had seemed to be in her father's good graces over the intervening Christmas season, strongly suggests that the banishment of Mary Tudor's maid was the unfortunate conclusion of an earlier quarrel with the young queen.

* * *

Catherine was still at Windsor, and her feud with Mary Tudor fermenting, when Francis Dereham returned to London. Despite having left the dowager duchess's service without her permission, he visited his old employer at Norfolk House, where a deal of sorts was struck; to piece together precisely what they agreed can only be done, and then imperfectly, by sifting through the transcripts of interrogations that took place in the autumn of 1541. At some point in 1540, the dowager had made discreet legal inquiries about the possible ramifications of a pre-contract like Francis and Catherine's and if there was any form of general pardon that might spare those involved.[15] She also seems to have asked for any written proof he had about his relationship with Catherine, including ballads she knew he had written about her. If this request was made, then Francis did not fully comply. All the documents were locked in a chest, which was kept at Norfolk House. Agnes knew where that chest was and that the papers were in it, strongly suggestive of a compromise between the two. Some members of the Privy Council believed, probably correctly, that this was how Francis kept the dowager's favour after abandoning her service.[16] We cannot know for certain if the dowager, with her long-standing affection for Francis, had encouraged him to leave London until Catherine was safely married, or if her story that he left without her knowledge is true. On the balance of probability, the latter seems more likely, especially in light of the Howards' subsequent uncertainty about what to do with him.

For most of 1540, Francis had ostensibly been earning his living as a merchant in Ireland. There were plenty of reasons for him to go to there, aside from the helpful sea separating him from Henry VIII. Dublin was the sixth largest city in the British Isles, and the island's eastern ports, such as the expanding Drogheda and Limerick, dubbed 'a little London' by a visitor in 1536, did a lively trade with their English and Welsh counterparts.[17] In the southern ports, fishing boats skimmed alongside trading ships to and from Europe. Ireland was also a society of ambiguity, a constant grinding mess of tensions and contradictions between de jure sovereignty, de facto authority, and outright criminality. The

Pale, which contained Dublin and her sister towns on the eastern coast, remained generally loyal to the Crown. In many ways, Dublin replicated the culture, architecture, mores, and mannerisms of any other Tudor city. Within its walls, the so-called Anglo-Irish, the descendants of long-ago settlers borne across the Irish Sea by the first English intervention in the twelfth century, were at their most influential and numerous. In the south and west of the island, the *Gaedhil* (natives) spoke a different language, dressed differently, and remained openly hostile to the Reformation. The Irish nobility were split between those headed by the Earl of Ormond, who espoused obedience to the monarchy, and other noble families who might have been prepared to acknowledge the feudal system that made Henry VIII their overlord, but who also continued to dominate their own ancestral lands and benefited from the ambiguities of life outside the Pale.[18]

Francis Dereham entered a land fuelled by the tense but dependent relationship between these two groups whose alleged ancestral differences were now largely imaginary after centuries of intermarriage. The east coast merchants provided the wine, salt and luxury items the Gaelic aristocracy wanted, while the Irish heartlands in return produced most of the goods exported from Dublin and the other ports. The Gaelic lords both preyed on and protected Irish merchant ships – in the harbours and straits where the government's control was lacklustre, the local lord expected a fee which could be paid by the captains or forcibly taken from them by the lord's retainers. Identifying what passed for unregistered trade, as opposed to smuggling or outright piracy, was thus nearly an impossible task that plagued Irish parliaments for years – the issue was still being debated in parliaments that met in the reigns of Elizabeth I and James I.[19] While he was in Ireland, Francis exploited this economic ambiguity to the extent that he was eventually accused of piracy.[20] Although he was not prosecuted for it, it may have been the reason he chose to return to Lambeth.

Upon hearing of his return, a Howard family servant who knew or suspected the truth about Francis and Catherine remarked to Lord William's wife, 'If I were Dereham I would never tell to die for it.'[21] The problem with that statement was that it presupposed a rational dignity that Francis quite simply did not possess. Something had to be done to buy his silence. He was impulsive, besotted, possessive, and loquacious.[22] Even the dowager's coy affection for him did not blind her to the fact that this was the worst possible combination of traits, and her harvesting of all the incriminating evidence from a man she knew to have the emotional equilibrium of a toddler gave the Howards possession of the documents that could have been used to push Catherine off the throne if they fell into the wrong hands.[23]

Francis wanted a job in Catherine's service. Refusing him or accepting him were both dangerous. The dowager duchess went to the queen to discuss it. Judging from subsequent queries, the Countess of Bridgewater supported her mother's suggestion that Catherine should grant an audience to Francis and perhaps show him some sign of her favour. Lord William Howard, who had known Francis for years, and his wife Margaret, who served as one of Catherine's ladies-in-waiting, would help facilitate a meeting at court, under the guise of reintroducing the queen to a family retainer. That was as far as the Howards were prepared to go; there is nothing to suggest that anyone else in the family even knew about the agreement with Dereham outside these four and the queen. Catherine had no affection for Francis, then or later, and he caused her nothing but anxiety from the moment he re-entered her life, but shortly before All Hallows' Eve, on a pre-arranged day, she asked her aunt Margaret where Dereham was. Lady Margaret curtseyed and answered, 'Madam, he is here with my lord.' Lord William, who did not leave on his embassy to France until January, had brought Francis to court that day as part of his retinue, which gave Catherine an opportunity to summon him without inviting suspicion. 'My lady of Norfolk hath desired me to be good unto him,' the queen answered, 'and so I will.'[24]

Most accounts of Catherine's career believe that at this point or shortly afterwards, Catherine made Francis her private secretary, but this long-established story is disproved by the household records.[25] A queen's private secretary managed her correspondence, took dictation from her, and drafted replies to any official letters she had to issue. It was a prestigious position, not just because it required intimate knowledge of the queen's affairs but also because the secretary was entitled to 'bouche of the court', meaning all his material needs met along with three stable places and four servants in residence of his own.[26] Sir William Paget had held the job of secretary for Anne of Cleves, in tandem with a German gentleman called Matthew.[27] Shortly after the divorce, Paget was recruited as clerk of the Privy Council, and a man called Thomas Derby took over as secretary for the new queen. Derby was still in the job by the middle of November 1540, nearly three weeks after Lord William brought Francis Dereham for his meeting with Catherine.[28] When Derby left his post, he was not replaced by Dereham but by a man called John Huttoft, who served Catherine until the end of her career.[29]

Francis was not appointed to her household staff in any capacity in November 1540, and the half-baked compromise that Catherine and some of her relatives came up with shows how uncertain they were about what to do with him. He could not be given an official post, certainly not as her secretary, since he was too young, unknown at court, and manifestly unqualified to serve as an officer of the queen's household, even if he had once taken some dictation for the dowager duchess of Norfolk. Everything about their actions in the early winter of 1540 supports a scenario in which the Howards, who had known and even liked Francis, decided to keep him close enough to control him through apparent acts of favour and the confiscation of his private papers, but not so close as to provoke speculation about his friendship with the queen. They must have known that it would not content Francis indefinitely, but a long-term plan is not always possible for those treading water. Unfortunately, Dereham, whose decision to keep the papers linking him to Catherine did not bode well for his future quiescence, had lost none of his flair for a public scene or his aggressive temper, and fleeting proximity to the girl he wanted to marry eventually proved too difficult for him.

Chapter 12

Jewels

Ceremony, though it is nothing in itself,
yet it doth everything ...

– William Cavendish,
1st Duke of Newcastle (1592–1676)

The king was in good spirits when he left Windsor Castle for Woking Palace on 23 November with his wife and a small retinue of about eighty people.[1] Despite its designation as a palace, Woking did not have space to hold the entire court. Half of its eight acres were taken up by manicured gardens, orchards, fish-ponds, and lawns that overlooked an area used for deer coursing, though it was from hawking, in season by late autumn, that the palace derived its reputation as an excellent hunting spot. For two weeks, Catherine and her entourage could look out from the great bay window in the queen's privy chamber onto the moat and the nearby River Wey.[2] After breakfast and morning prayers, they rode out hawking with the gentlemen and the king, who was thrilled to be hunting in the countryside again.

This trip was a break from the usual royal itinerary, which saw the king spend most of the colder months in London. The revitalised joie de vivre that so many people had noticed in the king after he married Catherine seems to have prompted the change in schedule, and he told a guest at Woking that 'he feels much better than when he resided all winter at his houses at the gates of this town'.³ The bracing winter winds that accompanied the king's new routine did not thrill his attendants quite as much as their master. Catherine's uncle William tried to turn it into a compliment when he praised the king for being 'so little in the house, but either hawking or hunting, were it never so cold, when divers of your servants had liever be home', but it is not difficult to detect the longing for warmth beneath William's praise for the king and the great outdoors.⁴

On 7 December, the courtiers had a new venue to shiver in when the hawking jaunt was extended by an eleven-day sojourn at Oatlands.⁵ When the party went out to hunt, servants were responsible for bringing the wooden frames, known as cadges, carrying hooded birds of prey that were then placed 'on the creep', that is, on the hunter's glove, and unhooded before they soared off to retrieve their targets. These birds used by the royal family and nobility were as prized and in many cases as expensive as good horses, if not more so. In wooded areas, hawks were generally used. The most desired falcons were the peregrines, with their rapid speed, and the beautiful white gyrfalcons. The cadge and the hoods were necessary to prevent the birds from unhelpfully attacking each other – a trait which, in a hunting party, was something of a liability.

On 18 December, the queen returned to Hampton Court on the same day that one of her ladies-in-waiting, Elizabeth Cromwell (born Elizabeth Seymour) became a baroness.⁶ Elizabeth's husband Gregory, Thomas's son, was raised to the peerage, which either suggested that the king did not intend to punish him for his father's wrongs or that Gregory Cromwell's matrimonial alliance with the Seymours had saved him from ruin by surname.⁷ Two days later, some of Thomas Cromwell's lands were given to Thomas Culpepper, in a gesture that showed Henry balancing the scales to remind everyone who was in charge.⁸

Lady Cromwell was one of Queen Jane Seymour's younger sisters, and she had spent most of her childhood at the Seymour family's home at Wulfhall in Wiltshire.⁹ Unusually, Elizabeth married before her elder sister.[10] Her first husband had been the much older Sir Anthony Ughtred, with whom she had a son and lived as chatelaine of the Château de Mont-Orgueil, home of the governors of Jersey, a post Ughtred was appointed to in 1532. Ughtred died in 1534 and his widow moved to the north of England. Elizabeth does not seem to have been close to her royal sister. She was not appointed to the household when Jane became queen in May 1536, and she was still living in the north in March 1537, though she did visit the court and took the opportunity to ask for Thomas Cromwell's help in acquiring land from some of the closed monasteries in Yorkshire. Cromwell subsequently helped the widow Ughtred by arranging her marriage to his son and heir, Gregory. Another of Elizabeth's suitors wrote, 'If I do tarry here in the country, I would have been glad to have had you likewise, but sure it is, that some Southern lord shall make you forget the North.'[11] Elizabeth and Gregory's wedding took place at Wulfhall in the summer of 1537. It was the start of a close and happy marriage, with a child a year for the first four, and when he was away from her – for example, serving as a member of the delegation sent to Calais to greet Anne of Cleves in 1539 – he playfully addressed his letters to 'my right loving bedfellow' and wrote, 'I am, thanks be to God, in health, trusting shortly to hear from you like news, as well of your self as also my little boys, of whose increase and towardness be ye assured I am not a little desirous to be advertised.'[12]

For Catherine, the return to Hampton Court meant beginning her public duties in earnest, and on 21 December she sat beneath the cloth of estate in her audience chamber to formally receive the incoming Hapsburg ambassador, Eustace Chapuys, a thin, middle-aged man with soft features and dark eyes.[13] Catherine was one of the few people at the English court who was unknown to Chapuys – he had served as the emperor's representative in London from 1529 to 1539. Chapuys would have preferred to stay in Europe, re-establishing a relationship with his bastard son Césare and busying himself with philanthropic projects such as setting up scholarships or funding the foundation of colleges and grammar schools in his hometown of Annecy.[14] His expertise and the emperor's command put those projects on hold, and he arrived back in London in the summer of 1540. Time away had not improved Chapuys's ever-diminishing opinion of Henry VIII. He returned at the same time as Cromwell was being beheaded, the apprentice boy Meekins was being fed to the flames, and Katherine of Aragon's former chaplain Dr Thomas Abel and Princess Mary's former tutor Father Richard Featherstone were being dragged through the city streets to be quartered for papism, alongside a fellow Catholic priest and three Protestant clergymen, who were butchered on charges of heresy so flimsy and imprecise that even the officiating sheriff could not answer the dying men's questions about why they were being executed. Ten men followed them four days later, on the same day as the last monk in England, Brother Thomas Epsam, was put on trial for treason at Newgate and had his habit torn from him in front of his judges.[15] 'This,' wrote his contemporary Edward Hall, 'was the last Monk that was seen in his clothing in England.'[16]

Chapuys was an intelligent man and passionate in his loyalties. He had been distressed by Henry's treatment of Katherine of Aragon but magnanimous enough to express horror at the fate of Anne Boleyn and her brother.[17] Many times in his career, Chapuys overstepped his brief from the emperor through acting as a confidant to Henry's eldest daughter. His advice to her was often flawed, but it was unfailingly given with the best intentions, and it is easy to understand why Mary Tudor regarded him with such affection. Chapuys's political views were suspected but unproven by most of his acquaintances in England, some of whom had accused him of supporting the Pilgrimage of Grace uprising; he told the emperor that he knew that he was being spied upon within weeks of his return.[18]

The court's tour of the best hunting spots in the south-east meant that 21 December was Chapuys's first opportunity to meet with the new queen, hence the need for a formal audience.[19] Catherine's reception of Chapuys was a prelude to his more important meeting with the king, who had not seen Chapuys since he returned to England. Struggling with the onset of gout, Chapuys bowed and walked towards Catherine's dais. He may have had mixed emotions about her. Even before they met, it was Chapuys who had warned Mary Tudor about Catherine's plans to dismiss two of her maids in retaliation for the princess's behaviour. On the other hand, for an imperialist, almost anyone was preferable to Anne of Cleves.

The king dined with his wife that day and then went to a council meeting, during which the ambassador visited the queen and chatted with the Earl of Hertford, who had been tasked with keeping Chapuys company until the king was free to discuss the ongoing trade dispute with the Netherlands. An account of that conversation took up most of Chapuys's subsequent letter to Maria of Austria, the emperor's governor in the Netherlands.[20] It was only after their second meeting, on the last day of Christmas, that Chapuys wrote about Catherine in detail.

Between their two encounters, Catherine's wardrobe had acquired several hundred new sparkles as Christmas turned into a deluge of gifts, a single one of which would probably have been enough to lift her father out of debt. A necklace of two hundred pearls was among the first gifts of the season, followed by a golden crucifix decorated with thirty-two diamonds and clusters of pearls. Another necklace, with six diamonds and five rubies interspersed in sequence by pearls, accompanied one made of sixteen diamonds. She received large square brooches for the front of her gowns, such as the one made of twenty-six clusters of pearls and twenty-seven diamonds, and a gold-and-diamond brooch that showed the king handing down true religion to his adoring, obedient subjects. Two more necklaces, thirteen golden girdles that matched the golden pomander to hang from her waist on a gold chain, flecked with thirty-two pearls and a smattering of rubies, and three more ornamental bejewelled books to alternate on her other pomanders arrived before Catherine could guard her hands against the January chill in a black velvet muff lined with sable that hung from her neck on a chain of thirty pearls held together by small pieces of gold. Thirty-eight rubies and another flourish of pearls decorated the exterior of the muff, lest the dark velvet and fur seem a tad austere. By Twelfth Night, she also had three new bodices to choose from, each decorated with eight diamonds and seven rubies.[21]

As the Earl of Sussex was shown into Catherine's presence on 4 January, what to wear was not her most pressing concern. Catherine was about to host Anne of Cleves in a charade designed to broadcast the king's insistence that his most recent divorce had been legal, amicable, and unavoidable. By mutual consent, at least officially, Anne was a member of the English royal family and thus accorded all the legal rights of a king's sister. Although New Year's Day was legally marked in England on 25 March, the nobility often observed the European date of 1 January as another excuse to give gifts during Yuletide, and Anne sent her ex-husband 'two fine and large horses caparisoned in mauve velvet, with trappings and so forth to match'.[22] She was invited to join the king and queen at Hampton Court on 4 January and was escorted to the palace gates by Catherine's uncle William, who had apparently accidentally met her retinue with his own while en route to Hampton Court and who 'could not well, for courtesy's sake, refuse to accompany her to the gates'.[23] The Duchess of Suffolk greeted her inside, sent at the head of a delegation by their new mistress to accompany their old to the apartments that had been prepared for her visit. Once Anne had viewed the rooms and her servants swarmed in to begin unpacking her things, the Duchess of Suffolk and the Countess of Hertford, who was not one of the queen's women, escorted Anne to the doors of the rooms she had never had the chance to enjoy during her own brief time as consort. There, they were asked to wait. The delay was not part of the schedule. Inside, Catherine was panicking.

She had sent for the Earl of Sussex, who was the king's Lord Great Chamberlain, and the Lord Chancellor, Lord Audley, to reassure her about the proper etiquette for greeting a woman in Anne's position.[24] Audley, who was the government's chief legal authority, might have been more used to deploying his skills in treason trials, a field where he was generally regarded as an expert, but his knowledge of the law was needed to shore up Sussex's mastery of decorum. Catherine's nerves were understandable. The two men must have struggled to find a precedent that could serve as a model for greeting Anne. This was not the same as greeting a dowager queen, since Anne was not Henry's widow or a former queen, a legal conundrum that had presented itself only twice in English history thus far.[25] The king insisted that Anne had never been his wife and, at least in public, she agreed. Etiquette is predicated on the idea of behaviour properly reflecting the situation of the interaction and the social position of the participating individuals. How did one treat a queen who had never been a queen? The two women who had endured similar limbo before, Elizabeth Woodville after her son's deposition in 1483 and Katherine of Aragon after her annulment in 1533, had refused to accept the legality of their demotion and because of it had not returned to court.[26] Even the obvious fallback of treating Anne with the decorum shown to one of Henry's sisters, one now dead and the other living in Scotland, was made difficult by the fact that for decades the procedure for greeting them had been based on the rank they acquired when they married their husbands. How Anne was received would not only reflect on Catherine personally, but it would also convey to the assembled guests, many of them representatives of foreign governments, the security of the king's most recent divorce. Henry's vanity and reputation were at risk.

Eventually, the queen and her advisers seem to have hit upon the idea of bending the rules in favour of lavish kindness. Catherine could smooth over any potential awkwardness by displays of spontaneity prompted by deep admiration for her guest. When the doors were at last opened and Anne was announced, it was apparent that she too had decided that no one ever erred in choosing the side of civility. She sank into the deepest curtsey possible and spoke to Catherine from her spot on the floor, from which she refused to budge despite the queen's pleas for her to stand. The manners one-upmanship continued when

Henry entered the room and made 'a very low bow to the Lady Anne', whom he embraced before they processed to supper. Protocol always has the potential to turn from a caress to a slap, particularly when its minutiae are adhered to at the expense of overall effect, and at the supper table that evening, Anne was given a spot near the bottom, though her face did not betray any sign of annoyance.[27]

Watching all this in the throng of courtiers and servants was Eustace Chapuys, whose government was initially perturbed to hear that Anne had been invited back to court. In a letter to the emperor's sister, Chapuys promised that if there was any sign of Anne's rehabilitation, 'I will seize every opportunity of indirectly thwarting it.'[28] As he observed the royal reunion, Chapuys unknowingly concurred with the French ambassador's assessment to his government that Anne's appearance at Hampton Court was a public relations' exercise and that rumours of her elevation, much less restoration, were baseless fantasies.[29] Since he did not regard Anne as a threat to the Hapsburg agenda, Chapuys could afford to be impressed by Catherine's handling of the situation and praised the 'favour and courtesy' she showed to her predecessor.

After supper, the king, the queen, and the ex-queen 'conversed for a while in the most gracious manner,' until the king retired for the night and left the ladies to lead the celebrations that were not due to stop for two more days. Catherine and Anne danced a duet together before the revellers were invited to join them. For the second dance, Catherine and Anne each chose a young man from the king's privy chamber staff as a partner. The privy chamber's gentlemen could be relied upon to know the steps and to keep up a steady flow of pleasant conversation as the musicians played into the night.

We do not know the name of Catherine's or Anne's male partners, and presumably they would have changed with each new dance, but whoever they were they were unlikely to have recognised Anne of Cleves as the shy, angular, tongue-tied princess in hideous pearl bonnets, whose one-year anniversary would have fallen on the same night as she was dancing with her replacement. She had put on weight, which suited her, and she filled out the numerous new dresses she had bought herself in retirement.[30] The woman who emerged from gilded seclusion in Düsseldorf with no language but German and a total ignorance of music, dancing, or cards was now fluent in English, sumptuously dressed, dispatching perfect gifts to her ex-husband, and pirouetting in public as if she was devoid of worries.[31]

On the second day of her visit, she had dinner with the king and queen and, according to Chapuys, 'there was again conversation, amusement and mirth, and on the king retiring to his apartments, as on the previous night, the queen and Lady Anne danced together'.[32] They were interrupted when a messenger knelt before Catherine to present her with two young lapdogs and a ring, gifts from her soon-to-be slumbering husband. Apparently, Catherine was as impressed as anyone with Anne's chutzpah and perhaps genuinely sympathetic to her situation, because she immediately passed the presents over to her.[33] After dinner, Anne, with her two new puppies, went to her apartments to oversee the packing, which took two more hours, before her horse was brought to one of the courtyards and she rode off to her own palace, six miles away, at Richmond. Knowing that she owed her position and continued freedom to Henry, Anne had behaved impeccably, and with more land due to be signed over to her on 17 January, her subservience at Hampton Court was shrewdly theatrical.[34]

The visit had been a success for Queen Catherine as well. She had managed to avoid any show of tasteless triumph, and her performance had impressed lifelong courtiers. The next few months saw Catherine in a mood of increasing confidence. It may have been around this time that she decided to reprimand her stepdaughter by making good on her threat to dismiss one of her maids. During Christmas, Chapuys told Maria of Austria that 'the Princess has not yet visited the new queen, though she has on this New Year's day sent her a present, at which the King, her father, has been much pleased'.[35] Henry's relief at Mary's gift to Catherine evidently did not last, and the fact that he sent her 'two most magnificent new year's gifts' in his name and Catherine's perhaps suggests that he organised the presents on his disgruntled wife's behalf.[36]

On 17 January, the same day as Anne of Cleves received her next batch of rent-generating lands, the poet, courtier, and diplomat Sir Thomas Wyatt was arrested and sent to the Tower on suspicion of treason. Wyatt, who was both repulsed by and addicted to life at court, had most recently served as Henry's ambassador to the Hapsburgs – despite his way with words, it was Wyatt who had caused a scene by thoughtlessly deploying the term 'ingratitude' in a conversation with the emperor – and before that he had been a close friend of Thomas Cromwell. His house was searched, one of his servants was imprisoned, and another wave of arrests was expected, plunging courtiers into dread as they remembered a similar environment three years earlier when Sir Geoffrey Pole was taken and the White Rose horror unfolded.[37] The news that the English ambassador in France, Sir John Wallop, was recalled from Paris the day after Wyatt's arrest deepened the chill. Wallop was as prominent a conservative as Wyatt was a reformist, provoking fears of a tit-for-tat game of reprisals from the respective sides which, as usual, would probably claim as collateral damage the lives or careers of hapless courtiers who spent their days treading the path of deliberate neutrality.[38]

On the surface, life continued as normal. Catherine was in good health and high spirits in the first week of February.[39] There was another round of official receptions, for Sir James Campbell, a Scottish diplomat travelling to represent his king at the Hapsburg court.[40] Catherine's chancellor, Sir Thomas Denys, who also oversaw the management of the Prince of Wales's estates, was defending himself before the Privy Council after a complaint was made against him by tenants on royal land in Dartmoor Forest.[41] All three of the main men in Catherine's life – her husband and two uncles – were preparing to leave her: the king and his councillors were going to conduct business in London for a few days, the Duke of Norfolk was heading north to inspect English fortifications on the border with Scotland, and her uncle William had been picked to replace Sir John Wallop as ambassador to France.[42] The government had clearly learned their lesson from Bonner's rudeness – William went with the reminder that he must use immaculate manners when dealing with the French royal family.[43]

Chapter 13

Lent

I have read in old books that some for as just causes
have by kings and queens been pardoned by the
suit of good folks.

– Mary Boleyn (d. 1543)

On 7 February 1541, the king and some of his councillors went into London for three days on business, while the queen stayed at Hampton Court with her household.[1] When he returned from the city, the king was irritated to hear that some of the defences built during the invasion scare of 1538–39 were already beginning to crumble. The ramparts near Dover, Portsmouth, Southampton, and various other points along the southern coastline, had already partially collapsed, and some of their sister structures had been damaged by the incoming tide which, considering their location, cannot have been an unanticipated factor. Their deterioration justified Charles de Marillac's earlier suspicion that more effort had gone into making the defences visually impressive than into making them durable.[2]

Worrying news was also coming from the north, where the Scottish Parliament was preparing to pass legislation that confirmed the kingdom's commitment to Roman Catholicism. The year before, Henry's representative in Edinburgh had reported conversations that seemed to indicate that the king, who was Henry's nephew, applauded some of his uncle's ecclesiastical policies, yet James V's government was now passing bills that stressed a traditional Catholic view of the seven sacraments, encouraged 'worship to be had of the Virgin Mary', declared 'that no man argue the Pope's authority', protected saints' images from Protestants who wished to destroy them, and outlined harsher punishments for heresy.[3] Scotland was too close to the parts of England where conservative religious sympathies had birthed the Pilgrimage of Grace for this development to pass without causing worry in London. It made the Duke of Norfolk's mission to inspect defences on the Anglo-Scottish border doubly pressing. Persuading James V to repudiate papal authority was an ongoing and unsuccessful feature of Henry VIII's foreign policy in the 1530s and early 1540s. The English consistently underestimated the depth of James's devotion to his faith and dismissed his protestations of piety as proof that he must be dominated by the Scottish episcopacy, with the result that they misinterpreted his motives and leapt on any ephemeral sign that he might change his mind by rebelling against his 'handlers'.[4]

At Hampton Court, the courtiers still lived under a pall. Thomas Wyatt and John Wallop remained in prison, more arrests were expected, and conversation in the palace antechambers predicted Wyatt's execution.[5] An observer wrote that 'although he is more regretted than any man arrested in England these three years, both by Englishmen and foreigners, no man is bold enough to say a word for him'.[6] It was tacitly understood that John Wallop was in less danger – although his conservatism was well known, he seemed to have been tossed into the Tower 'due to his having said something in favour of Pope Paul'.[7] Courtiers interpreted Wallop's spell in gaol as an attempt to teach him a lesson, rather than a prelude to his death. Still, memories of the White Rose intrigue were fresh. Many people were nervous, and the debates over the possible outcomes did nothing to soothe frayed nerves. Wallop might, like the Countess of Salisbury, be spared the axe to spend years in prison. When summoned home from his embassy to France, Wallop had suspected it was because he was in trouble with his king. Every courtier or member of the local gentry who encountered him on his journey from Dover to London was under strict and horrible instructions to 'let him pass on without suspicion' to make sure Wallop put himself into the government's hands without a fuss.[8] Desperate to prove his loyalty, the fifty-year-old Wallop tried to surrender himself to Sir Richard Long, who, remembering his orders, would not accept. Wallop broke down in tears in front of Long, terrified and confused that he might be considered a traitor.[9] By imprisoning a reformist and conservative at the same time, the king was reminding all his courtiers that both sides were at his mercy.

The king was voicing his intention to go south to inspect the disintegrating strongholds when he began to feel unwell.[10] He took to his bed with a fever, which de Marillac thought 'should rather have profited than hurt him, for he is very stout'.[11] Henry did not have time to sweat out the weight de Marillac thought he could stand to lose. He felt better by 23 February, when the council sent a letter to the Duke of Norfolk informing him that the king had recovered after a few days of sickness.[12] They were wrong. The fever was tertian, a malarial strain, that caused the king's leg ulcer to close over. He was in such pain that for a few days his entourage were genuinely afraid that he was going to die. The Privy Council and Privy Chamber worked together to stifle news of their master's infirmity. Discussions about rebuilding the southern defences and the fortifications at Calais continued in council, as if nothing were wrong, but ambassadors and courtiers knew that something was amiss. From her windows, the queen could see the effects of tightened security – the usual flow of petitioners and place-seekers trying to get into the palace met with questions about their intentions, and more often than not they were sent away. When the doctors finally managed to pierce the ulcer and alleviate some of his pain, Henry sank into what the French envoy called a *mal d'esprit*.[13] That unhappiness turned outwards and Henry began to threaten his advisers: he accused them of putting their own needs above his and undermining his policies with their flattery and greed. He missed Thomas

Cromwell, charging his no doubt terrified councillors that 'by false accusations, they made him put to death the most faithful servant he ever had'.[14] He also raged against his subjects' ingratitude. Having heard that 'his subjects in divers places murmured at the changes which, contrary to their ancient liberties, are imposed upon them, and at their ill treatment for religious opinions,' Henry ranted that 'he had an unhappy people to govern whom he would shortly make so poor that they would not have the boldness nor the power to oppose him.'[15] Either because he was embarrassed at his physical condition or in too low spirits to take comfort from her company, Henry ordered that Catherine was not allowed to visit him and the queen was left rattled by his decision.[16]

The king's temper did not improve during Shrove Tuesday. Usually a time of celebration before the penitential season of Lent began on Ash Wednesday, it was sometimes known as 'Fat Tuesday', or by its French translation 'Mardi Gras' and the English celebrated it with rich foods such as pancakes, which used up all the ingredients they would not be allowed during Lent. The court usually marked the holiday with feasting, cockfighting, plays, and dancing. In 1541, all those entertainments were cancelled. Courtiers were encouraged to go home, petitioners were still turned away, and an isolated Catherine, for the first time, felt the chill fear of uncertainty that so many of her husband's companions had endured for years. De Marillac wrote in a letter to his own king that Henry 'spent Shrovetide without recreation, even of music, in which he used to take as much pleasure as any prince in Christendom, and stayed in Hampton Court with so little company that his Court resembled more a private family than a king's train'.[17]

In observance of Lent, fish replaced meat, eggs and cheese were removed, sexual intercourse was discouraged, and examination of one's conscience was exhorted as the Church marked the temptation of Christ in the wilderness with a season of self-denial.[18] In the magnificent Chapel Royal at Hampton Court, the riot of colour was blotted out as sombre veils were hung through the chancel and over the lectern, statues, and altars.

Catherine may have used the Lenten fast as a time to examine her life. It is hard not to fall into the trap of undue speculation when writing about a historical individual. In Catherine's case, we can only infer from what happened next, since she left no record of her feelings at this time. All that can be said with confidence is that after her only Lent as queen, her behaviour altered significantly. She became more prone to insecurity but paradoxically began to behave more recklessly in the privacy of her own apartments. She veered between uncertainty, which bred unhappiness, and a dangerous overconfidence. It was possibly during her husband's brush with death that she realised for the first time that his love for her was no more consistent than his love for his country. Her husband had threatened to impoverish and punish his own people for having 'murmured' against his policies. She had stood on the sidelines during Thomas Cromwell's destruction, an event that Henry was now blaming on everyone but himself. She knew that her uncle and Bishop Gardiner were hated by Cromwell's supporters for ruining him, but neither of those men had been at the king's side at Shrovetide when he lashed out that he had been tricked into destroying 'the most faithful servant he ever had'. Norfolk was in the north and Gardiner on a diplomatic mission to Europe. She knew that there had been ample opportunity for Henry to save Cromwell, if he had wished to. Perhaps too the atmosphere among the agitated courtiers, even before the king took ill, had eventually affected her.

Henry VIII's court was a place riddled with espionage, where nothing was quite what it seemed and people listened behind the walls, peeped at keyholes, and whispered in alcoves. Its inhabitants exhibited a bizarre and unsettling mixture of bone-chilling fear alongside obsequious, and often genuine, loyalty. When John Wallop wept, it was not ostensibly because he was afraid that he was going to die, but rather that 'nothing grieved him so much as that your Majesty should think him a false man'.[19] Henry VIII was able to command an obedience within the walls of his palace that was total in comparison to the varying degrees of resentment that festered outside. Some writers have likened the courtiers' loyalty to a kind of Stockholm syndrome, and while modern labels like that are difficult to validate, they do nonetheless seek to explain why there was such sustained devotion to a man who caused a sword of Damocles to hang over the head of everyone he had ever known, liked, promoted, or loved and who ruled by playing them off against each other.[20]

The first six months of Catherine's queenship was a reduced version of it. She was only very briefly at one of the larger palaces at the start of August, when she was first proclaimed queen. Apart from that, Catherine moved from hunting lodge to hunting lodge with a reduced court that insulated her from the political reality of her new position – that her marriage had pitched her headfirst into a fraught and internecine environment where everyone had long, if silenced, memories of those who had already been destroyed by her husband. Her behaviour during Anne of Cleves's visit to Hampton Court showed how much store Catherine set by doing things properly, and that visit and her quarrels with her stepdaughter confirmed in different ways how disagreeable she found criticism. Her husband's dark mood, which resulted in her first moment in the shadows, must have unsettled her, as did the situation as described in de Marillac's letters – eerie silence and mounting panic in an enormous palace.

One touching anecdote about Catherine from this time unfortunately can now be disproved. The incarcerated Countess of Salisbury had complained about the cold blowing in off the Thames, and to alleviate her pain the queen's tailor, John Scutt, delivered two nightgowns, one trimmed with fur and the other with satin, a woollen kirtle, a bonnet, four pairs of hose, four pairs of shoes, and a pair of slippers. This is often ascribed to Catherine's generosity and her sympathy for the elderly and bereaved Lady Salisbury.[21] However, at the same time the king's tailor was asked to make or source an almost identical delivery for Lord Lisle, another royally descended prisoner in the Tower, and the order for both was issued by the Privy Council in a meeting held at Hampton Court on 1 March. The bill, for £11 6s 4d, was settled on 12 April.[22] Even in prison, Tudor concepts of social hierarchy were maintained – queens, dukes, and countesses were treated as their position demanded. They were to have everything they needed, except freedom. The queen's tailor was asked for the same reason the king's was commissioned for Lord Lisle's 'necessaries' – they were making clothes for the countess, who was King Edward IV's niece, and Lord Lisle, who was his illegitimate son.[23] Queen Catherine had nothing to do with the gift to the Tower in 1541. To have associated herself with someone like Lady Salisbury, whom the king loathed and whose son Reginald was still actively working against Henry in Europe, would have been unwise, to say the least.

On 8 March, the recovered king and his court left Hampton Court after nearly three months and sailed downriver to the Palace of Westminster.[24] They did not plan to stay for long – Westminster was an administrative hub and Parliament met there, but most of the royal apartments had been destroyed by fire in 1512 and never fully rebuilt. The decision to move there for just over a week was motivated by Catherine. Owing to the plague that had ravaged London after the summer drought, the queen had been kept away from the capital until the risk abated. She therefore had not made her ceremonial entry into the City, a queenly rite of passage during which City officials and by extension the commoners they represented would formally greet her and in doing so convey their support for her queenship. For this to happen, she had to formally cross London's boundaries. Hence, she would go to Westminster for eleven days, and then when the court travelled to Greenwich Palace on St Joseph's Day, the guilds and aldermen of London would acknowledge her in coordinated public ceremonies.

The business of government continued. Eustace Chapuys was unwell and had temporarily left London to recuperate in the countryside, and the French ambassador was busy quashing rumours that King Henry planned to initiate a rapprochement with the emperor by offering the hand of Princess Mary in marriage.[25] Plans were in motion to issue the necessary papers for summoning a parliament in Dublin, since Ireland had its own House of Lords and House of Commons, and two scarlet robes made from twenty-four yards of fabric were ordered from the king's tailor to be sent to the Earl of Desmond, the speaker of the Irish House of Lords, and McGilpatrick, who performed the same office for the House of Commons.[26] A dispute over trade tariffs with the regent of the Netherlands rumbled on, the Duke of Norfolk was expected back from the borders by the middle of Lent, and talk of the king travelling to Dover to see the dilapidated fortifications had revived now that Henry was in better health.[27]

While Catherine was at Westminster, a scandal involving seduction and larceny broke in court circles. With her sense of humour, it is hard to believe she did not find some of its details amusing. It had links to Catherine's establishment, and in fact its unusual resolution had much to do with that household. The affair began when a London-based goldsmith called William Emlar was brought before the Privy Council after silverware belonging to Eton College surfaced in the local markets. Eton had been founded just over one hundred years earlier by King Henry VI, Henry VIII's great-uncle, which meant that it had already endured a plundering of its resources when Edward IV deposed Henry VI in 1461. Building work on the still-incomplete school had resumed under the Tudors, and by 1541 the provost was Nicholas Udall, an Oxford scholar who had written a textbook called *The Floures for Latine Spekynge* that was used in English classrooms for most of the rest of the century, and who had also helped script most of the pageants for Anne Boleyn's coronation in 1533. The appearance of the Etonian plate and silver in London implied either corruption in the school or, more probably, theft. William Emlar told the council that he had received the items from a former student at Eton called John Hoorde, the nineteen-year-old son of a well-to-do Shropshire gentleman. Hoorde was brought in for questioning, during which he implicated his friend and co-conspirator Thomas Cheney, who was still in his final year at Eton. On 13 March 1541, Cheney was summoned to Westminster, where he confessed to stealing the plate. He also implied that Nicholas Udall, the provost, had been party to the scheme, so Udall was fetched from Windsor to answer questions about his role in the black-marketing of his school's possessions.

Udall, who was about thirty-four or thirty-five years old at the time, seemed an unlikely thief. During his early career, the Duke of Norfolk had apparently been one of many court lights who recognised his talent and promoted him. Udall's work for the 1533 coronation had managed to incorporate scenes that ranged from flattering juxtapositions of Anne Boleyn's physique, status, and heraldry ('Of body small, / Of power regal / She is, and sharp of sight; / Of courage hault, / No manner fault / Is in this falcon white …') to paeans to Queen Anne's patron saint and clever innuendoes about her coat of arms as it was incorporated into renderings of the Annunciation.[28] As a headmaster, Udall had maintained Eton's tradition of beating recalcitrant or underperforming students on Fridays or 'flogging days', yet he had still acquired a reputation as 'the best schoolmaster' during his seven years there.[29] He encouraged acting and drama at the school, for which it is still famous, and it is probable that he wrote his play *Ralph Roister Doister*, the earliest surviving theatrical comedy in the English language, for performance by a student cast.[30] His skills as one of the finest Latinists of his generation had stood him in good stead to lead a school where most of the lessons were still conducted in Latin and dunce caps were affixed to the heads of the *custos*, young gentlemen who talked too much in English in the classrooms, made more than three spelling mistakes in a lesson, or misquoted one of the rules of Latin grammar.

In his interrogation before the council at Westminster, Udall denied complicity in the theft but instead startlingly confessed to 'buggery with the said Cheney sundry times'.[31] According to Udall, the last time student and headmaster had sex was only eight days before Udall's testimony. There was no good reason for Udall to confess to the crime of sodomy to try to exculpate himself from one of larceny. The Buggery Statute of 1533 had made homosexual activity a capital offence. It had been one of the accusations laid against Lord Hungerford, who had been executed nine months before Udall confessed to similar behaviour. The only explanation for Udall's startling admission was that it was the truth. It is possible that Cheney had already confessed their liaison in the hope that Udall's senior age and position would drag attention off him for helping to steal the silver. The councillors in session that day – the Duke of Suffolk, the Earl of Southampton, the Earl of Sussex, Sir Anthony Wingfield, Sir Thomas Wriothesley, and Cromwell's onetime ward Sir Ralph Sadler – signed an order for Udall to be incarcerated in the Marshalsea prison in Southwark, which may indicate some sympathy for Udall or, just as likely, respect for his social position. Compared to other London prisons, the Marshalsea was relatively comfortable in the sixteenth century, and while prisoners were prepared to pay through the nose for its amenities, there were many other gaols where Nicholas Udall would have paid as much and suffered more.

The council sent messengers to Shropshire and Buckinghamshire for the fathers of the two Etonians involved to come to London. Thomas Cheney's father, Sir Robert Cheney, arrived a few days before Richard Hoorde, John's father. In the meantime, the Privy Council established a version of events in which Cheney and Udall had been sleeping together while Cheney and his friend Hoorde had worked with one of Udall's servants, a man called Gregory, to rob the college of various images, plate, and silver that they then attempted to sell in London. Udall, it seems, was not party to the scheme, though the fact that he had been in debt beforehand raises the possibility that he could have been. So while he would not be charged with theft, his sexual relationship with a male student, with which he may have been blackmailed to keep quiet about Cheney's theft, could still put a noose around his neck.

At this point, the affair goes quiet. Everyone involved ultimately escaped punishment. John Hoorde went home to Shropshire, where he eventually married a local woman called

Katherine Oteley and lived well into the reign of Queen Elizabeth I. Thomas Cheney married Frances Rotherham, a woman from his mother's home county of Bedfordshire. He died in the spring of 1554, when he was in his early thirties. Most unexpectedly of all, Udall was released from prison and was soon once again in favour with the great personalities of the court – he helped Princess Mary with her translation of a biblical commentary, *Paraphrases upon the New Testament*, was patronised by Henry VIII's final wife, Queen Katherine Parr, recruited to Bishop Gardiner's household, and after Princess Mary succeeded to the throne in 1553, Udall was appointed headmaster of Westminster School in London, where he served until his death two years later.

Three of the councillors who quizzed Emlar, Hoorde, Cheney, and Udall had wives in Catherine's service, but it was one in particular who had a vested interest in the case. Sir Thomas Wriothesley had, like Sir Ralph Sadler, risen to the Privy Council thanks to his ties to Thomas Cromwell, and again like Sadler, he had managed to avoid ruin when the minister fell in 1540. Holbein's portrait of Wriothesley shows a bearded man with auburn hair and, even allowing for artistic embellishment, piercing and watchful blue eyes.[32]

From prison, Nicholas Udall wrote a grovelling, hysterical letter to his 'Right worshipful and my singular good Master'. Apart from illustrating that Udall really did love Latin and the classics as much as his previous job had required him to – the text is peppered with references to Pliny, promises of rehabilitation couched in didactic examples from the lives of Greek philosophers, and Latin pieties about the value of mercy – his letter to Sir Thomas Wriothesley provides clues as to why a scandal that should, according to the law of the land, have taken Udall's life ended with him walking free. Udall's decision to throw himself on Wriothesley's good graces is the first oddity, for while the letter does hint that Wriothesley had patronised Udall before 1541, he was nonetheless a strange choice. Wriothesley did not exactly have the reputation of an angel of mercy. A few years later, he was nearly ruined when allegations surfaced that he had personally tortured a female prisoner on the rack by twisting the roller himself after the professionals at the Tower refused to keep going.[33]

The second point of interest is the plan that they concocted – or, to be more precise, Wriothesley offered and Udall gratefully acquiesced to. Udall's letter states that Wriothesley had tried to get him his old job back, 'my restitution to the room of Schoolmaster of Eton', then, once that ploy had failed, Udall begged for the opportunity to meet with Wriothesley in person to outline a strategy for Udall's rehabilitation that would enable him 'to shake it off within two or three years at the uttermost'. Judging by his subsequent relationships with Mary Tudor, Katherine Parr, and Stephen Gardiner, it evidently worked. This leaves the question of why Wriothesley was prepared to undertake 'travail, pains, and trouble' on Udall's behalf despite, as Udall wrote, being full of 'displeasure and indignation' at his actions.

The answer lies in the relationship between Thomas Cheney, the student at the centre of the outrage, and one of Catherine's ladies-in-waiting, Lady Jane Wriothesley, Sir Thomas's wife. Lady Wriothesley may have briefly left the court around the time of Catherine's marriage to give birth to a son, Anthony, who sadly died shortly afterwards. By the time the Eton affair was playing out in the council chambers at Westminster, Lady Wriothesley was back in the queen's service. Before her marriage, she had been Mistress Jane Cheney from Chesham Bois, the same manor in Buckinghamshire that eventually belonged to Thomas Cheney's father, Sir Robert. The exact familial relationship between Lady Wriothesley's father and Thomas Cheney's is difficult to specify, but given their respective ages and the fact that they both hailed from the same manor, the logical conclusion is that they were either siblings or first cousins. The affiliation between Sir Thomas Wriothesley's wife and the student who possibly seduced and certainly robbed Nicholas Udall explains why Wriothesley advocated the unthinkable suggestion of sending Udall back to Eton as if nothing had happened – because that was what the

Cheney–Wriothesley families wanted, so that their kinsman's name would not become associated with a buggery scandal. Lady Wriothesley was kin to Bishop Gardiner, in whose service Udall eventually began his climb back to steady employment and social respectability, and she was the half sister of the bishop's secretary, confidant and nephew Germaine Gardiner.[34] It was in the Wriothesleys' best interests to help Udall by sweeping the scandal under the rug. All the events in the affair support the conclusion of a cover-up based on who Thomas Cheney was related to.[35] Chatter about the flow of silver and scandal from Eton to London cannot have missed the alcoves and galleries of the queen's household. Even if, presumably, Lady Wriothesley might have preferred to stay tight-lipped about the whole thing, the Duchess of Suffolk and the Countess of Sussex both had husbands who were involved in the questioning of the associated parties.

Hoorde's and Cheney's fathers were still on their way to meet the council when the royal household left Westminster for Greenwich on the afternoon of 19 March. It was two years to the day since Catherine's father had died in debt and been thwarted in his dreams of a career at court. From the palace, Catherine walked down the steps to the royal barge. To mask the smell from the river, its decks were strewn with rosemary-scented rushes and herbs burned in sconces. The king and various members of her household accompanied Catherine, taking their places before the twenty-six oarsmen pushed off into the current.[36] As they sailed past the Tower, its heavy gates rising from the filthy waters of the Thames, salvoes of cannon fire rang out in salute. Directly ahead, they could see brightly decorated barges, hung with cloth and banners flapping from their masts. The Lord Mayor of London and his aldermen were on one of those boats, between Tower and London bridges, and they were rowed over to welcome Catherine to the City. Catherine Howard, the private gentlewoman, had been to London many times, but 'this was the Queen's Grace first coming to London since the King's Grace married her', and as a result 'the people of this city honoured her with a most splendid reception'.[37]

From the Tower, Catherine and Henry continued to Greenwich, where they disembarked at a wharf that led to a staircase exclusively for the royal family's use. At Greenwich, the king announced his intention to free Thomas Wyatt and John Wallop, a decision accredited to Catherine's influence. Queens traditionally interceded for compassionate causes, mirroring the Virgin Mary's role in Catholic theology whereby Mary acted as a conduit of mercy while God functioned as the font of justice. The trope of the intercessor queen featured heavily in medieval romances and popular tales. Earlier in Henry VIII's reign, his first wife had publicly begged him to free a group of xenophobic apprentice boys after they rioted against the presence of wealthy foreigners in London, and his second had asked him to intervene with the French government on behalf of a man condemned to burn for heresy.[38]

On several occasions, a queen's intervention seemed too well staged to be genuine – for instance, in the apprentice boys' case, Katherine of Aragon had fallen to her knees with Cardinal Wolsey and the court nobility following suit. The consort's role as mediatrix at the heart of government could be used by her husband as an acceptable reason to reverse a policy, lest he appear weak or inconsistent in doing so of his own volition. There were those on Henry's council who were worried at the prospect of putting Wyatt on trial, in case his eloquence resulted in embarrassment for the government, as George Boleyn's had at his trial in 1536. Pardoning Wyatt at the queen's behest, which was distinctly different to an exoneration, would allow the Crown to maintain that it had been right to imprison him, while avoiding any prospective fallout from his defence of himself. The Privy Council pretended that Wyatt's admission of guilt in return for mercy had been 'spontaneous', when it had been anything but.[39] Considering that Wyatt and Wallop's detentions look, in hindsight, like Henry reminding factions at his court of his dominance over them, it is possible that Catherine was asked to publicly beg for their lives as a touching dénouement to a scene that Henry had always intended to culminate with the two men walking free.

Yet comments from the Privy Council in a letter to the queen's uncle William, in France, a report written by Eustace Chapuys for Maria of Austria, and another by Charles de Marillac for King François I, all state that Catherine had been lobbying on the gentlemen's behalf for quite some time.[40] In a letter written one week after the king's decision, the council told Lord William that Wallop, his predecessor as ambassador to France, had been freed after 'great intercession was made for him and Wyatt by the Queen'. Chapuys wrote that after her official entry into London 'the Queen took occasion and courage to beg and entreat the King for the release of Master [Wyatt], a prisoner of the said Tower, which petition the King granted, though on rather hard conditions', and de Marillac, who had previously been almost certain that Wyatt would only leave the Tower in a coffin, praised Catherine for her 'great and continual suit' to have the two men pardoned. So while it is possible that Henry knew of Catherine's plans to ask for Wallop and Wyatt's liberty on the day of her official entry to London, it seems as if Catherine had been working on her husband for quite some time.

One of the men who had ended up in prison in the fallout of the Wyatt affair was John Leigh, a relative of Catherine's late mother. He had served in some of Wyatt's embassies and stood accused of papist sympathies.[41] Some of those who cared for Wyatt seem to have spoken to the queen in the hope that she would have the bravery and prominence lacked by other courtiers who were too afraid to plead on his behalf. Her kinsman's fate may have helped focus the queen's interest in the detentions.[42] Wyatt's most recent biographer has surmised that Catherine's cousin, Lord Surrey, may have been one of those who talked to Catherine about Wyatt's plight.[43] Surrey and Wyatt were close friends, and Surrey would eventually compose Wyatt's elegy in which he praised him as a man 'with virtue fraught, reposed, void of guile'.[44] Catherine had already shown herself indifferent or perhaps even hostile to the machinations of court faction through her friendliness towards Archbishop Cranmer, and she liked to help people. While she never risked her standing with her husband if she knew the case had been judged treasonous, it is clear that in this case she went to some effort for both men, regardless of their political backgrounds, and in doing so earned more admiration from diplomats and some courtiers.

Her influence had its limits, and Chapuys was right in describing 'hard conditions' on Wyatt's rehabilitation. Both men had to confess to wrongdoing for which the king was pardoning them, abandoning their previous protestations of innocence, and Wyatt was required to set up house with his estranged wife after living apart from her for fifteen years, allegedly after he had caught her in bed with a lover.[45] He also promised to separate from the two women he had been living in sin with, including the mother of his illegitimate children, and he was warned that if he did not resume 'a conjugal life' with his wife 'or should he be found to keep up criminal relations with one or two other ladies that he has since loved, he is to suffer pain of death and confiscation of property'.[46] Why the details of Wyatt's private life should have featured so prominently in his pardon is unclear. His wife's brother, Lord Cobham, may have asked the king to remove the separation as a stain on the family's honour or Henry may have wished to cast himself as a virtuous prince, capable of reforming morally errant subjects.

Wyatt's audience with the king took place at Dover Castle at the end of the month.[47] The king had gone to Kent to see the damaged defences while Catherine stayed behind with her women, which meant she did not have an opportunity to witness the ceremony that marked Wyatt's rehabilitation.[48] Instead, she spent the final weeks of Lent at Greenwich. Breaking the rules of the Lenten fast was a controversial topic in Henry's England, and traditionalists were upset by reformers' tendency to eat meat on the vigils of certain feast days. Shortly before Catherine became queen, the Bishop of Lincoln had complained when one of the Bishop of Worcester's servants ate buttered chicken on the eve of the Feast of the Assumption.[49] At court, the Lenten dietary rules were generally still adhered to, but that did not mean all exhortations for restraint were. Catherine and her husband may have continued sleeping together during the penitential season, and if not, they certainly had in the build-up to it. When Henry returned to Greenwich on 5 April after sixteen days in the south, Catherine informed him that she was pregnant.

Chapter 14

For They Will Look Upon You

A lady gave me a gift she had not;
And I received her gift which I took not;
She gave it me willingly, and yet she would not;
And I received it, albeit, I could not:
If she give it me, I force not;
If she take it again, she cares not.
Construe what this is, and tell not;
For I am fast sworn I may not.

– Sir Thomas Wyatt (d. 1542),
'A Riddle of a Gift Given by a Lady'

On Palm Sunday, Charles de Marillac had an audience with King Henry. The main topic of their conversation was English resentment against Scotland. Evidently, the ambassador talked also with courtiers or informers during his visit because in a subsequent letter to Constable de Montmorency in France he wrote: 'that this Queen is thought to be with child, which would be a very great joy to this King, who, it seems, believes it, and intends, if it be found to be true, to have her crowned at Whitsuntide. Already all the embroiderers that can be got are employed making furniture and tapestry, the copes and ornaments taken from the churches not being spared. Moreover, the young lords and gentlemen of this Court are practising daily for the jousts and tournaments then to be made.'[1]

It was hardly surprising that as soon as the idea of Catherine's coronation was floated, gentlemen dusted off their armour and lances to head for the tiltyards. Jousts that accompanied a coronation offered spectacular opportunities for athletic one-upmanship, and preparations for them typically began months in advance.[2] Whitsuntide, the suggested date for the coronation, was the seventh Sunday after Easter, which gave enough time for the court athletes to practise and for arrangements to be made to crown Catherine at a point when she would presumably be beginning to show her baby bump but long enough before it would be unwise for her to exert herself with the three or four days' worth of ceremonies that surrounded it.

A coronation would raise Catherine's prestige, and a child, even if she (preferably he) was only second in line after Prince Edward, could help her outshine Jane Seymour, her most successful predecessor. Jane's portrait still hung alongside images of Henry, his parents, and his late brother, Arthur, in his private collection. Even during Katherine Parr's reign, the spectral Queen Jane appeared in her place in dynastic paintings. Catherine's table was set with Jane's golden spoons, silver plates for spices, crystal glasses speckled with rubies, and a golden goblet, decorated with diamonds and pearls, that bore Queen Jane's maxim 'Bound to Obey and Serve', which, in terms of prostrating oneself at the shrine of a husband, might be the one motto that outdid Catherine's 'No Other Will But His'.[3] A baby would guarantee Catherine's future. If she had a son, as Duke of York and the future king's brother he would guarantee her position as a great lady. And if, for whatever reason, Prince Edward shared the fate of his late uncle Arthur and did not live long enough to either succeed or father an heir, then Catherine could find herself as queen mother and potentially regent, if her son succeeded to the throne as a minor, though given past precedent in England that job would likely go to one of her kinsmen.[4] In light of how much could change and be secured by a successful pregnancy, it is easy to understand why early modern queens consort were so earnest in their prayers for conception and safe delivery.

The court's Holy Week observances of 1541 seem to have been kept, like the king's offering on Good Friday, 'according to the ancient ordering in years past'.[5] Conservative prelates would have found nothing to make them uncomfortable in the rituals. To all outward appearances, Henry and Catherine presided over a 'Catholic' court. The royal family still kept gilt images of saints such as John the Baptist, Saint Andrew the Apostle, Gabriel the Archangel, Saint Mary Magdalene, and Saint James the Great. The Virgin Mary stood rooted in grief and rendered in silver at the base of their private crucifixes. The life of the Virgin's father, Saint Joachim, was displayed in tapestries at the Palace of Whitehall; her Assumption decorated the walls at Windsor; the scourging and Passion of her Son were popular topics for weavers. The king and queen also owned distinctly Catholic aids to morality, such as the allegorical tapestries of the seven deadly sins, which were commissioned by the royal household about three years after it repudiated the authority of the Vatican.[6]

The heavy presence of traditionalist art and ritual in the worship of Henry's court has led to a modern description of the Henrician Church as 'Catholicism without the Pope'. It is easy to see how that label has been taken as an aphorism. Henry's Church defended a Catholic view of the sacraments, particularly the belief that during Holy Communion, Christ's words of *hoc est corpus meum* became literally true through the miracle of transubstantiation.[7] It refused to promote the emerging Protestant view that salvation was a gift that could be acquired through faith alone and that via *sola fide* the redeemed would be born again through a spiritual catharsis that required them to accept Christ as their saviour, trusting in Him and no other to atone for their sins. Instead, the Henrician Church promoted the older interpretation that in a world where belief was almost universal there must also be actions to show one's faith, a kind of kinaesthetic spirituality that encourgaed pilgrimages, fasting, mortification of the flesh, and public and private acts of penance. The seven corporal deeds of mercy – to feed the hungry, give drink to the thirsty, clothe the naked, shelter the homeless, visit the sick and the imprisoned, and bury the dead – were seen as useful guides on the efficacy of good deeds in absolving oneself of certain sins.[8] The early Church of England would not, to the distress of many reformers, abolish prayers for the departed and, implicit through them, the country's belief in purgatory. Predestination, which was at this stage admittedly a fringe belief held only by the more extreme Protestant sects, drew even more ire – the idea that God had already chosen who was to be saved and who damned struck the majority of English Christians as a brutal, hope-destroying psychosis – and it led to Henry's Church vigorously asserting the contrary doctrine of free will. Henry VIII himself was in many ways a spiritual conservative. In his will, he specifically sought the intercession and protection of the Blessèd Virgin Mary. In 1538, dressed all in white, he personally presided over the heresy trial of a Lutheran preacher called John Lambert, and each time the Eucharist was mentioned during the proceedings, Henry reverently doffed his cap as a sign of respect; he debated with Lambert, refused to offer succour to heretics, and signed a death warrant consigning the preacher to the stake.

Yet if the outward appearance of English and Welsh Christian worship remained fairly similar to how it had been in the centuries before the schism, the experience was radically different. The subtitle of the Six Articles, usually taken as a legislative victory for traditionalists, was 'an act abolishing diversity of opinions', a reflection of the king's unhappiness as the after-effects of the break with Rome opened the floodgates to dozens of different interpretations of the Scriptures.

The one constant in Henry's religious policy was his sincere belief that he was rightfully head of the Church in England, the custodian and shepherd of the country's conscience, while the pope was the heir to centuries of usurpation. To Tudor loyalists, Henry VIII was not a revolutionary but a restorer of what had, and should always have, been. He was resurrecting the legacy of early Christian Roman emperors such as Constantine the Great and Justinian, who had presided over early Church councils and involved themselves in their theological disputes. With sublime self-belief, Henry accepted the propaganda that cast him as a latter-day Old Testament king-cum-spiritual-leader – Solomon building the Temple and Jehoshaphat casting down idols. It has been argued that the Buggery Statute of 1533 was partly inspired by Henry's fascination with Levitical law after his first divorce. His attempt to replicate the behaviour of King Jehoshaphat, who had attacked homosexual activity in various pagan cults, according to the Bible's first Book of Kings, was evidenced in the role that accusations of sodomy played in bringing down English monasticism in the 1530s.[9] The ransacking of the shrines and the abbeys also had an Old Testament precedent when, in the Books of Kings, one biblical monarch 'took all the sanctified things which … his fathers the kings of Juda[h] had dedicated to holy uses, and which he himself had offered: and all the silver that could be found in the treasures of the temple of the Lord' and put them to national use.[10]

All this scriptural justification for his ecclesiastical policies may endow Henry VIII with too much moral credit. After all, if Pope Clement VII had allowed him to marry Anne Boleyn, it is hard to foresee a set of circumstances that could have persuaded Henry to rebel against the Holy See at such enormous cost to himself and risk to his kingdom. Henry's inquisitiveness and changing views after 1531 gave both reformers and conservatives cause for hope and despair at different times. Yet whatever one might make of the morality or impact of his decisions, the one salient feature of his Reformation was the king's total belief that he was God's anointed. Having convinced himself of that, he never wavered. His moods and his theological debates pulled the Church in different directions, but they were always anchored by the Royal Supremacy. Henry was impressed by some reformist ideas and appalled by others. Thomas Cromwell wrote that Henry 'leaned neither to the right nor to the left hand'.[11] A more critical eye might dismiss the Henrician Church of England as a

syncretic misfire led by an erratic megalomaniac caught somewhere between the liturgical certainties of his childhood and the
storm-following-sunshine appeal of new and untested
philosophies.

For Catherine, as queen and wife to one of God's self-
appointed earthly lieutenants, Holy Week was a time when she
was expected to be on display by attending services in the Chapel
Royal at Greenwich. The ceremonies and customs of the week
were designed to inspire the faithful through relevant biblical
readings, symbolic gestures, and public processions. On Palm
Sunday, Catherine heard the story of Christ's entry into Jerusalem,
as told in the Gospel according to Saint John, followed by
anthems and a parading of the Blessed Sacrament. Priests and
choristers knelt and kissed the ground in front of the Sacrament's
resting place. Saint Matthew's version of the entry to Jerusalem
rang forth from the choir with the words of the evangelist, Christ,
and the crowd sung in different keys.

Holy Monday and Holy Tuesday generally stressed Christ's
role as the Messiah who fulfilled the prophecies of the Old
Testament. Rather than interpreting it as a linear narrative, a
sequential divine revelation, as Protestants increasingly came to
do, medieval Christian theology stressed the interconnectedness
of the Bible as a divinely inspired mirror that constantly reflected
itself in past and present. For adherents of this view, the Virgin
Mary's first mention was not in Saint Luke's Gospel, when she is
referenced by name, but in the third chapter of Genesis, when a
woman who will crush a serpent beneath her heel was foretold at
the fall of man.[12] In much the same way as defenders of transubstantiation insisted that the elevation of the Host during Mass
marked a moment out of time, Holy Week and Easter tried to
stress the concept that time was a human construct that, through
Christ's life, had interacted with something that was eternal,
neither past nor present.

From Wednesday, the ceremonies Catherine attended began to
centre more clearly on biographical details from the Gospel
narratives of the Passion of Christ – Judas's betrayal on the

Wednesday, the Last Supper on the Thursday.[13] The queen had been a passive observant for the first four days of Holy Week, but on the Thursday she was required to perform public acts of piety. Maundy Thursday took its name from Christ's command or *mandatum* at the Last Supper – *Mandatum novum do vobis: Ut diligatis invicem, sicut dilexi vos …* ('A new commandment I give unto you: That you love one another, as I have loved you …')[14] After the Supper, Christ had washed the feet of the twelve apostles to convey the importance of humility and serving others. In homage to this, since the reign of Edward I the English monarchy had performed a Maundy ritual on the Thursday of Holy Week in which various members of the royal family publicly washed the feet of the local poor.[15] Henry IV had established the custom of the number of attendees growing to reflect the monarch's age, and so, in 1541, fifty-one poor men[16] had their feet bathed by a kneeling Henry VIII, who then handed them purses of money.[17] We know less about Catherine's performance of the Maundy obeisance than we do about some of her predecessors', but Catherine would have followed the custom of having an apron tied around her gown as some of her ladies followed her with basins, cloths, and water that she used as she washed and wiped the feet of pauper women. Frustratingly, considering that we do not know Catherine's date of birth, the records do not state how many women were invited to the queen's Maundy ritual in 1541. If they had, we would know for certain what age Catherine was when it happened.

When Henry returned to his apartment and set down his black velvet-lined Mass book in the same little room next to his bedchamber where his two copies of the Great Bible were kept alongside a book of Aristotle, discussion turned from the betrayal of Christ to betrayal of the king.[18] A minor conspiracy against him, the Wakefield conspiracy, had been uncovered and foiled in the north. The news was circulating at court by Easter Sunday, when a council meeting was held to discuss it, which means it must have reached the king a day or so earlier. The details of the failed plot were vague. Rumours that the ringleaders had been in league with the Scottish government or Cardinal Pole were voiced, as was a story that they had planned to kidnap the king's deputy, the Bishop of Llandaff, president of the Council of the North. Some observers, such as Eustace Chapuys, were unsurprised that the north remained fertile soil for treachery after the region had been treated so terribly in the aftermath of the Pilgrimage of Grace: 'The people's indignation against the King has risen to a higher pitch since then,' he wrote, 'owing to the cruelties and exactions that followed the rebellion in the North.'[19] The discovery of the Wakefield conspiracy increased Henry's already lively sense of paranoia, and the presence of some very distant relatives of the Countess of Salisbury in the rebel cabal brought the imprisoned dowager back into his mind's eye.

A map of England hung in Henry's gallery at Greenwich.[20] It was as close as Henry had ever come to seeing the northern half of his kingdom. Unlike his parents, he had never visited it, but the collapse of the so-called 'Wakefield conspiracy' of 1541 prompted him to reconsider his entrenched residency in the south.[21] The Duke of Norfolk was back at Greenwich for the council meetings about the plot, and by Sunday the word round court was that the king, 'fearing lest [in] the North there should exist other conspiracies of the same kind, or perhaps more dangerous ones still, has announced his intention to go thither immediately after these festivities'.[22]

In her apartments on Maundy Thursday afternoon, after the public charity, the queen was handing out more gifts. Accompanied only by her chamberer Katherine Tilney and Lady Rochford, one of her privy chamber ladies, Catherine met her old beau Thomas Culpepper in the small corridor that linked the queen's public and private rooms. Since their flirtation in the weeks before Anne of Cleves's arrival had ended with Culpepper transferring his affections to another woman, Culpepper had remained in service in the privy chamber, where he was a great favourite of the king. Thomas and Catherine's earlier romance had apparently been so fleeting and inconsequential that Henry had never heard about it, but evidently Catherine remained fascinated. Lady Rochford had arranged the meeting on the queen's behalf, and Henry Webb, one of the queen's ushers, had gone to fetch Culpepper from the presence chamber. Culpepper already had two fine velvet caps that had been gifts from the king, but the queen's present of a cap was not given in the same spirit. She begged him to keep the cap under his cloak until he was back in his rooms, in case anyone saw it.[23] Culpepper flirtatiously bantered back, 'Alas, Madam, why did you not this when you were a maid?' This reference to Catherine's lack of enthusiasm for him when she first came to court as a single woman did not land well. She retorted, 'Is this all the thanks ye give me for the cap? If I had known ye would have these words you should never have had it.'

A flirtatious gesture met with a putdown or a reminder of contradictory past behaviour is always liable to embarrass, and Catherine did not summon Culpepper to her rooms for quite some time after his underwhelming reaction to the cap. Her response to his teasing and her own suggestion that he hide the cap when he left her apartments indicate that she had hoped for, and expected, praise and that she had not given him the hat with purely platonic intentions. This first meeting also conclusively disproves the absurd recent theory that Catherine only ever met with Thomas Culpepper in 1541 because he was blackmailing her with knowledge of her premarital private life.[24] Culpepper's mockery and Catherine's annoyance at it, as well as everything she said to him at their subsequent meetings, are obviously and without exception the behaviour of two outgoing, confident people who were both attracted to one another and accustomed to being the dominant partner in a romantic relationship.

That evening, Catherine was back in chapel to see the altar stripped of its coverings and ornaments. Christ's arrest had occurred after the Last Supper, and the symbolism of water and wine being poured over an altar that was then wiped clean by a stiff-twigged broom pointed to the forthcoming horror of the scourging and Crucifixion – the wine stood for Christ's blood, the water for the fluids that spilled from His side when it was pierced post-mortem by a Roman soldier's spear, and the sticks of the broom for the crown of thorns that was twisted into His head as the procession to Golgotha commenced. From the evening service on Spy Wednesday, Tenebrae saw all lights in the chapel being successively extinguished to the sound of chanted Psalms.

On Good Friday, the commemoration of the Crucifixion, the great spiritual theatre of Easter reached its apogee. Two pieces of linen decorated the otherwise stripped altar, and they were removed in homage to the fate of Christ's garments that had been gambled for by His executioners.[25] Henry and Catherine removed their shoes and led the congregation as they crept on their knees to kiss a crucifix held before them by two priests. 'Creeping to the Cross' on Good Friday was an ancient custom dismissed as superstition by most Protestants, but in 1541 it was still being practised by the majority of Henry's subjects. After the adoration, Henry moved to a square enclosure near the altar where he knelt to pray over platefuls of rings. The king as God's anointed was believed by many people to have sacerdotal powers, none in and of himself but rather as a vessel for God's blessing, and the rings, known as cramp rings, were anointed by the monarch in the hope that the wearer 'may be protected from the snares of Satan'.[26] Psalms were sung as the king lifted up each of the rings individually before they were sprinkled with holy water.[27]

In most churches, the venerated crucifix was carried with the consecrated Host to a small makeshift hearse, representing Christ's burial in the tomb of Saint Joseph of Arimathea, where candles were lit to burn in front of it until the following Friday. Christ was dead and the officiating cleric spoke words from the eighty-seventh Psalm, 'I am counted as one of them that go down to the pit.'[28] The ritual reminded the congregation not just of Christ's death on the cross and the subsequent 'Harrowing of Hell', through which the souls of the damned were liberated, but also of their own mortality. On Easter Sunday, the crucifix and sacrament were removed – Christ had risen – and the promise of eternal life and salvation was reiterated to the worshippers. Easter was one of the few occasions in the year when the majority were encouraged to take Holy Communion, which required fasting from the evening before and permission from one's confessor, since a state of grace by confession and subsequent atonement were necessary before partaking in the 'great mystery'. The cap for Culpepper was not something that the queen needed to seek absolution for. Their meeting was indiscreet, but it was not yet a sin.

By Easter, members of Catherine's household were noticing her preference for the company of Jane Boleyn, Dowager Viscountess Rochford, the lady of the privy chamber who had helped arrange the queen's private meeting with Thomas Culpepper on Maundy Thursday. Lady Rochford had been born Jane Parker, sometime around 1505, making her only a year or so younger than her future husband, George Boleyn.[29] Her father Henry, Lord Morley, was a bibliophile who had grown up in the household of Henry VIII's grandmother Margaret, Countess of Richmond, but kept away from court life as he grew older. He signed his letters as 'Harry Morley', and correspondents included European philosophers, scholars at Oxford and Cambridge, and fellow aristocrats.[30] Lord Morley's preference for his library over the corridors of power was not shared by his eldest daughter, although she later used her own wealth to become the 'most special patroness' of a scholar based at King's College, Cambridge.[31] Jane joined the court in her adolescence, and she never really left it. During the Shrovetide celebrations of 1522, she was given the role of 'Lady Constancy' in a masque called *Château Vert*, where she appeared alongside six other dancers, including the king's youngest sister and Anne Boleyn, who had recently returned from her education in France. She married Anne's brother George sometime between 1522 and January 1526, when Cardinal Wolsey authorised an extra £20 per annum to be granted to 'young Boleyn for him and his wife to live on'.[32]

Jane's marriage took place before her sister-in-law became the king's fiancée, and as Anne rose, Jane went with her. In 1532, she was chosen as one of Anne's companions on a trip to meet the

King of France at Calais, and three years later Anne turned to Jane for help when they concocted a plan that would force Henry's latest mistress to leave the court.[33] Unfortunately, Jane's enthusiasm for intrigues was not quite commensurate with her skill for them, a recurring problem in her career, and the king reacted by temporarily banishing her, rather than his mistress.[34] Queen Anne's decision to reach out to Jane discredits the historical tradition that the two women despised each other and that Jane was pathologically jealous of her.

By the 1530s, she enjoyed the courtesy title of Lady Rochford, since her husband was heir-presumptive to the earldoms of Ormond and Wiltshire. The couple were also given use of Beaulieu Palace in Boreham, Essex, a large country house that had once belonged to the Boleyns, before they sold it to the king for £1,000 in 1516.[35] She was a woman of great wealth and prominence, but her world came crashing down around her after her husband was arrested on 2 May 1536, for allegedly committing incest with his sister the queen. In their histories of the English Reformation, John Foxe, writing in the sixteenth century, and Gilbert Burnet, Bishop of Salisbury, writing in the seventeenth, both accused Jane of providing false evidence which condemned the Boleyn siblings to death. Their criticism stuck, but Jane's modern biographer Julia Fox has raised enough questions about the evidence linking Jane to perjury in 1536 to suggest that she did not betray her husband or actively seek his death.[36] George trusted her to speak to their friends at court on his behalf, which he is unlikely to have done if their marriage was as unhappy as is usually assumed.[37] If she did give any evidence during the fall of the Boleyns, then it is possible that she did so in her husband's defence and her testimony was later subverted by Thomas Cromwell at the queen's trial or Lord Rochford's. Either way, Jane found herself in dire straits after her husband's execution on 17 May 1536, and it was her natal family's connections that came to her rescue when she and they had to bring pressure to bear on her father-in-law, who was reluctant to give her the income owed to her as his son's widow.[38] When he was finally compelled to give in, he did so 'alone to satisfy the King's desire and pleasure' and in a letter peppered with complaints about Jane's extravagance and righteous reminders that when he was a young man he and his wife had lived on a lot less, with a growing family, than childless Jane was now demanding for life as a *feme sole*.[39]

In 1539, Jane was able to join the household of Anne of Cleves, where she had been one of the women who pressed the queen about her chances of conceiving and subsequently gave evidence about it during the royal annulment hearings.[40] Like most of her colleagues, Jane then transferred smoothly to Catherine's service, where, by the spring, she had established a firm friendship with the new queen.

Historians are divided on what to make of Anne Boleyn's sister-in-law and Catherine Howard's confidante. The assessment of one biographer, that Lady Rochford was 'a pathological meddler, with most of the instincts of a procuress who achieves a vicarious pleasure from arranging assignations', strikes a judgemental note, especially when compared to more recent sympathetic depictions of her as 'very much the grand lady … elegant, poised and animated'.[41] Unlike some of Catherine's other companions, Lady Rochford had lengthy experience of life at court, having been a member more or less constantly since 1522 and very possibly since 1520, but these two decades of life at Henry VIII's court do not seem to have translated into a prudent attitude towards its dangers. There is some evidence, though it may admittedly be hearsay, that in the mid-1530s she had discussed intimate information about the king's behaviour in bed.[42] She had been involved in intrigues in the households of Anne Boleyn and Anne of Cleves, and in both cases her discretion had been poor. Like many courtiers, she delighted in gossip and she had an addiction to palace life that predisposed her to participate in its plots, particularly if they raised her standing. Proximity to royalty was important in Henry's palace, but knowing their secrets gave a courtier even greater credit.

Lady Rochford's ascendancy in Queen Catherine's affections provoked curiosity in the household and then, after several months, hostility. She was not an obvious candidate for the queen's favour. By 1541, Jane Boleyn was about thirty-six years old, old enough to be the queen's mother by contemporary standards. Although they were distantly related to each other thanks to the Parkers' kinship to the Tilneys and the Boleyns' to the Howards, Catherine had far closer relatives in her household, including her sister Isabella, who was in the privy chamber with Lady Rochford and found herself being edged out of her sister's favour by the latter.[43] There was a childhood friend in Katherine Tilney or women closer in age, like Anne Bassett or the Duchess of Suffolk. The reasons for this unusual and damaging friendship are therefore difficult to determine, but given what happened next and what we know of both ladies' personalities, it does seem as if a shared love of scandal and intrigue brought them together – a conclusion supported by the fact that Jane was instrumental in arranging Catherine's secret Maundy meeting with Culpepper.

The queen's family were all in relatively good health that spring. Uncle William, although keen to come home, remained on his embassy in France, and gossip that Catherine's aunt would be reconciled with her estranged husband, the Earl of Bridgewater, had come to nothing. The earl was a wealthy man and the countess had secured enough money to maintain a townhouse of her own at Lambeth, while her sons were still wards of the dowager duchess, as Catherine had once been.[44] Catherine's brothers Charles and George continued to do well at court – the king made a grant to Charles during Lent.[45] On St George's Day, 23 April, the king went to Westminster for the annual chapter meeting of the Most Noble Order of the Garter, the highest chivalric order available to an English subject, a group of twenty-four 'companions' of the order, founded by Edward III in 1348 to promote chivalry, loyalty, and fraternity in battle. It was dedicated to England's patron saint, George, and on his feast day new members were usually brought in to fill any vacant stalls. There were three spaces available in April 1541, one of which went to Catherine's cousin, Lord Surrey.[46] His father was already a companion knight, as his grandfather and great-grandfather before him had been, meaning that Surrey's promotion had more to do with the favour the Howards stood in by the spring of 1541 than with a specific policy of rewarding the queen's family in light of her pregnancy. For the Howards, this was fortunate because by the time Catherine's brother George received a grant from the king in May, preparations for the queen's coronation had stopped along with any talk of her having a child.[47]

What precisely happened with Catherine's pregnancy is unclear, and a variety of explanations are all equally possible. The first is that the pregnancy had ended in miscarriage at a very early stage. A second possibility is that Catherine had, either of her own volition or at the instigation of others, invented the story in order to restore herself to the king's favour after the upset their relationship had suffered during his spell of poor health. She perhaps hoped to make her lie into a truth at the earliest available opportunity. At some point, biological chronology would have given her away, but by that stage Henry might have been so pleased with the anticipated arrival of a new Duke of York that he would have forgiven her earlier 'mistake'. There is a possible explanation as to why Catherine might have lied, found in Chapuys's correspondence. Chapuys believed that the deception started with the king, who had faked his illness at Lent to avoid seeing Catherine, because, for a few weeks, he had considered divorcing her and reported his suspicions in a letter to Maria of Austria: 'Last Lent I wrote to Your Majesty that this king, feigning indisposition, was ten or twelve days without seeing his queen or allowing her to come into his room; that during all that time there had been much consultation and talk of a divorce; but that, owing to some presumption that she was in the family way, or because the means and ways to bring about a divorce were not yet sufficiently prepared, the affair dropped.'[48]

Alternative correspondence, from the Privy Council to the Duke of Norfolk and Charles de Marillac to François I, confirms that Chapuys's suspicions about Henry's illness were unjustified. Henry was genuinely and seriously ill during Lent, as was

Chapuys himself at the same time, which might explain how he was confused about events later. It is possible that Catherine or some of her ladies feared the sickness was a ruse or that the king's decision to keep his distance from her while he was unwell encouraged Catherine to try to buy herself some time by claiming she was pregnant.[49] A third possibility is that Catherine, or those around her, made a genuine mistake in diagnosing her condition.

Whatever the truth, the fragility of the royal line of succession was brought home by shocking news from the Scottish court in May. At the same time as Catherine announced her pregnancy, the Scottish queen consort, Marie de Guise, was preparing to give birth. The child was a boy, a younger brother to King James's one-year-old heir, James, Duke of Rothesay. Some sources give the new prince's name as Arthur; others suggest that he was christened Robert.[50] Officially, he was referred to as the Duke of Albany in his eight short days alive. On 14 May, Sir Thomas Wharton, writing from the border as Deputy Warden of the West Marches, sent the news that not only had the newly born Albany died, but within a day his elder brother had also passed away.[51] De Marillac, who had a vested interest in Scottish news since Scotland was France's ally and its queen was a French noblewoman by birth, wrote that 'the queen of Scotland was brought to bed of her second son, but that, within eight days after, he died, and the eldest also, at which there was great sorrow there'.[52] According to Wharton, the catastrophe, at once a political and personal tragedy for the Scottish monarchy, 'perplexes all'. Queen Marie, who perhaps needless to say was 'very sickly and full of heaviness', wrote in anguished letters to her mother, Antoinette, Duchess of Guise, that the tragedy seemed so horribly improbable that she believed her babies must have been poisoned.[53]

Henry VIII was not close to his Scottish relatives. Leaving aside his political disagreements with his nephew, he refused to provide support or financial help to his sister Margaret, Queen Mother of Scots, who had remarried twice after her first husband's death at the Battle of Flodden and found herself permanently short of money. Her French daughter-in-law was doing her best to heal the rifts that Margaret's remarriages had created between her and her son King James, but in the meantime Margaret had written many times to her brother begging him for a pension so that she could 'live like a princess, as the King their father intended'.[54] The death of the two princes also coincided with English suspicions about the Scottish government's involvement in recent unrest in Ireland and the north of England, so it is perhaps unsurprising, if equally unlovely, that there was no trace of sympathy emanating from the Tudor court at the news.

Children were on Catherine's mind in May 1541. In the same week as Wharton's letter about the deaths in Scotland, Catherine visited her stepchildren. Until that point, she had only interacted with the eldest, twenty-five-year-old Mary, and she wanted to meet the other two. The visit to her stepson was discussed in one of Chapuys's letters to the Governor of the Netherlands, but he failed to mention – and perhaps did not know – that on Friday, 6 May the queen's barge brought her to Chelsea Old Palace, where she received the Princess Elizabeth.[55] The night before, Catherine had stayed at Baynard's Castle, her official residence in London, while the king visited his son's household in Essex, and it is interesting that Catherine took the opportunity to meet Elizabeth, away from the girl's father, before she was introduced to the Prince of Wales.[56]

The seven-year-old Elizabeth was the youngest, least loved, and most ignored of Henry's daughters. She had her mother's dark eyes, her father's colouring, and the long Tudor nose of her grandfather Henry VII. She was two-and-a-half when her mother was beheaded, and her first two stepmothers had respectively lacked the inclination or the opportunity to take much interest in her.[57] She spent most of her life in the smaller countryside palaces where royal children were housed to keep them safe from the noxious, harmful air in the city. Her mother's execution on charges of adultery cast a pall over Elizabeth's life, not just because it robbed her of the mother who had showered her with attention and gifts, but also because it left her legitimacy open to question. Chapuys, with a touch more spite than was excusable, consistently and pointedly referred to her in his letters as 'Anne Boleyn's daughter', rather than as 'the King's bastard', which was the official government line after legislation removed her from the line of succession in 1536. A few months after her mother's death, Elizabeth's then governess wrote to Thomas Cromwell to explain that Elizabeth had outgrown all her clothes and needed new ones, which could not be bought because the court had forgotten to pay the ex-heiress's bills. Elizabeth's modern biographers who read this as the result of forgetful neglect in the excitement of her father's third marriage rather than deliberate cruelty are probably right. It may have been that Queen Anne was more involved than Henry in the management of their daughter's household and it took Lady Bryan's complaint for Cromwell to realise that no one had stepped into the void to make sure Elizabeth had everything she needed. Even with those explanations, it is a poor reflection on Henry VIII's interest in his younger daughter, and although she, like her elder sister, had her own suite of rooms at Greenwich Palace, she was seldom invited to court, on account of her age, and her father did not visit her in her own houses after Queen Anne's execution. Despite this, Elizabeth impressed nearly everyone she met, and even at this early stage in her life observers were quick to notice her self-possession and her intelligence. A year earlier, Sir Thomas Wriothesley had gone to see her and written that when he spoke to her, Elizabeth replied 'with as great gravity as she had been 40 years old. If she be no worse educated than appears she will be an honour to womanhood.'[58]

Elizabeth was to be better educated and substantially so. Within a few years of Wriothesley's observations, her schooling was farmed out to tutors like the regius professor of Greek at Cambridge. In 1541, when Catherine met her presumably for the first time, Elizabeth's accomplishments were largely due to the intelligence and forcefulness of her governess, Katherine Champernowne.[59] Katherine, whom Elizabeth and nearly everyone else referred to as Kat, was determined to make the most of

Elizabeth's natural aptitude and pushed ahead with a rigorous programme despite objections from some of the princess's staff, who compared her style of teaching to a servant pouring too much wine into too small a goblet. Elizabeth regarded Kat Champernowne as a second mother and in later life praised her for providing most of the love and encouragement she could remember from her childhood.[60]

Kat may have been part of the reason for the meeting between her charge and Queen Catherine at Chelsea, because her sister Lady Joan Denny was one of Catherine's ladies-in-waiting. Kat shared her sister's brains and her Protestant sympathies. Later, Joan's husband used his position in the king's privy chamber to suggest men known to favour religious reform as potential tutors for Elizabeth and her younger brother, something that played a significant role in the two siblings' future commitment to a Protestant England, albeit to varying degrees. Kat was also ambitious for and protective of her ward, and she knew that the favour of the queen could help Elizabeth's future prospects, which must, given her position, be made or broken by the king's goodwill. It is possible that the relationship between Elizabeth's governess and Catherine's lady-in-waiting saw Lady Denny lobbying for a meeting on Elizabeth's behalf.

Catherine's own familial bond to Elizabeth may also explain why she went out of her way to meet her at Chelsea. The trip from Baynard's was unusual enough in itself; despite being the queen's official London residence, the castle was hardly ever used for overnight stays by Tudor queens consort, but it was clearly used as a base for Catherine to talk with Elizabeth, who moved to Chelsea by barge on 5 May, the day before Catherine was taken there by her twenty-six oarsmen.[61] On her mother's side, Elizabeth was Catherine's second cousin – Elizabeth's maternal grandmother, the late Countess of Ormond, had been Edmund Howard's younger sister and Anne Boleyn's mother. In relative terms, the necklaces Catherine gave to Elizabeth as a gift were not remarkably expensive and paled in comparison to the rubies Princess Mary had received from their father at Christmas, but it was more than Catherine had ever given to Mary personally or willingly.

Four days afterwards, Catherine rejoined her husband to accompany him to Waltham Holy Cross in Essex, where the Prince of Wales was staying with the Princess Mary and their respective households. When she saw him for the first time, Edward was three years old, 'handsome, well-fed and remarkably tall for his age', and waddled over to her in an infant-sized man's doublet set off with a floor-length skirt.[62] Royal and noble-born boys were generally dressed in feminine clothes from the waist down until around the age of seven, when they were 'breached' and began wearing clothes similar in style to an adult's. Edward was not breached until his sixth birthday, so he would still have worn the clothes of an aristocratic infant in May 1541.[63] A squad of well-born boys kept him company in the schoolroom, including Barnaby Fitzpatrick, the young man who became the prince's closest friend.[64] Barnaby was the son of an Irish lord who had a distant bloodline claim to one of the ancient Irish sub-kingdoms but wanted to trade that in for a title in the contemporary Anglo-Irish nobilities. The invitation for Barnaby to join the Prince of Wales's household was a boon for the Fitzpatricks, and it indicated that the king was interested in rehabilitating potentially rebellious Irish nobles by bringing certain families into more regular contact with the court. One month after Catherine's visit to Waltham, Barnaby's father was created Baron Fitzpatrick of Upper Ossory.

Edward, who became Edward VI upon his father's death, died shortly before his sixteenth birthday, which resulted in subsequent descriptions of him as a sickly child. The irony of the sought-after son being the least healthy in the litter is one too tempting for many writers to ignore, but Edward's death in 1553 was probably the result of a short-term illness.[65] As a teenager, he was physically robust, with a passion for jousting and hunting that rivalled his father's as a young man. In his childhood, there were spells of ill health, inevitable and often exacerbated by those who were tasked with protecting him. When Catherine first met her most valuable stepchild, she saw a boy who had been cosseted in a household that went to obsessive and self-defeating lengths to keep him away from any potential infection. From time to time, this cloistering mixed badly with the servants' tendency to give the heir whatever he asked for and produced a lifestyle that a court physician described as 'gross and unhealthy'.[66]

That Edward was the king's sole surviving son and legitimate child was never far from the minds of servants or courtiers, many of whom feared the chaos that would be unleashed if the son predeceased the father. After Henry I's only son was lost at sea in 1120 and the beautiful young Queen Adeliza failed to produce a new heir, the country had descended into a generation-long civil war when the king died in 1135. Since then, there had been four kings who succeeded their fathers because elder brothers had died before them. Henry VIII was one of them.[67] The conversation the ladies-in-waiting had with Anne of Cleves about the absence of a duke of York revealed how much the spare to the heir was on everyone's mind, as did the joyous rush to prepare for Catherine's coronation once the king believed she was pregnant, and the subsequent abandonment of the ceremony when it was discovered that she was not.

The visit into Essex to see the little heir was judged a success. It ended with the king inviting Mary back to court, and 'the Queen has countenanced it with a good grace'.[68] Mary had been pressing for her father to visit Edward more often – she was over twenty years older than her brother and she had a protective and caring attitude towards him. However, Chapuys was quite clear in his letter to the emperor that the deciding factor was Catherine's enthusiasm for the trip – he told Charles V that Henry and Catherine had gone 'to visit the Prince at the request of the Princess, but chiefly at the intercession of the Queen herself'.[69] This implies that Catherine was eager to meet with all three of Henry's children and apparently to be reconciled with the eldest. Her different attitudes towards the two Tudor sisters leaves little doubt about which one she preferred, while the 'good grace' that she displayed when Mary was invited back to London was another example of her tendency towards kindness once she had calmed down about an earlier slight.

Catherine's rapprochement with Mary may have had pragmatic motivations as well. It is speculative, but two months later the Duke of Norfolk revealed in conversation with the French ambassador that there were 'secret' plans to restore Mary to the line of succession.[70] For the good of the realm, there would have to be a clearly designated second-in-line. Since three of Henry VII's offspring had lived long enough to produce children of their own and Henry VIII had bastardised two of his, the issue was murky, with too many claimants, none of whom was in a strong enough position to succeed without a challenge. Henry's matrimonial and diplomatic escapades had even managed to raise doubt in Catholic Europe about Edward's legitimacy, on the grounds that he was the son of an excommunicate, conceived at a time when England was in schism from the Holy See.[71] This admittedly was a minority view, and both the emperor and François I recognised Edward as Henry's heir apparent, but who would come after him was nonetheless a fraught question. The pursuit of the answer was liable to prove bloody. Henry VII had seven acknowledged and uncontested grandchildren alive in 1541: James V, King of Scots and his half sister, Lady Margaret Douglas, were the children of Henry VII's eldest daughter, Margaret Tudor, Queen of Scots; there were also Henry VIII's three children by three different wives and the two surviving daughters of Henry VII's youngest daughter Mary, Duchess of Suffolk – Frances Grey, Marchioness of Dorset, and Eleanor Clifford, Countess of Cumberland. Of those seven, only Frances had children of her own – so far, two girls. There were thus ten direct bloodline claimants to the English throne, who could be divided into three groups: the direct Tudor line in Henry's children; the Stewart or Scottish line via Queen Margaret's; and the Suffolk line in the late duchess's daughters and granddaughters.

If Catherine bore any children, they would rank after Edward but before his sisters, regardless of their gender, but until that happened who followed Edward was frighteningly ambivalent.

Since both Henry's daughters had been declared illegitimate after their respective mothers' demotions, James V and any future descendants could plausibly claim the English inheritance if Edward died without heirs. James, after all, was a man and the product of an uncontested royal marriage. It seemed unlikely that either of the Suffolk sisters would try to advance their lineage at the expense of their Tudor cousins, though as events were to prove in the next decade the improbable could happen. A fracas with Scotland seemed likely. To resolve the ambiguity, Henry planned to put his two daughters after Edward and any heirs he might father, with Mary as the eldest ranking above Elizabeth. These plans were not formalised until 1544, but the French ambassador's correspondence proves they were being discussed as early as 1541. It may be that Catherine knew of her stepdaughter's rising prominence – even if Mary never became queen, acknowledging her as second-in-line was a clear sign of her restoration to her father's favour – and decided that it would be sensible to remain on good terms with her. Mary's rumoured restoration and Catherine's attempts to build a better relationship with her, and her younger sister, occurred shortly after the end of Catherine's alleged pregnancy. It is possible that the debacle forced Catherine to realise that, if she did not have children of her own, her future as a widow would be determined by one of her stepchildren. The rumours of Mary's return to the line of succession may also have arisen from Henry's doubts about Catherine's fecundity, after the embarrassment at Easter.

Perhaps what is most telling about the visit with Elizabeth at Chelsea and then with Edward and Mary at Waltham Holy Cross four days later was when it took place. Catherine did not rush into the role of loving stepmother. From the evidence left to us, she first met Elizabeth and Edward ten months after she married their father. The only reason she knew Mary was that she was the only one old enough to live at court. Going to see Edward did not carry any great risks, but the trip to meet Elizabeth does seem to have required some organisation and genuine interest on Catherine's part. So much of her behaviour in spring 1541 can only be explained by accepting that she was growing in confidence and that her successful execution of her duties as queen during the Christmas at Hampton Court had bolstered her self-esteem. Catherine had always liked to organise people; she was friendly, charming, and had the kind of charisma that aimed to make people smile while remaining the centre of attention. The intercession for Wyatt and Wallop, the brief rendezvous with Thomas Culpepper, the meeting with Elizabeth Tudor, and then the trip to Waltham are all the actions of a woman who felt that she could get away with more and began to behave accordingly.

That is not to say that a sense of insecurity vanished completely. Her husband's brush with death during Lent and the fiasco of her alleged pregnancy were not things that a childless queen was likely to remain unaffected by. Alongside the confidence, there was also a jitteriness to Catherine which occasionally expressed itself through what she was prepared to believe. A week after their visit to the Prince of Wales, Henry noticed that Catherine was in low spirits, and when he asked her why 'she said it was owing to a rumour that he was going to take back Anne of Cleves'. That story was not new – it had circulated in London in September – but this time, Catherine reacted to it and even, in her weaker moments, found it credible. Henry's comforting of his wife made up in sincerity for what it lacked in finesse: 'The King told her she was wrong to think such things, and even if he were in a position to marry he had no mind to take back Anne.'[72]

Reading between the lines, the Cleves rumour seems to have been resuscitated by Scottish involvement in the Wakefield conspiracy. Chapuys thought that whoever was spreading the story must know nothing about Henry VIII's personality 'as his love never returns for a woman he has once abandoned' and that whispers of Anne's restoration at Catherine's expense arose because 'many thought he would be reconciled to her for fear of the King of France making war on him at the solicitation of the duke of Cleves and the king of Scotland'.[73] Since the divorce, France had allied with Cleves. On the same day as Catherine's visit to her stepson, Lord William had written from Paris with the news that the Duke of Cleves was at the French court as a guest of the royal family.[74] If Henry were reconciled with Anne of Cleves, it might negate the possibility of France's alliance with Scotland and Cleves causing problems.

Fortunately for England, Lord William's reports from France made it clear that the Duke of Cleves had no intention of risking his diplomatic credibility on his sister's behalf. The two men met at a supper party hosted in the duke's honour by the King and Queen of France – Duke Wilhelm embraced the English ambassador, asked after the health of King Henry, and said absolutely nothing about his sister.[75] Of course, those chatting about the merits of putting Anne of Cleves back on the consort's throne did not have access to the ambassador's letters to know how unimportant Anne's position was to Cleves's foreign policy, but a lack of precise information did not stop them talking or Catherine from listening. Her brief unhappiness reflected the power of the rumour mill at court and the speed with which members of the household could bring almost absurd stories to their mistress's ears.

There were other problems facing Catherine in 1541, arising from the realm of public opinion, where she was intermittently accused of low morals and wild spending. Catherine's tactfulness, deportment, and her kindness to Anne of Cleves, Thomas Wyatt, and John Wallop were praised at court and in diplomatic correspondence, as was her desire to see her stepchildren. A member of the Privy Council later described Catherine's behaviour in public as that of 'a very virtuous and chaste creature', but others were less enamoured.[76] The demotion of Anne of Cleves had not been popular in the capital, which was a tribute to her public persona, since she had had very little time to establish herself as queen before she was divorced, and Catherine had first come to the wider population's notice as a potential mistress receiving surreptitious nighttime visits from the king on his barge. Talk in London had already referred to her as a harlot and a woman of 'poor character'. Accusations of whoredom were an occupational hazard for royal women, who held a place in people's imaginations that was usually either patriotic or prurient. Vices were not so much magnified as imagined. Anne Boleyn had been referred to as 'a strong whore' and 'a goggle-eyed whore'; it was assumed that Jane Seymour could not be a virgin because of her age when she married; and in 1511 a man was imprisoned for implying that Katherine of Aragon's newborn son was illegitimate.[77]

Catherine's high spirits also encouraged criticism. What might appear as vivacious loveliness to some can be interpreted as irritating garrulousness by others. A Spanish merchant living in London, who admittedly never let fact stand in the way of a good story, claimed later that 'the King had no wife who made him spend so much money in dresses and jewels as she did, who every day had some new caprice'.[78] She certainly liked to have a good time and in her apartments Catherine 'did nothing but dance and rejoice'.[79] A defence of her spending can be mounted by pointing out that it does not seem so great when set in its wider context. Her jewellery acquisitions in the summer and winter of 1540, for instance, compare favourably in cost to those commissioned by or for Anne Boleyn, even before she became queen.[80] However, Catherine's extravagance was not balanced by any particular displays of piety or memorable largesse, as it had been by some of her predecessors.

The unkind attacks on Catherine's morals were illegal under the Treason Act of 1534, but they only constituted a threat if they came from someone who actually knew something specific about her involvement with Francis Dereham. In May 1541, comments about her sexuality could be dismissed as the febrile ramblings of bored and ill-informed commoners, while mutterings about her spending and dancing simply did not matter. Wisely, given the nature of her rise to prominence, Catherine's focus continued to be her husband. To please him was the only way to guarantee her position.

It is interesting that after a period when she felt real doubt and insecurity, Catherine threw herself into the role of a model queen consort – conduit of royal mercy, stepmother, suppressor of discord – and found herself to be very good at it. At the same time, she began to pine for some of the excitement she had known as a younger woman, with men like Thomas Culpepper. It would be tempting to identify this as the point at which Catherine's behaviour underwent a definitive change and argue that after it she acted either with greater circumspection or greater recklessness. The truth is that she did both. Human beings are a mass of contradictory emotions. If one were to try to summarise Catherine's life from this point on, it would be that she excelled in public but made more and more mistakes in private. She was aware of the tenuousness of her position, yet met in quasi-secret with an old admirer. She interceded for prisoners such as Thomas Wyatt and John Wallop, but did not help others who posed too great a risk to become involved with. She continued to respond to the hearsay being fed to her by her ladies, and she inflamed the household's volatile atmosphere by favouring Lady Rochford over other women of the privy chamber, including her sister. Catherine was the most observed woman in the country. Her every move was watched and judged by the courtiers and servants around her. When she mentioned that Thomas Culpepper continued to stare at her, even after she had made it very clear that she wanted nothing more to do with him because of his rudeness to her on Maundy Thursday, Lady Rochford answered with an observation that could be true of the nature of queenship – 'Yet must you give men leave to look, for they will look upon you.'[81]

Chapter 15

The Errands of Morris and Webb

To have beheld him naked as he stood,
Ready to leap into the silver flood;
But might not: for the laws of heaven deny,
To shew men's secret to a woman's eye:
And therefore was her sad and gloomy light
Confin'd unto the secret-keeping night.

– Francis Beaumont,
Salmacis and Hermaphroditus (1602)

On the morning after Chapuys wrote to the emperor's sister about Catherine's fears regarding Anne of Cleves, the sixty-seven-year-old Margaret Pole, Countess of Salisbury, was wakened in her rooms at the Tower of London with the news that the king had decided she was to be executed in the next few hours. She had been condemned by Act of attainder during the White Rose intrigue, which meant the death sentence against her could be enacted whenever the king saw fit. Throughout her interrogation in 1538, the countess had consistently refused to confess to treason. The Earl of Southampton, one of her inquisitors, remarked that in defence of herself and her family Lady Salisbury 'showed herself so earnest, vehement and precise that more could not be'.[1] She was in a similar spirit when they told her about her execution. She argued with her gaolers and demanded to know the justification for her impending death. It was only once she realised that there was no way out that she went quietly out of the Tower to a green near Tower Hill called East Smithfield.[2] There was no scaffold, only a small block that rested on the ground, and there were 150 witnesses, including the lord mayor. After the pious old lady had entrusted her soul to the mercy of God, she prayed for Catherine and all the other members of the royal family, with the exception of Elizabeth, whose legitimacy she had never acknowledged. Her prayers for the king, the queen, and the Prince of Wales seemed more duty than inclination when compared to those for her goddaughter Princess Mary, whose mother she had once served as a lady-in-waiting and to whom Lady Salisbury had remained loyal until her death from cancer in 1536.[3] She was not allowed to continue much longer. Her handlers rushed her through her speech, chivvying her to hurry up and put her head on the block. It was reported later that she refused them because she was not a traitor, and therefore had to be wrestled into place by her executioner, but that story originates from the seventeenth century. Such extraordinary behaviour would have been commented on by her contemporaries, none of whom mention it in their accounts of her death.

When Lady Salisbury turned to submit herself to her executioner, she saw 'a wretched and blundering youth' instead of the usual headsman, who had been dispatched north to deal with the men convicted of complicity in the recent plot against the king. She placed her head on the block. When the first blow of the axe fell, it was clear just how inexperienced the stand-in executioner was. A horrified Chapuys heard from eyewitnesses that the headsman 'literally hacked her head and shoulders to pieces in the most pitiful manner'. When, at last, the deed was done, her remains were taken for swift interment in the chapel of St Peter-ad-vincula inside the Tower. On the same day, three men were hanged, drawn, and quartered in the city for their role in the northern intrigue.[4]

The Countess of Salisbury's execution had been carried out with no advanced warning, and later that afternoon many people in London still doubted that it had happened. Once the news was confirmed, it was not well received. Even reformers who had abhorred the ultra-conservative Lady Salisbury's refusal to let her servants read the Bible in English were uncomfortable with what had happened.[5] It looked as if she had been dispatched to punish her for a failed rebellion that she had no part in. If she had been spared at the time of her eldest son's execution, then what could she possibly have done as a prisoner in the Tower? The inescapable conclusion was that she had suffered because the king hated her greatly, her son Reginald even more so, and that he wanted, in de Marillac's view, to empty the Tower before he went on his prolonged visit to the north.[6]

Predictably, the international reaction was stronger. What Chapuys described as 'the very strange and lamentable execution of Mme de Salisbury' intensified many western Europeans' already low opinion of Henry VIII. In Italy, Henry was accused of having 'wrongfully murdered the Cardinal's mother, his brother, and so many other nobles that it should all be too long to rehearse'.[7] To defend Henry, the best that loyal Englishmen could come up with when foreigners asked them how they could possibly obey such a tyrant was that Lady Salisbury's death was 'nothing so marvellous nor so cruel as it is made [to sound] here in Italy'.[8] As Cardinal Pole's mother, the countess had a reputation as 'a most virtuous and honourable lady', and comments were passed on the disparity between Henry's presentation of himself as God's instrument and the ways his concept of justice had 'come to women and innocent children'.[9] Lady Salisbury's grandson Henry and Lord Exeter's fourteen-year-old son remained in custody in the Tower. Cardinal Pole, who was widely respected in Catholic Europe as a man 'whose virtue and learning seemeth rare unto the world', described Henry as comparable in wickedness to Herod, Caligula, and Nero.[10] Long after it had happened, Henry's continental critics were still citing Lady Salisbury's horrible end, alongside the executions of Cardinal Fisher and Thomas More in 1535, or Queen Anne's in 1536, as unanswerable examples of his tyrannical nature.[11]

Four days after Lady Salisbury's death, Catherine and the king went to Westminster while Greenwich Palace was cleaned. The decomposing heads of traitors usually jutted out from pikes on Tower Bridge, but they had all been taken down 'in order that the people may forget those whose heads kept their memory fresh'.[12] De Marillac, still repulsed by the countess's execution, surmised that it would not be long before the old heads were replaced by new ones.

Shortly after Catherine's return to a refreshed Greenwich, two of her husband's guards were convicted of robbery and hanged 'in example of all other'.[13] *Pour encourager les autres* was very much the maxim of Henry's government – that summer more obviously than ever before. De Marillac was not alone in thinking that more deaths would follow the countess's; Chapuys told the emperor's sister that Lady Salisbury's grandson was no longer allowed to take the air in the Tower courtyards and 'it is supposed that he will soon follow his father and grandmother. May God help him!'[14]

The government swung between reprieve and repression, confounding those who tried to guess the next move. The day after the two guards were executed, a courtier called Sir Edmund Knyvet was surrounded by officers of the king's household as they prepared to cut off his hand as punishment for brawling within the confines of the court. He had punched Thomas Clere, a young poet attached to the household of Lord Surrey, on 27 April, when the two men had come to blows at the palace tennis courts.[15] Whether he had caused a nosebleed or thrown a punch that packed more force than expected, Knyvet was in real trouble owing to the fact that he had technically 'shed blood' in the precincts of the court, a misdemeanour that required the courtier to lose his right hand as the price of his rehabilitation. The king's surgeon was standing by with his instruments, an official from the woodyard had brought in the block, the king's master cook had provided the knife, another serjeant from the household stood by with the irons heating in the fire to cauterise the wound after the amputation, and officers from the king's cellar and ewery had organised beer, wine, ale, basins, and towels for the ceremony, when Sir Richard Long, a gentleman of the Privy Chamber, entered to say that the king wanted Knyvet's hand to be cut off after dinner. Knyvet was Catherine's first cousin – his mother, Muriel, who died in childbirth when Edmund was about four years old, was another of Edmund Howard's sisters and given his name, Catherine's father may even have stood as one of Edmund Knyvet's godfathers. It may have been Catherine's influence that saved him from the cleaver, though it did not spare him the game of cat and mouse that accompanied any of Henry's reprieves. Knyvet, who begged that his left hand should be severed so he could still use the right to wield a sword in the king's service, was fully pardoned after dinner and allowed to keep both hands with the warning that there would be no reprieve if he repeated his offence, or mercy for anyone else who behaved in the same way.[16]

Despite his ties to the queen, the case against Edmund Knyvet had proceeded so far that many people were surprised when he was forgiven, hands intact. With equal confidence, observers expected Lord Dacre of the South to walk free after he and a group of friends accidentally killed a man as they set out on a poaching expedition in Sussex. They had met in Lord Dacre's mansion to plot their illegal hunting trip, which technically put him in the position of ringleader. On their way, they encountered two men called James Busebryge and Richard Somener. Fearful that they might tell people about a crew of young men with hunting dogs and nets, Lord Dacre's group attacked them. How much force they intended to use was contested, but eight against two resulted in some rough blows falling on the innocent bystanders, and Busebryge later died as a result. At his trial, Lord Dacre denied that they had ever intended to take a life, but he was told that the over-excitable conversations in his home and the unnecessary violence used against the two men constituted 'sufficient and probable evidence'. Accepting the point, Lord Dacre changed his plea to guilty and threw himself on the king's mercy. The clerk of the Privy Council, Sir William Paget, brought the news of

Dacre's supplication to the king 'hoping thereby to move his Majesty to pardon'.[17] Dacre's judges, who had wept as they sentenced him to death as the law required, went as a group to beg the king to spare his life. Chapuys, who confused Dacre with Knyvet when he described him as 'son of the duke of Norfolk's sister, and cousin of this queen', recorded other courtiers' hopes that Dacre would be pardoned. There was a general feeling that as horrible and undeserved as Busebryge's death had been, it had not been intended nor had it been the fault of the entire group. Chapuys heard that Dacre's crime was 'having belonged to a set of eight rakish youths, one of whom had killed a poor old man in a sudden unpremeditated affray'. That the twenty-five-year-old Lord Dacre was considered 'the handsomest and best bred man that could be seen here in England' certainly helped his standing with his peers.[18]

Less than twenty-four hours after Lord Dacre's trial, his kinsman John Mantell, who had served in the king' guard, six of their companions, and two huntsmen, were hanged for their part in the poaching and manslaughter.[19] The following day, in defiance of the usual protocol that gave aristocrats an axe instead of the noose, Lord Dacre was dragged through the streets of London to 'the most ignominious gibbet possible'. It was a calculated degradation that culminated in quite possibly one of the nastiest and most deliberate twists in any Tudor execution. As with Edmund Knyvet, at the very last minute a messenger arrived from the king ordering them to delay the execution until after two o'clock that afternoon. At three, the crowd's expectation of a pardon ended when the trapdoor was opened.[20] The deliberately mercurial nature of royal justice could not have been more clearly displayed. 'But the most strange thing, and one at which people were wonderfully taken aback, was that on the very same day on which Milord Dacres [sic] was hung,' wrote Chapuys, 'another young man, son of the treasurer of the Royal household, who was one of the lot, and had also been present at the old man's death, was freely pardoned by the king, though he had already been tried for some like misdemeanour, whereas his friend and companion

Dacres met, as I have related, such a piteous death.'[21] The fact that the royal demesnes benefited from the confiscation of Lord Dacre's estates was also commented upon by Londoners. In the same week, Lord Leonard Grey, the former Lord Deputy of Ireland, who had been questioned by the Duke of Norfolk in November, was condemned to death for treason. One of several charges against him was that he had allowed his pro-papal nephew to escape Ireland for Europe rather than arrest him. Grey was beheaded three days after the verdict.

A Tudor courtier had to cultivate a studied indifference in the face of such horrors and the possibility that family, acquaintances, and friends could be removed at a moment's notice. Queen Catherine's household kept its reputation for gaiety and extravagance, a place where the musicians accompanied the dancing as often as the queen's passion for it required. The delicious, titillating rustle of gossip and innuendo accompanied the men of the privy chamber who called on the queen's ladies to flirt, tease, converse, and dance. Queen Catherine was supposed to occupy the role of goddess among the nymphs, an object of collective adoration, but never a participant. For a time, she lived vicariously through her women and tolerated far more than her predecessors might have. Even if we accept that Catherine did not know or may not have been certain about what was happening with her brother and Lady Margaret, there is still her failure to halt another affair embarked upon by her latest maid of honour, Dorothy Bray.

At the age of twenty-seven, the blond and blue-eyed William, Lord Parr, had all the accomplishments needed for life as a middle-of-the-road courtier – fluent in French, a skilled hunter and musician, elegant in his manners, and a patron of the arts. He was only a boy when his father died, and his mother had worked hard to get him an heiress for a wife. Lady Maud Parr must have been tenacious, because William went down the aisle aged thirteen with ten-year-old Lady Anne Bourchier, the only surviving child of the Earl of Essex. As Anne's husband, William stood a good chance of succeeding her father to become an earl *suo uxoris*.

Due to the bride's youth, the marriage had still not been consummated when its matchmaker died in 1531, though even in death Maud took no chances with her son's future and left Anne a substantial amount of jewellery, which would be hers 'when she lieth with my son'.[22] The bequest was not enough to bring sparkle to a miserable union. William wanted to spend his life in the corridors of power, and he gravitated towards the company of bright clever young courtiers such as the Earl of Surrey, while his wife went to court rarely and reluctantly. In their prayers, William leaned towards Protestantism, like his sisters and Lord Surrey; his wife was a religious conservative. Alas, the rosary was not enough to lasso Lady Parr away from sin when she ran off with a penniless clergyman, conceived a bastard child with him, and told her husband, in no uncertain terms, 'that she never loved him, nor never would'. Lord Parr had no choice but to wear his horns in public, since Anne defied nearly all the social conventions for aristocratic women and proclaimed that 'she would take her pleasure and do as she listed'.[23] William Parr may have been unfaithful to his wife before this scandal. If he had not been, he considered that her departure freed him of his obligations, and he fell into bed with Dorothy Bray, who was about sixteen or seventeen at the time.

Given that Queen Catherine was supposed to be acting as the guardian of her maids' reputations and future marital prospects, her failure to censure Bray's relationship with a married man is revelatory. That she knew about Dorothy Bray's affair and may even have found it entertaining is made quite clear by a conversation she had later with her own admirer, Thomas Culpepper. The fury of Anne Boleyn, Mary I, and Elizabeth I when their ladies' moral standards slipped stands in stark contrast to Catherine's indifference or obliviousness.[24] A servant's actions reflected on her mistress, and a queen who was incapable of controlling the morals of her staff was likely to be considered incapable of governing her own. To have allowed Dorothy Bray to indulge in the same kind of activity which she and her friends had undertaken whilst living at Horsham indicates that Catherine did not realise or did not care that, as queen, she could not encourage, and certainly could not indulge in, the behaviour of her adolescence.

Following their tiff on Maundy Thursday, Catherine kept away from Thomas Culpepper for a short period of time, until the attraction that had prompted her to send for him through Lady Rochford and the usher Henry Webb reasserted itself. After standing on the water's edge for months, she dipped her toe in. At some point when they were back at Greenwich, between either 12 and 31 May or 4 and 18 June, Culpepper was ill for a few days and Catherine sent one of her pageboys, Morris, with dinners for the patient.[25] Young Morris went several times with food from the queen's kitchens, meat most days and fish on Fridays or holy days. Morris was only a page, whose main function in the palace was running errands, and Catherine was not technically doing anything wrong, but sending dinner trays to a sickly man's room was a flirtatious kind of charity.

In some aspects, the previous year had been a difficult one for Thomas Culpepper. He had lost both his parents, Sir Alexander and Lady Constance Culpepper, who died within a year of each other.[26] On the positive side, he was still benefiting from the king's fondness for him, expressed through gifts, grants of land, and get-out-of-jail-free cards for him and his servants.[27] In March, royal indulgence had helped one of Culpepper's servants, William Brice, escape punishment after he was reprimanded by the Privy Council for brawling in Southwark.[28] Far more seriously, the king may also have intervened to save Thomas from the consequences of his actions a few years earlier, when he was accused of rape and murder.

The only surviving account of this case is in a letter written in 1542 by an English Protestant merchant called Richard Hilles to the Swiss theologian Heinrich Bullinger. On this subject Hilles claimed that Culpepper:

> two years before, or less, had violated the wife of a certain park-keeper in a woody thicket, while, horrid to relate!, three or four of his most profligate attendants were holding her at his bidding. For this act of wickedness, he was,

notwithstanding, pardoned by the king, after he had been delivered into custody by the villagers on account of this crime, and likewise a murder which he had committed in his resistance to them, when they first endeavoured to apprehend him. God, who is just, will not always suffer wickedness, either here or elsewhere, to go unpunished.[29]

Hilles, who fled England on account of his Protestant faith in 1540 or 1541 and had settled in Strasbourg by the time he wrote this letter, dates the attack to two or so years before early 1542, either when he was still living in London or had only very recently left. He also provides enough anecdotal detail about the affray and the king's role in quashing the charges to suggest that it had happened. Culpepper's servants appear in the other records helping him pick locks, arranging potentially sexual assignations, or brawling in the streets. It is therefore, unfortunately, not beyond possibility that they held down a married woman at their employer's behest or that they helped him take down one of his opponents when he was apprehended. If it did happen as Hilles described, it would have been around the time of Culpepper's first romance with Catherine, which makes it difficult to believe she did not hear about it.

Hilles's story can be questioned on three points, the first being that it is not mentioned anywhere else, even in subsequent criticisms of Culpepper by Parliament or the French ambassador. The second is that Hilles could have confused Culpepper with somebody else, which was easily done because Culpepper had an elder brother with the same Christian name. Admittedly, the two Culpepper brothers were usually differentiated in grants or court documents concerning them, but these were official communications, not city gossip.[30] It is possible that the elder Thomas Culpepper was responsible for the crime described in Richard Hilles's letter and that his younger brother used his influence to have him pardoned.

There are enough alternative explanations to Hilles's version of what happened to prevent its acceptance as fact about the Thomas

Culpepper associated with Catherine Howard. Equally, there are too many details for it to be dismissed as a fabrication, and short of the discovery of new documents, a satisfactory conclusion on Hilles's story is likely to remain elusive.

We can be more confident in describing Culpepper as unashamedly promiscuous with consensual partners. He seems to have had a mildly flirtatious relationship with Lord Lisle's wife when he served in their household, and Lady Rochford acknowledged how attractive he was. Several of his partners are alluded to, and one named, in the surviving documents that mention him. The named lady was Elizabeth Harvey, usually referred to as Bess. She had been Culpepper's mistress for some time when he began his late-night conversations with the queen. She had once been attached to Anne Boleyn's household, from which she had been dismissed on grounds that may have had something to with her alleged immorality. She remained at court, perhaps in some other lady's service, although she was retired from the queen's household with an annual pension of £10, the salary of a maid of honour. She was still at court in 1540–41, when she became Culpepper's latest mistress.

Catherine had spent most of her married life on the move, and she was already familiar with the upheaval that came with each relocation, but the progress to the north in 1541 was a new experience not just for the queen but for everyone around her. Most of the royal family's residences were in the Thames Valley and accessible by water, the court's preferred mode of transport, and those that were not tended to be smaller and within riding distance. The tour of 1541 took them to houses that most of the court had never visited, in parts of the country that the king had never seen. Everything would have to be moved by land, making their journey more dependent on the weather than if they had been travelling on the Thames.

Each department of the royal household had carts, chariots, and horses, as nearly everything that belonged to it moved with it from place to place – clothes, jewels, books, carpets, linens,

furniture, even the irons for the king and queen's fires were transported. Catherine's officers and councillors went north with her,
as most of the Privy Council did for the king, since government
was located with the king's person. A rump council was left
behind in London as caretakers of the capital. Some officers rode
ahead to liaise with local suppliers to ensure the court had
everything it needed by the time it arrived. The Surveyor of the
King's Works went with a team to inspect the next stop and repair
anything that had fallen apart since the last time the house was
visited, and Henry's personal locksmith, Henry Romains, travelled with his assistants to check the locks, before handing over a
set of keys to the king and queen, whose chosen privy attendants
would have copies made for the duration of their stay. The queen's
servants unpacked her furniture, and the maids and women
pointed out where it needed to be put; fires were made, beds
dressed, and clothes unpacked.[31]

The size of the royal party as it moved north from Westminster
on 30 June was also unusual. With about four to five thousand
horses, compared to the usual thousand, two hundred tents, and
artillery sent from London by sea to the north-east, it looked
more like a military operation than a royal progress, and it intensified speculation that Henry was rediscovering his aspirations
for battle.[32] As de Marillac watched the preparations, including
the renewed interest in the southern and northern defences, and
restrictions placed on the movements of foreigners living in
London, he told his government, 'whether for offence or defence,
the English are thinking of war'.[33]

It had always been in France that English armies had won their
most memorable victories. As well as this legacy, Henry VIII was
also heir to an antique claim that had been repeated at his coronation in 1509, when he had been crowned 'Henry, By the Grace
of God, King of England, France, and Lord of Ireland'. The roots
of this claim went back to the fourteenth century, when Edward
III, a grandson of King Philippe IV of France on his mother's
side, believed that he was his grandfather's heir to the French
throne after a run of dynastic ill fortune so improbably

catastrophic that it fuelled a legend that Philippe's entire immediate family had been cursed. The different claimants eventually sparked a war that ran on and off for the next 116 years. Its later name, the Hundred Years War, is thus technically a misnomer, poetic rather than pedantic.

The great moments of the Hundred Years War entered into the English imagination as an integral part of their identity. The naval victory at Sluys, the sieges of Harfleur and Rouen, the Black Prince's capturing of King Jean the Good after victory at Poitiers, and the battles of Crécy and Agincourt acquired a totemic value in the national memory. An imperfect comparison today might be the ways in which the evacuation of Dunkirk, the cracking of the Enigma code, 'Blitz spirit', and George VI and Queen Elizabeth's visits to a bomb-flattened East End of London have become something which most British people know about, however imprecisely. In America, it might be the crossing of the Delaware, the firing on Fort Sumter, or the Gettysburg Address – complex events separated by years or even decades yet still understood as important parts of the communal narrative. They may be lovingly if imprecisely remembered by many, and through that they continue to matter and vitally so. Today, all this may appear as ludicrous; the English claim that their monarchs were the lawful sovereigns of France might seem like an exercise either in absurdity or fanciful nostalgia, depending on how charitable the interpretation – something that might have been a joke had it not cost so many lives – but the early modern view of war fuelled its cultural importance. Pursuing a rightful claim was part of the cult of chivalry. For many of Henry VIII's subjects, particularly the upper classes, that was justification in itself, and they rode into battle with minds unencumbered by later generations' doubts that a just war might be a paradox.

Henry's advancing age – he turned fifty in June 1541 – the reminder of his mortality at the start of Lent, and the fact that he might soon be too old to pursue dreams of securing his posthumous reputation on the battlefield also helped focus attention on an invasion of France in the near future. If that happened, the potential for Scottish involvement in the north of England had to be negated. The last time Henry had attacked France, James IV's campaign against England ended in defeat at Flodden. Thanks to the king's mishandling of the Pilgrimage of Grace and the trail of broken promises in its wake, the north remained England's unbolted back door. A royal visit would, as Catherine's uncle Norfolk believed, give the king an opportunity to get his house in order before he attacked somebody else's.

Henry and Catherine's four-month progress was tied in many different ways to these aspirations. The Wakefield conspiracy and rumours of Scottish involvement in it made peace in the north a priority as it had never been at any other point in Henry's reign, even when most of it had been convulsed by rebellion in 1536. The Duke of Norfolk had been encouraging the king to go on progress there for four years. Henry agreed whenever the idea was mentioned, but it inevitably vanished into the ether. Norfolk's report that English defences on the border with Scotland required repairs had received similar agreement followed by amnesia until his trip during Lent in 1541, when he was accompanied by a military engineer called Stefan van Haschenperg, who was charged with strengthening the fortifications. Norfolk had also visited two of the great northern magnates – Ralph Neville, Earl of Westmorland, who had previously helped suppress disorder in the region, and Henry Clifford, Earl of Cumberland, who as governor of Carlisle Castle, ten miles from Scotland, had the responsibility of preserving peace on the western sections of the border. Norfolk left the two earls to be ready if the Scottish threat materialised.[34]

Increasing English military presence on the border would hopefully intimidate the Scottish government, while an impressive royal progress would stimulate loyalty and obedience in the northern English. For the visit itself, a policy of honey and vinegar would be enacted, whereby the king would forgive those who had sided with the rebellion in 1536, after they or their representatives formally prostrated themselves in a public ceremony which acknowledged their collective faults. These ceremonies made a virtue out of necessity, since in the aftermath of the Pilgrimage of Grace, if the government had punished all the uprising's supporters or those who had allowed the unrest to happen, either through fear of the rebels or sympathy with their aims, then the entire governing class of most of the northern counties would have vanished at a stroke.

Catherine was thus being marched into a situation that had the potential to end in disaster. Her uncle and those pushing for the tour could be wrong in their predictions that it would revitalise royal control over the region. The precautions taken to protect the royal party were extensive. Significant and loyal northerners were told not to travel to greet the king and queen, but to stay in their localities to suppress any signs of trouble.[35] Like Catherine herself at this stage in her queenship, the progress embodied the juxtaposition of arrogance and insecurity.

One of Catherine's companions on the journey was her eldest stepdaughter.[36] Physically, Mary Tudor resembled her father, most noticeably around the mouth. Charles de Marillac joked that Mary's voice was as unexpectedly low for a woman's as her father's was high for a man's.[37] She had an excellent complexion which made her look five or so years younger than she was. Marillac thought she looked about eighteen or twenty in 1541, when she turned twenty-five that February. The long days of the progress did not strain a woman who kept herself physically active with two- or three-mile walks most mornings, weather permitting. Emotionally, she was less robust. She suffered from depression, what de Marillac called her 'ennuy' when he heard about it from her servants, who noticed that it lifted when she was no longer out of favour with her father, a state so horrible it had the power to break a woman known for her courage and determination.[38] Like her late mother, Katherine of Aragon, Mary was deeply religious, but unlike Katherine she had ended her rustication from court by swearing oaths that acknowledged her father's headship of the Church and, equally painful, her own illegitimacy. Mary Tudor's motto was 'Truth, the daughter of Time'; in her case, an apt declaration since twelve years later she led England's brief resubmission to papal authority. As with many people on the progress to the north and even more of those watching as it passed by, Mary's religious views corresponded with the rebels' of 1536, something which she was intelligent enough to keep hidden for the time being.

In the sixteenth century, likenesses of royalty and glimpses into the lifestyle of the privileged and famous were few. The procession of the king, the queen, and their court through the towns, villages, and hamlets of the provinces offered a spectacle that most people north of London had never seen. The progress trooped along the Great North Road which ran like a spine through England, connecting London with the capital of Scotland. Accounts told of the court's transports and baggage train sinking into mud as the roads turned to sludge because 'the rains have since been so great and incessant, and the weather so unseasonably cold and stormy'.[39] Crops were damaged and diseases spread. Catherine saw little of the observers curious or loyal enough to brave the weather and line the road to see her pass by. As the rain thumped on the canopy of her horse-drawn litter, Catherine suffered with each jolt. The weather had made her so unwell that some people thought the progress would or should be called off.[40] It was saved by the amount of preparation that had gone into it, which made the prospect of cancellation too horrible to actualise, and by the time the queen left Grafton manor in Northamptonshire, the last stop that she was familiar with, the decision to press ahead with the visit to the north had been taken.[41]

Chapter 16

The Girl in the Silver Dress

O, you wake then! come away,
Times be short, are made for play;
The humorous moon too will not stay ...

– Ben Jonson, *Oberon,
the Faery Prince: A Masque* (1611)

On 7 July 1541, while she was still at Dunstable, Catherine received a new title when heralds at Greenwich proclaimed her the first queen consort of Ireland.[1] The Irish Parliament had been summoned in spring, met from 13 June to 20 July, and its first statute was a proposal to change Henry's title from lord to King of Ireland. The bilingual Earl of Ormond translated the relevant speeches into Irish, to the 'contention' of fellow lords who did not speak English, and the motion was 'joyously agreed to by both Houses'.[2] Those hearing the news on the streets of Dublin could not have been more emphatically supportive. Prisoners were pardoned; the council dispensed free wine to the revellers who danced and lit bonfires in the streets; Dubliners organised celebratory feasts in their homes, and two thousand people attended a thanksgiving Mass at St Patrick's Cathedral.[3] The kings of England had been styled lords of Ireland for the last three centuries since the reign of Henry II, when his intervention after a series of local disputes culminated with him being acknowledged as overlord by Ireland's local kings and chieftains, and the apparent blessing of the papacy.[4]

The Irish Parliament wanted to use the Crown of Ireland Act to fix a plethora of problems facing their country, and while many foreigners, and historians, assumed that the kingly elevation in Ireland was Henry's idea, it was an initiative born in Dublin. In his capacity as Lord of Ireland, Henry had ruled on the vicious side of indifference – when he did involve himself in the island's issues, it was seldom pleasant. The first reason for proposing a change in his title was that a king had a certain set of expected responsibilities, far more clearly defined than a lord's and, as king, Henry would be expected to work harder at the island's good government.

It was also quite clear to everyone in sixteenth-century Dublin that the country could not prosper if the Crown's authority was obeyed by some Irishmen and ignored by others. Everyone who interacted with Irish politics and possessed a modicum of intelligence could see that the country was in urgent need of reform. The Duke of Norfolk, who had been the king's Viceroy for Ireland from 1519 to 1523, and later Thomas Cromwell had both put forward plans for an overhaul of the system.[5]

The Irish Council had an ambitious programme to accompany the act, which included bringing the estranged Gaelic nobility into the fold by granting them titles in the Anglo-Irish peerage while confirming their ancestral grants of land or making new ones. Through a process of assimilation, the Irish Parliament hoped to neutralise the tensions, and threats of rebellion, that had plagued the island and dominated the Irish aristocracy. A representative of the Irish Privy Council told his English colleagues that 'being accepted as subjects, where before they were taken as Irish enemies … is the chiefest mean, by good wisdom, to continue them in peace and obedience'.

Henry acted on their advice with poor grace and pointed reluctance. When one Irish nobleman asked to receive the title of an earl, Henry reminded him of the 'vile and savage life' he and his ancestors had lived, despite the fact that the man's fidelity and character had been vouched for by Henry's viceroy and councillors. The insult was even more gratuitous for being couched in a half-acceptance of the man's petition, which Henry granted with the title of a viscount on grounds that 'the honour of an earl is so great that it is never conferred except by the king in person. If he desires it so much he must repair hither, where it shall gladly be given. If he will be content with the honour of a viscount or a baron, which may be given by letters patent, he shall have it.'[6]

Henry's nitpicking over the Irish legislation dragged on for most of the summer, with messengers bouncing back and forth between London, Dublin and wherever the court moved on its progress. Some of the paperwork was brought to him when he and Catherine were at Pipewell in Northamptonshire, near to property owned by Dorothy Bray's lover, and the king was clearly displeased by what he read.[7] Would granting the proposed lands to the Irish who lived beyond the Pale secure their obedience or simply provide them with resources to fund future rebellions? A few weeks later, Henry complained that the parliamentary legislation made it sound as if the Irish lords and commons were granting him a title; he wanted every relevant piece of documentation to contain a 'plain setting forth of his old right and inheritance'.[8] Discussion of the exact wording of the title dragged into the autumn and it was only in January that it was finally settled upon.[9] The Irish got much of what they wanted, although perhaps not enough, and their proposal that the Kingdom of Ireland should now be bumped up to stand after England and before France in the king's official style was rejected, despite the fact that English royal presence in Ireland was arguably older and certainly more tangible.[10]

The king's irritation over the Irish proposals aside, he and Catherine were enjoying themselves. On 14 July, the king hunted and killed a great stag and two fat bucks, which he then sent as personal gifts to the Lord Mayor of London.[11] Two weeks later, the queen gave her chamberer Margaret Morton a note to deliver to Lady Rochford's rooms.[12] Morton, noticing that the queen's letter was unaddressed and devoid of any seal, handed it over to

Lady Rochford, who asked her to tell the queen that she would have a response for her in the morning. The next day, when Margaret went to fetch the reply, Lady Rochford sent it with a warning for 'her Grace to keep it secret and not lay it abroad'. Morton, who disliked Lady Rochford intensely, thought the errand and the viscountess's subsequent instructions about the queen needing to be careful with her correspondence were odd. She remembered both anomalies later.

The queen had been in 'merry' spirits when she entered Northamptonshire on 21 July, the first county on the progress that Catherine had never visited before; but it was not a cheering experience for everyone travelling with her.[13] Henry's advisers were often tasked with settling one of the many questions of precedence created by the progress. At Collyweston Palace, where they arrived on 1 August, the dispute was between competing representative bodies of the county of Northamptonshire against those from the towns of Peterborough and nearby Stamford about who should welcome the king and queen, and in what order.[14] At their earlier stay at Ampthill, the councillors had examined a local man called Richard Taylor who was accused of papism, and at Pipewell a man was examined, then released, after it was alleged that he had not blotted the pope's name out of his prayer book. Upon examination, the council discovered that he had erased the pontiff's name, but not as thoroughly as his neighbours had.[15] Other messengers travelling to and from Collyweston included Eustace Chapuys's secretary, who arrived with more letters about the still unresolved trade dispute with the empire, and those bearing invitations from the king to three Italian shipwrights who were experts in the construction of war galleys.[16]

Collyweston Palace had originally been owned by the king's paternal grandmother Margaret, Countess of Richmond, and her coat of arms could still be seen in the palace's four great bay windows with their fine views over the nearby Welland Valley. Following the devout countess's death in 1509, the palace had been maintained but seldom lived in until it was passed over to the king's bastard son. Catherine was staying in a house that still reflected the tastes of its original owner. She had access to summerhouses reached by gravel paths that ran through herb gardens and beside ponds. By the woods and near the orchard, there was a little clearing where the countess had once listened to outdoor concerts given by her choristers, who had been taught in the now-abandoned schoolroom beside the chapel. Catherine's apartments, originally built for Henry's mother Elizabeth of York when she visited, overlooked the gardens, which she could access by a private staircase. The palace had a fortified jewel house where Catherine's treasure trove could rest as securely as the countess's had half a century earlier.[17]

From Collyweston, the court moved into the county of Lincolnshire to spend three days at Grimsthorpe Castle, the recently renovated and expanded home of the Duke and Duchess of Suffolk.[18] Grimsthorpe was part of the duchess's inheritance but it became the duke's at the time of their marriage, since before 1870 a married woman could not own any property in her own right under English law. The couple who stood outside to greet them were very familiar to the king and queen. The duke, born Charles Brandon, had by 1541 become the greatest landowner in Lincolnshire.[19] The son of a man who had fallen for the Tudor cause at Bosworth, Brandon had seen service on land and sea in Henry's wars and he had scaled the ranks of the nobility through a combination of valour and devotion. Since then, he had gone to seed in the same direction, if not quite with the same speed, as his king. He too had grown fat, his hair was grey and when he went to the House of Lords he had to remain seated for most of the time.[20] Nearly thirty years earlier, Suffolk had caused one of the great scandals of the reign by eloping with the king's youngest and recently widowed sister, Mary. A *mea culpa*, accompanied by lavish gifts from Mary's inheritance from her first husband, King Louis XII of France, helped soothe royal outrage, and the couple had four children, three of whom lived past infancy.

In his determination to increase the family's position as magnates, Suffolk bought the wardship of young Katherine Willoughby, heiress to the deceased Lord Willoughby de Eresby.

The duke brought Katherine to the Suffolk household with the intention of marrying her to his son once they were both of age. Gossip in the household of Anne Boleyn, who was then on the rise and never much enamoured with the duke or his wife, made arch hints that the duke's interest in his son's fiancée was not entirely proper – an accusation that turned out to be a polished arrow when Suffolk's wife died of tuberculosis in June 1533 and he broke off his son's engagement to Katherine and married her himself that September.[21] When the son also died of tuberculosis a year later, Queen Anne and her clique were not slow to exploit the duke's private failings in order to undermine his position at court.[22]

By contemporary standards, Brandon and Willoughby's marriage had been successful in that the new duchess provided her husband with two sons to replace the one who died in 1534. The twenty-two-year-old hazel-eyed duchess was one of Queen Catherine's more outspoken and intelligent ladies-in-waiting. Although her Spanish mother had been a childhood friend of Katherine of Aragon, and the duchess had been named in the old queen's honour, she did not share her namesake's devotion to the old religion.

After the chamberers had unpacked everything at Grimsthorpe, the queen directed Katherine Tilney to find Lady Rochford and ask her if she had the thing she had promised her. Lady Rochford promised to bring her word herself when it arrived, an odd and cryptic answer to a similar question, both sent through a confused chamberer.[23] The queen and her favourite had talked about Thomas Culpepper throughout the progress. Lady Rochford told the queen that another of the king's Privy Chamber gentlemen, Thomas Paston, was also captivated by her.[24] Paston, who was twenty-four – about Culpepper's age – and single, would two years later marry Catherine's niece, Agnes Leigh, daughter of her much older half brother, Sir John Leigh of Stockwell. Like most Privy Chamber gentlemen, Paston and Culpepper were both permitted to socialise with the queen's ladies in her apartments, when off duty, during the day, and it was presumably there that

Lady Rochford noticed Paston's interest in the queen. Flirtation was a way of life in most Renaissance courts – a way of passing time and advertising one's nimbleness in speech. Courtly love was a fashion that made it very difficult to tell when the usual patter, perhaps like Paston's, had been replaced by the real thing, as seemed to be happening with Thomas Culpepper.

Catherine was not interested in Paston, but she was becoming obsessed with Culpepper. Since their conversation at Greenwich messages and gifts had passed between them. Catherine had worried about Culpepper when he was unwell. But there had been no opportunity for them to meet privately. Lady Rochford had been tasked with arranging a meeting and, if the wording recalled by Margaret Morton and Katherine Tilney about the two ladies' messages was correct, the widowed viscountess promised to do so. Every time they arrived at a new house Lady Rochford would inspect the stairs leading to and from the queen's rooms to see if there was a suitable venue for the discreet conversations her mistress and Culpepper desired. Thus far, she had not found anything suitable and, if she had, Culpepper could not be absent from the Privy Chamber if he was on duty that night or if the king demanded his company.

The day before they left Suffolk's house at Grimsthorpe for the county capital, the kingdom's other duke arrived. Norfolk had said his farewells to Henry and Catherine shortly before they left London with the intention of joining them at Lincoln, after he made another round of inspections of the border. His return may not have been welcomed by Catherine, since there is strong evidence that her relationship with her uncle had deteriorated. Her quarrel with Norfolk is mentioned in a history of the English Reformation penned a century later by the Bishop of Salisbury, who wrote, 'The king went in progress with his queen, who began to have great influence on him; and, on what reason I do not know, she withdrew from her uncle, and became his enemy.'[25]

It would be possible to remain sceptical about Bishop Burnet's version of events, except for two facts in its favour. Burnet's *The History of the Reformation* was researched and published in 1679 and he had access to many original documents about the Tudor court that were later and sadly lost in a fire at the Cotton Library in London in 1731. Where Burnet quoted or discussed documents that were available in his time and have survived to ours, we can see that he generally reproduced them faithfully. That documents recording a chill between the queen and her uncle in 1541 may have existed only to be lost in the eighteenth century is seemingly corroborated by a lengthy, self-pitying and vitriolic letter written by the Duke of Norfolk five years later. By that point, he had temporarily lost royal favour and he used his letter as an opportunity to accuse everyone around him of betraying him over the last two-and-a-half decades. He specifically mentioned his two nieces 'that it pleased the king's highness to marry' for the 'malice' they had both shown to him, which 'is not unknown to such ladies ... as my lady Herbert, my lady Tyrwhit, my lady Kingston, and others, which heard what they said of me'.[26] Norfolk, whose ability to play the victim was matched by a determination never to play the role quietly, had once complained that Queen Anne Boleyn drove him from her presence with words that one would not use to a dog, which if nothing else was inaccurate on the basis that she liked her dogs far more than she did her uncle.[27]

Anne Boleyn's feud with Norfolk is better documented than Catherine's, but the three ladies-in-waiting mentioned by the duke prove that Burnet was truthful when he wrote that Catherine also came to dislike her uncle. Anne Herbert was in both queens' households, Lady Mary Kingston only waited on Queen Anne in the final weeks of the latter's life, but Elizabeth Tyrwhitt was a lady in Catherine's service, never Anne Boleyn's. The inclusion of her name on Norfolk's list confirms that at some point she, and quite possibly Anne Herbert, heard Catherine's plummeting opinion of the Howard patriarch.

Why Catherine turned against the duke is unclear. The most obvious conclusion is that as she grew more comfortable in her role as queen, she felt she needed him less. It has been suggested here that the duke's role as Catherine's Svengali in the early days of her marriage has been exaggerated, which undermines the image of the ingénue turning against her patron. Nor was Catherine the only member of the family to develop an animosity towards the duke. Along with Queen Anne Boleyn, the Countess of Bridgewater's first husband 'confessed', in Norfolk's words, 'that of all men living he hated me most'.[28] Norfolk's second wife despised him and later gave evidence against him. At various times, his relationships with his surviving children were strained. The Duke of Norfolk was not the feeble-minded ogre of popular legend; in biography and fiction he is so often presented as a cretinous boor pining for wars against France or a return to the Wars of the Roses, with nothing to commend him to Henry VIII's government except his title. It is easy to forget that the duke could be charming, engaging and courteous. He was also a Francophile with real military skill but little hunger for war. On many occasions, his advice should have been listened to, for example on Ireland in 1520, the north in 1536, or the Anglo-Scottish border in 1539. Yet he was also prone to faintly hysterical reactions and he was incapable of admitting he was in the wrong – when defending himself in 1546, he did not mimic many of his contemporaries by acknowledging his own wretchedness in disappointing the king, but instead hit back with, 'In all times past unto this time, I have shewed my self a most true man to my sovereign lord' – and when he lost his temper, he was accusatory, offensive and aggressive. He tried too hard to control members of his family, which they resented, objected to and rebelled against. There are enough quarrels with his other relatives throughout Norfolk's life to lend credence to the stories – told by Elizabeth Tyrwhitt, and probably by Anne Herbert as well, referenced by Norfolk in 1546 and then repeated in 1676 by Bishop Burnet – that by the time they met again at Grimsthorpe Castle in August 1541, Catherine was contemptuous of her uncle and discussed those feelings in front of her women.

The royal party left Grimsthorpe on the morning of 8 August and travelled to the market town of Sleaford, roughly halfway in the forty miles between Grimsthorpe and Lincoln.[29] The local manor had once been the patrimony of the Hussey family, until

Lord Hussey of Sleaford was beheaded for supporting the Pilgrimage of Grace. The visit to his home may have brought up unpleasant memories for Mary Tudor, since Lord Hussey had been one of her chamberlains. The next morning the court headed to Temple Bruer, a spot about seven miles from Lincoln, where the cavalcade stopped to have dinner and send messengers to inform the authorities in Lincoln that the king and queen were about to arrive. When Catherine, in a crimson velvet gown, rode toward the walls of Lincoln she could see a forest of red robes, swaying into bows as she approached. They were Lincoln's mayor, burgesses and aldermen, who stood as representatives of the commoners of the region, while the gentry's delegation sat on horseback near a tent that had been erected for Henry and Catherine to change in before their ceremonial entry to the city itself. Henry, resplendent if enormous in green velvet – the Tudors' colour, but also, by happy coincidence, one traditionally associated with Lincoln – listened to an address in Latin delivered by the cathedral's archdeacon, dean and clergymen, after which the priests rode off to the minster to prepare for the service Henry and Catherine were due to attend after receiving gifts from the other castes, who admitted their wrongdoing in 1536 in return for gestures of pardon from the king.

Catherine and Henry remained on their horses throughout the clergy's presentation, then rode over to their tent, where Henry changed into a dazzling outfit of cloth of gold and Catherine donned a dress cut from cloth of silver. After pieces from her jewellery collection were wrapped around her throat and waist, and slotted into her ears and onto her fingers, the little queen shimmered from head to toe as she walked out on her husband's arm. Their servants helped them back onto their horses and as soon as they were mounted, the heralds put on their coats, the trumpets sounded and the procession into Lincoln began.

Before they passed into the city, Lincoln's other representatives prostrated themselves as the clergy had done. The city's serjeant-at-law and recorder, Mr Misseldon, was tasked with the first greeting, which he delivered in English and then presented a copy to the king, who passed it to the Duke of Norfolk, riding near enough behind him as the highest-ranking aristocrat present. The gentry and the mayor's party alike knelt before the king and twice shouted, 'Jesus save your Grace!' Before he began his speech, the mayor kissed the mace, the symbol of his office, passed it to the king, who also kissed it, and then handed it back. The initial gesture symbolised the mayor's position as representative of the city's liberties, which were granted by the king; the king's return of the mace, carried by the mayor for the rest of the ceremony, in turn underlined the monarchy's obligation to respect and preserve the rights it had long ago bestowed on its subjects.

The court nobility did not generally have a high opinion of Lincolnshire's landed classes. A few years earlier, Thomas Cromwell had received a report that referred to them as 'a sight of asses, so unlike gentlemen as the most part of them be', but that might have been nothing more than a blast of geographical snobbery.[30] On 9 August, the leaders of the local gentry acquitted themselves well in a ceremony that was not only partly humiliating but also nerve-racking and rife with potential for a mistake to be made or offence given. The gentry from the nearby Lindsey region pleaded for absolution and gave Henry a purse that contained £300; the Lincoln authorities handed over £40.[31] Through this, the fruits of the county were being offered to the sovereign, who accepted his subjects' gifts in the same way his government accepted their taxes. Again the underlying imagery was one of submission in return for protection, obedience and tribute that was supposed to bring with it certain freedoms and privileges. Under Henry VIII, that bargain had long ago been stretched to its limits, but the theatre of politics continued with the script used in past centuries. The symbolism was continued with the city's offerings to Catherine – she was given local fish for her table, including pike and carp.[32] This may sound like a lacklustre souvenir in comparison to the king's purses of gold, but food was a staple of present-swapping within the aristocracy – Cardinal Wolsey had sent Anne Boleyn fish for her supper table during Lent and Lady Lisle sent baked partridge to Sir Brian Tuke.[33]

Rising to their feet with the king's permission, Lincoln's leaders took their place at the front of the procession and escorted it through Stonebow, the main gate, where a statue of the Virgin Mary, the city's patron saint, watched down on the arrivals, in the company of a carved Saint Gabriel. On the other side of Stonebow, the king's coat of arms had been erected after a manic two-day cleaning spree in which everyone in the city was ordered to help clear away dunghills and filth from the streets, which were then coated with sand. All Lincoln's church bells rang out in welcome, including those of the Cathedral Church of the Blessed Virgin Mary of Lincoln, an architectural wonder built in the eleventh century on the site of an earlier place of worship, expanded and beautified throughout the Middle Ages. Its 520-foot spire might have been the tallest building constructed between the time of the Great Pyramid of Pharaoh Khufu and the completion of the Washington Monument in 1884.[34] In the afternoon light, the hilltop cathedral was an awe-inspiring sight, dwarfing both its bishop's palace, which nestled in the first southern indents of the hill, and the local castle that lay directly ahead of the great western door. Here Henry and Catherine dismounted to be met by John Longland, Bishop of Lincoln, who moved forward from a sea of choristers to greet the king and queen.

If the suppression of the Pilgrimage of Grace had shown the government at its most firm, the reception at Lincoln Cathedral was an attempt to wipe the sting of repression away with rosewater and perfume. Henry in gold and Catherine in silver knelt on prayer cushions covered in more cloth of gold and clasped their hands in prayer as Bishop Longland presented a bejewelled crucifix for them both to kiss. Incense curled forth into the air from golden censers to bless Catherine and her husband, who knew the bishop well, since he had once served as the king's confessor. Bishop Longland's loyalty to his king, however, was not as strong as his zeal for the Queen of Heaven: a golden statue of the Virgin had been hidden in the cathedral's vaults when

Thomas Cromwell's commissioners came to gut the Church of its 'idols'.[35]

Another of the bishop's preoccupations was saving his flock from the perils of lust, a concern shared by his episcopal predecessors – and one of many scenes immortalised in stone by earlier masons on Lincoln Cathedral's west front. If Catherine saw it, it is possible she missed its significance, especially since it was part of a series of carvings that also showed the torment of the damned in Hell, Daniel in the lions' den, and the expulsion of Adam and Eve from Eden. When the king and queen had been blessed, clergy held the canopy used for processions of the Blessed Sacrament over Henry and Catherine as they walked into the cathedral and over to the choir, where they again knelt in prayer as the choristers sang a Te Deum as part of a thanksgiving service for the couple's safe arrival. The area where they prayed was a broad space, with only the few sturdy beams bracing the transepts giving any clue to how far the long-dead architects had been willing to push their craft when it came to building the cathedral.

Two of Henry's ancestresses were buried, or partially buried, in Lincoln Cathedral. A few feet from where he and Catherine knelt was the tomb of his three-times great-grandmother Katherine, Duchess of Lancaster, who had also been a sister-in-law of Geoffrey Chaucer.[36] Ahead of them, bathed in the light streaming through the stained glass of the great east window, was the visceral tomb of Henry's six times great-grandmother, Queen Eleanor of Castile, whose viscera had been interred at Lincoln after she died nearby in 1290.[37] An elaborate funerary procession had brought her body back to Westminster for burial and as with many medieval royal funerals some of her organs, which were removed during embalming, were buried near to the site of her death. Eleanor's position as the king's ancestress and a former Queen of England had not saved her monument from damage during the gutting of the cathedral fourteen months earlier, when the head shrine of Saint Hugh of Lincoln, a twelfth-century Bishop of Lincoln, was dismantled. The head shrine's name was literal – after his canonisation, the cathedral staff had tried to move Saint Hugh's body to a new resting site, but the skull became detached during the exhumation which led to a separate shrine for it in the early fourteenth century.[38] Over the next two centuries, the head shrine had been visited so many times that the pilgrims' knees had worn a groove into the step directly in front of it.[39] In 1540, the royal commissioners ordered that 'a certain shrine and divers feigned relics and jewels, with which all simple people be much deceived and brought into great superstition and idolatry' should be destroyed and melted down; 2,621 ounces of gold and 4,285 ounces of silver, along with 'a great number of pearls and precious stones', were stripped from the cathedral.[40]

Oddly, the shrine to a local nine-year-old who had vanished in 1255 was left intact by Henry's Reformation.[41] The child, known as 'Little Saint Hugh of Lincoln', despite the fact that he had never formally been canonised, had been found murdered at the bottom of a well. His death was used as one of the most infamous examples of the 'blood libel' against the local Jewish community, who were accused of enticing the child to his capture, feeding him up, then ritually torturing and crucifying him before dumping the body. Fantastic stories claimed that every Jew in England had been invited to the Christian child's execution. The fact that there was no evidence to suggest that little Hugh had suffered a death anywhere near as traumatic as the blood libel story claimed did not prevent it being repeated in a climate of anti-Semitic hatred that lasted long after the entire Anglo-Jewish community were expelled from England in 1290. There is no clear reason why 'little Saint Hugh's' shrine was spared when the cathedral's other shrines were gutted. Perhaps the commissioners hesitated to pillage a spot associated with a child or spared it because it did not have the same material value of the other Saint Hugh's. For whatever reason, the grizzly reminder of the ruthless exploitation of a boy's death was still on display when Catherine entered the cathedral in August 1541.

The arrival in Lincoln and her public prayers at its cathedral was one of the high points of Catherine's queenship. Throughout the progress, she carried out her public duties perfectly. Accounts of the tour, written years later, referred to her as Henry's 'fair and beloved queen'. Catherine was a flawlessly behaved consort – content to dazzle as a supporting player, clothed in silver next to Henry's cloth of gold, never pulling focus or openly pursuing her own agenda. After a rapid and unexpected rise, she had successfully negotiated her first few months on the consort's throne. She had weathered rumours of a rival's restoration at her expense and the embarrassment of an alleged pregnancy, some details of which had leaked to the public. She was credited with saving the lives of two prisoners, at least one of whom had been expected to die; she had established her pre-eminence over a disgruntled and respected stepdaughter and won praise from diplomats and courtiers for her tact and dignity.

But beyond the Lincoln Cathedral choir, half-hidden in the bracket of a dark pillar on the left of the dismantled shrine and Eleanor of Castile's dented memorial, just above the carved face of a bearded saint, long-dead masons had rendered the image of a demonic imp – a visual reminder to worshippers that evil, sin and failure lurked close to all human triumphs, just as it had in Eden and through the betrayal of Judas Iscariot at the Last Supper.[42]

When they had finished their prayers, the king and queen blessed themselves and processed out of the cathedral. They were escorted 'straight to their lodgings for the night', down the hill to Bishop Longland's palace.[43] Twenty fat oxen and a hundred fat muttons had been provided for the visiting entourage by the city, cooked in the palace's cavernous fireplaces.

The fatigue of a long day was eased by the layout of the rooms set aside for Catherine. Lady Rochford's bedroom was at the top of a narrow little flight of stairs leading from the queen's. Jane was the queen's preferred lady-in-waiting and a member of her Privy Chamber, so the location of the dowager viscountess's rooms was not suspicious; however Catherine's announcement that she wanted a late-night chat in those rooms was distinctly odd. Members of the royal family did not call on anybody. Katherine Tilney and Margaret Morton accompanied Catherine up the staircase until she dismissed them and went in alone. Once they thought they were alone, Catherine and Lady Rochford went to the back entrance to the apartments and waited for Thomas Culpepper to arrive.

Light spilled in as one of the guardsmen on watch approached and saw an unlocked door in the dead of night leading into the queen's apartments. Catherine and Lady Rochford ducked out of view and the guard relocked the door. He had then mercifully moved on before Culpepper arrived, accompanied by one of his servants, who was also told to wait outside. Apparently very pleased with himself, Culpepper had picked the lock and slipped through the door. Catherine was frightened by the near-miss and Culpepper had to be his most charming self to calm her down. The three of them relocated to the queen's lavatory, a large room with enough space for Lady Rochford to doze in the corner while the two she had brought together had 'fond communication'. With frankness and humour, they chatted about past lovers. It must have been refreshing for Catherine, daringly liberating, to talk about Manox and Dereham, or other men like Roger Cotes and Thomas Paston who might have harboured unreciprocated feelings for her, with a man like Culpepper, who was handsome and amused by her stories. He had a few of his own, including his dalliance with Bess Harvey. He seems to have been quite clear to Catherine about the nature of his relationship with Bess and about his less than chivalrous treatment of her. Bess's wardrobe was not that of a kept woman. She had the notoriety but not the rewards. Thomas and Catherine's conversations became more flirtatious when the queen teased him with boasts of her skills as a lover: 'If I listed [wanted], I could bring you into as good a trade as Bray hath my lord Parr in.' Thomas replied that he did not think of her as the same kind of woman as the flighty Dorothy, but Catherine was not put off and replied, 'Well, if I had tarried still in the maidens' chamber I would have tried you.'[44]

The two talked for hours, until about two or three o'clock in the morning, which makes Lady Rochford's subsequent claim that she fell asleep much more believable. Katherine Tilney had the same idea and climbed into the bed she shared with Mistress Frideswide, another chamberer. A disgruntled Margaret Morton, who had seen other examples of odd behaviour from Catherine during the last few weeks, went back to see if the queen was still with Lady Rochford. When she returned to the chamberers' room, Tilney asked, 'Jesus, is not the Queen abed yet?' Morton answered, 'Yes, even now', and went to bed.[45]

The next morning, the king, accompanied by Catherine, went to inspect Lincoln Castle. The queen learnt of the case of a local spinster called Helen Page who had been condemned for various minor felonies. We do not know what Helen Page's crimes were, or her sentence, or who brought it to the queen's attention, but Catherine evidently heard enough to feel moved and she spoke to the king, who agreed to pardon the woman.[46] Charitably, but less appropriately, Catherine also had one of her servants deliver a damask gown to Bess Harvey, and then sent Lady Rochford with an innuendo-heavy joke to Culpepper to tell him about the dress, which the queen claimed she gifted to save Thomas's reputation for having allowed 'his tenement to be so ill repaired'.

Despite how late she had gone to bed the night before, that evening the queen asked Katherine Tilney to accompany her on another visit to Lady Rochford. This time Tilney was told to wait in an alcove outside the room, where she sat with Lady Rochford's maid for hours. On the other side of the door, the queen and Lady Rochford again slipped out of another exit from the room and went down to the stool house, where Culpepper joined them. Opportunities to meet had proved sparse since they left London, so even after the frightening brush with the guardsman the previous night, they did not want to miss the chance to talk. The queen was in a more serious humour than before, when she had fired out witty quips and suggestive gifts. She was agitated, jumping with fear when she heard a noise and dashing into the shadows. The first night they had talked of the past; on the second evening, conversation turned to the present and Catherine told Culpepper that she was in love with him. Culpepper felt the same: 'bound' to her, because he 'did love her again above all other creatures'.

As he left, he kissed Catherine's outstretched hand and told her it was the only physical intimacy he could allow himself.[47]

The declaration of love at Lincoln was a rubicon moment between Catherine and Thomas. They had been indiscreet before – servants had been sent on unusual errands, open doors had been noticed, risqué gifts had been exchanged, Culpepper had been invited in daylight to the corridor leading to Catherine's private rooms – but after Lincoln, their behaviour, and particularly Catherine's, spiralled out of control. There could be, and was, no more pretence that they were meeting as friends to joke about long-ago romantic mishaps. The possibility that the queen might commit adultery with Culpepper had shifted to a probability and the only explanation for why she was prepared to run such a terrible risk was the obfuscating lunacy of having fallen in love with an arrogant, risk-taking womaniser who, it seems, had actually developed feelings for her, which were either too strong or too weak for him to take the wisest course of action and avoid any further nocturnal meetings.

A suggestion that Catherine hoped to use Culpepper as a stud for the heir she could not get from her husband is often raised in conversations about Henry's marriages. Henry VIII's sexual problems may have been exaggerated and it has already been argued here that if he was impotent for prolonged periods of time, his wife's safest option was to remain barren. For a queen with an impotent husband, prayer and patience were the only courses of action open to her. Neither does the chronology of Catherine's liaison with Culpepper imply that her goal was pregnancy. She was in her stool house with him at Lincoln for hours on end, talking. Had she later slept with Culpepper and if the proficiency in contraception she had boasted of during her relationship with Francis Dereham had let her down, she probably would have been able to pass the child off as Henry's, but her behaviour does not suggest that a child was part of her plan or that she approached Culpepper in the spring and summer of 1541 with anything other than feelings of deep attraction that evolved into addling love.

Thomas Culpepper's motivation is less clear. He said all the right things when he was with her, but it is difficult to believe that he was as romantically infatuated with Catherine as she was with him. Later, nobody suggested that it was Culpepper who was the initiating party. The preposterous idea that he was blackmailing her into meeting with him is impossible to credit from a documentary point of view. Nothing Culpepper or the queen said, then or later, corroborates that interpretation. A theory that gained currency in the years immediately after their deaths was that it had been a grand love affair, somewhere between the star-crossed hopelessness of the next generation's Romeo and Juliet and the destructiveness of Helen and Paris. The vignette of Culpepper kissing his queen's hand in the pre-dawn darkness after professing his love for her and gallantly refusing to go further for honour's sake is arresting. It happened. It was not, however, the conclusion.

The most mercenary explanation for Culpepper's entanglement with Catherine is not that he was blackmailing her. Rather, he knew, like all the gentlemen in the Privy Chamber, that the king's health was unpredictable, his weight was increasing, his ulcer remained the great unknown that could close over and kill him at any moment, and he had seen at first hand how close Henry had come to dying during the scare in February. When Henry went, Catherine would be left as one of the wealthiest women in the country, even if she did not have children. Widowed queens had remarried before: after Henry I died, his childless widow Adeliza of Louvain married a former officer of the royal household called William d'Aubigny. When great widows married, they often did so to men far beneath them in the social hierarchy, with the differences in class helping to offset the legal inequality created by gender. Two of Henry VIII's great-grand-mothers, Queen Catherine de Valois and Jacquetta of Luxembourg, had eloped with handsome servants after their respective first husbands, a king and his younger brother, predeceased them. His aunt Cecily, Lady Welles, both of his sisters, and his sister-in-law Lady Mary Carey, had done the same. Along with perhaps some genuine romantic feelings for Catherine, Culpepper potentially had his eye on the long-term advantage of marrying a young and attractive woman, who was likely to become a dowager queen before she was much older. That is speculation, of course, and while it is unlikely that Catherine's future never crossed Culpepper's mind, we cannot know if the queen's future financial and social desirability outweighed her current personal attraction.

Chapter 17

The Chase

I would put amber Bracelets on thy wrists,
Crownets of Pearl about thy naked Arms:
And thou sitst at swilling Bacchus feasts
My lips with charms would see thee from all harms:
And when in sleep thou tookst thy chiefest Pleasure,
Mine eyes should gaze upon thine eye-lids Treasure.

– Richard Barnfield,
The Affectionate Shepherd (1594)

After three days in Lincoln, Catherine and the court made the eighteen-mile trip to the town of Gainsborough for another round of receptions, gifts, and reconciliations.[1] Lincolnshire was often marshy terrain, and it did not have enough bridges to make transport easy, so the household had to cross the Humber by ferry in what must have been a lengthy process.[2] It is unclear where Catherine stayed during her four-day visit to Gainsborough; the most likely spot was Gainsborough Old Hall, home of the cantankerous Lord Burgh, an explosively temperamental Protestant sympathiser who had once served as Lord Chamberlain to the queen's household before retiring to his home county, where a lot of his time seemed to be occupied with making life difficult for his family and servants.[3] Local legend has it that Henry and Catherine slept in the upper bedchamber of

Gainsborough Old Hall's tower. It is certainly possible that Catherine stayed in that room, which can still be seen today, but wherever they stayed the king and queen would have been given separate bedrooms as a matter of established protocol.

From Gainsborough, they followed the Great North Road to a manor house in Scrooby in Nottinghamshire, where they stayed for two nights.[4] At smaller towns or villages like this, the royal arrival was scaled back – the king, the queen, and Princess Mary rode down streets that had been cleaned and decorated, escorted by inhabitants 'going before him on their little geldings in their ordinary clothes', with about seventy archers, bows pointedly drawn, marching behind the courtiers.[5] The next major stage of the progress would be the king's entry into Yorkshire, which, with Lincolnshire, had formed the heartland of the 1536 uprisings. Before Yorkshire, Henry and Catherine stopped for a long hunting weekend at Hatfield Chase, an area of prime hunting land that straddled the county border.[6] Between Thursday 18 August and Sunday 21 August, a steady stream of guests joined the king, his gentlemen, and his nobles for long days hunting, shooting, and fishing. Both dukes were there, and Norfolk took the opportunity to talk for the first time in weeks with Charles de Marillac, who had also been invited, a gesture appreciated by the French king, who could be forgiven if he hoped it was an indication that de Marillac's recent assessment that England was preparing for a war had either been wrong or presaged a strike against the emperor.[7] The papal nuncio in France judged that the French court's view of Henry was best summarised as 'if not their friend, he is not their enemy'.[8]

De Marillac's personal and political rival, Eustace Chapuys – the two loathed one another and their feud spiralled into each man telling increasingly inventive lies about the other – had been asked to join the king and queen at Collyweston in July, but had to decline the invitation on grounds of poor health.[9] De Marillac was pleasantly surprised by the level of luxury he experienced at Hatfield – he confessed in a letter to François that he had not expected any comfort in the 'barbarous and mutinous' provinces

– so the effort the king's servants went to on his behalf was doubly appreciated.[10] The weekend passed in an orgy of organised slaughter. Two hundred stags were felled on the first day, a similar number on the second. The greyhounds took down many of the deer, which were then served at the guests' dinner tables. Courtiers were rowed out onto the Chase's ponds and marshes, where they caught young swans and two boatfuls of river birds, and fished for pike. De Marillac joined Henry for dinner in his tent, where his host leaned on him to give a full report in his next letter to François of the good hunting he had experienced. The ambassador was genuinely impressed by the scale of the hunt and Henry's wealth. He told François that there were so many bucks at Hatfield that Henry regarded them 'as if they were mere cattle'. He did not know that shortly before the progress arrived, the Earl of Shrewsbury had been tasked with moving more stags into the area, in return for which he angled for, but did not receive, the honour of hosting the king and queen as guests.[11]

When de Marillac took the opportunity to talk with Catherine's uncle, Norfolk did not mention his strained relations with the queen. At their last meeting, back in London, the duke and the ambassador had discussed ways to solidify the peace between their two countries. At the hunt, Norfolk shot down French interest in marrying one of King François's sons to Princess Elizabeth. Since Elizabeth was his great-niece, Norfolk told de Marillac that he could not publicly support any attempt to arrange such an advantageous match for her, since he would be suspected by other councillors of seeking to aggrandise his house.[12] Instead, he suggested de Marillac focus on a betrothal between Princess Mary and François's second son, the Duke of Orléans, something which he knew the French royal family had been keen on for some time. He also revealed, allegedly confidentially but doubtless with Henry's permission, the plans to restore Mary to the line of succession. She would be second after her little brother, and it would remain a 'great secret' until it was announced. Norfolk omitted to say that Elizabeth would also be restored, as third in line.

De Marillac did not see much of the queen during his visit. He barely mentioned her in his letters, and she seems to have spent much of her time with her ladies back at the house, rather than out in the field. She was in her rooms one day when she saw Culpepper on his way to or from the hunt. Margaret Morton, who was standing nearby, 'saw her look out of her chamber window on Mr Culpepper after such sort that she thought there was love between them'.[13] Margaret had been curious about the queen's behaviour since she left London, but before Hatfield Chase she seems to have put it down to her fondness for Lady Rochford. Once she saw the look Catherine gave Culpepper, she had an explanation that made more sense and struck more dread. If she kept this observation to herself, Morton might have been the only one to understand why the queen issued an unusual and insulting order that no one was allowed to come into her bedchamber unless she specifically summoned them, except, of course, Lady Rochford.[14]

At this point during the progress, the king's developing relationship with Scotland forced a change in the itinerary.[15] By 1541, Anglo-Scottish tensions were at breaking point over Scottish encouragement of Irish and English rebels, as well as its asylum for political, and especially religious, English exiles. The latter group of exiles were a particular gripe for Henry, since James promised that if he found any English political refugees in his kingdom he would hand them over, but refused to violate sanctuary claimed by a clergyman. In retaliation, Henry refused to extradite Scottish criminals. The Duke of Norfolk's recent inspections and the subsequent building work on defences in border towns like Berwick and Carlisle alarmed the Scottish government, as did King Henry's arrival with a large retinue of armed guards in the north of England. In the hope of applying pressure on James about the religious émigrés to Scotland, Henry's underlings encouraged English raids on Scottish property just across the border. This suggests that in 1541 Henry VIII was pursuing three interrelated policies when it came to Scotland: to intimidate

James, through the border raids and partial mobilisation of forces commanded by northern magnates such as the earls of Cumberland and Westmorland, into negotiations about papist clergy who had fled to Scotland from England; to bolster, through Norfolk's inspections, England's defences against possible Scottish attacks during any future war; and to pacify the north of England, through the progress, in the hope that there would be no more English rebels looking to Scotland for support.

Fearful of the danger this put them in, the Scottish government decided on a strategy of preparing for the worst while hoping for the best. Cardinal Beaton, one of the most influential men at James V's court, was sent to Paris, where he sought, and received, the backing of their French allies, who promised to help Scotland if England attacked. At the same time, the Scottish court dispatched Thomas Bellenden, a justice clerk, to meet Henry during the progress.[16] At his audience, Bellenden unexpectedly offered the possibility of a meeting between his king and Henry, something Henry had been trying to arrange for the best part of a decade only to have the plans frustrated every time by James's steady stream of excuses. It is unclear if Bellenden, who belonged to a set at the Scottish court who thought the two British monarchs should meet, had overstepped his brief in suggesting the conference or if he had been told to do so in the hope of throwing the English off course long enough for Scotland to arrange for her defence in conjunction with France.[17]

Henry was pleased. A face-to-face encounter with his nephew would give Henry the chance to encourage James to imitate the English Reformation and reject papal authority. There were absolutely no signs that James had any inclination towards a schism with Rome, as his defence of English priests, monks, and nuns who sought asylum in Scotland should have made clear. James had been so repulsed by the religious views expressed in one of his uncle's letters that he threw it into the fire.[18] Henry's diplomats were frequently ordered to deliver communications from Henry that sounded more like scolding or lecturing; King James had once responded that he had no need to take his uncle's advice since he was adequately obeyed, respected, and loved in his own kingdom.[19] Considering the Pilgrimage of Grace, that was quite a jab at Henry's own political record. However, James V was also careful never to go too far in alienating his southern neighbours, and although the Scottish court was split on the issue, Henry knew from his informers that James sided with those who did not want another war with England.[20] In light of the current tensions, a pro-peace James seemed prepared to cross the border and meet his uncle. To facilitate this, Henry rescheduled his arrival in York to a later date and planned to stay longer.

Immediately after the Chase, Catherine went to Pontefract Castle, famous and infamous as one of the great English castles, for a twelve-night stay, one of the longest stops in the progress. Pontefract was pronounced 'Pomfret' in Catherine's era.[21] Shakespeare had it that way in his plays, and its name is written phonetically in most accounts of the 1541 progress. When Catherine and her retinue rode into it on 23 August, they saw that, up close, Pontefract had a slightly dilapidated air. A report from three years earlier had recommended extensive repair work.[22] The tiny chapel dedicated to Saint Clement, which dated from the eleventh century, was showing its age, and another makeshift chapel had sprung up for the castle's regular inhabitants in the meantime. Pontefract stood on a rocky outcrop, its nine towers rising five or six storeys around a series of courtyards built over the course of the last four centuries. Edward I had once called it 'the key to the North', and a painting of the castle by Alexander Keirincx in its last years gives some idea of its size.[23] At its height in the Middle Ages, the key to the North ordered 2,140 dishes for a household of about 400. It had bakeries, breweries, and bowling greens, with stone benches set into the garden walls for spectators.

Pontefract's dungeons were to become the stuff of horror stories after the civil war in the next century, and even in Catherine's lifetime, the castle had a notorious reputation. Shakespeare characterised it as a 'bloody prison / Fatal and ominous' after Richard II died there in 1400.[24] Richard, whose court was beautiful but his policies less so, was overthrown by his cousin Henry, Duke of Lancaster, Pontefract's master, in 1399. It was through the latter's succession that Pontefract became a property of the Crown. The deposed Richard was sent to his rival's impregnable castle, where plots which aimed to free him and restore him to the throne were foiled. These were enough to frighten Henry of Lancaster, by then Henry IV, into ordering his cousin's death. The weight of evidence suggests that the horror of regicide, spilling the quasi-sacred blood of God's anointed, was technically avoided by inflicting an even more terrible death: the prisoner at Pontefract was simply denied adequate food until he starved to death. Thus, Richard II was not technically murdered on Henry IV's orders. Instead, he died of 'natural' causes. The Victorians believed the deed was done in the Gascoigne Tower. It would have been macabre poeticism to kill a king born in Gascony in a tower named after his natal province, but although the nineteenth-century version of Richard's death is still preserved in the modern tourist signs at Pontefract Castle, it is far more likely that Richard was taken to lodge and die in the King's Tower, where Henry VIII stayed in 1541.[25] Catherine was the first queen consort to reside in the Queen's Tower, which had been named in honour of Henry IV's stepmother.[26] Catherine and Henry's accommodations at Pontefract were probably linked to the castle's Great Hall and, through it, to each other. Although they had seen better days, the still-impressive royal apartments had a privy kitchen, and once the servants had unpacked their possessions, Henry and Catherine would not have lacked for comfort.

Catherine's old mixture of overconfidence and nervous insecurity had been magnified by the successes and strains of the progress. In the privacy of her apartments, her mood was irascible. She was jumpy, tired, heedless of how strangely she was behaving, and she was treating her servants terribly, snapping at them and issuing orders that confused or upset them. Katherine Tilney was sent to Lady Rochford with messages so imprecise and puzzling that she did not know how to word them; the queen's sister Isabella was one of the privy chamber staff unceremoniously shoved from the privilege of entering the queen's bedchamber, as privy women were supposed to do, and the chamberers were being dragged around back stairwells to spend half the night waiting in alcoves. Two of the chamberers, Margaret Morton and Mistress Luffkyn, had been on the receiving end of the queen's frayed nerves when she thought they were spying on her. Luffkyn in particular irritated the queen greatly.[27]

On 25 August, Francis Dereham arrived unexpectedly at Pontefract. His papers were still locked in a chest at Norfolk House, and whatever he had been promised in return for them, even implicitly, was evidently a debt too long delayed in Dereham's eyes. His arrival presented Catherine with a crisis, which she had to move quickly to neutralise. Francis had come to her of his own volition after the dowager duchess's patience finally reached breaking point. They had quarrelled, and in her fury she had thrown him out of her house, perhaps, although we do not know for certain, because he made demands about joining Catherine's service. The fact that he made straight for the touring court after he stormed away from Norfolk House indicates where his priorities lay. Catherine could not afford to alienate him, certainly not after her grandmother had come so close to doing so. There was no obvious vacancy in the household, but necessity gave birth to invention, and after speaking to him privately in her quarters at Pontefract, Catherine introduced Francis to the rest of her staff as a newly appointed gentleman usher, who had previously worked for the dowager duchess of Norfolk.

Unfortunately, Catherine's anxiety about Francis's ego and temper proved justified. He boasted to his friend Robert Damport, who was still in service at Norfolk House, that many people at court hated him because of the favour Catherine showed him at and after Pontefract. More accurately, the queen's other servants could not understand why Catherine tolerated such boorish behaviour from one of her retainers or why he had been appointed in the first place. Their suspicion and resentment were compounded by Dereham's remorselessly unappealing manners. He argued with another one of Catherine's gentlemen ushers, Mr Johns, who objected to Dereham's habit of lingering at the table after supper, a privilege reserved for members of the Queen's Council. One evening, after he heard that Dereham was once again still at the table long after the meal had finished, Johns sent a pageboy to order him away, with the sarcastic inquiry 'whether he were of the Queen's Council?' Dereham retorted, 'Go to Mr Johns and tell him I was of the Queen's Council before he knew her and shall be when she hath forgotten him.'[28] The exchange between the two men shows not only the recklessness of Dereham's personality by alluding to some former intimacy with the queen, but also the importance attached to etiquette within an environment like the queen's household. It also highlights how even relatively minor members were constantly being watched by one another. Catherine resorted to personally pressing occasional gifts of money into Francis's hands, £3 here or £10 there, theoretically in return for 'sending [him on] Errands, and writing of letters when her Secretary was out of the way', in reality to get him, as she begged during one exchange of money, to 'take heed what words you speak'.[29]

Throughout the spring and summer of 1541, Catherine's household was festering with private tensions. The indiscretion of Francis Dereham provoked the suspicions of its male members, the ascendancy of Lady Rochford provoked the jealousy of their female equivalents, and Margaret Morton and Luffkyn both thought they were going to be dismissed to make way for two girls suggested by the dowager viscountess.[30] At the same time as this dangerous dynamic of internal suspicion and self-scrutiny was developing, Catherine's focus was fixed on Thomas Culpepper, who came to her rooms most evenings at Pontefract and either left to help the king undress for the night or came to her again once the king was in bed and one of Thomas's colleagues had been tasked with sleeping in the king's bedchamber.

Most nights at Pontefract, the queen locked the doors to her bedroom and only Lady Rochford was allowed to attend her.

When Mistress Luffkyn either disobeyed or misunderstood the instructions and tried to enter one evening, Catherine was so angry that she threatened to dismiss both her and Margaret Morton.[31] When one of the king's servants came with a message for the queen, he found the door bolted on the other side. Like the queen's staff, the gentleman said nothing at the time but remembered it later. Lady Rochford ensured that certain doors were left open, and Catherine sent Culpepper the note, 'As ye find the door, so to come', a note which was subsequently used to imply that she had considered inviting him into her bed.

She occasionally feared that they might be lured into a trap, that her husband might already suspect something and set a watch to catch Culpepper in her rooms.[32] They were briefly separated in the second week of September when Culpepper accompanied the king while he inspected the north-eastern port of Hull, an unscheduled visit and one of several that was now made possible by the promise to remain in the north until Henry's summit with King James. It does not seem as if Catherine or her ladies accompanied the jaunt to Hull, since she is not mentioned in the accounts of the king's arrival there.[33] Even in her glistening silence, a demure and beautiful accessory at Henry's side, the queen was too important a person to be omitted in accounts of a royal reception if she had been present.

Her reunion with her husband on 15 September was also her chance to resume her midnight meetings with Thomas. Catherine begged him never to confess what they were doing to a priest. One of Catherine's twentieth-century biographers accredited this plea to Catherine's vigorous credulity in believing that her husband, as God's anointed, might actually have some kind of magical power to hear what was said between priest and penitent.[34] More probably, Catherine jittered at the fact that her husband was head of the Church, with vast and as yet poorly understood powers. If Henry asked a priest to break the vow of secrecy that usually surrounds the sacrament of confession, or if the cleric felt duty-bound to tell him, the old rules of confidentiality might no longer apply. Culpepper, who was no more the wide-eyed bumpkin than Catherine, promised her that he would never tell anyone about them, even a priest.

In her more relaxed and happier moments, Thomas made Catherine laugh and vice versa. One night when they were at York, he arrived through the usual open door and the queen joked that she had a whole 'store of other lovers at other doors as well as he'. Thomas batted back that he had no doubt about that. She sent him bracelets to keep his arms warm, a private joke between them that, before her, his arms had been kept warm by other women. Now he needed the bracelets because, according to the promises he had made to her in Lincoln, there was no one but the queen.

Chapter 18

Waiting for the King of Scots

Driven by desire I did this deed,
To danger myself without cause why,
To trust the untrue not like to speed,
To speak and promise faithfully.

– Sir Thomas Wyatt (d. 1542),
'On Trusting Suddenly'

On 18 September, Queen Catherine had her first sight of York, described by a visitor in the next generation as 'the second city of England, the finest of this region and indeed of the whole North, as well as its principal fortress. It is pleasant, large, and strongly fortified, adorned with private as well as public buildings, crammed with riches and with people, and famous as the seat of the archbishop.'[1] Two miles of walls encircled the religious and administrative capital of the north, home to the king's Council in the Northern Parts, regional branches of the Star Chamber, and an archdiocese that served about one in ten of the English Christian population. Five fortified gateways led into York from the farmland and marshes surrounding it; the bridges over the Ouse and Foss rivers were, like similar conduits in London, crammed with multi-storeyed residences, shops, taverns, and small chapels. It was an impressive and important city that had felt keenly the insult of no royal visit since that of Henry VIII's father in 1487. That arrival had managed to win over a city that had hitherto remained defiantly loyal to 'their' king, Richard III, head of the House of York at the time he fell and recalled in the city records as 'the most famous prince of blessed memory King Richard late deceased'.[2] The Duke of Norfolk, who knew and understood the north far better than Henry VIII did, hoped that Henry VIII's arrival in his kingdom's second city might have the same effect, banishing lingering regional resentment against the Royal Supremacy. In October 1536, the city gates had been opened to the rebellion, with no more than a halfhearted pretence at resistance. Incense and Latin chants had floated through the air in the city's cathedral, York Minster, praying for the Pilgrims of Grace to be successful in turning back the tide of dissolutions and religious revolution. The uprising's Council of War had met in York, and when it failed its most famous leader, Robert Aske, had been hoisted outside its castle to die of exposure.[3] York had willingly handed itself over to the Pilgrimage, and retrospective protestations by its officials that it had done so only because it feared the rebels' numbers looked even weaker in light of the collapse of the Wakefield conspiracy of 1541, when eleven of its supporters were brought back to their home town of York to be executed.[4]

York had been, if not the origin, the eventual centre of the rebellion, and so Catherine's journey towards it through its county of Yorkshire was paved with more public prostrations. At every stage, in each new locality, she saw hundreds (on one occasion, thousands) on horseback or on their knees, describing themselves as 'wretches', vowing never to swerve again in their loyalty or their prayers for the long life and happy reign of King Henry of 'bountiful heart and liberal grant', his queen, and his heir.[5] Supplicants were split into two groups – those who had supported the rebellion, 'grievously, heinously and wantonly', and those who had remained loyal. The Archbishop of York, Edward Lee, approaching sixty and the highest-ranked churchman in the land after Thomas Cranmer, sank into the grass with 300 offending priests, passed £600 into Henry's ring-heavy hands, and lauded him for the mercy he had shown to them. Archbishop Lee was the most famous of the Yorkshire ambiguous. He was ranked with those who had rebelled, even though he insisted and the government claimed to believe that he had only tolerated the uprising's presence at York because he was terrified at what might happen to innocent people if it was defied. His letters from 1536, which had been sent to the king and his councillors, revealed where his sympathies had lain, when he expressed his happiness in a mistaken belief that the rebels had been pardoned and some of their demands listened to by London.[6] Those whose thoughts remained more opaque but who had offered little resistance to the rebels were generally ordered to kneel with the 'guilty' side of the submissions. The treason laws introduced to stifle opposition to the break with Rome had criminalised disloyal thoughts. Even knowledge of another's misdeeds or animus towards the king was categorised under the lethal, catch-all legal term 'misprision of treason'.

Henry, Catherine, and their courtiers listened as York's reception committee praised the 'inspiration of the Holy Ghost replete with mercy and pity as evidently hath been shewed by your grace to your Subjects later offenders in these North parts'.[7] In the distance, they could see the spires of York Minster, a cathedral dedicated to the patronage of Saint Peter, 'Prince of the Apostles', a project that had taken thousands of hands 242 years to build.[8] Its white-and-gold vaulted ceiling soared above Catherine's head as an ecclesiastical procession welcomed her when she and Henry arrived there. Shafts of royal purple and blue light shone on the floor, alongside a green so dark it was almost emerald. Catherine and her husband passed a statue of King John, participant in the most famous English royal quarrel with the papacy before Henry VIII, on their left, and his reverent son Henry III on their right. The Plantagenet monarchs formed part of a set that fanned out from the entrance screen and showed every King of England in chronological order from William the Conqueror on the far left to Henry VI on the opposite right. After his murder in 1471, the latter had been venerated as a martyr by many of his former subjects. Suspicious of populist cults, Thomas Cromwell's commissioners had ordered Henry VI's image to be removed from the carved line-up at York Minster. If Catherine had had time to really examine the twelfth plinth, she might therefore have noticed that poor Henry VI's statue was wooden, a rushed job in comparison to his stone-and-gold ancestors. Henry VI was Henry VIII's great-uncle, and his posthumous popularity had been an early plank of Tudor justifications for seizing the throne from the House of York. On Henry VIII's orders, the image of the last Lancastrian king had been put back where he belonged. The stand-in would suffice until a new statue could be carved or, as events outmanoeuvred human plans, until Protestants gained the upper hand again in the next decade and had 'Saint' Henry VI scattered on a rubbish heap for a second time.

Following the service, Henry and Catherine rode the two or three minutes from the minster down Petergate and over to the closed Benedictine abbey of St Mary, where the dismissed abbot's red-brick mansion would serve as their home while they stayed in York. The street from the minster to Petergate was one of the most prosperous parts of the city, home to skilled craftsmen, many of whom worked for the archdiocese. On their way into York, even any last-minute attempts to spruce up the ramshackle collection of timber houses and unpaved roads could not have hidden the narrow quarters and filthy streets. York's collective memory looked back on the century preceding the Wars of the Roses as their 'golden age', after which the city had slipped into decline. Richard III had blamed trouble from the Scots for retarding the area's prosperity; Henry VII suspected incompetence in the mayor and his officials. Numerous plague outbreaks, frequent and virulent in the first decade of the sixteenth century, had accelerated the city's deterioration. The York aldermen encountered by Henry VII in 1487 may have been inept, but there were signs that the degeneration was happening across the north. Both Hull and Lincoln had informed the king in 1541 that they were facing similar problems.[9] The half-sung requiem for York turned out to be obsequies over an empty bier – its fortunes revived significantly under Elizabeth I – though when Catherine alighted at a gutted St Mary's, halfway on its own road to ruin, she and the Yorkers accompanying her could have been forgiven for thinking that the rot was terminal and that King Henry did not necessarily regard that as a negative development.

In the queen's rooms at St Mary's, Lady Rochford showed Catherine a ring belonging to Culpepper, which he had sent after stealing one of the batch of holy cramp rings that had been blessed by the king at Greenwich on Good Friday. When Lady Rochford told her of the good-natured larceny, Catherine sent Thomas another one from the batch she, as queen consort, had been handed during the Easter ceremonies. One evening when they were together, Catherine also brought up his betrayal of her when she was a maid, to which he tried to use the dishonest defence that he had not slept with any other women until it was clear Catherine was going to marry the king. For someone who was usually so proud and preferred brittle one-upmanship in her flirtations, Catherine was unashamedly forthright with Culpepper when she told him about how she had wept in front of the other maids of honour when she heard he 'loved another'.[10]

At some point on the progress, probably at York, Culpepper was again unwell and Catherine wrote to him. It has been conjectured that this letter, which is the only one of Catherine's known to survive in full, might date from Culpepper's sickness at Greenwich earlier in the summer, but with its tone and details, including the fact that she cannot see him every day and the open declarations of love, it seems to belong to a later date in the summer. The queen mentions that he will 'depart from me again', which could place it in the first week of September, after Pontefract and either just before or after the king's trip to Hull, when Culpepper would have been gone with his master for just over a week:

Master Culpeper,

I heartily recommend me unto you, praying you to send me word how that you do. It was showed me that you was sick, the which thing troubled me very much till such time that I hear from you praying you to send me word how that you do, for I never longed so much for a thing as I do to see you and to speak with you, the which I trust shall be shortly now. That which doth comfortly me very much when I think of it, and when I think again that you shall depart from me again it makes my heart die to think what fortune I have that I cannot be always in your company. Yet my trust is always in you that you will be as you have promised me, and in that hope I trust upon still, praying you that you will come when my Lady Rochford is here for then I shall be best at leisure to be at your commandment, thanking you for that you have promised me to be so good unto that poor fellow my man which is one of the griefs that I do feel to depart from him for then I do know no one that I dare trust to send to you, and therefore I pray you take him to be with you that I may sometime hear from you one thing. I pray you to give me a horse for my man for I had much ado to get one and therefore I pray send me one by him and in so doing I am as I said afor, and thus I take my leave of you, trusting to see you shortly again and I would you was with me now that you might see what pain I take in writing to you.

Yours as long as life endures,
Katheryn.

One thing I had forgotten and that is to instruct my man to tarry here with me still for he says whatsomever you bid him he will do it.

The Scottish visit remained the priority on either side of the first visit to Hull. The rendezvous between the two kings in York would be the first time Catherine had met fellow royalty or

'The English Nero': King Henry VIII, painted in the year of his marriage to Catherine.

O ·ÆTATIS·   ·SVA

This miniature, once identified as Catherine, may be a likeness of her eldest stepdaughter, Mary Tudor. They were not particularly friendly towards one another, a fact which became painfully evident during Catherine's first Christmas as queen.

Eustace Chapuys, the Hapsburg Emperor's ambassador in London. He first met Catherine at Hampton Court Palace in December 1540 and later wrote detailed reports on her downfall.

As queen, Catherine was credited with saving the life of the poet, courtier and diplomat Sir Thomas Wyatt, following his arrest and imprisonment.

By the time they were reunited at Grimsthorpe Castle as guests of the Duke and Duchess of Suffolk in 1541, Queen Catherine had developed feelings of dislike for her uncle Norfolk and some of her ladies-in-waiting apparently repeated her remarks to him.

The ruins of the Bishop's Palace in Lincoln, where Catherine
also stayed as a guest and where she held one of her
nocturnal meetings with Thomas Culpepper.

Magnificent Lincoln Cathedral where Catherine, wearing
a silver gown, publicly prayed on 9 August 1541,
as part of the royal tour of the north.

Pontefract Castle, painted by Alexander Keirincx, shortly before it was demolished as a consequence of serving as a royalist stronghold during the English Civil War. Pontefract was allegedly where Catherine had planned adultery with Thomas Culpepper and where she was reunited with Francis Dereham.

The ruins of Catherine's apartments at Pontefract.

James V, King of Scots, whose trip to York was to have been Catherine's first experience of a state visit as queen. The invitation came at a time of rapidly deteriorating relations between England and Scotland.

The entrance to Hampton Court Palace, where Catherine's downfall began, one day after she was publicly praised for the happiness she had brought to the king.

Thomas Cranmer, Archbishop of Canterbury, Catherine's reluctant but relentless interrogator. He had romantic secrets of his own – namely an illegal wife and family – but he doggedly pursued the details of Catherine's mistakes and he was the first man to suggest to the king that Catherine might have committed adultery.

Catherine Howard being conveyed to the Tower – by the nineteenth century, when this drawing was made, Catherine had become an object of fascination and, often, sympathy. In 1877, her grave was marked for the first time, on the orders of Queen Victoria.

Catherine spent the last three nights of her life at the Tower of London, where the constable Sir John Gage treated her with the courtesy and honours due to a queen.

interacted with social equals since her wedding. James would probably bring his wife, who, like Catherine, had been born into the nobility and married into royalty.[11] The last time Henry had hosted a foreign monarch was during a short visit to Calais in 1532 when he and Anne Boleyn met with François I. Impressing the Scottish visitors with displays of English wealth was a matter of national pride. The court would be beneath the spotlight in front of an audience many of whom would be predisposed to find fault where they could, and as its leading lady everything Catherine did, said, and wore would be critiqued by her Scottish guests.

For Catherine, the preparations for James V's arrival likely proved stressful. They were certainly noisy. In the courtyards and land around St Mary's, about twelve hundred workmen toiled night and day to spruce up anything that had been damaged during the dissolution. Tents and pavilions were erected to house James's entourage as messengers were sent south to fetch some of the court's best tapestries, plate, and outfits from the royal wardrobes. Even the archers and privy chamber servants were to have their finest liveries for James's visit. If there was any doubt about the fact that Henry valued impressing James more than impressing his own people, it was dispelled by the flow of accoutrements that arrived in York, all of which had apparently been judged too good to risk transporting for procession in front of the northerners, but were considered necessary to dazzle foreign visitors. Orders were given to draw up letters guaranteeing safe conduct for King James and any Scots who accompanied him. The gentry were told to stand down the armed men that they had fielded from their estates in case of trouble from Scots or northern malcontents.[12] Since the visit had still not been announced publicly, the work at St Mary's and the arrival of treasures from storerooms in the south gave rise to talk in York that Catherine was going to be crowned in a ceremony at the minster or even that she was pregnant and might stay long enough to give birth to a future duke of York in his 'home' city.[13]

Some of those watching the activity in York guessed that an interview between the kings was being organised. Charles de

Marillac, who had followed the court to York as its guest after the Hatfield hunt, had heard enough from his contacts at the French court to predict that James V did not want to travel into England. A few men in Henry's retinue, too shrewd to state their views publicly in light of how much time and money their king had spent in preparation for it, discreetly shared de Marillac's belief that the conference would never take place.

They were right. The expense at St Mary's was confidence attempting to create a reality. Henry had already sent letters asking James to make a firm commitment about when he would arrive in York. As Henry told his nephew, the meeting would have to take place before the end of September, at the very latest, in view of 'our distance from the parts where we accustom most to live, with also the time of the year which will shortly much impair the ways, which should be much tedious specially for the carriage of ladies and gentlewomen being here with us'.[14] Henry also had it from his spies, and from his sister, that James's court was riddled with political divisions that had already successfully torpedoed several proposed visits. The Dowager Queen Margaret had warned Henry of the strength of the clerical lobby on James's council, who, for perfectly obvious reasons, were strongly opposed to their monarch meeting with the excommunicated heretic across the border.[15] Scottish councillors who saw merit in a meeting generally preferred that it take place in a town closer to the border, like Newcastle, so that James did not have to travel far into his uncle's territory.[16] Even those who had previously promised to lobby for peace or a meeting, like Queen Marie, who had politely spoken to English delegates about it in 1540, did not raise their voices in favour of a visit as far south as York.[17] The French government had also made it very clear to James's envoy, Cardinal Beaton, that they would not support any conference between James and Henry unless François was also invited, a caveat that intentionally rendered the proposal all but impossible.[18] James, who was a canny politician, may have counted on these oppositions preventing him from ever meeting Henry, no matter how many times he personally promised to do so. However deeply the game of manipulation ran, the truth was that even if James had sincerely wanted to talk face to face with his uncle at York, and there is precious little evidence that he did, he would have been opposed every step of the way by most of his courtiers, clergymen, and councillors.

Earlier signs that contradicted Henry's confidence in the conference taking place had been ignored. On 3 September, Sir Thomas Wharton had written from the borders to the council and told them that there was no possibility of James coming to York in person. James and his wife had in fact gone north, away from the border, to stay at Falkland Palace.[19] Wharton's warning was partly confirmed by a subsequent letter from James to Henry, addressed from Falkland, in which James discussed the old issue of prisoners, without mentioning a visit.[20] When the point was pressed by the English, the Scots cited the distance from Edinburgh to York, which was countered by English councillors at York when they loyally tackled James's representative by pointing out that a few years earlier James had visited the French court and asked if 'the king's highness your master might with a great deal less danger repair hither than he lately went into France, having no sea to pass as he then had, no going to a stranger but to his natural uncle, who can not but love and tender him'.[21] King James later claimed that there were disturbances that required his attention in Scotland, a story that Henry, correctly, interpreted as a polite lie. If the Scottish government had told Bellenden to offer a meeting in the hope of knocking the English off their aggressive course, they failed to anticipate how badly Henry wanted to see his nephew in person. Henry's decision to alter the progress's schedule, wait at York, and spend a great deal of money preparing accommodation for visitors who never intended to arrive meant that when the 'promise' of a meeting fell through, the English king's attitude to Scotland hardened into open and murderous hatred. On the other hand, if Bellenden had simply casually mentioned the possibility of a conference at some unspecified point in the future and that was then jumped upon by an over-eager Henry, accustomed to getting his own way and bent on intimidating the elusive James, then Henry's subsequent anger stemmed from embarrassment and pique.

Henry finally accepted in the last week of September that the King of Scots was not coming.[22] A wryly amused de Marillac headed back to the south separately from the court, which planned to meander home over the course of the next four weeks. It was the time of year for magnates to visit their estates, and they were allowed to leave at the same time as de Marillac. To the queen's presumable relief, that included her uncle, Norfolk, who planned to stay at Framlingham Castle after one more tour of the border, which had again become a priority after James V's failure to visit.[23]

Anglo-Scottish relations went into a tailspin after York. Scotsmen on the borders took matters into their own hands and launched retaliatory attacks on their English counterparts. Henry fired off angry letters about it to James, which did not acknowledge that his own subjects had been behaving with equally lawless aggression for the past few months.[24] James, trying to balance preservation of the peace with independence from his uncle's agenda, sent a courtier called Adam Logan to Henry with a gift of falcons.[25] In the meantime, the Duke of Norfolk answered a series of questions from officials who had been ordered to expel any Scots living on the English side of the border, ostensibly because of the recent raids, but more probably because of James's apparent snub. If a Scotsman had married an Englishwoman and they had a child together, what was to be done with the family? Were they to be banished? Did employment make any difference? Were Scottish servants or apprentices to be sent away? What about Scotsmen who had married Englishwomen but did not have children? Was that different? Who was to seize their goods when they were expelled, since, presumably, they were not to be allowed to take them? What would happen with regard to any debts the refugees might have? Also, were those selected for deportation to be marked or perhaps branded and, if so, in what way?[26]

Other questions were discussed at the court in transit as well. Important news arrived for the king, still in a foul mood over the

Scottish fiasco, in a letter from a Hapsburg courtier, the Dutch nobleman Baron Jeorjus ab Heideck, who informed him that a force commanded by the emperor's younger brother, the Archduke Ferdinand, had suffered a terrible defeat at the hands of an Ottoman army outside Budapest.[27] Henry broke the news to de Marillac before he left the court and asked him if he had heard about the disaster in Budapest, which he had not.[28] Only France hated the Hapsburgs enough to want to see them lose against the sultan's forces. The eastern borders of their empire allowed the Hapsburgs to don the mantle of defenders of Christendom against the unbelievers who, not a century before, had conquered the Christian city of Constantinople. Byzantium's greatness was long behind it in anything except architectural beauty and Christian imagination when it fell, but that did not stop a chill of fear shooting through the West at the thought that the Ottoman sultans would soon be able to build mosques within riding distance of Vienna – 'the Turkish beast coming into Europe', in Chapuys's hardly impartial turn of phrase.[29] Henry also demanded an apology from his councillors left behind in London after he heard that they had put men caught burgling Windsor Castle in an ordinary gaol. Henry felt they should have gone to the Tower and that a run-of-the-mill prison implied stealing from the king was an unremarkable crime, when it was clearly an example of petty treason.[30] The council in Dublin received an irate letter from their sovereign, who had found a new reason to vent his spleen about their generous proposals for land distribution to the Irish peers, established, disgraced, and aspirant.[31]

Catherine's uncle William was about to end his embassy in France and had been summoned home, possibly with the intention of sending him to represent the king at another court, but in the meantime he would reside in London with his wife, children, and royal niece.[32] Lord William Howard had wanted to leave France for some time, but his letters, which balanced politics with titbits from the Valois court, had been appreciated by the king and his entourage. Thanks to William's reports, the women of the French royal household could provide fodder for conversation as

Catherine travelled back to the capital at a snail's pace. Now that she had recovered, the French court revealed that Queen Eleanor had been so unwell for most of the summer that her doctors feared for her life.[33] The old and new generations of the French royal household were also butting heads in their Loire valley châteaux – the king's mistress, the Duchess of Etampes, had developed a powerful dislike for Diane de Poitiers, who, despite being a decade older than the duchess and just past her forty-second birthday, had become the mistress of the king's twenty-two-year-old heir. Pro-Inquisition Diane, with her cloud of blonde hair and statuesque elegance, was described as one of the most beautiful women of her generation by all but the most blinkered of her opponents; she espoused radically different politics to the soft-on-Protestantism Duchess of Etampes. Gliding around the French palaces in her monochrome gowns of black and white, a demure expression of virtuous widowhood, Diane's sedate grace struck her glittering rival as rank hypocrisy, and the two women's prosecution of a stealthy feud had already given diplomats, and foreign courtiers, a giggle. Perhaps less amusing was the story that the dauphin's Italian wife, another Catherine, was stoically trying to face down threats of divorce because, after eight years of marriage, the royal nursery remained empty.[34]

The route south brought Queen Catherine to places she knew from the outward journey, like the stopover at the Suffolks' home at Grimsthorpe Castle and then two nights at Collyweston, as well as royal residences that she had never seen before, such as Richard III's birthplace at Fotheringhay Castle, where they rested behind its grey walls for two nights.[35] From 24 October, she spent two nights as a guest of the Lord High Admiral, the privy coun-cillor in charge of the Royal Navy. The grey-bearded John, Lord Russell, welcomed the king and queen into his lovely and recently completed red-brick home, Chenies Manor House, where he introduced them to Lady Russell and their teenage son, Francis, who would soon begin his studies at Cambridge.[36]

On the court's second day at the Russells', Alice Wilkes, now Mrs Alice Restwold, was brought into Catherine's presence by

Francis Dereham – acting as an usher – and Katherine Tilney, both of whom, like Alice, had once been servants to the dowager duchess of Norfolk. Catherine greeted Alice with lavish charm, raised her to her feet, kissed her, and invited her to stay as her guest with Katherine Tilney and the other chamberers. While Alice acclimatised herself to her former friend's change in circumstances, Lady Rochford arrived with jewellery, French hoods, and dresses trimmed with gold thread for her – gifts from the queen.[37] At Chesworth House, Alice had once asked to switch beds rather than sleep next to Catherine and Dereham's rambunctious lovemaking. Quite possibly, Francis's admittance to her service prompted Catherine to think of other loose ends from her girlhood. Alice had been helped and patronised by members of the Howard clan before, specifically Catherine's uncle William, who had helped find her a new job after she was married, but Catherine's generosity, and the two people she chose to fetch Alice, suggest a desire to buy the support and silence of another potential witness.[38]

Chenies was followed by a stop at the recently burgled Windsor Castle.[39] By the time they reached it on 26 October, Henry and Catherine would have received the news from the council in London that Henry's only surviving sibling, Queen Margaret, had died at Methven Castle near Perth eight days earlier. The queen mother had suffered a 'palsy', a stroke, on a Friday evening four days before her death.[40] She had left all her possessions to her daughter Lady Margaret Douglas, but if Henry's court went into mourning for his sister and the mother of Catherine's highest ranking lady-in-waiting, there is no record of it and they were not wearing it by the time they reached Hampton Court Palace ten days after Margaret passed away.[41] Henry had ordered public Masses and eleven days of black in honour of the Empress Isabella in 1538; for the sister he had exploited and ignored, who had been the daughter, niece, and granddaughter of kings of England, the English court cannot have expressed anything but the most perfunctory mourning.

Henry was far more upset to hear that his son was bedridden with a fever. He summoned some of the best doctors in England to inspect Edward, and they agreed that the fever was serious enough to put the prince's life in danger. It was at this point that the king began to notice the indulgence of the heir's servants in feeding him not just too often but also with whatever food the child demanded, even if it was not good for him. De Marillac managed to bribe one of the doctors into telling him 'that, apart from this accident, the Prince was so fat and unhealthy as to be unlikely to live long'.[42] The physician was wrong. Edward recovered, but his establishment was subsequently subjected to more frequent inspections by the king's councillors.

Catherine returned to her enormous high-ceilinged apartments at Hampton Court on 28 October. In three days' time, she would be on public display again at Mass in the Chapel Royal for All Saints' Day, followed by All Souls' Day a day later, when the departed were commemorated in prayer. All Saints' Day, which honoured every Christian who had died, was also known in England as All Hallows, from the Anglo-Saxon word for holy. The vigil or eve of the feast, All Hallows' Eve or Hallowe'en, was the start of three days when superstition held that the souls of those trapped in purgatory wandered the Earth and the living and the dead stood side by side.

Chapter 19

Being Examined by
My Lord of Canterbury

Who is this? and what is here?
And in the lighted palace near
Died the sound of royal cheer;
And they cross'd themselves for fear,
All the knights at Camelot ...

– Alfred, Lord Tennyson,
The Lady of Shalott (1833)

A day or so after they returned to Hampton Court, Katherine Tilney stepped into Lady Rochford's presence: the queen had sent her to ask if 'she should have the thing she promised her'. Tilney was sent back with a message which was difficult to interpret but easy to construe as something secret or inappropriate – that Lady Rochford 'sat up for it, and she would next day bring her word herself'.[1] The last part of Lady Rochford's sentence may have been a subtle plea for Catherine to rein in an impatience that was causing her to send chamberers on errands bound to provoke their curiosity. The incident proves that Catherine's relationship with Culpepper had not been a summer passion. Regardless of the dangers of meeting him in a palace like Hampton Court, where any anomalies in locked doors or behaviour could not be put down to the court residing in an unfamiliar building, Catherine intended to keep seeing Thomas. Lady Rochford dutifully waited up in the hope that Culpepper might be able to slip away from his colleagues in the privy chamber for long enough to visit the queen. It was frustrating for Catherine, though there was potentially good news for her as well – the Duke of Norfolk, one man she did not want to see, was asked to stay away from court for fifteen days when, genuinely this time, one of his servants died from the plague.[2]

At the All Saints' Mass in the Chapel Royal, Catherine received a public tribute from the king for her behaviour in the north. The celebrant was the king's confessor and one of the couple's progress hosts, John Longland, Bishop of Lincoln, and in his prayers for All Saints he had been asked on the king's behalf to 'give thanks with him for the good life he led and hoped to lead with [the queen]'.[3] The next day, All Souls' Day, Catherine went through her morning toilette and either heard Mass in her apartments or progressed to the Chapel Royal for a second public service. The sources do not say. All Souls' Mass was not usually considered a public 'holy day' in the same way as All Saints. Had she gone, Catherine would have not seen much of her husband anyway. At services in the Chapel Royal, the queen arrived with her ladies, processed to light candles, prayed at the altar rail, then exited a different way from the king, who sat in a gallery on the second floor. As a young girl, Catherine had seen petitioners and inferiors leave notes, letters, and written requests in her grandmother's pews at Horsham and Lambeth. The same thing typically happened for the king, although access to his in-tray was more tightly controlled. For the second time in her life, Catherine's private life was about to be upended by a letter left for a relative during Mass. This time, no amount of determined charm would save her from the consequences.

Archbishop Cranmer and the two colleagues left behind with him in London during the progress, the Lord Chancellor Sir Thomas Audley and Edward Seymour, Earl of Hertford, had spent most of the council meeting on All Saints' Day informing the other councillors of what had happened in their absence, hearing and reporting any news that had been left out of their many letters during the tour of the north, and discussing the situation with Scotland.[4] There was one item of new business that the three men did not share with the rest of the Privy Council – an audience that Cranmer had granted to an evangelical called John Lascelles, who had arrived at Lambeth Palace, the archbishop's official London residence, asking to speak with him.

Cranmer might reasonably have expected Lascelles to have news about the religious radicals he knew and admired, several of whom had relocated to Germany after Thomas Cromwell's execution. Instead, Lascelles told the archbishop that his younger sister Mary, now Mary Hall, had once worked as a servant at Norfolk House, the dowager duchess's residence that was about a two-minute walk from Lambeth Palace's gatehouse. Mary, a married woman living in Sussex by 1541, had been a nursemaid to Lord William Howard's eldest daughter and then a chamberer to the dowager when the future Queen Catherine lived in the same household as a ward. During a recent visit to his sister and brother-in-law, Lascelles encouraged Mary to petition for a place in Catherine's household. A year earlier, Lascelles had lamented Cromwell's downfall and worried that the ascent of a Howard queen consort might seriously damage the English Reformation. His fears had apparently abated, and he could not understand why Mary would not take advantage of her earlier ties with the queen. Mary answered that she would not be comfortable serving a woman with Catherine's morals, because she was 'light, both in living and conditions'. She offset her criticism with the caveat that although she disapproved of her she 'was very sorry for the Queen'. Lascelles, naturally, pressed her to be more specific, and Mary rewarded his curiosity with the story of Catherine's romances with Henry Manox and Francis Dereham. It had been Mary who tried to warn Manox off his pursuit of Catherine and was rewarded with his charming boast 'I have had her by the cunt', which, according to Manox, he would recognise amongst a hundred. Lascelles put it a tad more delicately when he told the archbishop that Manox 'knew a privy mark on her body', perhaps a birthmark on her thigh or near her vagina.[5]

Lascelles had consulted with friends, who agreed that it was his duty to bring Mary's revelations to somebody on the Privy Council. Lascelles's religious enthusiasm and his choice of Cranmer as a confidant fuelled suspicions later that he divulged the information as part of a political agenda to unseat a queen associated with a conservative family. It cannot be ruled out as part of his motivation – one could fairly speculate if Lascelles would have dashed to Lambeth with the same urgency had his sister told him similar things about a reformist queen. Where that speculation should end is with Cranmer, whose involvement in the case was, from start to finish, thorough, slightly regretful, and never motivated by a desire to embarrass Catherine.

Cranmer too discussed the story with friends, in his case Audley and Hertford, who gave the archbishop the same advice John Lascelles's friends imparted to him: he had no choice but to pass on what he knew. If it ever emerged that the queen had been unchaste before her marriage and the Archbishop of Canterbury knew but did not pass the information on to the king, Cranmer would probably find himself disgraced or imprisoned by association. With the tact he was known for, and just the faintest whiff of the cowardice his enemies often accused him of, Cranmer wrote the whole thing down and left it for the king to pick up after divine service on All Souls' Day.

The prelate's fear of how the king would take it must have been exacerbated when he heard Bishop Longland praise the queen, quite literally, to the heavens the day before Cranmer was due to drop Lascelles's bombshell. Henry sent for Cranmer once he had read the missive, and the king seemed perfectly calm as he stated that the story must have been fabricated, either by Lascelles or by Lascelles's sister. The other men in the room with Cranmer and the king were some of the latter's favourite and most trusted advisers – William Fitzwilliam, Earl of Southampton and Lord Privy Seal; Lord Russell, the Lord Admiral who had hosted the king and queen at his house only a week earlier; the king's Master of the Horse, Sir Anthony Browne; and Sir Thomas Wriothesley.

Writers who assume Henry initially entertained no suspicion against his wife are perhaps taking too seriously his protestations of good faith and apparent confidence that Lascelles's story was a lie.[6] In the same interview, Henry ordered the men to ascertain the truth and remarked that 'he could not believe it till the certainty was known'.[7] Whilst Henry may not have entirely believed the contents of Cranmer's letter, to order the investigation at all suggests that on some level he did not find the charges against Catherine as risible as he initially claimed. Regardless of any conflicting feelings, Lascelles's story had to be verified. Either he was breaking the law by defaming the queen, or the king's marriage might have to be annulled. Henry's only other stipulation to the five men in his chamber was that all their inquiries were to be handled with the utmost discretion, a condition which suggested that any suspicions Henry had were still outweighed by the hope or belief that it would turn out to be a misunderstanding or a malicious lie.

Catherine remained in her apartments for the rest of the day with no idea of the disaster hurtling towards her. As the chosen councillors went about their business on the king's behalf, they did not give any clue that something was wrong. Sessions of the whole Privy Council adhered to workaday agendas – a crackdown on smuggling was discussed later on All Souls' Day, enlarging the king's hunting demesnes on the Hampton Court Chase the day after, and the Crown of Ireland Act the day after that.[8] Meanwhile, the investigators worked quickly and within seventy-two hours had interviewed all the witnesses mentioned in Mary Hall's story.

Lord Southampton went into London to quiz Lascelles, who confirmed the archbishop's précis of his declaration, 'saying he had made it only for the discharge of his duty'. A day or so later, Mary Hall and her husband were interrupted at home in Sussex by a group of hunters, who asked if they could break their ride at the Halls'. The double-chinned Southampton managed to get the lady of the house on her own long enough to reveal that their hunting trip was a ruse to prevent her husband from knowing that the king had sent them.[9] He asked Mary if she would stand by what she had told her brother about the queen. She would. Meanwhile, Wriothesley had left Hampton Court for Lambeth, where he found Manox's house and asked him to tell his version of events. Wriothesley, accompanied by Archbishop Cranmer, did not get Manox until the 5th, three days after he was asked to – either it took time to discover where he was living or the king's desire for secrecy meant that Saturday the 5th was the first point Wriothesley could get away from the palace without attracting unwanted attention. Cranmer's sources in Lambeth may have helped locate Manox's home.

The gentle-mannered archbishop and the intimidating Wriothesley were the archetypal good and bad inquisitors. In their presence, Manox did not just confirm what Mary Hall had said, first to her brother and then to the Earl of Southampton, he also provided information so excruciatingly anecdotal that it was impossible to disbelieve him. He told them which rooms in the duchess's house he and Catherine had used for their trysts, he told them about the tip-off he sent to the dowager about men being invited to the maidens' chamber after sunset, then of Catherine's theft of that letter and Manox's subsequent tussle with Francis Dereham. He gave a list of everyone he could remember who had known about his fling with Catherine – the duchess's maid Dorothy, who had carried love tokens between him and Catherine; Katherine Tilney; Francis's partner in seduction, Edward Waldegrave, who had gone on to serve in the Prince of Wales's establishment; the dowager's sister-in-law Malyn Tilney; and Joan Bulmer, or Joan Acworth as she had been then, against whom Manox seemed to nurture a special grudge, since he told Cranmer and Wriothesley the slightly unnecessary biographical detail that Joan had also been sexually involved with Francis at some point during their time at Chesworth.[10] Manox also mentioned Mary Hall in his list of people to contact as witnesses, which implies that Cranmer and Wriothesley did not tell him who their original source was, in case Manox tailored his confession to suit what he thought Mary might know. When pressed on how far he had gone with Catherine, Manox momentarily played coy and admitted that he 'had felt more than was convenient'. They encouraged him to return to his earlier frankness and believed him when he insisted, over and over again, that he and Catherine had never gone beyond foreplay. Manox's version of events, which was confirmed by everyone else interviewed, was that he had wanted to take Catherine's virginity and had suggested it to her many times; she had refused, he had been angry and indiscreet, and she had moved on to Francis Dereham.[11]

Francis was their next point of attack. He had already been apprehended, probably on the 3rd or possibly late on the 2nd.[12] Since he was one of the queen's ushers and his detention might alert his employer, they put about the story that they were re-investigating old claims that he had participated in piracy during his time in Ireland. The questions they put to Francis once they had him were more focused on why he had gone to Ireland in the first place and why he had returned, not what he had done while he was there. Francis's appointment to Catherine's service after she became queen rang alarm bells for Wriothesley and the archbishop, even at this stage. Francis told them that he been invited into Catherine's privy apartments and about the gifts of money she had given him, along with her pleas to 'take heed what words you speak'.[13] He confessed that 'he had known her carnally many times' when they lived under the dowager duchess's roof and, as with Manox, the details he provided were intimate and specific enough to banish any doubt that he was only telling his questioners what he thought they might want to hear – he could remember that he was 'in his doublet and hose between the sheets' when they first began to touch each other, later 'in naked bed', and the female friends who had seen him and Catherine making love.[14] If they did not question in him in the Tower by the 5th, they sent him there not long afterwards.

Corroboration was sought from the others mentioned by Mary Hall and Henry Manox. Initially, they did not have time to get to all of them, but Sir Ralph Sadler wrote a few weeks later that 'eight or nine' were questioned and that they all 'sang with one tale'.[15] Two of Catherine's women – her aunt, Lady Margaret Howard, and her friend, Katherine Tilney – were asked what they knew. Lady Margaret admitted that she had suspected a liaison between her niece and Dereham before the former came to court, and yes, since then she had heard a few servants gossiping about what would happen if the truth ever came out. Tilney provided a testimony that unknowingly confirmed some of Mary Hall's testimony and most of Francis Dereham's. Dereham's friend Edward Waldegrave was fetched from the Prince of Wales's household and, like Tilney, told a story similar in detail to the others. Two of the dowager duchess's former maids, Margaret Benet and Alice Restwold, the recent recipient of the queen's generosity, were summoned. Neither of them offered anything radically different.[16] Sadler was generalising but not misleading when he said they all sang the same song – the slight variations only helped convince those asking the questions that the story was true in essence.

On 6 November, the councillors went to the king to tell him what they had learned. They had interviewed and dismissed another young man who had been at Chesworth House at the same time as Catherine, Roger Cotes, who had also once been romantically interested in her. From what they could tell, Catherine had not reciprocated Cotes's intentions and he was guilty of absolutely nothing beyond hoping for a job at court after she became queen.[17] There was no reason to doubt that Mary Hall had told the truth about the queen and the other two men. It would have been impossible for her, her brother, Manox, and Dereham to plan a conspiracy of deception – they lived too far apart and had not seen each other in years – and in any case, even if they had been lying, they should have told any story but the one imparted. As their findings were relayed to him, the king sat in a thunderously loud silence that dragged on until he began to weep, a sight that few of the councillors had witnessed before and one 'which was strange in his courage'.[18] Orders were dispatched to the quarantine Duke of Norfolk, demanding his return to court, and to the Duke of Suffolk, who had recently been granted permission to stay at home at Grimsthorpe Castle until Christmas.[19]

The next few council meetings ran at odd hours, with the king in attendance. Both facts were unusual enough to set tongues wagging, especially when Norfolk, who had not been expected back for at least another week, emerged from the sessions noticeably anxious and unsettled. Eustace Chapuys thought Norfolk had come back for more discussions with de Marillac about Princess Mary's proposed marriage to the Duke of Orléans.[20] Others thought there had been trouble in Ireland or that there was about to be a declaration of war against Scotland.[21] Clergymen could be seen arriving at Hampton Court, reminding courtiers and servants of the fate of Anne of Cleves a year earlier. Despite the best efforts of the piracy subterfuge, Dereham's apprehension, like the summoning of the theologians, intensified and focused speculation on the queen. Andrew Pewson, one of the Dowager Duchess of Norfolk's retainers, was either running errands to Hampton Court for his mistress or had been sent there on that pretence once she heard rumours that Dereham had been taken. Servants to Catherine's Master of the Horse were able to confirm to him that Francis had been detained – news which Pewson carried back posthaste to Norfolk House. The pall of present uncertainty and approaching disaster settled over the queen's apartments as Catherine was asked to keep to her rooms for the time being. De Marillac heard that 'whereas, before, she did nothing but dance and rejoice, and now when the musicians come they are told that it is no more the time to dance'.[22]

Council meetings were held in various members' residences, perhaps to confuse suspicion about the topic of conversation. One session took place at Cranmer's London residence, Lambeth Palace, on Saturday, the 5th, and like most over the past few days, it ran late into the evening. As he was preparing to leave Lambeth, Norfolk was approached by one of the dowager's servants, Robert Damport, who had brought an invitation for the duke to spend the night at Norfolk House, since it was too late for the

journey back to London.[23] Norfolk sent polite regrets to his stepmother, with an explanation that he must return to court on the
king's business, regardless of the hour. The dowager's offer of
hospitality almost certainly had an ulterior motive. She wanted to
know what was happening with the queen. Robert Damport
returned to a household cracking under the first signs of panic.
The dowager had summoned her chaplain, Father Borough; her
comptroller, Robert Damport; a servant called William Ashby,
who also knew Dereham; and her sommelier, a man called Dunn,
'who played the smith's part' and broke open the locks on Francis
Dereham's coffers.[24] The dowager, with a candle in her hand,
reached into the chest and took out every piece of paper she could
find, then retreated to her bedroom and would not let any of the
servants see them. The tattle-tale note from Henry Manox was
there, still in Dereham's possession three years after Catherine
had stolen it from her grandmother and passed it over to him;
there were ballads, too, sheets of music, and letters. The men she
had summoned saw the dowager 'cast back into the chest the
writings she liked not', and it was a few nights later that she
handed some of the retrieved paper trail to Ashby with the
instruction to deliver it to the duke.[25] The dowager appeared to
be helping the council's investigation, but neither Ashby, Dunn,
Damport, or Father Borough could be certain later if she had not
incinerated the most damning pieces before handing over ephem-
era to her stepson.[26]

In front of her servants, Agnes gave the appearance of a woman
who would commit misprision of treason without a qualm if it
would save her or her granddaughter. The dowager clung to the
meagre comfort that if a pre-contract was proved, the queen
would be stripped of her title and humiliated, but after that the
principle of *De minimis non curat lex* would save her from further
repercussions for her youthful affair with Francis. The night she
sent him to the archbishop's palace, the dowager told Damport
on several occasions that no matter what was said about them,
Catherine and Francis would escape with their lives, since
premarital sex was not a crime that carried the death penalty. She

wondered if Catherine would be divorced and then 'shall become [un]to me home again'.[27]

The next day, the king went on a hunting trip in the Chase, and that night he made for the empty Palace of Whitehall. An old legend, preserved in tours of Hampton Court, has it that when Catherine realised the danger she was in, she made a dash from her apartments and down the gallery that ran past the king's entrance to the Chapel Royal and the Privy Council chamber. She was caught by her guards and dragged away screaming before she could reach her husband. If it happened, and it remains an unknown, then it took place before or during Mass on Sunday, the 6th, by which point three or four days of nervous uncertainty had combined to push her over the edge. Her brother Charles had been kept away from her rooms and then banished from court without a reason given; Francis Dereham had been taken in for questioning, ostensibly about Ireland, but he had not returned and was rumoured to be kept as a prisoner in the Tower.[28]

It was on the Sunday that Catherine received the first official confirmation of what was wrong. Archbishop Cranmer asked to see her as part of a delegation that consisted of the Lord Chancellor, the dukes of Norfolk and Suffolk, and Bishop Gardiner, recently returned from his embassy to the emperor. They told her that information had come to their attention that indicated she had been pre-contracted to Francis Dereham, a man who had since served in her household and who might very well have a legal claim to being her husband. The queen, still dressed as the first lady of the realm and sitting beneath her canopy of estate, brazened it out, denied everything, and refused to discuss the matter further.[29] The deputation left, but Cranmer, perhaps guessing that they were unlikely to get the truth from the queen if she was expected to divulge it in front of a room full of people, came back to see her several times over the next twenty-four hours.[30] Somehow, he got her to confess.

He was two years older than her husband, although with his trim build and a clean-shaven face he looked far younger. His warm brown eyes, with lines and crow's-feet only just beginning to show, watched her as she spoke, then with his long pale fingers, his signet ring on the first finger of his left hand, he wrote down what she divulged.[31] The archbishop was surrounded by a haze of ambiguity, perhaps appropriately so in a man christened with the name of a saint famous for his capacity to doubt. He seemed kinder than most of Henry's councillors, but he had a reputation for spinelessness, which had not prevented him, on several occasions, from behaving with great bravery. Cranmer was one of the great survivors of the Henrician court, *un homme de son temps* in his evolving religious views, possessing a conscience capable of acrobatic flexibility when confronted with the king's latest horror. He was one of the few courtiers courageous enough to try to defend Anne Boleyn when she was arrested. He had wept on the day of her execution and a few hours later signed the necessary paperwork permitting Henry's marriage to Jane Seymour. He had likewise befriended, defended, and reluctantly abandoned Thomas Cromwell. He had only become archbishop thanks to papal bulls authorising his elevation, which he had accepted with the intention of destroying the pope's authority in England.

A grammar school boy from Lincolnshire, Cranmer had been earmarked by his devout father for a life in the clergy, for which he gained his bachelor's and master's degrees at Jesus College, Cambridge, only to give it all up when he fell in love and married shortly after graduating. He returned to college and cloth when his wife and their baby died in childbed. Ordained a priest and with a doctorate in Divinity, Cranmer came to the attention first of Cardinal Wolsey, who sent him as part of a diplomatic delegation to Charles V in 1527, and then Anne Boleyn's father, the Earl of Ormond, who showed favour to the reform-sympathising doctor who argued so cogently for the king's right to divorce Katherine of Aragon. Boleyn patronage launched Cranmer faster and higher than he seems to have wanted and coincided with his own spiritual development towards Protestantism. He visited the German city of Nuremberg, where Lutheran clerics had already abandoned vows of chastity in favour of matrimony, and what he saw there persuaded him to take the great risk of marrying a young Lutheran lady, called Margaret, despite the fact that clerical marriages were still illegal in England. As with Catherine, a romantic indiscretion worthy of censure was magnified by a subsequent meteoric rise to prominence; in Cranmer's case, when he received news that his court backers had successfully nominated him to succeed William Warham as Archbishop of Canterbury, the highest-ranking cleric in England. He left Margaret in Germany and returned to be invested, crown Anne Boleyn, and stand as godfather to her daughter Elizabeth.

He had become Archbishop of Canterbury with a terrible secret hanging over him, but he did not abandon Margaret, and at great risk to himself and to her, he brought her to live with him in England, where they started a family, only for Margaret Cranmer and their children to be sent away to Germany for four years when the Six Articles, which Cranmer had spoken against in the House of Lords, intensified the penalties for married priests. With his own complex and potentially ruinous romantic past, Cranmer might have been expected to, and did, sympathise with Catherine, yet that did not stop him from doing his duty. Cranmer was at heart the kind of Cambridge don who smiled warmly and offered encouragement in his tutorials, but left savagely honest critiques on a student's written work. In his interactions with people, the archbishop more often than not was courteous, considerate, and gentle, but when it came to the pursuit of what he had decided was right, he was doggedly pragmatic.

His own account of his meetings with Queen Catherine describe how he began with the intention of stressing her misdemeanours to the point of exaggeration, in the hope that fear of the possible consequences might nudge Catherine into making a full and honest confession. As soon as he crossed the threshold of the queen's apartments, he realised that his pre-planned strategy would be both counterproductive and cruel. The poor woman was in the grips of dramatic mood swings, and when the pendulum swung to the point of total hysteria, as it did frequently,

Cranmer could not get any kind of coherent response from her. He tactfully left in the hope Catherine would calm down, but the queen's servants told him on his return that her paroxysms had continued unabated. 'At my repair unto the Queen's Grace, I found her in such lamentation and heaviness, as I never saw no creature, so that it would have pitied any man's heart in the world, to have looked upon her,' he wrote in his report for the king, 'and in that vehement rage she continued (as they informed me which be about her,) from my departure from her, unto my return again; and then I found her, as I do suppose, far interred towards a frenzy.'[32] A total shattering, the culmination of her 'dangerous ecstasy', was only narrowly avoided, in Cranmer's opinion, when a messenger arrived from the king, who had doubtless been informed of his wife's initial refusal to greet the accusation with anything but defiant scorn, promising her that if she would confess and tell the truth, then Henry would be merciful.

Catherine flung her hands in the air and 'gave most humble thanks unto Your Majesty' for showing her more kindness than she claimed she had any right to ask for. After that, Cranmer said her mood settled 'saving that she still sobbed and wept'. The respite gave way when the queen collapsed again 'into a new rage, much worse than she was before'. But as Cranmer soothed Catherine, he managed to tease out the truth that could ruin her. There is something gross about the archbishop's letter in which he described his cool and meticulous approach to breaking Catherine:

Now I do use her thus; when I do see her in any extreme braids, I do travail with her to know the cause, and then, as much as I can, I do labour to take away, or at least to mitigate the cause ... I told her, there was some new fantasy come into her head, which I desired her to open unto me; and after a certain time, when she had recovered her self, that she might speak, she cried and said, 'Alas, my Lord, that I am alive, the fear of death grieved me not so much before, as doth know the remembrance of the King's goodness, for when I remember how gracious and loving a Prince I had, I can not but sorrow; but this sudden mercy, and more than I could have looked for, showed unto me, so unworthy, at this time, maketh mine offences to appear before mine eyes much more heinous than they did before; and the more that I consider the greatness of his mercy, the more I do sorrow in my heart, that I should so misorder my self against His Majesty.'

Cranmer again worked on soothing her and, saving another upset at six o'clock when she remembered that this was the time when one of the king's gentlemen usually came to call on her with a message from her husband if they had not seen each other that day, he was able to put to her the information divulged by the others.

Catherine's first confession does not survive, but the second one, apparently confirming more or less what she had said previously to Cranmer, perhaps during one of his initial visits, does. This confession is cited far less frequently than her final heart-rending one, which is in large part responsible for the popularity of the theory over the last decade that she was a survivor of childhood abuse. Cranmer retained a vital sense of scepticism about those claims, and this earlier document, full of precise detail and seemingly frank admittance of hazy memories, shows why. The letter below was transcribed by the Bishop of Salisbury in the seventeenth century. It appears in his *The History of the Reformation of the Church of England*, first published in 1679, fifty-two years before the original was lost in the Cottonian fire. It is worth quoting in full, not simply as an object of historical curiosity, but also because so much of it contradicts Catherine's subsequent, less precise, and more frequently referenced version of events:

Being examined by my lord of Canterbury of contracts and communications of marriage between Dereham and me: I shall here answer faithfully and truly, as I shall make answer at the last day of judgement; and by the promise that I made in baptism, and the sacrament that I received upon Allhallows-day last past. First, I do say, that Dereham hath many times moved unto me the question of matrimony; whereunto, as far as I remember, I never granted him more than before I have confessed: and as for these words, *I promise you, I do love you with all my heart*, I do not remember that I ever spake them. But as concerning the other words, that I should promise him by my faith and troth, that I would never have other husband but him, I am sure I never spake them.

Examined what tokens and gifts I gave Dereham, and he to me: I gave him a band and sleeves for a shirt. And he gave me a heart's-ease of silk for a new-years-gift and old shirt of fine Holland or Cambric, that was my lord Thomas['s] shirt, and my lady did give it to him.[33] And more than this, to my remembrance, I never gave him, nor he to me, saving this summer ten pounds about the beginning of the progress.

Examined whether I did give him a small ring of gold upon this condition, that he should never give it away. To my knowledge I never gave him no such ring, but I am assured upon no such condition.

Examined whether the shirt, band, and sleeves were of my own work. They were not of my own work; but, as I remember, Clifton's wife of Lambeth wrought them.

And as for the bracelet of silkwork, I never gave him none; and if he have any of mine, he took it from me.

As for any ruby, I never gave him none to set in a ring, nor for other purpose. As for the French fennel, Dereham did not give it me, but he said there was a little woman in London with a crooked back, who was very cunning in making all manner of flowers. And I desired him to cause her to make a French fennel for me, and I would pay him again when I had money. And when I first came to court, I paid him as well for that, as for diverse other things, to the value of five or six pound. And truth it is, that I durst not wear the said French fennel, until I had desired my lady Breerton to say that she gave it to me.[34]

As for a small ring with a stone, I never lost none of his, nor he gave me none.

As for the velvet and satin for billyments, a cap of velvet with a feather, a quilted cap of sarcenet and money, he did not give me, but at my desire he laid out money for them to be paid again. For all which things I paid him, when I came into the court. And yet he bought not for me the quilted cap, but only the sarcenet to make it of. And I delivered the same to a little fellow in my lady's house, as I remember, his name was Rose, an embroiderer, to make it what work he thought best, and not appointing him to make it with Freer's knots, as he can testify, if be a true man. Nevertheless, when it was made, Dereham said, 'What wife here be Freer's knots for France.'

As for the indenture and obligation of an hundred pound, he left them in my custody, saying, that if he never came again, he gave them clearly unto me. And when I asked him whether he went, he said he would not tell me until his return.

Examined whether I called him husband, and he me wife. I do answer, that there was communication in the house that we two should marry together; and some of his enemies had envy there at, wherefore, he desired me to give him leave to call me wife, and that I would call him husband. And I said I was content. And so after that, commonly he called me wife, and many times I called him husband. And he used many times to kiss me, and so he did to many other commonly in the house. And, I suppose, that this be true, that at one time when he kissed me very often, some said that were present, they trowed that he would never have kissed me enough. Whereto he answered, 'Who should let him kiss his own wife?' Then said one of them, 'I trowe this matter will come to pass as the common saying is. What is that?' quoth he. 'Marry,' said the other, 'That Mr Dereham shall have Mrs Katherine Howard.' 'By St John,' said Dereham, 'you may guess twice, and guess worse.' But that I should wink upon, and say secretly, 'What and this should come to my lady's ear?' I suppose verily there was no such thing.

As for carnal knowledge, I confess as I did before, that diverse times he hath lain with me, sometime in his doublet and hose, and two or three times naked: but not so naked that he had nothing upon him, for he had always at least his doublet, and as I do think, his hose also, but I mean naked were his hose were put down. And diverse times he would bring wine, strawberries, apples, and other things to make good cheer, after my lady was gone to bed. But that he made any special banquet, that by appointment between him and me, he would tarry after the keys were delivered to my lady, that is utterly untrue. Nor I never did steal the keys my self, nor desired any person to steal them, to that intent and purpose to let in Dereham, but for many other causes the doors have been opened, sometime over night, and sometime early in the morning, as well at the request of me, as of other. And sometime Dereham hath come in early in the morning, and ordered him very lewdly, but never at my request, nor consent.

And that Wilkes and Baskerville should say, what shifts should we make, if my lady should come in suddenly. And I should answer, that he should go into the little gallery. I never said that if my lady came he should go into the gallery, but he hath said so himself, and so he hath done indeed.

As for the communication of my going to the court, I remember that he said to me, that if I were gone, he would not tarry long in the house. And I said again, that he might do as he list. And further communication of that matter, I remember not. But that I should say, it grieved me as much as it did him, or that he should never live to say thou hast swerved, or that the tears should trickle down by my cheeks, none of them be true. For all that knew me, and kept my company, knew how glad and desirous I was to come to the court.

As for the communication after his coming out of Ireland, is untrue. But as far as I remember, he then asked me, if I should be married to Mr Culpepper, for so he said he heard reported. Then I made answer, 'What should you trouble me therewith, for you know I will not have you; and if you heard such report, you heard more than I do know.'[35]

When he left her apartments after sunset, Cranmer asked Sir John Dudley to deliver a message to the king. On his return to the queen's rooms, Sir Edward Baynton told Cranmer that 'after my departure from her, she began to excuse, and to temper those things, which she had spoke unto me, and set her hand thereto'.[36] Catherine's new and thoroughly unbelievable version of events was that Francis Dereham had repeatedly raped her and that at no point in her time in the dowager's household had Catherine been a willing partner to either of her alleged lovers. Cranmer's incredulity seeps through the sign-off in his letter 'To the King's Majesty', where he promises 'at my coming unto Your Majesty, I shall more fully declare by mouth; for she saith, that all that

Dereham did unto her, was of his importune forcement, and, in a manner, violence, rather than of her free consent and will'.[37]

There had been honest mistakes in Catherine's previous letter – for instance, she seemed to forget when Francis had gone to Ireland – but the confession quoted below was nothing more than a tissue of lies told in trying and fearful circumstances. Catherine tried to downplay how long they had been a couple, in the process unknowingly or uncaringly contradicting eight or nine affidavits from other witnesses, all of whom had deliberately been kept separate from one another by the councillors sent to the question them. And either with callous pragmatism or, more likely, morbid terror, she threw Francis Dereham to the wolves while trying to save herself. Cranmer possibly helped her draft this letter too, as he had been tasked with assisting her, and it was dated Monday 7 November:

> I, your Grace's most sorrowful subject and most vile wretch in the world, not worthy to make any recommendation unto your most excellent Majesty, do only make my most humble submission and confession of my faults. And where no cause of mercy is given on my part, yet of your most accustomed mercy extended unto all other men undeserved, most humbly on my hands and knees do desire one particle thereof to be extended unto me, although of all other creatures I am most unworthy either to be called your wife or subject.
>
> My sorrow I can by no writing express, nevertheless I trust your most benign nature will have some respect unto my youth, my ignorance, my frailness, my humble confession of my faults, and plain declaration of the same, referring me wholly unto Your Grace's pity and mercy. First, at the flattering and fair persuasions of Manox, being but a young girl, I suffered him a sundry times to handle and touch the secret parts of my body which neither became me with honesty to permit, nor him to require. Also, Francis Dereham by many persuasions procured me to his vicious

purpose, and obtained first to lie upon my bed with his doublet and hose, and after within the bed, and finally he lay with me naked, and used me in such sort as a man doth his wife, many and sundry times, and our company ended almost a year before the King's Majesty was married to my Lady Anne of Cleves and continued not past one quarter of a year, or a little above.

Now the whole truth being declared unto Your Majesty, I most humbly beseech you to consider the subtle persuasions of young men and the ignorance and frailness of young women. I was so desirous to be taken unto your Grace's favour, and so blinded by with the desire of worldly glory that I could not, nor had grace to consider how great a fault it was to conceal my former faults from your Majesty, considering that I intended ever during my life to be faithful and true unto your Majesty ever after. Nevertheless, the sorrow of mine offences was ever before mine eyes, considering the infinite goodness of your Majesty toward me from time to time ever increasing and not diminishing. Now, I refer the judgment of my offences with my life and death wholly unto your most benign and merciful Grace, to be considered by no justice of your Majesty's laws but only by your infinite goodness, pity, compassion and mercy, without which I acknowledge myself worthy of the most extreme punishment.

Acting on tips that the queen's household was the cause of the unusual events of the past week, Charles de Marillac set spies to watch the palace, with instructions to pay special attention to Catherine's ladies-in-waiting. His watchers saw Cranmer leave Hampton Court on the Monday evening, a development they rightly reported as potentially significant, although they did not realise that Cranmer was carrying the queen's confessions to the king at Whitehall, along with his own assessment of her stories.[38] Three things stood out as jarring to the archbishop: the first the change in her interpretation of events, from a foolish romance to coercive exploitation. Secondly, that Francis Dereham had been appointed to Catherine's service in August, despite her alleged distaste for him. Thirdly, the queen's stunning blunder in one of the earlier confessions, when she recalled: '… he then asked me, if I should be married to Mr Culpepper, for so he said he heard reported. Then I made answer, "What should you trouble me therewith, for you know I will not have you; and if you heard such report, you heard more than I do know."'

Whether Catherine had simply honestly recalled a conversation with Dereham in late 1539 or early 1540, or tactically included it to throw Cranmer off the scent, is unknowable. As much as he pitied her, Cranmer believed the queen had lied to him at least once, and that made him suspect everything else she said. Why would she have mentioned Culpepper in relation to Dereham and the question of marriage unless there was something between them? Why would she appoint a man she claimed had repeatedly assaulted her to her household more than a year after she became queen? And how could she expect Cranmer to believe that all her initial memories of her time with Dereham, of flirtatious gifts and affectionate questions, had been untrue?

In the unnatural quiet of her apartments, Thomas was on Catherine's mind far more than Francis. For the time being, she still had her staff and she took every available opportunity to speak privately with Lady Rochford. She veered from confidence to fear over what would happen if the council found out about her nocturnal meetings with Culpepper. Lady Rochford loyally promised 'to be torn with wild horses' rather than betray her queen.[39]

Outside the palace, events moved quickly to a seeming conclusion that would see Catherine's marriage annulled on grounds of pre-contract. Robert Damport was brought in for questioning. As soon as he was taken from her house, the dowager had his chests smashed open as well to see if he had hidden anything about Francis's relationship with Catherine.[40] She gave her servant Ashby a white silk jacket that she found in Dereham's coffers as recompense for the money Ashby had once loaned him.[41] She sent her grandson Gruffydd, the Countess of Bridgewater's eldest boy, to fetch a book of statutes to see if she or any of her relatives could be held accountable for Catherine's premarital dalliances.[42] She fretted about her son William returning from his embassy in France without any prior knowledge of what he was walking into. Her servants had to talk her out of sending a warning to him, because, if caught, such a message would give the appearance that they had a secret to hide.[43]

By Tuesday Hampton Court was under close guard, as preparations were made within to send Catherine's ladies-in-waiting home or to the houses of nearby friends.[44] The queen was to be moved to Syon Abbey, a disused Bridgettine convent on the north bank of the Thames, where she was to be housed 'till the matter be further ordered'. While there, she was to be treated with 'the state of a Queen', but the council stipulated that her furniture was to be modest and her household cut dramatically. She was allowed to pick four gentlewomen and two chamberers, with the condition that one woman be her sister Lady Isabella Baynton, whose husband was sent to manage the queen's household-in-exile, as it were. They would depart on Monday, the 14th.[45]

The government prepared letters to send to its ambassadors in Europe. The officials who would be sent in to disband the queen's establishment were briefed on what to say, namely to condemn her morality but leave out any specifics in case it swayed future testimonies against her. Rumours, each with a unique tethering to reality, flew unchecked through the court. The queen was to be divorced. Physicians had discovered that she was barren. Anne of Cleves was to be restored. The queen had previously been married to another man. The queen had enjoyed eight or nine lovers before her marriage. In a letter sent on the 11th, its first half having been written three days earlier, de Marillac concluded, 'Nothing is certain except that these troubles are on her account.'[46]

Then, sometime between the orders being given to move Catherine from Hampton Court to Syon Abbey, and the dispatching of the official notifications to the English embassies abroad, the case shifted. That it was still an investigation into Catherine's unchaste adolescence as late as the evening of the 11th is suggested by the fact that it was then that the directive was given to move the queen, but by the evening of the 12th the council were hinting in their letters that 'an appearance of a greater abomination' was imminent.[47] In a letter to Paris, written on the 22nd, Charles de Marillac wrote that the change in the investigation had been initiated by an unexpected revelation from Francis Dereham, who, 'to show his innocence since the marriage, said that Culpepper had succeeded him in the Queen's affections'.[48] Thomas Culpepper had gone hawking on the 11th, seemingly and perhaps deliberately oblivious to the events unfolding around Catherine. He was summoned to his first interrogation two days later.[49] In a letter written on the evening of the 12th and sent to the clerk of the Privy Council, Sir William Paget, the council summed up their collective attitude to the queen: 'Now may you see what was done before the Marriage; God knoweth what hath been done sithence.'[50]

Chapter 20

A Greater Abomination

Thus spoke that inscription. He stood intent on the hidden
meanings of the cryptic words: meanwhile he heard the
wind continually moaning among the leaves and
undergrowth of the wood, and drawing from them a
sound that seems a plaintive harmony of human sobs
and sighs, and instils in his heart, I know what mingled
sense of pity, fear, and sorrow.

– Torquato Tasso,
Jerusalem Liberated (1581)

On Saturday, 12 November, Catherine was visited by Cranmer,
her uncle, Norfolk, the earls of Southampton, Sussex, and
Hertford, Lord Russell, and five other members of the Privy
Council, including Sir Anthony Browne, Sir Ralph Sadler, and Sir
Thomas Wriothesley.[1] The council asked the queen about three
nocturnal meetings she had allegedly had with Thomas Culpepper
during the royal progress, at which point Catherine abandoned
Lady Rochford with the same alacrity she had Francis Dereham.
She tossed all the blame onto her lady-in-waiting: 'The Queen
saith that my lady Rochford hath sundry times made instance to
her to speak with Culpepper declaring him to bear her good will
and favour, whereupon she did at the last grant he should speak
to her, my lady of Rochford affirming that he desired nothing else

but to speak with her and that she durst swear upon a book he meant nothing but honesty.'[2]

It is possible that this was how Culpepper's interest in Catherine first came to her attention – through the prattling of Lady Rochford – but she omitted the extent of her own attraction to him or their previous premarital entanglement. Catherine admitted to meeting with Culpepper privately and late at night in Lincoln, Pontefract, and York, and exchanging flirtatious gifts with him, including the velvet cap, a chain, and a cramp ring from her own finger. She also confirmed Lady Rochford's role in organising their meetings and repeatedly implied that she had been the initiating party by advising Catherine, 'Yet must you give men leave to look, for they will look upon you,' and refusing Catherine's request to chaperone them more efficiently during the late-night meetings, when the queen had apparently asked, 'For God's sake madam, even nearer us.' Catherine admitted that Lady Rochford had hunted out rooms or back stairs at every stop on the progress for the queen's meetings with Culpepper but failed to mention her own frequent insistence for news about when she and Culpepper could next meet. She remembered trivial things, like the gossip from Lady Rochford that Culpepper's colleague in the Privy Chamber, Thomas Paston, was also romantically interested in her, a memory which looks like a deliberate divulgence to cast the Culpepper relationship in an equally innocent light. Catherine claimed that she had tried to end the relationship when she told both Culpepper and Lady Rochford that she wished to hear no more about it, but Culpepper had refused and in response to his protests Catherine had called him 'little sweet fool'. Even though it was wholly at odds with her behaviour in the north, the latter claim could credibly refer to her temporary anger at Culpepper after his rudeness to her on Maundy Thursday. She also told the councillors that she had lived in fear since the investigations into her private life began at the start of November and that Lady Rochford advised her never to tell about their conversations with Culpepper. This version of events was repeated later by Lady Rochford, who did not cause too much of a surprise when she remembered it was the queen who advised silence and initiated most of the earlier meetings.

It is often assumed that at this juncture Catherine was simply responding to the details of the confession made by Dereham, and that faced with his singling out of Culpepper's name, she had no choice but to admit her involvement with him.[3] Yet Dereham could not possibly have known firsthand of the queen's meetings with Culpepper on the progress, since he did not join Catherine's household at Pontefract until 26 August. Nor could he have known of the gifts she had given Thomas. Equally, confusion over the dates of the interrogations of Lady Rochford and Thomas Culpepper have led to the assumption in some accounts that Catherine's confessions of 12 November were provoked by evidence of her transgressions being laid before her.[4] However, Lady Rochford was not questioned until 13 November, and Culpepper's rooms were not searched, nor was he arrested, until 14 November.[5] The missing link is the multiple testimonies of Katherine Tilney, who was questioned for the first time with regard to the queen's premarital liaisons on 5 November, then once the investigation had shifted focus to her alleged adultery on 13 November and again on 30 November.[6]

Katherine Tilney could not have been the direct source of the information the government set in front of the queen on the 12th, since she was questioned about it a day after, but she had almost certainly been the source for Dereham. Unlike him, Tilney had been present throughout the progress, and the records provide a tantalising glimpse of the two old acquaintances being sent on errands by the queen on the long journey from Pontefract.[7] Dereham had few other friends in Catherine's household, and he certainly did not make any with his eye-watering manners. It cannot be ruled out that he heard whispers about Culpepper from somebody else, but that scenario does not fully explain how, between 11 and 12 November, the council were able to confront Catherine with relatively accurate details of her recent encounters with Thomas Culpepper.

Two scenarios are possible. The first is that the narrative reported by de Marillac, which places the blame on Dereham attempting to exonerate himself from the charge of intending to resume sexual relations with the queen after her marriage, is correct but incomplete, as has been mentioned. Secondly, there is the possibility either that the chamberer Margaret Morton's testimony pre-dates Katherine Tilney's and Lady Rochford's on 13 November or that other depositions, now lost, were taken from other members of the household. One of those lost revelations, made either to Dereham or the council, presumably came from a retainer fairly close either to the queen or to Lady Rochford, or one who was eagle-eyed, who then divulged information about the queen's activities at Lincoln, Pontefract, and York. Katherine Tilney had been sent on numerous unusual errands by the queen during the progress, and she had felt disgruntled or confused enough to discuss it with Margaret Morton, which strongly suggests she may have done so with others, particularly someone she already knew, like Francis Dereham.

Katherine Tilney's first formal interrogation on 5 November had been conducted by Sir Thomas Wriothesley and focused exclusively on the queen's youthful romances.[8] A month later, after the first spate of executions, it was Wriothesley who, oddly, tried to save Tilney from ruin alongside the others with the unusual phrase in a letter to the council, 'My woman Tilney hath done us good service.'[9] The language used and their lack of previous connection make it clear that some sort of deal must have been made between Tilney and her first inquisitor. It is possible, on the most tenuous and speculative level, to discern something exploitative and possibly sexual in the phrase 'my woman', but that is neither the most obvious nor perhaps the most probable explanation.

Of everyone bar the principals, Katherine Tilney stood in the most appalling danger and, like Nicholas Udall and Thomas Cheney in March, without Wriothesley she faced more than an outside chance of ending her life on the scaffold. Tilney was the only one, apart from the queen, who could be said with a confidence approaching certainty to know all that had transpired before Catherine married the king. She had been at Chesworth House when the Manox fling took place. She had, at least once, been in the bed when Catherine and Francis slept together. She had heard the talk in the house of their betrothal. She had carried messages from the queen to Lady Rochford which she may not have fully understood but nonetheless had suspicions about. She had accompanied Catherine to her first post-marital rendezvous with Culpepper at Greenwich Palace on Maundy Thursday. She was the servant chosen to accompany Catherine on both her night-time visits to Lady Rochford's rooms at Lincoln. The queen's favour towards Tilney had been noticed by other chamberers, such as Mistresses Morton and Luffkyn.

If Wriothesley had worked his magic to rescue Udall and Cheney from hanging for sharing a bed with each other, he might be able to save Katherine Tilney for having been in the same one as Catherine Howard and Francis Dereham. For Wriothesley, who prided himself on getting results from his suspects, a plea bargain for Katherine Tilney, to use a modern term, was tactical good sense. She knew the most, and if they wanted her to tell them that information, which could be used to condemn her to death for misprision of treason, they would have to offer her something. We know from his behaviour during a later interrogation of a condemned female heretic that Wriothesley did use the strategy of offering help in return for information.[10] Tilney's role as a passive observer rather than an initiator in most of the key episodes of the case against the queen may have made it easier for Wriothesley to praise her 'good service' as the scandal drew to a close and make good on any promise to her.

It would be unfair to see Katherine Tilney as an unprincipled snitch. She may have been indiscreet in her conversations with Margaret Morton and Francis Dereham, and she certainly helped Wriothesley and his colleagues, yet it is difficult to see what else she could have done when she was first asked about the queen's behaviour in the north. Once questions about the progress were put to Tilney, to deny everything entirely could risk her being accused of complicity. To Tilney's credit, she seems to have avoided telling the councillors what they wanted to hear. When they were feverishly hunting evidence that the Dowager Duchess of Norfolk knew that Catherine's relationship with Francis had been consummated either at Chesworth or Lambeth, Tilney stuck to her belief that the dowager 'only knew that there was love between them'.[11]

Katherine Tilney's multiple interrogations signpost a split in the questioning after 12 November. The investigations into Queen Catherine can broadly be divided into three successive phases. The first, which took place from 2 November to late on 11 November, was an inquiry prompted by the revelations by Mary Hall via John Lascelles of the queen's alleged binding pre-contract to Francis Dereham, which could have made her legally ineligible to marry anyone else. The second, from 12 November to about 1 December, sought to establish if the queen had committed adultery, either with Francis Dereham or Thomas Culpepper. This was inaugurated by the confessions of Francis and then, within twenty-four hours, of the queen, whose testimony was then used to bounce Katherine Tilney into testifying, who quite probably completed the circle by having been the source of the information about Culpepper that was originally imparted to the Privy Council in self-preserving panic by Francis Dereham. The third thrust of the prosecution, which gathered momentum from 1 to 22 December, but had been discussed, debated, and investigated intermittently since early November, was to determine how much the Howards had known and if, as a result of that knowledge, they had conspired to commit treason by encouraging Catherine to hire Dereham, her former lover. It was during that phase of proceedings that so many of the witnesses from the first round were called back, often several times.

The second stage, the quest to discover what had happened with Culpepper, was settled by the questioning of Thomas and Lady Rochford. It is impossible to judge if Thomas Culpepper decided that only honesty could save him or if he was an almost-ingenious liar. Admittedly, he did not have much leeway for denial. Inspired by how often he had been mentioned by others in the last few days, the council had searched his rooms and discovered the letter the queen had sent to him when he was unwell. If it was foolish for Catherine to have written it, it was even more so for Culpepper to have kept it. At his interview on Sunday, the 13th, he told the aghast councillors about everything from the meeting at Greenwich on Maundy Thursday to the queen's pleas that he not divulge their relationship when he made confession.

Thomas's memory had the queen and Lady Rochford as equal partners in the affair, urging one another on, but he did not say this to paint himself as their pawn or dupe. He knew that meeting at night in a lavatory did not suggest the purest intent. He and the queen had not, he claimed, committed treason by sleeping together. According to Culpepper, 'he intended and meant to do ill with the Queen and that likewise the Queen was so minded with him'.[12] That claim, that they would have slept together at some point in the future, is the crux of deciding if Culpepper was confessing honestly or pursuing a strategy of a lie that sounded so shameful that his accusers might have assumed it must be the truth. Adultery with a queen or with a Princess of Wales was treason, because it endangered the succession. Culpepper had, physically, not yet endangered the royal bloodline. If he hoped that this claim would save him, he evidently did not have the sharpest legal mind. Misprision of treason pertained to the intention to commit the act, whether it be through withheld knowledge of another's traitorous desires or one's own harbouring of treasonous thoughts. In response to Culpepper's account, the Earl of Hertford replied, 'That is already too much.' Thomas was sent to the Tower and his goods and houses inventoried, a sign that the Tudor court usually took as a credible token of approaching death.[13]

Lady Rochford's testimonies had more in common with the queen's than with Culpepper's. Despite her vow, it took a lot less than wild horses for her to spill a confusing mixture of half-truths, unprovable improbabilities, and complete lies. Like Catherine, Lady Rochford asked too much of credulity in claiming ignorance and thus innocence of things that no human in her position could have missed. She may have been telling the truth when she said she had slept through most of Thomas's after-hours reunions with the queen, when she apparently 'heard or saw nothing of what passed', but that sat uneasily with her only significant deviation from the testimonies of Culpepper and the queen – 'She thinks Culpepper has known the Queen carnally.'[14]

Afterwards, Lady Rochford was also sent to the Tower and her goods were inventoried.[15] Her alternative tale – wisely prefixed with the caveat that it was only in her opinion that Catherine and Thomas had sexual intercourse at some point in the late summer or early autumn based on how she had seen them act towards one another – did not make much difference to the councillors, who remained sceptical about Catherine's claim that the farthest they had gone was a kiss on the hand, and Thomas's that they intended to consummate their relationship at a later date. As far as the councillors were concerned, Lady Rochford was not telling them anything they did not already know. For the historian, her suggestion is more interesting and complicating. She cannot be dismissed as a liar intent on stirring up trouble for the queen. Had she been thinking clearly and willing to fib her way out of it, Jane's surest bet lay in parroting the line that no physical intimacy had ever taken place. Of course, she may have been bounced into her statement through intimidation or intimations of mercy by the councillors. She may have told them of her own volition what she thought they wanted to hear. Or perhaps she told the truth.

Lady Rochford's veracity is undercut by her mental state. When she was sent to the Tower of London, where her husband and sister-in-law were buried close to the recently interred Lady Salisbury, Jane suffered a nervous breakdown. Three days into her incarceration, she was 'seized with a fit of madness by which her brain is affected'.[16] As it was illegal to execute the insane, Jane was moved out of her prison and into the care of the Lord Admiral's wife, Anne, Lady Russell, who took her to Russell

House, one of the fine mansions along the Strand.[17] Lady Russell's task as ward and nurse was the inverse of Hippocrates. Chapuys told the emperor that 'the King takes care that his own physicians visit her [Lady Rochford] daily, for he desires her recovery chiefly that he may afterwards have her executed as an example and warning to others'.[18] She was nursed and tended like a calf being fattened for the slaughter.

In the next phase of the interrogations, many previous witnesses were brought back for another round of questioning. The reason for the ghastly caprice with which the queen's downfall continued to play out lay in what Henry VIII and his councillors came to believe had happened. It was only in the first stage of the investigation and in the early days of the second that they were genuinely responding to information as it came to them. It has already been mentioned that Catherine's inconsistent *mea culpas* on the 6th and 7th convinced Cranmer and the council that she had been promiscuous before her marriage and unfaithful after it, and if she had not been, it was only because she had not yet found the opportunity. When Cranmer delivered Catherine's testimony of 12 November, in which she admitted meeting Culpepper in the dead of night and in secret, Henry VIII did not believe that the closest physical contact his wife had ever had with Thomas Culpepper was a kiss on the hand. One of Henry's principal private secretaries wrote on the king's behalf that the queen 'hath not, as appeareth by her confession, so fully declared the circumstances of such communications as were betwixt her and Culpepper; at their sundry meetings, as His Majesty would have'.[19]

For the council, the issue of whether or not the queen had slept with Culpepper was settled relatively quickly. The questions about their relationship were asked in the course of seventy-two hours and tidied away by 16 November, at the very latest. There was proof, and one confession, of intent, and that was enough to condemn them. For the government, the unanswered question was not what Catherine had done or hoped to do with Culpepper but rather what had gone on with Dereham. The king was certain, as indeed were many of his councillors, that the queen's decision to employ him, and her relatives' apparently friendly interest in him, torpedoed Catherine's improbable claims of rape and instead suggested a conspiracy to allow Francis back into her bed. This was why several witnesses who had no real way of knowing how Catherine had behaved after she left Lambeth were fetched following 13 November. By pursuing anyone linked to the case, the council hoped that 'many things may appear and come to light, which be not yet discovered'.[20] The king wanted proof of just how much the Howards, specifically the dowager duchess, Lord William, and the Countess of Bridgewater, 'knew of the former naughty life betwixt the Queen and Dereham', and therefore 'that his coming again to the Queen's service, was to an ill intent of the renovation of his former naughty life'.[21]

On 13 November, Alice Restwold and Mary Hall were summoned to appear before certain councillors at Whitehall 'upon pain of their lives'.[22] The servants were divided into pairs recorded in a neat list in Wriothesley's handwriting – the Duke of Norfolk and Sir John Gage, Comptroller of the Royal Household and Constable of the Tower of London, got Joan Acworth, whose wish to be summoned to London had not come true in quite the way she had hoped in 1540; Alice Restwold; the dowager duchess's elderly porter; two of her grooms; three of her chamberers; and Robert Damport. The Earl of Hertford and Sir Thomas Audley were sent in to deal with the queen's sister-in-law Anne Howard, wife of her brother Henry; Edward Waldegrave; and the queen's chamberers Margaret Morton and Katherine Tilney.[23]

The witnesses indicted friends, relatives, and themselves. One of the dowager's servants, Andrew Maunsay, remembered seeing Catherine in bed with Francis at Lambeth and told the councillors that Katherine Tilney could verify his story. The government had compartmentalised the respective testimonials so well that Maunsay had no way to know how unnecessary his revelation about Tilney was. He recalled the old laundry woman, Bess, who knew some of Catherine's secrets.[24] In front of the other panel, Tilney was imparting what she could recall of Lincoln and

Margaret Morton's backstairs snooping when the queen was gone for hours in Lady Rochford's bedroom.[25] Morton herself proved a gold mine. She remembered everything: the queen's out-of-character and foul-tempered rants against some of the chamberers towards the end of the progress, the adoring look she had given Culpepper when they were at the Hatfield Chase, the locked doors night after night at Pontefract. Despite Catherine's less than commendable tantrums in the north, Morton still refused to blame her and instead described Lady Rochford as 'the principal occasion of her folly'. Margaret Morton's evidence survives today, and at the very bottom of the transcript one can see a small, touching sign of how frightened she must have been. It was only on the third attempt that her handwriting is back to a normal size, unblemished and legible. She smudged her own signature twice.[26]

Other detainees, like Joan Bulmer, only corroborated what the government already knew. Lord William Howard's wife, Lady Margaret, relayed some suspicions and idle palace gossip. Alice Restwold's recollection of the queen's recent invitation to join her at Lord and Lady Russell's house, en route back from the north, and her generosity struck the council as yet another poor reflection on the queen's honesty about her earlier life. Initially, they did not seem to hold Restwold culpable for being the recipient of apparent blackmail.[27] They even sent a note to her husband Anthony's employers asking them to excuse him for a few more days, since he was chaperoning his wife while she was questioned.[28]

The chief victims of the councillors' attempts to squeeze the participants or witnesses for evidence of treason were Francis Dereham and the wholly innocent Robert Damport, both of whom were tortured. In Francis's case, on numerous occasions. In early December, the council ordered that 'both he [Damport], and Dereham shall be seriously examined again'. 'Seriously examined' was usually a euphemism for torture; admittedly, in this case, it was also used in instructions for 'the serious examination of the Duchess of Norfolk', who certainly was not tortured.[29] Unusually, the records of Dereham and Damport's imprisonment specifically mention torture on several occasions, and it is hard to believe that they were referring to psychological pressure. When Damport claimed to remember a comment that Dereham had made in 1540 about marrying Catherine if the king died, the council were suspicious since when they had originally asked him to confess about any conversations on that subject, Damport 'would not do it for any torture he could before be put to'.[30] Francis seems to have been subjected to sporadic bouts of torture from mid-November until the first week of December. At the earlier date, the king wrote to Archbishop Cranmer encouraging 'persevering in your diligence to attain knowledge of the truth, by all ways and means', and Henry personally authorised torture to be used on the two friends on 6 December.[31] How they were savaged is unknown. The rack seems the most likely, particularly in Dereham's case, but a story that was still doing the rounds in court circles a decade later had it that Robert Damport had his teeth pulled out one by one until he confessed his crime of knowing his friend had once slept with a girl who went on to become Queen of England.

Between 13 and 24 November, the Privy Council waged a war for control of the story. They could not afford to be delicate, even if some people in London thought it was unusual or inappropriate for the full details of the queen's behaviour to be publicised as they were.[32] The secrecy and inconsistencies in the case against Anne Boleyn had convinced even some of her bitterest enemies of her innocence. The same reaction had been generated by the downfall of the Pole family. In Catherine's case, the government was working with more information, which had the unfamiliar benefit of plausibility. They took full advantage of the opportunity 'to open and make manifest the King's Highness's just cause of indignation and displeasure, so as the world may know and see that which is hitherto done, to have a just ground and foundation'.[33] As Lord Chancellor, Sir Thomas Audley officially broke the news to all the king's other councillors and advisers, most of whom probably already knew that the source of the recent tension in the palace was 'the abominable demeanour of the Queen'. As per his instructions, Audley was careful not to mention specifics, especially Catherine's alleged pre-contract with Francis Dereham, 'which might serve for her defence' by giving anyone inclined to help Catherine a tip on the government's case against her.

The same policy was adopted when the queen's household were gathered into one room at Hampton Court and officially disbanded. The servants would be paid an advance of a quarter year's worth of wages and sent to the homes of family or friends. Mary Tudor was asked to reside with her brother's household temporarily. Sir John Dudley was to escort her there 'with a convenient number of the Queen's servants' who did not have anywhere to go. Lady Margaret Douglas, whose mother had recently died in Scotland, was to accompany Catherine's cousin, the Dowager Duchess of Richmond, to stay as a guest of the Duke of Norfolk in his mansion at Kenninghall.[34] After the official announcement was made, Lady Margaret was taken to one side by Archbishop Cranmer, who apparently had not yet been set free from his recent task of reprimanding royal ladies. Margaret's flirtation with the queen's brother Charles may have been winked at while Catherine was still in the ascendant, but with her gone and Charles banished, the king was displeased. The day before, Henry had ordered one of his secretaries to send instructions to the archbishop that:

His Majesty's pleasure is, also, that tomorrow, after this declaration made, ye shall call a part unto you my Lady Margaret Douglas; and first declare unto her, how indiscreetly she hath demeaned herself towards the King's Majesty, first with the Lord Thomas, and now secondly with Charles Howard; in which part ye shall, by discretion, charge her with overmuch lightness, and finally give her advice to beware the third time, and wholly apply herself to please the King's Majesty, and follow and obey that shall be His Highness's will and commandment; with such other exhortations and good advices, as, by your wisdom, ye can devise to that purpose.[35]

Governments abroad were next on Henry's list. By carefully controlling the information sent to foreign courts, the Privy Council hoped to prevent any contrary versions of events, especially any which might harm the king's reputation. The queen's uncle William, still due to return from his stint as ambassador in France, apparently remained in the dark about the situation as late as 15 November. His mother's anxiety about his ignorance was justified. No one had dared warn him and he was due home within the fortnight. On 12 November, he wrote home with news that the Duchess of Etampes was basking in political victory after she had secured the restoration to favour of one of her protégés, Admiral de Brion.[36] Three days later, William's correspondence to the Privy Council was taken up with musings on the Franco-Scottish alliance.[37] Four days after that, blissful ignorance was dispelled either during or shortly before his audience with King François, who had just received letters from England about Queen Catherine's 'wondrously lewd' behaviour. William Howard's colleague in France, Sir William Paget, ruefully reported that French courtiers who promoted closer ties with the emperor were having a field day laughing at Henry's expense.[38]

Explanatory letters were dispatched to England's other representatives abroad, who then in turn had to make a full report to foreign heads of state.[39] In London, Norfolk was sent to discuss the case with Charles de Marillac, who joked in his letters home that Culpepper had once shared the king's bed as one of the men of the privy chamber but 'apparently wished to share the Queen's too'. Before questioning some of those who had served his stepmother and niece, Norfolk had somehow got hold of the story that Catherine had enjoyed eight or nine lovers before her marriage. When he spoke to de Marillac again on Monday, the 14th, he confirmed that they only had proof that she had slept with Dereham before and Culpepper after. His eyes filled with tears as he told Marillac about the queen's activities at Lincoln.[40]

The Hapsburg embassy was accorded the courtesy of a visit by Lord Russell, who told the ambassador's secretary on Thursday, the 17th, that Dereham, Culpepper, and Lady Rochford had all been sent to the Tower, because Dereham had known the queen carnally before her marriage and Lady Rochford helped arrange meetings and 'many loving presents' between Thomas and Catherine over the last two months. A day later, the Earl of Southampton called on Chapuys personally to confirm what he had heard through his secretary. Southampton thought Catherine might make it out alive, though he told Chapuys that if she did it would be despite her uncle Norfolk, not because of him. Norfolk had worked himself up into a rage at a scandal that had blindsided him and threatened to weaken his position through a niece he was not even particularly close to. In his account to the emperor of Southampton's visit, Chapuys could not hide his disdain for the Duke's attitude: 'The duke of Norfolk has declared – God knows why – that he wishes the Queen to be burnt alive.'[41]

On Monday, the 14th, Catherine was escorted from the queen's apartments at Hampton Court. The rooms were stripped after she left, and Sir Thomas Seymour arrived to inventory Catherine's jewellery collection. She walked past the stone lions, yales, and unicorns towards the barge that bore her to Syon, once the wealthiest abbey in England, now a vast nothing. Its famous library had been gutted by Henry's antiquarians. Its masonry from the previous century bore little cracks, incipient proof of its neglect. Catherine walked through the same gatehouse the sisters had left by two years earlier when they became one of the few monastic communities to choose collective exile to the Hapsburg Empire rather than disbandment via the dissolution. Back at Hampton Court, Thomas Seymour made his list of the queen's jewels, relinquished to his temporary custody by Anne Herbert, who was now, like all the other women of the household, technically unemployed. Catherine left her sable muff on its ruby-and-gold chain, pearls counted in their hundreds, diamonds dotting

scenes from the life of Noah, golden girdles, bejewelled crucifixes, all their sister pieces, the glittering detritus of a failed life,
and walked into three sparsely furnished rooms in an abandoned
monastery. On the council's orders, there was no cloth of estate
over her chair, and she was not allowed access to her wardrobe.
Six dresses had been provided for her, in silk, damask, and velvet,
with six French hoods trimmed with gold thread and 'such things'
as usually went with a lady's wardrobe. But, again by specific
instruction, none of them were to be augmented by pearls or
precious stones. The king's secretary had helpfully sent a book on
etiquette to guide Sir Edward Baynton and the remaining servants in how they should serve her.

Catherine thought she would be left alone at Syon, but the
anaesthetic of life in the Middlesex convent was denied her when
the councillors came to confront her with the constant drip of
information provided by her servants. As with Lady Rochford,
but to a lesser extent, the steady thump of harassment caused a
collapse. De Marillac heard that 'she thought that after her free
confession they would not enquire further; but, finding the
contrary, refuses to drink or eat and weeps and cries like a
madwoman, so that they must take away things by which she
might hasten her death'.[42] On 22 November, a proclamation was
issued from Hampton Court that stripped Catherine of her royal
title on the grounds that 'she had forfeited her honour, and should
be proceeded against by law, and was henceforth to be named no
longer Queen, but only' as Catherine Howard.[43]

The final scene now looked as if it could have no venue bar the
scaffold. Catherine's confessions had not convinced. The government would press ahead with a charge of adultery, either in deed
or intent, with Thomas Culpepper and, if they could find the
proof they were searching for, with Francis Dereham as well.
Catherine's reputation had been torn asunder by courtiers. Her
uncle Norfolk, who described her in one conversation as little
better than a prostitute, led the charge. She was also betrayed
closer to home by her brother-in-law and her sister Isabella. The
Bayntons were with Catherine at Syon throughout that odd

winter. Sir Edward, who ate with the other servants in one of Catherine's three rooms, had been sent with the instruction that 'the King's pleasure' was that Baynton 'should attend upon the Queen, to have the rule and government of the house'.[44]

Isabella had been questioned earlier in the month. As the queen's half sister and a lady of the privy chamber, she was naturally under suspicion. She was saved by the favour Catherine had shown to Lady Rochford over the previous months. De Marillac reported to Paris that 'the Queen's sister is released as innocent', though he overstated the reasons for her acquittal and assumed Isabella had actually been dismissed from Catherine's service for Lady Rochford, when they had remained colleagues throughout.[45] It was not compassion that prompted Henry to send the Bayntons to Syon with Catherine. Sir Edward's willingness to assist the council in their investigations of Queen Anne Boleyn in 1536 and his antipathy towards the household he served made him a reliable gaoler and a trustworthy informant. Baynton was the one who told Cranmer how Catherine behaved when the archbishop left her rooms in the first few days of her disgrace. In the same month as she was questioned and released, Isabella received from the king the grant of a small parcel of land in Wiltshire, which, rather than being the usual lifetime bequest, was to pass 'to the heirs of the body of the said Isabella'.[46] Henry's men did not doubt Isabella Baynton's innocence, but that he gifted Isabella with land in the same month as her half sister was incarcerated and their brother Charles was banished from court leads to a conclusion that she had done far more than clear herself of complicity. Edward Baynton's appointment to Syon and the grant to Isabella suggest that they sent the Privy Council reports on Catherine's behaviour.

The information coming out of Syon painted a bleak picture: Catherine's appetite had vanished, her moods were volatile, and she was often hysterical. When he was quizzed later about his involvement with Catherine, Thomas Culpepper reported, with far more literal accuracy than he intended, that Catherine 'pined for him, and was actually dying of love for his person'.[47] By the end of November, when the arrangements for his trial were under way, it did not look as if she would be the first or the only victim of their infatuation.

Chapter 21

The King Has Changed His Love into Hatred

Why should the private pleasure of some one
Become the public plague of many more?

– William Shakespeare,
The Rape of Lucrece (1594)

Culpepper and Dereham were escorted into the Great Hall at the Guildhall, centre of London's civic government, on Thursday 1 December by Sir John Gage, Constable of the Tower, where they had spent the last few weeks. As Lord Mayor of London, Michael Dormer presided over the trial, in conjunction with, amongst others, Lord Chancellor Audley; Lord Russell; the earls of Southampton, Hertford and Sussex; the Duke of Suffolk and the Duke of Norfolk. Knights from the counties where the queen's crimes were allegedly committed had been summoned as petty juries. Also present was John Sackville, sheriff in Lambeth, where Catherine and Dereham's affair had taken place years earlier, as was a jury from Kent, Culpepper's native county and the location of Greenwich Palace, where his first inappropriate meeting with the queen had taken place back in April. In a show of solidarity, every privy councillor attended, including the queen's cousin, Lord Surrey.

Both men pleaded not guilty. The queen's deposition, which claimed a coerced sexual relationship with Dereham but none with Culpepper, was read aloud to the court. The details gleaned from the interrogations about her premarital romance with Dereham and summer interactions with Culpepper were also relayed. The allegation that Dereham had intended to resume his affair with the queen after he joined her household at Pontefract was lent unfortunate credence by a joke Catherine had made about Culpepper to Lady Rochford during the progress, when she had apparently said that if Culpepper did not visit her that night, she could find another man behind a door who, in de Marillac's early modern French, was '*ung aultre qui ne demandoit pas meilleur party*', which could translate either as another who would cause less hassle or someone who represented a 'making the best of things' choice. The queen had made similar jibes when she teased Culpepper that she had a store of lovers waiting to replace him in York. In the hands of a skilled prosecutor, those words could be twisted and magnified as an allusion to Francis Dereham, who denied any aspirations to treasonable adultery, despite the torture he had endured, and admitted only to sleeping with Catherine in the dowager duchess's establishment in the belief that he and Catherine were betrothed.

Next to him, Culpepper claimed that although the queen had 'pined for him', encouraged to do so by an interfering Lady Rochford, they had never gone to bed together. Nonetheless, his admission before the council two weeks earlier that he had 'intended and meant to do ill' was enough to damn him. The charges against Thomas were made capital from the ambiguity of his testimony. They focused on the fact that although he had not passed beyond words with the queen, he had confessed his intention to do so, and that even if he had never consummated his relationship with her, such conversations between a subject and a queen 'deserved death'. The specifications of where they had met to plan their adultery were kept vague. The indictments did not state that adultery had taken place, but played a safer game in focusing on Culpepper's admission of intent. Queen Catherine had, 'on the 29 Aug. 33 Henry VIII., at Pomfret, and at other times and places before and after, with Thos. Culpepper, late of

London, one of the gentlemen of the king's privy chamber, falsely and traitorously held illicit meeting and conference to incite the said Culpepper to have carnal intercourse with her; and insinuated to him that she loved him above the king and all others. Similarly the said Culpepper incited the Queen.'[1] Thomas's prosecutors did not have much truck with the idea that there had been an instigator and a passive recipient in the relationship.

After the jury retired, they returned a verdict that 'sufficient and probable evidence' had been produced to justify the death sentence. With that, each prisoner chose to follow the well-established script of submission. One could not say the law, the foundation of order, was unjust and so Dereham and Culpepper changed their pleas to acknowledge that they had been found guilty. Full prostration before the Crown was their only chance at salvation once a jury had reached that decision. Since neither of them was an aristocrat, there was no legal precedent for any other kind of traitor's death sentence than hanging, drawing, and quartering, which is what they received. Even his friends could not conceal their disapproval at the sight of Norfolk laughing as the sentence was handed down.[2]

What had they really been condemned to die for? Dereham and Culpepper were trapped not by what they had done but what they had planned to do. Their actions – in Culpepper's case the covert meetings and in Dereham's, joining Catherine's household – were taken, not unreasonably, as proof that they both had the goal of seducing the king's wife. Dereham was also guilty of withholding knowledge of Catherine's treasonous conduct, because he had not alerted the government to their pre-contract and her unsuitability to be queen at the time of her marriage. The documents about Dereham's last two weeks alive are frustratingly imprecise. De Marillac, who, like all the other major embassies in London, had accepted the Privy Council's invitation to send witnesses to the Guildhall trial, only confirms that Dereham confessed after the jury had found him guilty. Yet it seems unlikely that he confessed, as Culpepper did, to a plan to become the queen's lover. Although de Marillac does not specify,

Dereham's submission at the end of the six-hour trial probably related to his failure to alert the Privy Council to Catherine's lack of virginity. This left Dereham in a legal grey area. It was, after all, also illegal to slander the queen consort. Which law should he have broken? The situation was further complicated by Catherine's insistence that any talk of marriage between them had been a joke. Francis's death sentence could only be fully justified if it was proven beyond reasonable doubt that he had hoped for something unambiguously treasonous because of his feelings for Catherine – either that the king would die or that Catherine would consent to an adulterous relationship. The king harboured no doubts that Francis had entertained one or both of those thoughts, despite the fact that no amount of torture could bring Francis to admit to either.

With his own trial fast approaching, Robert Damport buckled and asked to see some of the Privy Council. They visited him in his cell in the Tower, as Catherine's three brothers rode through the streets of London with Lord Surrey and Thomas Culpepper's brother to advertise that they were free men, untainted by suspicion of their kinsman's treason, an absolution on horseback.[3] Damport told his visitors that when the king's affair with Catherine first began, Dereham fell into despair during which he reflected hopefully that if the king died, he might be able to resume his relationship with Catherine. The exact words he reported were: 'I could be sure to Mistress Catherine, and I would; but I dare not. The King beginneth to love her; but, and he were dead, I am sure I might marry her.'[4] The councillors were sceptical, considering that both Damport and Dereham had been pressed for such information before and denied it. Damport also made this revelation on 6 December, five days after Francis was condemned to death, quite possibly after the verdict against his friend sufficiently frightened him into telling a lie. If Francis was going to perish anyway, perhaps by perjuring himself Damport might live. His story was, almost certainly, a fabrication. He had not admitted it while he was tortured the first time, Francis denied it up to the very end, and even the councillors, who had wanted this testimony earlier, seemed surprised at Damport's revelation after Dereham had already been condemned. There is also the fact that the chronology of Francis's visit to Ireland does not quite fit with Damport's claim. According to Damport, Dereham was distraught because the king began 'to love' Catherine, which would place the conversation in the spring or early summer of 1540. Every other piece of evidence relating to Francis's decision to leave London suggests that their last quarrel had been over Thomas Culpepper.[5]

The circumstances of Damport's revelation and the tenacity with which Dereham, who had admitted his earlier romps with Catherine, stuck to his denial even when the king, inspired by Damport's claim, ordered both men to be subjected to another round of torture, also suggests that Damport's final, desperate revelation was a fabrication.[6] Even as Francis's family ransacked their resources for an offering to the government that might have their son acquitted or his sentence at least commuted to beheading, and he was reduced to begging for the latter, he would not budge from his claims that he had never hoped for or planned the king's death, nor had he planned to commit adultery with the queen. De Marillac expected Dereham and Culpepper to be executed on the Saturday two days after their trial. Instead, some of Francis Dereham's last few days alive were spent at the mercy of torturers and another round of questions.

The information, or lack of, provided by the torture sessions was sent to Henry by his nervous councillors, who had persuaded him to decamp to the countryside until the affair was resolved, with only musicians, one or two advisers, and privy chamber gentlemen for company. De Marillac heard that 'this King has changed his love for the Queen into hatred', and the councillors bore the brunt of his mood swings as he grappled with the realisation that his wife had preferred another man to him. There was no repetition of the nighttime river banquets that had occurred when Anne Boleyn was imprisoned in 1536 or the cheery plays Henry had penned about it and shown to a discomfited Bishop of Carlisle. In 1541, he was absolutely certain that Catherine had deceived him, and his grief was so severe that at one point his entourage feared for his sanity. He lurched from his seat at the council table with a sudden call for horses without any indication of where he was planning to go. He cried for a sword so that he could kill 'that wicked woman' himself and vowed that he would have her tortured to death to ensure she felt as much pain in her demise as she had delight in her lust. There were echoes of the Lenten rants about Cromwell as he blamed his councillors for their poor service and less threatening yet still uncomfortable scenes during which the king wept in front of his servants.[7]

Despite this erratic behaviour, Henry remained in control of the case against his wife and her family, even from his rural retreats. His guiding hand can be seen throughout the paperwork, where phrases such as 'This is His Majesty's opinion ...' and instructions to wait 'till the King's pleasure should be further known' proliferate, along with his orders of whom to arrest, whom to pardon, why and when; his citation of previous legal cases to convince the judges that treason had taken place; his sanctioning of the use of torture on Robert Damport and Francis Dereham; his interest in sending his own physicians to nurse Lady Rochford back to health to secure her execution; and his direct involvement in arranging the seizure of Howard goods and the relocation of the clan's dependants.[8] His grief did not touch everyone. The King of France sent several letters which were, on the surface, comforting but on closer reflection seem masterfully patronising. François's platitude that 'the lightness of women cannot bind the honour of men' reads like a reassurance designed to accentuate what it claimed to dispel.[9] Eustace Chapuys, who had seen too many of Henry's matrimonial misdemeanours, was even less sympathetic. In a letter to the young Bishop of Arras, one of Maria of Austria's councillors, Chapuys gave his unvarnished assessment of Henry's mood that December:

> The king has wonderfully felt the case of the Queen, his wife, and that he has shown greater sorrow and regret at her loss than at the faults, loss, or divorce of his preceding wives. In

fact, I should say that this king's case resembles very much that of the woman who cried more bitterly at the loss of her tenth husband than she had cried at the death of the other nine put together, though all of them had been equally worthy people and good husbands to her: the reason being that she had never buried one of them without being sure of the next, but that after the tenth husband she had no other one in view, hence her sorrow and her lamentations. Such is the case with the King, who, however, up to this day does not seem to have any plan or female friend to fall back upon.[10]

Two days after Chapuys wrote this, an unstable Catherine received a delegation at Syon who wanted to know more specifically why she had allowed Francis back into her service.[11] Considering that Francis was already condemned to death, the queries sought evidence to incriminate her family as the case against them gathered momentum, as per the king's instructions. The ex-queen was part of a group who found themselves unexpectedly pestered in their prison cells or homes. Joan Bulmer and Alice Restwold were brought back, the former to answer questions mostly pertaining to the dowager duchess's knowledge of the affair and the latter pressed on what Lord William, who had helped find her a job after she left Norfolk House, knew or suspected. The two women endured three days of interrogation, spread out over a nine-day period.[12] Edward Waldegrave trawled his memory to provide answers about Dereham's intentions towards Catherine and actions after she became queen.[13] The dowager duchess's maids were asked if they had witnessed her incinerating any of Dereham's papers, a charge which the dowager consistently denied, heightening the king's suspicions since he could not understand why the duchess had Francis's coffers broken into unless it was 'to conceal letters of treason'.[14] Katherine Tilney and her former colleagues William Ashby and Andrew Maunsay were also quizzed about the dowager, who had taken to her bed in Norfolk House with the claim that she was too ill to receive visitors, much less be moved for questioning.[15]

By this point, two new faces had joined the regular roll call of inquisitors – Richard Rich, the middle-aged chancellor of the Court of Augmentations, a man unencumbered by any discernible principles and never too far away from charges of corruption, and the king's solicitor general, Henry Bradshaw. Rich, Bradshaw, and the councillors had heard enough examples of the dowager's titanic idiocy, including jokes she had allegedly made about Dereham fleeing to Ireland 'for the Queen's sake' in front of the queen's servants, to see her as easy prey, an impression apparently confirmed when they arrived at Norfolk House 'as if only to visit and comfort her' and found that the dowager was nowhere near as ill as she had pretended – until they told her that the Lord Chancellor wanted to question her and she immediately began to complain of pains in her chest. Honeyed lies persuaded Agnes to have her barge prepared to call on Lord Chancellor Audley, and the men left her for Sir Thomas Wriothesley's house, also in Lambeth, where they waited by a window until they saw the duchess sail by. They immediately sent men over to Norfolk House to shutter it and make arrangements for the disbanding of the household on the assumption that Agnes would never return.[16]

At the Lord Chancellor's, the dowager showed a magnificent gravitas. There was no sign here of the twittering gossip making ill-advised bons mots in front of servants. Instead, the councillors wrote to the king's secretary with an apologetic request that 'you signify unto the King's Majesty, that, according to our last advertisement, we travailed all yesterday in the examination of my Lady of Norfolk; who made herself so clear from all knowledge of the abomination between the Queen and Dereham, that she would confess no mistrust or suspicion of their love, or unseemly familiarity'. They gave 'her scope and liberty, without interruption, to say what she would', but she took that opportunity to deny everything. Only a day before, the council had wrung three or four sheets of affidavits from her gentleman, William Ashby, and received a set of questions to put to her, annotated by the king himself, none of which seemed to perturb the duchess.[17] No, she had never suspected anything improper between her granddaughter and Francis Dereham. She had only opened the latter's coffers in November to provide her stepson the duke with evidence to help the Privy Council's inquiries. Her desire to send a word of warning to her son William in France had not been to obfuscate, but rather to alert him of an unhappy turn of events. She had never made jokes about Francis Dereham's sojourn in Ireland, and she had no idea why he had gone there in the first place. She had never been overly generous to Francis; rather, she was munificent with all her servants, despite the fact that her wealth had in fact been exaggerated. No, she had never sent her grandson to fetch legal advice about possible loopholes that would free them all from suspicion of treason.[18] Agnes's performance was one part poor widow to one part great lady; it, and 'her extreme denial', riled and reluctantly impressed her opponents, who described her as 'old and testy' and immovable, regardless of the small mountain of contrary evidence they could put in front of her.[19]

Similar admiration was not generated by Lord William Howard, who, like his predecessor, Sir John Wallop, had been lured back to London with everyone who met him under specific instructions not to inform him that he was under suspicion. William mirrored his mother in denying any knowledge of his niece's romance with Francis. What made his story credible was not the fact that it was the truth, more that there was just enough truth in it to raise doubts in the councillors' minds. It was plausible for an uncle, even one in the same household, to have missed how far his niece's love affair had progressed. He had confronted Henry Manox for his anonymous note to the dowager. Could that not have been the result of anger at Manox stirring up trouble on what Lord William presumed then to be a false premise? They had evidence from Alice Restwold and other servants that the dowager had worried about her son finding out, which indicated either that he did not know or she did not know that he knew. The council had leapt down the rabbit hole with the Howard investigation by trying to give precise, ascertainable meanings to half-remembered conversations, truths, lies, differing interpretations, and genuine mistakes, when in fact any number of conclusions were possible. Lord William's 'stiff manner' irked Wriothesley, who perhaps expected the same kind of fear and contrition shown by William's wife, Margaret, who tottered on the verge of full collapse. The councillors began to pity the 'simple woman' as she endured a horrible epiphany, that the gossip she remembered from her visits to Norfolk House had come to constitute treason.[20]

Her sister-in-law did not buckle. Instead, at her interrogation at Westminster on the Feast of the Immaculate Conception, the Countess of Bridgewater gave the impression of a woman who, staring down the barrel of a loaded gun, shrugged. Ten men sat opposite her – the Archbishop of Canterbury, Lord Chancellor Audley, the Duke of Suffolk, the Earl of Southampton, into whose custody she had been placed until they had enough evidence to send her to the Tower, the earls of Hertford and Sussex, the Constable of the Tower, Wriothesley, and Rich. Bishop Gardiner was also there.[21] Norfolk was not. The woman who had once incited large parts of southern Wales into quasi-rebellion to protect her family was unfazed by the censorious line-up on the other side of the table. The councillors had recently taken her maid, Mistress Philip, and one of William's gentlemen to arm them with more information, which they fired at the countess in the form of twenty-six questions about Catherine's upbringing.[22] Had the countess ever heard talk of late-night romps or picnics in the maidens' chamber? Had she ever seen anything in Catherine's attitude to Dereham that might have indicated a romance? Had she ever rebuked Catherine or given her advice about her behaviour at Chesworth House or Norfolk House? Had she ever witnessed something that she had considered wanton between the young couple? They wanted her to admit to the role she had played in persuading Catherine to take Dereham into her service, that she had known about a pre-contract between them and taken steps to cover it up since the queen's wedding, that she had aided her mother's surreptitious attempts to seek legal advice, and that she had known of, or helped, with the smashing of the controversial caskets at Norfolk House. With every answer, 'she sheweth herself to be her mother's daughter; that is, one that will by no means confess anything that may touch her'.[23]

The reports went to Oatlands, where the king had retreated to end his marriage in the same place it had been solemnised. On the same day as the countess's interrogation, the king's team at Oatlands wrote to the councillors in London. Lord Russell, Sir Anthony Browne, Sir Ralph Sadler, and Sir Anthony Wingfield had spoken to the king about the council's assessments of the dowager duchess, her two children, and her daughter-in-law, and their conclusion that even further torture would bring no new revelations from Dereham:

> Touching Culpepper and Dereham, if your Lordships do think that ye have gotten as much of Dereham as would be had, that then ye shall (giving them convenient respite and warning of the time, that they may prepare themselves to God for the salvation of their souls,) proceed to their execution, in such sort as hath been signified unto you before, accordingly.
>
> Thus the Holy Trinity preserve Your good Lordships in long life and good health.
>
> At Oatland, this present Feast of the Conception of Our Lady. By your Lordship's loving friends ...

The next day, fourteen people were shipped to the Tower because 'misprision of treason is proved against' them. The gates opened through the murky, freezing river water for the Dowager Duchess of Norfolk; the Countess of Bridgewater; Lord William Howard and his wife, Katherine Tilney; Alice Restwold; Joan Bulmer; William Ashby; the ex-queen's sister-in-law Anne Howard; the dowager's former maid Margaret Benet; Agnes's sister-in-law Lady Malyn Tilney; Edward Waldegrave; and even the original informant, Mary Hall. A broken Robert Damport was, of course, already incarcerated. Every single one was expected to have their worldly goods and possessions confiscated as a prelude to 'their bodies [sentenced] to perpetual prison'.[24] The Countess of Bridgewater's children were taken from their grandmother and from one another to be committed to separate wardship – her daughter, Anne, was sent to the Countess of Oxford's household;[25] the elder boy, Gruffydd, was passed to Archbishop Cranmer's household; and his younger brother, Thomas, went north to the Bishop of Carlisle's.[26] Faced with the confiscation of his goods, William claimed that his best plate and silver had been washed overboard on his return voyage from France. His mother's claims that her wealth had been magnified by rumour had already been dented by the discovery of £800 in silver hidden in Norfolk House, and the old lady's panic at the thought she would be put in a dungeon when she reached the Tower. A prisoner had to pay for their own upkeep, which prompted the frightened revelation from the dowager that she had at least a further £1,000 than she had admitted to. There had been storms in the Channel that prompted sailors on one boat to kill Lord William's poor horses and toss their bodies into the swell in a desperate attempt to keep the ship afloat, yet in light of his mother's brazen mendacity, the king and the Privy Council suspected that William was trying to swindle Henry out of what would soon be rightfully his – 'Word was brought unto the King's Majesty,' wrote the Privy Council, 'that all of Lord William's stuff, plate, and apparel, which he had with him in France, should now be perished and lost on the sea; which, whether it be matter of truth or (the cast standing as it doth) devised by some crafty means to embezzle the same' would be resolved by their inquiries.[27] Captains were sent to search every castle and house William had stayed at on his way back from France to see if he had hidden the treasure there. It was never found.

One person immune to grief, horror, revulsion, and pity that winter was Anne of Cleves. Three days after Catherine was shipped off to Syon, Anne set up residence at Richmond Palace. Richmond had been the greatest prize tossed at her during the annulment bonanza of the previous year, and it was also the house closest to the Hampton Court Chase, where the king was moving from house to house in wounded, prickly sorrow. Although it was one of the seven great English royal palaces, by the time Richmond was signed over to Anne of Cleves it was infrequently visited by the court. It had been built on the orders of Henry VIII's father in the first decade of the century as one of the finest examples of Renaissance architecture in northern Europe.[28] Its many towers and three storeys overlooked the Thames, and galleries intersected its orchards and gardens, stuffed full of carved and gilded heraldic beasts. A fountain splashed in its stone-and-marble inner courtyard; gold or stone crests dotted its glass-windowed corridors. It had fallen out of favour not because it lacked splendour or luxury, more because its style seemed hopelessly outdated by the 1530s. The layout of the rooms still reflected the decade of its construction, when there had been a large royal family with king, queen, and titled, unambiguously legitimate children. In Richmond's chapel, the closets for a king, a queen, and their progeny stood empty.[29] If their emptiness stung Anne, she did not always hide it well. In the last decades of the twentieth century, a myth grew up about Anne that became as convincing, in its own way, as the old canard of her as the repellent 'Flanders Mare'. Anne of Cleves has been presented as the great survivor in a world organised to kill, the one who got away, the lady who had the last laugh in a story that saw a 'narcissistic buffoon foiled by a woman with common sense'.[30] Unfortunately, this inspirational Anne is the product of projection rather than reality. Incredible as it might seem to us, especially in the light of what was happening to Catherine and the harsh crudities that had been used against Anne herself a year earlier, the ex-queen or, to be legally precise, the queen-who-never-was was poised and eager for Henry to take her back.[31]

London buzzed with speculation that Cleves would be restored, and one woman was even imprisoned when a conversation was reported in which she had suggested Queen Catherine's adultery was God's punishment on the king for divorcing the virtuous Anne.[32] Eustace Chapuys was somewhere between distressed and irate at the rumours, and his mood was hardly helped by de Marillac's public taunt that 'the young duke of Cleves would soon be one of the most highly connected princes in the world'. The emperor was emphatic on what Chapuys's response should be on the subject of Anne: 'You must watch the affair, since you know how injurious it would be for Us were the King to effect a reconciliation with her. If it be so, you must try all means in your power to dissuade the King from it, and, if possible, prevent him from taking her back.'[33] Chapuys's informants managed to get him some of de Marillac's correspondence and codes to his ciphers. From what he knew of Henry's personality, Chapuys did not think he could ever reunite with someone he had discarded, but nonetheless he agreed with the emperor that 'means ought to be found to prevent it'.[34] Those means, whether intentionally planted by the imperial embassy or simply the product of idle unfounded gossip, soon broke in London with a story that Anne had recently given birth to a bastard child.[35] A housewife called Frances Lilgrave was imprisoned for suggesting that the father was the king, and officers from Anne's household were summoned to court to answer the Privy Council's questions on the matter after the king was told of the rumours on the Feast of the Immaculate Conception.[36]

Chapuys, who forgot it was poor form to continue punching after the fight was won, characterised Anne as a plump, garish, over-the-hill alcoholic in his conversations with Henry's courtiers, in which he turned Anne's post-marital rejuvenation of herself on its head by arguing that because of 'her being fond of wine, and of indulging in other excesses, as they might have had occasion to observe, it was natural enough to suppose that she had failed' as a suitable candidate for queenship.[37] De Marillac had initially written to King François for instructions on whether or not to promote Anne's candidacy in light of Catherine's ruin, but on the day that Catherine was stripped of her title he penned a letter advising the French government that, in his opinion, Anne's fortunes were unlikely to change.[38]

None of this perturbed the resilience of the Clevian embassy, who wrote on Anne's behalf to courtiers whom they erroneously believed to be sympathetic to her cause, including the Earl of Southampton and Archbishop Cranmer, and then to the entire Privy Council.[39] Their persistence reached a point where Cranmer had to cut them off mid-conversation with a protestation that he could not discuss something so intimate without the king's permission. Even with that, the matter was not laid to rest until February, when the king, after pointedly refusing to allow his barge to sail anywhere near Richmond Palace, sent a curt note to Anne asking her to send back the ring from the royal collection that she had received as a Twelfth Night gift from Catherine in 1541.[40] A year later, Anne was distraught when Henry married another woman who was not only older than her but also, as she bitterly insisted to her servants, far less attractive.[41]

The council was dispelling the rumours about Anne's love child at the same time as they reached the decision that Francis Dereham was beyond the point of usefulness following the latest bout of torture. In accordance with the king's wishes, both men could now be executed. The king had rejected Dereham's plea that his sentence be commuted to beheading, a mercy which, inexplicably, he had granted to Culpepper who was 'only to lose his head'.[42] Thomas's death warrant survives in the National Archives at Kew, a short and perfunctory piece of parchment that stipulated that in light of how heinous the offence, the men should die publicly at Tyburn. The council signed it on the king's behalf, their signatures visible in neat black ink – Archbishop Cranmer heads the list, followed by Audley and then everyone else present, in ranking order: the Duke of Suffolk; the earls of Southampton, Sussex, and Hertford; Bishop Gardiner; Sir John Gage; Sir Thomas Wriothesley; and Richard Rich.[43] The warrants were signed on the 9th and the sentence carried out the next day when the two men were tied to wooden or wicker hurdles which were pulled from the Tower by horses that dragged them the four miles through the city and its crowds to Tyburn gallows.

No one recorded their speeches, which indicates that they were short and conventional. Thomas, standing on the ground in front of the gallows, asked the spectators to pray for his soul. It is tempting to wonder if Dereham was in a fit state to make an eloquent farewell after the torture he had endured in prison, since no account mentions his final words, even in passing. Thomas Culpepper knelt down in the dirt, positioned his neck on the block, and an axe cut through his neck. A noose was placed over Francis's throat and he was dropped just enough to cut off the air supply. The victim's legs kicked, the body began to spasm against the trauma and then the rope was severed so that Francis, still alive, could be stretched out for the knives to slice into his flesh, first to castrate him, and then for his intestines and other viscera to be drawn from him.[44] Only then was his head struck off like Thomas's and taken to be impaled on the spikes that jutted out over London Bridge.[45] Dereham's body did not receive a proper Christian burial, since it was hacked into quarters which were also displayed in various parts of the City.[46] One would almost certainly have gone to Lambeth, his home parish and the site of his original crimes. Where the others went is not recorded.

Meanwhile, the Tower's administrators were struggling with the influx of gently born prisoners, since there were not enough appropriate rooms to hold all of them.[47] The London mansions and country manors of the dowager duchess, Lord William, and the countess had all been seized, stripped, locked up, and handed over to court-appointed stewards.[48] On 22 December, Lord William and Lady Margaret Howard, Lady Malyn Tilney, Anne Howard, Katherine Tilney, Alice Restwold, Joan Bulmer, William Ashby, Margaret Benet, Robert Damport, and Edward Waldegrave were brought to be arraigned for misprision of treason.[49] The king had intervened to pardon Mary Hall, the original informant, on the grounds that she had never sought to work in Catherine's employment and when confiding the secrets of Lambeth to her brother had expressed 'sorrow for His Majesty'. Henry also explained that freeing Mary Hall was to encourage others to report friends or family to the government in the future without fear of collateral retribution. The dowager duchess and the countess were excused since, as the only two members of the group who held aristocratic titles by right of marriage rather than a courtesy lordship given to the sons of noblemen (as was the case for Lord William), they could only properly be tried by their peers. As with Catherine and Lady Rochford, their arraignment would have to wait until Parliament reconvened in January.

At the hearing, none made the same mistake as Culpepper or their onetime companion Francis in trying to plead their innocence. Frightened, demoralised, and in Lady Margaret's case, tottering on the edge of a breakdown, all of them showed themselves to be suitably contrite, even the formerly defiant Lord William. They were all found guilty and received the anticipated sentences of life imprisonment. But, as of yet, there were no more executions scheduled. The mood in the capital towards the Howards and their servants had also subtly shifted. Although criticism of Catherine had not abated:

> [it] was thought extreme cruelty to be so severe to the queen's kindred for not discovering her former ill life: since the making of such a discovery had been inconsistent with the rules of justice or decency. The old duchess of Norfolk, being her grandmother, had her of a child; and it was said, for her to have gone and told the king, that she was a whore, when he intended to marry her, as it was an unheard-of thing, so the not doing of it could not have drawn so severe a punishment from any but a prince, or that of a king's temper.[50]

Catherine was absent from this progression of misery. After she was questioned on 5 December, she was left at Syon. She was at once the subject of most conversations and half-forgotten. Her husband stayed away, travelling through the Chase in peripatetic misery, refusing to discuss affairs of state.[51] There is no account of how she received the news of Thomas and Francis's deaths, but the incarceration and ruin of her closest family members seems to have distressed her. Unlike her uncle Norfolk, who had washed his hands of her conspicuously and thoroughly, the dowager duchess and Lady Bridgewater had, despite their poor advice in days past, done their best not to implicate Catherine. A cynic might point out that to indict Catherine was to damn themselves, but they could have exonerated one another by painting Catherine as a duplicitous harlot who had hoodwinked them all into believing she was a model of virtue. The condemnations of Catherine by others who were questioned were recorded; the dowager and the countess seem to have made none.

There were moments in the crumbling ornateness of the convent by the river when Catherine's attendants heard that 'she believes that her end will be on the scaffold', yet there were also prolonged spells of defiant, manic gaiety. Chapuys heard that Catherine had recovered her appetite and her habit of command, which she used to torment the disloyal servants who had been appointed by others to watch over her. Catherine was 'more imperious and commanding, and more difficult to please than she ever was when living with the King, her husband'. In the second kingdom of Syon, the great purgatorial wait for a horrible finale, Catherine was once again 'taking great care of her person'. Like a candle flaring before it went out, she had apparently never been more beautiful than she was during that winter at Syon. Staring death in the face in a mood of hubristic hedonism, she became as preoccupied with her toilette as she had been at Hampton Court. She made the most of her denuded wardrobe, dressing and coiffing herself, donning her few remaining jewels, waiting for the opening of Parliament on 16 January, when the matter would be settled. Preening in her loveliness, Catherine kept her pulse beating at Syon with the appearance of someone who might live for ever; but in her more sombre moments, when no amount of make-believe could distract her, Chapuys heard from her servants that 'her only prayer is that the execution be secret, and not in public'.[52]

Chapter 22

Ars Moriendi

The body is but earth, ashes and worm's meat … Serpents,
worms and toads, shall grow, eat, and devour thy beautiful
face, thy fair nose, thy clear eyes, thy white hands, thy
goodly body. Remember this thou lord and lady.
Remember this thou Christian man and woman.
Remember this once a day.

– John Longland, Bishop of Lincoln (d. 1547),
Henry VIII's confessor

After Christmas, the emperor wrote to Chapuys, 'With regard to
the queen of England and the King's fresh divorce We have nothing to say, except that We thank you for the news, and shall be
glad to hear what is to become of the Queen, and other events of
that country.'[1] After the frenzied activity of the inquiries and the
king's corresponding reluctance to engage with government, the
silence that had cocooned Catherine at Syon seemed to have
settled over the case. It was back to business as usual for the Privy
Council in January: the issues surrounding the Crown of Ireland
Act had been resolved, and the council also had time to investigate four citizens suspected of Judaism, which had been illegal in
England ever since Edward I expelled the entire Anglo-Jewish
community in 1290.[2] Rumours floated about that, despite de
Marillac's summertime bonhomie with the Duke of Norfolk, the

French were actually angling for the Duke of Orléans's betrothal to the emperor's niece, Maria of Portugal, a suggestion that the imperialists were keen to downplay since the emperor was now interested in resurrecting a Hapsburg alliance with the Tudors to balance the scales against France's unsettling friendliness towards the sultan. This in part explained the emperor's non-comment on what he mistakenly described as Henry's 'latest divorce'. Regardless of the sniggering and eyebrows raised almost to the ceiling at the Hapsburg court, officially Charles V avoided offending a man he sought a treaty with. He could not, however, disguise his interest in Catherine's fate, and Chapuys diligently hunted down the relevant information, which he was putting into a report for his master when he was interrupted by the news that Catherine had been condemned to death:

A few days ago the assembly of Parliament, or the States of this kingdom, began its sessions. The chief point of the Chancellor's speech relates to the Queen's misdeeds, which that official exaggerated and aggravated without measure. After some four days' discussion, the members, lords, and prelates sitting in the said Parliament have declared the Queen, as well as Mme de Rochefort, guilty of high treason and *lèse-majesté*. As to the dowager duchess of Norfolk and her daughter, they are sentenced to perpetual imprisonment with confiscation of property, on the same plea and for the same reason that milord, his wife and the rest of the accomplices, had been condemned. Within two days the said resolution and award will be brought forward before the deputies of the people and Commons.

At this very moment, whilst I am writing these lines, some one comes to tell me that this very morning the Commons have passed a similar resolution on the Queen's, Mme de Rochford's, and the other two ladies' cases. It is, therefore, to be apprehended that the Queen will soon be taken to the Tower. She is still in Syon House.[3]

Ten days before the emperor sent his request for more information about Catherine, a new session of Parliament had been opened by the king, who watched from his throne as Lord Chancellor Audley gave the maiden speech during which, according to Chapuys, he launched into a tirade on Catherine's crimes that struck the ambassador as a gross distortion. Unfortunately, there is no direct record of what he said, but we do know that Audley concluded by contrasting Catherine's failures with Henry's 'three shining qualities: in the perfect knowledge of the Word of God, the chiefest glory in a king; in the exact understanding of the art military, which is the second virtue in a prince; and in politic knowledge, which holds the third place, as bringing the greatest good to the republic'.[4]

Writs to summon this Parliament had been issued on 23 November, the same week that preparations for the juries and trial of Francis Dereham and Thomas Culpepper took place, which lends credence to the view that the Parliament of 1542 was initially fetched specifically to deal with Catherine.[5] Here too was a significant contrast to the affair of Anne Boleyn, when Parliament had actually been dissolved a few weeks before she fell. With Catherine, where there was more evidence, the government were determined that everything should be done openly to allow any kind of scrutiny and spare the king the charge of unfairly executing a second wife. Chapuys's letters to the emperor capture something of the stop-and-start nature of Catherine's final month alive, when events could move quickly only to halt and be followed by stasis before the next burst of activity.

At the first session of the House of Lords, the clerical caste, the Lords Spiritual, were headed by the archbishops of Canterbury and York, joined by twenty-three bishops, whose position entitled them to sit in the Lords. The dukes of Norfolk and Suffolk were the highest-ranking members of the Lords Temporal, with the earls of Oxford, Arundel, Southampton, Sussex, Rutland, Hertford, Westmorland, Shrewsbury, Derby, Worcester, Cumberland, Huntingdon, and Bath; the countess's estranged husband, the Earl of Bridgewater; and twenty-five viscounts and barons, including Lady Rochford's father, Thomas Cromwell's son, and Katherine Parr's husband.[6]

The Lords had no intention of defending Catherine, especially since 'the lasciviousness of her former life made people incline to believe any ill thing that could be reported of her', but there was a spasm of discomfort at the proceedings.[7] Different accounts suggest different origins for the decision to offer the queen a trial. Bishop Burnet believed the proposal came from the king via Lord Chancellor Audley, 'that there might be no ground of suspicion of complaint, he proposed, that some of their number should be sent to examine the queen'.[8] The *Journal of the House of Lords* implies that blue-blooded solidarity, or self-protection, inspired the offer, after the Lords murmured that to condemn the former queen by an Act of attainder was an affront to the state. Keen to secure unity, Audley made the offer on 21 January on the grounds that the 'queen was in no sense a mean [average or unimportant] and private person but an illustrious and public one'.[9] A deputation with the gentle but deadly presence of Archbishop Cranmer, gouty Suffolk, Lord Southampton, and the Bishop of Westminster were announced at Syon. They informed Catherine that the House of Lords considered it 'just that a princess should be tried by equal laws', that is, with trial by her peers, as Queen Anne Boleyn, her brother, Lord Montagu, the Marquess of Exeter, and the Duke of Buckingham had been.[10]

At this juncture, Catherine made another possible error when she declined the offer of a trial.[11] Her preoccupation with her pride may have encouraged her to avoid the shame of having the details of her private life read out in court. She may also have gambled on the fact that it was only by abasing herself before her husband, appealing to his alleged sense of mercy, that she stood any chance of escape. The gateway to absolution was confession, and in her conversation with her visitors, Catherine did confess to her sinfulness, through which she insisted that she deserved death.[12]

In declining a trial, she threw herself at her husband's feet and he trampled on her. An act of attainder was prepared against her in Parliament, couched as a petition that begged the king 'not to be troubled at the matter, since that might be a means to short[en] his life', to pardon anyone who had been detained or punished for criticising Queen Catherine since July 1540, that Catherine and her surviving accomplices, principally 'the bawd, lady Rochford' be attainted for high treason since 'it appeared what she [Catherine] had intended to do', and that 'the king should not trouble himself to give his assent to this act in his own person, but grant it by letters patent under his hand and great seal'.

At Syon, Catherine had begged the Duke of Suffolk to pass on her plea that none of her relatives should suffer on her account, but although he gave a speech acknowledging her request, the legislation did not reflect it. Instead, it suggested that 'the dowager duchess of Norfolk, countess of Bridg[e]water, the lord William Howard and his lady, four other men, and five women, who were already attainted by the course of common law, (except the Duchess of Norfolk and the Countess of Bridg[e]water,) that knew the queen's vicious life, and had concealed it, should be all attainted of misprision of treason'.[13] A law was also enacted that made it a criminal offence for anyone to withhold information about a royal bride if they knew she was not 'a pure and clean maid'. It proved deeply unpopular as 'a piece of grievous tyranny: since if a king, especially one of so imperious a temper as this was, should design such an honour to any of his subjects, who had failed in their former life, they must either defame themselves, by publishing so disgraceful a secret, or run the hazard of being afterwards attainted of treason'.[14]

The king's men had served him well through orchestrating the last stage of the queen's downfall, absolving Henry of all responsibility by casting it as a request from the peers of the realm. The clause specifying that Catherine's death warrant could come into effect through a kind of rubber stamp rather than Henry's own signature further distanced the king from a second act of uxoricide. The dowager duchess and the countess were condemned to perpetual imprisonment and the loss of all their worldly goods by acts of attainder and, on 4 February, Parliament made itself even more convenient by approving a new law that permitted the execution of those who 'after their confessions or convictions of treason shall happen to fall mad or lunatic'.[15] Everything necessary to grant the act of attainder's request 'that the queen and the lady Rochford should suffer the pains of death' had been prepared.

Since the act and his wife's condemnation, the king's malaise had lifted. On the night of 29 January, the day the act was passed in Parliament, Greenwich Palace echoed with the sounds of 'a grand supper' given by the king, who flirted with Thomas Wyatt's wife Elizabeth, another young woman related to Sir Anthony Browne, and with Anne Bassett.[16] If Catherine had gambled on clemency, she may have suspected that she had made a poor bet when Sir John Gage arrived at Syon on 7 February to dismiss her remaining servants. It took him a few days to make arrangements on where they were to go and to settle their wages. Chapuys told the Hapsburgs, 'In two or three days the matter will be cleared up, and it will be known what will become of her.'[17]

Three days later, that Friday, the last of Catherine's illusions were snatched from her when most of her servants left and she was informed that barges had arrived to take her to the Tower. She descended into a blind panic at the very sight of the councillors who had arrived as her escort. They begged her to be reasonable, but she was so terrified that she could only move to struggle. Eventually, they lost their patience and manhandled Catherine into the waiting barge. She cut a pathetic figure in her black velvet dress and French hood as they manoeuvred her towards the smallest of three boats. Lord Southampton, escorted by a large retinue of servants, represented the government in the first; the Duke of Suffolk sat in the final barge, which was full of armed men. Catherine was put in a covered boat, with four waiting women, the last of her servants, a group that quite probably included her sister Isabella, and four sailors, who pushed off in the fading afternoon light.

By the time they passed under London Bridge, where Thomas and Francis's heads remained on display, the sun had already set. Southampton and Suffolk waited with Sir John Gage on the steps of the Tower to greet her 'with the same honour and ceremonies as if she were still reigning'.[18] Catherine was escorted to her apartments, which may very well have been the fine set of rooms where Anne Boleyn had spent the last two-and-a-half weeks of her life in 1536. Somewhere in the vast fortress, Lady Rochford had been brought back into custody, and she 'had shewn symptoms of madness until the very moment when they announced to her that she must die'.[19] Perhaps she had been exaggerating and prolonging her alleged ill health after the first breakdown in the hope of saving herself, or perhaps the sentence shocked her into sanity. If all that was left was death, it had to be done well.

At Westminster, the MPs from the House of Commons were summoned to hear the queen and Lady Rochford's sentences on Saturday, the 11th. The lords, dressed in their robes, either clerical colours or the rich reds of the secular noblemen, gave their assent and Catherine and Jane passed beyond the chance of reprieve.[20] There could be no executions on the Sabbath, when Catherine was told in the evening to prepare her soul since she was to be beheaded early the next morning. A thirty-one-year-old clergyman called John White was brought to her rooms to take her last confession. White, who eventually succeeded Stephen Gardiner as Bishop of Winchester, had read divinity at New College, Oxford, eight years earlier and was a religious traditionalist, with a strong belief in the sacrament of confession and the existence of purgatory.[21] As she knelt and prayed with White, Catherine reiterated what she had done with Henry Manox and Francis Dereham, but 'took God and His angels to be her witnesses, upon salvation of her soul, that she was guiltless of that act of defiling the sovereign's bed'.[22] Catherine then made a curious request which could not be refused – she wanted to see the block that she would die on. Her marriage had begun on the day when Cromwell's death was botched; she had been queen when Lady Salisbury was all but hacked apart on the scaffold. She explained to her gaolers that she wanted the opportunity to practise 'by way of experiment', and she did so, over and over again, laying her slender neck into the wooden curvature.[23]

The Tower is always locked and sealed at sundown. Catherine heard the gates shutting and the locks turning as she faced her last night. At about seven o'clock in the morning, the privy councillors arrived to witness her execution. Her cousin, Lord Surrey, attended, just as he had Thomas Cromwell's death eighteen months earlier, though not in the same boisterous spirits. The only councillors to miss it were the Duke of Suffolk, who had been compelled to sit for health reasons during most of his recent speeches in the House of Lords and whose ill health may have been exacerbated by the expedition on the freezing river to fetch Catherine on Friday, and her uncle Norfolk, who had abandoned not only her but Lady Rochford, his niece by marriage, and his brother, sister, sister-in-law, and 'ungracious' stepmother in a letter to the king in which he disavowed all affection for them and knowledge of their crimes.[24] Norfolk had attended sessions of the Privy Council the day before the beheading, so it was apparently a diplomatic choice to stay away from Catherine's death.[25]

She was escorted out into the chilly morning air and led to a scaffold that stood on the same site where Anne Boleyn had been executed.[26] Catherine's hope that the execution would be private was not granted, although the decision to hold it within the confines of the Tower saved her from dying in front of a crowd as large as Cromwell's and Lord Hungerford's. One of the men watching her was Ottwell Johnson, a London-based merchant with family ties to Calais, where Catherine's father had sought refuge in the twilight of a dwindling life. Edmund, who had endured so much humiliation, had fathered a daughter aggressively averse to it. Now, a demure and fragile figure in a dark gown, her feet moved up the steps to the scaffold. Johnson watched Catherine with admiration as she made steady progress towards the headsman. He did not write down her exact words, but he told his brother two days later that she died well.* That

---

* The story that she proclaimed, 'I die a Queen, but I would rather die the wife of Culpepper', is apocryphal and comes from an account which claimed Catherine had been interrogated by Thomas Cromwell.

day, at the palace, her husband was bouncing from room to room overseeing preparations for the guests who had been invited to attend a banquet with him the day after, the feast of St Valentine. Catherine's marriage ended as it had begun, with a celebration and a slaughter. For her last performance, she was, as ever when in public, note perfect. She spoke of Christ and the redemption promised to all who believed. She urged the crowd to learn from her example and effusively praised the justice of her sentence and the good government of the king. There were no last-minute protestations of love, nor was there admission of guilt for the adultery she was suspected of but had not formally been condemned for.

A few women from her suite stood by to perform their last service for Catherine, who sank to the straw and nuzzled her neck, bare and exposed, into the embrace of the block. She had made it familiar. She would leave with dignity. The feared final humiliation was avoided as the axe rose into the air, then descended at rapid speed to slice through Catherine's neck with one clean and merciful stroke. Blood gushed forth onto the scaffold; the dead woman's head thudded into the straw; the ladies moved forward with a cloak that they threw over the little body and then they lifted it, and the head, over to one side of the scaffold. Jane Boleyn, Lady Rochford, was brought out to follow her mistress. She sang from the same hymn sheet – she was a wretched sinner, as all Christians were, she begged for mercy from God and prayers from the bystanders, she praised the king – and knelt down. For her too the end was swift. A whistle in the air, a momentary trauma, and the play was over.

No one recorded Jane's final speech either, but Ottwell Johnson wrote: 'I saw the Queen and the Lady Rochford suffer within the Tower, the day following, whose souls (I doubt not) be with God, for they made the most godly and Christians' ends, that ever was heard tell of (I think) since the world's creation; uttering their lively faith in the blood of Christ only, and with goodly words and steadfast countenances.'[27] Had Catherine lived out a normal span and died with the title she acquired on her wedding day, representatives of London guilds would have lined the route her coffin took through the city. Hundreds of flaming torches would have flickered in the darkness over the many days it took to inter her. One maiden for each year of her earthly life would have carried a taper, while anthems and requiems rang out to pray for her soul's entry into paradise. Mountains of black cloth would have been issued to every member of the royal households, down to the pageboys, all of whom would have appeared in the procession, honouring their departed mistress. Hundreds of poor folk, encouraged to pray for her soul, would have moved with knights and noblemen on horseback, carrying displays of Catherine's heraldry and images of her patron saints. While her bier rested in the chapel, six women would have kept vigil, on rota, kneeling throughout. Alms would have been issued in the dead queen's name. All the panoply and pomp of monarchy would have accompanied her off the face of the earth. Bishops would have blessed her grave before her body was lowered into it, after which her chamberlain, his deputies, the officers of her household, and her gentlemen ushers would have broken their staffs, symbols of their office, and hurled the broken pieces into the grave to symbolise that their service to the queen was at an end.[28]

Instead, her body was taken, with Lady Rochford's, to the chapel of St Peter-ad-vincula a few yards away, and the stones beneath the altar were prised up. Jane Boleyn and Catherine Howard were buried quickly next to the mouldering remains of Lady Salisbury, Thomas More, Jane's husband, and another queen of England. The prayers for the faithfully departed were hastily intoned, the cannons fired out over London, the stones were returned, the few attendees genuflected to the altar and walked out of the little church into the courtyard, where the scaffold still stood. The body of Catherine Howard was left to a vast silence. In all probability, she had not yet reached her twenty-first birthday.

Chapter 23

The Shade of Persephone

Her?
Don't even mention her – she no longer exists.

– Sophocles, *Antigone* (*c.*441 BC)

Twelve days after Catherine's death, Maria of Austria wrote to Eustace Chapuys. The majority of the letter was occupied by a précis of her brothers' activities in the Hapsburg Empire. On English affairs, the queen regent told the ambassador, 'We cannot do otherwise than thank you most cordially for the good service you are doing by continually informing Us of occurrences in that country.'[1] This was Maria's only oblique reference to Catherine's death. The former queen had already passed beyond relevance. Glaziers were paid to remove her arms from the windows and niches of the English royal palaces, and seventeen months later, Henry married Katherine Parr, an elegant and intelligent widow in her early thirties.[2]

The apparent desire to draw a veil over an embarrassing incident, now that a blood sacrifice had been offered in atonement, saved Catherine's friends and family from their sentences of life imprisonment. All were pardoned and set free, most in May 1542. After that, the majority of those servants and friends who had known Catherine, and come perilously close to dying with her, vanished into the safety of anonymity. Francis's friend Edward

Waldegrave even managed to return to service for the Prince of Wales, and by 1545 he had sufficient good standing at court for the new queen to refer to him as 'our well-beloved Edward Waldegrave, servant to our most dear and entirely beloved son the lord prince'.[3] Waldegrave married a Chesworth alumna, Francis's former lover and Catherine's friend, Joan Bulmer, after she became a widow. Her first marriage had never been a happy one and, after her imprisonment, her first husband had refused to be reconciled with her.[4] She and her second husband had five children together and retired to a manor house in Warwickshire, purchased by Edward.[5] He died there in 1584, and Joan outlived him to die on 10 December 1590, the forty-ninth anniversary of Francis Dereham's execution. The couple are still buried in St Mary's Church in Lawford; their tomb bears the inscription: 'The end of the just is peace'.[6]

The Dowager Duchess of Norfolk also left the Tower in the spring of 1542 and after she died in 1545 she was buried next to her husband, whom she had outlived by just over two decades. In her grave, Tudor politics managed to disturb Agnes one last time. With the last of the priories and monasteries closing, the Howards moved her body to St Mary-at-Lambeth, the church near Norfolk House. Agnes's bones remain there, but because of significant Victorian renovations to the church, which is now a museum, her resting place, along with that of Anne Boleyn's mother, who was buried there in 1538, is no longer marked.[7]

The diplomatic crisis, of which Catherine had witnessed the acceleration in the summer and autumn of 1541, culminated with English invasions of Scotland and France, wars that changed, or ended, the lives of many whom Catherine had known. Her brother-in-law Sir Edward Baynton, who had served and then abandoned her, died in the French campaign. Sensibly, Baynton made a will before he crossed the Channel, which included bequests to Archbishop Cranmer and Richard Rich. In France, Baynton was in charge of overseeing the transport home of sick and wounded soldiers. It is possible that he contracted an illness from this work that resulted in his death on 27 November 1544.[8]

Catherine's sister Isabella subsequently married the MP Sir James Stumpe, who had been her stepson-in-law until his first wife, Bridget Baynton, died. Isabella, who married again after Stumpe's death, passed away in 1573.[9]

Thanks to Henry's wars, the Countess of Bridgewater was never able to reunite her family. Her daughter Anne seems to have returned to her care and was eventually betrothed to Lord Stourton, who died before they were married, though as proof of his affection he left Anne 'all my plate of silver gilt'.[10] The countess's son Gruffydd took up his mother's quest to have his father posthumously pardoned; he became an MP and one of his sons, Walter, fought for Elizabeth I.[11] Her youngest son Thomas did not return. At the time of the countess's arrest, the Crown had placed Thomas in ward to the Bishop of Carlisle and sent him north to join the bishop's household. Evidently, Thomas detested his time there, because he ran away and, to ensure he was not sent back, crossed the border and offered his services to the Scottish Crown. He had inherited the Howard skill on the battlefield, and in 1544 he commanded 200 men at the Battle of Blar-na-leine. The skirmish, which aimed to crush an insurrection, 'began', in one contemporary's account, 'with the discharge of arrows at a distance; but when their shafts were spent both parties rushed to close combat, and, attacking each other furiously … a dreadful slaughter ensued'.[12] The countess's son was, at the age of about nineteen or twenty, among the dead. Like his cousin Catherine, he was buried without pomp, and today his remains probably rest somewhere near the ruins of Beauly Priory in Aird, Scotland.

We know very little of Charles Howard's movements following his rustication in 1541, but one seventeenth-century account states that he was killed fighting in France three years later.[13] None of Catherine's brothers seems to have fathered children, and the same source states that Henry Howard died at a relatively young age. The only brother to grow old was George, who soldiered in the war against Scotland, where, like his father long before him, he was knighted.[14] He successfully revived his career at court, where he remained until his death in May 1580. He served as a gentleman usher to his second cousin, Queen Elizabeth I, was elected a Member of Parliament for the new constituency of Reigate in 1563, and, like his father, became a justice of the peace.[15]

In the months and years after Catherine's death, Henry VIII's moods acquired a new unpredictability. His health collapsed as his weight increased, and he died, morbidly obese, at the Palace of Whitehall on 28 January 1547, aged fifty-five. The snow and ice made the roads to the palace almost impassable, and by the time Cranmer made it to Henry's bedside, there was no time for the last rites. Instead, the archbishop cradled the king's hand as he passed away. His will, which confirmed his self-created position as 'in earth immediately under God the Supreme Head of the Church of England and Ireland', passed the throne to his nine-year-old son as King Edward VI.[16] Henry's body was interred at Windsor Castle, next to that of the new king's mother, Queen Jane Seymour. During the journey to Windsor, the procession stopped for a night at crumbling Syon, the abbey where Catherine had spent her last winter. A story circulated later that as Henry's coffin rested in Syon's chapel, a putrid liquid leaked from it and local dogs sniffed around it the next morning, fulfilling, in some Catholics' view, a prophecy made against Henry that dogs would one day lick his blood, as they had with Ahab, a wicked and idolatrous king in the Old Testament.[17] Henry left instructions for a magnificent sepulchre to be constructed at Windsor, but his children lacked either the funds or inclination to complete it. Henry's grave is marked today by a plain black marble slab, installed in the reign of the nineteenth century's William IV.

Henry's death saved Catherine's uncle Norfolk from following her to the scaffold by a matter of hours. In the last year of his reign, Henry had turned on the Howards again, having convinced himself that the family's patriarch and heir were both plotting against him. Catherine's cousin, the Earl of Surrey, had led one of the English armies to defeat at the Battle of Saint-Etienne in France. Surrey was so aghast at his actions that he apparently begged his companions to 'stick their swords through his guts and make him forget this day', but his contrition and shame did not stop a burst of suicidal egotism when he commissioned a portrait of himself with a coat of arms clearly advertising the Howards' descent from Saint Edward the Confessor and King Edward III.[18] It looked, to a paranoid Henry, as if the Howards were planning to snatch power from him or his son, and Surrey was executed for treason on 19 January 1547, the last political casualty of Henry's torturous reign. His father was condemned by act of attainder on the 27th, but with the king's death a day later, the guardians of the new regime were too nervous to open the reign with the execution of the country's highest-ranking peer.[19] Instead, Norfolk was kept in the Tower.

As with Surrey, the violent vagaries of contemporary politics claimed many of those involved in Catherine's story. One of her brothers-in-law, Sir Thomas Arundell, was executed for treason on 26 February 1552. Both the Seymour brothers met similar ends – Thomas, who had inventoried Catherine's jewels when she fell, was beheaded on 20 March 1549, and clever Edward Seymour, Earl of Hertford, the first man to tell Thomas Culpepper that his thoughts about the queen were enough to condemn him to death, on 22 January 1552.[20] Catherine's former master of the horse, Sir John Dudley, became the most powerful man in Edward VI's government as Duke of Northumberland; he was executed for treason on 22 August 1553. John Lascelles, the devout evangelical whose conversation with Archbishop Cranmer in 1541 had set in motion Catherine's downfall, was burned for heresy on 16 July 1546. Ten years later, Cranmer, Catherine's most reluctant but zealous interrogator, perished when the government of Catherine's stepdaughter, Queen Mary I, condemned him to burn in the centre of Oxford. The site of his stake is marked by a small metal cross on Broad Street.[21]

Mary Tudor's succession, after the death of her half brother Edward VI at the age of fifteen in 1553, was hard won. Mary was popular and tenacious enough to defeat a coup that aimed to disinherit her in favour of her young and conveniently Protestant cousin, Lady Jane Grey. Anne of Cleves, still a mistress in the art of pragmatic supplication, waited quietly in the countryside to see if Mary or Jane would emerge victorious, swore loyalty to Mary, and received a state funeral at Westminster Abbey when she died, possibly from cancer, in 1557.[22] Until the very end, she was praised for her generosity to her servants, her cheerfulness, and the good table she offered as a hostess.[23]

Cardinal Reginald Pole, the son of the butchered Countess of Salisbury, returned to England after decades in exile. In Henry VIII's time, Reginald had been referred to as 'the Archtraitor Reginald Pole, enemy to God's word and his natural country'; in 1556 he replaced Cranmer as Archbishop of Canterbury, and he served Mary until his death in 1558.[24] Mary's reign also benefited two clergymen closely associated with Catherine's queenship. Her uncle's ally Stephen Gardiner, Bishop of Winchester, had languished in prison for most of Edward VI's reign. Under Mary, Gardiner became Lord Chancellor, a post he held until he died of natural causes at his episcopal palace in Southwark in November 1555. Edmund Bonner, the bishop who had married Catherine to Henry in 1540, was less lucky. He used the Marian regime's crackdown on radicals to pursue anyone suspected of Protestant sympathies, earning himself the nickname of 'Bloody Bonner' in the process. When Mary died in November 1558, her sister and successor, Elizabeth, was so revolted by Bonner's behaviour that she had him degraded from his diocese and imprisoned. He died as an inmate in the Marshalsea prison in 1569.

Mary's triumph in 1553 brought relief for the Duke of Norfolk, who had lived in the Tower for six years by the time she set him free, as she did most of her father's and brother's prisoners. The duke did not enjoy his liberty for long. He died in his mansion at Kenninghall on 25 August 1554, at the age of eighty, the same age as his late father when he had expired in the very different world of 1524. Mary I also, unintentionally, gave a kind of reprieve to Catherine. As a young woman, Mary had lost some of her closest friends and allies to acts of attainder, the notorious legal mechanism which allowed for execution without a trial. When she became queen, she retrospectively annulled en masse the condemnations that her father's government had secured through attainder, meaning that Catherine Howard was legally pardoned by the member of the royal family who had disliked her the most. Mary's actions brought a husband to Catherine's former colleague and then her maid, Anne Bassett, whose prospects had been ruined by her stepfather's arrest in 1540. Bassett had remained single until June 1554, when she married Walter Hungerford, the son of the peer executed on Catherine's wedding day. Queen Mary danced at Anne's wedding celebrations, and she restored several of the late Lord Hungerford's confiscated estates to the newlyweds.[25]

By the time Elizabeth I succeeded to the throne in 1558, natural deaths had carried off many of the other men involved in Catherine's career. Sir Edmund Knyvet, the cousin whose hand she was credited with saving, fulfilled his vow to use his sword-wielding hand in the Crown's service. He helped suppress a rebellion in Norfolk in 1549 and died at his London town house on 1 May 1551. The two courtiers who were pardoned during the celebrations that marked Catherine's official entry into London, Sir Thomas Wyatt and Sir John Wallop, returned to royal service, but Wyatt did not survive for long. He had been tasked with escorting a diplomatic mission, and then the Earl of Tyrone, to London when he caught a fever and died eight months after Catherine's execution. Wallop served in the wars against France and was inducted into the Order of the Garter in 1543. He died in 1551, and his will dutifully acknowledged Edward VI as rightful head of the Church, although, true to the Catholic sympathies which had earned him a spell at the Tower in 1540, it also asked for the intercession of the Virgin Mary in easing his soul's passage into Heaven.

Charles de Marillac, whose correspondence provides so much of our knowledge about English court life during Catherine's career, was recalled as the relationship between the two countries deteriorated. In France, he acquired the favour of King Henri II, who succeeded to the throne in 1547, and during Henri's reign de Marillac's careers as clergyman, courtier, and diplomat continued to flourish. He represented his king on embassies to the Hapsburg Empire, the papal states, and the Swiss cantons, and he rose through the Church hierarchy to become Archbishop of Vienne. The last act of his public life was a speech in 1560 in which he begged for toleration for France's growing number of Protestants. The two pillars of a successful monarchy, he said, were 'the integrity of religion and the benevolence of the people. If they are strong, it is not necessary to fear that obedience will be lost.'[26] After this advice, given on the eve of France descending into a generation-long trauma with eight religious wars, de Marillac retired, and he died on 2 December 1560. His former adversary, Eustace Chapuys, had passed away in Louvain in January 1556.[27]

The sectarian divide, evident in both countries during Catherine's time as queen, intensified in the decades after her death. Most of her former ladies-in-waiting spent quiet lives as women of property, but in terms of how religion and politics divided and shaped her generation, the fates of Lady Margaret Douglas and the Duchess of Suffolk are revealing.

After her second brush with disgrace for her liaison with Catherine's brother, Margaret Douglas wisely reinvented herself as an icon of royal propriety. She submitted to an arranged marriage with the pretty Earl of Lennox in 1544 as part of her uncle's manoeuvres to increase English influence in Scotland.[28] Lennox was a French-educated, pro-English Scottish émigré, and Henry provided generously for the couple. Fortunately for Margaret, it was a happy marriage, and the couple also agreed on religion. Whatever her levels of piety during her uncle's reign, by the time her cousin Mary succeeded to the throne, Margaret was a zealous Roman Catholic.

Where she had once enjoyed romantic intrigues, a more mature Margaret occupied herself with political aims, usually with the same energy and lack of long-term success. Her faith, her ancestry, and her two healthy sons briefly made her seem like a more attractive candidate as heiress to the throne than her cousin, Princess Elizabeth. Margaret's favoured position at Mary I's court fuelled her delusional belief that she might succeed her as queen, but Mary had come to power on the argument that it was fundamentally wrong to tamper with the succession. In the meantime, Margaret allowed confidence to master good sense when she took to taunting Elizabeth, who suffered from migraines and was notoriously sensitive to strong smells and loud noises, by installing her kitchens immediately above Elizabeth's apartments at court. The strategy did not pay dividends when Elizabeth became queen and promptly made it clear that Margaret was no longer welcome at court. The animosity between the cousins intensified, and Margaret found herself imprisoned in the Tower for the second time in her life when her eldest son, Lord Darnley, visited Scotland and married Mary, Queen of Scots, a move which Elizabeth interpreted to be the result of his mother's ambition and a threat to her own position.

The rest of Margaret's life was stalked by tragedy. Darnley was detested in Scotland, and at the age of twenty-one his body was found in the smoking ruins of an Edinburgh townhouse. Scottish politics then claimed the life of Margaret's husband, who was shot dead by his opponents four years later, and their only surviving child, Charles, died in his early twenties. Despite their animosity, Queen Elizabeth visited Margaret to break the news of her husband's death in person, and she paid for Margaret's state funeral when she died in 1578.[29]

Margaret Douglas's former colleague in the queen's household, Katherine Brandon, Duchess of Suffolk, outlived her by two years. Katherine had become as fervent in her Protestantism as Margaret was in her Catholicism. Under Edward VI, she was a generous patroness to evangelical preachers and scholars, delighted in the disgrace of Bishop Gardiner, and described Edward's reign as a time when 'it was merry with the lambs'.[30] She endured almost unimaginable heartbreak in 1551 when her only two sons, Henry and Charles, died within hours of each other. They were both students at Cambridge when they contracted the sweat, a strain of the plague that was famous for the speed with which it could claim a victim.[31] Katherine, left a widow after the duke's death in 1545, married one of her gentleman ushers, and they had two children together, Susan and Peregrine. The family left England in 1555 when Katherine came under pressure from Mary I's government to convert to Catholicism. They were living as guests of King Sigismund II Augustus of Poland when they heard the news of Elizabeth's accession and returned home. In old age, Katherine increasingly sympathised with the Puritan cause and despaired at Elizabeth I's attempts to reach a religious compromise.

Elizabeth I, who died unmarried and childless after a reign of forty-five years in 1603, may have been indirectly and partly influenced by Catherine in one of the most significant decisions of her life. Elizabeth's favourite, Robert Dudley, Earl of Leicester, whose father had served as Catherine's master of the horse, told a diplomat in the 1560s that he and Elizabeth 'had first become friends before she was eight years old. Both then and later (when she was old enough to marry) she said she never wished to do so. Thereafter he had not seen her waver in that decision.'[32] Although this admission is often paraphrased to say that Elizabeth developed her aversion to marriage specifically in reaction to Catherine's death, and it would be unwise to see Catherine's end as the crucible of the Virgin Queen, Elizabeth was eight years old at the time of Catherine's execution. Leicester's remarks indicate that it may, quite naturally, have affected her, even if only as a childish vow which, in light of her subsequent refusal to marry, Leicester chose to regard as decisive.

For the Howards and the Tudors, Catherine remained persona non grata for the rest of the century. There seems to have been a consensus, even among those charitable enough to view her with pity, that Catherine's behaviour had destroyed herself and unfairly damaged others. From the sanctuary of his beloved library, Lady Rochford's father, Lord Morley, translated a fourteenth-century text, *De claris mulieribus*, from Latin into English. The book structured its chapters around individual lives, in this case the great or notorious women of history and mythology. Lord Morley picked forty-six from the original text's roster of 104, and his daughter's modern biographer, Julia Fox, has convincingly argued that in the section on the Trojan princess Polyxena, Morley made a subtle validation of his daughter and condemnation of her mistress. In most places, Morley's translation is word perfect, but in his account of Polyxena, who was sacrificed to atone for the mistakes of the adulterous Helen of Sparta, he inserted a sentence bemoaning that 'so sweet a maiden should be devoured by the hands of Pyrrhus for to satisfy for another woman's offence'.[33]

As far as we know, only one courtier wrote a full and unambiguous reflection on Catherine's downfall. In retirement, George Cavendish, a talented writer who had once served as a gentleman usher to Cardinal Wolsey, composed a series of first-person monologues which he put into the mouths of the Henrician court's most famous casualties, each of which attempted to impart the truth of the person, as Cavendish had known or perceived them, with a wider moral point about why they had fallen. Cavendish, whose brother William had remained at court long after he retired, included the figures of Catherine and Culpepper in his *Metrical Visions*. Although we do not know if Cavendish ever met either of them, his portraits of Thomas and Catherine are detailed enough to suggest that he had access to firsthand information about them. Culpepper was dismissed as an impious rogue, who 'drowned in the depth of my own outrage'.[34] With Catherine, Cavendish focused almost exclusively on her physical beauty, which he blamed for leading her into sin. Comments on Catherine's appearance were frequent and effusive in nearly every near-contemporary account of her downfall: when Nikander Nucius, a Greek-born diplomat in service to the Hapsburg emperor, visited London in 1545, the skulls of Culpepper and Dereham were still being displayed over London Bridge, and Nucius was told that they had perished for falling in love with a queen who had been 'the most beautiful woman of her time'.[35] For George Cavendish, Catherine's loveliness was 'the chief cause of my mischief'. Yet, his text does show restrained compassion towards her by suggesting that while beauty inevitably incited lust, which in its turn brings ruin, these dangers are commonplace among the young. Cavendish's interpretation of Catherine was of a youthful siren damned for adolescent mistakes. His spectre of Catherine plaintively admits that it is 'hard for youth against vice to fight: for youth is blind and hath no sight'.[36] *Metrical Visions* suggested that Catherine's epitaph should be:

> By proof of me, none can deny
> That beauty and lust, enemies to chastity,
> Have been the twain that hath decayed in me,
> And hath brought me to this and untoward;
> Some time a queen, and now a headless Howard.

There was, of course, no epitaph on a grave that remained unmarked. Nor could the Howards have erected a memorial to an attainted traitor, even if they had desired to do so.[37] As one of Edward VI's privy councillors wrote, 'He that dieth with honour liveth for ever, / And the defamed dead recovereth never.'[38] For many, Catherine remained as Cavendish saw her – a beautiful but promiscuous young woman who committed adultery and paid for that mistake with her life. Compared to queens like Anne Boleyn or Katherine of Aragon, who tangibly and deliberately mattered, Catherine has been depicted as an irrelevance, the author of a shallow yet profane queenship.

It has been argued here that Catherine probably did not commit physical adultery with Thomas Culpepper and that her denials of it were probably truthful, but that adultery would likely have taken place had their liaison not been discovered in November 1541. Despite how often she is described as a queen executed for committing adultery, the treason laws under Henry VIII meant that she could be, and was, condemned for her intention, rather than her actions. A privy councillor wrote later that 'before her marriage, she had contaminated her virginity, and afterwards committed or, at the leastwise, sought means to commit adultery'.[39] As for her promiscuity, the copious evidence left to us indicates that she had two sexual partners – her first love and her husband.

Her story is, like so many lives, one which was predominantly shaped not by intention or design, but by the unquantifiable power of luck. This may be frustrating when we try to construct an easily understood narrative, but Catherine, whose life is often seen as one moulded and ended by conspiracy, exemplifies the impact of the unpredictable and the improbable. It was improbable luck that first brought her to the king's attention in 1539–40, and it was appalling circumstance that led from Mary Hall's revelations to Catherine's execution four or five months later. Had Mary retracted her statement, if John Lascelles had decided it was too dangerous to bring to Cranmer, or Henry had dismissed the latter's letter, had Culpepper burned Catherine's note, Francis Dereham stayed in Ireland, or if he had not quarrelled with the dowager duchess and travelled to Pontefract in August 1541, had Lady Rochford withheld gossip about Culpepper's infatuation, if Catherine had held her nerve and not attempted to lie so clumsily during her interrogations, or had Henry decided not to prosecute her to the end, when even some in the House of Lords were uncertain about the merits of executing her – if any of these had played differently, the outcome of the scandal might have been disgrace or survival, rather than death.

In Greek myth, Persephone was the daughter of Spring, snatched from the land of the living by the god of death to keep him company. As queen, Catherine made many mistakes, but it was not a foregone conclusion that she should pay for those errors with her life. At every stage of Catherine's fall, after the first revelation, her husband's hand can be seen guiding her into the grave as punishment for her betrayal and humiliation of him. Catherine's career offers a window into the mesmerising brutality of Henrician England as it lurched through the final decade of Henry's reign and the first of the English Reformation. In this world, Catherine Howard did not have the impact of other English queens, before or after, and it would be disingenuous to claim otherwise, but that augments, rather than lessens, her particular tragedy. Looked at in detail, the portrait that emerges of Henry's fifth wife is of an elegant, beautiful, and vivacious young woman. Her faults were obvious, but usually trivial. She could be vain, quick-tempered, egotistical, reckless, and when in a temper, capable of great rudeness. Catherine was mediocre in everything, except her appearance and her charm. She was a girl whom many of us may know or have known.

In his letter to his brother and family in Calais, in which he gave them, and us, the only extant eyewitness account of Catherine Howard's final moments, the merchant Ottwell Johnson added a postscript: 'I pray you let them be made partakers of this news, for surely the thing is well worth the knowledge.'[40]

Appendix I

The Alleged Portraits of Catherine Howard

There are three key problems confronting any assessment of Catherine's portraiture. Firstly, after her execution there is a good chance that any images of Catherine would have been destroyed or ignored, until their identity became a subject of debate to later generations. A miniature alleged to show Catherine as painted by Hans Holbein was sold at Antwerp in 1668, then vanished from history.[1] The allure of the lost is always potent, but even this portrait may have been mislabelled, as there is no documentary evidence that Catherine ever had her portrait painted – the second serious difficulty – and so it may be that Brett Dolman was correct in his recent paper when he argued that in searching for a surviving likeness of Catherine Howard we may very well be hunting for the impossible.[2] The paperwork could, of course, have been lost, in which case one could argue that a surviving portrait or portraits would be the most obvious pieces of evidence that Catherine did indeed sit for an artist.

The third problem is the enthusiasm with which collections and patrons hope to own or view an image of one of Henry VIII's six wives. Most people would rather discover a portrait of Queen Catherine Howard than one of Elizabeth Cromwell or Baroness Monteagle. The changing identifications of many Tudor portraits is thus a proverbial game of musical chairs. For example, a miniature allegedly showing Anne Boleyn by Lucas Horenbout has absolutely nothing to support that identification.[3] The sitter's brooch, once cited as the Ormond falcon and thus proof that it is a portrait of a Boleyn, is in fact too tiny, even upon magnification, to show anything clearly. The same miniature had previously been identified as Jane Seymour and then Katherine of Aragon, before it was floated as a potential likeness of Mary Boleyn, or her sister-in-law, Lady Rochford.

There are six original images, most with copies or derivatives, which have been identified as likenesses of Catherine. An incomplete Holbein sketch in the Royal Collection that shows a pretty young woman with auburn hair and a gentle smile was first formally identified as Catherine in 1867 on no compelling ground beyond optimism. There was no tradition placing it as Catherine before the eighteenth century and precious little in the way of documentary support afterwards.[4] There is also a miniature currently held at the Yale Center for British Art in New Haven that has been suggested as a potential portrait of Catherine.[5] The sitter's clothes place it at approximately the right time for it to be Catherine, and the current tentative reattribution to Lucas Horenbout rules out earlier hypotheses that it depicts either Elizabeth I or Lady Jane Grey, since Horenbout was dead before either queen was of the right age; the lady in the Yale miniature does bear a certain physical resemblance to the future Mary I.[6] It cannot, of course, absolutely be ruled out as a likeness of Catherine, especially given the style of costume, but there are other candidates whom the Yale miniature is far more likely to depict.

In the chapel of King's College, Cambridge, the east window is one magnificent stained-glass monument among many. It shows the scene 'The Queen of Sheba Bringing Gifts to Solomon', and the marked physical similarities between the biblical king, sitting on his golden throne beneath a cobalt-blue canopy, and Henry VIII, prompted the theory that the face of the queen of Sheba was inspired by Catherine.[7] The stained-glass queen wears a gown of green and white, the Tudor colours, with ruby, pink, and gold details. Gold bands rope around her dress like chains as she prostrates herself at Solomon/Henry's feet, proffering a golden vessel in tribute and flanked by her sturdy guards and ladies-in-waiting in amethyst fur-lined robes and ruby gowns. The presence of the traditional crest and motto of the Prince of Wales elsewhere in the same window means that it must have been completed after Edward's birth in 1537, while the presence of the initials 'HK' gives us a date between July 1540 and January 1547, the period after Edward's birth when Henry was married to women called Catherine/Katherine. It also rules out recent speculation that the queen of Sheba's face might have been inspired by Anne Boleyn's.[8] It is possible that the east window at King's was finished during Henry's sixth marriage, to Katherine Parr, and even if it was completed during his time with Catherine Howard, as seems probable, the depiction of the queen of Sheba is neither clear nor detailed enough to provide us with much of an idea of the young queen's appearance.

Perhaps the most famous portrait of 'Catherine' is a half-length by Hans Holbein, about twenty-nine inches tall, of a lady in a high-necked dark dress and a white French hood trimmed with gold braid. She wears a golden necklace, waist chain and rings, and a large pendant that seems to depict the angels leading Lot's family from the biblical destruction of Sodom.[9] On either side of the sitter's head, Holbein has added the biographical detail 'ETATIS SVÆ 21' ('AGED 21'). The original is owned by the Toledo Museum of Art in Ohio, which acquired it in 1926, and copies are housed at the National Portrait Gallery in London and Hever Castle in Kent.[10]

It was identified as Catherine by the art historian Sir Lionel Cust in 1909, after he was asked to examine it by its owners, the Cromwell family. The portrait's association with the Cromwells is enough to prove beyond reasonable doubt that whoever sat for this portrait in the sixteenth century, it was not Catherine Howard. Few families had less of a reason to keep a portrait of her than Thomas Cromwell's, nor did the family have a tradition of regarding the unidentified lady as one of Henry VIII's queens. Up to about 1817, they seemed to think it might show Oliver Cromwell's mother, Elizabeth, but the clothing is at least a generation too early for that.[11] Later in the nineteenth century, the rather magnificently named Avarilla Oliveria Cromwell believed it was a likeness of Henry VIII's youngest sister, Mary, an interpretation shared and promoted by the talented amateur artist and historian Sarah Capel-Coningsby, Countess of Essex.[12]

Lionel Cust's findings, published in the *Burlington Magazine* in 1910, enjoyed wide acceptance for the next forty years, which might explain why the Toledo portrait still crops up on so many souvenirs commemorating Catherine and Henry VIII's other family members.[13] However, as early as 1953 it was being questioned at a Liverpool exhibition, whose organisers preferred to showcase it as an *Unknown Lady*, a conclusion shared today by its curators in Toledo, who label it as a *Portrait of a Lady, probably a Member of the Cromwell Family*.[14] When one of its copies was sold in a Christie's auction room in 1961, it was tentatively marketed to prospective buyers under Avarilla Cromwell's suggestion of Henry's sister Mary Tudor, Queen of France and Duchess of Suffolk.[15] Eight years later, Sir Roy Strong, director of the National Portrait Gallery, argued that it was a portrait of Catherine's lady-in-waiting Lady Elizabeth Cromwell, Gregory's wife and Queen Jane's sister. The style of the sleeves suggests it was painted between 1535 and 1540 which, with the sitter's age given as twenty-one, would put her date of birth between 1513 and 1519. Elizabeth Seymour's date of birth is usually given either as circa 1513 or circa 1518. As a wealthy married woman and then as Cromwell's daughter-in-law, she was in a position to afford a portrait by Holbein. Some viewers detect facial similarities, particularly around the mouth, chin, and nose, between the sitter and Queen Jane in a portrait by the same artist, and Elizabeth was a member by marriage of the family who owned the portrait from the sixteenth until the early twentieth century.[16]

Recent attempts to push Catherine's date of birth back to the late 1510s are largely motivated by the desire to validate this portrait.[17] The dress, though clearly appropriate for a member of the upper classes, is not quite grand enough for a queen, which has prompted some defenders of the portrait's authenticity to advance a chronology wholly untenable with what we know of Catherine's biography, namely that it must have been painted before she became queen, around the time she joined the court. This would date the portrait to a time in Catherine's life when she was paying back Francis Dereham the money she had borrowed to buy a few silk flowers, and require her to have been born between 1516 and 1518, which makes her almost a decade older than some of the other maids of honour in 1539, and negates every piece of evidence we have from her childhood. Holbein painted the great and the good, and he did not come cheap. Even if the Howards had paid the fee during the time Catherine was Henry's mistress, an unlikely scenario considering the secrecy surrounding the affair and the lengths Henry went to in lying about the reasons for his frequent visits to Lambeth, accepting that this portrait showed Catherine Howard before she became queen requires us to disregard almost everything we know about her life before 1540.

Although its two copies were once dismissed as later reproductions, analysis of the Hever Castle copy's panelling dates it possibly to the mid-sixteenth century, which again lowers the likelihood of it being Catherine, since after her execution copies of her image were hardly in high demand. Before coming to Hever, that copy was owned by the Dukes of Sutherland, who counted Henry VIII's youngest sister as one of their ancestresses. The dress is too late in terms of its style for the portrait to be of the elder Princess Mary, but it is from the right time period to show one of her daughters – Frances Grey, Marchioness of Dorset, who was twenty-one in 1538–39, or her younger sister Eleanor Clifford, Countess of Cumberland, who was the same age in 1540–41. Frances Grey inherited her father's title on her husband's behalf in 1545 and became Duchess of Suffolk, an ancestress of the Dukes of Sutherland and one of the most prominent figures at the courts of her uncle Henry VIII and cousin Edward VI.[18] Unlike Queen Catherine, Frances Grey was the right age and background and was connected to families who might want a copy of her portrait. Who the lady in the Toledo

Holbein is cannot be said with certainty. Elizabeth, Lady Cromwell, and Frances Grey, later Duchess of Suffolk, are the most likely candidates, with the available circumstantial evidence supporting either candidate, while none of it supports it being a likeness of Catherine.[19]

Another alleged portrait of Catherine is a miniature of a lady in a golden dress with furred sleeves and a large ruby-pearl-and-emerald necklace. Two versions exist – one in the Royal Collection and the other in the collection of the Duke of Buccleuch and Queensberry.[20] A description that closely matches it places it as one of the items recovered by the royal household after the restoration of the monarchy in the 1660s, and it seems to have been one of the pieces perhaps initially accumulated a generation earlier in the treasure trove of Thomas Howard, 21st Earl of Arundel. Lord Arundel was fascinated by his ancestors, especially those who had lived at the court of Henry VIII, and he went to great lengths to acquire portraits of them and their contemporaries.[21] Many of his Tudor pieces were inherited from the collection of Lord Lumley, a Catholic peer born in Henry VIII's reign and a brother-in-law of the 4th Duke of Norfolk, who managed to acquire full-length portraits of Anne Boleyn and Christina of Denmark (Boleyn's, unfortunately, vanished in 1773, shortly after it was damaged by fire).[22] However, it is not clear when this miniature was first identified as a likeness of Catherine. If it did come into the Royal Collection from Lord Lumley via the Earl of Arundel, the absence of a label identifying it as Catherine Howard is problematic in light of Lord Lumley's ties to the Howards in the generation after Catherine's death. When it was inventoried by the royal household in 1661, it was described as an unknown lady in the dress of Henry VIII's era, but by the 1740s the Buccleuch copy had inspired the image of Catherine in a pictorial guide to British history by Thomas Birch called *The Heads of Illustrious Persons of Great Britain*.[23] When the version in the Royal Collection was catalogued again, around 1837, the popular identification had stuck and it was listed as Catherine.[24]

More recently, the necklace, which is almost identical to one worn in Holbein's portrait of Jane Seymour, also once part of the Arundel collection and now housed at the Kunsthistorisches Museum in Vienna, has become the key piece of evidence in the debate on the sitter's identity. The necklace in question is listed in the jewellery collections of Catherine Howard and Katherine Parr, and on that basis David Starkey has suggested that the miniature is of Queen Catherine, perhaps painted to celebrate her wedding in 1540.[25] With queens often loaning pieces of their jewellery to friends for special occasions, such as having one's portrait painted, Susan James has countered that the lady in the miniature may be Lady Margaret Douglas, who would have been in a position to borrow jewellery from Queen Anne Boleyn or Catherine, or from Katherine Parr after 1543, quite possibly in preparation for her own wedding.[26] There is another candidate: Mary, Lady Monteagle – the Duke of Suffolk's daughter, who was one of Jane Seymour's ladies-in-waiting and who sat for a sketch by Holbein that now hangs in the Royal Library at Windsor Castle.[27] The woman in this sketch does have certain physical similarities to the lady in the miniature, although it is difficult to tell since they are shown from opposite angles. There is unfortunately not evidence enough either to rule the miniature out or to prove that it is Catherine, and the current reference used for it by the Royal Collection, *Portrait of a Lady, perhaps Catherine Howard*, seems the fairest conclusion on it.

A final work, currently housed at the Metropolitan Museum of Art in New York, shows a young girl with auburn hair, dark eyes, pale skin, and full lips.[28] Her low-cut navy dress has golden pins holding together its sleeves, which are interspersed with crimson, and a gold-decorated French hood sits so far back on her head it requires a strap beneath her chin, like a bonnet. Like Holbein's probable portrait of Elizabeth Cromwell or Frances Grey, where the same style is worn, the headdress trend helps date the portrait, along with the lower cut of the bodice and the shape of the sleeves. The Metropolitan portrait seems to have originated from the workshop of Hans Holbein the Younger between circa 1540 and 1545. The museum, which acquired the portrait along with the rest of the Jules Bache collection in 1949, identifies it as *Unknown lady, c. 1540–5, aged 17*, a piece of information provided in original gold lettering on either side of the girl's head.

The latter detail fits with other circumstantial evidence of Catherine's life. If the Metropolitan portrait is of her, the age given puts her date of birth at circa 1523; it supports de Marillac's assessment of a graceful and pretty young woman, and there are some physical similarities to other women in the extended Howard family, noticeably to Catherine's cousin, the Dowager Duchess of Richmond.[29] The details on the dress, decorated with pearls and gold and set off by a matching brooch and necklaces, narrows down the pool of who it could be to someone wealthy enough to dress this way, and to retain Holbein as a seventeen-year-old member of Henry VIII's court in the early-to-mid-1540s. Some of the possible alternatives, such as Lady Elizabeth Fitzgerald, the Earl of Kildare's daughter, are ruled out by their other portraits, which show no similarity to the woman in the Metropolitan Museum's piece.[30] Others, like Anne Bassett, who turned seventeen sometime around 1539, would not have had enough money for this kind of portrait, following her stepfather's incarceration. Lady Anne Manners, the eldest daughter of the Earl and Countess of Rutland, and the baronesses Bray and Sheffield, respective daughters of the earls of Shrewsbury and Oxford, were of the right age and background, though none of them was regularly at court in the last decade of Henry's reign, which leaves Catherine as a possible, if by no means definite, candidate.

Brett Dolman's suggestion that searching for Catherine's portrait may be a futile quest given the transience of her career is depressing but inescapably fair.[31] Of the six images associated with her, only two, the Royal Collection's Holbein miniature and the Metropolitan Museum's Holbein half-length, stand up to scrutiny and, tantalisingly, might show us the face of Catherine Howard.

Appendix II

The Ladies of Catherine Howard's Household

An asterisk indicates where the lady described is, in the author's opinion, the most likely candidate, but not a certainty.

The Great Ladies of the Household

LADY MARGARET DOUGLAS (1515–78), daughter of Archibald Douglas, 6th Earl of Angus (d. 1557), and Margaret Tudor, Dowager Queen of Scots (d. 1541). Subsequently, Countess of Lennox and mother-in-law to Mary, Queen of Scots.

MARY FITZROY, Dowager Duchess of Richmond and Somerset (c.1519–55), daughter of Thomas Howard, 3rd Duke of Norfolk (d. 1554), and widow of Henry Fitzroy, 1st Duke of Richmond and Somerset (d. 1536).

KATHERINE BRANDON, Duchess of Suffolk (1519–80), daughter of William Willoughby, 11th Baron Willoughby de Eresby (d. 1526), and wife of Charles Brandon, 1st Duke of Suffolk (d. 1545).

MARY RADCLYFFE, Countess of Sussex (d. 1557), daughter of Sir John Arundell of Lanherne (d. 1545), and wife of the Lord Great Chamberlain Robert Radclyffe, 1st Earl of Sussex (d. 1542). Subsequently, Countess of Arundel.

LADY MARGARET HOWARD (*c.*1515–81), Queen Catherine's aunt by marriage, daughter of Sir Thomas Gamage of Glamorgan, and wife of Lord William Howard (d. 1573). Subsequently, Baroness Howard of Effingham.

* ELIZABETH FIENNES DE CLINTON, Lady Clinton (*c.*1500–40), daughter of John Blount (d. 1531), widow of Gilbert, 1st Baron Tailboys (d. 1530), wife of Edward Fiennes de Clinton, 9th Baron Clinton and Saye (d. 1585), and mother of the late Henry Fitzroy, 1st Duke of Richmond and Somerset (d. 1536).

The Ladies and Gentlewomen of the Privy Chamber

ELEANOR MANNERS, Countess of Rutland (d. *c.*1551), daughter of Sir William Paston (d. 1554), and wife of the queen's chamberlain Thomas Manners, 1st Earl of Rutland (d. 1543).

JANE BOLEYN, Dowager Viscountess Rochford (*c.*1505–ex. 1542), daughter of Henry Parker, 10th Baron Morley (d. 1556), and widow of George Boleyn, Viscount Rochford (ex. 1536).

LADY KATHERINE EDGECOMBE (d. 1553), daughter of Sir John St John of Bletsoe, widow of Sir Gruffydd ap Rhys of Carmarthen (d. 1521) and of Sir Piers, sometimes given as Peter, Edgecombe (d. 1539).

LADY ISABELLA BAYNTON (d. 1573), Queen Catherine's sister, daughter of Sir Ralph Leigh and Lady Joyce Howard (née Culpepper, prev. Leigh), and wife of the queen's vice chamberlain Sir Edward Baynton (d. 1544).

MRS ANNE HERBERT (*c.*1513–52), daughter of Sir Thomas Parr (d. 1517), wife of William Herbert (d. 1570), and sister of the future queen consort, Katherine Parr (d. 1548). Subsequently, Countess of Pembroke.

MRS ELIZABETH TYRWHITT (d. 1578), daughter of Sir Goddard Oxenbridge (d. 1531) and wife of Robert Tyrwhitt (d. 1572).

MRS JOYCE LEE (d. *c.*1586), daughter of Edward Sutton, 2nd Baron Dudley (d. 1531), widow of Sir John Leighton (d. 1532), and wife of Richard Lee (d. *c.*1558).

MRS SUSANNA GILMYN (d. 1554), daughter of Gerard Horenbout (d. 1541), widow of John Parker (d. 1537), and wife of John Gilmyn (d. 1558).

The Ladies and Gentlewomen Attendant

ELIZABETH, LADY CROMWELL (d. 1563), daughter of Sir John Seymour (d. 1536), widow of Sir Anthony Ughtred (d. 1534), wife of Gregory, 1st Baron Cromwell (d. 1551), and sister of the late queen consort, Jane Seymour (d. 1537). Subsequently, Baroness St John.

LADY JANE DUDLEY (*c.*1508–55), daughter of Sir Edward Guildford (d. 1534) and wife of the queen's Master of the Horse, Sir John Dudley (ex. 1553). Subsequently, Duchess of Northumberland and mother-in-law to Queen Jane (née Grey).

* LADY ELIZABETH ARUNDELL (d. 1564), daughter of Gerald Danet (d. 1520) and wife of Sir John Arundell of Lanherne (d. 1557).

LADY JOAN DENNY (d. 1553), daughter of Sir Philip Champernowne (d. 1545) and wife of Sir Anthony Denny (d. 1549).

LADY JANE WRIOTHESLEY (*c.*1511–74), daughter of William Cheney and wife of Sir Thomas Wriothesley (d. 1550). Subsequently, Countess of Southampton.

LADY KATHERINE HENNEAGE (d. 1575), daughter of Sir John Skipwith (d. 1518) and wife of Sir Thomas Henneage, a gentleman of the king's privy chamber (d. 1553).

* LADY ANNE KNYVET (d. 1563), daughter of Sir John Shelton (d. 1532) and wife of Sir Edmund Knyvet (d. 1551).

LADY ELEANOR WROUGHTON (*c.*1510–90), daughter of Edward Lewknor (d. 1522) and wife of Sir William Wroughton (d. 1559).

MRS JANE MEWTAS (née Astley) (d. *c.*1550), parentage unknown, wife of Peter Mewtas (d. 1562).

The Maids of Honour

LADY LUCY SOMERSET (1524–83), daughter of Henry Somerset, 2nd Earl of Worcester (d. 1549). Subsequently, Baroness Latimer.

DOROTHY BRAY (*c.*1524–1605), daughter of Edmund, 1st Baron Bray (d. 1539). Subsequently, Baroness Chandos.

ANNE BASSETT (1521–57), daughter of Sir John Bassett (d. 1528) and stepdaughter of Arthur Plantagenet, 1st Viscount Lisle (d. 1542). Subsequently, Lady Anne Hungerford.

MARGARET GARNEYS (d. 1599), probably a daughter of Mr John Garneys. Subsequently, Viscountess Hereford, and then Baroness Willoughby of Parham.

MARGARET COPLEDIKE (b. *c.*1524), daughter of Leonard Copledike. Very little is known of her life after 1541.

DAMASCIN STRADLING (1524–67), daughter of Sir Thomas Stradling. Very little is known of her life after 1541, except that she left England with Jane (née Dormer), Countess of Feria, after the death of Queen Mary I and subsequently died in Spain.

Appendix III

The Fall of Catherine Howard

November 1541

2   All Souls – the Archbishop of Canterbury informs the king of John Lascelles's claims about the queen's premarital romances.

3   Either today or the day before, John Lascelles is questioned.

4   Mary Hall is questioned in her home by the Earl of Southampton.

5   Henry Manox is questioned at his home in Lambeth.
    Francis Dereham is detained, ostensibly to answer questions about his alleged piracy in Ireland.

6   The queen is informed of the allegations against her, and she is questioned by Archbishop Cranmer for the first time.
    The king leaves Hampton Court and spends the night at Whitehall.

7   The queen confesses her involvement with Francis Dereham to Cranmer.

8   Rumours circulate in the court that the queen is barren and that Anne of Cleves may be rehabilitated.

11 Orders are given to move the queen to Syon Abbey.

12 The Lord Chancellor informs the rest of the Privy Council of the charges against the queen.

13   Mary Hall and Alice Restwold are summoned to
            Westminster to answer questions about the queen's
            activities before her marriage. Katherine Tilney is
            questioned by Sir Thomas Wriothesley.
                Thomas Culpepper is interrogated for the first time.

14   The queen is moved to Syon Abbey.
                The queen's household is disbanded.
                Jane, Lady Rochford, is questioned and states that
            she believes the queen has committed adultery.
                Margaret Morton is asked about the queen's
            behaviour during the progress to the north.
                Thomas Culpepper's goods are inventoried.

15   Lady Margaret Howard testifies about the queen's
            intimacy with Francis Dereham, before her marriage.
                Andrew Maunsay is interviewed.

16   Lady Rochford's goods are inventoried.

17   Lady Rochford is entrusted to the care of Lady
            Russell, after suffering a nervous breakdown.
                Lord Russell informs Eustace Chapuys that the
            queen is suspected of adultery with Culpepper.

19   Rumours are circulating that the queen will be
            pardoned.

20   The King of France discusses the scandal with the
            English ambassadors.

22   Catherine is stripped of her title as queen.

23   The King of France writes to Henry VIII with
            commiserations on Catherine's behaviour.
                Writs are issued to summon Parliament.

24   The first indictment against the queen is published.

30   Katherine Tilney is questioned again, this time about
            the queen's behaviour in the north.

December

1   Trial of Francis Dereham and Thomas Culpepper at
            the Guildhall, London.

2   Catherine's brothers and the Earl of Surrey ride
       through the streets of London to advertise their lack
       of complicity.

3   Robert Damport is questioned for the second
       consecutive day.

4   The Dowager Duchess of Norfolk is taken in for
       questioning.

5   The interrogation of the dowager duchess. The
       Countess of Bridgewater is committed to the
       wardship of the Earl of Southampton.
           At Syon, Catherine is once again questioned about
       how Francis Dereham entered her household.

6   Norfolk House is locked up.
           Robert Damport alleges that Francis Dereham
       hoped that the king would die, so he could marry
       Catherine.
           The Countess of Bridgewater's maid is among
       those questioned.

7   The order is given to torture Robert Damport and
       Francis Dereham.

8   The Feast of the Immaculate Conception –
       interrogation of the Countess of Bridgewater.
           Mary Hall is pardoned.

9   Thomas Culpepper's death warrant is signed.
           Lord William Howard offends his interrogators
       with his 'stiff' manner.
           The goods of Lord William Howard and the
       Countess of Bridgewater are inventoried.

10   Execution at Tyburn of Thomas Culpepper and
       Francis Dereham

11   The Dowager Duchess of Norfolk is sent to the
       Tower.
           Anne of Cleves's chamberlain, Sir William Goring,
       and her house steward are ordered to appear before
       the Privy Council to answer allegations that Anne
       had given birth to a bastard child.

13	Caretakers are appointed for the Howards' seized London properties.
	The Countess of Bridgewater's three children are committed to ward.
15	The Duke of Norfolk writes a letter disowning his imprisoned relatives.
22	Lord William Howard, his wife Margaret, Katherine Tilney, William Ashby, Robert Damport, and Margaret Benet are all arraigned for treason.

January 1542

16	Opening of Parliament.
	The queen's prosecution is discussed in the House of Lords.
	The Dowager Duchess of Norfolk and the Countess of Bridgewater are attainted for treason.
26	The Emperor Charles V orders Eustace Chapuys to prevent Anne of Cleves's restoration, if rumours about it prove to be accurate.
28	The House of Lords proposes sending a delegation to Syon to offer Catherine the opportunity to stand trial.
29	The queen and Lady Rochford are condemned to death by act of attainder.

February

1st week	Catherine rejects the offer of a trial by her peers.
7	Sir John Gage visits Syon to disband what remains of Catherine's household.
10	Catherine is taken to the Tower.
11	Catherine and Lady Rochford's death sentences are read out to both houses of Parliament.
12	The former queen makes her last confession.
13	Catherine Howard and Jane, Lady Rochford, are beheaded at the Tower.

ACKNOWLEDGEMENTS

In the course of writing this book, I have incurred debts as numerous and difficult to repay as Edmund Howard's, though far more pleasurable to shoulder. My agent and friend, Brettne Bloom, made all of this possible; it is a privilege to work with her. The same is true of Dr James Davis, who supervised and encouraged my dissertation on Catherine's household in 2011; Professor Catherine Clinton, who was the first to suggest that there might be a book in it, and Dr Steve Gunn, my undergraduate tutor on the sixteenth century, who again gave so generously of his time as I was returning to the subject of Thomas Cromwell, the Howards, and sixteenth-century graves.

My wonderful editor at Harper Collins, Arabella Pike, has my sincere gratitude, as does everyone who worked on *Young and Damned and Fair* in London and New York.

My thanks to the staff at the Ashmolean Museum, Oxford; the Bodleian Library, Oxford; the British Library, London; the Garden Museum, London; Hawkwise Falconry, Nuneaton; Hever Castle, Kent; the McClay Library, Belfast; the Metropolitan Museum of Art, New York; the National Archives, Kew; Pontefract Castle, West Yorkshire; the Royal Collection Trust; the Scala Archives; Sotheby's; the Toledo Museum of Art, Ohio; the Yale Center for British Art; and at the cathedrals of Lincoln and York.

Colleagues, professionals, and academics who graciously lent their time were Alan Brown, Dana Chernock, Dr James

Corke-Webster, Dr T. Alexander Desmond, Michael Charles Foote, Rachel Franks at King's Manor (York), Becky Friar, Dr Sarah George, Isabel Holowaty, Dr Georgy Kantor, Professor Diarmaid MacCulloch, Lauren Mackay, Dr Lawrence W. Nichols, Philip Norman, Alison Palmer, Lauren Ritz, Professor Maggie Snowling, President of St John's College, Oxford, Dr Eleanor Standley, Timothy Stead at York Minster, Dr Edward Town, Dr Christopher Warleigh-Lack, Kathryn Warner, Colin Weston, and Joseph Zigmond.

My family have been supportive and encouraging throughout this process, and long before, they cheerfully endured years of an ever-increasing mountain of books on the sixteenth century in my childhood home. My deepest thanks, as always, to them and also to the friends who helped in different ways along the road to this book's completion – Laura Bradley, Lauren Browne, Cailum Carragher, Scott De Buitléir, Robbie Dagher, Nina Foster, Claire Handley, Aoife Herity, Dan Kelly, Rebecca Lenaghan, Stephanie Mann, Stephen McCombe, Dr Hannah McCormick, Ryan Nees, Jim De Piante, Alexa Stewart Reid, Tim and Claire Ridgway, Mary-Eileen Russell, Eric Spies, Alex Steer, Emma Elizabeth Taylor, my editor in the U.S. Trish Todd, Angharad Williams, and the Woodward family.

Gareth Russell
Belfast
Lent, 2016

BIBLIOGRAPHY

Printed Primary Sources and Sources Published Before 1731

A collection of ordinances and regulations for the government of the royal household, made in divers reigns: from King Edward III to King William and Queen Mary, also receipts in ancient cookery (London: Society of Antiquaries of London, 1790)

Alba, Jacobo Fitz-James Stuart, 10th Duke of Berwick and 17th Duke of (ed.), *Correspondencia de Gutierre de Fuensalida* (Madrid: privately published, 1907)

Anglo, Sydney (ed.), *The Great Tournament Roll of Westminster: a collotype reproduction of the manuscript* (Oxford: Clarendon Press, 1968)

Archaeologia: or Miscellaneous Tracts relating to Antiquity, Published by the Society of Antiquaries of London (London: J. B. Nichols and Son, 1834)

Ascoli, Georges, *La Grande-Bretagne devant l'opinion française au XVIIe siècle* (Geneva: Slatkine, 1971)

Ashton, John (intro.), *A Ballade of the Scottyshe Kynge, written by John Skelton, Poet Laureate to King Henry the Eighth* (London: Elliot Stock, 1882)

Aungier, George James, *The History and Antiquities of Syon Monastery, the Parish of Isleworth and the Chapel of Hounslow* (London: J. B. Nichols and Sons, 1840)

Bannerman, W. Bruce (ed.), *The Visitations of the County of Surrey made and taken in the years 1530, by Thomas Benolte, Clarenceux King of Arms; 1572, by Robert Cooke, Clarenceux King of Arms, and 1623, by Samuel Thompson, Windsor Herald, and Augustin Vincent, Rouge Croix Pursuivant, Marshals and Deputies to William Camden, Clarenceux King of Arms* (London: Harleian Society, 1899)

— *The Visitations of Kent, taken in the years 1574 and 1592 by Robert Cooke, Clarenceux* (London: Harleian Society, 1924)

Beadle, Richard, and Colin Richmond (eds), *Paston Letters and Papers of the Fifteenth Century: Part III* (Oxford: Oxford University Press, 2005)

Boase, C. W. (ed.), *Register of the University of Oxford: Volume I (1449–63; 1505–71)* (Oxford: Clarendon Press, 1885)

Burnet, Gilbert, *The History of the Reformation of the Church of England* (Oxford: Oxford University Press, 1829)

Calendar of Inquisitions Post Mortem and other analogous documents preserved in the Public Record Office: Henry VII (London: Eyre and Spottiswoode, 1898)

Calendar of the Manuscripts of the Marquis of Bath preserved at Longleat, Wiltshire (Dublin: Historical Manuscripts Commission, 1907)

Castiglione, Baldesar, *The Book of the Courtier*, George Bull (trans.) (London: Penguin, 1976)

Cavendish, George, *The Life of Cardinal Wolsey, by George Cavendish, his Gentleman Usher, and Metrical Visions*, Samuel Weller Singer (ed.) (Chiswick: Harding, Triphook, and Lepard, 1825)

Cessolis, Jacobus de, *Game and Playe of Chesse*, William Caxton (trans.), W. E. A. Axon (ed.) (St Leonards-on-Sea: British Chess Magazine Classics Reprints, 1969)

Cherbury, Edward, 1st Baron Herbert of, *The Life and Raigne of Henry the Eighth* (London: M. Clark, 1683)

Chester, Joseph Lemuel, and George J. Armytage (eds), *Allegations for Marriage Licenses issued by the Bishop of London, 1520 to 1610* (London: Harleian Society, 1887)

Clifford, Henry, *The Life of Jane Dormer, Duchess of Feria*, Joseph Stevenson (ed.) (London: Burns and Oates, 1887)

Commynes, Philippe de, *The Memoirs of Philip de Comines* (London: J. Brotherton et al., 1723)

Cramer, J. A. (ed. and trans.), *The Second Book of the Travels of Nicander Nucius, of Corcyra* (London: Camden Society, 1841)

Crawford, Anne (ed.), *Letters of the Queens of England, 1100–1547* (Stroud: Sutton, 1997)

Dashwood, G. H. (ed.), *The Visitation of Norfolk in the year 1563 taken by William Hervey, Clarenceux King of Arms* (Norwich: Miller and Leavins, 1878)

Davis, Norman (ed.), *Paston Letters and Papers of the Fifteenth Century* (Oxford: Oxford University Press, 1971)

Devey, Joseph (ed.), *The Moral and Historical Works of Lord Bacon, including his Essays, Apophthegms, Wisdom of the Ancients, New Atlantis, and Life of Henry the Seventh* (London: Henry G. Bohn, 1854)

Dugdale, William, *The Baronage of England, or An Historical Account of the Lives and most Memorable Actions of Our English Nobility in the Saxons' time, to the Norman Conquest; And from thence, of those who had their rise before the end of King Henry the Third's Reign. Deduced from Publick Records, Antient Historians, and other Authorities* (London: Thomas Newcomb, 1675)

Durling, Richard J. (ed.), *A Catalogue of Sixteenth Century Printed Books in the National Library of Medicine* (Bethesda, MD: US Department of Health, Education, and Welfare, 1967)

Ellis, Henry (ed.), *Original Letters, Illustrative of English History* (London: Harding, Triphook, and Lepard, 1824)

— *Original Letters of Eminent Literary Men of the Sixteenth, Seventeenth, and Eighteenth Centuries* (London: Camden Society, 1843)

Frowde, Henry, *The Historical Register of the University of Oxford being a supplement to the Oxford University Calendar* (Oxford: Clarendon Press, 1900)

Gairdner, James (ed.), *Memorials of King Henry the Seventh* (London: Longman, Green, Longman, & Roberts, 1858)

Hall, Edward, *Hall's Chronicle: Containing the History of England During the Reign of Henry IV and the Succeeding Monarchs to the End of the Reign of Henry VIII*, Henry Ellis (ed.) (London: Johnson et al., 1809)

Hamilton, Hans Claude (ed.), *Calendar of the State Papers relating to Ireland, of the Reigns of Henry VIII., Edward VI., Mary, and Elizabeth, 1509–1573* (London: Longman, Green, Longman, & Roberts, 1860)

Hannay, R. K., R. L. Mackie, and Anne Spilman (eds), *The Letters of James the Fourth, 1505–1513* (Edinburgh: Scottish Historical Society, 1953)

Hannay, Robert Kerr, and Denys Hay (eds), *The Letters of James V* (Edinburgh: Her Majesty's Stationery Office, 1954)

Hinds, Allen B., *Calendar of State Papers and Manuscripts Relating to English Affairs Existing in the Archives and Collections of Milan* (London: His Majesty's Stationery Office, 1912)

Holinshed, Raphael, *The Third Volume of Chronicles, Beginning at Duke William the Norman, Commonlie called the Conqueror; and Descending by Degrees of Yeeres to all the Kings and Queenes of England in their Orderlie Successions* (London: Johnson et al., 1808)

Howard, Henry, *Indications of Memorials, Monuments, Paintings, and Engravings of Persons of the Howard Family, and of their Wives and Children, and of those who have married Ladies of the Name, and of the Representatives of some of its Branches now extinct* (Corby Castle: privately published, 1834)

Hume, Martin A. S. (ed.), *Chronicle of King Henry VIII of England, being a contemporary record of some of the principal events of the reigns of Henry VIII and Edward VI, written in Spanish by an unknown hand* (London: George Bell and Sons, 1889)

Jones, Emrys (ed.), *The New Oxford Book of Sixteenth Century Verse* (Oxford: Oxford University Press, 1991)

Journal of the House of Lords, Beginning Anno Primo Henrici Octavi (London: s. n., 1771)

Kaulek, Jean Baptiste Louis (ed.), *Correspondance politique de mm. de Castillon et de Marillac, ambassadeurs de France en Angleterre (1537–1542)* (Paris: Félix Alcan, 1885)

Letters and Papers, Foreign and Domestic of the Reign of Henry VIII, preserved in the Public Record Office, the British Museum, and Elsewhere, R. H. Brodie et al. (eds), (London: Her Majesty's Stationery Office, 1862–1932)

MacGeagh, Henry F., and H. A. C. Sturgess, *Register of Admissions to the Honourable Society of the Middle Temple: From the Fifteenth Century to the year 1944* (London: Butterworth & Co., 1949)

Maclean, John (ed.), *The Berkeley Manuscripts: The Lives of the Berkeleys, Lords of the Honour, castle and manor of Berkeley, in the County of Gloucester, from 1066 to 1618, with a description of the Hundred of Berkeley and its inhabitants, by John Smyth, of Nibley* (Gloucester: John Bellows, 1883–85)

Madden, Frederic, *Narrative of the Visit of the Duke of Najera to England, in the Year 1543–4, Written by his Secretary, Pedro de Gante* (London: Society of Antiquaries, 1831)

The Manuscripts of His Grace the Duke of Rutland, G. C. B., Preserved at Belvoir Castle (London: Historical Manuscripts Commission, 1888)

Maxwell Lyte, H. C., et al. (eds), *Calendar of the Patent Rolls, Henry VII: Volume 1, A.D. 1485–1494* (London: His Majesty's Stationery Office, 1914)

Merriman, Roger Bigelow (ed.), *Life and Letters of Thomas Cromwell* (Oxford: Clarendon Press, 1902)

More, Thomas, *The Complete Works of St Thomas More: The History of King Richard III*, Richard S. Sylvester (ed.) (Forge Village, MA, and London: Yale University Press, 1963)

Muller, James Arthur (ed.), *The Letters of Stephen Gardiner* (Cambridge: Cambridge University Press, 1933)

Myers, A. R., *The Household of Edward IV: The Black Book and the Ordinance of 1478* (Manchester: Manchester University Press, 1959)

Nicolas, Nicholas Harris (ed.), *Testamenta vetusta: illustrations from wills, of manners, customs, etc., from the reign of Henry the second to Queen Elizabeth* (London: Eyre & Spottiswoode, 1826)

— *Proceedings and Ordinances of the Privy Council of England* (London: Eyre & Spottiswoode, 1834–37)

Proceedings of the Society of Antiquaries of Scotland, proceedings 1866–67– 1867–68 (Edinburgh: Neill and Company, 1870)

Pronay, Nicholas, and John Cox (eds), *The Crowland Chronicle Continuations: 1459–1486* (London: Sutton, 1986)

Rebholz, R. A. (ed.), *Sir Thomas Wyatt: The Complete Poems* (New Haven and London: Yale University Press, 1978)

Rickert, Edith, and Israel Gollancz (eds), *The Babees' Book: Medieval Manners for the Young: Done into Modern English from Dr. Furnivall's Texts* (New York: Cooper Square Publishers, 1966)

Robinson, Hastings (ed.), *Original Letters Relative to the English Reformation, written during the reigns of King Henry VIII., King Edward VI., and Queen Mary: Chiefly from the Archives of Zurich* (Cambridge: Cambridge University Press, 1846)

Rowland, Beryl (trans.), *Medieval Woman's Guide to Health: The First English Gynecological Handbook* (Kent, OH: Kent State University Press, 1981)

St Clare Byrne, Muriel (ed.), *The Lisle Letters* (Chicago and London: University of Chicago Press, 1981)

Sander, Nicholas, *Rise and Growth of the Anglican Schism*, David Lewis (trans.) (London: Burns and Oates, 1877)

Sandford, Francis, *A genealogical history of the kings and queens of England, and monarchs of Great Britain, etc. From the conquest, Anno 1066. to the Year 1707* (London: M. Jenour, 1707)

Silva, Alvaro de, (ed.), *The Last Letters of Thomas More* (Grand Rapids, MI: William B. Eerdmans Publishing, 2000)

Slavin, Arthur J. (ed.), *Thomas Cromwell on Church and Commonwealth: Selected Letters, 1523–1540* (New York: Harper & Row, 1969)

Smith, Thomas, and Mary Dewar (eds), *De Republica Anglorum* (Cambridge: Cambridge University Press, 1982)

Spont, Alfred (ed.), *Letters and Papers Relating to the War with France, 1512– 1513* (London: Navy Records Society, 1897)

Starkey David, Alasdair Hawkyard, Maria Hayward, and Philip Ward (eds), *The Inventory of Henry VIII* (London: Society of Antiquaries of London, 1998–2012)

Sterry, Sir Wasey, *The Eton College Register, 1441–1698* (Eton: Spottiswoode, Ballantyne & Co., 1943)

Stevenson, W. H. (ed.), *Report on the Manuscripts of Lord Middleton, Preserved at Wollaton Hall, Nottinghamshire* (Hereford: Historical Manuscripts Commission, 1911)

Strachey, J., et al. (eds), *Rolls of Parliament* (London: Records Commission, 1767–1832)

Strype, John, *Ecclesiastical Memorials; Relating chiefly to Religion and the Reformation of it, and the emergencies of the Church of England, under King Henry VIII. King Edward VI and Queen Mary the First* (London: John Wyat, 1721)

Thomas, William, *The Pilgrim: A Dialogue on the Life and Actions of King Henry the Eighth*, J. A. Froude (ed.) (London: Parker, Son, and Bourn, 1861)

Thomson, Thomas, and Cosmo Innes, *The Acts of the Parliaments of Scotland* (Edinburgh: Record Commission, 1814–75)

Vivian, J. L. (ed.), *The Visitations of Cornwall, Comprising the Heralds' Visitations of 1530, 1573, and 1620* (London: Golding and Lawrence, 1887)

Weever, John, *Ancient Funerall Monuments within the united Monarchie of Great Britain, Ireland, and the Islands adjacent, with the dissolved Monasteries therein contained: their Founders, and what eminent Persons have beene in the same interred. As also the Death and Buriall of Certaine of the Bloud Royall; the Nobilitie, Gentrie of theses Kingdoms entombed in forraine Nations. A work reviving the dead memory of the Royall Progenie, the Nobilitie, Gentrie, and Communaltie, of these his Majesties Dominions* (London: Thomas Harper, 1631)

Williams, C. H. (ed.), *English Historical Documents, 1485–1558* (London: Routledge, 1996)

Windeatt, B. A. (trans.), *The Book of Margery Kempe* (London: Penguin, 2004)

Wriothesley, Charles, *A Chronicle of England During the Reigns of the Tudors*, William Douglas Hamilton (ed.) (London: Camden Society, 1875)

Secondary Sources

Adams, Simon, *Leicester and the Court: Essays on Elizabethan Politics* (Manchester and New York: Manchester University Press, 2002)

— and David Scott Gehring, 'Elizabeth I's Former Tutor Reports on the Parliament of 1559: Johannes Spithovius to the Chancellor of Denmark, 27 February 1559', *English Historical Review* (2013)

Aikin, Lucy, *Memoirs of the Court of Queen Elizabeth* (London: Stratham and Spottiswoode, 1818)

Allen, Willoughby C., *A Critical and Exegetical Commentary on the Gospel According to S. Matthew*, third edition (Edinburgh: T. & T. Clark, 1922)

Alvarez, Manuel Fernández, *Charles V: Elected Emperor and Hereditary Ruler*, J. A. Lalaguna (trans.) (London: Thames and Hudson, 1975)

Amussen, Susan Dwyer, *An Ordered Society: Gender and Class in Early Modern England* (Oxford: Basil Blackwell, 1988)

Anglo, Sydney, 'The Evolution of Early Tudor Disguising, Pageant, and Mask', in *Renaissance Drama* (Chicago: University of Chicago Press, 1968)

Archer, John Michael, *Sovereignty and Intelligence: Spying and Court Culture in the English Renaissance* (Stanford, CA: Stanford University Press, 1993)

Armstrong, Edward, *The Emperor Charles V* (London: Macmillan, 1902)

Aston, Margaret, *The King's Bedpost: Reformation and Iconography in a Tudor Group Portrait* (Cambridge: Cambridge University Press, 1993)

Aylmer, G. E., and Reginald Cant (eds), *A History of York Minster* (Oxford: Clarendon Press, 1977)

Bak, János M. (ed.), *Coronations: Medieval and Early Modern Monarchic Ritual* (Berkeley, CA: University of California Press, 1990)

Baldwin, David, *Elizabeth Woodville: Mother of the Princes in the Tower* (Stroud: Sutton Publishing, 2002)

— *Henry VIII's Last Love: The Extraordinary Life of Katherine Willoughby, Lady-in-Waiting to the Tudors* (Stroud: Amberley, 2015)

Baumgartner, Frederic J., *Henry II: King of France, 1547–1559* (Durham, NC, and London: Duke University Press, 1988)

Beckingsdale, B. W., *Thomas Cromwell: Tudor Minister* (London: Macmillan Press, 1978)

Beer, Barrett L., *Northumberland: The Political Career of John Dudley, Earl of Warwick and Duke of Northumberland* (Kent, OH: Kent State University Press, 1973)

Beier, A. L., D. Cannadine, and J. M. Rosenheim (eds), *The First Modern Society: Essays in English History in Honour of Lawrence Stone* (Cambridge: Cambridge University Press, 1989)

Bell, Doyne C., *Notices of the Historic Persons Buried in the Chapel of St Peter ad Vincula, in the Tower of London: With an Account of the Discovery of the Supposed Remains of Queen Anne Boleyn* (London: J. Murray, 1877)

Bellamy, John, *The Tudor Law of Treason* (London: Routledge & Kegan Paul, 1979)

Benham, William, *Old St Paul's Cathedral* (London: Selby and Co., 1902)

Bernard, G. W., *The Power of the Early Tudor Nobility: A Study of the Fourth and Fifth Earls of Shrewsbury* (Brighton: Harvester Press, 1985)

— (ed.), *The Tudor nobility* (Manchester and New York: Manchester University Press, 1992)

— *The King's Reformation: Henry VIII and the Remaking of the English Church* (New Haven and London: Yale University Press, 2005)

— *Anne Boleyn: Fatal Attractions* (New Haven and London: Yale University Press, 2010)

Betteridge, Thomas, and Suzannah Lipscomb (eds), *Henry VIII and the Court: Art, Politics and Performance* (Farnham: Ashgate, 2013)

Biddle, Martin, *Nonsuch Palace: The Material Culture of a Noble Restoration Household* (Oxford: Oxbow Books, 2005)

Bindoff, S. T. (ed.), *The House of Commons, 1509–1558* (London: Secker & Warburg, 1982)

Bingham, Caroline, *Darnley: A Life of Henry Stuart, Lord Darnley, Consort of Mary Queen of Scots* (London: Constable and Co., 1995)

Birch, Thomas, *The heads of illustrious persons of Great Britain, engraven by Mr. Houbraken, and Mr. Vertue. With their lives and characters* (London: John and Paul Knopton, 1747)

Bloch, Marc, *The Royal Touch: Sacred Monarchy and Scrofula in England and France*, J. E. Anderson (trans.) (Montreal, QC, and Kingston, ON: McGill-Queen's University Press, 1973)

Borman, Tracy, *Thomas Cromwell: The Untold Story of Henry VIII's Most Faithful Servant* (London: Hodder and Stoughton, 2014)

Bowker, Margaret, *The Henrician Reformation: The Diocese of Lincoln Under John Langland, 1521–1547* (Cambridge: Cambridge University Press, 1981)

Braddick, Michael J., and John Walter (eds), *Negotiating Power in Early Modern Society: Order, Hierarchy and Subordination in Britain and Ireland* (Cambridge: Cambridge University Press, 2001)

Bradshaw, Brendan, *The Irish Constitutional Revolution of the Sixteenth Century* (Cambridge: Cambridge University Press, 1979)

Brady, Ciarán, and Raymond Gillespie (eds), *Natives and Newcomers: Essays on the Making of Irish Colonial Society, 1534–1641* (Newbridge, Ireland: Irish Academic Press, 1986)

Brandi, Karl, *The Emperor Charles V: The Growth and Destiny of a Man and a World-Empire*, C. V. Wedgewood (trans.) (London: Jonathan Cape, 1965)

Bray, Alan, *Homosexuality in Renaissance England* (New York: Columbia University Press, 1995)

Breitenberg, Mark, *Anxious Masculinity in Early Modern England* (Cambridge: Cambridge University Press, 1996)

Brenan, Gerald, and Edward Philips Statham, *The House of Howard* (London: Hutchinson & Co., 1907)

Brigden, Susan, *New Worlds, Lost Worlds: The Rule of the Tudors, 1485–1603* (London: Penguin, 2000)

— *Thomas Wyatt: The Heart's Forest* (London: Faber and Faber, 2012)

Brinch, Ove, 'The Medical Problems of Henry VIII', *Centaurus* (1958)

Brown, Jonathan, *Kings and Connoisseurs: Collecting Art in Seventeenth-Century Europe* (Princeton, NJ: Princeton University Press, 1995)

Brown, Raymond E., Joseph A. Fitzmyer, and Roland E. Murphy, *The Jerome Biblical Commentary* (London: Geoffrey Chapman, 1968)

Bruce, Marie Louise, *Anne Boleyn* (London: Pan Books, 1972)

Brundage, James A., *Law, Sex, and Christian Society in Medieval Europe* (Chicago and London: University of Chicago Press, 1987)

Buchanan, Colin, et al., *Tower of London Local Setting Study: An Assessment of the Local Setting of the Tower of London and Guidelines for Its Management* (Bristol: Land Use Consultants, 2010)

Buchanan, Patricia, *Margaret Tudor, Queen of Scots* (Edinburgh and London: Scottish Academic Press, 1985)

Buck, Mark, *Politics, Finance and the Church in the Reign of Edward II: Walter Stapeldon, Treasurer of England* (Cambridge: Cambridge University Press, 1983)

Burke, Bernard, *A Genealogical History of the Dormant, Abeyant, Forfeited, and Extinct Peerages of the British Empire* (London: Harrison, 1883)

Bush, M. L., 'The Lisle–Seymour Disputes: A Study of Power and Influence in the 1530s', *Historical Journal* (1966)

Byrne, Conor, *Katherine Howard: A New History* (Lúcar, Spain: MadeGlobal Publishing, 2014)

Cameron, Jamie, *James V: The Personal Rule, 1528–1542*, Norman Macdougall (ed.), (East Lothian: Tuckwell Press, 1998)

Campbell, Lorne, *Renaissance Portraits: European Portrait-Painting in the 14th, 15th and 16th Centuries* (New Haven and London: Yale University Press, 1990)

Campbell, Lorne, and Susan Foister, 'Gerard, Lucas and Susanna Horenbout', *Burlington Magazine* (1986)

Caraman, Philip (ed.), *The Other Face: Catholic Life Under Elizabeth I* (London: Longmans, Green and Co., 1960)

Card, Tim, *Eton Established: A History from 1440 to 1860* (London: John Murray, 2001)

Carley, James P., *The Books of King Henry VIII and His Wives* (London: British Library, 2004)

Carlson, Eric Josef, *Marriage and the English Reformation* (Oxford: Blackwell Publishers, 1994)

Cartwright, Julia, *Christina of Denmark, Duchess of Milan and Lorraine, 1522–1590* (London: John Murray, 1913)

Carus-Wilson, E. M., *Medieval Merchant Ventures* (London: Methuen & Co., 1954)

Chalmers, C. R., and E. J. Chaloner, '500 Years Later: Henry VIII, Leg Ulcers and the Course of History', *Journal of the Royal Society of Medicine* (2009)

Chamberlin, Frederick, *The Private Character of Henry the Eighth* (London: John Lane, 1932)

Chambers, Roger Wilson, *Thomas More* (London: Jonathan Cape, 1948)

Chaney, Edward (ed.), *The Evolution of English Collecting: Receptions of Italian Art in the Tudor and Stuart Periods* (New Haven and London: Yale University Press, 2003)

Cherry, Clare, and Claire Ridgway, *George Boleyn: Tudor Poet, Courtier, and Diplomat* (Lúcar, Spain: MadeGlobal, 2014)

Childs, Jessie, *Henry VIII's Last Victim: The Life and Times of Henry Howard, Earl of Surrey* (London: Vintage Books, 2008)

Clark, Peter, *English Provincial Society from the Reformation to the Revolution: Religion, Politics and Society in Kent, 1500–1640* (Hassocks: Harvester Press, 1977)

Cockerill, Sara, *Eleanor of Castile: The Shadow Queen* (Stroud: Amberley, 2014)

Collins, Stephen L., *From Divine Cosmos to Sovereign State: An Intellectual History of Consciousness and the Idea of Order in Renaissance England* (Oxford: Oxford University Press, 1989)

Conway Davies, James, *The Baronial Opposition to Edward II: Its Character and Policy – A Study in Administrative History* (London: Frank Cass & Co., 1967)

Cook, Alan, 'The Oatlands Palace Excavations, 1968, interim report', *Surrey Archaeological Collections* (1969)

Copinger, W. A., *The Manors of Suffolk: Notes on Their History and Devolution* (London: T. Fisher Unwin, 1905)

Cowan, Ross, 'Flodden: Scotland's Greatest Defeat', *Military History Monthly* (2013)

Crawford, Anne, *Yorkist Lord: John Howard, Duke of Norfolk, c. 1425–1485* (London: Continuum, 2010)

Cressy, David, 'Kinship and Kin Interaction in Early Modern England', *Past and Present* (1986)

Crompton, Louis, *Homosexuality and Civilization* (Cambridge, MA, and London: Harvard University Press, 2003)

Cross, Beverley, *Catherine Howard: A play* (London: Samuel French, 1973)

Currie, Andrew. S., 'Notes on the Obstetric Histories of Catherine of Aragon and Anne Boleyn', *Edinburgh Medical Journal* (1888)

Cust, Lionel, 'A Portrait of Queen Catherine Howard, by Hans Holbein the Younger', *Burlington Magazine for Connoisseurs* (1910)

Denny, Joanna, *Anne Boleyn: A New Life of England's Tragic Queen* (London: Portrait 2004)

— *Katherine Howard: A Tudor Conspiracy* (London: Portrait, 2005)

Dimock, Arthur, *The Cathedral Church of Saint Paul: An Account of the Old and New Buildings with a Short Historical Sketch* (London: George Bell & Sons, 1900)

Dodd, Gwilym, and Anthony Musson (eds), *The Reign of Edward II: New Perspectives* (Woodbridge: York Medieval Press, 2006)

Dodds, Madeleine Hope, and Ruth Dodds, *The Pilgrimage of Grace, 1536–1537, and the Exeter Conspiracy, 1538* (Cambridge: Cambridge University Press, 1915)

Donaldson, Gordon, *All the Queen's Men: Power and Politics in Mary Stewart's Scotland* (London: Batsford Academic and Educational, 1983)

Doran, Susan, and Thomas S. Freeman (eds), *Mary Tudor: Old and New Perspectives* (London: Palgrave Macmillan, 2011)

Duffy, Eamon, *The Stripping of the Altars: Traditional Religion in England, c.1400–c.1580*, second edition (New Haven and London: Yale University Press, 2005)

Dyer, Alan, *Decline and Growth in English towns, 1400–1650* (Cambridge: Cambridge University Press, 1991)

Dyer, Christopher, *Standards of Livings in the Later Middle Ages: Social Change in England, c. 1200–1520* (Cambridge: Cambridge University Press, 1989)

Eames, Penelope, *Furniture in England, France and the Netherlands from the Twelfth to the Fifteenth Century* (London: Furniture History Society, 1977)

Edgerton, William L., *Nicholas Udall* (New York: Twayne Publishers, 1965)

Edwards, H. L. R., *Skelton: The Life and Times of an Early Tudor Poet* (London: Jonathan Cape, 1949)

Edwards, John, *Archbishop Pole* (Farnham: Ashgate, 2014)

Elliott, J. H., and L. W. B. Brockliss (eds), *The World of the Favourite* (New Haven and London: Yale University Press, 1999)

Ellis, Steven G., *Ireland in the Age of the Tudors, 1447–1603: English Expansion and the End of Gaelic Rule* (London: Longman, 1998)

— and Sarah Barber (eds), *Conquest and Union: Fashioning a British State, 1485–1725* (London: Longman Group, 1995)

Elwes, Dudley G., and Charles J. Robinson, *A History of the Castles and Manors of Western Sussex* (London: Longman & Co., 1876)

Emerson, Kathy Lynn, *Wives and Daughters: The Women of Sixteenth Century England* (Troy, NY: Whitston, 1984)

Enterline, Lynn, *The Tears of Narcissus: Melancholia and Masculinity in Early Modern Writing* (Stanford, CA: Stanford University Press, 1995)

Euler, Carrie, *Couriers of the Gospel: England and Zurich, 1531–1558* (Zurich: Theologischer Verlag Zurich, 2006)

Everett, Michael, *The Rise of Thomas Cromwell: Power and Politics in the Reign of Henry VIII* (New Haven and London: Yale University Press, 2015)

Fagan, Brian, *The Little Ice Age: How Climate Made History, 1300–1850* (New York: Basic Books, 2000)

Fitzgerald, Teri, 'Elizabeth Seymour', *Tudor Life* (2014)

Fleming, Peter, 'Culpeper family (per. c.1400–c.1540)', *Oxford Dictionary of National Biography* (Oxford: Oxford University Press, 2004)

Forge, J. W. Lindus, *Oatlands Palace* (Walton-on-Thames: Walton and Weybridge Local History Society, 1982)

Fox, Julia, *Jane Boleyn: The Infamous Lady Rochford* (London: Weidenfeld & Nicolson, 2007)

Fox, Vivian C., and Martin H. Quitt, *Loving, Parenting and Dying: The Family Cycle in England and America, Past and Present* (New York: Psychohistory Press, 1980)

Foyle, Jonathan, *Lincoln Cathedral: The Biography of a Great Building* (London: Scala Arts & Heritage Publishers, 2015)

Fraser, Antonia, *The Six Wives of Henry VIII* (London: Arrow Books, 1998)

Froude, James Anthony, *History of England from the Fall of Wolsey to the Death of Elizabeth* (London: John W. Parker and Son, 1858)

Fuller, Reginald C., Leonard Johnston, and Conleth Kearns (eds), *A New Catholic Commentary on Holy Scripture* (London: Thomas Nelson and Sons, 1969)

Glenne, Michael, *Catherine Howard: The Story of Henry VIII's Fifth Queen* (London: John Long, 1948)

Goldberg, P. J. P., *Women, Work, and Life Cycle in a Medieval Economy: Women in York and Yorkshire, c. 1300–1520* (Oxford: Clarendon Press, 1992)

Gooch, Leo, *A Complete Pattern of Nobility: John, Lord Lumley (c.1534–1609)* (Rainton Bridge: University of Sunderland Press, 2009)

Goodman, Ruth, *How to Be a Tudor: A Dawn-to-Dusk Guide to Everyday Life* (London: Viking, 2015)

Gordon, Bruce, and Peter Marshall (eds), *The Place of the Dead: Death and Remembrance in Late Medieval and Early Modern Europe* (Cambridge: Cambridge University Press, 2000)

Gordon, Dillian, Lisa Monnas, and Caroline Elam (eds), *The Regal Image of Richard II and the Wilton Diptych* (London: Harvey Miller, 1997)

Gower, Graham, and Kieron Tyler, *Lambeth Unearthed: An Archaeological History of Lambeth* (London: Museum of London, 2003)

Gregory, Donald, *The History of the Western Highlands and Isles of Scotland, from A. D. 1493 to A. D. 1625* (London and Glasgow: Hamilton, Adams, and Co., etc., 1881)

Griffiths, Ralph A., *The Reign of Henry VI: The Exercise of Royal Authority, 1422–1461* (London: Ernest Benn, 1981)

— *Sir Rhys ap Thomas and his Family: A Study in the Wars of the Roses and Early Tudor Politics* (Cardiff: University of Wales Press, 1993)

Grove, Jean M., *The Little Ice Age* (London: Routledge, 1990)

Gunn, S. J., *Charles Brandon, Duke of Suffolk, c. 1484–1545* (Oxford: Basil Blackwell Ltd, 1988)

Gunn, Steven J., *Early Tudor Government, 1485–1558* (London: Macmillan Press, 1995)

— *Henry VII's New Men and the Making of Tudor England* (Oxford: Oxford University Press, 2015)

Guy, John, *The Children of Henry VIII* (Oxford: Oxford University Press, 2013)

Gwyn, Peter, *The King's Cardinal: The Rise and Fall of Thomas Wolsey* (London: Pimlico, 1990)

Hackett, Francis, *Henry the Eighth* (London: Jonathan Cape, 1929)

Hamilton, Dakota Lee, 'The Household of Queen Katherine Parr' (Unpublished DPhil thesis submitted to the History Faculty Board, University of Oxford, 1992)

Hanawalt, Barbara A., *Growing Up in Medieval London: The Experience of Childhood in History* (Oxford: Oxford University Press, 1993)

— and Kathryn L. Reyerson (eds), *City and Spectacle in Medieval Europe* (Minneapolis, MN, and London: University of Minnesota Press, 1994)

Harris, Barbara J., *Edward Stafford, Third Duke of Buckingham, 1478–1521* (Stanford, CA: Stanford University Press, 1986)

— 'Women and Politics in Early Tudor England', *Historical Journal* (1990)

— 'The Fabric of Piety: Aristocratic Women and Care of the Dead, 1450–1550', *Journal of British Studies* (2009)

Hasler, P. W. (ed.), *The House of Commons, 1558–1603* (London: Her Majesty's Stationery Office, 1981)

Head, David M., *The Ebbs and Flows of Fortune: The Life of Thomas Howard, Third Duke of Norfolk* (Athens, GA, and London: University of Georgia Press, 2009)

Heal, Felicity, 'The Archbishops of Canterbury and the Practice of Hospitality', *Journal of Ecclesiastical History* (1982)

— *Hospitality in Early Modern England* (Oxford: Clarendon Press, 1990)

Heard, Kate, and Lucy Whitaker (eds), *The Northern Renaissance: Dürer to Holbein* (St James's Palace: Royal Collection Enterprises, 2011)

Hicks, Michael, *Richard III: The Man Behind the Myth* (London: Collins & Brown Ltd, 1991)

Hill, J. W. F., *Tudor and Stuart Lincoln* (Cambridge: Cambridge University Press, 1956)

Hilton, Lisa, *Queens Consort: England's Medieval Queens* (London: Weidenfeld & Nicolson, 2008)

— *Elizabeth I: Renaissance Prince* (London: Weidenfeld & Nicolson, 2014)

Hoak, Dale (ed.), *Tudor Political Culture* (Cambridge and New York: Cambridge University Press, 1995)

Holmes, Frederick, Grace Holmes, and Julia MacMurrough, 'The Death of Young King Edward VI', *New England Journal of Medicine* (2001)

Horrox, Rosemary, *Richard III: A Study of Service* (Cambridge: Cambridge University Press, 1989)

Houlbrooke, R. A., *The English Family, 1450–1700* (London: Routledge 1984)

Hoyle, R. W., *The Pilgrimage of Grace and the Politics of the 1530s* (Oxford: Oxford University Press, 2001)

— and J. B. Ramsdale, 'The Royal Progress of 1541, the North of England, and Anglo-Scottish Relations, 1534–1542', *Northern History* (2004)

Hui, Roland, 'Two New Faces?: The Horenbolte Portraits of Mary and Thomas Boleyn' (tudorfaces.blogspot.co.uk, 2011)

Hume, Martin, *The Wives of Henry the Eighth and the Parts They Played in History* (London: Eveleigh Nash, 1905)

Hutchinson, Robert, *The Last Days of Henry VIII: Conspiracy, Treason and Heresy in the Court of the Dying Tyrant* (London: Phoenix, 2006)

Hutton, Ronald, *The Rise and Fall of Merry England: The Ritual Year, 1400–1700* (Oxford: Oxford University Press, 1994)

Ingram, Martin, *Church Courts, Sex and Marriage in England, 1550–1640* (Cambridge: Cambridge University Press, 1987)

Ives, E. W., R. J. Knecht, and J. J. Scarisbrick (eds), *Wealth and Power in Tudor England: Essays Presented to S. T. Bindoff* (University of London: Athlone Press, 1978)

Ives, Eric, 'A Frenchman at the Court of Anne Boleyn', *History Today* (1998)

— 'Norris, Henry (b. before 1500, d. 1536)', *Oxford Dictionary of National Biography* (Oxford: Oxford University Press, 2004)

— *The Life and Death of Anne Boleyn: The Most Happy* (Oxford: Blackwell Publishing, 2004)

Jacquart, Danielle, and Claude Thomasset, *Sexuality and Medicine in the Middle Ages*, Matthew Adamson (trans.) (Princeton, NJ: Princeton University Press, 1988)

James, M. E., 'Obedience and Dissent in Henrician England: The Lincolnshire Rebellion 1536', *Past & Present* (1970)

James, Mervyn, *Family, Lineage, and Civil Society: A Study of Society, Politics and Mentality in the Durham Region, 1500–1640* (Oxford: Clarendon Press, 1974)

James, Susan E., 'Lady Margaret Douglas and Sir Thomas Seymour by Holbein: Two Miniatures Re-identified', *Apollo* (1998)

— *Kateryn Parr: The Making of a Queen* (Aldershot: Ashgate Publishing, 1999)

— and Jamie S. Franco, 'Susanna Horenbout, Levina Teerlinc and the Mask of Royalty' (Antwerp: Jaarboek Koninklijk Museum voor Schone Kunsten, 2000)

Jarrett, Bede, *The Emperor Charles IV* (London: Eyre and Spottiswoode, 1935)

Jarrold, Walter, *Henry VIII and His Wives* (London: Hutchinson & Co., 1933)

Johnson, Paul, *Elizabeth: A Study in Power and Intellect* (London: Weidenfeld and Nicolson, 1974)

Jones, Michael K., and Malcolm G. Underwood, *The King's Mother: Lady Margaret Beaufort, Countess of Richmond and Derby* (Cambridge: Cambridge University Press, 1992)

Kelly, Henry Ansgar, *The Matrimonial Trials of Henry VIII* (Stanford, CA: Stanford University Press, 1976)

Kelly, Morgan, and Cormac Ó Gráda, 'Change Points and Temporal Dependence in Reconstructions of Annual Temperature: Did Europe Experience a Little Ice Age?', *Annals of Applied Statistics* (2014)

— 'The Myth of Europe's Little Ice Age', *Vox* (2015)

Kent, H. R. H. Princess Michael of, *The Serpent and the Moon: Two Rivals for the Love of a Renaissance King* (New York: Simon & Schuster, 2004)

King, Edmund, *King Stephen* (New Haven and London: Yale University Press, 2010)

Kipling, Gordon, *Enter the King: Theatre, Liturgy, and Ritual in the Medieval Civic Triumph* (Oxford: Clarendon Press, 1998)

Kirby, J. L., 'Edgcumbe, Sir Richard (c.1434–1489)', *Oxford Dictionary of National Biography* (Oxford: Oxford University Press, 2004)

Kleineke, Hannes, *Edward IV* (New York: Routledge, 2009)

Knecht, R. J., *The Rise and Fall of Renaissance France, 1483–1610* (London: Fontana Press, 1996)

Knowles, David, *Bare Ruined Choirs: The Dissolution of the English Monasteries* (Cambridge: Cambridge University Press, 1976)

Kramer, Kyra, *Blood Will Tell: A Medical Explanation of the Tyranny of Henry VIII* (Bloomington, IN: Ash Wood Press, 2014)

— 'A Not So Little Ice Age', *Tudor Life* (2015)

Kussmaul, Ann, *Servants in Husbandry in Early Modern England* (Cambridge: Cambridge University Press, 1981)

Lake, Peter, with Michael Questier, *The Antichrist's Lewd Hat: Protestants, Papists and Players in Post-Reformation England* (New Haven and London: Yale University Press, 2002)

Laslett, Peter, *The World We Have Lost – Further Explored* (London: Methuen, 1983)

Laynesmith, J. L., *The Last Medieval Queens: English Queenship, 1445–1503* (Oxford: Oxford University Press, 2004)

Lehmberg, Stanford E., *The Later Parliaments of Henry VIII, 1536–1547* (Cambridge: Cambridge University Press, 1977)

Lennon, Colm, *The Lords of Dublin in the Age of Reformation* (Dublin: Irish Academic Press, 1989)

— *Sixteenth-Century Ireland: The Incomplete Conquest*, second edition (Dublin: Gill & Macmillan, 2005)

Levin, Carole, Debra Barrett-Graves, and Jo Eldridge Carney (eds), *'High and Mighty Queens' of Early Modern England: Realities and Representations* (New York: Palgrave Macmillan, 2003)

Licence, Amy, *The Six Wives and Many Mistresses of Henry VIII* (Stroud: Amberley, 2014)

— *Cecily Neville: Mother of Kings* (Stroud: Amberley, 2015)

Lindsey, Karen, *Divorced, Beheaded, Survived: A Feminist Reinterpretation of the Wives of Henry VIII* (Cambridge, MA: Da Capo Press, 1995)

Lipscomb, Suzannah, *1536: The Year That Changed Henry VIII* (Oxford: Lion Hudson, 2009)
— *The King Is Dead: The Last Will and Testament of Henry VIII* (London: Head of Zeus, 2015)
Lisle, Leanda de, *The Sisters Who Would Be Queen: The Tragedy of Mary, Katherine and Lady Jane Grey* (London: HarperPress, 2009)
— *Tudor: The Family Story* (London: Chatto & Windus, 2013)
Lloyd, T. H., *England and the German Hanse, 1157–1611: A Study in Their Trade and Commercial Diplomacy* (Cambridge: Cambridge University Press, 1991)
Loach, Jennifer, *Edward VI*, George Bernard and Penry Williams (eds) (New Haven and London: Yale University Press, 1999)
Loades, David, *Mary Tudor: A Life* (Oxford: Basil Blackwell, 1989)
— *The Tudor Navy: An Administrative, Political and Military History* (Aldershot: Scolar Press, 1992)
— *The Politics of Marriage: Henry VIII and his Queens* (Stroud: Alan Sutton Publishing, 1994)
— *John Dudley, Duke of Northumberland, 1504–1553* (Oxford: Clarendon Press, 1996)
— *Catherine Howard: The Adulterous Wife of Henry VIII* (Stroud: Amberley, 2012)
Lyons, Mary Ann, 'Thomas ('Silken Thomas') FitzGerald', *Dictionary of Irish Biography* (Cambridge: Cambridge University Press and the Royal Irish Academy, 2009)
MacCulloch, Diarmaid (ed.), *The Reign of Henry VIII: Politics, Policy and Piety* (Basingstoke: Macmillan Press, 1995)
MacCulloch, Diarmaid, *Thomas Cranmer: A Life* (New Haven and London: Yale University Press, 1996)
MacDougall, Norman, *James IV* (Edinburgh: John Donald Publishers, 1989)
Mackay, Lauren, *Inside the Tudor Court: Henry VIII and his Six Wives through the writings of the Spanish Ambassador, Eustace Chapuys* (Stroud: Amberley, 2014)
MacMahon, Luke, 'Ughtred, Sir Anthony (d. 1534), soldier', *Oxford Dictionary of National Biography* (Oxford: Oxford University Press, 2004)
MacNalty, Arthur S., *Henry VIII: A Difficult Patient* (Norwich: Christopher Johnson, 1952)
Manning, Roger, *Village Revolts: Social Protest and Popular Disturbance in England, 1509–1540* (Oxford: Clarendon Press, 1988)
Marsh, Christopher, *Popular Religion in Sixteenth-Century England: Holding Their Peace* (Basingstoke: Macmillan Press, 1998)
— *Music and Society in Early Modern England* (Cambridge: Cambridge University Press, 2013)
Marshall, Peter, *Religious Identities in Henry VIII's England* (Aldershot: Ashgate Publishing, 2006)
Marshall, Rosalind K., *Mary of Guise* (London: Collins, 1977)
Maxwell-Lyte, H. C., *A History of Eton College, 1440–1875* (London: Macmillan and Co., 1877)
McDermott, James, 'William Howard, first Baron Howard of Effingham (*c.*1510–1573)', *Oxford Dictionary of National Biography* (Oxford: Oxford University Press, 2004)
McFarlane, K. B., *The Nobility of Later Medieval England* (Oxford: Clarendon Press, 1973)

McGrigor, Mary, *The Other Tudor Princess: Margaret Douglas, Henry VIII's Niece* (Stroud: History Press, 2015)

McLean, Teresa, *The English at Play in the Middle Ages* (Slough: Kensal Press, 1983)

Merriman, Marcus, *The Rough Wooings: Mary Queen of Scots, 1542–1551* (East Linton: Tuckwell Press, 2000)

Mertes, Kate, *The English Noble Household, 1250–1600: Good Governance and Politic Rule* (Oxford: Basil Blackwell, 1988)

Merton, Caroline Isabelle, 'The Women who served Queen Mary and Queen Elizabeth: Ladies, Gentlewomen and Maids of the Privy Chamber, 1553–1603' (unpublished PhD dissertation submitted to the University of Cambridge, 1991)

Mikhaila, Ninya, and Jane Malcolm-Davies, *The Tudor Tailor: Reconstructing sixteenth-century dress* (London: Batsford, 2006)

Miller, Helen, *Henry VIII and the English Nobility* (Oxford: Basil Blackwell, 1986)

Mollat, Michel, *The Poor in the Middle Ages: An Essay in Social History*, Arthur Goldhammer (trans.) (New Haven, CT, and London: Yale University Press, 1986)

Morris, Christopher, *The Tudors* (London: Collins, 1955)

Morris, Sarah, and Natalie Grueninger, *In the Footsteps of Anne Boleyn* (Stroud: Amberley, 2015)

Mortimer, Ian, *The Perfect King: The Life of Edward III, Father of the English Nation* (London: Vintage, 2008)

— *The Time Traveller's Guide to Medieval England: A Handbook for Visitors to the Fourteenth Century* (London: Vintage, 2009)

Muir, Kenneth, *Life and Letters of Sir Thomas Wyatt* (Liverpool: Liverpool University Press, 1963)

Murphy, Beverley A., *Bastard Prince: Henry VIII's Lost Son* (Stroud: History Press, 2010)

Mustakallio, Katariina, and Christian Laes (eds), *The Dark Side of Childhood in Late Antiquity and the Middle Ages: Unwanted, Disabled and Lost* (Oxford: Oxbow Books, 2011)

Nicholson, William, *Katherine Howard: A play* (London: Samuel French, 1999)

Niles, Philip, 'Baptism and the Naming of Children in Late Medieval England', *Medieval Prosopography* (1982)

Norton, Elizabeth, *Anne of Cleves: Henry VIII's Discarded Bride* (Stroud: Amberley, 2010)

— *Bessie Blount: Mistress to Henry VIII* (Stroud: Amberley, 2013)

— *The Boleyn Women: The Tudor Femmes Fatales Who Changed English History* (Stroud: Amberley, 2014)

O'Hara, Diana, *Courtship and Constraint: Rethinking the making of marriage in Tudor England* (Manchester and New York: Manchester University Press, 2000)

Orme, Nicholas, *From Childhood to Chivalry: The education of English kings and aristocracy, 1066–1530* (London: Methuen, 1984)

— *Medieval Children* (New Haven and London: Yale University Press, 2003)

Page, William (ed.), *The Victoria History of the Counties of England* (London: Constable and Company, 1920)

— *A History of the County of Kent* (London: Constable and Company, 1926).

Palliser, D. M., *Tudor York* (Oxford: Oxford University Press, 1979)

Payer, Pierre J., *The Bridling of Desire: Views of Sex in the Later Middle Ages* (Toronto: University of Toronto Press, 1993)

Perry, Maria, *Sisters to the King: The Tumultuous Lives of Henry VIII's Sisters – Margaret of Scotland and Mary of France* (London: André Deutsch, 1998)

Philips, Kim M., *Medieval Maidens: Young Women and Gender in England, 1270–1540* (Manchester and New York: Manchester University Press, 2003)

Pierce, Hazel, *Margaret Pole, Countess of Salisbury, 1473–1541: Loyalty, Lineage and Leadership* (Cardiff: University of Wales Press, 2003)

Pine, L. G. (ed.), *Burke's Genealogical and Heraldic History of the Peerage, Baronetage & Knightage*, 101st edition (London: Burke's Peerage, 1956)

Plowden, Alison, *The House of Tudor* (New York: Scarborough Books, 1976)

Pollard, A. F., *Henry VIII* (Aberdeen: Longmans, Green and Co., 1951)

Pollmann, Judith, 'Of Living Legends and Authentic Tales: How to Get Remembered in Early Modern Europe', *Transactions of the Royal Historical Society* (2013)

Pollnitz, Aysha, *Princely Education in Early Modern England* (Cambridge: Cambridge University Press, 2015)

Porter, Linda, *Mary Tudor: The First Queen* (London: Piatkus, 2009)

Poulton, Richard, Simon Thurley, and Alan Cook, 'Excavations at Oatlands Palace, 1968–1973 and 1983–84' (Surrey County Archaeological Monograph, 2010)

Prestwich, Michael, *Edward I* (London: Methuen, 1990)

Prior, C. M., *The Royal Studs of the Sixteenth and Seventeenth Centuries* (London: Horse and Hound Publications, 1935)

Rankin, Mark, Christopher Highley, and John N. King (eds), *Henry VIII and his Afterlives: Literature, Politics, and Art* (Cambridge: Cambridge University Press, 2009)

Redesdale, Algernon Freeman-Mitford, 1st Lord, *A Tragedy in Stone: and Other Papers* (London: John Lane, 1912)

Redworth, Glyn, *In Defence of the Church Catholic: The Life of Stephen Gardiner* (Oxford: Basil Blackwell, 1990)

Renier, Hannah, *Lambeth Past: Kennington, Vauxhall, Waterloo* (London: Historical Publications, 2006)

Rex, Richard, *Henry VIII and the English Reformation* (London: Macmillan Press, 1993)

Roberts, Ian, and Ian Downes, *Pontefract Castle: Key to the North*, second edition (Wakefield: West Yorkshire Archaeology Service, 2013)

Robinson, John Martin, *The Dukes of Norfolk: A Quincentennial History* (Oxford: Oxford University Press, 1982)

Rollo-Koster, Joëlle (ed.), *Medieval and Early Modern Ritual: Formalized Behavior in Europe, China and Japan* (Leiden, Netherlands: Brill, 2002)

Rosenthal, Joel T., *Nobles and Noble Life, 1295–1500* (London: George Allen & Unwin, 1976)

— *Patriarchy and Families of Privilege in Fifteenth-Century England* (Philadelphia: University of Pennsylvania Press, 1991)

Ross, Charles, *Edward IV* (London: Eyre Methuen Ltd, 1974)

— (ed.), *Patronage, Pedigree and Power in Later Medieval England* (Gloucester: Alan Sutton Publishing, 1979)

Ross, James, *John de Vere, Thirteenth Earl of Oxford (1442–1513): 'The Foremost Man in the Kingdom'* (Woodbridge: Boydell Press, 2011)

Rosser, Gervase, *Medieval Westminster, 1200–1540* (Oxford: Clarendon Press, 1989)

Rushton, M. A., 'Anne Mowbray's Teeth', *British Medical Journal* (1965)

Russell, Gareth, 'Catherine Howard and the Queen's Household in England, 1540–1' (unpublished MA thesis submitted to Queen's University, Belfast, 2011)

Saaler, Mary, *Anne of Cleves: Fourth Wife of Henry VIII* (London: Rubicon Press, 1995)

Sadleir Stoney, F., *A Memoir of the Life and Times of the Right Honourable Sir Ralph Sadleir* (London: Longmans, Green, & Co., 1877)

Sayer, M. J., 'Norfolk Visitation Families: A Short Social Structure', *Norfolk Archaeology* (1975)

Scarisbrick, J. J., *Henry VIII*, second edition (New Haven and London: Yale University Press, 1997)

Schutte, Kimberly, *A Biography of Margaret Douglas, Countess of Lennox (1515–1578)* (Lewiston, NY: Edwin Mellen Press, 2002)

Scott, Anne M. (ed.), *Experiences of Charity, 1250–1650* (Farnham: Ashgate Publishing, 2015)

Sharpe, Kevin, *Selling the Tudor Monarchy: Authority and Image in Sixteenth-Century England* (New Haven and London: Yale University Press, 2009)

Siddons, Michael Powell, *Heraldic Badges in England and Wales* (Woodbridge: Society of Antiquaries of London, 2009)

Skidmore, Chris, *Edward VI: The Lost King of England* (London: Weidenfeld & Nicolson, 2007)

Smith, Bruce R., *Homosexual Desire in Shakespeare's England: A Cultural Poetics* (Chicago and London: University of Chicago Press, 1991)

Smith, Lacey Baldwin, *A Tudor Tragedy: The Life and Times of Catherine Howard* (London: Reprint Society, 1962)

— *Henry VIII: The Mask of Royalty* (London: Jonathan Cape, 1971)

Somerville, C. John, *The Rise and Fall of Childhood* (Beverly Hills, CA: Sage Publications, 1982)

Stanton, Pamela Y., 'Arundell family (*per.* 1435–1590)', *Oxford Dictionary of National Biography* (Oxford: Oxford University Press, 2004)

Starkey, David (ed.), *The English Court: from the Wars of the Roses to the Civil War* (London: Longman, 1987)

— *Elizabeth: Apprenticeship* (London: Vintage, 2001)

— *Six Wives: The Queens of Henry VIII* (London: Vintage, 2004)

— et al., *Lost Faces: Identity and Discovery in Tudor Royal Portraiture* (exhibition catalogue, London: Philip Mould Ltd, 2007)

Stewart, Alan, *Close Readers: Humanism and Sodomy in Early Modern England* (Princeton, NJ: Princeton University Press, 1997)

Strickland, Agnes, *Lives of the Queens of England from the Norman Conquest* (Bath: Cedric Chivers, 1972)

Strong, Roy, *Tudor and Jacobean Portraits: Volume 1, Text* (London: Her Majesty's Stationery Office, 1969)

— *Splendour at Court: Renaissance Spectacle and Illusion* (London: Weidenfeld and Nicolson, 1973)

— *The English Renaissance Miniature* (London: Thames and Hudson, 1984)

Sutter Fichner, Paula, 'Dynastic Marriage in Sixteenth-Century Habsburg Diplomacy and Statecraft: An Interdisciplinary Approach', *American Historical Review* (1976)

Sutter, W. D., *Catherine Howard: A Romantic Drama in Three Acts* (London: Samuel French, 1855)

Swanson, R. N., *Catholic England: Faith, Religion and Observance Before the Reformation* (Manchester and New York: Manchester University Press, 1993)

Tabori, Paul, *Alexander Korda* (London: Oldbourne, 1959)

Tentler, Thomas N., *Sin and Confession on the Eve of the Reformation* (Princeton, NJ: Princeton University Press, 1977)

Terry, Francis (ed.), *A Guide to the History, Architecture, and Current Proposals for the Church of St Mary-at-Lambeth, London* (London: Vauxhall Society and the Tradescant Trust, 1980)

Thurley, Simon, *The Royal Palaces of Tudor England: Architecture and Court Life, 1460–1547* (New Haven and London: Yale University Press, 1993)

Tjernagel, Neelak Serawlook, *Henry VIII and the Lutherans: A Study in Anglo-Lutheran Relations from 1521 to 1547* (Saint Louis, MO: Concordia Publishing, 1965)

Tremlett, Giles, *Catherine of Aragon: Henry's Spanish Queen* (London: Faber and Faber, 2010)

Tucker, Melvin, *The Life of Thomas Howard, Earl of Surrey and Second Duke of Norfolk* (The Hague: Mouton and Co., 1964)

Urban, Sylvanus, *The Gentleman's Magazine and Historical Chronicle* (London: John Nichols, 1797)

Van Patten, Jonathan K., 'Magic, Prophecy, and the Law of Treason in Reformation England', *American Journal of Legal History* (1983)

Von Staats, Beth, 'Thomas Cranmer: Were his recantations driven by Stockholm Syndrome?', *Tudor Life* (2014)

Visser, Margaret, *The Rituals of Dinner: The Origins, Evolution, Eccentricities, and Meaning of Table Manners* (London: Viking, 1992)

Walker, Greg, *John Skelton and the Politics of the 1520s* (Cambridge: Cambridge University Press, 1988)

— 'Rethinking the Fall of Anne Boleyn', *Historical Journal* (2002)

Walker, Nigel, *Crime and Insanity in England* (Edinburgh: Edinburgh University Press, 1968)

Wall, Barry L., *Long Melford through the ages: A guide to the buildings and streets* (Ipswich: East Anglian Magazine Ltd, 1986)

Waller, Gary, *Walsingham and the English Imagination* (Farnham: Ashgate Publishing, 2011)

Ward, Jennifer (trans. and ed.), *Women of the English Nobility and Gentry, 1066–1500* (Manchester and New York: Manchester University Press, 1995)

Ward, Jennifer C., *English Noblewomen in the Later Middle Ages* (London: Longman Group, 1992)

Warner, Kathryn, *Edward II: The Unconventional King* (Stroud: Amberley, 2014)

Warnicke, Retha M., *The Rise and Fall of Anne Boleyn: Family politics at the court of Henry VIII* (Cambridge: Cambridge University Press, 1989)

— 'Henry VIII's Greeting of Anne of Cleves and Early Modern Court Protocol', *Albion* (1996)

— *The Marrying of Anne of Cleves: Royal protocol in early modern England* (Cambridge: Cambridge University Press, 2000)

— 'Katherine [Catherine; née Katherine Howard], queen of England and Ireland, fifth consort of Henry VIII', *Oxford Dictionary of National Biography* (Oxford: Oxford University Press, 2004)

Watkins, Sarah-Beth, *Lady Katherine Knollys: The Unacknowledged Daughter of King Henry VIII* (Alresford: Chronos Books, 2015)

Way, Twigs, *The Tudor Garden, 1485–1603* (Oxford: Shire Publications, 2013)

Wayment, Hilary, *Corpus Vitraeum Medii Aevi: The Window of King's College, Cambridge* (London: British Academy and Oxford University Press, 1972)

Weir, Alison, *The Lady in the Tower: The Fall of Anne Boleyn* (London: Jonathan Cape, 2009)

— *Mary Boleyn: 'The Great and Infamous Whore'* (London: Jonathan Cape, 2011)

— *The Lost Tudor Princess: A Life of Margaret Douglas, Countess of Lennox* (London: Jonathan Cape, 2015)

Welsford, Enid, *The Court Masque: A Study in the Relationship Between Poetry and the Revels* (New York: Russell & Russell, 1962)

Westervelt, Theron, 'The Woodvilles in the Second Reign of Edward IV, 1471–83' (unpublished MPhil thesis submitted to Cambridge University, 1997)

Wheeler, Elisabeth, *Men of Power: Court Intrigue in the Life of Catherine Howard* (Glastonbury: Martin Wheeler, 2008)

Whistler, Laurence, *The English Festivals* (London: William Heinemann Ltd, 1947)

White, Michelle Anne, *Henrietta Maria and the English Civil Wars* (Aldershot: Ashgate, 2006)

Whitelock, Anna, *Mary Tudor: England's First Queen* (London: Bloomsbury, 2010)

Whitron, C. A., 'The Coinage of Henry VIII and Edward VI in Henry's Name: Part 2', *British Numismatic Journal* (1949–51)

Wilding, Peter, *Thomas Cromwell* (London: William Heinemann, 1935)

Wilkinson, Josephine, *Mary Boleyn: The True Story of Henry VIII's Favourite Mistress* (Stroud: Amberley, 2009)

Wilson, Barbara, and Francis Mee, *St Mary's Abbey and the King's Manor, York: The Pictorial Evidence* (York: York Archaeological Trust, 2009)

Wilson, Derek, *The Uncrowned Kings of England: The Black Legend of the Dudleys* (London: Constable & Robinson, 2005)

— *A Brief History of Henry VIII: Reformer and Tyrant* (London: Constable & Robinson, 2009)

Wolffe, Bertram, *Henry VI* (London: Eyre Methuen, 1981)

Wood, Andy, *Riot, Rebellion and Popular Politics in Early Modern England* (Basingstoke: Palgrave, 2002)

Woodcock, Thomas, and John Martin Robinson, *The Oxford Guide to Heraldry* (Oxford: Oxford University Press, 1988)

Woods, L. L. B. Martin, *The Winthrop Papers* (Boston, MA: Massachusetts Historical Society, 1931)

Woolgar, C. M., *The Great Household in Late Medieval England* (New Haven and London: Yale University Press, 1999)

Wunderli, Richard M., *London Church Courts and Society on the Eve of the Reformation* (Cambridge, MA: Medieval Academy of America, 1981)

Young, Elizabeth, and Wayland Young, *Old London Churches* (London: Faber and Faber, 1961)

NOTES

The following abbreviations are used in the Notes:

Acts and Monuments – John Foxe, *The Acts and Monuments of John Foxe: A New and Complete Edition*, ed. Rev. S. R. Cattley (London: Seeley and Burnside, 1837–41)

BL – British Library (manuscripts)

Cal. S. P. Milan – *Calendar of State Papers and Manuscripts in the Archives and Collections of Milan 1385–1618*, ed. A. B. Hinds (London: His Majesty's Stationery Office, 1912)

Cal. S. P. Span. – *Calendar of letters, despatches, and state papers relating to the negotiations between England and Spain*, ed. G. Bergenroth, et al. (London: Longman, Green, Longman & Roberts, 1862–1954)

HMC Bath – *Calendar of the Manuscripts of the Marquis of Bath: preserved at Longleat, Wiltshire* (London: His Majesty's Stationery Office, 1907)

HMC Rutland – *The Manuscripts of His Grace the Duke of Rutland G. C. B., preserved at Belvoir Castle* (London: Her Majesty's Stationery Office, 1888)

Household Ordinances – *A collection of ordinances and regulations for the government of the royal household, made in divers reigns: from King Edward III to King William and Queen Mary, also receipts in ancient cookery* (London: Society of Antiquaries of London, 1790)

Inventory – *The Inventory of Henry VIII*, ed. D. Starkey, et al. (London: Society of Antiquaries of London, 1998–2012)

Journal of the House of Lords – *Journal of the House of Lords, Volume I, 1509–1577* (London: s. n., 1771)

Kaulek – *Correspondance politique de mm. de Castillon et de Marillac, ambassadeurs de France en Angleterre*, ed. Jean Baptiste Louis Kaulek (Paris: Félix Alcan, 1885)

LP – *Letters and Papers, Foreign and Domestic of the Reign of Henry VIII*, ed. J. S. Brewer, et al. (London: Her Majesty's Stationery Office, 1862–1932)

MS Ashmole – Bodleian Library (manuscripts)

Original Letters – *Original Letters, illustrative of English History*, ed. Henry Ellis (London: Harding, Triphook, and Lepard, 1824)

Proceedings of the Privy Council – *Proceedings and Ordinances of the Privy Council of England, 1386–1542*, ed. Sir Nicholas Harris Nicolas (London: Eyre and Spottiswoode, 1834–37)

RCIN – Royal Collection Identification Number

SP – *State papers domestic 1547–1649* (National Archives)
State Papers – State Papers, King Henry VIII (London, 1830–52)
Surrey Archaeological Collections – Surrey Archaeological Collections, relating to the History and Antiquities of the County (London: Various, 1858–)
The Cause Papers Database – Cause Papers in the Diocesan Courts of the Archbishopric of York, 1300–1858
The Spanish Chronicle – Chronicle of King Henry VIII of England, being a contemporary record of some of the principal events of the reigns of Henry VIII and Edward VI, written in Spanish by an unknown hand, ed. M. A. S. Hume (London: George Bell and Sons, 1889)

Introduction

1. Gareth Russell, 'Catherine Howard and the Queen's Household in England, 1540–1' (unpublished MA dissertation submitted to Queen's University, Belfast, 2011).
2. William Thomas, *The Pilgrim: A Dialogue on the Life and Actions of King Henry the Eighth* (London: Parker, Son, and Bourn, 1861), p. 59.
3. Lacey Baldwin Smith, *A Tudor Tragedy: The Life and Times of Catherine Howard* (London: Reprint Society, 1962), p. 11.
4. The only queen consort's household to receive significant attention was Katherine Parr's, see Dakota Lee Hamilton, 'The Household of Queen Katherine Parr' (unpublished DPhil thesis, submitted to the University of Oxford, 1992).
5. SP 1/168, f. 13.
6. David Starkey, *Six Wives: The Queens of Henry VIII* (London: Vintage, 2003).
7. *Original Letters*, I, ii, 121.
8. David Loades, *The Politics of Marriage: Henry VIII and his Queens* (Stroud: Alan Sutton Publishing, 1994), p. 132.

Chapter 1: The Hour of Our Death

1. At the time of his downfall, Cromwell was Chancellor of the Exchequer, the king's Principal Secretary, Lord Privy Seal, Governor of the Isle of Wight, and Lord Great Chamberlain.

2. Edward Hall, *Hall's Chronicle: Containing the History of England, during the Reign of Henry the Fourth, and the Succeeding Monarchs, to the End of the Reign of Henry the Eighth* (London, 1809), p. 840; Edward, 1st Lord Herbert, *The Life and Raigne of King Henry VIII* (London, 1683), p. 525.
3. Alan Stewart, *Close Readers: Humanism and Sodomy in Early Modern England* (Princeton, NJ: Princeton University Press, 1997), p. xvi. Another woman, called 'Mother Huntley', had been questioned about 'certain grave misdemeanours' alleged against Lord Hungerford, see LP, XV, 784.
4. LP, XV, 926; Retha M. Warnicke, *The Marrying of Anne of Cleves: Royal protocol in early modern England* (Cambridge: Cambridge University Press, 2000), p. 228.
5. *Cal. S. P. Span.*, V, ii, 55.
6. Eric Ives, *The Life and Death of Anne Boleyn: The Most Happy* (Oxford: Blackwell Publishing, 2004), p. 357.
7. Author's visit, July 2011. The monument visible today is a reconstruction from the original designs and materials, which were saved by the conservationist Alexandre Lenoir when the basilica was ransacked by supporters of the French Revolution in 1793. During that attack, the original tomb of Louis XII and Anne of Brittany

was vandalised and their bodies were thrown into a mass grave, along with most of the other cadavers at Saint-Denis. Although the bones were past the point of recovery, the grave was pieced back together following the restoration of the monarchy.

8. Lancelot de Carles, Bishop of Riez, in Georges Ascoli, *La Grande-Bretagne devant l'opinion française au XVIIe Siècle* (Geneva: Slatkine, 1971), lines 1002–12.

9. *Acts and Monuments*, VII, pp. 155–56.

10. LP, XV, 811.

11. My thanks to the wonderful Dr Mark Whittow for a walking tour of Oxford as part of an archaeology module. I was subsequently unable to get the medieval name out of my head when en route to Oriel or Corpus Christi, via what is now 'Magpie Lane'.

12. Hall, *Hall's Chronicle*, p. 840.

13. More described Anne Boleyn this way in a letter to Thomas Cromwell, dated 5 March 1534. In modern translations, the description is sometimes given as 'really anointed queen', meaning 'truly or legally'. In the original, it reads as 'rially', which could mean either 'really' or 'royally'. Either way, it does not much change the meaning of More's letter, since he referred to Anne as Henry's wife and added a pious hope that they would soon have children for 'rest, peace, wealth, and profit' of the realm. See Alvaro de Silva (ed.), *The Last Letters of Thomas More* (Grand Rapids, MI: William B. Eerdmans Publishing, 2000), pp. 48–56, 151.

14. Roger Wilson Chambers, *Thomas More* (London: Jonathan Cape, 1948), p. 331.

15. *Acts and Monuments*, V, p. 605.

16. Oatlands was part of a property swap with a local landowner called William Reed, sometimes given as 'Rede'.

17. This physical description of Oatlands is the result of combining the research in Alan Cook, 'The Oatlands Palace Excavations, 1968, interim report', in *Surrey Archaeological Collections* (1969), LXVI, pp. 1–9; Simon Thurley, *The Royal Palaces of Tudor England: Architecture and Court Life, 1460–1547* (New Haven and London: Yale University Press, 1993), pp. 60–6; J. W. Lindus Forge's *Oatlands Palace* (Walton-on-Thames: Walton and Weybridge Local History Society 1982); Anton van den Wyngaerde's sketch of the palace from early in the reign of Queen Elizabeth I, and Robert Poulton, Simon Thurley and Alan Cook, *Excavations at Oatlands Palace, 1968–1973 and 1983–84* (Surrey County Archaeological Unit Monograph, 2010).

18. Gilbert Burnet, Bishop of Salisbury, *The History of the Reformation of the Church of England* (Oxford: Oxford University Press, 1829), III, p. 556.

19. LP, XVI, 12.

20. Ibid., XV, 902.

21. Ibid., 926.

22. Peter Wilding, *Thomas Cromwell* (London: William Heinemann, 1935), p. 319; Herbert, *Life and Raigne*, pp. 598–601.

23. Hall, *Hall's Chronicle*, p. 839.

24. The Latin quote is from the Last Words of Christ on the Cross as given in Luke 23:46.

25. Raphael Holinshed, *The Third Volume of Chronicles, Beginning at Duke William the Norman, Commonlie called the Conqueror; and Descending by Degrees of Yeeres to all the Kings*

and Queenes of England in their Orderlie Successions (London: Johnson et al., 1808), p. 818.

26. Jessie Childs, *Henry VIII's Last Victim: The Life and Times of Henry Howard, Earl of Surrey* (London: Vintage Books, 2008), p. 150.

27. LP, XV, 942, grant 21.

28. Ibid., XVI, 1407, 1433.

29. Hall, *Hall's Chronicle*, p. 839.

30. Revelation 12:1. The official teaching of Roman Catholicism remains that the verse pertains to the Virgin Mary and this position was confirmed by the use of papal infallibility to promulgate *ex cathedra* the dogma of the Assumption in 1950 under Pope Pius XII. See *Munificentissimus Deus* (1 November 1950), the Apostolic Constitution, available in full via the Vatican Archives online.

Chapter 2: Our Fathers in Their Generation

1. The order for mandatory records, 'Every parson, vicar or curate within this diocese shall for every church keep one book of register wherein you shall write the day and year of every wedding, christening and burial made within your parish,' was given on 5 September 1538, through Thomas Cromwell.

2. The will of Dame Isabel Leigh (née Worsley, prev. Culpepper), P. C. C. 18 Porch in *Surrey Archaeological Collections*, LI, p. 88.

3. Mary Howard may have been something of a favourite to her grandmother – another goddaughter, Joyce Wellbeck, received twenty shillings.

4. All the available sources listing Lord Edmund's children place Mary after Catherine, not just Isabel's will, when it could be argued that Mary was named after and separately from her sister because she was a goddaughter.

5. The will of Sir John Leigh of Stockwell, Knight of the Bath, P. C. C. 15 Bodfield, in *Surrey Archaeological Collections*, LI, pp. 87–8. The family's surname is variably spelled 'Legh', 'Leigh', and 'Leygh' in the documents.

6. For example, see Joanna Denny, *Katherine Howard: A Tudor Conspiracy* (London: Portrait, 2005), pp. 5–9.

7. LP, XVI, 1426. De Marillac claimed that her romance with Francis Dereham had ended when she was eighteen. We know that the liaison ended in 1539, but de Marillac was still getting fragmentary information about the affair when he wrote this letter on 7 December 1541.

8. A letter from Charles de Marillac to King François I, dated 5 January 1540, trans. J. A. Froude and published in Thomas, *The Pilgrim*, App., p. 135.

9. De Marillac was wrong on other occasions. In a letter to King François I of 29 May 1541 (LP, XV, 868), he described the late Countess of Salisbury as being well past her eightieth birthday, when in reality she was sixty-seven. The Countess of Salisbury had been a prisoner since before de Marillac's arrival in England, but it does further the possibility that he was making his comments based on the ladies' appearances or on gossip, rather than on specific knowledge of their birthdates.

10. Katherine Carey's most recent biographer and her mother's place her birth in 1524 – see Sarah-Beth Watkins, *Lady Katherine Knollys* (Alresford: Chronos Books, 2015), pp. 10–11; Josephine Wilkinson, *Mary Boleyn* (Stroud: Amberley, 2009), pp. 79, 87; and Alison Weir, *Mary Boleyn* (London:

Jonathan Cape, 2011), pp. 140–41, 147–48.

11. The aforementioned codicil to Sir John Leigh's will was added on 26 August 1523, in which Leigh gave permission 'for part of the land to be used in marriage settlements'. This might, on a highly tentative basis, suggest that another girl had been added to the family at some point between the first draft and the addition of the codicil, once it became clear that the Howards would need to provide more dowries in the future.

12. Her grandmother's will mentions locations in Surrey on seven occasions, and her bequests for the improvements of local roads and to local housewives are all for Stockwell, which was within the parish of Lambeth. At the time of her downfall Catherine was also referred to in LP, XVI, 1395, as 'late of Lambeth, Surrey', which could admittedly refer to the time she spent there immediately before coming to court.

13. LP, I, App, 1a.

14. Gerald Brenan and Edward Philips Statham, *The House of Howard* (London: Hutchinson & Co., 1907), I, p. 79; Henry Howard, *Indications of Memorials, Paintings, and Engravings of Persons of the Howard Family* (Corby Castle: privately published, 1834), p. 13.

15. Norfolk House was demolished in the 1780s. The site where it stood is now mostly covered by a Hotel Novotel at 113–29 Lambeth Road. The only remains from Catherine's lifetime are a few foundations. Author's visit, 20 June 2015.

16. Brenan and Statham, *House of Howard*, I, p. 79.

17. Today, the porch, like most of the former church, has been greatly altered, but much of the stonework dates from the fourteenth century and surviving illustrations suggest it stands on much the same site as it did in the 1520s.

18. A custom dating from the sixth century, when the Body of Civil Law encouraged Christians to adopt nonparents as their child's godparents.

19. Mark 7:32–37.

20. Nicholas Orme, *Medieval Children* (New Haven and London: Yale University Press, 2003), p. 28.

21. A reference to the Second Coming of Christ, when both the living and the dead would be judged. See Matthew 25:1–13.

22. Each time a peerage is created, the incumbents are numbered. If the title falls into disuse and is subsequently revived, the numbering starts anew. For instance, there have been six 1st earls of Sussex – the title was awarded to members of the de Warenne, Radclyffe, Savile, Yelverton, and royal families under Edward I, Henry VIII, Charles I, Charles II, George I, and Queen Victoria, respectively. In each case, the title had previously gone into abeyance following the extinction of the direct line of inheritance.

23. The surviving children in 1524 were Thomas, Earl of Surrey; Sir Edmund Howard; Lady Elizabeth Boleyn; Lord William Howard; Lord Thomas Howard; Anne de Vere, Countess of Oxford; Lady Katherine Howard; Lady Elizabeth Howard; and Lady Dorothy Howard.

24. LP, II, 1269.

25. Elizabeth Howard the younger married Henry Radclyffe, 2nd Earl of Sussex (1507–57). His father was elevated in 1529 to the earldom, which he inherited in 1542.

26. The duke's mortuary monument indicates that Katherine and Rhys were betrothed but not yet married at the time of her father's death.

27. Their children were typically referred to by the anglicised surname of 'Rice'.

28. John Weever, *Ancient Funerall Monuments within the united Monarchie of Great Britain, Ireland, and the Islands adjacent* (London: Thomas Harper, 1631), p. 840. Lady Dorothy Howard's husband was Edward Stanley, 3rd Earl of Derby (c.1509–72). He had already inherited the title at the time of their marriage.

29. This was another difference between the gentry and the nobility. Some landed families in the gentry felt comfortable endowing younger sons, as well as the heir – for instance, in 1435 Sir John Arundell helped found a collateral branch of the family by leaving enough for his younger son Thomas to set up his own household in nearby Tolverne. This, coupled with the cost of maintaining a certain level of public pomp, helps explain why several great gentry families declined peerages in the Tudor era.

30. Brenan and Statham, *House of Howard*, I, p. 79; Henry Ellis, 'Copy of an Order made by Cardinal Wolsey as Lord Chancellor, respecting the Management of the Affairs of the young Earl of Oxford', in *Archaeologia*, XIX (1821).

31. James Ross, *John de Vere, Thirteenth Earl of Oxford (1443–1513): 'The Foremost Man in the Kingdom'* (Woodbridge: Boydell Press, 2011), pp. 161–62.

32. John de Vere, 14th Earl of Oxford (1499–1526). He did not outlive his father-in-law by long, and the title passed to his second cousin. His widow survived him by three decades.

33. Weever, *Funerall Monuments*, p. 835.

34. Christopher Dyer, *Standards of Living in the Later Middle Ages: Social change in England, c.1200–1520* (Cambridge: Cambridge University Press, 1989), p. 215. The example used is a thatcher, who in the 1510s was on an average income of fivepence farthing a day.

35. Adeliza of Louvain was queen consort of England through her marriage to King Henry I (d. 1135). That marriage was childless, and the Howards were descended from the offspring of her subsequent marriage to William d'Aubigny, 1st Earl of Arundel and Lincoln (d. 1176).

36. Howard, *Indications*, p. 49.

37. Brenan and Statham, *House of Howard*, I, pp. 7–8; James Conway Davies, *The Baronial Opposition to Edward II: Its Character and Policy – A Study in Administrative History* (London: Frank Cass & Co., 1967), p. 275; Alistair Tebbit, 'Household Knights and Military Service Under the Direction of Edward II', in *The Reign of Edward II: New Perspectives*, Gwilym Dodd and Anthony Musson (eds) (Woodbridge: New York Medieval Press, 2006), p. 89; Mark Buck, *Politics, Finance and the Church in the Reign of Edward II: Walter Stapeldon, Treasurer of England* (Cambridge: Cambridge University Press, 1983), p. 185n.

38. Weever, *Funerall Monuments*, p. 835.

39. Ibid., p. 833.

40. John de Vere, 13th Earl of Oxford (1442–1513) was a Lancastrian who escaped captivity to join Henry VII's cause, when the latter was still in exile. After Bosworth, he was awarded many

roles at court, including Lord Great Chamberlain, and stood as godfather to Arthur, Prince of Wales.

41. Weever, *Funerall Monuments*, p. 835.

42. H. C. Maxwell Lyte et al. (eds), *Calendar of Patent Rolls, Henry VII: Volume I* (London: His Majesty's Stationery Office, 1914) p. 314.

43. Catherine's biological grandmother – Elizabeth (née Tilney) (*c.*1444–97), daughter of Sir Frederick Tilney, a Norfolk landowner, and lady-in-waiting to queens Elizabeth Woodville, Anne Neville, and Elizabeth of York. Her first husband was Sir Humphrey Bourchier, who was killed at the Battle of Barnet on 14 April 1471. She married Thomas Howard on 30 April 1472. By her first marriage, she was the mother of John, 2nd Baron Berners.

44. David M. Head, *The Ebbs and Flows of Fortune: The Life of Thomas Howard, Third Duke of Norfolk* (Athens, GA, and London: University of Georgia Press, 2009), p. 20.

45. By 1476, the vagaries of ill health and bad luck had pruned the Mowbray family tree until the only Mowbray left to inherit the dukedom of Norfolk in the direct line was four-year-old Lady Anne de Mowbray. The kinsman with the strongest claim after her seemed to be John Howard. However, when a sudden childhood infection killed Anne at the age of eight, Edward IV showed absolutely no qualms at snatching away the birthright of the man who had served him so faithfully on the battlefields. The royal family co-opted the Mowbrays' title, estates and vast income for themselves. The Norfolk prize was given to King Edward's youngest son, Richard of Shrewsbury, whom he had fortuitously married off to the late Anne de Mowbray, despite the fact that Church law prohibited marriages between infants. In 1483, John backed the coup that put Richard III on the throne at the expense of Edward IV's son. In return for his support, Richard made John the first Howard to hold the title of Duke of Norfolk, and Richard of Shrewsbury vanished into the Tower of London, where he and his elder brother, Edward V, disappeared from the records within weeks of Richard III's accession.

46. Henry VIII and Elizabeth Stafford shared a set of great-grandparents – their grandmothers, Queen Elizabeth Woodville and Katherine Woodville, Duchess of Buckingham, were sisters. The sixteenth century had an elastic definition of the word 'cousin'.

47. K. B. McFarlane, *The Nobility of Later Medieval England* (Oxford: Clarendon Press, 1973), pp. 144–45.

48. This list excludes courtesy titles enjoyed by a peer's heir apparent and does not count as separate different titles held by the same person. They were Thomas Howard, 2nd Duke of Norfolk (d. 1524); Charles Brandon, 1st Duke of Suffolk (d. 1545); Thomas Grey, 2nd Marquess of Dorset (d. 1530); Thomas FitzAlan, 17th Earl of Arundel (d. 1524); John de Vere, 14th Earl of Oxford (d. 1526); James FitzGerald, 10th Earl of Desmond (d. 1529); Gerald FitzGerald, 9th Earl of Kildare (d. 1534); Henry Percy, 5th Earl of Northumberland (d. 1527); George Talbot, 4th Earl of Shrewsbury and 4th Earl of Waterford (d. 1538); Ralph

Neville, 4th Earl of Westmorland (d. 1549); Richard Grey, 3rd Earl of Kent (d. 1524); Edward Stanley, 3rd Earl of Derby (d. 1572); Henry Bourchier, 2nd Earl of Essex (d. 1540); Henry Courtenay, 2nd Earl of Devon (ex. 1538); Henry Stafford, 1st Earl of Wiltshire (d. 1523); and Charles Somerset, 1st Earl of Worcester (d. 1526).

49. Another example was the prominence of men at court like Sir William Compton (d. 1528) or Henry Norris (ex. 1536), the latter of whom was part of a gentry family from Berkshire and a great-grandson of one of the earls of Oxford on his paternal grandmother's side. He married Mary Fiennes, daughter of the 8th Baron Dacre, and was one of the most respected and influential men at court between 1526 and 1536. At the time of his death, Norris's annual income was about £1,327 15s 7d, making him wealthier than many nobles. Through his ascent at court, Compton managed to increase his annual income from £10 to £1,700, constructing a significant base of those dependent on his patronage and support. In practical terms, the crucial difference seems to have been proximity to the court, rather than a strict division between gentry and aristocracy.

50. LP, V, 238.

51. Ibid., I, 20, 81–2, 257, 698, 707.

52. Weever, *Funerall Monuments*, p. 839.

53. Revelation 5:5.

54. At the earliest, the monument must have been completed in June 1525. It refers to the duke's daughter as 'the Lady Elizabeth wife to the count Rochford' (Weever, *Funerall Monuments*, pp. 839–40). Thomas Boleyn was elevated to the viscounty of Rochford in June 1525.

Chapter 3: Lord Edmund's Daughter

1. 'A Contemporary Account of the Battle of Flodden, 9th September 1513. From a Manuscript in the Possession of David Laing, Esq., L.L.D., V.P.S.A. Scot', in *Proceedings of the Society of Antiquaries of Scotland* (Edinburgh, 1870), VII, p. 148.

2. Hall, *Hall's Chronicle*, p. 511.

3. Sydney Anglo, 'The Evolution of Early Tudor Disguising, Pageant, and Mask', in *Renaissance Drama* (Chicago: University of Chicago Press, 1968), pp. 14–15.

4. Hall, *Hall's Chronicle*, pp. 510–11.

5. Sir Henry F. MacGeagh and H. A. C. Sturgess (eds), *Register of the Admissions to the Honourable Society of the Middle Temple: From the Fifteenth Century to the Year 1944* (London: Butterworth and Co., 1949), I, p. 3, gives 3 February '1510–11' for the admission of 'Edmund Hayward, son of the Earl of Surrey'. The date of Edmund's failed legal career is sometimes confusingly given as 1510 – Smith, *A Tudor Tragedy*, p. 36. However, the English legal new year did not commence until the Feast of the Annunciation on 25 March, meaning that when he was admitted on 3 February it was still legally classed as 1510, but 1511 in most other countries and to subsequent histories.

6. Hall, *Hall's Chronicle*, p. 508.

7. Ibid., p. 517.

8. Sydney Anglo (ed.), *The Great Tournament Roll of Westminster: a collotype reproduction of the manuscript* (Oxford: Clarendon Press, 1968), p. 56.

9. MS Ashmole 1116, f. 110.

10. Ibid., f. 109.

11. Hall, *Hall's Chronicle*, p. 517.

12. Hall, *Hall's Chronicle*, p. 519.

13. R. K. Hannay, R. L. Mackie, and Anne Spilman (eds), *The Letters of James the Fourth, 1505–1513* (Edinburgh: Scottish Historical Society, 1953), p. 550.

14. There is some mystery over these two sons. Details of their tombs are recorded in Howard, p. 11. Charles Howard's grave read: '*Hic jacet Carolus Howard unus filiorum Thome Howard Comitis Sur; qui quidem Carolus obiit tertio die Martii Ao. Dni Millemo quingetesimo duo decimo cujus anime propitietur deus. amen.*' The grave of Henry Howard, who died on 22 February 1514 (NS), read: '*Hic jacet Dns Henricus Howard, filius serenisimi, Ducis Norfolckiæ qui obiit xxiii. die Februarii, Ao. Dni. Millemo vcxiij., cujus anime propitietur Deus amen.*' They seem to have been two sons born to the duke's second marriage and who died in infancy, mentioned with their siblings in Melvin Tucker, *The Life of Thomas Howard, Earl of Surrey and Second Duke of Norfolk, 1433–1524* (The Hague: Mouton and Co., 1964), p. 26.

15. *Proceedings of the Society of Antiquaries of Scotland*, p. 143.

16. Norman MacDougall, *James IV* (Edinburgh: John Donald Publishers, 1989), p. 271.

17. *A Ballade of the Scottyshe Kynge*, written by John Skelton, Poet Laureate to King Henry the Eighth, John Ashton (intro.), (London: Elliot Stock, 1882), p. 81.

18. Ashton, *Ballade*, p. 63.

19. LP I, ii, 2246.

20. *Proceedings of the Society of Antiquaries of Scotland*, pp. 145–48.

21. Ashton, *Ballade*, p. 73; Hall, *Hall's Chronicle*, p. 562.

22. Ashton, *Ballade*, pp. 73–4.

23. Hall, *Hall's Chronicle*, p. 562. This was the same Heron who had murdered Sir Robert Ker, Scottish Warden of Middle March, in 1508, and whose pardon from the English government featured in James IV's grievances against his southern neighbours. Heron was the bastard son of an English noble with estates near the Anglo-Scottish border. See LP, I, ii, 4406, for the pardon, and MacDougall, pp. 252–54, for the Scottish government's complaints about him.

24. Ashton, *Ballade*, p. 74.

25. LP, I, ii, 2283. The casualty figures for Flodden are still unclear, with estimates varying between five and ten thousand on the Scottish side.

26. Hall, *Hall's Chronicle*, p. 563.

27. Ashton, *Ballade*, p. 87.

28. William Dugdale, *The Baronage of England* (London: Thomas Newcomb, 1675), II, p. 272; LP, I, ii, 2283.

29. *Original Letters*, I, i, 32.

30. Hall, *Hall's Chronicle*, p. 567.

31. Ibid., p. 564.

32. LP, I, ii, 2246.

33. Ibid., 3325.

34. Ibid., 3348.

35. Ibid., 2090.

36. Ibid., 2090; LP, Add. I, 33, 430.

37. Joyce had five children from her first marriage, as mentioned at length in the wills of her mother and stepfather: Ralph, John, Isabel, Joyce, and Margaret.

38. Lady Joyce's date of birth was around 1480–81, based on evidence provided from the settling of her father's estate in November 1493, when she was described as 'Joyce wife of Ralph Legh, aged 12 or more', when her younger sister was listed as 'Margaret Culpepyr, aged 11 or more'. While the supplement of 'or more' seems vague, or catch all, the difference of a year between the sisters suggests that there was an attempt to be

relatively specific. *Calendar of Inquisitions Post Mortem and other analogous documents preserved in the Public Record Office: Henry VII* (London: Eyre and Spottiswoode, 1898), I, p. 820.

39. LP, I, ii, 3484.

40. Sir Thomas Elyot's *Boke Named the Governor* (1531) cit. Andy Wood, *Riot, Rebellion and Popular Politics in Early Modern England* (Basingstoke: Palgrave, 2002), p. 26.

41. Wood, *Rebellion and Popular Politics*, p. 26.

42. Hall, *Hall's Chronicle*, pp. 599–600.

43. *Archaeologia: or Miscellaneous Tracts relating to Antiquity, Published by the Society of Antiquaries of London* (London, 1834), XXV, p. 376.

44. *Surrey Archaeological Collections*, LI, pp. 87–8.

45. LP, IV, ii, 3732.

46. Thomas Lamb and 'Lord Howard's servant George', who may have been the same as another servant of his, George Shaw – LP, I, ii, 2090; LP, Add. I, 1148; Muriel St Clare Byrne (ed.), *Lisle Letters* (Chicago and London: University of Chicago Press, 1981), III, 798.

47. LP, V, 1757.

48. *Original Letters*, III, i, 64.

49. W. Bruce Bannerman (ed.), *The Visitations of the County of Surrey made and taken in the years 1530... 1572 ... and 1623* (London: Herleian Society, 1899), XLIII, p. 21.

50. *Surrey Archaeological Collections*, LI, pp. 87–8.

51. It is not true that Joyce died giving birth to Catherine, since both women are mentioned in the will of Isabel Leigh. Cf. Denny, *Katherine Howard*, pp. 10–11. Joyce must have been alive in 1527, when she is mentioned as a beneficiary in her

mother's will, and equally she must have been dead for some time by May 1530, when Edmund's second wife made her will (see *Surrey Archaeological Collections*, III, p. 174).

52. LP, V, 220, grant 14.

53. His appointment was given at Windsor Castle on 1 April 1531 – LP, V, 220, grant 14.

54. LP, V, 1757.

55. LP, Add., I, 746.

56. The friendship between Arundell and Northumberland was close enough for some to suggest a romantic relationship. For discussions on their relationship and the debate, see R. W. Hoyle, 'Henry Percy, Sixth Earl of Northumberland, and the Fall of the House of Percy, 1527–1537', in G. W. Bernard (ed.), *The Tudor Nobility* (Manchester: Manchester University Press, 1992), pp. 180–211, and Gareth Russell, 'His Dear Bedfellow: The Debate over Henry Percy', in *Tudor Life* (2016).

Chapter 4: The Howards of Horsham

1. Weever, *Funerall Monuments*, p. 834.

2. Stewart, *Close Readers*, p. 94.

3. Ibid., p. 87.

4. Ann Kussmaul, *Servants in Husbandry in Early Modern England* (Cambridge: Cambridge University Press, 1981), p. 3; Peter Laslett, *The World We Have Lost: Further Explored* (London: Methuen, 1983), pp. 13–16.

5. Chesworth House, or Chesworth Place, became property of the Crown following the 4th Duke of Norfolk's attainder and execution for treason in 1572. As a result, it was examined by a parliamentary commission in 1650 following the temporary abolition of the monarchy. The physical

description of the house is taken from the commission's findings, which are detailed in Dudley G. Elwes and Charles J. Robinson, *A History of the Castles and Manors of Western Sussex* (London: Longman & Co., 1876), pp. 119–20.

6. In 1531, Agnes ranked behind the queen, her daughter Princess Mary, and the king's younger sister Mary, Duchess of Suffolk and Dowager Queen of France. Her only immediate equal was her daughter-in-law Elizabeth (née Stafford), Duchess of Norfolk.

7. A. R. Myers, *The Household of Edward IV: The Black Book and the Ordinance of 1478* (Manchester: Manchester University Press, 1959), p. 94.

8. Kate Mertes, *The English Noble Household, 1250–1600: Good Governance and Politic Rule* (Oxford: Basil Blackwell, 1998), p. 1.

9. Chesworth House, which is privately owned, currently contains part of the brickwork that Catherine would have known, including a southeast range built in brick between 1514 and 1524. However, owing to neglect in the seventeenth century, the house today is very different to the one which Agnes Howard occupied, with additions from the seventeenth, eighteenth, and twentieth centuries.

10. 'John Russell's Book of Nurture', quoted in Edith Rickert and Israel Gollancz (eds), *The Babees' Book: Medieval Manners for the Young: Done into Modern English from Dr. Furnivall's Texts* (New York: Cooper Square Publishers, 1966), p. 63.

11. *State Papers*, I, 180; LP, XI, 17; Ralph A. Griffiths, *Sir Rhys ap Thomas and his Family: A Study in the Wars of the Roses and Early Tudor Politics* (Cardiff: University of Wales Press, 1993), p. 113.

12. 'The Babees' Book or A Little Report on how young people should behave', quoted in *The Babees' Book*, p. 4.

13. 'John Russell's Book of Nurture', in *The Babees' Book*, p. 57.

14. Felicity Heal, *Hospitality in Early Modern England* (Oxford: Clarendon Press, 1990), p. 71.

15. LP, IV, ii, 4710. On Agnes's patronage of John Skelton historians are divided, owing to the cryptic nature of Skelton's dedications and debates over dating his work. H. L. R. Edwards, *Skelton: The Life and Times of an Early Tudor Poet* (London: Jonathan Cape, 1949), pp. 206–07, believes Agnes was one of Skelton's patrons. Tucker, pp. 9, 74n, argues that the Howards' connection to Skelton was the 2nd duke's first wife Elizabeth, Countess of Surrey, and Greg Walker, *John Skelton and the Politics of the 1520s* (Cambridge: Cambridge University Press, 1988), pp. 15–32, believes the Howard links to Skelton have been exaggerated.

16. LP, IV, ii, 4710.

17. Ibid., XVI, 1317, 1398, 1461; Ibid., Add. I, 367.

18. Ibid., VI, 212, 1111.

19. Elwes and Robinson, *Castles and Manors*, p. 120.

20. MS Ashmole 61, fol. 20.

21. 'The Babees' Book or A Little Report on how young people should behave', quoted in *The Babees' Book*, p. 3.

22. Sir John Maclean (ed.), *The Berkeley Manuscripts* (Gloucester: John Bellows, 1883), II, pp. 384–86.

23. 'The Babees' Book or A Little Report on how young people

should behave', quoted in *The Babees' Book*, pp. 3–4.

24. Ibid.

25. 'John Russell's Book of Nurture', in *The Babees' Book*, p. 47.

26. Maclean (ed.), *Berkeley Manuscripts*, II, p. 382. The compliment referred to Catherine's second cousin Katherine (née Howard), Lady Berkeley, daughter of Henry Howard, Earl of Surrey, and wife of Henry Berkeley, 7th Baron Berkeley.

27. 'The Boke of Nurture, or School of Good Manners for Men, Servants, and Children, with Stans Puer Ad Mensam, newly corrected, being necessary for all youth and children', quoted in *The Babees' Book*, p. 132; 'The Little Children's Little Book', quoted in *The Babees' Book*, pp. 16–19; 'The Young Children's Little Book', quoted in *The Babees' Book*, p. 25; Penelope Eames, *Furniture in England, France and the Netherlands from the Twelfth to the Fifteenth Century* (London: Furniture History Society, 1977), p. 57.

28. 'The Little Children's Little Book', quoted in *The Babees' Book*, p. 16.

29. Agnes Strickland, *Lives of the Queens of England from the Norman Conquest* (Bath: Cedric Chivers, 1972), III, p. 105.

30. *The Babees' Book*, p. 4.

31. 'John Russell's Book of Nurture', quoted in *The Babees' Book*, p. 50.

32. *The Babees' Book*, p. 2012.

33. Joan Bulmer (née Acworth) was born c.1519 and later married 'young Bulmer'. Others, like Katherine Tilney, seem to have been younger and were still unmarried and in the dowager's service when Catherine became queen.

34. Originally published in French as *L'enfant et la vie familiale sous l'Ancien Régime* (Paris: Plon, 1960).

35. The tradition arose from a popular legend that the logs that were burned to warm the stable in Bethlehem at the time of Christ's birth had been from ash trees.

36. Laurence Whistler, *The English Festivals* (London: William Heinemann, 1947), pp. 59–60.

37. Matthew 2:1–11.

38. *Cal. S. P. Span.*, IV, ii, 323.

39. LP, III, 1675.

40. Griffiths, *Sir Rhys ap Thomas*, pp. 91–2.

41. Ibid., p. 92.

42. Ibid., p. 98.

43. LP, VIII, 230.

44. *Proceedings of the Privy Council*, VII, p. 282–83.

45. LP, IX, 577.

46. Griffiths, *Sir Rhys ap Thomas*, p. 113.

47. Muriel (ed.), *Lisle Letters*, IV, p. 10.

48. LP, IX, 576–77.

49. Ibid., XVI, 1414, 1469.

50. Ibid., VIII, 1103.

51. Ibid., IX, 577. This seems to disprove the contemporary rumour, either repeated or invented by the imperial ambassador, that Katherine's first husband had been targeted partly because he was anti-Boleyn and that 'had it not been for the Lady, who hated him because he and his wife had spoken disparagingly of her, he would have been pardoned and escaped his miserable fate'. The speed with which Katherine remarried, her favour with the queen, and the attempts made to safeguard Katherine's finances during her husband's downfall suggest that Rhys's fall was not linked to the question of the king's remarriage. Cf. Cal. S.P., Span., IV, ii, 323;

Griffiths, *Sir Rhys ap Thomas*, pp. 104–11.

52. LP, X, 911.

53. Griffiths, *Sir Rhys ap Thomas*, pp. 94–5.

54. Later in life, Elizabeth I publicly defended her mother on several occasions, even going into relatively precise details of her life to do so. Given that her mother died before Elizabeth's third birthday, and many of her childhood servants were appointed by Queen Anne, including Elizabeth's governess Katherine Ashley (née Champernowne) and her future Archbishop of Canterbury, Matthew Parker, they remain the most likely source for Elizabeth's information about her mother. It is not true that Elizabeth seldom mentioned her, and accounts from her sister's reign, when it would have been more diplomatic to avoid the conversation, describe the topic in a way that suggests Elizabeth had discussed it frequently – see Lisa Hilton, *Elizabeth I: Renaissance Prince* (London: Weidenfeld & Nicolson, 2014), pp. 84–5.

55. Between May 1536 and October 1537, there was no clear heir to the English throne. All three of the king's biological children were legally illegitimate, either because they had been born in bastardy or because they had been declared so after the annulment of their mothers' marriages. As a result, Margaret Douglas's place in the line of succession was ambiguous but undeniable.

56. *Original Letters*, III, iii, 208.

57. Muriel (ed.), *Lisle Letters*, III, 221; LP, XIII, i, 295.

58. LP, X, 371.

59. Ibid., XI, 636.

60. Ibid., Add., I, 1148.

61. Ibid., XVI, 1398; W. A. Copinger, *The Manors of Suffolk: Notes on Their History and Devolution* (London: T. Fisher Unwin, 1905), I, p. 221. Manox was also thought to have been related to Edward Waldegrave, another young man on the dowager's staff, and a close friend of Manox's future rival, Francis Dereham.

62. SP 1/167, f. 117.

63. See in particular R. M. Warnicke, 'Katherine [Catherine; *née* Katherine Howard] (1518x24–1542), queen of England and Ireland, fifth consort of Henry VIII', in *Oxford Dictionary of National Biography* (Oxford: Oxford University Press, 2004), and Denny, *Katherine Howard*, pp. 86–9, 115–24. This particular interpretation rests strongly on Denny's belief that Catherine was born *c*.1525. Variants of this narrative of Catherine as a victim of long-term sexual abuse have been repeated elsewhere.

64. Paul Johnson, *Elizabeth: A Study in Power and Intellect* (London: Weidenfeld and Nicolson, 1974), pp. 25–7; David Starkey, *Elizabeth: Apprenticeship* (London: Vintage, 2001), pp. 67–70.

65. Martin Ingram, 'Child sexual abuse in early modern England', in Michael J. Braddick and John Walter (eds), *Negotiating Power in Early Modern Society: Order, Hierarchy and Subordination in Britain and Ireland* (Cambridge: Cambridge University Press, 2001), pp. 81–3.

66. B. A. Windeatt (trans.), *The Book of Margery Kempe* (London: Penguin, 2004), p. 59.

67. See chapter 19.

68. LP, XVI, 1321.

69. Ibid., XVI, 1320.

70. Ibid., XVI, 1321.

71. Ibid.

72. Dating Mary's arrival requires combining her own imprecise memories with the itinerary of

her first mentioned employer, Lord William Howard. On 5 November 1541, Mary dated her arrival to 'three or four years past' (LP, XVI, 1320), provisionally meaning 1537 or 1538. In the same statement, she mentions that her first job was as a nursemaid to Lord William's daughter Agnes, the future Marchioness of Winchester. Agnes must have been born before 1535, the year of her mother's death, but Mary's own recollections make it clear that she had not served the girl from birth. Mary also states that much of her early employment was spent in Lord William's household and that it was only later that she gradually began to spend more time at the dowager duchess's. After the Prince of Wales's christening in October 1537, William was sent to France to report back on a rumoured marriage negotiation between the Scottish king, James V, and Marie de Guise, Dowager Duchess of Longueville (LP, XII, ii, 1004). The proposed union worried the English, and William was ordered to remain in France until a final announcement was made. That announcement arrived in January 1538, which, when set alongside Mary's statement from November 1541, supports the idea that she became familiar with both households after that – in early or mid-1538. Testimonies from other servants, who dated the beginning of Catherine's affair with Francis Dereham to mid-1538, suggest that Mary arrived in 1538, since she had certainly arrived before the end of the liaison with Manox.

73. LP, XVI, 1320.
74. SP 1/167, f. 129.
75. Ibid., f. 130.
76. Ibid., f. 117.
77. Ibid., 1/168, f. 85.

Chapter 5: Mad Wenches

1. Kim M. Philips, *Medieval Maidens: Young Women and Gender in England, 1270–1540* (Manchester University Press, 2003), p. 6.
2. Smith, *A Tudor Tragedy*, p. 138.
3. George Cavendish, *The Life of Cardinal Wolsey, by George Cavendish, his Gentleman Usher, and Metrical Visions* (Chiswick: Harding, Triphook, and Lepard, 1825), II, p. 64. The author had retired from court in 1530, but he remained tied to it through his brother, William.
4. LP, XVI, 1317.
5. Ibid., 1321.
6. Ibid.
7. In 1536, the dowager duchess gave him money to purchase a livery – LP, XVI, 1398.
8. Francis Dereham's date of birth is difficult to determine. G. H. Dashwood (ed.), *The Visitation of Norfolk in the year 1563 taken by William Hervey, Clarenceux King of Arms* (Norwich: Miller and Leavins, 1878), I, family tree 84, p. 228, provides dates of birth for Francis's siblings of ranging from late in Henry VII's reign to early in Henry VIII's, but they seem out of order and there are gaps for several of the younger siblings. More concretely, a family will indicates that Francis was under twenty-one in 1529, two years before his father's death. How far under twenty-one is not clear, but it weakens the suggestion he was born c.1508. He may have been a decade or so older than Catherine, but his entry into the dowager's service in 1536 raises the possibility of a date of birth of c.1515, or perhaps sometime after.
9. LP, XVI, 1398, 1416; Dyer, *Standards of Living in the Later Middle Ages*, p. 55.

10. Dyer, *Standards of Living*, pp. 58–63.

11. Burnet, *History of the Reformation*, IV, p. 71.

12. LP, XVI, 1321; Burnet, *History of the Reformation*, IV, p. 71.

13. Burnet, *History of the Reformation*, IV, p. 71.

14. SP 1/167, ff. 130, 161.

15. Burnet, *History of the Reformation*, IV, p. 71.

16. LP, XVI, 1337; *Proceedings of the Privy Council*, VII, p. 354.

17. SP 1/167, f. 131.

18. Ibid.

19. LP, XVI, 1320.

20. Teresa McLean, *The English at Play in the Middle Ages* (Slough: Kensal Press, 1983), p. 3.

21. Susan E. James, *Kateryn Parr: The Making of a Queen* (Aldershot: Ashgate Publishing, 1999), plate 9.

22. Beryl Rowland (trans.), *Medieval Woman's Guide to Health: The First English Gynecological Handbook* (Kent, OH: Kent State University Press, 1981), p. 87; James A. Brundage, *Law, Sex, and Christian Society in Medieval Europe* (Chicago: University of Chicago Press, 1987), p. 491.

23. Brundage, *Law, Sex, and Christian Society*, p. 504.

24. Ibid., p. 535.

25. Thomas Tentler, *Sin and Confession on the Eve of the Reformation* (Princeton, NJ: Princeton University Press, 1977), p. 143.

26. Rowland, p. 167.

27. SP 1/167, f. 137.

28. LP, XVI, 1321.

29. Ibid., 1469.

30. SP 1/167, ff. 130, 137. Whoever that family was it was not the 'Lord Bayment' mentioned in Smith, *A Tudor Tragedy*, p. 50. There was no family with that title in the Anglo-Irish peerages in 1539.

31. LP, XVI, 1469.

32. Ibid., 1385, 1424.

33. Ibid., 1337 (2).

34. Ibid., 1330, 1337 (2).

35. Ibid., 1469.

36. Ibid.

37. LP, XVI, 1348. Maunsay told a member of the Privy Council on 15 November 1541 that Bess 'could also speak of this', at a time when they were inquiring after the queen's alleged sexual indiscretions at Horsham and Lambeth. If she was subsequently questioned, Bess's testimony sadly has not survived, but because he identified her, Maunsay must have known that she had some specific and relevant information.

38. LP, XVI, 1385.

39. Ibid.

40. LP, XVI, 1414.

41. Burnet, *History of the Reformation*, IV, p. 71.

42. Burnet, *History of the Reformation*, IV, p. 71.

43. Catherine only referred to 'my lady Breerton'. Elizabeth Brereton (née Somerset), daughter of Charles, 1st Earl of Worcester, and widow of William Brereton (ex. 1536) could have been the lady she was referring to, but there is no firm evidence that her late husband had ever been properly knighted. The only definite Lady Brereton in 1539 was Lady Eleanor Brereton (née Brereton), wife of Sir William Brereton, who became Lord Justice of Ireland in April 1540. Her husband was in England between 1536 and November 1539, which leaves Eleanor as the only Lady Brereton in the right place and time.

44. For one instance among hundreds, the twelfth-century case of the disinheritance of Mabel de Francheville by her cousin Richard de Antsey, who challenged her legitimacy in the

hope of confiscating her lands, which would then fall to him. Pope Alexander III eventually ruled in de Antsey's favour. In living memory for Catherine's parents, the bastardising of Edward V and his siblings in 1483 on the grounds of his father's alleged pre-contract with Lady Eleanor Talbot helped bring the Duke of Gloucester to the throne as Richard III. A pre-contract would also later be used to annul Henry VIII's fourth marriage.

45. He may have retired from his job in Calais shortly before his death, quite possibly for health reasons. Plans were in motion to appoint a replacement by 31 January, although the intention may have been to make the appointment only after Edmund retired or was dismissed. LP, XIV, i, 172; 906, grant 17; Sylvanus Urban, *The Gentleman's Magazine and Historical Chronicle* (London: John Nichols, 1797), p. 543.

46. Margaret Jennings was not subsequently attached to Catherine's household, as was suggested in the nineteenth century and repeated in the twentieth and twenty-first centuries. The sources make it clear that the Lady Howard in question was Catherine's aunt.

47. *Archaeologia: or Miscellaneous Tracts Relating to Antiquity* (London: J. B. Nichols and Son, 1883), XLVII, p. 326.

48. LP, XII, ii, 463.

49. Muriel (ed.), *Lisle Letters*, IV, 998.

50. LP, XIII, I, 395.

51. Muriel (ed.), *Lisle Letters*, V, 1139. The Countess of Bridgewater acted as chief female mourner. Elizabeth Boleyn had died at a house near Baynard's Castle in London and her body was taken from there to Lambeth on a barge, with burning torches and banners from each of the barge's corners.

52. Burnet, *History of the Reformation*, IV, p. 71.

Chapter 6: The King's Highness Did Cast a Fantasy

1. LP, XII, ii, 1004.
2. Ibid.
3. LP, XIII, ii. 77.
4. There is some evidence that a middle sister, Louise, was also briefly considered. She later married Charles II, Prince de Chimay.
5. LP, XII, ii, 1172, 1187; Julia Cartwright, *Christina of Denmark, Duchess of Milan and Lorraine, 1522–1590* (London: John Murray, 1913), pp. 149–54.
6. Cartwright, *Christina of Denmark*, pp. 192–94.
7. LP, XIII, i, 583; LP, XIV, ii, 400; Cartwright, *Christina of Denmark*, pp. 192–94.
8. LP, XIII, ii, 1087. The final straw seemed to be the despoliation of the shrine of Saint Thomas Becket and St Augustine's monastery, both in Canterbury.
9. LP, XIV, i, 953, 1005, 1245; XV, 142. There were already concerns about the Scottish government's possible role in encouraging aristocratic dissent in Ireland.
10. Susan Brigden, 'Henry VIII and the Crusade against England', in Thomas Betteridge and Suzannah Lipscomb (eds), *Henry VIII and the Court: Art, Politics and Performance* (Farnham: Ashgate, 2013), pp. 215–23.
11. LP, XIV, i, 940; XIV, ii, 35.
12. The white rose was the heraldic crest most popularly associated with the House of York, the branch of the Plantagenets who ruled England immediately before the Tudors.
13. Hall, *Hall's Chronicle*, p. 842.
14. Hazel Pierce, *Margaret Pole, Countess of Salisbury,*

1473–1541: Loyalty, Lineage, and Leadership* (Cardiff: University of Wales Press, 2003), pp. 36–7.

15. LP, XIII, ii, 695.

16. *The Spanish Chronicle*, p. 132. This is accepted by Pierce, *Margaret Pole*, p. 128.

17. Muriel (ed.), *Lisle Letters*, V, 1259; LP, XIV, i, 191.

18. LP, XVI, 74.

19. Burnet, *History of the Reformation*, VI, pp. 258–59; LP, XXI, ii, 554.

20. LP, XIII, i, 1124.

21. Ibid., i, 37.

22. Ibid., 233, 280.

23. Madeleine Hope Dodds and Ruth Dodds, *The Pilgrimage of Grace, 1536–1537, and the Exeter Conspiracy, 1538* (Cambridge: Cambridge University Press, 1915), II, pp. 321–22.

24. LP, XIV, i, 815, 1009, 1035.

25. Ibid., 940, 953, 1005, 1245, 1288.

26. Manuel Fernández Alvarez, *Charles V: Elected Emperor and Hereditary Ruler* (London: Thames and Hudson, 1975), p. 115.

27. Charles Wriothesley, *A Chronicle of England During the Reigns of the Tudors*, William Douglas Hamilton (ed.) (London: Camden Society, 1875), pp. 97–9.

28. LP, XIV, ii, 1137.

29. An example being Francis Dereham's trip to Ireland: the majority of the sources suggest that he went there without the dowager duchess's permission or knowledge, but there is one which implies she told Lady Isabella Baynton that she knew Dereham had gone there. On the balance of probability, especially given the doubt expressed in the latter anomalous source, the majority version that remembered him leaving England without taking leave of the Howard family beforehand

seems the most probable – SP 1/168, f. 53; LP, XVI, 1409 (8), 1416.

30. LP, XIV, ii, 300.

31. Ibid., i, 955.

32. Ibid., ii, 275.

33. *Original Letters*, I, ii, 146.

34. LP, XIV, ii, 469.

35. Burnet, *History of the Reformation*, VI, p. 233.

36. SP 1/167, ff. 110, 131; LP, XVI, 1334, 1379.

37. SP 1/168, f. 14.

38. Ives, *Life and Death*, p. 9.

39. SP 1/168, f. 8.

40. Ibid., f. 53. The framing of the questions put to Agnes during the interrogations also makes it clear that the dowager was not present at the time and that the information was passed on to her by another source.

41. Ibid.

42. *Inventory*, II, pp. 58–9.

43. 2 Samuel 11:1–27.

44. LP, XIV, ii, 221.

45. Anne of Cleves may have had as many as seven maids of honour, based on BL – Additional MS 45, 716a, f. 16. At least at the start of her queenship, Catherine had five, excluding the mother of the maids, based on SP 1/157, f. 16. Katherine Parr's were back up to seven in 1547, with their mother – Hamilton, 'Household of Queen Katherine Parr', pp. 30–1.

46. LP, XIV, i, 1088.

47. Muriel (ed.), *Lisle Letters*, III, 574; IV, 899; VI, 1653.

48. Lord Lisle was an acknowledged illegitimate son of King Edward IV, Henry VIII's maternal grandfather.

49. LP, XV, 1030 (52); Muriel (ed.), *Lisle Letters*, V, 1558.

50. *Original Letters*, I, ii, 146.

51. LP, XV, 215.

52. Ibid., 229.

53. LP, XIV, ii, 33; XV, 215

54. 'John Russell's Book of Nurture', in *The Babees' Book*, p. 66.

55. *Household Ordinances*, p. 156; Thurley, *Royal Palaces*, pp. 123–27.
56. Ninya Mikhaila and Jane Malcolm-Davies, *The Tudor Tailor: Reconstructing sixteenth-century dress* (London: Batsford, 2006), p. 23.
57. Muriel (ed.), *Lisle Letters*, IV, 161–62, 191, 894; Burnet, *History of the Reformation*, VI, 72.
58. BL, Harleian MS 6807, ff. 10v–11.
59. Thurley, *Royal Palaces*, p. 172.
60. Ibid., pp. 172–76.
61. G. W. Bernard, *The Power of the Early Tudor Nobility: A Study of the Fourth and Fifth Earls of Shrewsbury* (Brighton: Harvester Press, 1985), p. 173.
62. Susan Brigden, *Thomas Wyatt: The Heart's Forest* (London: Faber and Faber, 2012), p. 521; Thurley, *Royal Palaces*, p. 50; LP, XIV, ii, 718.
63. LP, XIV, ii, 718.
64. Thurley, *Royal Palaces*, pp. 50–8.
65. LP, XIV, ii, 340.
66. Ibid., i, 970; 1208; XV, 330.
67. SP 1/168, f. 48.
68. Head, *Ebbs and Flows*, pp. 251–52.
69. Childs, *Henry VIII's Last Victim*, pp. 92–3.
70. Ibid., p. 17.
71. Ibid., pp. 133–34. His wife was Lady Frances de Vere, daughter of the 15th Earl of Oxford and his second wife Elizabeth (née Trussell).
72. Ibid., p. 3.
73. Beverley A. Murphy, *Bastard Prince: Henry VIII's Lost Son* (Stroud: History Press, 2010), p. 176.
74. Ibid., pp. 221–22.
75. Mary Howard had three titles in 1539 – her late husband Henry Fitzroy (1519–1536) had been Duke of Richmond and Somerset and Earl of Nottingham. It was only later in the reign, when the Seymour match was suggested again, that Surrey apparently claimed that marrying a Seymour was beneath a Howard.
76. *Household Ordinances*, p. 155.
77. LP, IX, 612.
78. SP 1/167, f. 148.
79. Ibid.
80. Ibid.
81. Burnet, *History of the Reformation*, VI, 72.
82. SP 1/168, f. 53.
83. LP, XIV, ii, 256.
84. The Hapsburg Netherlands covered what is now the kingdoms of Belgium and of the Netherlands, the grand duchy of Luxembourg, and part of the French region of Nord-Pas-de-Calais. Daughters or sisters of the monarch ruled the Netherlands as extremely capable deputies for most of the sixteenth century.
85. LP, XIV, ii, 314, 360, 553, 591.
86. Ibid., 622.
87. Ibid., 718.
88. Ibid., 677.

Chapter 7: The Charms of Catherine Howard

1. The account of Anne of Cleves's arrival, including the weather and her ladies' outfits, is taken from *Hall's Chronicle*, pp. 834–36. Edward Hall's mania for the details of Tudor court pageantry is a historian's delight.
2. LP, XIV, i, 490.
3. Hall, *Hall's Chronicle*, pp. 834–36.
4. The Feast of the Epiphany is still counted as the last day of Christmas in Catholic countries, like Spain, where as 'Kings' Day' it is the main gift-giving day of the season.
5. The first recognisably 'modern' royal wedding, taking place in a cathedral and accompanied by processions through the streets

and media attention, was that of Mary, the Princess Royal, to Henry Lascelles, the future 6th Earl of Harewood, in February 1922.

6. Hall, *Hall's Chronicle*, p. 837.

7. Hall, *Hall's Chronicle*, p. 836.

8. LP, XV, 86. A report of the punishment of a criminal mentions that they were pelted with snowballs by local children.

9. Hall, *Hall's Chronicle*, p. 837.

10. LP, XV, 822; letter from Charles de Marillac to the Constable de Montmorency, 5 January 1540, cit. Thomas, *The Pilgrim*, pp. 135–36.

11. Warnicke, *The Marrying of Anne of Cleves*, pp. 183–84.

12. The famous portrait of Anne of Cleves by Hans Holbein, which now hangs in the Louvre, is usually blamed for misleading the king. However, Holbein did not go to Schloss Düren to paint Anne's portrait until August 1539 and it was not complete until September, by which point the negotiations for the marriage were almost concluded.

13. Retha M. Warnicke, 'Henry VIII's Greeting of Anne of Cleves and Early Modern Court Protocol', in *Albion* (1996), pp. 580–82.

14. The habit of a disguised royal bridegroom spying on his fiancée was a trope borrowed from numerous romances, but one which actual princesses seemed to find both offensive and annoying. Three years after Anne's marriage, Princess Maria Manuela of Portugal shielded her face with a fan when she heard her betrothed was dressed as a commoner in the crowds as she entered Salamanca.

15. LP, XV, 179.

16. The comments on Anne's appearance tally with de Marillac's assessment, although it is possible that Eleanor had also heard reports on Anne of Cleves from her sister Maria, Dowager Queen of Hungary, who had sent a nobleman to escort Anne on her journey through the Netherlands. The sisters were in regular enough contact that when a messenger was absent from the dowager queen's court, it was assumed he had taken a message to the Queen of France – LP, XV, 837, and a letter from Charles de Marillac to King François I, 5 January 1540, cit. Thomas, *The Pilgrim*, p. 135.

17. The title was held by Edward's family before their seizure of the crown in 1461, and it was given to his younger son, Richard, in 1473. Ironically, given its customary designation as a title for the monarch's second surviving son, five of the men invested with the title since then later succeeded to the throne – Henry VIII, Charles I, James II, George V, and George VI were all dukes of York during their fathers' or brothers' lifetimes. In the eighteenth century, the title was also joined with the duchy of Albany and awarded to younger brothers of kings George I, George III, and George IV. The duchies were separated for a son and grandson of Queen Victoria and have not been coupled together since.

18. John Strype, *Ecclesiastical Memorials* (London: John Wyat, 1721), App., pp. 315–16.

19. LP, XIV, ii, 33.

20. Ibid., XV, 925. De Marillac's experience of England typically meant London.

21. Ibid., 243. This message was carried verbally by one of Anne's compatriots, making it more likely that the sentiment was genuine.

22. Ibid., 776.

23. Ibid., 976.

24. Ibid., 823.

25. Diarmaid MacCulloch, *Thomas Cranmer: A Life* (New Haven and London: Yale University Press, 1996), p. 258.
26. LP, XV, 822.
27. The English interest in maintaining the alliance with Cleves is suggested by the Duke of Norfolk's embassy to France, in which his mission was to persuade François I to default on his treaty with Charles V in favour of a tripartite alliance with England and Cleves – LP, XV, 233.
28. LP, XV, 652.
29. Ibid., 38.
30. Ibid., 189.
31. *Cal. S. P. Span.*, VI, 160.
32. LP, XV, 154.
33. Ibid., 121.
34. Ibid., 115.
35. Hall, *Hall's Chronicle*, p. 837; LP, XV, 209. For the weather, a letter from Sir John Gage records that the weather was improving by the middle of February – LP, XV, 218.
36. LP, XV, 239, 240.
37. Ibid., 115, 224.
38. Ibid., 223.
39. Ibid., 223, 253, 412; Roger Bigelow Merriman, *Life and Letters of Thomas Cromwell* (Oxford: Clarendon Press, 1902), II, p. 338.
40. LP, XVI, 1332.
41. Michael Everett, *The Rise of Thomas Cromwell: Power and Politics in the Reign of Henry VIII* (New Haven: Yale University Press, 2015), pp. 58–61.
42. SP 1/121, f. 131.
43. Burnet, *History of the Reformation*, VI, pp. 258–59.
44. LP, XIV, ii, 379.
45. Ibid., 383.
46. Hall, *Hall's Chronicle*, p. 838.
47. Ibid., p. 840.
48. LP, XV, 414.
49. Ibid., 259, 269.
50. Ibid., 179.
51. Wriothesley, *Chronicle*, p. 115.
52. LP, XV, 1025.
53. Glyn Redworth, *In Defence of the Church Catholic: The Life of Stephen Gardiner* (Oxford: Basil Blackwell, 1990), pp. 119–20.
54. LP, XV, 822.
55. SP 1/168, ff. 64–5.
56. Ibid., f. 8.
57. Ibid., f. 80.
58. LP, XV, 612, grant 12.
59. Ibid., 686; *Inventory*, II, 155.
60. Hastings Robinson (ed.), *Original Letters Relative to the English Reformation* (Cambridge: Cambridge University Press, 1846), I, pp. 201–02.
61. Robinson (ed.), *Original Letters*, I, pp. 201–02.
62. LP, XV, 648, 737.
63. Burnet, *History of the Reformation*, V, p. 276.
64. LP, XV, 442.
65. Ibid., 719, 737.
66. Ibid., 749; Stanford E. Lehmberg, *The Later Parliaments of Henry VIII, 1536–1547* (Cambridge: Cambridge University Press, 1977), p. 127.
67. Redworth, *In Defence of the Church Catholic*, pp. 105–06.
68. LP, XV, 833.
69. Wriothesley, *Chronicle*, p. 118.
70. LP, XV, 737.
71. Ibid., 823.
72. Ibid., 332.
73. Ibid., 418.
74. LP, XV, 412.
75. Ibid., XIV, ii, 389; XV, 171. Even on occasions when they were declaring the opposite, as in conversations with Charles de Marillac, the English courtiers' conversations suggested a degree of concern about the Duke of Cleves's actions – LP, XV, 651.
76. Ibid., XV, 161, 662, 665.
77. Ibid., 676.
78. Ibid., 712.
79. Ibid., 811, 901.
80. Ibid., 703.
81. *Cal. S. P. Span.*, XI, 337.

82. Strype, *Ecclesiastical*, I, App., p. 313.

83. LP, XV, 850 (11) seems to show Cromwell's sluggishness or reluctance to press ahead with the annulment, despite Wriothesley's panic.

84. Ibid., 776.

85. Ibid., 766 – the French ambassador was told by an unnamed gentleman of the court that the primary reason for the king's anger was Cromwell's religious policy.

86. Ibid.

87. Ibid., 767.

88. In a twist of fate, Anne's childhood fiancé eventually married Christina of Denmark, the emperor's niece who had avoided Henry's advances in 1538–39.

89. LP, XV, 267.

90. Ibid., XIV, i, 1193.

91. Ibid., XV, 825, 850 (13).

92. *Original Letters*, II, ii, 141.

93. LP, XV, 844.

94. HMC Rutland, I, p. 27.

95. LP, XV, 850 (5, 7, 9, 13, 14).

96. Ibid., 850 (7).

97. Burnet, *History of the Reformation*, II, pp. 307–08; LP, XV, 823.

98. LP, XV, 860, 861.

99. H. A. Kelly, *The Matrimonial Trials of Henry VIII* (Stanford, CA: Stanford University Press, 1976) p. 273.

100. There is some debate over legislation passed to facilitate Catherine's marriage, with suggestions that some of it indicates that Catherine had made some half-confession about having being attached to someone in a relationship that involved discussion of marriage but no consummation. However, it seems far more likely that the legislation was designed to free Henry from any difficulty regarding the annulment of his marriage to Anne of Cleves;

Kelly, *Matrimonial Trials*, pp. 261–64.

101. LP, XV, 845.

102. Ibid., 899.

103. Ibid., 883.

104. Ibid., 991.

105. Ibid., 925 (ii).

106. Ibid., 901.

107. MacCulloch, *Thomas Cranmer*, p. 271.

108. Burnet, *History of the Reformation*, I, pp. 569–70.

109. Thurley, *Royal Palaces*, p. 190.

110. David Starkey, 'Intimacy and innovation: the rise of the Privy Chamber, 1485–1547', in David Starkey (ed.), *The English Court: from the Wars of the Roses to the Civil War* (London: Longman, 1987), p. 82.

Chapter 8: The Queen of Britain Will Not Forget

1. LP, XIV, i, 1303; Thurley, *Royal Palaces*, p. 60.

2. Hall, *Hall's Chronicle*, p. 840. This might explain why writers later in the century and in the Stuart era mistakenly dated Catherine's wedding to 8 August, for instance Burnet, *History of the Reformation*, II, p. 449.

3. LP, XV, 902.

4. Emperor Charles IV (d. 1378) was survived by his fourth wife, Elisabeth of Pomerania (d. 1393), the mother of Anne of Bohemia, queen consort of England (d. 1394). Charles is buried in St Vitus's Cathedral in Prague, in a sepulchre that houses the Empress Elisabeth's remains and those of his first three wives – Blanche of Valois (d. 1348), Anna of Bavaria (d. 1353), and Anna of Swidnica (d. 1362). Technically, King Philippe II of France (d. 1223) was also married four times, but twice to the same woman. Henry VIII's record as the most married European sovereign was beaten in the next generation by Tsar Ivan IV ('the

Terrible') of Russia (d. 1584), who wed seven times.

5. *Cal. S. P. Span*, VI, i, 115.

6. The Bulmers were a prominent family in York; *The Cause Papers Database*, G.360 – a case regarding a tithe dated to the Church Courts at York on 7 October 1540 gives a John Bulmer's age and occupation, when he was named as one of the plaintiffs. Holinshed gives the name of Joan's husband as Anthony Bulmer, but John Roche Dasent et al. (eds), *Acts of the Privy Council* (London: Her Majesty's Stationery Office, 1890–1964), I, pp. 46–8, explicitly gives his Christian name as William. There is nothing to support the narrative that Joan and William were married while she was still in service to the Dowager Duchess of Norfolk, since the *Acts of the Privy Council* only refer to an estrangement between the couple after February 1542. The suggestion that William Bulmer stopped Joan joining Queen Catherine's household in 1540 is speculative and it is difficult to believe that a counter-command from the queen would not have secured Joan's place.

7. *LP*, XV, 875.

8. Antonia Fraser, *The Six Wives of Henry VIII* (London: Arrow Books, 1998), p. 329; Denny, *Katherine Howard*, pp. 166–67.

9. E101/422/16, f. 63v; SP 1/157, ff. 15–16.

10. SP 1/167, f. 110.

11. James, *Kateryn Parr*, p. 152.

12. *LP*, XVI, 1321.

13. Ibid., 1334.

14. Ibid., 1394, 1422. Potentially contrary evidence is that the king granted a pardon to Mary Lascelles on the grounds that she had refused to join the queen's service and that by pardoning her it would encourage others to

tell the truth in future. Joan was not included in this pardon, but that may simply be because she had not willingly revealed the information about Catherine's past, as Mary had, or because in July 1540 she had sought employment in Catherine's household.

15. SP 1/168, f. 80.

16. *Original Letters*, I, ii, 121.

17. Griffiths, *Sir Rhys ap Thomas*, p. 90.

18. The countess's quest to prove that the witnesses against her husband had acted from greed or fear resulted in future generations' resilience in trying to overturn what they saw as a miscarriage of justice. The last attempt to have Rhys's verdict posthumously revoked was through a petition to King James I in 1607. For Llwyd, see Griffiths, *Sir Rhys ap Thomas*, pp. 127–28.

19. Smith, *A Tudor Tragedy*, p. 155.

20. That it was a sustained policy is supported by the fact that they sought out Alice Restwold in October.1541 – see SP 1/167, f. 136.

21. See chapters 11 and 17.

22. SP 1/167, f. 117.

23. *LP*, XIII, ii. 695

24. Andrew S. Currie, 'Notes on the Obstetric Histories of Catherine of Aragon and Anne Boleyn', in *Edinburgh Medical Journal* (1888), pp. 1–34; Ove Brinch, 'The Medical Problems of Henry VIII', in *Centaurus* (1958), pp. 339–69.

25. Sir Arthur Salusbury MacNalty, *Henry VIII: A Difficult Patient* (Norwich: Christopher Johnson, 1952), pp. 159–63, which retracts in detail an earlier lecture given by the author in support of the theory that the king had syphilis. For the recent resurrection of the theory, see Joanna Denny, *Anne Boleyn* (London: Portrait, 2004),

pp. 119, 227–28, and the same author's *Katherine Howard*, pp. 160–61.

26. Frederick Chamberlin, *The Private Character of Henry the Eighth* (London: John Lane, 1932), pp. 268–76 for the medical experts' responses, and pp. 276–82 for Chamberlin's own debunking of the syphilis myth.

27. Derek Wilson, *A Brief History of Henry VIII: Reformer and Tyrant* (London: Constable & Robinson, 2009), p. 106. This is one of the best books to explore and promote the idea that Henry's impotence significantly affected his performance as king, along with Ives, *Life and Death*, pp. 190–92.

28. Ives, *Life and Death*, p. 191.

29. Ibid.

30. Michelle Anne White, *Henrietta Maria and the English Civil Wars* (Aldershot: Ashgate, 2006), pp. 23–4.

31. Derek Wilson, *The Uncrowned Kings of England: The Black Legend of the Dudleys* (London: Constable & Robinson, 2005), p. 109.

32. C. M. Prior, *The Royal Studs of the Sixteenth and Seventeenth Centuries* (London: Horse and Hound Publications, 1935), pp. 2–3; *Inventory*, II, pp. 98–9.

33. Thurley, *Royal Palaces*, pp. 63–5.

34. Martin Biddle, *Nonsuch Palace: The Material Culture of a Noble Restoration Household* (Oxford: Oxbow Books, 2005), pp. 1–3.

35. Thurley, *Royal Palaces*, p. 38.

36. Ibid., p. 51.

37. LP, XIV, ii, 35.

38. Hall, *Hall's Chronicle*, p. 840.

39. One such procession was organised in London by Edmund Bonner.

40. LP, XIV, i, 1239.

41. Ibid., XII, i, 923; XIV, ii, 378; XV, 985, 1015.

42. Susan Brigden, *New Worlds, Lost Worlds: The Rule of the Tudors,* *1485–1603* (London: Penguin, 2000), p. 233; LP, XV, 82.

43. Hall, *Hall's Chronicle*, p. 841; Burnet, *History of the Reformation*, I, pp. 599–600. Wriothesley, *Chronicle*, I, p. 126, incorrectly places Meekins's execution on 30 July 1541.

44. LP, XVI, 20. Swinerton or Swynerton came from the parish of Swineshead, most likely the one which is now in Bedfordshire. He was summoned to appear before the Privy Council at Ampthill, also in Bedfordshire. If he had been from the Lincolnshire village of the same name, he would have been taken to the Council of the North. Until the reign of George III, Swineshead was an exclave of Huntingdonshire, but it was enclosed as part of Bedfordshire by Parliament in 1803.

45. LP, XIV, ii, 11.

46. LP, XV, 202; Kaulek, 347; *Cal. S.P. Span*, VI, i, 135.

47. Brigden, *Thomas Wyatt*, pp. 515–21.

48. The constable was, in effect, the King of France's chief minister, and all the other Great Officers of the French Crown were subordinate to him.

49. LP, XV, 954.

50. Holinshed, *Chronicles*, III, p. 819.

51. Hall, *Hall's Chronicle*, p. 840.

52. LP, XV, 976.

53. J. J. Scarisbrick, *Henry VIII* (New Haven and London: Yale University Press, 1997), p. 353.

54. Herbert, *Life and Raigne*, p. 532.

Chapter 9: All These Ladies and My Whole Kingdom

1. *The Spanish Chronicle*, pp. 75–6.

2. Hamilton, pp. 15–16.

3. James, *Kateryn Parr*, p. 122.

4. LP, XV, 21.

5. Elizabeth Norton has suggested that the Lady Clinton in attendance was Jane (née

Poynings), Elizabeth Blount's mother-in-law. However, by 1540, Jane had remarried to Sir Robert Wingfield, and despite his death, it would be unusual to see her referred to by her previous marital name – see Elizabeth Norton, *Bessie Blount: Mistress to Henry VIII* (Stroud: Amberley, 2013), pp. 301–04. I believe it was Elizabeth (née Blount) who served in the household as Lady Clinton in 1540, but I am convinced by Norton's suggestion, based on her analysis of family wills, that Elizabeth probably died giving birth to a daughter. This child was christened Catherine, which, on an admittedly tenuous basis, may have been a tribute to the queen Elizabeth served at the time of her death.

6. *The Babees' Book*, p. 4.
7. *Household Ordinances*, p. 38.
8. Margaret Visser, *The Rituals of Dinner: The Origins, Evolution, Eccentricities, and Meaning of Table Manners* (London: Viking, 1992), p. 334.
9. 'John Russell's Book of Nurture', in *The Babees' Book*, p. 64.
10 The gentlewomen of the privy chamber were generally members of the gentry, perhaps linked to the aristocracy on their mothers' sides and married to up-and-coming court-based knights or expectant sons. Once a husband was knighted, his wife could style herself a lady.
11. Julia Fox, *Jane Boleyn: The Infamous Lady Rochford* (London: Weidenfeld & Nicolson, 2007), p. 333; S. T. Bindoff (ed.), *The House of Commons, 1509–1558* (London: Secker & Warburg, 1982), III, pp. 255–58; J. L. Kirby, 'Edgcumbe, Sir Richard (c.1443–1489)', *Oxford Dictionary of National Biography*. Lady Edgecombe's parents, Sir John St

John of Bletsoe and Sybil (née Morgan), had started their family in the late 1490s. Lady Edgecombe's brother, who had the same name as her father and served as one of the MPs for Bedfordshire, was married by 1521 and she by 1525. She was widowed on 14 August 1539.

12. Norman Davis (ed.), *The Paston Letters and Papers of the Fifteenth Century* (Oxford: Oxford University Press, 1971), I, 116, 117, 165, 231.
13. LP, XIV, i, 1312; XV, 236.
14. S. J. Gunn, *Charles Brandon, Duke of Suffolk, c.1484–1545* (Oxford: Basil Blackwell, 1988), p. 205; Barbara J. Harris, 'Women and Politics in Early Tudor England', in *Historical Journal* (1990), p. 265.
15. Muriel (ed.), *Lisle Letters*, IV, 882; *Original Letters*, II, ii, 106.
16. Wriothesley, *Chronicle*, I, p. 124; LP, XIV, i, 965; XIV, ii, 753, 1121; XV, 1, 215, 229, 947.
17. LP, XIV, ii, 188.
18. Muriel (ed.), *Lisle Letters*, V, p. 1393.
19. LP, XVI, 1389.
20. Ibid.
21. BL: Addit. MS 46, 348, ff. 167b, 169b, 170a.
22. Ibid., f. 168b.
23. Ibid., f. 172b.
24. LP, XVI, 1389; BL: Addit. MS. 46, 348, f. 171b.
25. James P. Carley, *The Books of Henry VIII and his Wives* (London: British Library, 2004), pp. 134–35.
26. RCIN 912256.
27. James, *Kateryn Parr*, p. 11.
28. LP, XII, ii, 167, 424, 1060. William Herbert's father, Sir Robert Herbert, was the illegitimate son of the 1st Earl of Pembroke, who died in 1469. The title had been surrendered to the Crown in the reign of Edward IV as part of a deal by the 2nd earl. It was one of the

titles used by King Edward V prior to his accession in 1483, and after his death it merged with the Crown until it was revived and elevated for Anne Boleyn, who became Lady Marquess of Pembroke in 1532. With her death, the title was again in abeyance, and William Herbert hoped to have it restored in his favour. This was achieved in the reign of Edward VI, and the title is currently held by William and Anne's descendant, William Herbert, 18th Earl of Pembroke and 15th Earl of Montgomery.

29. The identity of the Mistress Lee as Joyce Lee is by a process of elimination, with all the gentlewomen with that surname in 1540–41, with husbands attached to the court.

30. Lorne Campbell and Susan Foister, 'Gerard, Lucas and Susanna Horenbout', in *Burlington Magazine* (1986), pp. 719–27.

31. Elizabeth Norton, *Anne of Cleves: Henry VIII's Discarded Bride* (Stroud: Amberley, 2010), p. 63.

32. 'John Russell's Book of Nurture', pp. 66–7; 'Francis Seager's School of Virtue', p. 143; both quoted in *The Babees' Book*.

33. Thurley, *Royal Palaces*, pp. 169–70.

34. Mikhaila and Malcolm-Davies, *Tudor Tailor*, p. 24.

35. James, *Kateryn Parr*, p. 127.

36. Hamilton, 'Household of Queen Katherine Parr', pp. 171–72.

37. Thurley, *Royal Palaces*, pp. 171–76; Hamilton, 'Household of Queen Katherine Parr', pp. 45, 172.

38. 'John Russell's Book of Nurture', in *The Babees' Book*, pp. 64–6.

39. An Act of Parliament in 1540 gave the newly married couple the right to inherit the Oxfordshire manor.

40. LP, XVI, 1389.

41. Ibid., 1339.

42. The identities of Lucy, the two Margarets, and Damascin are reached after research, since in Lucy's case only her first name and title are used in the surviving documentation, and in Damascin's and the Margarets', only their surnames. They are the only girls of the right age and background in 1540–41 whose details correlate with what survives in LP, XV, 21.

43. Margaret Somerset (née Courtenay), Countess of Worcester, was the daughter of Katherine Courtenay, Countess of Devon, a younger daughter of King Edward IV and Queen Elizabeth Woodville.

44. Stewart, *Close Readers*, pp. xv, 178.

45. LP, XV, 21.

46. Hamilton, 'Household of Queen Katherine Parr', p. 29; Thurley, *Royal Palaces*, p. 143.

47. James, *Kateryn Parr*, pp. 154–55, 323.

48. David Baldwin, *Henry VIII's Last Love: The Extraordinary Life of Katherine Willoughby, Lady-in-Waiting to the Tudors* (Stroud: Amberley, 2015), p. 72.

49. In her will, Jane Dudley, by then Dowager Duchess of Northumberland, confessed, 'I have not loved to be very bold afore women', as part of a stipulation that she should not be autopsied, due to her modesty.

50. Thurley, *Royal Palaces*, p. 140.

51. Scarisbrick, *Henry VIII*, pp. 13–14.

52. Leviticus 20:21.

53. Deuteronomy 25:5. Her parents' pact with Portugal was maintained by marrying Katherine's sister Maria to King Manoel I, after the death in childbed of his first wife,

Katherine and Maria's eldest sister.

54. James Gairdner (ed.), *Memorials of King Henry the Seventh* (London: Longman, Brown, Green, Longmans, and Roberts, 1858), p. 232.

55. Jacobo Fitz-James Stuart, 10th Duke of Berwick and 17th Duke of Alba (ed.), *Correspondencia de Gutierre de Fuensalida* (Madrid: privately published, 1907), p. 449.

56. Lisa Hilton, *Queens Consort: England's Medieval Queens* (London: Weidenfeld & Nicolson, 2008), p. 411.

57. Eleanor of Austria (1498–1558) was Charles V's eldest sister and the widow of King Manoel I of Portugal when she married King François I of France in 1530.

58. Scarisbrick, *Henry VIII*, pp. 13–14; LP, I, 2391.

59. Giles Tremlett, *Catherine of Aragon: Henry's Spanish Queen* (London: Faber and Faber, 2010), p. 159.

60. Scarisbrick, *Henry VIII*, pp. 21–39.

61. Hall, *Hall's Chronicle*, p. 515.

62. RCIN 403368; Mark 16:15.

63. R. W. Hoyle, *The Pilgrimage of Grace and the Politics of the 1530s* (Oxford: Oxford University Press, 2001), p. 454.

64. The best argument for a shift in 1536 can be found in Suzannah Lipscomb, *1536: The Year That Changed Henry VIII* (London: Lion Hudson, 2006).

65. For the theories on Henry's health, see in particular Robert Hutchinson, *The Last Days of Henry VIII: Conspiracy, Treason and Heresy at the Court of a Dying Tyrant* (London: Phoenix, 2006), and Kyra Kramer, *Blood Will Tell: A Medical Explanation of the Tyranny of Henry VIII* (Bloomington, IN: Ash Wood Press, 2014), the latter of which tackles the debate from the perspective of medical anthropology.

66. C. R. Chalmers and E. J. Chaloner, '500 Years Later: Henry VIII, Leg Ulcers and the Course of History', *Journal of the Royal Society of Medicine* (2009), pp. 514–17.

67. Strype, *Ecclesiastical*, I, App., p. 313.

68. *Household Ordinances*, p. 144; BL Harleian MS 6807, f. IIv.

69. Tremlett, *Catherine of Aragon*, pp. 134–39; Retha M. Warnicke, *The Rise and Fall of Anne Boleyn: Family politics at the court of Henry VIII* (Cambridge: Cambridge University Press, 1989), p. 229n.

70. *Household Ordinances*, pp. 151–52.

71. SP 1/167, f. 136.

72. Muriel (ed.), *Lisle Letters*, IV, 155–56; LP, XIV, ii, 1026.

Chapter 10: The Queen's Brothers

1. BL: Addit. MS 46, 348, f. 6b.

2. Burnet, *History of the Reformation*, I, p. 568, mentions consternation in Parliament at the king's request. LP, XV, 697 states that the request was granted without open complaint.

3. Matilda of Boulogne, whose husband seized the throne as King Stephen in December 1135, was crowned separately at Easter 1136, since her husband's coronation was probably intended to directly mirror that of his predecessor, Henry I – see Edmund King, *King Stephen* (New Haven: Yale University Press, 2010), pp. 47–8, 56–7. The reasons for Marguerite of France never being crowned are unclear, since by all accounts her marriage to Edward I was a happy one. He commissioned a goldsmith, Thomas de Frowick, to make a crown for her to wear after her wedding, but the decision to skip a coronation

may have had something to do with the prominence of Edward's first wife, Eleanor of Castile, who was mother to the living heir apparent, the future Edward II. There is no other logical explanation for Philippa of Hainault's coronation being delayed for nearly two years except at the instigation of the queen regent, Isabella of France.

4. David Starkey, *Six Wives: The Queens of Henry VIII* (London: Vintage, 2004), p. 602.

5. She arrived at Windsor on 17 August and did not return to Hampton Court until 18 December – LP, XV, 963; XVI, 325.

6. LP, XVI, 60, 311.

7. Ibid., XV, 963, 996; XVI, 26, 112, 114, 124, 179.

8. Ibid., XV, 259.

9. Ibid., XVI, 503, grant 25.

10. Sarah Morris and Natalie Grueninger, *In the Footsteps of Anne Boleyn* (Stroud: Amberley, 2015), pp. 87–90.

11. LP, XVI, 1389.

12. Kaulek, 246.

13. Supper was the name generally used for a later meal.

14. Morris and Grueninger, *In the Footsteps of Anne Boleyn*, pp. 131–32.

15. Thurley, *Royal Palaces*, p. 193.

16. Ibid.

17. LP, XVI, 11. De Marillac was born between 1510 and 1513.

18. Cavendish, *Life of Cardinal Wolsey*, II, p. 66.

19. Thomas, *The Pilgrim*, p. 58.

20. LP, XVI, 12.

21. In 2009, the then Wales Herald Extraordinary, Dr Michael Powell Siddons, could find no information on any specific heraldic device or beast associated with Catherine, in contrast to all five of Henry's other queens – see Michael Powell Siddons, *Heraldic Badges in England and Wales*

(Woodbridge: Society of Antiquaries of London, 2009), Volume I, p. 116; Volume II, part I, pp. 21–25, 132.

22. *Inventory*, II, 94; Hall, *Hall's Chronicle*, p. 834.

23. LP, XVI, 12.

24. Strickland, *Lives of the Queens of England*, III, p. 122.

25. For the coin debate, see Starkey, *Six Wives*, p. 810.

26. LP, XVI, 1389.

27. Ibid., 32.

28. Ibid., 60.

29. Mikhaila and Malcolm-Davies, *Tudor Tailor*, pp. 16–19.

30. LP, XVI, 60.

31. Ibid., 41, 61, 62.

32. Ibid., 284, 286. Lord Grey became 1st Viscount Grane in the Irish peerage in 1536, but he was still referred to as Lord Leonard Grey by many of his contemporaries by 1540.

33. Ibid., 334.

34. *Cal. S. P. Milan*, I, 131.

35. J. L. Laynesmith, *The Last Medieval Queens: English Queenship, 1445–1603* (Oxford: Oxford University Press, 2004), p. 182.

36. Hamilton, 'Household of Queen Katherine Parr', p. 127.

37. LP, XVI, 27.

38. Ibid., 128; Burnet, *History of the Reformation*, IV, p. 64.

39. LP, XVI, 128.

40. SP 1/167, f. 131.

41. Henry is named first in Sir John Leigh's will from 1524, but Charles precedes him in Dame Isabel Leigh's in 1527. W. Bruce Bannerman (ed.), *The Visitations of the County of Surrey* (London: Harleian Society, 1899), XLIII, p. 21, is the only source which puts George first, however it omits Henry entirely. W. Bruce Bannerman (ed.), *The Visitations of Kent* (London: Harleian Society, 1924), LXXV, i, p. 81, gives Henry as the eldest and Charles as the youngest.

42. Burnet, *History of the Reformation*, IV, p. 64.

43. LP, XVI, 1056, grant 16.

44. Patricia Buchanan, *Margaret Tudor, Queen of Scots* (Edinburgh and London: Scottish Academic Press, 1985), p. 255.

45. Frederic Madden, '*Narrative of the Visit of the Duke of Najera to England, in the Year 1543–4*' (London: Society of Antiquaries, 1831), p. 352; Thurley, *Royal Palaces*, p. 131. Other people allocated double lodgings at all the palaces included Thomas Cromwell and the future Queen Mary I.

46. LP, XIII, ii, 622.

47. *Original Letters*, III, iii, 309.

48. Hall, *Hall's Chronicle*, p. 819.

49. Kimberly Schutte, *A Biography of Margaret Douglas, Countess of Lennox (1515–1578)* (Lewiston, NY: Edward Mellen Press, 2002), p. 27.

50. Brenan and Statham, *House of Howard*, I, pp. 305–07, which also includes fanciful descriptions of Catherine's 'tearful entreaties' in 1540 for the pair to be allowed to marry. Schutte, *Margaret Douglas*, pp. 72–3, dates the affair to 1541 but repeats the story that Margaret was sent to Syon. Later in her life, when Margaret listed her previous detentions, she made no mention of being rusticated for her involvement with Charles Howard. Alison Weir's biography of Lady Margaret Douglas was published after this manuscript was first submitted, but before publication; Weir also concludes that there is no evidence to support that the affair was discovered and punished in 1540 – Alison Weir, *The Lost Tudor Princess: A Life of Margaret Douglas, Countess of Lennox* (London: Jonathan Cape, 2015), pp. 89–93.

51. LP, XVI, 1067, grant 16.

52. Ibid., 183.

53. Ibid., 91.

54. Baynton hosted Anne Boleyn at his home in August 1535, but this should not necessarily be taken as a sign of affection or intimacy between the pair – likewise, their shared sympathies for religious reform. The queen most likely used her visit as a base for her charitable operations in the area, see Ives, *Life and Death*, p. 262.

55. Ives, *Life and Death*, p. 326.

56. Bindoff (ed.), *House of Commons*, I, p. 402.

57. LP, VI, 613. It seems highly unlikely that the letter regarding celebrations after the queen's coronation in 1533 was a veiled reference to sexual activity, especially when it is remembered that the letter was written to the queen's brother and she was pregnant at the time – see Ives, *Life and Death*, pp. 182–83. Cf. G. W. Bernard, *Anne Boleyn: Fatal Attractions* (New Haven and London: Yale University Press, 2010), pp. 185–86.

58. Tremlett, *Catherine of Aragon*, pp. 167–68; Sir Anthony Browne was the king's Master of the Horse during Catherine's tenure. At the time of his quarrel with his sister, the office was held by Sir Nicholas Carew. Browne's interrogation of his sister has resulted in a recent academic dispute and, quite possibly, in its exaggeration. For the argument that it is central to explaining Anne Boleyn's downfall see Bernard, *Anne Boleyn*, pp. 152–55. For the suggestion that the disagreement between the siblings has been exaggerated and conflated with the downfall of the queen later that summer, see Ives, *Life and Death*, pp. 331–35, and Warnicke, *Rise and Fall*, p. 299n.

59. LP, V, 748; XIII, 450.
60. Ibid., XVI, 223.

Chapter 11: The Return of Francis Dereham

1. It is unclear if Catherine also received the extra twenty-eight manors that were given to Katherine Parr later in her marriage. Hamilton, 'Household of Queen Katherine Parr', p. 141–42, believes both queens had the same amount of property, which would give Catherine 133 manors in twenty counties; fifteen boroughs; six castles; and other related properties.
2. LP, I, I, 94 (35); VII, 419 (25); Hamilton, 'Household of Queen Katherine Parr', p. 142.
3. LP, XVI, 503, grant 25.
4. Ives, *Life and Death*, pp. 214–16; Hamilton, 'Household of Queen Katherine Parr', pp. 147–62.
5. LP, XV, 21; XIX, ii, 165, 534, 677, 749, 767; Add., 1694, 1742, 1735.
6. LP, XIX, ii, 165.
7. *Proceedings of the Privy Council*, VII, pp. 105–07.
8. LP, XVI, 423.
9. *The Birth of Mankind* was first published in German in 1533. It was the work of Eucharius Roeslin (d. *c.*1554), and its first English translation was by Richard Jonas in 1540. Richard J. Durling, *A Catalogue of Sixteenth Century Printed Books in the National Library of Medicine* (Bethesda, MD: US Department of Health, Education, and Welfare, 1967), pp. 503–04.
10. MacCulloch, *Thomas Cranmer*, p. 272.
11. LP, XVI, 316.
12. Aysha Pollnitz, 'Religion and Translation at the Court of Henry VIII: Princess Mary, Katherine Parr and the *Paraphrases of Erasmus*', in Susan Doran and Thomas S. Freeman (eds), *Mary Tudor: Old and New Perspectives* (London: Palgrave Macmillan, 2011), pp. 132–36.
13. *Cal. S.P. Span.*, VI, 143.
14. Ibid., 151.
15. SP 1/168, f. 53.
16. LP, XVI, 1409.
17. Steven G. Ellis, *Ireland in the Age of the Tudors, 1447–1603* (London: Longman, 1998), pp. 36–7.
18. Ciarán Brady, 'Comparable histories?: Tudor reform in Wales and Ireland', in Steven G. Ellis and Sarah Barber (eds), *Conquest and Union: Fashioning a British State, 1485–1725* (London: Longman Group, 1995), p. 66.
19. Mary O'Dowd, 'Gaelic Economy and Society', in Ciarán Brady and Raymond Gillespie (eds), *Natives and Newcomers: Essays on the Making of Irish Colonial Society, 1534–1641* (Bungay, Ireland: Irish Academic Press, 1986), pp. 120–47; Colm Lennon, *The Lords of Dublin in the Age of Reformation* (Dublin: Irish Academic Press, 1989), pp. 105, 195.
20. Herbert, *Life and Raigne*, p. 534.
21. SP 1/167, f. 136. Lady Margaret Howard gave the man's name as 'one Stafford', but it is unlikely that this was Katherine Carey's stepfather, William Stafford. If it had been, he would have been specified by name.
22. SP 1/168, f. 53 supports the idea that it was Dereham who first suggested it though, frustratingly, the answers of the Dowager Duchess of Norfolk and the Countess of Bridgewater have not survived.
23. Why they were not destroyed as soon as they were handed over is an intriguing question, and perhaps the safest answer is the aforementioned theory of buying Dereham's silence.

24. SP 1/168, f. 85.
25. An exception is Starkey, *Six Wives*, pp. 661–62, who describes Dereham as a member of the household. The rest generally build on Smith, *A Tudor Tragedy*, pp. 148–49, that Dereham was appointed as the queen's private secretary in August 1541.
26. *Household Ordinances*, p. 199.
27. Mary Saaler, *Anne of Cleves: Fourth Wife of Henry VIII* (London: Rubicon Press, 1995), p. 78.
28. LP, XVI, 268.
29. Bindoff (ed.), *House of Commons*, II, p. 429; SP 1/157, fos. 13–14; LP, XV, 21.

Chapter 12: Jewels
1. LP, XVI, 325.
2. Morris and Grueninger, *In the Footsteps of Anne Boleyn*, pp. 95–97.
3. Kaulek, 246.
4. LP, XVI, 528.
5. Ibid., 325.
6. Ibid., 379, grant 34.
7. Ibid., XV, 940.
8. Ibid., XVI, 503, grant 14.
9. For Elizabeth Seymour, see Luke MacMahon, 'Ughtred, Sir Anthony (d. 1534), soldier', in *Oxford Dictionary of National Biography*; Teri Fitzgerald, 'Elizabeth Seymour', in *Tudor Life* (December 2014), pp. 43–51; Tracy Borman, *Thomas Cromwell: The Untold Story of Henry VIII's Most Faithful Servant* (London: Hodder and Stoughton, 2014), pp. 282–84.
10. Some estimates put Lady Cromwell's birth in *c.*1500–05, which would have made her older than Jane, who was born *c.*1508. Other evidence would suggest *c.*1513.
11. Borman, *Thomas Cromwell*, pp. 282–83.
12. *Original Letters*, III, iii, 354.
13. This physical description of Chapuys is based on portraits of him at the Musée-château and Lycée Berthollet, both in Annecy, France – see plates 1 and 18 in Lauren Mackay, *Inside the Tudor Court: Henry VIII and His Six Wives Through the Writings of the Spanish Ambassador, Eustace Chapuys* (Stroud: Amberley, 2014). The latter image is reproduced in this book, by kind permission of Lauren Mackay.
14. Mackay, *Inside the Tudor Court*, pp. 18–19, 202–03.
15. Hall, *Hall's Chronicle*, p. 840; LP, XV, 953.
16. Hall, *Hall's Chronicle*, p. 840. Holinshed, *Chronicles*, III, p. 819, describes him as the last 'till queen Maries [Mary I] daies'.
17. Mackay, *Inside the Tudor Court*, pp. 168–72.
18. Ibid., pp. 182–83, 202–03; *Cal. S. P. Span.*, VI, i, 135.
19. *Cal. S. P. Span.*, VI, i, 144.
20. Ibid.
21. For Catherine's jewellery collection and the dates of the gifts from the king, see LP, XVI, 1389.
22. *Cal. S. P. Span.*, VI, i, 149.
23. Ibid.
24. LP, XV, 1012, grant 12.
25. After the deposition of King Richard II in 1399, his widow, Isabelle de Valois, was regarded as a former queen consort rather than a widow, due to the non-consummation of her marriage, and she was eventually sent home to her parents in France. Margaret of Anjou was tentatively classed as a former queen by Yorkists following her husband's first deposition in 1461.
26. By the time Elizabeth Woodville was received back at court, during the reign of her son-in-law Henry VII, her title and

position as queen had been legally restored by Act of Parliament.

27. This account of Anne of Cleves's visit is based on a letter from Eustace Chapuys to Maria of Austria of 8 January 1541 – *Cal. S. P. Span.*, VI, i, 149.

28. *Cal. S. P. Span.*, VI, i, 148. Chapuys had been sceptical of the need to do so, because he doubted that Henry would ever take back someone he had dismissed, but he remained vigilant during Anne's visit, as the length of his letter about it indicates.

29. LP, XVI, 374.
30. Ibid., XV, 976.
31. Norton, *Anne of Cleves*, p. 115.
32. *Cal. S. P. Span.*, VI, i, 149.
33. Chapuys and most of the courtiers concluded that the dogs and jewel were given to Anne by Catherine on her own initiative, rather than as part of an elaborate gift-giving orchestrated by the king, who had already separately presented Anne with an increase to her annual income.
34. LP, XVI, 503, grant 32.
35. *Cal. S. P. Span.*, VI, i, 149.
36. Ibid., 151, 161.
37. Ibid., 150; LP, XVI, 482, 534.
38. *State Papers*, VIII, 514.
39. LP, XVI, 517.
40. Ibid., 511.
41. Ibid., 481.
42. Ibid., 482, 528, 529; *Cal. S. P. Span.*, VI, i, 151.
43. LP, XVI, 649.

Chapter 13: Lent
1. LP, XVI, 529.
2. Ibid., XIV, ii, 35; XVI, 533, 590; Kaulek, 274.
3. Ibid., XV, 114; *Acts of the Parliament of Scotland*, II, p. 368.
4. LP, XV, 248; Jamie Cameron, *James V: The Personal Rule, 1528–1542* (East Lothian: Tuckwell Press, 1998), p. 289.

5. LP, XVI, 534.
6. Kenneth Muir, *Life and Letters of Sir Thomas Wyatt* (Liverpool: Liverpool University Press, 1963), p. 167.
7. LP, XVI, 541; *Cal S. P. Span.*, VI, i, 155.
8. LP, XVI, 595.
9. Ibid., 597.
10. Ibid., 533.
11. Ibid., 589; Kaulek, 273.
12. Ibid., 558.
13. Kaulek, 273.
14. Ibid., 274.
15. LP, XV, 589; Kaulek, 273.
16. *Cal. S. P. Span.*, VI, i, 204.
17. Ibid.
18. Luke 4:1–13.
19. LP, XVI, 597.
20. Hoyle, *Pilgrimage of Grace*, p. 545; for the Stockholm syndrome analogy, Beth von Staats, 'Thomas Cranmer: Were his recantations of faith driven by Stockholm Syndrome?', in *Tudor Life* (November 2014), pp. 2–14.
21. Strickland, *Lives of the Queens of England*, III, pp. 127–28, seems to have been the origin of the story; for one modern repetition of it, see Denny, *Katherine Howard*, p. 186.
22. *Proceedings of the Privy Council*, pp. 146–47; LP, XVI, 1489.
23. *Proceedings of the Privy Council*, p. 146.
24. LP, XVI, 598.
25. Ibid., 606.
26. Ibid., 631, 658. McGilpatrick was replaced as speaker by Thomas Cusack.
27. *Cal. S. P. Span.*, VI, i, 134, 154; LP, XVI, 589, 607 – de Marillac mistakenly concluded that the discussions about the inspections had ceased, but the tour began twelve days later.
28. Ives, *Life and Death*, pp. 222–23.
29. Ibid., p. 219; Sir Henry C. Maxwell-Lyte, *A History of Eton College* (London: Macmillan & Co., 1877), p. 114.

30. *Ralph Roister Doister* (c.1553) was probably written during his time as headmaster of Westminster School, though Tim Card, *Eton Established: A History from 1440 to 1860* (London: John Murray, 2001), pp. 38–9, suggests that it may have been written earlier or give a flavour of the kind of plays encouraged at Eton in Udall's time.

31. A sympathetic biographer of Udall attempted to argue that the word 'buggery' was mistranslated in the publication of the Privy Council records in the nineteenth century and that the original read 'burglary'. This is untrue. Cf. William L. Edgerton, *Nicholas Udall* (New York: Twayne Publishers, 1965), pp. 37–40.

32. Metropolitan Museum of Art, New York, 25.205.

33. MacCulloch, *Thomas Cranmer*, p. 354.

34. Redworth, *In Defence of the Church Catholic*, p. 82n.

35. For the Udall–Cheney affair at Eton, the relevant pieces of evidence are *Proceedings of the Privy Council*, VII, pp. 152–58; LP, XII, I, 1209; Bindoff (ed.), *House of Commons*, I, pp. 12, 663; Sir Henry Ellis (ed.), *Original Letters of Eminent Literary Men of the Sixteenth, Seventeenth, and Eighteenth Centuries* (London: Camden Society, 1843), pp. 2–7; Maxwell-Lyte, pp. 114–16, 143–44; Sir Wasey Sterry, *The Eton College Register, 1441–1698* (Eton, 1943), pp. 70, 179.

36. LP, XVI, 804.

37. Wriothesley, *Chronicle*, I, p. 124; *Cal. S. P. Span.*, VI, i, 155.

38. LP, II, 3204; E. W. Ives, 'A Frenchman at the Court of Anne Boleyn', in *History Today* (1998), pp. 21–6.

39. LP, XVI, 678, grant 41.

40. *State Papers*, VIII, 544 (LP, XVI, 1660); *Cal. S. P. Span.*, VI, i, 155; Brigden, *Thomas Wyatt*, p. 547.

41. Brigden, *Thomas Wyatt*, pp. 515–66.

42. LP, XVI, 517.

43. Brigden, *Thomas Wyatt*, p. 547. On the subject of John Leigh, Wyatt may ironically have had a hand in setting up Leigh's arrest before he himself was taken.

44. Childs, *Henry VIII's Last Victim*, p. 167.

45. Brigden, *Thomas Wyatt*, pp. 92–3.

46. *Cal. S. P. Span.*, VI, i, 155.

47. *State Papers*, VIII, p. 544.

48. LP, XVI, 650 (2).

49. Ibid., XIV, ii, 71.

Chapter 14: For They Will Look Upon You

1. Kaulek, 289. It does not seem as if Henry told de Marillac personally.

2. The jousts for Elizabeth Woodville's coronation in 1465 were the result of months of preparation by the organisers and contestants; Laynesmith, *Last Medieval Queens*, p. 109.

3. *Inventory*, I, 55, 57, 112–55, 1096–97.

4. In France, the precedent for the king's mother to serve as regent during her son's minority was more established – approximately a century on either side of Catherine Howard's life, the regency in France was held by Louise of Savoy, Catherine de Medici, Marie de Medici, and Anne of Austria. However, a dowager queen had never successfully served as regent for her son in England – an attempt to do so by Elizabeth Woodville in 1483 ended in disaster, and previous queens, such as the mothers of Henry III, Richard II, and Henry VI, had all been sidelined in favour of a council of guardians.

5. LP, XVI, 774.

6. *Inventory*, II, p. 49.

7. Luke 22:19–20.

8. Matthew 25:34–40; the Book of Tobias, sometimes known as the Book of Tobit, 1:19–20 and 2:6–9.

9. Richard Rex, *Henry VIII and the English Reformation* (London: Macmillan Press, 1993), pp. 173–74. A contemporary defence of Henry's actions on the grounds that it mirrored Old Testament kings, such as Hezekiah, can be found in Thomas, *The Pilgrim*, p. 40. For the biblical precedent of Jehoshaphat, see 1 Kings 22:46. In the Old Testament, Jehoshaphat's actions specifically pertain to expelling male prostitutes associated with worship in various pagan cults. The theory that the Buggery Act may have been partly inspired by this relies also on the act's alleged purpose in intimidating English monks on the eve of the Dissolution.

10. 4 Kings 12:18 (Douay-Rheims translation); 2 Kings 12:18 (the King James Version).

11. Rex, *Henry VIII and the English Reformation*, p. 172.

12. Luke 1:27; Genesis 3:15.

13. Matthew 26:14–29.

14. John 13:34.

15. Edward I's grandfather, King John, performed the ceremony twice, in 1210 and 1213, and fragmentary evidence survives about Henry III's participation in the ritual, which he seems to have conducted on several dates throughout the year. It was in the reign of the latter's son, Edward I, that it became a more regular occurrence for English kings. See Virginia A. Cole, 'Ritual Charity and Royal Children in Thirteenth-Century England', in Joëlle Rollo-Koster (ed.), *Medieval and Early Modern Ritual: Formalized Behavior in Europe, China and Japan* (Leiden, Netherlands: Brill, 2002), pp. 228–43.

16. The number was based on one for each year of the sovereign's life, thus despite the fact he turned fifty in 1541, it was Henry VIII's fifty-first year.

17. LP, XVI, 1488 (183b).

18. *Inventory*, I, 9513, 9514, 9515.

19. *Cal. S. P. Span.*, VI, i, 158.

20. *Inventory*, I, 9543.

21. Henry VII visited the north of England after his succession. Elizabeth of York had spent time residing in Lancashire and Yorkshire before becoming queen.

22. LP, XVI, 733; *Cal. S. P. Span.*, VI, i, 156.

23. SP 1/167, f. 148.

24. Catherine's conversations with Culpepper were very different in setting, tone, and dynamic to her more fraught dealings with Francis Dereham. A hat, however dashing, did not constitute a down payment for hush money. Equally, her request that he hide it undercuts recent arguments that, at this stage, their relationship was purely platonic.

25. Psalm 21:19 in the Douay-Rheims translation; Psalm 22:18 in the King James Version; Matthew 27:35.

26. The custom of blessing the cramp rings on Good Friday was discontinued by Henry's younger daughter, Elizabeth I.

27. For Easter, Eamon Duffy, *The Stripping of the Altars*, second edition (New Haven and London: Yale University Press), pp. 22–37. For the cramp rings ceremony: Marc Bloch, *The Royal Touch: Sacred Monarchy and Scrofula in England and France* (Montreal, QC, and Kingston, ON: McGill-Queen's

University Press, 1973), pp. 105–06.

28. Psalm 87:5 in the Douay-Rheims translations of the Bible; Psalm 88:4 in the King James Version.

29. Fox, *Jane Boleyn*, pp. 8, 333.

30. *Original Letters*, III, iii, 278.

31. Fox, *Jane Boleyn*, pp. 120–21, suggests that she may also have partially or fully paid for William Foster, the scholar's, education at Eton.

32. LP, IV, 1939.

33. Ibid., V, 1109; VIII, 263.

34. Ibid., VII, 1257.

35. Thurley, *Royal Palaces*, pp. 44–5.

36. Fox, *Jane Boleyn*, pp. 315–26.

37. Ibid., pp. 191–92; Clare Cherry and Claire Ridgway, *George Boleyn: Tudor Poet, Courtier and Diplomat* (Lúcar, Spain: MadeGlobal, 2014), pp. 232–33.

38. *Original Letters*, I, ii, 124.

39. Ibid., III, iii, 265.

40. Warnicke, *The Marrying of Anne of Cleves*, pp. 233–34.

41. Smith, *A Tudor Tragedy*, p. 154; Fox, *Jane Boleyn*, pp. 120, 329.

42. LP, X, 908.

43. Ibid., XVI, 1366.

44. Ibid., XIV, I, 927; XV, 217; XVI, 824; *Proceedings of the Privy Council*, VII, pp. 282–83. The rumours that the Bridgewaters might reunite were reported in February of the previous year, but there was never a formal reconciliation between them. The documents are clear that both Lady Bridgewater's sons were living with the dowager, but they do not specify if her daughter Anne was with the dowager or still residing with her mother.

45. LP, XVI, 678, grant 38.

46. Ibid., 751.

47. Ibid., 878, grant 49.

48. *Cal. S. P. Span.*, VI, i, 204.

49. Two of Henry's previous wives, Katherine of Aragon in 1510 and Anne Boleyn in 1534, had been accused of concocting pregnancies – see Starkey, *Six*

Wives, pp. 116–18; Tremlett, *Catherine of Aragon*, pp. 168–71; Ives, *Life and Death*, pp. 191–92; Warnicke, *Rise and Fall*, pp. 173–78. Cf. Bernard, *Anne Boleyn*, pp. 74–6.

50. Cameron, *James V*, p. 265, gives it as Arthur.

51. LP, XVI, 832.

52. Ibid., 852.

53. Ibid., 832; Rosalind K. Marshall, *Mary of Guise* (London: Collins, 1977), pp. 87–8.

54. LP, XVI, 573.

55. Ibid., 804.

56. Ibid., 816.

57. Starkey, *Six Wives*, p. 602; Hilton, *Elizabeth I*, pp. 43–4.

58. LP, XIV, ii, 697.

59. Katherine Ashley following her marriage in 1545.

60. Starkey, *Elizabeth*, pp. 25–6.

61. LP, XVI, 804.

62. Kaulek, 302.

63. Mikhaila and Malcolm-Davies, *Tudor Tailor*, pp. 16–18.

64. Jennifer Loach, *Edward VI* (New Haven and London: Yale University Press, 1999), p. 12.

65. A variety of theories have been put forward on the causes of Edward VI's death – Loach, *Edward VI*, pp. 160–62, suggests renal failure; Frederick Holmes, Grace Holmes, and Julia McMorrough, 'The Death of Young King Edward VI', in *New England Journal of Medicine* (2001) argue for tuberculosis; Linda Porter, *Mary Tudor: The First Queen* (London: Piatkus, 2009), pp. 184–86, suggests a bacterial pulmonary infection that left Edward defenceless against secondary infections.

66. Chris Skidmore, *Edward VI: The Lost King of England* (London: Weidenfeld & Nicolson, 2007), p. 28.

67. The others were Richard I in 1189, Edward II in 1307, and Henry V in 1413.

68. *Cal. S. P. Span.*, VI, i, 161.

69. *Cal. S. P. Span.*, VI, i, 161.
70. LP, XVI, 1122.
71. Thomas, *The Pilgrim*, p. 75.
72. LP, XVI, 111.
73. *Cal. S. P. Span.*, VI, i, 163.
74. LP, XVI, 823.
75. LP, XVI, 823.
76. Thomas, *The Pilgrim*, p. 58.
77. Steven J. Gunn, *Early Tudor Government, 1485–1558* (London: Macmillan Press, 1995), pp. 194–95; Bernard, *Anne Boleyn*, p. 184; Starkey, *Six Wives*, pp. 584–85.
78. *The Spanish Chronicle*, p. 77.
79. LP, XVI, 1332.
80. LP, V, 276.
81. HMC Bath, ii, pp. 9–10.

Chapter 15: The Errands of Morris and Webb

1. LP, XIII, ii, 855.
2. This means that the countess did not die on Tower Green, though her name is included in the memorial plaque there. Both Eustace Chapuys and the court herald Charles Wriothesley record that she was taken out of the Tower, which means that the site of Lady Salisbury's death is probably now covered by the A100 road.
3. LP, I, i, 81.
4. For contemporary descriptions of the execution, see *Cal. S. P. Span.*, VI, i, 166, and Wriothesley, *Chronicle*, I, p. 124. For the site of East Smithfield, Colin Buchanan et al., *Tower of London Local Setting Study* (Bristol: Land Use Consultants, 2010), pp. 20–21.
5. Thomas, *The Pilgrim*, p. 61.
6. LP, XVI, 868.
7. Thomas, *The Pilgrim*, p. 12.
8. Ibid., p. 61.
9. LP, XIV, ii, 212.
10. Thomas, *The Pilgrim*, p. 12; LP, XVI, 1060, 1081–83, 1204.
11. Thomas, *The Pilgrim*, pp. 10–11.
12. LP, XVI, 868.
13. Hall, *Hall's Chronicle*, p. 842; Wriothesley, *Chronicle*, I, p. 125. Hall gives Damport and Chapman's execution date as 9 June 1541, while Wriothesley writes that it took place on the 19th.
14. *Cal. S. P. Span.*, VI, i, 166.
15. LP, XVI, 760.
16. Wriothesley, *Chronicle*, I, p. 125; Holinshed, *Chronicles*, III, p. 820.
17. LP, XVI, 932.
18. *Cal. S. P. Span.*, VI, i, 168.
19. Wriothesley, *Chronicle*, I, pp. 125–26; LP, XVI, 941.
20. Wriothesley, *Chronicle*, I, p. 126.
21. The freed member of the gang was John Cheney (killed in battle in 1544), son of Sir Thomas Cheney, treasurer of the royal household from 1539 to 1558. For the Dacre case, see *Cal. S. P. Span.*, VI, 166; LP, XVI, 760, 932, 941; Wriothesley, *Chronicle*, I, pp. 125–26.
22. James, *Kateryn Parr*, p. 59.
23. Ibid., p. 98; LP, XVIII, i, 66.
24. Ives, *Life and Death*, pp. 278–79; Henry Clifford, *The Life of Jane Dormer, Duchess of Feria* (London: Burns and Oates, 1887), pp. 167–68; Johnson, *Elizabeth*, pp. 112–14.
25. LP, XVI, 832, 873, 905, 911.
26. Barbara J. Harris, 'The Fabric of Piety: Aristocratic Women and Care of the Dead, 1450–1550', in *Journal of British Studies* (April 2009), p. 316.
27. LP, XVI, 503, grant 14; 625.
28. *Proceedings of the Privy Council*, VII, p. 154; LP, XVI, 625.
29. Hastings Robinson (ed.), *Original Letters Relative to the English Reformation* (Cambridge: Cambridge University Press, 1846), pp. 266–67.
30. LP, XVI, 678; 947, grant 2.
31. *Household Ordinances*, p. 41; Thurley, *Royal Palaces*, pp. 70–4, 83.
32. LP, XVI, 941.

33. Ibid., 763.
34. *Proceedings of the Privy Council*, VII, pp. 192, 195–96.
35. LP, XVI, 1130.
36. Ibid., 1089.
37. Kaulek, 347.
38. Ibid.
39. LP, XVI, 1011.
40. Ibid.
41. Ibid., 1002, 1011, 1016.

Chapter 16: The Girl in the Silver Dress

1. LP, XVI, 974.
2. Ibid., 631, 901, 926.
3. Ibid., 912. Brendan Bradshaw, *The Irish Constitutional Revolution of the Sixteenth Century* (Cambridge: Cambridge University Press, 1979), p. 265.
4. The papal blessing was allegedly given by Pope Adrian IV in 1155 and confirmed by Pope Alexander III in 1172. This is, perhaps needless to say, a controversial episode in Anglo-Irish history and the existence of papal endorsement has been contested. Henry VIII's repudiation of the Vatican's authority continually stressed that Rome had no right to interfere in the sovereignty of any Christian country, a claim that simultaneously made him head of the Church in England and damaged the legitimacy of his rule over Ireland.
5. The Duke of Norfolk in question was Catherine's uncle, not her grandfather who died in 1524. Norfolk was still Earl of Surrey when he served as viceroy of Ireland.
6. LP, XVI, 784.
7. Ibid., 1030.
8. Ibid., 1058, 1061.
9. Bradshaw, *Irish Constitutional Revolution*, pp. 231–38.
10. LP, XVI, 1159.
11. Wriothesley, *Chronicle*, I, p. 127.
12. The court was at Loddington when Morton was given the errand, dating it to between 28–31 July – LP, XVI, 1053, 1061; SP1/167, f. 133.
13. LP, XVI, 1019.
14. Ibid., 1061, 1066.
15. Ibid., 992, 1035.
16. Ibid., 1005, 1071.
17. Michael K. Jones and Malcolm G. Underwood, *The King's Mother: Lady Margaret Beaufort, Countess of Richmond and Derby* (Cambridge: Cambridge University Press, 1992), pp. 83–6, 154–56.
18. LP, XVI, 1074.
19. Gunn, *Charles Brandon*, pp. 170–74.
20. *Journal of the House of Lords*, I, p. 164.
21. *Cal. S. P. Span.*, IV, ii, 765.
22. Gunn, *Charles Brandon*, p. 119; Ives, *Life and Death*, pp. 140–41.
23. SP1/167, f. 131.
24. Fox, *Jane Boleyn*, p. 298.
25. Burnet, *History of the Reformation*, V, p. 295.
26. Ibid., VI, p. 259.
27. Head, *Ebbs and Flows*, pp. 124–25.
28. Burnet, *History of the Reformation*, VI, pp. 258–59.
29. LP, XVI, 1077.
30. Ibid., XI, 888.
31. Hall, *Hall's Chronicle*, p. 842.
32. Hill, p. 51.
33. Ives, *Life and Death*, p. 111; LP, XIV, i, 965.
34. Jonathan Foyle, *Lincoln Cathedral: The Biography of a Great Building* (London: Scala Arts & Heritage Publishers, 2015), p. 104.
35. It was not discovered until repairs were carried out in 1586. J. W. F. Hill, *Tudor and Stuart Lincoln*, p. 50n.
36. By counting the king's descent from Katherine via his father – Katherine (often known by her first married surname of Swynford), Duchess of Lancaster (d. 1403) was the mother of John Beaufort, 1st Earl of Somerset (d.

1410), father of John Beaufort, 1st Duke of Somerset (d. 1444), father of Margaret Tudor, Countess of Richmond and later Derby (d. 1509), mother of King Henry VII.

37. Eleanor of Castile had numerous descendants by the sixteenth century and this relationship is made by counting back from Henry's mother. Describing Eleanor as Henry VIII's ancestress comes from firmly disagreeing with popular theories that the connecting family members of Edward III and Edward IV were illegitimate. For a good discussion of why, see Kathryn Warner, *Edward II: The Unconventional King* (Stroud: Amberley, 2014), p. 68; Ian Mortimer, *The Perfect King: The Life of Edward III, Father of the English Nation* (London: Vintage, 2008), pp. 17–25; Hannes Kleineke, *Edward IV* (New York: Routledge, 2009), pp. 28–9.

38. Saint Hugh died in 1200, he was canonised by Pope Honorius III in 1220, the body was moved in 1280 and the head shrine completed c.1340, Foyle, *Lincoln Cathedral*, p. 93.

39. Author's visit, 30 June 2015.

40. LP, XV, 772. The cathedral's shrine to Saint John of Dalderby was also destroyed.

41. Foyle, *Lincoln Cathedral*, p. 85.

42. Author's visit, 30 June 2015.

43. LP, XVI, 1088.

44. Ibid., 1339.

45. SP1/167, f.131.

46. LP, XVI, 1391, grant 18.

47. SP1/167, f. 159.

Chapter 17: The Chase

1. LP, XVI, 1094.

2. Hill, *Tudor and Stuart Lincoln*, pp. 1–3.

3. Anne Herbert's elder sister, Katherine, had been married to Lord Burgh's eldest son, and after his premature death she had married another northern nobleman, Lord Latimer.

4. LP, XVI, 1102.

5. Ibid., 1089.

6. They arrived on Thursday 18 August 1541, and left on Monday 22 August. The Hatfield Chase is not to be confused with Hatfield Palace in Hertfordshire, the main residence of the future Elizabeth I for most of her childhood.

7. LP, XVI, 1114.

8. Ibid., 1138.

9. Ibid., 1071; Mackay, *Inside the Tudor Court*, p. 207.

10. This account of the long weekend at Hatfield is based on de Marillac's account of it – LP, XVI, 1130.

11. LP, XVI, 972. Francis Talbot, 5th Earl of Shrewsbury, 5th Earl of Waterford, and 11th Baron Talbot (d. 1560).

12. LP, XVI, 1122.

13. SP 1/167, f. 133.

14. SP 1/167, f. 133.

15. R. W. Hoyle and J. B. Ramsdale, 'The Royal Progress of 1541, the North of England, and Anglo-Scottish Relations, 1534–1542', in *Northern History* (September 2004), pp. 253–54.

16 James V sent Thomas Bellenden on 9 July.

17. Cameron, *James V*, p. 289.

18. Ibid.

19. LP, XVI, 766; XVII, 61; Cameron, *James V*, p. 264.

20. LP, XVI, 832, 990 (5).

21. It is still pronounced this way among a dwindling number of denizens of a particular strain of Received Pronunciation, who have historically used it and a thousand other anti-phonetic nomenclatures as linguistic bear traps to weed out conversational interlopers and demarcate the tribe. It is not generally pronounced that way in Pontefract itself, although the

survival of the alternative form elsewhere preserves a link to the Tudors and Shakespeare.

22. Ian Roberts and Ian Downes, *Pontefract Castle: Key to the North* (Wakefield: West Yorkshire Archaeology Service, 2013), p. 22.

23. Roberts and Downes, *Pontefract Castle*, p. vi.

24. William Shakespeare, *Richard III*, Act III, scene iii.

25. My thanks to the extremely kind and helpful staff at Pontefract Castle for pointing this out and answering my queries about it. Author's visit, 2 July 2015.

26. Constanza of Castile, Duchess of Lancaster, (1354–94) was the daughter of Pedro the Just, King of Castile and León. Her husband pursued her claim to the Castilian throne, which is why 'her' tower at Pontefract was referred to as the Queen's Tower.

27. SP 1/167, f. 133.

28. LP, XVI, 1339.

29. SP 1/167, f. 136; Herbert, *Life and Raigne*, p. 535.

30. SP 1/167, f. 133.

31. Ibid.

32. LP, XVI, 1339.

33. Ibid., 1172, 1176, 1211.

34. Smith, *A Tudor Tragedy*, p. 141.

Chapter 18: Waiting for the King of Scots

1. D. M. Palliser, *Tudor York* (Oxford: Oxford University Press, 1979), p. 1.

2. Lorraine Attreed, 'The Politics of Welcome: Ceremonies and Constitutional Development in Later Medieval English Towns', in Barbara A. Hanawalt and Kathryn L. Reyerson (eds), *City and Spectacle in Medieval Europe* (Minneapolis, MN, and London: University of Minnesota Press, 1994), p. 219.

3. York Castle was not something Catherine had to see except from a distance during her visit. The castle, built in the reign of William I, was not in a good enough condition to host the king and queen in 1541. By that stage, it was primarily used for musters of troops and public events.

4. For York in 1541, see Hoyle, *Pilgrimage of Grace*, p. 2; Gordon Kipling, *Enter the King: Theatre, Liturgy, and Ritual in Medieval Civic Triumph* (Oxford: Clarendon Press, 1998), pp. 183–84; Palliser, *Tudor York*, pp. 1–5, 24–9, 207–08.

5. Hoyle, *Pilgrimage of Grace*, p. 2; LP, XVI, 1130, 1131.

6. Hoyle, *Pilgrimage of Grace*, p. 2.

7. Kipling, p. 40n.

8. For the minster in 1541, see John Harvey, 'Architectural History from 1291 to 1558', pp. 149–92, and David E. O'Connor and Jeremy Haselock, 'The Stained and Painted Glass', p. 324, both in Aylmer and Cant (eds), *History of York Minster*; Palliser, *Tudor York*, p. 238.

9. LP, XVI, 1229.

10. Ibid., 1339.

11. Marie de Guise (1515–60) was the daughter of Claude of Lorraine, Duke of Guise, and Antoinette of Bourbon, Duchess of Guise. Her first husband was Louis II, Duke of Longueville. After his death, she married King James V of Scots. She was the mother of Mary, Queen of Scots, and served as her regent in Scotland from 1542 to 1560.

12. Hoyle and Ramsdale, 'The Royal Progress of 1541', p. 253.

13. LP, XVI, 1183.

14. Hoyle and Ramsdale, 'The Royal Progress of 1541', p. 255.

15. Ibid., p. 261.

16. *State Papers*, V, pp. 44–5.

17. LP, XV, 248.

18. Ibid., XVI, 1181–82.

19. Ibid., 1143.

20. Ibid., 1163.

21. Hoyle and Ramsdale, 'The Royal Progress of 1541', p. 255.
22. LP, XVI, 1253.
23. Ibid., 1229.
24. Ibid., 1202, 1207.
25. Ibid., 1251.
26. Ibid., 1205 (2).
27. Ibid., 1260.
28. Kaulek, 347.
29. *Cal. S. P. Span.*, VI, i, 209.
30. LP, XVI, 1261.
31. Ibid., 1194.
32. Ibid., 1253.
33. Ibid., 1252.
34. A divorce did not take place. The dauphine gave birth to her son, the future King François II, in January 1544.
35. LP, XVI, 1266, 1269.
36. That Catherine was at Chenies Manor House is my own supposition, based on a consultation of relevant maps of the area, comments made in LP, XVI, 1278 and 1287, and in SP 1/167, f. 136.
37. LP, XVI, 1339.
38. The impetus for inviting Alice to Chenies may have been her husband Anthony's job in Calais. The couple appear to have been visiting England in late 1541, which may have prompted Catherine to take the opportunity of trying to buy Alice's loyal silence. Equally, it may have been a generous gesture which she decided to make during the opportunity afforded by Alice's trip back to England.
39. LP, XVI, 1289.
40. Ibid., 1307.
41. Ibid., 1297.
42. Kaulek, 350.

Chapter 19: Being Examined by My Lord of Canterbury

1. LP, XVI, 1339.
2. Ibid., 1332.
3. SP 1/167, f. 127; Burnet, *History of the Reformation*, I, pp. 623–24, writes that the king gave thanks personally after receiving the Sacrament.
4. LP, XVI, 1310.
5. Ibid., 1334.
6. Smith, *A Tudor Tragedy*, pp. 165–66.
7. LP, XVI, 1334.
8. Ibid., 1312, 1314.
9. The physical description of the Earl of Southampton is based on the sketch of him by Holbein, currently housed in the Royal Collection.
10. The wording used in the transcripts of Manox's interview on 5 November 1541 describe Joan as 'also entertained' by Dereham. This could mean that she received financial rewards or support from him, possibly bribes in return for access to Catherine. However, elsewhere in the interrogation records Wriothesley used 'entertained' to mean sexual intercourse, and he also recorded Joan's relationship with Francis immediately after a description of Dereham's involvement with Catherine. In that context, 'also entertained by' can only have a sexual connotation.
11. SP 1/167, f. 117.
12. Dereham's first interrogation is recorded on 5 November. However, he must have been taken beforehand. Andrew Pewson, one of the Dowager Duchess of Norfolk's servants, mentioned in his interview 'his going to Hamptoncourte after Derams apprehencion' on Friday 4 November. The delay raises the possibility that Dereham was tortured even at this early stage, between All Souls' Day and Saturday, the 5th.
13. SP 1/167, f. 136.
14. Ibid., f. 136v.
15. Ibid., f. 127.
16. LP, XVI, 1339.
17. SP 1/167, f. 109.
18. LP, XVI, 1334.

19. Ibid., 1332.
20. *Cal. S. P. Span.*, VI, i, 201.
21. LP, XVI, 1332.
22. Ibid.
23. SP 1/168, f. 48.
24. *State Papers*, I, p. 697.
25. SP 1/168, f. 96.
26. Ibid., f. 98.
27. Ibid., f. 14.
28. LP, XVI, 1332; *Cal. S. P. Span.*, VI, i, 204.
29. SP 1/167, f. 127.
30. *Cal. S. P. Span.*, VI, i, 204.
31. This description of Archbishop Cranmer is based on the portrait of him by Gerlach Flicke, painted in 1545.
32. *State Papers*, I, p. 689.
33. Most probably Catherine's uncle Lord Thomas Howard the younger, who died of a fever in the Tower in October 1537. It could also have referred to her first cousin, Lord Thomas Howard, who was the 3rd duke's youngest surviving son and later created 1st Viscount Howard of Bindon by Elizabeth I.
34. See Chapter 5 for discussion of Lady Brereton.
35. Burnet, *History of the Reformation*, VI, document 72.
36. *State Papers*, I, p. 689.
37. Ibid.
38. LP, XVI, 1332.
39. HMC Bath, II, p. 10.
40. SP 1/168, f. 80.
41. LP, XVI, 1416, 2.ii.
42. SP 1/168, f. 80.
43. Ibid.
44. LP, XVI, 1332; *State Papers*, I, pp. 691–92.
45. *State Papers*, I, p. 691.
46. LP, XVI, 1332.
47. *State Papers*, II, p. 694.
48. LP, XVI, 1366.
49. HMC Bath, II, p. 10; SP 1/167, f. 136.
50. Herbert, *Life and Raigne*, p. 535.

Chapter 20: A Greater Abomination

1. Their visit suggests that de Marillac's version of events, which has Dereham confessing and naming Culpepper in an attempt to exonerate himself, is the correct one. Here, the traditional chronology of Catherine's downfall is inconsistent with a closer examination of the sources. It is not so much that de Marillac's account is incorrect, but rather that it is incomplete.
2. HMC Bath, II, pp. 9–10.
3. Smith, *A Tudor Tragedy*, pp. 173–74; Denny, *Katherine Howard*, pp. 223–36.
4. Smith, *A Tudor Tragedy*, pp. 171–74.
5. LP, XVI, 1339.
6. SP 1/167, f. 131; 1/168, f. 8.
7. LP, XVI, 1339. Tilney and Dereham were sent by the queen to fetch Alice Restwold when Catherine was staying at Lord and Lady Russell's in the last week of October.
8. SP 1/167, f. 136.
9. LP, XVI, 1438.
10. He seems to have made an offer to Anne Askew when she was tortured for information about the queen's household in 1546.
11. SP 1/168, f. 8.
12. SP 1/167, f. 136.
13. SP 1/167, f. 148; LP, XVI, 1366, 1371.
14. LP, XVI, 1339.
15. *Cal. S. P. Span.*, VI, i, 207; SP 1/167, f. 147.
16. *Cal. S. P. Span.*, VI, i, 209.
17. Fox, *Jane Boleyn*, p. 302.
18. *Cal. S. P. Span.*, VI, i, 209.
19. *State Papers*, I, p. 694.
20. *State Papers*, I, p. 708.
21. Ibid., p. 700.
22. *Proceedings of the Privy Council*, VII, p. 267.
23. LP, XVI, 1337.2.
24. SP 1/167, f. 161.
25. Ibid., f. 131.
26. Ibid., f. 133.
27. Ibid., f. 136.
28. *Proceedings of the Privy Council*, VII, p. 279.

29. *State Papers*, I, pp. 698, 708.
30. Ibid., p. 698.
31. Ibid., pp. 691, 701.
32. LP, XVI, 1326.
33. *State Papers*, I, p. 692.
34. Ibid., pp. 692–94.
35. Ibid., pp. 694–95.
36. SP 1/167, f. 129.
37. Ibid., f. 166.
38. Ibid., f. 162.
39. *Proceedings of the Privy Council*, VII, p. 267.
40. LP, XVI, 1332, 1342.
41. *Cal. S. P. Span.*, VI, i, 207.
42. LP, XVI, 1342.
43. Ibid., 1366. De Marillac gives her name as 'Katharine de Auvart'.
44. For the arrangements at Syon, see *State Papers*, I, pp. 691–95.
45. LP, XVI, 1366.
46. Ibid., 1391, grant 59.
47. *Cal. S. P. Span.*, VI, i, 209.

Chapter 21: The King Has Changed His Love into Hatred

1. The date refers to the thirty-third year of the monarch's reign, a common English dating technique in the medieval and early modern period.
2. For the trial of Dereham and Culpepper, see *Proceedings of the Privy Council*, VIII, p. 276; LP, XVI, 1395; Kaulek, 379, 380; *Cal. S. P. Span.*, VI, i, 209.
3. SP 1/168, ff. 14, 48; Kaulek, 380.
4. *State Papers*, VIII, p. 698.
5. Gossip about the king's early appreciation of Catherine's appearance was current in Norfolk House in late 1539, though it does seem quite a stretch for Francis to describe the king as being in love with Catherine and for that to prompt his own departure for Ireland. The king's second wave of romantic interest in Catherine in early 1540 could have coincided with the end of her flirtation with Culpepper, around the same time as jealousy over one or both of those men provoked Francis's quarrel with her and his subsequent decision to leave the dowager's service. However, given Dereham's admission of his sexual relationship with Catherine, without the threat of torture, and his refusal to corroborate Damport's story, even when he was repeatedly tortured, the weight of evidence still suggests Damport's claims were untrue.
6. SP 1/168, f. 100.
7. LP, XVI, 1426.
8. SP 1/168, ff. 100, 110; *State Papers*, VIII, p. 700; *Proceedings of the Privy Council*, VII, p. 283; LP, XVI, 1422, 1430; *Cal. S. P. Span.*, VI, i, 209.
9. LP, XVI, 1372, 1396.
10. *Cal. S. P. Span.*, VI, i, 211.
11. LP, XVI, 1422.
12. SP 1/168, ff. 13, 14, 100; *Proceedings of the Privy Council*, p. 277; *State Papers*, VIII, p. 706.
13. LP, XVI, 1416 (2).
14. *State Papers*, VIII, p. 700.
15. SP1/168, f. 80.
16. Ibid., f. 51.
17. Ibid., ff. 80, 112.
18. Ibid.
19. *State Papers*, VIII, p. 702; SP 1/168, f. 112.
20. *State Papers*, VIII, pp. 701–02; *Proceedings of the Privy Council*, pp. 280–81; LP, XVI, 1416 (2); SP 1/168, f. 122.
21. *Proceedings of the Privy Council*, VII, p. 280.
22. LP, XIV, 1422; SP 1/168, f. 53.
23. *State Papers*, VIII, p. 706.
24. LP, XVI, 1422.
25. It is unclear which Countess of Oxford this was, as there were two alive in 1541. It could have been Lady Bridgewater's younger sister Anne, Dowager Countess of Oxford, or Dorothy (née Neville), Countess of Oxford. The latter had a larger household and neither of the Lady Bridgewater's sons was sent to close relatives. However,

it cannot be ruled out that young Anne was briefly sent to the home of her aunt, the Dowager Countess.

26. *Proceedings of the Privy Council*, pp. 280–81.

27. *State Papers*, VIII, p. 709.

28. Richmond Palace reverted to the Crown in 1557 and Elizabeth I died there in 1603. It was demolished and sold as raw materials after the abolition of the monarchy in 1649.

29. Thurley, *Royal Palaces*, pp. 27–32, 53.

30. Karen Lindsey, *Divorced Beheaded Survived: A Feminist Reinterpretation of the Wives of Henry VIII* (Cambridge, MA: Da Capo Press, 1995), p. 137.

31. Anne's decision to move to Richmond and remarks she made in 1542–43 strongly suggest that she wished to be reinstated as queen after Catherine's fall – see Norton, *Anne of Cleves*, pp. 119–28.

32. LP, XVI, 1332, 1407.

33. *Cal. S. P. Span.*, VI, i, 227.

34. Ibid., 204.

35. Ibid., 213.

36. *Proceedings of the Privy Council*, VIII, p. 279, 282; SP 1/168, f. 100.

37. *Cal. S. P. Span.*, VI, i, 209.

38. LP, XVI, 1332, 1366.

39. SP 1/167, f. 168; LP, XVI, 1387, 1457.

40. *Cal. S. P. Span.*, VI, i, 232.

41. Norton, *Anne of Cleves*, pp. 128–29.

42. *State Papers*, VIII, pp. 704, 708–09; SP 1/168, f. 80.

43. SP 1/168, f. 117.

44. There is some debate about what the 'drawn' part of the sentence referred to, whether the mode of transport or the extraction of the vital organs. In Francis Dereham's case, his sentence stipulated he was to be hanged, then disembowelled, beheaded, and then quartered. The sentence was carried out and confirmed in Wriothesley, *Chronicle*, I, p. 131.

45. *Cal. S. P. Span.*, VI, i, 213.

46. Thomas Culpepper is buried in the Church of the Holy Sepulchre in Newgate. Also known as St Sepulchre-without-Newgate, the church is the largest parish church in London and it has been a living of St John's College, Oxford, since the seventeenth century. The walls and tower remain, but the Great Fire in 1666 gutted the interior and the porch seems to be the only original interior feature left standing from 1541. Culpepper's body lies in the same church as John Smith, Governor of Virginia, who acquired posthumous fame owing to his association with Pocahontas.

47. SP 1/168, f. 112.

48. *Proceedings of the Privy Council*, pp. 280, 281, 283–4.

49. Hall, *Hall's Chronicle*, pp. 842–43.

50. Burnet, *History of the Reformation*, I, pp. 626–67.

51. *Cal. S. P. Span.*, VI, i, 215.

52. Ibid., 223.

Chapter 22: *Ars Moriendi*

1. *Cal. S. P. Span.*, VI, i, 227.

2. *Proceedings of the Privy Council*, VIII, p. 304.

3. *Cal. S. P. Span.*, VI, i, 223. The original translators' use of 'lese Majesty' and 'Sion House' have been adapted in this citation. Chapuys's phonetic rendering of Lady Rochford's name was left as 'de Rochefort' in the original.

4. Lehmberg, *Later Parliaments of Henry VIII*, p. 141. Lehmberg (pp. 142–43) credibly suggests that the Lord Chancellor's discussion of Catherine was deliberately left out of transcripts, with orders perhaps given to the clerks beforehand that they were not to record a

specific discussion of the queen's vices.

5. Lehmberg, *Later Parliaments of Henry VIII*, pp. 128–29.
6. *Journals of the House of Lords*, I, p. 166.
7. Burnet, *History of the Reformation*, I, p. 627.
8. Ibid., p. 625.
9. *Journal of the House of Lords*, I, p. 166.
10. Ibid.
11. *Cal. S. P. Span.*, VI, i, 232.
12. Bishop Burnet (*History of the Reformation*, I, p. 626) noted: 'How much she confessed to them is not very clear, neither by the journal nor the act of parliament; which only says that she confessed without mentioning the particulars.' The charges against her did not subsequently change to ones of adultery, which suggests that she reiterated her earlier confessions. For Catherine's insistence that she deserved to die, *Cal. S. P. Span.*, VI, i, 232.
13. Burnet, *History of the Reformation*, I, pp. 626–27.
14. Ibid., p. 627. The law was unpopular enough to be repealed in the reign of Henry's son, Edward VI.
15. Lehmberg, *Later Parliaments of Henry VIII*, p. 147.
16. *Cal. S. P. Span.*, VI, i, 230.
17. Ibid.
18. Ibid.
19. Ibid.
20. Hall, *Hall's Chronicle*, p. 843; *Cal. S. P. Span.*, VI, i, 232.
21. Burnet refers to him as 'Dr White', although he did not return to study for his doctorate until the reign of Mary I.
22. Burnet, *History of the Reformation*, I, p. 624.
23. *Cal. S. P. Span.*, VI, i, 232.
24. SP 1/168, f. 48.
25. *Proceedings of the Privy Council*, VIII, pp. 304–05.
26. The spot on Tower Green, still exhibited to tourists today and marked with a memorial plaque, is almost certainly not the site of the actual scaffold on which Catherine perished. It was shown by a colourful yeoman to Queen Victoria, who had a fascination with Anne Boleyn and Lady Jane Grey, and the actual spot of Anne and Catherine's scaffolds lay on what is now the parade ground near the White Tower. *Cal. S. P. Span.*, VI, i, 232, stipulates the scaffolds for the respective queens were erected on the same site.
27. *Original Letters*, I, ii, pp. 128–29.
28. This description is based on the funeral of Elizabeth of York (d. 1503). See Laynesmith, *Last Medieval Queens*, pp. 119–26.

Chapter 23: The Shade of Persephone

1. *Cal. S. P. Span.*, VI, i, 233.
2. Siddons, *Heraldic Badges*, I, p. 116.
3. LP, XIX, ii, 613.
4. *Proceedings of the Privy Council*, pp. 46–8, 81–2, 148. Bulmer was still refusing to be reconciled with Joan in October 1542, five months after she was released from the Tower. Bulmer himself was imprisoned in Fleet prison, on financial charges, in February 1543 and the couple were officially separated by June of that year.
5. He should not be confused with his kinsman Sir Edward Waldegrave, the Catholic courtier imprisoned for hearing Mass in Elizabeth I's reign. Joan Waldegrave's children were called Edward, Anne, Mary, Bridget, and Margery.
6. Barry L. Wall, *Long Melford through the ages: A guide to the buildings and streets* (Ipswich: East Anglian Magazine Ltd, 1986); L. L. B. Martin Woods,

The Winthrop Papers (Boston, MA: Massachusetts Historical Society, 1931).

7. The Countess of Bridgewater was also interred there, in 1554.

8. Bindoff (ed.), *House of Commons*, I, p. 403.

9. Evidence from family wills raises the possibility that Isabella may not have been close to any of her surviving siblings. Despite the fact that George Howard was his half brother, while Isabella was his full sibling, John Leigh left bequests to the former and not the latter when he died in 1563. He also left a benevolence to his nieces and nephews from other Leigh siblings, including their late sister Margaret, but no mention is made of Isabella whatsoever – see *Surrey Archaeological Collections*, LI, p. 90.

10. Sir Nicholas Harris Nicolas (ed.), *Testamenta Vetusta: Being Illustrations from Wills of Manners, Customs, etc.* (London: Eyre & Spottiswoode, 1826), pp. 729–30. There is debate over whether their relationship began in the lifetime of Lord Stourton's first wife, Elizabeth (née Dudley), sister of Catherine's former Master of the Horse.

11. For Gruffydd ap Rhys's career, see Griffiths, *Sir Rhys ap Thomas*, pp. 117–25. Elizabeth I made more substantial grants to Gruffydd than Mary I did, perhaps partly because of his Howard blood and his son's service to her.

12. Donald Gregory, *The History of the Western Highlands and Isles of Scotland, from A. D. 1493 to A. D. 1625* (London and Glasgow: Hamilton, Adams, and Co., etc., 1881), p. 161.

13. Dugdale, II, p. 272.

14. Ibid.

15. Bindoff (ed.), *House of Commons*, I, p. 403.

16. Suzannah Lipscomb, *The King Is Dead: The Last Will and Testament of Henry VIII* (London: Head of Zeus, 2015), p. 171.

17. Hutchinson, pp. 229–30.

18. Childs, *Henry VIII's Last Victim*, p. 243.

19. Scarisbrick, *Henry VIII*, pp. 495–96.

20. Edward Seymour is better known to history as Duke of Somerset, the title he enjoyed between 1547 and 1552.

21. Many of the leaders and victims of the Tudor state were buried in the same chapel as Catherine and Lady Rochford. Lady Jane Grey was interred there after her execution in 1554. Cardinal Fisher, Thomas More, the Countess of Salisbury, and Catherine's kinsman Philip Howard, 20th Earl of Arundel, who died imprisoned for his faith in 1595, rest in St Peter's, as does Thomas Cromwell, both of the Seymour brothers, John Dudley, Catherine's brother-in-law Thomas Arundell, and two more of her kinsmen – the 4th Duke of Norfolk, executed for treason in 1572, and William Howard, 1st Viscount Stafford, beheaded during the anti-Catholic hysteria of the Popish Plot in 1680. Catherine is thus buried in a chapel that houses the remains of three saints, two beatified Catholic martyrs, three dukes, one marquess, four earls, and three queens.

22. Norton, *Anne of Cleves*, pp. 159–62.

23. Saaler, *Anne of Cleves*, pp. 91–2.

24. Hall, *Hall's Chronicle*, p. 828.

25. Muriel (ed.), *Lisle Letters*, VI, pp. 277–79.

26. R. J. Knecht, *The Rise and Fall of Renaissance France, 1483–1610* (London: Fontana Press, 1996), p. 335.

27. Mackay, *Inside the Tudor Court*, p. 246.

28. Bindoff (ed.), *House of Commons*, I, p. 403.; *Cal. S. P. Span.*, VIII, I, 206.

29. Rosalind K. Marshall, 'Douglas, Lady Margaret, Countess of Lennox (1515–1578)', in *Oxford Dictionary of National Biography*.

30. *Acts and Monuments*, VIII, p. 570.

31. Baldwin, *Henry VIII's Last Love*, pp. 97–101. The brothers had attempted to escape the epidemic in Cambridge and both died at Buckden Palace in Cambridgeshire.

32. Letter, dated 6 August 1566, from Jacob de Vulcob to Jacques Bochetel de La Foret, cit. Simon Adams, *Leicester and the Court: Essays on Elizabeth Politics* (Manchester University Press, 2002), p. 139.

33. Fox, *Jane Boleyn*, pp. 312–13.

34. Cavendish, *Life of Cardinal Wolsey*, II, p. 69.

35. *The Second Book of Travels of Nicander Nucius of Corcyra*, J. A. Cramer (ed. and trans.) (London: Camden Society, 1841), p. 48.

36. Cavendish, *Life of Cardinal Wolsey*, II, pp. 65–8.

37. Catherine's grave was not marked with a plaque until the reign of Queen Victoria. During renovations of the chapel, the queen ordered that those buried there should be commemorated. Excavations were carried out on the chancel at the same time, but Catherine's body was not among those exhumed.

38. Thomas, *The Pilgrim*, p. 3.

39. Thomas, *The Pilgrim*, p. 58.

40. *Original Letters*, I, ii, p. 129.

Appendix I: The Alleged Portraits of Catherine Howard

1. Kate Heard and Lucy Whitaker (eds), *The Northern Renaissance: Dürer to Holbein* (St James's Palace: Royal Collection Enterprises, 2011), p. 83.

2. Brett Dolman, 'Wishful Thinking: Reading the Portraits of Henry VIII's Queens', in Betteridge and Lipscomb (eds), *Henry VIII and the Court: Art, Politics and Performance*, pp. 124–26.

3. Roland Hui, 'Two New Faces?: The Horenbolte Portraits of Mary and Thomas Boleyn' (tudorfaces.blogspot.co.uk, 2011).

4. Sir Roy Strong, *Tudor and Jacobean Portraits* (London: Her Majesty's Stationery Office, 1969), I, p. 43. A coloured version of the sketch, described as Catherine Howard, was printed by Francesco Bartolozzi in 1797, and in the 1850s, Strickland (III, p. 124) accepted the sketch as a likeness of Catherine and based her description of her appearance on it, which seems to have been the origin of the myth that Catherine was curvaceous, repeated in many subsequent histories.

5. Susan E. James and Jamie S. Franco, 'Susanna Horenbout, Levinia Teerlinc and the Mask of Royalty' (Antwerp: Jaarboek Koninklijk Museum voor Schone Kunsten, 2000).

6. It was acquired by the Yale Center for British Art in 1970 via a sale at Sotheby's. I am grateful to Dr Edward Town for his extremely kind help with my questions about the miniature. For the Yale miniature, see Sir Roy Strong, *The English Renaissance Miniature* (London: Thames and Hudson, 1984), p. 44; David Starkey et al., *Lost Faces: Identity and Discovery in Tudor Royal Portraiture* (Exhibition Catalogue, London: Philip Mould Ltd, 2007), pp. 79–83.

7. Christopher Morris, *The Tudors* (London: Collins, 1955), fig. 15; Fraser, *Six Wives of Henry VIII*, p. 315, is more tentative on the Sheba attribution, describing it as a possible 'tantalising glimpse'.

8. The period between November 1541 and July 1543, when Henry VIII was unmarried, can also tentatively be dismissed – though glaziers were not always thorough in reflecting the latest instalment in the matrimonial misadventures of the royal household. For the suggestion that the queen of Sheba might have been inspired by Anne Boleyn, see Bernard, *Anne Boleyn*, p. 198.

9. Genesis, 19:15–26; Strong, *Tudor and Jacobean Portraits*, I, p. 43. The details in the brooch are difficult to see, but it does show a figure leading individuals away from scenes of destruction. It could also represent the moment Lot's wife was turned into salt for her disobedience.

10. Toledo Inventory 1926.57; National Portrait Gallery, Portrait 1119; 'Portrait of King Henry VIII's Fifth Wife Catherine Howard Is Found', *The Times* (4 March 2008).

11. Oliver Cromwell was Thomas's great-great-great-nephew, via the latter's sister Katherine. Her son, Sir Robert Williams (d. 1544), preferred to go by the Cromwell name, a move imitated by his descendants.

12. Lot 45 at Christie's auction on 27 October 1961; *Portrait of Mary Tudor, Queen of France and Duchess of Suffolk*, drawn by Sarah Capel-Coningsby, Countess of Essex, in Lucy Aikin, *Memoirs of the Court of Queen Elizabeth* (London: Stratham and Spottiswoode, 1818).

13. Sir Lionel Cust, 'A Portrait of Queen Catherine Howard, by Hans Holbein the Younger', in *Burlington Magazine for Connoisseurs* (July 1910), pp. 193–99.

14. Courtesy of the Toledo Museum of Art, correspondence with the author, 2015.

15. Henry VIII's youngest sister, Mary (d. 1533), married King Louis XII of France and, after his death, Charles Brandon, 1st Duke of Suffolk. They were the maternal grandparents of Lady Jane Grey.

16. Fraser, *Six Wives of Henry VIII*, p. 315n; Kathy Lynn Emerson, *Wives and Daughters: The Women of Sixteenth Century England* (Troy, NY: Whitston, 1984), pp. 114–15, 197.

17. Starkey et al., *Lost Faces*, pp. 73–5, is the best modern argument in favour of the Toledo portrait and its derivatives as depictions of Catherine Howard.

18. Frances Grey's appearance is not incompatible with this attribution. She is usually described as an obese lady, based on the misidentification of a portrait by Eworth of Lady Dacre and her son. This has been convincingly refuted, and Frances's appearance is discussed, in Leanda de Lisle, *The Sisters Who Would Be Queen: The Tragedy of Mary, Katherine and Lady Jane Grey* (London: HarperPress, 2009), pp. 167–68.

19. Strong, *Tudor and Jacobean Portraits*, I, p. 43.

20. RCIN 422293.

21. Jonathan Brown, *Kings and Connoisseurs: Collecting Art in Seventeenth-Century Europe* (Princeton, NJ: Princeton University Press, 1995), pp. 22–3, 65. The portrait of Anne of Cleves by Holbein that now hangs in the Louvre was also part of the Arundel collection and was subsequently purchased by the French Crown in 1671.

22. Leo Gooch, *A Complete Pattern of Nobility: John, Lord Lumley (c.1534–1609)* (Rainton Bridge: University of Sunderland Press, 2009), pp. 115–16; Ives, *Life and Death*, p. 43. The Boleyn portrait was apparently last recorded intact during a sale of John West's (d. 1772) collection.

23. 'Catherine Howard, Queen of K. Henry VIII', in Thomas Birch, *The Heads of Illustrious Persons of Great Britain* (London: John and Paul Knopton, 1747).

24. Heard and Whitaker (eds), *Northern Renaissance*, p. 83.

25. Starkey et al., *Lost Faces*, pp. 70–3; Starkey, *Six Wives*, p. 651.

26. Susan E. James, 'Lady Margaret Douglas and Sir Thomas Seymour by Holbein: Two Miniatures Re-identified', *Apollo* (1998), pp. 15–20.

27. RCIN 912223; RL 12223.

28. *Unknown Lady, c. 1540–5, aged 17*, Metropolitan Museum of Art, New York, 49. 7.30.

29. It cannot be Mary Fitzroy herself owing to her age. For arguments in favour of the Metropolitan portrait as a portrait of Catherine, see James and Franco, 'Susanna Horenbout', p. 124, and Conor Byrne, *Katherine Howard: A New History* (Lúcar, Spain: MadeGlobal Publishing, 2014), pp. 118–20.

30. National Gallery of Ireland 1195. Katherine Knollys (née Carey) was also unlikely on the basis of her subsequent portraiture and the uncertainty of her husband's financial situation. A case over his inheritance was not settled until 1545; Yale Center for British Art B1974.3.22.

31. Dolman, 'Wishful Thinking', pp. 124–26.

INDEX